Cambridge Studies in Modern Economic History 6

The Balkan economies c. 1800–1914

The Balkan economies c. 1800–1914 is a strongly revisionist book which compares the economic progress of Serbia, Bulgaria, Bosnia, Montenegro and Macedonia in the century before World War I. Michael Palairet draws heavily on native language primary sources to argue that these territories probably experienced economic decline rather than growth, at least from the mid nineteenth century. This comprehensive study of the economic development of the Balkans is divided into two parts, the first covering the 1790s to 1878 when most of the Balkan area except Serbia was subject to Ottoman rule. The second deals with the period 1878 to 1914 when Bulgaria and Bosnia had been prised from Ottoman rule. Dr Palairet points out that, far from being a drag on development, Ottoman rule made possible more progress than the arrangements which accompanied self-government. Thanks to the in-depth research which he conducted during the writing of this book, it now promises to be the definitive economic history of the Balkans.

Cambridge Studies in Modern Economic History

Series editors
Charles Feinstein
All Souls College, Oxford

Patrick O'Brien
The Institute of Historical Research, London

Barry Supple
The Leverhulme Trust

Peter Temin
Massachusetts Institute of Technology

Gianni Toniolo
Università degli Studi di Venezia

Cambridge Studies in Modern Economic History is a major new initiative in economic history publishing, and a flagship series for Cambridge University Press in an area of scholarly activity in which it has long been active. Books in this series will primarily be concerned with the history of economic performance, output and productivity, assessing the characteristics, causes and consequences of economic growth (and stagnation) in the western world. This range of enquiry, rather than any one methodological or analytic approach, will be the defining characteristic of volumes in the series.

The first titles in the series are:

1 *Central and Eastern Europe 1944–1993: detour from the periphery to the periphery*
  Ivan Berend
  ISBN 0 521 55066 1

2 *Spanish agriculture: the long Siesta 1765–1965*
  James Simpson
  ISBN 0 521 496306

3 *Democratic socialism and economic policy: the Attlee Years 1945–1951*
  Jim Tomlinson
  ISBN 0 521 55095 5

4 *Productivity and performance in the paper industry: labour, capital and technology, 1860–1914*
  Gary Bryan Magee
  ISBN 0 521 58197 4

5 *An economic history of the silk industry, 1830–1930*
  Giovanni Federico
  ISBN 0 521 58198 2

6 *The Balkan economies c. 1800–1914: evolution without development*
  Michael Palairet
  ISBN 0 521 58051 X

The Balkan economies c. 1800–1914

Evolution without development

Michael Palairet

University of Edinburgh

CAMBRIDGE UNIVERSITY PRESS

PUBLISHED BY THE PRESS SYNDICATE OF THE UNIVERSITY OF CAMBRIDGE
The Pitt Building, Trumpington Street, Cambridge, United Kingdom

CAMBRIDGE UNIVERSITY PRESS
The Edinburgh Building, Cambridge CB2 2RU, UK
40 West 20th Street, New York NY 10011–4211, USA
477 Williamstown Road, Port Melbourne, VIC 3207, Australia
Ruiz de Alarcón 13, 28014 Madrid, Spain
Dock House, The Waterfront, Cape Town 8001, South Africa

http://www.cambridge.org

© Vesna Palairet 1997

First published 1997
First paperback edition 2002

Typeface Plantin 10/12 pt.

A catalogue record for this book is available from the British Library

Library of Congress Cataloguing in Publication data
Palairet, M. R. (Michael)
The Balkan economies c. 1800–1914: evolution without development
/ Michael Palairet.
p.   cm. – (Cambridge studies in modern economic history: 6)
Includes bibliographical references and index.
ISBN 0 521 58051 X (hardback)
1. Balkan Peninsula – Economic conditions.   I. Title.   II. Series.
HC401.P35   1997
330.9496–dc21   96-48210   CIP

ISBN 0 521 58051 X hardback
ISBN 0 521 52256 0 paperback

For Rowland, father, son

Contents

Contents   ix

Illustrations

Tables

Preface

In 1891, Belgian consular agents in the Balkans were ordered to leave their comfortable quarters in the capital cities and undertake commercial 'voyages of exploration' in the provinces. They did a fine job. This book seeks to emulate them by exploring the economic experience of the Balkan territories through the observations of contemporaries, and setting these within a deductive framework of economic logic. It makes minimal use of the inductive approach, the insertion of the data within a mould of (under-) development theory, because of the author's scepticism of the validity of the typologies on offer.

There is no universally accepted definition of what 'the Balkans' comprise, but for the purpose of our study, we define it as the area displayed on map 1 p. 35, comprising the territories bounded by the sea to west, south and east, and by the line of the rivers Sava and Danube to the north. In terms of the jurisdictions of 1885–1912, the area included Bosnia-Hercegovina, Montenegro, Serbia, Bulgaria and Ottoman Europe (excluding the city of Constantinople). Romania, lying within the Carpathian zone, is not included within this study.

A number of the statistical tables are sourced to 'Balkstat statistics'. This is because the data were drawn from numerous sources, usually with a number of adjustments, which would have taken up excessive space. The Balkstat data are held on disk by the author at the Department of Economic and Social History, University of Edinburgh, and are available on request.

Acknowledgement is owed especially for help, enlightenment, comment and criticism to Ian Blanchard, John Lampe, Joel Halpern, Danica Milić, and to Donald Quataert, who reviewed the work internally for Cambridge. Financial assistance was granted by the ESRC, and the Carnegie Trust for the Universities of Scotland.

Glossary

aba   heavy peasant woollen cloth
ayans   notables
beg   Ottoman landowner
chiflik (čiflik, čitluk, čiftlik)   landed estate
cizye   head-tax on non-Moslems
čorbadžija (çorbaci)   rich Christian
dan'k   tithe on crops
dünüm   0.092 hectares
gajtan (gaytan)   braid, piping
gospodarl'k   doubled tithe
Hambarya   Ottoman uniform factory, Constantinople
iltizam   tithe farming
kolibi   hill cottages
kaza   district
kmet   in Bosnia, a tenant farmer
k'rdzhaliya   bandit
mirieh   uncultivated and untaxed land
mulk   cultivated, taxed land
nizam   Ottoman regular army
opština (obshtina)   equivalent to French *commune*
pečalbars   migrant workers
pašaluk   province ruled by pasha, military governor
reaya   non-Moslem
shajak (šajak)   carded woollen cloth (=Austrian *Loden*)
spahija (sipahi)   Ottoman feudal cavalryman, owner of a *spahiluk*
spahiluk (sipahilik)   Ottoman territorial fief
Tanzimat   Ottoman reform era, 1839–56
tapija (tapu)   Ottoman cultivating lease
vak'f   untaxable property
yamaks   irregular soldiery controlled by the Janissaries
yaylak   privileged pasture rights

Abbreviations

AAE   Paris, Archive du Ministère des Affaires étrangères
ACG   Cetinje, Arhiv Crne Gore
AHOI   Acta Historico Oeconomica Iugoslaviae
AN   Paris, Archives nationales
AS   Belgrade, Arhiv Srbije
BAE   Brussels, Archive du Ministère des Affaires étrangères
BOUCA   Austria-Hungary. *Berichte der Österr.-Ung. Consular-Ämter*
GBC   Great Britain, consular reports
GSUD   Glasnik srpskog učenog društva
IAB   Belgrade, Istorijski arhiv Beograda
IČ   Istorijski Časopis
IKKS   Industrijska komora kraljevine Srbije
IUBH   Bosnia Hercegovina, *Izvještaj o upravi Bosne i Hercegovini,*
   1906–1911
JEcH   Journal of Economic History
JEEcH   Journal of European Economic History
LRO   Preston, Lancashire Record Office
Michoff [II (1924)]   *La population de la Turquie et de la Bulgarie* II
   (Sofia, 1924)
Michoff, Nicolas V. [I(1941)]   *Contribution à l'histoire du commerce*
   bulgare, I, Rapports consulaires belges (Sofia, 1941)
Michoff [II/1 (1943)]   *Beiträge zur Handelsgeschichte Bulgariens, II,*
   Österreichische Konsularberichte (Part 1) (Sofia, 1943)
Michoff [III (1950)]   *Contribution à l'histoire du commerce de la Turquie*
   et de la Bulgarie. III, Rapports consulaires français (Svishtov, 1950)
Michoff [II/2 (1953)]   *Beiträge zur Handelsgeschichte Bulgariens, II,*
   Österreichische Konsularberichte (Part 2) (Sofia, 1953)
Michoff [V (1967)]   *Naselenieto na Turtsija i B'lgarija prez XVIII i XIX*
   v V (Sofia, 1967)
MuS   Smederevo, Muzej u Smederevu
NBKM   Narodna biblioteka Kiril i Metodi (M/S dept.)
NiPS   Naselja i Poreklo Stanovništva

NSZ   Naselja srpskih zemalja
PRO   London, Public Record Office
PS   *Periodichesko spisanie na b'lgarskoto knizhnovnoto druzhestvo*
RC   Belgium. *Recueil consulaire*
SGBTs   *Statisticheski godishnik na B'lgarskoto Tsarstvo*
SGKS   *Statistički godišnjak kraljevine Srbije*
SKS   *Statistika kraljevine Srbije*
SN   *Srpske Novine*
Sp.BID   *Spisanie na B'lgarskoto Ikonomichesko Druzhestvo*
TsDIA   Sofia, Tsentralen D'rzhaven Istoricheski Arhiv

Part I

The Balkan economies during the Ottoman period to 1878

The Balkan countries were not drawn into the main stream of European economic development before 1914. It is nevertheless common currency that even this most retarded of European regions was slowly modernizing, and that from the end of the nineteenth century, the hitherto infinitesimal tempo of change was speeding up, and resulting in slow, faltering, but still significant economic growth.[1] This book takes a different view. The Balkan economies were subject to a distinct evolutionary dynamic which was not intrinsically developmental, but this dynamic was overlaid in the different territories studied by changing institutional arrangements which temporarily caused performance to deviate from a long-run declining trend. The book is divided chronologically into two parts, the first covering the period from the 1790s to 1878, when most of the Balkan area except Serbia remained subject to Ottoman rule and institutions. Part II deals with the period 1878–1914, when Bulgaria and Bosnia had been prised from Ottoman rule. Emphasis shifts to examining the changes which took place under new institutional arrangements: in Bulgaria, like Serbia and Montenegro, under those of self-rule, in Bosnia as a dependency of Austria-Hungary.

In the period before 1878, it will be argued, Ottoman institutions, in particular agrarian arrangements, engrained themselves deeply into the organization of economic life. The institutions themselves were undergoing radical changes which had a profound effect on economic life and on its evolution, especially in Bulgaria.

In an overwhelmingly agrarian economy, changes in the density of settlement were bound to have far-reaching effects on economic change, so Chapter 1 identifies population trends and the distribution of population between urban and rural communities. For simplicity its content covers the entire period to 1914.

---

[1] The consensus is well defined in R. Preshlenova, 'Austro-Hungarian Trade and the Economic Development of Southeastern Europe before World War I', in *Economic Transformations in East and Central Europe*, ed. David F. Good (London, 1994), p. 232.

Chapter 2 examines the institutional evolution of Ottoman Europe, and the economic responses elicited in Bulgaria and southern Macedonia. Chapter 3 looks in greater depth at the outcome both for agriculture and manufacturing in Bulgaria. The evidence produced will indicate that the responses to improving opportunities were sufficiently strong and sustained for Bulgaria to become the most productive and dynamic of all the Ottoman territories.

This contrasts with the experience of Serbia, liberated since 1815 from Ottoman rule. Serbia (Chapter 4) became a country of universal peasant landownership and low taxation, a combination which resulted in an economy dominated by subsistence farming. So far from providing the basis for the free formation of capitalist mechanisms, Serbia, it will be shown, retrogressed economically, and chapter 4 explores why this retrogression occurred.

Pre-1878 economic trends in the dinaric zone, in Ottoman Bosnia and the then tiny Montenegrin state, form the subject of Chapter 5. Institutional arrangements in Bosnia differed from those in Bulgaria, as did the outcomes. The chapter attempts to analyse why this was so, and uses the sketchy evidence available for the period on Montenegro to bring out some characteristics of dinaric economic life which both (uneasily) shared.

Economic performance is ultimately determined by entrepreneurial response to changes in externalities. Chapter 6 explores economic aspects of the Bulgarian 'renaissance' of the mid nineteenth century, and contrasts the diffusion of an indigeneous Bulgarian enterprise culture with the near-absence of any equivalent culture in Bosnia or Serbia.

The Balkan economic experience in the period before 1878 provides the clues needed to understand performance between 1878–1914, as covered in Part 2. In particular it shows why it would be misleading to view the earlier period in Ottoman Europe as a phase of feudal stagnation. Rather, it will be argued, the removal of Ottoman rule led to deepening economic retardation, except in Bosnia, where a rather inefficient tyranny was exchanged for a more efficient one.

Of course, the Balkan countries were much more sophisticated institutionally in 1914 than they had been in the 1860s, but they were probably, with the exception of Bosnia, poorer and less productive. It is not argued that the institutions created by the new Balkan states were directly responsible for economic decline, but it is argued that those pertaining in the Ottoman lands before 1878 had provided a more effective offset.

1 Balkan population 1790–1914

Throughout the century before World War I, Balkan economic life was based on low productivity farming. Population growth would alter the relationship between land and population in a way critical to the evolution of the Balkan economies. As population trends for the Balkans have not yet been satisfactorily charted, we aim to establish a working estimate of Balkan population and its growth over the period 1790–1910.

Population trends in Ottoman Europe

The most serious gaps in our demographic knowledge concern the experience of the Ottoman provinces. These comprised 76 per cent of the peninsula (by area) till 1877–8, and 37 per cent subsequently. Nineteenth-century Ottoman population trends have been 'a perplexing problem to students of modern Ottoman history'.[1] Properly speaking, the Porte did not enumerate the population, but from the 1830s onwards its system for registering population was subjected to periodic updating; it is these updates which pass for censuses.[2] The Porte appears to have revised its registers in 1831, 1835, 1838, 1844 and 1857, and probably in 1864. However, these revisions were not published, and several have yet to be rediscovered. Only one of these documents, which was begun in 1831, has been examined by historians, but even this is of limited usefulness. We know something of the contents of later revisions from information leaked to European observers who made their own estimates, but these varied widely. Different territories were registered at different times, areas would wholly or partly escape the count, and even within individual territories, registration was a protracted affair which could go on for years. Sins of omission, double counting and plain bad arithmetic were rife. Moreover, the authorities were primarily interested in identifying the

[1] Stanford J. Shaw, 'The Ottoman Census System and Population 1831–1914', *International Journal of Middle East Studies [IJMES]* IX (1978), p. 325.
[2] Justin McCarthy, *The Arab World, Turkey, and the Balkans (1878–1914): A Handbook of Historical Statistics* (Boston, MA, 1982), p. 53.

adult manpower population, or the number of taxable hearths, and this introduces problems in converting their figures into estimates of absolute population. The very dating of revisions is elusive since they were never intended to provide a snapshot of population at any precise date, and when new registers were released to replace older ones, the new statistics could be derived partially from old registers. The quality of the surviving material improves from the 1870s onward, but still leaves much to be desired. Recent research has been devoted to analysing some of the registers in static terms, most notably by Kemal Karpat.[3]

Our presentation of Balkan population trends is therefore subject to an indeterminate margin of error, and some statistics we have used could be misleading. Nevertheless, it is common ground among the historians, having warned of the shortcomings of the statistics, to proceed to a more favourable evaluation of their quality. The underlying figures were relied upon by the authorities for the vital purposes of taxing and ascertaining military strength, and some of the Europeans who used them knew enough about the Ottoman administrative system to draw reasonable conclusions from them.[4] Thus it appears worthwhile to apply the estimates they made, for such purposes as do not require a high degree of accuracy.

In c. 1530 population in the Balkans was about 5.4 million (4.3 million within our reference area).[5] The following three centuries have till recently remained a dark age for Ottoman population statistics. Hearth tax records suggest a continuous population decline from 1650 through to 1834,[6] and contemporary comment did nothing to convey an alternative impression. For example, it was claimed in 1798 that 'without going farther back in time than the memory of persons now living, it is easy to prove that depopulation has been, at least in latter times, astonishingly rapid'.[7] Stavrianos and Stoianovich treat the entire early modern period as one of plague-racked demographic decline.[8]

However, the hearth tax records lost their significance from 1691 when the basis of taxation was changed. McGowan analysed the registers

[3] Kemal Karpat, *Ottoman Population 1830–1914. Demographic and Social Characteristics* (Madison, Wis., 1985); Karpat, 'Ottoman Population Records and the Census of 1881/2–1893', *IJMES*, IX (1978).

[4] Karpat, 'Ottoman Population Records', pp. 239, 240, 244.

[5] Calculated from information in Omer Barkan, 'Essai sur les données statistiques des régistres de récensement dans l'empire Ottoman aux XVe et XVIe siècles', *Journal of the Economic and Social History of the Orient*, I (1957–8).

[6] Peter F. Sugar, *Southeastern Europe under Ottoman Rule 1354–1804* (Seattle, 1977), p. 222.   [7] W. Eton, *A Survey of the Turkish Empire* (1798), p. 254.

[8] Traian Stoianovich, 'L'économie balkanique aux XVIIe et XVIIIe siècles' (unpublished doctoral thesis, Faculté des lettres, University of Paris, 1952), pp. 19–20; L. S. Stavrianos, *The Balkans since 1453* (New York, 1958), pp. 134–5.

for the new *cizye* tax system, for 1700, 1718, 1740, 1788 and 1815, and concluded that the massive population fall experienced by the Ottoman Empire in the late seventeenth century was partially reversed during the eighteenth.[9] *Cizye* was chargeable on all non-Muslim males of 15 years and over,[10] or more precisely of 15–60 years of age.[11] McGowan estimates that men of this age group would constitute one in three of the population of a pre-industrial society, but this proportion may be a little high. Our calculations from the Serbian census of 1863 indicate that 29.3 per cent of villagers and 34.5 per cent of townspeople fell into the taxpayer category, in this 94.45 per cent rural country, or 29.5 per cent of the population (1 in 3.385). We lack information as to the Muslim population of the area, but Karpat's statistic for the elayets of Rumeli and Silistra from the 1831 census shows that Muslim males were 58.8 per cent as numerous as non-Muslim males. We will not go far wrong in applying the same proportions to McGowan's statistics. McGowan abstains from translating his *cizye* totals into explicit population estimates, since his purposes are served by demonstrating a trend rather than estimating absolute numbers, but he considers the records to be roughly reliable. The *cizye* figures for 1815 may not have been entirely up to date, especially for the Greek lands,[12] so to allow for omissions from the registers, an 8 per cent upward adjustment would probably be appropriate.[13] McGowan's reference area includes the Dobrudzha which later statistics indicate had a population of 220,000 or about 2 per cent of that of our own reference area, and it excludes the Greek Aegean islands which had a population of 390,000 around 1850.[14] As a result, we add a further 1.7 per cent to our revision of McGowan's basic material. McGowan's data and our estimates from it are set down in Table 1.1.

The next landmark is the registration of male population which began in 1831. A table of findings from the registers was published by Akbal in 1951, but large areas in Albania, Macedonia and Thessaly were largely or wholly excluded from the statistics, presumably because the records were lost.[15] Territorially, male population has been grouped by Todorov as follows:[16]

[9] Bruce McGowan, *Economic Life in Ottoman Europe. Taxation, Trade and the Struggle for Land, 1600–1800* (Cambridge, 1981), p. 103.   [10] McGowan, *Economic Life*, p. 82.
[11] Karpat, *Ottoman Population*, p. 20.   [12] McGowan, *Economic Life*, pp. 82–5.
[13] Karpat, *Ottoman Population*, p.10.
[14] [E. Boré], *Almanach de l'Empire Ottoman pour l'année 1850, avec une statistique politique et religieuse...* (Galata, 1850) reproduced in Michoff, II (1924), p. 4.
[15] Fazila Akbal, '1831 Tarihinde osmanli imparatorlugunda idari taksimat ve nufus', *Belletin*, XV (1951).
[16] Nikolai Todorov, *The Balkan City, 1400–1900* (Seattle, 1983), p. 311.

Danube 477,862
Edirne 421,721
Salonica 240,411
Bitola 208,222

Total 1,348,216

Table 1.1 *Population of Ottoman Europe 1700–1815*

Year	*cizye* payers	Population estimate (000)
1700	635,835	3,755
1718	683,316	4,035
1740	756,949	4,470
1788	868,648	5,130
1815	932,322	5,506

Source: McGowan's *cizye* figures multiplied here by 5.905, to allow for family members, Muslims, under-recording, deduction of Dobrudzha, and addition of the Aegean islands, see text p. 5.

These figures have been modified by Karpat, though as his total for Rumeli and Silistra elayets together is close to that of Akbal, the figures are still not credible in aggregate, for they imply an unrealistically small population for Rumeli of less than 3 million.[17] The lost Ottoman revision of 1844 for the European provinces provided the basis for population estimates by Ubicini, Heuschling, Boré and Michelsen.[18] Despite their common source, these writers differed widely in their estimates for the population of Ottoman Europe, and expressed their findings in round figure terms, which they defined to regions of indeterminate extent. All appear to have over-corrected grossly for what they knew to be problems of under-recording in the original documents. Ubicini estimated the population of Rumeli at 7.5 million, Boré at 5 million. Later observers agree that these figures were too high.[19] If taken at face value, they would

[17] It is not clear whether a full count was made of male children under the taxable age. See Karpat, *Ottoman Population*, p. 20.

[18] A. Ubicini, *Letters on Turkey* (tr. Lady Easthope, London, 1856), I, pp. 18–20; Xavier Heuschling, *L'Empire de Turquie* (Brussels, 1860), pp. 52–54; (Boré) *Almanach*, in Michoff, II (1924), p. 4; Edward H. Michelsen, *The Ottoman Empire and its Resources* (London, 1853), p. 47.

[19] Engin Akarli, 'Ottoman Population in Europe in the Nineteenth Century: its Territorial, Racial, and Religious Composition' (MA Thesis, University of Wisconsin, 1972), p. 44.

show an implausibly rapid rate of population growth between 1815 or 1831 and 1844 followed by a sharp decline into the 1860s and 1870s. Karpat's view is that there was more or less continuous population growth throughout the first two-thirds of the nineteenth century, and this certainly seems more probable.[20] A further (lost) revision of the registers was undertaken in 1857,[21] though I know of no estimates composed from it. In Bosnia, which seems to have missed the count in 1831 and 1844, an enumeration was undertaken in 1851/2, which provides a reasonably solid figure.[22]

After the Crimean War an increasing flow of material became available. Akarli thinks a census (or updating of the registers) was taken in 1864. This seems to have provided a new crop of figures which were probably derived from calculations by Vladimir Jakšić, chief of the Serbian statistical department.[23] However, no trace of the document has been discovered, nor did Jakšić publish data directly from it. For the period 1864–76 we have disaggregated statistics for Danube, Edirne (Adrianople) and Bosnia vilayets, for which our sources give mutually compatible figures. However, the aggregative figures for Ottoman Europe as a whole vary unacceptably, mainly because of wild divergences in estimates for the areas comprised today by Albania, Kosovo, the Pindus and Macedonia. The authorities probably disposed few satisfactory records for these anarchic tribal areas because of the weakness of the local administrative machinery. In Table 1.2, we set out the most consistent evidence for the population of the various territories of Ottoman Europe.

In Bosnia-Hercegovina (which then included the sanjak of Novi pazar and territories seized in 1877–8 by Montenegro), population probably rose from 1.078 million in 1851 to 1.264 million in about 1875, that is to say, by 1.1 per cent per annum. McGowan's figures for Bosnia and part of the sanjak in 1815 (an area for which he regards the enumeration as sound)[24] show 114,230 *cizye* payers. This suggests a population of 675,000, and implies growth to 1851 at 1.3 per cent per annum. So the population estimate given by Chaumette des Fosses, of 1,074,000 at the end of the eighteenth century[25] looks exaggerated, and it is unlikely that Bosnia uniquely experienced no population growth during the first half of the nineteenth century.

Northern Bulgaria (Danube vilayet) and Thrace (Edirne vilayet) are more of a problem. Danube vilayet seems to have experienced sustained 2.1 per cent annual population growth between 1864 and c. 1875. Growth

[20] Karpat, *Ottoman Population*, p. 11.   [21] Shaw, 'Ottoman Census System', p.327.
[22] Djordje Pejanović, *Stanovništvo Bosne i Hercegovine* (Belgrade, 1955), pp. 29–30.
[23] Akarli, 'Ottoman Population', p. 14.   [24] McGowan, *Economic Life*, p. 90.
[25] Stoianovich, 'L'économie balkanique', pp. 8–9.

Table 1.2 *Territorial population estimates for Ottoman Europe 1864–1881 (000s)*

Source	relates to	Edirne	Danube (with Niš)
1. Behm-Jakšić	1864	1,355	1,995
2. Salname (Tuna), 1868	1866?		2,047[a]
2. Salname (Tuna), 1869	?		2,067[a]
3. Samo	1872	1,304	2,016[b]
3. Salname (Tuna), 1874	?		2,313[ac]
4. Ravenstein	?	1,306	2,303
5. Salname (Devlet), 1877	?	1,305	2,496[a]

			Bosnia-Hercegovina
6. Census	1851		1078
7. Jones	1857–9		1150
8. Thömmel	?		1212
9. Salname (Bosna), 1870	?		1242[a]
10. Ubicini-Courteille	1871		1232[a]
6. Salname, 1876	?		1264

			Salonica, Prizren, Monastir, Shkodër, Yanina
11. Boré, 1850	1844		4,200
12. Bowen, 1852	?		1,930
13. Michelsen, 1853	?		2,600
14. Ubicini, 1856	1844		3,900
15. Heuschling, 1860	1844		3,900
1. Behm-Jakšić	1864		3,080
16. Salaheddin, 1867	?		4,787
10. Ubicini-Courteille	1871–2		3,342
3. Samo	1872		3,374
17. Cammerer, 1875	?		3,575
4. Ravenstein, 1876	?		2,176
5. Salname, 1877	?		2,509[a]
18. Census	1881		2,978

Notes:
[a] Double of male population listed in original.
[b] Niš may not be included.
[c] Figure for Niš, 1869, added.

Sources:
1 Behm, *Bevölkerung*, in Michoff, II (1924), p. 28. Behm's figure is specific to 1864, and is credited to Jakšić.
2 Karpat, *Ottoman Population*, p. 116.

Table 1.2 *Notes (cont.)*

3 Ibid. p. 117.

4 Ravenstein, 'Distribution of Population', pp. 260–1.

5 Ubicini, 'L'empire Ottoman', p. 107.

6 Pejanović, *Stanovništvo Bosne*, pp. 29–30, 37, and table.

7 GBC Bosnia 1858.

8 Gustav Thömmel, *Beschreibung des Vilajet Bosniens* (Vienna, 1867), p. 102.

9 *Salname-i vilayet-i Bosna*, Defa V, sene 1287 (=1870) p. 144. This figure was repeated in several successive yearbooks, which is why it was used by Samo for 1872.

10 Ubicini and Courteille, *Empire Ottoman*, p. 19.

11 Extract from *Almanach de l'Empire Ottoman pour l'année 1850...* in Michoff, II (1924), p. 4.

12 Bowen, *Mount Athos*, p. 249.

13 Michelsen, *Ottoman Empire*, p. 139.

14 Ubicini, *Letters on Turkey*, I, p. 18.

15 Heuschling, *Empire de Turquie*, pp. 51–2.

16 Salaheddin, *Turquie*, p. 210.

17 Cammerer, *Handbuch*, in Michoff, II (1924), p. 70.

18 Karpat, 'Ottoman Population Records', pp. 258–74.

at this high rate was quite possible, because heavy immigration augmented natural increase. This immigration included numerous Bulgarians, as well as Tatars and Circassians who were driven from the Russian Empire. Of the Circassians alone, about 600,000 were resettled in the Balkans, mainly in northeast Bulgaria between 1860 and 1876, and the Tatar immigration may have been of comparable size.[26] Population in Edirne vilayet, on the other hand, was either static or falling between 1864 and 1875. Our main difficulty in setting these figures in a long-term trend is the dearth of satisfactory figures prior to 1864 with which to link them. For Edirne elayet in 1844, Ubicini gave a figure of 1.8 million, but Heuschling indicated that this included Constantinople and environs. Ubicini estimated Constantinople's population at 891,000, including 116,000 non-residents, but the enumeration of that year showed but 213,693 males resident in the city.[27] We therefore infer a population for Edirne elayet of 1.0–1.4 million at this time, and take a mean of 1.2 million.[28] For Northern Bulgaria, however, the only estimate which lies within the range of plausibility is Boré's, of 2 million (for 1844) but this is probably too high.[29] If we assume that the rate of population growth was similar to that of Bosnia (1.1 per cent per annum) then an 1851 population of 1.73 million is indicated.

[26] Karpat, *Ottoman Population*, pp. 64–9.   [27] Ibid., p. 203.

[28] G. F. Bowen, *Mount Athos, Thessaly and Epirus* (London, 1852), p. 249 estimates its population at 1,020,000, but his figures were in general implausibly low.

[29] Ubicini, Heuschling and Salaheddin all gave 3 million, and Michelsen 4 million, but these are as far outside the bounds of probability as Bowen's 560,000. Salaheddin Bey, *La Turquie à l'exposition universelle de 1867* (Paris, 1867), p. 210.

For the problem area of the southwest Balkans in the third panel of Table 1.2, we reason as follows. The 1881 revision indicated a population of 2.98 million and was reliable to within 10 per cent even in the remotest areas.[30] Territorial losses to Serbia and Montenegro had slightly reduced the population of this area since the previous revision. We should therefore be looking for a pre-1878 population somewhat in excess of 3 million. Thus the von Samo, Ubicini-Courteille, and Cammerer figures[31] fall into the right range,[32] implying that population in c. 1872 was of about 3.4 million. Most of the earlier figures are therefore improbably high, especially that of Salaheddin, which is widely regarded as exaggerated. The figure Behm attributed to Jakšić, stated to relate specifically to 1864, is obviously compatible,[33] as is that of Michelsen (presumably for 1844) an estimate which is much lower for the territory than that of Ubicini or Boré. If we take the southwest Balkans as having 3.08 million inhabitants in 1864 and 3.4 million in 1872, implying growth at 1.2 per cent per annum, then this growth projected backwards implies a population in 1844 of 2.41 million. This makes the Michelsen figure, if for 1844, the most acceptable estimate, which will therefore be adopted.

These are the figures which we will use as the basis of calculation. However, we must introduce two basic modifications, one to adjust for sex ratios, the other for general undercounting. The estimates we have quoted for total population were derived from registers of male population, whose numbers were doubled. These can be improved on, since all enumerations in the nineteenth-century Balkans which counted women showed male population to have been significantly in surplus. The censuses of Bulgaria and Eastern Rumelia of 1880 and 1884 showed a 4.05 per cent surplus of males,[34] and that for Bosnia in 1879 showed a surplus of 10.4 per cent.[35] The Greek census of 1861 showed a surplus of 7.1 per cent,[36] and the one true census taken in Montenegro in 1911 disclosed a

[30] Karpat, 'Ottoman Population Records', p. 56.
[31] A. Ritter zur Helle von Samo, *Die Völker des Osmanischen Reiches* (Vienna, 1877) cited in Karpat, *Ottoman Population*, p. 117; A. Ubicini and Pavet de Courteille, *Etat présent de l'Empire Ottoman* (Paris, 1876), p.19; A. A. Cammerer, *Handbuch der neueste Erdkunde* (1875), cited in Michoff, II, p. 70.
[32] The Ravenstein and the 1877 *Salname* figures seem far too low. E. G. Ravenstein, 'Distribution of the Population in the Part of Europe Overrun by the Turks', *Geographical Magazine*, III (1876), pp. 260–1; for *Salname* 1877 figures see A. Ubicini, 'L'Empire Ottoman, ses divisions administratives et sa population', *L'économiste français*, V-e année, II, 30 (28 July 1877), pp. 106–8.
[33] E. Behm, *Die Bevölkerung der Erde* (Gotha, 1875), cited in Michoff, II (1924), p. 28.
[34] *SGBTs*, I, 1909, p. 16.
[35] *Ortschafts und Bevölkerungs-Statistik von Bosnien und Hercegovina* (Sarajevo, 1880), p. 4.
[36] *Statesman's Yearbook*, 1865, p. 296.

male surplus of 8.8 per cent.[37] Some authorities attribute these results to the under-recording of females,[38] but they may also have reflected reality. My research on the Serbian census of 1863 indicates a 6.6 per cent male surplus for the rural areas. It established that this surplus was probably not caused by under-recording females, but existed in reality.[39] The Serbian experience was not exceptional. Marija Todorova, who worked with 1860s Ottoman data for three towns in North Bulgaria, showed a male surplus among a relatively small sample of ethnic Bulgarians of as much as 11 per cent, and considers her results to be statistically admissible.[40] Obviously, an unevenly successful census, such as the 1881–93 Ottoman revision, the first in which women were included, could well 'lose' additional women through under-recording. Karpat's work on this document disclosed a male surplus for the European territories of 17.7 per cent, which looks implausibly wide, but when Kosovo vilayet is eliminated, the gap is reduced to a more realistic 9.2 per cent.[41] Therefore, since we treat the male surplus as real, and not the result of defective enumeration, we have revised downward all figures which have been generated by the doubling of male population, by 3.1 per cent for Serbia, 4.7 per cent for Bosnia, 2.2 per cent for Bulgaria, 4.0 per cent for Montenegro and 4.2 per cent for the other provinces of Ottoman Europe. For Danube vilayet (including Niš) a further downward adjustment of 9.55 per cent is needed (on the basis of Ravenstein's figures) to eliminate Tulçea sanjak, which subsequently passed to Romania.

A second basic modification is needed to account for general under-recording of both sexes and is inevitably crude. As far as can be gauged, the estimates for 1864 and later were drawn more or less directly from the population registers (unlike those for 1844) and were corrected for under-enumeration. These have therefore been adjusted upward, like the earlier data, by 8 per cent across the board. Table 1.3 summarizes our estimates for the population of the Ottoman provinces in Europe between 1844 and 1875.

We can now unite these estimates with those based on McGowan's

---

[37] Pavle S. Radusinović, *Stanovništvo Crne Gore do 1945 godine* (Belgrade, 1978), p. 133.

[38] Shaw, 'Ottoman Census System', p. 337.

[39] This is because there was no male surplus among the lowest age group (0–4 years), in which the scope for female underenumeration was greatest. Rather there was a male deficit of 2.21 per cent. The deficit of adult females arose through differential mortality in adolescence. See M. Palairet, 'Rural Serbia in the light of the census of 1863', *JEEcH*, XXIV (1995), pp. 56–8.

[40] Maria Todorova, 'Population Structure, Marriage Patterns, Family and Household (According to Ottoman Documentary Material from North-Eastern Bulgaria in the 60s of the 19th Century)', *Etudes Balcaniques* (Sofia), I (1983), pp. 63–4 attributes male surplus to the overexploitation of women's labour.

[41] Calculated from summary table in Karpat, 'Ottoman Population Records'.

Table 1.3 *Territorial division of population: Ottoman Europe 1844–1875 (millions)*

Year	Bosnia	Danube	Edirne	SW Balkans
1844	–	–	1.26	2.69
1851	1.11	1.65	–	–
1857	1.19	–	–	–
1864	1.25	1.90	1.44	3.19
1866	–	1.95	–	–
1869	1.27	1.98	–	–
1871	1.26	–	–	–
1872	–	2.21	1.38	3.52
1874	–	2.20	1.38	–
1875	1.30	2.39	1.38	–

Note:
For sources and method of estimation see text above (p. 11). SW Balkans includes the area which comprises Salonica, Monastir, Yanina and Shkodër vilayets in 1876.

work and displayed in Table 1.1. The latter include territories which by 1844 had become Greece and Serbia. The population of Greece in 1844 was 930,295, and in 1861, 1.097 million.[42] That of Serbia in 1850 was 976,000 if allowance is made for an estimated 8,000 gipsies and 11,000 Ottoman subjects who were not included in the enumeration.[43] If all these figures are interpolated to 1850, the population of Ottoman Europe that year was 6.88 million, and that of Serbia and Greece was 1.96 million, making a total of 8.33 million for an area with 5.51 million in 1815. Implied annual population growth is 1.36 per cent. Now the population of the 1850 territory of Serbia in 1815 is estimated at 480,000,[44] and that of Greece in 1815 at 851,000.[45] If we deduct 1.33 million (the population of Serbia and Greece) from our 1815 estimate for Ottoman Europe, the 1815 population of the territory the Ottomans held in 1850 was 4.175 million. Therefore between 1815 and 1850 population in this territory grew at 1.44 per cent per annum. This is probably excessively high, and suggests that a higher margin for under-recording than 8 per cent should have been applied to the McGowan *cizye* figures. His belief that they under-record for Greece seems to be confirmed. However, further mutilation of this data would render any conclusions more arbitrary, so the figures have

[42] See below, Table 1.7.
[43] Vladimir Stipetić, 'Stanovništvo uže Srbije u 19 vijeku i prvi srpski ustanak', *Glas CCXCIV Srpske akademije nauka i umetnosti* (Belgrade, 1975), pp. 231, 238.
[44] Stipetić, 'Stanovništvo uže Srbije', p. 253.   [45] By interpolation. See below, Table 1.7.

Table 1. 4 *Population of Ottoman Europe 1885–1912*

Vilayet	1885	1896	1897	1906	1912
1 enumerated figures					
Edirne	836	955	986	1,334	1,027
Çatalca	59	59	61	79	258
Salonica	990	1,010	1,039	921	–
Kosovo	721	721	756	672	–
Monastir	664	664	712	825	–
Yanina	516	512	517	517	–
Total	3,787	3,921	4,070	4,347	3,953
2 estimate derived from enumerated figures					
Edirne	903	1,031	1,065	1,441	–
Çatalca	64	66	66	85	–
Salonica	1,069	1,091	1,122	995	–
Kosovo	931	959	961	949	–
Monastir	717	765	769	891	–
Yanina	557	553	558	611	–
Total	4,241	4,465	4,541	4,972	5,176[a]

Note:
[a] In 1910, see text p. 14.
Sources for panel 1: 1885–1906: Karpat, *Ottoman Population*, pp. 148–9, 158–61, 168–9.
Karpat also presents figures for 1894 and 1895, but for the European provinces it appears that the registers were not revised. 1912: Greek estimates are from McCarthy, *Arab World*, pp. 94, 95.
For panel 2 see text, p. 14.

been left to stand, subject to the reservation that they are probably too low, and that the implied 1815–50 population growth rate is probably too high.

After the Ottoman military and diplomatic disasters of 1877–8, the truncated lands of Ottoman Europe (Albania, Epirus, Macedonia, Old Serbia and part of Thrace) seem, after a pause, to have increased in population, as shown in Table 1.4. The first panel transcribes the raw data from Karpat.[46] These figures are still less than wholly reliable. However, the registration of population was now linked with the issue of personal identity cards, which made it difficult for men, if not for women, to escape the count. Shaw considers (a little optimistically) that the censuses were now 'probably as good as contemporary efforts in the other nations of

[46] Karpat, *Ottoman Population*, pp. 148–9, 158–61, 168–9.

Europe'.[47] The first figure relates to registrations which were carried out in the European provinces between 1882 and 1888.[48] It has been ascribed to the mid-point date of 1885.

In the second panel, the figures in the first have been adjusted to improve them. Firstly, we note the partial failure to record females in Kosovo vilayet, which resulted in apparent male surpluses of 65.8 per cent in 1885, 59.7 per cent in 1897 and 70.5 per cent in 1906. In the second panel, female numbers have been raised for Kosovo to give the same male surplus of 9.2 per cent that was shown by the other European provinces in 1885. Where figures from previous registers were obviously carried forward unchanged, interpolated figures are substituted. The resulting figures have then all been rounded up by 8 per cent. The final figure, a Greek estimate for 1912, is clearly too low and has been rejected, in favour of extrapolating the 1897–1906 trend to 1910.

Panel 2 signals that the population of Ottoman Europe grew by about 22 per cent between 1885 and 1910. This 0.8 per cent annual growth rate was significantly lower than that for the ex-Ottoman Balkans, and indicates that population growth in the imperial possessions decelerated. The reason may have been continuous emigration, partly to other areas of the Ottoman Empire and the Balkans, partly overseas.

Population trends in the non-Ottoman Balkans

Most population statistics for the Balkan states and the Habsburg provinces emanate from published abstracts of censuses which were taken at frequent intervals, and are reasonably reliable. One serious exception to this rule (though admittedly a small one) was the Principality of Montenegro, for which population trends were not easy to determine.

A recent study of Montenegro's population before 1945 admits defeat for the pre-1914 period, because of the inconsistency of the data.[49] Censuses were secret documents, because the authorities wanted the outside world to overestimate the size of Montenegro's exiguous population, and to overrate the country's combat strength. So *all* officially sanctioned figures were spurious. For example a figure of 196,238 souls was claimed in a semi-official publication, and purported to be the result of a census made in 1863/4. The compiler was obliged to recant an earlier (and still inflated) estimate he had previously published, of 100,000.[50]

[47] Shaw, 'Ottoman Census', pp. 334, 338, appendix 2.
[48] Karpat, 'Ottoman Population Records', pp. 254, 255–6.
[49] Radusinović, *Stanovništvo Crne gore*, p. 132.
[50] 'Najnoviji statistički podatci o Crnoj-gori', in *Orlić: Crnogorski godišnjak za ... 1865*, ed. J. Sundečić (Cetinje, n.d.; reprint, Cetinje, 1979), p. 75 and note 1.

Table 1.5 *Population of Montenegro 1800–1911*

Year	Population
1800	29,000
1838	47,000
1868	67,486
1875	72,386
1879	117,495
1880	144,967
1881	152,494
1889	165,628
1900	185,558
1911	211,909

Note:
Separation lines indicate discontinuities arising from
territorial gains in 1820, 1859, 1878, 1879 and 1880.

Although independent contemporaries were aware of this falsification, even their own figures were usually unwittingly biased upward. A Serbian estimate published in 1872 disregarded the 'census' figure and gave population at 123,000.[51] Such figures, as we shall see, were still wild exaggerations. The annexations of 1878–81 provided further scope for muddying the waters; a German observer of 1882 dismissed the figure of 250,000 – 300,000 inhabitants which was being bandied around as a military bluff, and revised it (with unusual accuracy) to 160,000.[52]

The only way to establish the true population of Montenegro is to consult the original documents which had been so jealously withheld from contemporaries. Unfortunately, few have survived. Of census material, an incomplete fragment exists for 1879,[53] and a summary list for 1911. The 1879 census fragment produced the useful fact that family size was 4.975, and the 1911 summary can be adapted to give a solid figure for that year.[54] But the best way to calculate a time series is to use the *dacija* (direct tax) registers from which figures can be obtained for the

---

[51] Nićifor Dučić, *Književni radovi* (Belgrade, 1893), III, p. 10.
[52] Bernhardt Schwarz, *Montenegro. Schilderung einer Reise durch das Innere* (Leipzig, 1883), p. 146.
[53] ACG MUD VII-1 and VII-2 (Statistički odsjek – Popis svega Stanovništva po okružjima, varošima, selima 1879, I and II).   [54] Radusinović, *Stanovništvo Crne gore*, p. 133.

number of families. From these (multiplied by 1879 family size) we have assembled estimates for 1868 to 1911. If family size changed markedly over time, these figures will be unreliable, but we have reason for thinking it was fairly stable. We also reproduce some less secure independent estimates for the earlier part of the nineteenth century.[55]

Though Serbia produced good censuses, especially from 1866 onwards, its population before 1834 has not been definitively established. It is thought that population density in the eighteenth century was extremely low. Serbian sources claim that in 1721 the 12 *nahijas* of the Belgrade *pašaluk* had only 50,000 – 60,000 inhabitants, but that rapid population growth during the eighteenth century raised this to 120,000 – 150,000 in about 1790. The same area is reckoned to have had a population of 192,500 at the time of Miloš Obrenović's uprising in 1815. Revolutionary Serbia in 1815 however comprised an additional 6 *nahijas* and a combined territory of 24,440 km². Its total population has been estimated at 322,500–342,000 souls.[56] In 1833, further territory was annexed, which raised the number of tax-heads between the spring and autumn collection lists by 41.9 per cent; the following year's census showed a population of 668,000.[57] There were also about 34,000 unenumerated Turks and Gipsies.[58] Assuming that 495,000 of these people lived in the pre-annexation area at this time, its population expanded at 2.1 per cent per annum between 1815 and 1834. This high growth rate is not surprising, for immigrants and re-immigrants were pouring into a thinly settled territory with free land for settlement, so we will accept the 1815 estimate as reasonably solid. However the 1721 and 1790 figures (above) for the Belgrade *pašaluk* are probably too low, while the growth rate between these dates is overstated.[59] McGowan's figures show non-Muslim taxpayer numbers growing in the 'north west zone' of Ottoman Europe, of which Serbia formed part, from 154,670 in 1718 to 280,015 in 1788 and 307,407 in 1815. That is to say, non-Muslim population grew at 0.85 per cent per annum between 1718 and 1788, then at 0.35 per cent per annum to 1815.[60] If the *pašaluk* had 192,500 inhabitants in 1815, then on the basis of McGowan's figures it would have had about 176,000 inhabitants in 1788 and 98,000 in 1721. Natural increase between 1804 and 1815 was offset by excess war mortality and emigration of 133,000

[55] Sources and calculation are explained in Michael Palairet, 'The Culture of Economic Stagnation in Montenegro', *Maryland Historian*, XVII (1986), pp. 17–21. Although the Porte claimed Montenegro as a province before 1878, we have not deducted its population from that of the empire, since the Ottomans lacked access to register its inhabitants.
[56] Stipetić, 'Stanovništvo uže Srbije', pp. 233, 237, 238.
[57] Zavod za statistiku i evidenciju N. R. Srbije, *Stanovništvo N R Srbije od 1834–1953* (Belgrade, 1953), pp. 3–4.   [58] Stipetić, 'Stanovništvo uže Srbije', p. 231.
[59] McGowan, *Economic Life*, p. 90.   [60] Ibid., p. 103.

Table 1.6 *Population of Serbia 1718–1874 (000s)*

Year	Territory	Area (km²)	Population
1718	⎫	n.a.	98
1788	⎬ *pašaluk*	n.a.	176
1815	⎭	n.a.	192
1815	Serbia	24,440	332
1834	old frontier	24,440	495
1834	new frontier	37,511	702
1846	⎫	37,511	924
1859	⎬ Serbia		1,084
1866	⎮		1,218
1874	⎭		1,353

Sources: 1815–74, Stipetić, 'Stanovništvo uže Srbije', pp. 226–53; *Stanovništvo NR Srbije,* pp. 3–13. For earlier figures, see text p. 16.

persons,[61] (from within a wider area than the *pašaluk* itself), so the 176,000 figure (based on McGowan) looks more appropriate for 1788 than the 120,000 – 150,000 figure for 1790. Population continued to grow between 1834 and 1846 at 2.2 per cent per annum, after which growth decelerated to 1.4 per cent per annum up to 1874. We assemble our best estimates for Serbia's population 1718 to 1874 in Table 1.6.

Greece (and the Ionian islands) and Dalmatia are peripheral to our study, and population figures are included primarily to round out the analysis of Balkan population. Enumeration data, as reproduced in secondary works, are presented below as Table 1.7.[62] The Ionian islands were under British administration till ceded to Greece in 1864. Greece acquired no territory in 1878, but Thessaly, previously under Ottoman rule with a population of 294,000, was awarded to Greece in 1881.[63] For

---

[61] Stipetić, 'Stanovništvo uže Srbije', p. 241.

[62] The first solid Greek census was conducted in 1834. Comparison with previous counts in 1821 and 1828 shows a fall ascribed to excess mortality and emigration, caused by wars, Todorov, *Balkan City,* pp. 327–8. Felix-Beaujour, in *Tableau du commerce de la Grèce formé d'après une année moyenne, depuis 1787 jusqu'en 1797* (Paris, 1800), pp. 22–3 had estimated the population at 520,000 in 1797, a figure we have adjusted to 634,000 to allow for the Cyclades. For the Ionian islands the earliest population figure, said to relate to 1807–15, is of 193,720 (*Encyclopaedia Britannica* 7th edn, 1842). Bory de Saint Vincent, in his *Histoire et description des Iles Ioniennes* (Paris, 1823), pp. 324, 350, 352, 364, 368, 375, 381, 386, 391 indicated a population of 179,000. Returns for 1836 showed a population of 204,242, and for 1850, of 225,736 see GBC Ionia 1851, p. 172; *Encyclopaedia Britannica,* 8th edn (1856). Back extrapolation suggests that Saint Vincent's figures relate to about 1818 and that the 1807–15 estimate is probably too high. Back projection to 1800 would indicate a population of about 158,000, the figure adopted in Table 1.9.

[63] A. Andreades, *Les progrés économiques de la Grèce* (Paris, 1919), p. 8.

Table 1.7 *Population of Greece 1797–1907*

Year	Area (km²)	GREECE	Populations	IONIA
1797	?	634,000		–
1807–15				193,720
1818				179,000
1821	?	938,765		–
1828	?	753,400		–
1834		651,233		–
1836				204,242
1839		823,773		–
1842		853,005		–
1845		960,236		–
1848		986,731		–
1850	48,976			225,736
1851				226,698
1853		1,035,527		–
1856		1,062,627		–
1860				232,426
1861		1,096,810		–
1870	51,321		1,457,894	
1879			1,679,470	
1889	64,641		2,187,208	
1896			2,433,806	
1907	64,296		2,631,952	

Sources: Greece 1821, 1828, 1839–79: Todorov, *Balkan City,* pp. 328–9; for 1834 and 1889–1907 land areas, see Andreades, *Grèce,* p. 7. In 1797, the population of mainland Greece was estimated at 520,000, see Félix-Beaujour, *Tableau,* pp. 22–3. In 1821 mainland population was estimated at 769, 465, and islands at 169,300 (Todorov, *Balkan City,* p. 328), so the 1797 figure is prorated accordingly.

Ionian islands 1807–15 estimate: *Encyclopaedia Britannica,* 7th edn (1842); 1818 estimate: Saint Vincent, *Iles Ioniennes,* pp. 334, 350, 352, 364, 368, 375, 381, 386, 391; 1836 population returns: *Encyclopaedia Britannica,* 8th edn (1856); 1850 and 1851 population returns, in GBC Ionia 1851, p. 172. Population in 1860: *Statesman's Yearbook,* 1865, p. 297.

Table 1.8 *Population of Dalmatia 1771–1869*

1771	223,765
1798	256,902
1808	256,864
1814	299,501
1837	382,285
1848	417,110
1857	405,514
1862	432,945
1869	442,796

Sources: 1771–1808: I. Erceg, 'Stanovništvo Dalmacije na prijelazu iz 18 u 19 st.', p. 25; 1814, 1848, 1869: Jakšić, 'Nestajanje srbskoga naroda u Ugarskoj', p. 138; 1857–62: Austria. *Statistisches Jahrbuch 1863.*

Dalmatia, administered by the relatively strong Austrian bureaucracy, we have reasonably solid figures extending into the eighteenth century. These are displayed as Table 1.8.

Balkan population and population density

The population estimates discussed above, when combined with more reliable census material for Bosnia, Bulgaria, Austria, Serbia and Greece for 1879 onwards, enable us to present a long-run overview of Balkan population trends, in panel (1) of Table 1.9 below. The second panel expresses these figures in terms of population density, to give a clearer (though still imperfect) view of underlying trends in this area of frequently shifting frontiers.

Over the 120 year period 1790–1910, the population of the Balkans expanded at 0.97 per cent per annum. Growth in Ottoman Europe was slower at a mean 0.80 per cent. After slow growth at around 0.5 per cent per annum until the 1820s, Balkan population grew till mid-century at around 1.3 per cent per annum. These indications depend on the rightness of our estimates for Ottoman population growth, because as late as 1870 the Ottoman lands accounted for 71.3 per cent of the population of the definitional area. From mid-century to 1880, growth probably decelerated to 0.9 per cent per annum for the Balkans as a whole, the slowdown resulting mainly from a fall to 0.7 per cent per annum for the Ottoman lands. Subsequently, between 1880 and 1910, Serbia experienced very rapid population growth at 1.63 per cent per annum, Bosnia, 1.58, and Bulgaria 1.37 per cent. These rates of population growth are

Table 1.9 Balkan population and population density 1790–1910

(1) Population of the Balkans c. 1790–1910

Year	Serbia	Montenegro	Ionian Islands	Greece	Bosnia	Bulgaria	E. Rumelia	Dalmatia	Total	Turkey	Balkans
1790	177ᵃ	28	153					247	428	5,157	5,585
1800	183	29	158	634				257	444	5,294	5,738
1810	189	30	169					270	469	5,434	5,903
1820	369	38	182	939	720			319	908	5,511	6,419
1830	455	43	195	718				355	1,766	5,560	7,326
1840	805	48	210	850				391	2,304	6,075	8,379
1850	971	54	226	1,009	1,100			415	2,675	6,880	9,555
1860	1,102	62	232	1,090	1,220			422	2,905	7,520	10,428
1870	1,284	69		1,458	1,260	2,022	747	459	3,270	8,130	11,400
1880	1,803	145		1,706	1,186	2,008	816	476	8,140	4,437	12,577
1890	2,185	167		2,221	1,447	3,247		518	9,785	4,341	14,126
1900	2,529	186		2,504	1,671	3,744		585	11,219	4,680	15,899
1910	2,922	212		2,689	1,898	4,338		637	12,696	5,176	17,872

(2) Density of Balkan population c. 1790–1910 (persons per km²)

Year	Serbia	Montenegro	Ionian Islands	Greece	Bosnia	Bulgaria	E. Rumelia	Dalmatia	Turkey	Balkans
1790	–			–	–			19.3	12.1	12.5
1800	–		67.4	–				20.0	12.4	12.9
1810	–		72.1	–				21.0	12.8	13.2
1820	15.1		77.6	19.2	11.7			24.9	13.7	14.4
1830	18.6		83.2	14.7				27.7	15.8	16.4
1840	21.5		89.6	17.4				30.5	17.9	18.8
1850	25.9		96.4	20.6	17.9			32.3	20.3	21.4
1860	29.4	12.0	98.9	22.3	19.9			32.9	22.2	23.4
1870	34.2	13.4		28.4	20.1	33.2	20.8	35.8	24.0	25.6
1880	37.3	–		33.2	23.2	32.9	22.7	37.1	25.1	28.2
1890	45.2	19.4		34.4	28.3	34.1		40.4	26.3	31.7
1900	52.4	21.6		38.9	32.6	39.3		45.6	28.3	35.7
1910	60.5	24.6		41.8	37.1	45.6		49.6	31.3	40.1

Note:

[a] Italicized figures are for areas while still under Ottoman rule, and are included in totals for Turkey.

Sources: Ottoman Europe: Tables 1.3 and 1.4.

Serbia: 1790–1810 Belgrade *pašaluk* only; 1820–70: Table 1.6; 1880: extrapolated from censuses of 1890 and 1884, for 1884 census see *Državopis*, XVI, pp. i–xliii; 1890–1910: *Prethodni rezultati popisa stanovništva i domaće stoke u Kr. Srbiji 31 Dek 1910 godine*, p. 4.

Montenegro, from Table 1.5.

Greece and Ionian Islands, from Table 1.7.

Bosnia: figures for 1820 and 1850–70 represent population of Bosnia, as estimated from McGowan's *cizye* figure of 1815 and from Table 1.3 above. Pejanović reduces his figure for Ottoman Bosnia in 1876 by 16.6 per cent to make it comparable to census figures for the area under Austrian occupation between 1878 and 1918. The density figures for the Ottoman period in panel 2 have been estimated by making the same assumption. For population 1879–1918 see Pejanović, *Stanovništvo Bosne*, Table 1.

Northern Bulgaria (Danube vilayet less Tulçea sanjak plus Sofia sanjak) and Eastern Rumelia (Plovdiv and Sliven sanjaks) in about 1875: Ubicini, 'L'Empire Ottoman', pp. 106–9; figures adjusted for female population and under-recording as in text above (p. xxx). Bulgaria 1880–1910: *SGBTs*, III (1911), p. 21.

E. Rumelia 1880: Statelova, *Iztochna Rumelija*, p. 14.

Dalmatia: Table 1.8 and *Österreichisches Statistisches Handbuch 1913*, pp. 4–5. Land areas in km[2].

Greece pre-1864: 48,976, 1864–81: 51,321, 1881–97: 64,641; 1897–1912: 64,296. Andreades, *Grèce*, p. 7.

Ionian islands: 2,345. Andreades, *Grèce*, p. 7.

Montenegro 1859–76: 5,150. Pejović, *Iseljavanja crnogoraca*, p. 247; 1881–1912: 8,629, Cvetić, 'Površina, i granična linija Crne Gore', pp. 483–5.

Bosnia: 51,200. *Rezultati popisa žiteljstva u Bosni i Hercegovini od 10 Okt 1910*, p. xxv.

Dalmatia: 12,830, *Österreichisches Statistisches Handbuch*, 1913, p. 1.

Serbia to 1833: 24,440; 1833–78: 37,511; 1878–1912: 48,303, Statelova, *Iztochna Rumelija*, p. 14 (subsequently 34,261 km[2] as in 1886 K'rdzhali *okolija*, 1,640 km[2], was ceded to the Ottomans), *SGBTs*, 1911, p. 1.

Eastern Rumelia 1878–85: 35,901, Statelova, *Iztochna Rumelija*, p. 14 (subsequently 34,261 km[2] as in 1886 K'rdzhali *okolija*, 1,640 km[2], was ceded to Romania in 1878. Balkan area as a whole was 445,698 km[2].)

Bulgaria, 1886–1912: 95,223. *SGBTs*, 1911, p. 6. Therefore, between 1879 and 1885, its land area, excluding Eastern Rumelia, was 60,962 km[2].

Ottoman Europe: calculated by adjusting backward through accessions and losses of the Balkan states and Bosnia-Hercegovina, from the 1897–1912 figure of 165,353 km[2] in *Statesmans Yearbook*, 1904, p. 1195. Thus area in 1885–97: 165,008; 1881–85: 163,368; 1878–81: 176,688; 1833–78: 338,941; 1827–33: 352,012; 1815–27: 400,988; 1790–1815: 425,292. (This does not include the area of Tulçea sanjak ceded to Romania in 1878. Balkan area as a whole was 445,698 km[2].)

claimed as the fastest ever recorded in Europe.[64] However, population growth in the Balkan area as a whole was less rapid, because of relatively slow growth in Greece, Dalmatia and Montenegro, all of which were affected by heavy external migration, while the annual growth rate in the Ottoman lands recovered only to 0.7 per cent.

Balkan population densities in the early nineteenth century were extremely low. In 1830, only coastal and island areas supported densities in excess of 20 persons per km^2. Leaving these aside, let us look at what low population density implied for Serbia, with 18.6 persons per km^2, slightly above the Balkan average. In 1840, population density was around 36 per cent of that of France.[65] Conditions in 1835 were vividly if briefly described by the author of *Eothen*. On leaving Belgrade, he rode 100 miles through 'the great Servian forest' – the *Šumadija* – a silent wilderness of virgin oak, whose inhabitants lived in occasional hamlets, such as one in which he passed a night, consisting of 'a dozen clay huts, standing upon a small tract of ground hardly won from the forest'.[66] Analogous comments concerning desolation and the underutilization of fertile plains were commonplace among contemporary writers on most Balkan territories; even on the fertile north coast of the Aegean, wild horses roamed and grazed unhindered.[67] Certain areas, often uplands, were more densely populated (at least in relation to their endowment of fertile land) but taken as a whole, the Balkans in the early nineteenth century were endowed with generous reserves of uncultivated waste. Small wonder then that the Ottoman state and the government of Serbia both pursued energetic immigration policies, providing settlers with land grants, tax holidays and promises of religious tolerance.[68]

The density of Balkan settlement in the early nineteenth century was too low to permit an efficient division of labour in utilizing the natural endowment. Communications varied from the bad to the non-existent but their low utilization provided little incentive to improve them. Under these circumstances, peasants engaged in subsistence farming, and procured cash through the sale of livestock. This could be raised cheaply on open pasture and extensive pastoralism corresponded best with their resource endowment. The heavy costs of moving even livestock to distant markets, and of bringing in exchange goods on a petty scale imposed

[64] Marvin R. Jackson, 'Comparing the Balkan Demographic Experience, 1860 to 1970', *JEEcH*, XIV (1985), p. 223.

[65] Georges Castellan, *La vie quotidienne en Serbie au seuil de l'indépendance, 1815–1839* (Paris, 1967), p. 94.   [66] Alexander Kinglake, *Eothen* (Icon, London, 1963), pp. 26–7.

[67] Georgi Chichovski, *Srednorodopski problemi* (Asenovgrad, 1935), p. 14.

[68] Karpat, *Ottoman Population*, p. 62.

unfavourable terms of trade on producers. Therefore peasants avoided raising crops for surplus, because of the problems of disposal.

However, the resulting low level equilibrium could be modified by superimposing institutional constraints upon the relationship between land and its population, causing the balance of activity to shift towards cereal production for the market, and cottage manufacturing. In Chapter 2, I shall argue that institutional intervention under Ottoman administration raised the level of specialization and the volume of market transactions above its equilibrium level, and, as a result, enhanced the productivity of the labour force.

The growth in the density of settlement during the nineteenth century would have similar effects, as empty spaces were filled by the expansion of existing holdings and the creation of new ones. This curtailed the extensive livestock economy, and forced farmers to replace a declining income from livestock with enhanced earnings from arable agriculture. The increasing subdivision of holdings in the more congested areas would shift labour increasingly into proto-industries. It would also make worth while the improvement of communications (by road-building and river navigation).

Of all the Balkan territories, it was in Serbia that the density of settlement grew the most rapidly (at 1.55 per cent per annum between 1820 and 1910). By the 1880s, the former forested wilderness of the Šumadija had vanished. It had become an agricultural area, which attracted inward migration on account of its fertile soil and improved communications. By the beginning of the twentieth century, when population densities in Bulgaria and Serbia had risen to above 40 persons per km^2, more intensive and market orientated forms of agriculture began belatedly to offset the dwindling resource of marginal land. Assisted by the growth of the domestic market, and in some degree by protection, modernized manufacturing industry began to expand with surprising rapidity.

The pace of population growth in the Balkans was high even by the demanding standards of nineteenth-century Europe. Balkan population growth during 1810–60 averaged 1.14 per cent per annum, and between 1860 and 1910 averaged 1.08 per cent. A full investigation of the causes of this growth lies outside the ambit of this study, but it was powered (at least in the latter years of the period) by an extraordinarily high birth rate, of over 40 per 1,000, (well above the 30 per 1,000 rate characteristic of pre-industrial Europe). This was a response to the facility with which marginal land could be brought under the plough, and the produce disposed of on international markets.[69] For Serbia, at least, a contribution

[69] Jackson, 'Balkan Demographic Experience', pp. 223–4.

was also made by an equally rapidly falling trend in mortality between 1862 and 1910.[70]

Even earlier in the century, the acceleration of population growth from the 1820s may have been caused by improving mortality trends. One after another, epidemic diseases abated in their ferocity, in some measure through the improvement of administration. Our evidence on this point relates mainly to Serbia, and insofar as population trends in the Ottoman lands were less favourable, they may reflect the lesser effectiveness of Ottoman organs in the field of public health.

Along with epidemic disease, famine took its toll of lives, at least in more isolated areas. Nevertheless, at least in Serbia, famine probably diminished from the 1830s onwards. Under Miloš's first government (1815–38) the Serbian state established a system of communal maize granaries. This technique was borrowed from Hungary, and was not applied in the Ottoman provinces. Each *opština* (local authority) compulsorily had to maintain granaries, which were opened in time of dearth.[71] Contemporary observers believed this system to operate effectively,[72] and it had an important role to play in Serbia, because bad communications hindered the circulation of grain between areas of surplus and deficit. It may account in part for the greater population growth of Serbia relative to that of other Balkan territories. The system was not readily exportable to the Ottoman provinces, because maize was the staple foodstuff of Serbia, and was much easier to store on a small scale than the bread-grains which predominated elsewhere. A negative insight into the (potential) efficacy of the communal granary system may be gained from a report of 1880 from Niš, the largest town in Serbia's annexed territory of 1878. Before the opening of the railway (which reached Niš in 1884) bad communications rendered prices too low for peasants of the fertile plains round Niš to raise grain for surplus, and the communal granary system had yet to be established there. In the aftermath of drought, a bad maize harvest caused acute distress, because there were no reserves. The state sought to relieve the people by buying in and distributing emergency supplies.[73] Subsequently the communal granary system was extended to the annexed territories, and proved its worth as late as 1909 when the opening of the communal granaries in the Niš district 'saved many from dying of hunger'.[74]

[70] Ibid., p. 269.   [71] Ami Boué, *La Turquie d'Europe* (Paris, 1840), III, pp. 38–9.

[72] J. Mallat, *La Serbie contemporaine* (Paris, 1902) II, pp. 15n, 142–3.

[73] PRO FO 105 14. No. 15 comm. 16 Jan. 1880.

[74] *Izveštaji podneseni Ministru narodne privrede o radu na unapredjenju domaće privrede za god. 1908 i 1909,... i merama za dalji rad u tome pravcu* (Belgrade, 1911), p. 1011.

Urban and rural population

Up to 1914, the Balkans had that great rural preponderance of settlement which was the hallmark of under development. In the Ottoman successor states, urban population grew rather more rapidly than total population, though from a low base level. Yet this process was slow and discontinuous, and in the territories which remained under Ottoman rule till 1913, it is doubtful whether there was any urbanization at all. In Table 1.10, we have disaggregated urbanization in the Balkans as far as possible according to territory, though the paucity of reliable and comprehensive figures before the 1860s means discussion of the earlier nineteenth century must be couched in qualitative terms. For the purpose of this section the urban sector is limited to towns of 2,000 inhabitants and over (for Montenegro, 1,000 and over).

In the Ottoman provinces the urban population was relatively large in relation to the general level of economic development. Take Macedonia in the 1880s and 1890s, where towns accounted for 27 per cent of population. The same proportion of population dwelt in towns in the Ottoman administered districts which were annexed by Montenegro in 1878–81. Elsewhere in the Ottoman Balkans, in Bosnia and Bulgaria in the 1860s, the urban proportion was in the 15–18 per cent range, and was probably higher in Eastern Rumelia. At the lower end of the Ottoman urbanization range, the *pašaluk* of Niš (annexed by Serbia in 1878) contained in about 1868 five substantial towns with 47,600 inhabitants.[75] As the population of the *pašaluk* in 1868 included 154,935 males[76] (implying a population of about 300,000) the urban proportion in this territory was around 15.9 per cent.

Independent Greece was urbanized to about the same extent, but unlike the Ottoman territories which were largely urbanized in the interior, most of the larger towns of Greece were seaports, reflecting the commercial orientation of this maritime state. By way of contrast, self-governing Serbia had 7–8 per cent of its population in towns, while Montenegro before 1878 functioned with a single town, the national capital, Cetinje. Only in 1847 had this town begun to form around the monastery from which the country was governed.[77]

The relatively high urbanization of Ottoman Europe in the 1880s was a phenomenon of long standing, rather than the product of nineteenth-century growth. Estimates for the size of towns in Ottoman Europe in the

[75] Obruchev, *Voenno-statisticheski sbornik na 1868 god.* in Michoff, V (1967), pp. 100–1.
[76] Karpat, *Ottoman Population*, p. 116.
[77] Dučić, *Književni radovi*, III, p. 25. It counted but 734 inhabitants in 1879. ACG MUD VII. 1.

Table 1.10 *Proportion of Balkan population living in towns of 2,000 or more inhabitants*

Year	Towns number	Towns population	Percentage of population
Northern Bulgaria			
1866	39	299,387	15.3–18.4
1880	45	344,799	17.2
1892	50	413,973	19.2
1900	53	482,754	18.3
1910	53	556,331	18.8
Eastern Rumelia			
1884	23	211,463	22.4
1892	24	234,066	23.7
1900	24	256,852	23.4
1910	25	269,484	21.7
Bosnia-Hercegovina			
1864	35	184,115	17.7
1879	30	133,424	11.5
1885	30	156,114	11.7
1895	38	206,295	13.2
1910	44	247,339	13.0
Serbia			
1834	7	27,509	4.1
1863	19	77,606	7.0
1874	22	113,871	8.4
1890	36	251,692	11.6
1900	39	299,189	12.0
1910	40	315,366	10.8
Montenegro			
1868	0	0	0
Ottoman Montenegro			
1870s	4	23,000	27.1
Montenegro			
1881	5	10,114	6.6
1887	5	12,012	7.4
1900	5	15,530	8.4
1911	5	18,907	8.9
Greece			
1853	23	160,687	15.5
1861	24	184,467	16.8
1879	32	310,902	18.5
1895 Salonica vilayet	30	324,946	27.9

Table 1.10 (cont.)

Year	Towns number	Towns population	Percentage of population
1894 Skopje vilayet	11	117,355	27.9
1888 Monastir vilayet	18	156,018	23.5
1888–95 Macedonia	59	598,319	26.6

Sources:

Northern Bulgaria, 1866: calculated from Todorov, Balkan City, pp. 345, 360. A small sample analysed by Todorov shows 956 females per 1,000 males. Where only male population is quoted, the appropriate 1.956 multiplier has been applied. In a few cases figures are for 1873. Some categories of male population are not included in the taxpayer list, and Todorov indicates that true population may have been 20 per cent above that indicated by the statistics (p. 344). This 20 per cent addition represents the upper end of the range tabulated. Population of towns in Bulgaria and Eastern Rumelia 1880–1900 is tabulated in SGBTs, I, 1909, pp. 22–4. 1910: SGBTs, III, 1911, pp. 30–3.

Bosnia-Hercegovina, 1864. The figure includes only territories within this province after occupation by Austria-Hungary. Towns of Nikšić, Novi Pazar, Nova Varoš, Plevlje and Prijepolje are omitted. According to Pejanović, of Bosnia's population in 1876, 83.38 per cent fell to the territory subsequently annexed by Austria-Hungary. Town population of 184,115 is expressed as a percentage of our estimate of 1864 population reduced pro rata. 1860s: Johann Roškiewicz, Studien über Bosnien und die Hercegovina (Leipzig, 1868) pp. 96–126; Thömmel, Beschreibung, pp. 119–34. We have taken the mean figure given by these sources where they differ. 1879: Ortschafts-Bevölkerungs-Statistik von Bosnien und Hercegovina (Sarajevo, 1880); 1885: Ortschafts- und Bevölkerungs-Statistik von Bosnien und der Hercegovina ... 1 Mai 1885 (Sarajevo, 1886); 1895: Civil population – Glavni rezultati popisa žiteljstva u Bosni i Hercegovini ot Aprila 1895 ... (Sarajevo, 1896). 1910: Civil population – Rezultati popisa žiteljstva u Bosni i Hercegovini od 10 Okt 1910 (Sarajevo, 1912).

Greece: Todorov, Balkan City, p. 335.

Macedonia 1888–95: Communities of 2000 or more listed in bold print in Vasil K'nchov, Izbrani proizvedenija (Sofia, 1970), II, pp. 440–581.

Serbia 1834 and 1863: Stanovništvo NR Srbije, p. 54; 1874: Državopis, X, pp. 1–153. 1900: SGKS, 1904; 1910: (permanently resident population) Prethodni rezultati popisa Stanovništva i domače stoke u Kr. Srbiji 31 Dek 1910 godine (Belgrade, 1911), pp. 74–5.

Montenegro. See Palairet, 'Stagnation in Montenegro', p. 20.

earlier part of the nineteenth century are of varying accuracy, but they suggest that, if anything, towns were expanding less rapidly than the population of their hinterlands. Chaumette's figures for the urban and total population of Bosnia in 1808 imply an urban proportion of 13.5 per cent (when neighbouring Serbia was probably 5 per cent or less urban).[78] In northern Bulgaria, 11 towns with a census population of about 103,000 in 1866 were estimated by Boué in the 1840s to have had 109,000 inhabitants.[79] If Boué is reliable, this would imply that in the 1840s over 21 per cent of the people of northern Bulgaria were urban dwellers. If population in the southwestern provinces of Ottoman Europe grew at a rate similar to that of the rest, then it roughly doubled in density between 1820 and 1910. At least one large town, Skopje, probably grew faster than this (from 10,000 – 15,000 in 1812–40, to 29,000 in 1898 and 47,000 in 1910)[80] but Salonica barely kept pace (with 60,000 inhabitants in 1807, 65,000 in 1840 and 118,000 in 1910),[81] Monastir, Prizren, Ohrid and Kastoria barely grew at all,[82] and Veles and Yanina seem to have been in outright decline.[83] So it seems likely that the established institutional and economic structure of Ottoman Europe produced significantly higher urbanization than that which pertained in the successor territories.

As the characteristically high urbanization of Ottoman Europe reflected institutional structure rather than economic complexity, the dissolution of Ottoman institutions by the successor states could cause rapid deurbanization. This process occurred in its most striking form in Serbia. In the eighteenth century, Ottoman Serbia was highly urbanized, but during the wars and the revolutionary upheaval of 1789–1815, the Serbian towns experienced a precipitous decline. In 1777, there were reportedly some 6,000 houses in Belgrade,[84] from which a population of 30,000 – 55,000 may be estimated. By about 1800, the town had shrunk to around 3,000 houses with 25,000 inhabitants,[85] and in 1834 the

[78] Stoianovich, 'L'économie balkanique', pp. 8–9. Both urban and total population may be exaggerated in this statistic.

[79] Ami Boué, *Recueil d'Itinéraires dans la Turquie d'Europe* (Vienna, 1854), I, pp. 91, 96, 97, 108, 109, 114, 117, 136, 289, 291, 298.

[80] Jovan Hadži-Vasiljević, *Skoplje i njegova okolina* (Belgrade, 1930), pp. 58–62; Dimit'r Iaranoff, *La Macédoine économique* (Sofia, 1931), p. 192.

[81] Dančo Zografski, *Razvitokot na kapitalističkite elementi vo Makedonija za vreme na Turskoto vladeenje* (Skopje, 1967), p. 201; Iaranoff, *Macédoine*, p. 189.

[82] Berissav Arsitch, *La vie économique de la Serbie du sud au XIXe siècle* (Paris, 1936), pp. 105, 115; Jovan Cvijić, *Osnove za geografiju i geologiju Makedonije i Stare Srbije* (Belgrade, 1911), III, pp. 1034–5, 1036.

[83] Arsitch, *Vie économique*, p. 112; Cvijić, *Osnove*, III, pp. 987–8.

[84] Srpska Akademija Nauka i Umetnosti (Odeljenje istorijskih nauka), *Istorija Beograda*, I, *Stari srednji i novi vek* (Belgrade, 1974), p. 653.

[85] Tihomir Djordjević, *Srbija pre sto godina* (Belgrade, 1946), p. 154.

number of houses had fallen further to 769.[86] Late-eighteenth-century Užice had 2,900 Muslim houses; this indicates a population of around 20,000, for when the last 3,834 Muslims were driven from the town in 1862, they vacated 550 houses.[87] Tihomir Djordević put the population of Užice in the late eighteenth century still higher, at 12,000 houses with about 60,000 inhabitants. By 1860, when Užice's population was 4,100, but still overwhelmingly Muslim, the effects of the town's decline were all too visible, the bazaars 'rotting and ruinous', and 'whole streets which stood here before the Servian revolution . . . turned into orchards'.[88] In 1863, after the expulsions, there remained in the town a population of some 2,490. Valjevo in the 1770s was also a substantial place with 3,000 Muslim and 200 Christian houses. At least 5 other towns had 200 – 500 houses each.[89] Given the low population density of Ottoman Serbia, a remarkably high proportion of its inhabitants were town dwellers. Belgrade *pašaluk* in the late eighteenth century had 376,000 Serbian and 40,000 – 50,000 Turkish inhabitants.[90] On this basis, the two largest towns alone would have accounted for 11–27 per cent of the population of the *pašaluk*. The urban proportion could have been higher still, for a number of smaller towns dwindled into villages on the departure of the Ottomans.[91]

The Serbian revolutions overturned the Ottoman institutional structure there so fundamentally as to make the existing town system redundant to the successor state. So it is worth questioning whether the annexations which followed the Russo-Turkish war of 1877–8 had a similar effect on the urban structure of territories which passed from Ottoman rule.

Such was unquestionably the case with Montenegro. The annexed districts had contained 4 towns which previously had about 23,000 inhabitants.[92] In 1881, the population of these towns was 9,114. As in Serbia, so also in Montenegro, urban depopulation was linked closely to the withdrawal or expulsion of the Muslims. In the late 1850s, 62.5 per cent of the 4,000 inhabitants of Bar had been Muslim, as were 70 per cent of the 6,600 inhabitants of Podgorica.[93] Annexation caused a haemorrhage of Muslim town dwellers whose land had been expropriated, or who feared

---

[86] Belgrade in 1834 had 9.1 inhabitants per house. *Istorija Beograda*, II, *Devetnaesti vek*, pp. 271, 274.   [87] S. Ignjić, *Užice i okolina* (Titovo Užice, 1967), pp. 8–9.

[88] A. A. Paton, *Researches on the Danube and the Adriatic* (London, 1862), I, pp. 76–7.

[89] Tihomir Djordjević, *Iz Srbije Kneza Miloša. Stanovništvo – naselja* (Belgrade, 1924), p. 277. Djordjević, *Srbija*, p. 155.

[90] Danica Milić, 'Ekonomski potencijal ustaničke Srbije', in *Istorijski značaj srpske revolucije 1804 godine* (Belgrade, 1983), pp. 163, 164.   [91] Djordjević, *Iz Srbije*, p. 300.

[92] Mirčeta Djurović, *Trgovački kapital u Crnoj gori u drugoj polovini XIX i početkom XX vijeka* (Cetinje, 1958), p. 109.   [93] Radusinović, *Stanovništvo Crne Gore*, pp. 134–5.

1. Montenegrins at the marketplace, Cetinje, Montenegro

maltreatment at the hands of the Montenegrins. Yet even those residents who remained in Montenegro's annexed towns were not, in the majority, Montenegrin. Bar, left with 1,823 inhabitants, was 30.9 per cent Muslim, and 24.6 per cent (Albanian) Catholic.[94] Podgorica, which lost 66 per cent of its inhabitants on annexation remained 86.6 per cent 'Turkish' in 1879.[95] There was no inrush of Montenegrins to take the places of those who had left. Right up to World War I, trades and commerce were 'the monopoly of Muslims and Albanian Catholics'.[96] Despite accumulating the trappings of a modern state, Montenegro's capital, Cetinje, probably had but 3,900 inhabitants in 1911.[97] In the same year, the urban population of the annexed area had recovered only to 15,000, still far short of the pre-annexation figure, despite the 84 per cent growth of national population since 1881.

De-urbanization may have occurred in Bosnia-Hercegovina after occupation by the Austrians. According to our estimates in Table 1.10, the urban proportion contracted from 17.7 per cent in the mid-1860s to 11.5 per cent in 1879. In particular, the population of Sarajevo purportedly diminished from 40,000 in the 1860s to 21,377 in 1879. The 1860s figures are not wholly reliable and the Austrian authorities, who had expected the city to have 45,000 inhabitants, attributed this downturn in part to exaggeration in the earlier estimate; but this did not exclude the probability of a significant real population loss.[98] As in Montenegro, there was a Muslim exodus from Bosnia, partly because of limitations on land rights, partly because of an abrupt decline in urban commerce. The incoming Austro-Hungarian administration soon employed five times the number of officials that the departed Ottomans had governed with,[99] but despite this, subsequent reurbanization was slight, and was concentrated mainly on Sarajevo, whose population grew to 51,919 by 1910.

Annexation of the *pašaluk* of Niš by Serbia caused little immediate diminution of the urban sector in this territory, although it was significantly larger than in the rest of the country. Here as elsewhere, there was a forced Muslim exodus, and the Muslims tended to be urban dwellers. Certainly they were the dominant ethnic group in Niš itself.[100] The Muslims who remained claimed that (an exaggerated) 150,000 of them had been chased from their homes and properties.[101] Partly in consequence, in 1879 the 5 substantial towns had diminished in population

[94] ACG MUD VII-2. 'Popis svega stanovništva . . . 1879.'
[95] ACG MUD VII-17. This document shows 575 'Turkish' and 89 'Christian' tax heads.
[96] 'Montenegrin Economics – I', *Montenegrin Bulletin*, no. 4–6 (1 Sept. 1918), p. 9.
[97] Palairet, 'Economic Stagnation', p. 20, Table 1.   [98] GBC Bosnia 1879, p. 298.
[99] Peter F. Sugar, *Industrialization of Bosnia-Hercegovina, 1878–1918* (Seattle, 1963), p. 29.
[100] Sevdelin Andrejević, *Ekonomski razvoj Niša od 1830 do 1946 godine* (Niš, 1970), p. 9.
[101] PRO FO 105 37. Protest by the Mussulmans of Servia, 24 Apr. 1882.

from their 1866 figure of 47,600 to 41,691. As the population of the territory as a whole was stable, the result was a fall in the urban proportion from 15.9 per cent to 13.9 per cent.[102] These towns quickly replaced their population losses, as settlers from the north flooded into the territory, but Serbia had difficulty in the longer term in providing an economic basis for its southern towns. While Serbia's urban population climbed 62.3 per cent between 1884 and 1910, the five towns of the south grew 24.7 per cent, or by much less than the growth of national population.[103]

The Bulgarian provinces probably retained the urban proportion inherited from Ottoman rule. The figures in Table 1.10 for Northern Bulgaria indicate that if there was any post-liberation decline it was small and speedily reversed. Eastern Rumelia may however have experienced some deurbanization. Figures for the pre-liberation period are fragmentary and unreliable. If we use More's figures for 1876 then no change in urban population occurred between then and 1884.[104] Other sets (relating to 1854–6 and 1871) do however show population falls. For the city of Plovdiv, a population of 26,670 is indicated in around 1875, while the census of 1880 disclosed 24,053,[105] and that of 1884, 33,442. Plovdiv, however, boomed as the capital of the newly constituted autonomous province, so its recovery may be unrepresentative. In the longer run, between 1884 and 1910, the urban proportion in this part of Bulgaria did decline. No such decline occurred in the former Danube vilayet, but that was largely thanks to the growth of Sofia.

We shall nevertheless argue that although they suffered no collapse of population, many of the towns of Bulgaria suffered an acute economic recession following the liberation, while others – above all, Sofia – expanded under the influence of the newly established state bureaucracy.[106] The same argument applies also to the towns in the annexed territories of Serbia. Niš, for example, became a seat of government, and as a key junction on the Trans-Balkan railway system after 1888, acquired new commercial functions, even though in the short run this failed to stimulate its commerce.[107] Leskovac was to flourish on the basis of a burgeoning textile industry rooted in the abundance of cheap labour in its environs. Taken as a whole, however, the towns of the region

---

[102] Excluding Vlasotinci as no population estimate was given for 1868. For 1879, see Milan Dj. Milićević, *Kraljevina Srbija. Novi Krajevi* (Belgrade, 1884), p. xvi.

[103] *SGKS* (1906), pp. 32, 34–5; *Prethodni rezultati popisa Stanovništva i domaće stoke u kr. Srbije 31 Dek 1910*, p. 76; *Stanovništvo N R Srbije od 1835–1953*, p. 54.

[104] On the basis of six major towns. R. J. More, *Under the Balkans* (London, 1872), p. 17.

[105] *Statisticheski svedenija na direktsijata na finantsiite na Istochna Rumelija*, p. 1.

[106] See John R. Lampe, 'Modernization and Social Structure: the Case of the pre-1914 Balkan Capitals', *Southeastern Europe*, V (1979), esp. pp. 25–7.

[107] PRO FO 105 79. No. 2 commercial of 3 Jan. 1889.

probably experienced a decline rather than a gain in activity. As in Bulgaria, this decline was associated with a shift towards agriculture by the urban population, and a run down of many long-established crafts, but it seldom led to outright population loss. In contrast to the case of Serbia in the early years of the century, the six decades of population growth since 1820 established a relatively high pressure on landed resources. This inhibited the flow back into the rural areas; moreover, the towns of Bulgaria and Serbia were less heavily Muslim than they had been earlier, and at least in Bulgaria, the Muslims, though not well treated, were not placed under such acute pressure to emigrate as they were in Montenegro.

2   The Balkans under the Ottomans 1800–1860s: institutional change and economic progress

In this chapter we examine the evolution of institutional structures and commercial trends in the Ottoman Balkans, especially in Bulgaria and Macedonia during the latter years of Ottoman rule. Far-reaching changes in the institutional environment facilitated economic expansion after about 1830. The scattered statistics for the period are drawn from sources which are pre-modern in type and not very reliable for interpreting aggregative trends, but the evidence affords grounds for an optimistic appraisal of economic performance. In the farming sector, the cultivated area appears to have expanded significantly more rapidly than population, as commerce in agricultural and livestock produce began to displace subsistence farming. Alongside this an upsurge of proto-industrial manufacturing made Bulgaria the industrial heartland of the Ottoman Empire.

We are not arguing that Ottoman institutions, as they emerged in the latter decades of Ottoman rule, had a consciously development-inducing role, or that the occasional exercises by the state in explicit interventionism were more constructive than they were harmful. The argument is that institutional collapse in the early years of the nineteenth century had stifled the interplay of market forces, but the replacement structure which subsequently emerged permitted economic progress within a market framework. Enterprise responded to a more favourable environment with remarkable vigour.

The breakdown of Ottoman feudalism c. 1700–1814

Ottoman government had long rested on a controlled feudal symbiosis between the Sublime Porte and the provincial elites. The feudatories, in origin, a military caste – were awarded the tenure for life of a fief (*spahiluk*) on which they were obliged to live. They were responsible for raising feudal levies in time of war, and for gathering a tithe on the crops and livestock within their fiefs on behalf of the Sultan. In return, a *spahija* exercised the right to grant leases on cultivable land within the *spahiluk*,

34

Map 1 The Balkans in the 1860s

from which he was allowed to collect feudal dues.[1] He could also maintain a small home farm or *chiflik* for his personal needs, amounting in
northern Bulgaria to 10–15 hectares of arable, and demand labour services to cultivate it from anybody who held a cultivation lease within his
spahiluk.[2] Despite numerous smaller perquisites owed by the peasant
population to the *spahija*, the system imposed a fairly shallow level of
exploitation upon the labour of the peasantry, and upon the usufruct of
the land. This was wholly intentional, as it limited the ability of the *spahija*
to command resources which might render him independent of the
Sultan.[3]

The Porte had devoted a large part of its revenue to the maintenance of
its army, including the corps of Janissaries, traditionally the elite fighting
arm of the Sultan. This arrangement not only increased the effectiveness
of the Ottoman state in its external wars, but also provided an instrument

[1] Michoff, II/1 (1943), p. 115.
[2] N. Konstantinov, 'Zemedelieto v B'lgarija predi osvobozhdenieto', *Sbornik na narodni
umotvorenija*, XXVI (1912), p. 27.
[3] Peter F. Sugar, *Southeastern Europe under Ottoman Rule, 1354–1804* (Seattle, 1977),
pp. 96–9.

for enforcing its hegemony over its feudatories. By the eighteenth century this system had fallen into manifest decay. The fiefs had become hereditary, and this in itself weakened the hold of the Porte over their holders. The Janissaries had themselves become a hereditary caste, and no longer provided the centre with a counter-balance against the centrifugal tendencies of the periphery. Yet they still drew salaries which bore heavily on the treasury. Moreover, the reward system of an expanding empire, that is the capacity of the crown to create new *spahiluks* on conquered territories, was no longer operative, for expansion had long since ceased.

The *spahijas* therefore tried to deepen the exploitation of their existing fiefs, by increasing the size of their *chifliks*, and correspondingly increased their demands on the peasantry for the labour services to cultivate them. They were not alone in this, for the acquisition of cultivating leases attracted a growing class of Muslim notables (*âyans*) who were intent on carving out *chifliks* of their own. The formal distinctions between the holding of fief and holding land in *chiflik* tenure became blurred among the more powerful Muslims, since there were few sanctions upon their dispositions. The *âyans* were men whose perquisites depended on their local power and prestige rather than on the delegated authority of the Porte. The Janissaries should certainly be included in their number.

Incentive to acquire *chifliks* was provided in the eighteenth century by the rising international demand for grain, tobacco, and later cotton, which made large-scale farming an attractive proposition, especially on the Danubian and Black Sea plains, in Thrace, and in the Vardar valley.[4] To facilitate their expropriations and defend their gains, many provincial *âyans* established private armies, or operated protection rackets, often with the assistance of the Albanian tribes. The Janissaries maintained their own gangs of *yamaks*, which operated in similar fashion, and represented a peculiarly disruptive element.[5] Most seriously from the point of view of central government, the *spahijas* increasingly treated the imperial tithes as their own perquisites, so in peripheral areas where central authority was least secure, the revenues to the Porte diminished, weakening its authority still further.

The breakdown of the old system of government accelerated during the period of campaigning against Austria and Russia between 1787 and 1792. These campaigns were not successful, and the Porte, lacking an effective centrally controlled army, came to depend increasingly on the efforts in the field of the *âyans* and their private armies. Lacking other means of enforcing their loyalty, the Porte had to buy their service with

---

[4] T. Stoianovich, 'Land Tenure and Related Sectors of the Balkan Economy', *JEcH*, XIII (1953), pp. 398–411.   [5] Sugar, *Southeastern Europe*, p. 242.

bribes, and to abstain from harassing *spahijas* over their failure to remit the tithe. The proliferation of private armies and hired gangs of brigands led to warlordism. Powerful *âyans* fought each other as they endeavoured to bring territories under their control,[6] while lands that lay beyond the sway of any powerful lord were swept time and again by armed gangs of marauders, the *k'rdzhalijas* and *da'alijas*, whose plundering and despoliations were to remain a serious problem for many years to come.[7]

Among the most successful of the *âyans* were Ali Pasha Tepeleni of Yanina (1788–1822) and his son Veli who ruled from Tirnavos in Thessaly, Pasvanoglu of Vidin (1799–1807) Karafeiz of Tr'n and his son Alibeg.[8] All these men established strong statelets of their own. They professed no loyalty to the Porte, save when it suited their purposes. Nevertheless, they alone possessed the capacity to protect the subject populations from the prevailing anarchy, and at best ruled as enlightened despots. Pasvanoglu ran Vidin and its environs as a prosperous ministate, though his forces and those of his *yamak* allies created mayhem in the surrounding provinces.[9] Edip Aga, *âyan* of Kjustendil, felt confident enough of his peasants to arm them, and successfully repulsed three *k'rdzhalija* armies.[10] Veli, son of Ali Pasha, was proud to administer what he regarded as an oasis of 'incipient civilization and security' in a desert of barbarism.[11]

Under his rule, industries flourished at T'rnavos and Ambelakia, especially the dyeing of cotton which had been raised on the *chifliks* round Seres, for export to central Europe.[12] Yet the stability that the greater *âyans* provided was transient, because the Porte was usually able with an effort to topple these potential successor states by the expedient of divide and rule, even though it was unable to govern the provinces after it had recovered them.[13] Indeed it was with the decline of warlord power that banditry became most intense.

The period of warlordism and banditry, whose intensity peaked early in the nineteenth century, is often referred to in the literature as the time of the *k'rdzhalijas*. It was associated with population shifts which were to become of profound significance in shaping the evolutionary path of the Balkan economy. Although some *âyans* might succeed in attracting

---

[6] Ami Boué, *La Turquie d'Europe* (Paris, 1840), III, pp. 182–3.

[7] Deena R. Sadat, 'Rumeli Ayanlari: the Eighteenth Century', *Journal of Modern History*, XLIV (1972), pp. 359–60.

[8] About whom see Konstantin Irechek, *Knjazhestvo B'lgarija* II (Plovdiv, 1899), pp. 515–16.   [9] Sugar, *Southeastern Europe*, p. 239.   [10] Irechek, *B'lgarija*, II, p. 562.

[11] [J. R. Jolliffe], *Narrative of an Excursion from Corfu to Smyrna...* (London, 1827), p. 80.

[12] M. R. Palairet, 'Désindustrialisation à la périphérie: études sur la région des Balkans au XIXe siècle', *Histoire, économie et société*, IV (1985), pp. 253–74.

[13] Sugar, *Southeastern Europe*, pp. 240–1.

immigrants to their territories, it was more usually the other way about. They needed to maximize their revenues, and therefore raised their exactions on the peasants, often taking over erstwhile free villages and converting them into *chifliks*. Alibeg of Tr'n simply enserfed the local population to work as labourers on his estates, and paid them in kind.[14]

Caught between the exactions of the *âyans* and the fear of marauding armies, the peasant populations tended to withdraw to remote areas, where the Ottoman presence was slightest. Most of these were uplands, which were unattractive for *chiflik* farming.[15] 'As a rule', says More, writing of southern Bulgaria, 'the villagers residing on the plains received harsher treatment at the hands of the government than those living in the mountains, the former being more accessible.'[16] In particular, there were a number of upland settlements which ranked as direct vassals of the Sultan, without the intermediary of any *spahija*, and enjoyed tax and other privileges as 'soldier' or 'pass-defender' villages. These settlements offered the subject population the best hope of security from arbitrary intervention by agents of the state.[17]

Even the privileged villages were not wholly secure, for neither *âyan* nor bandit concerned himself over their putative rights.[18] Despite this, they provided their residents with mutual self-defence. Most were plundered at least once by *k'rdzhalijas* but the peasants would escape to their *kolibi*, cabins in the mountains, to return when safe.[19] Besides this, the hills provided an adequate environment for stockraising and subsistence agriculture. The withdrawal of population into the hills, particularly during the seventeenth and eighteenth centuries, was not prompted solely by insecurity or oppression in the lowlands. When population density was low or falling and land abundant, the hills offered a more salubrious climate than the marshy lowlands, their soil was easier to clear, and supplies of water and timber more ample.[20] The produce of the hill economy was augmented by long-established domestic industries. It cannot be accidental that many of the liveliest later centres of industry in Bulgaria, including Panagjurishte, Koprivshtitsa, Kotel, Kalofer, Zheravna, Sliven,

[14] D. Ilkov, 'Grad Tr'n', *B'lgarska istoricheska biblioteka*, III (1930), p. 202.
[15] George W. Hoffman, 'Transformation of Rural Settlement in Bulgaria', *Geographical Review*, LIV (1964), p. 54.
[16] Robert J. More, *Under the Balkans. Notes of a Visit to the District of Philippopolis in 1876* (London, 1877), p. 245.   [17] Konstantinov, '*Zemedelieto*', p. 29.   [18] Ibid.
[19] Irechek, *B'lgarija*, II, p. 82.
[20] *Izveštaj o radu odeljenja za poljsku privredu i veterinarstvo* (Serbia. *Izveštaji podneseni ministru narodne privrede*, Belgrade, 1907), pp. 227–8; J. Hadži Vasiljević, *Južna Stara Srbija* II, *Preševska oblast* (Belgrade, 1913), pp. 89–90; W. S. Vucinich, *A Study in Social Survival: Katun in the Bileća Rudine* (Denver, CO, 1975), pp. 80, 116.

Chiprovtsi and Tr'n enjoyed (or claimed to enjoy) pass-defender, or 'soldier' privileges.[21]

Because of the shrinkage of the peasant population in the plains, the *âyans* lacked sufficient labour to cultivate their terrain; some went to the lengths of bringing in serf settlers to cultivate abandoned lands.[22] This shortage of labour provided money earning opportunities for the hill villages. They sent out migrants, usually bands of teenage girls, to harvest on the *chifliks*, which were desperately in need of their services. Consequently, the girls were usually well cared for, and protected in transit. Pre-agreed collective contracts were scrupulously observed. The work was hard, but the migration was surrounded by a carnival atmosphere, which led to sexual liaisons which were more or less tolerated.[23]

This expedient was of great advantage to the hill villages for the access it provided them to the usufruct of the plains, but despite the spread of the *chifliks*, plains agriculture remained restricted in extent. Huge tracts lay unworked both for want of labour, and because of the lack of security for the cultivator. In Thessaly after the fall of Veli Pasha, and as late as 1840, land was sold for a pittance. 'Anyone who can afford to watch and guard [the crop] may sow wherever he pleases, and when the time of the harvest comes he may reap it, if it has not been stolen before that.'[24] At about the same time, it was reckoned that only a fifth of the arable in Vidin province was being cultivated.[25] Parallel with this partial depopulation of the plains, hill agriculture, especially in central Bulgaria, became relatively intensive, since land was in short supply.[26] However, the prevailing want of commercial security constrained economic activity to a depressed level.

The worst of the disorders affected the western and central Balkans, including western Bulgaria, while the Bulgarian lands nearer to the centre of Ottoman power enjoyed relative stability. Even so, no area was immune to visitation by *k'rdzhalijas* or the passage of armies. Sofia was sacked and plundered by Alibeg of Tr'n as late as 1832.[27] Furthermore, banditry was not confined to *k'rdzhalija* gangs: a Russian traveller of 1829 warned that the Christian Bulgars of the uplands were 'ferocious brigands . . . who rob and mutilate their victims'.[28]

---

[21] Konstantin Irechek, 'P'tni belezhki za Srednja gora i za Rodopskite planine', *PS*, IX (1884), pp. 13, 14, 24; Ilkov, 'Tr'n', p. 204.   [22] Stoianovich, 'Land Tenure', p. 402.
[23] D. Usta-Genchov, 'Zhetvarskite zadrugi niz T'rnovsko', *Sbornik za narodni umotvorenija nauka i knizhnina* (Sofia) VII (1892), pp. 485–94; E. M. Cousinery, *Voyage dans la Macédoine* (Paris, 1831), pp. 93–6.
[24] J. J. Best, *Excursions in Albania* (London, 1842), pp. 154–5.
[25] Michoff, II/2 (1953), p. 115.   [26] Michoff, III (1950), p. 159.
[27] Irechek, *B'lgarija*, II, p. 27.
[28] G. Eneholm, *Notice sur les villes au dela du Balkan occupées par les troupes russes pendant la glorieuse campagne de 1829* (St Petersburg, 1830), p. 48.

Even in the fertile plains of the Black Sea littoral, the bread basket of Constantinople, where the authority of the Porte was more effective, agriculture was at a low ebb. Here market production of cereals was depressed because of intervention by the authorities to hold the price of bread down in Constantinople,[29] and to secure supplies for the armed forces. Grain exports were forbidden, and military contractors exercised the right to pre-empt produce at prices which may have been as low as a quarter of those prevailing on the free market.[30]

It was a long time before the Porte was able to restore an efficient administration, and re-establish order over such parts of Europe as remained to it after the loss of Serbia and Greece. Stability, the suppression of banditry and warlordism, and the enforcement of property rights awaited the reassertion of central authority over the provinces. The initial efforts of the Porte at recovering its authority in the 1790s aimed at putting the clock back by restoring feudal discipline. This could not succeed. The provincial magnates could not be brought to heel, nor could the Janissaries be reconstituted as an efficient and loyal fighting force. What was needed was a strong central administrative apparatus to take over the civil functions of the feudatories, and a new standing army as a counterpoise to the territorial power of the *âyans*. Only gradually did the Porte flounder towards this system of enlightened absolutism.

During the reign of the unfortunate Sultan Selim III (1792–1808) the first serious efforts were made to bureaucratize Ottoman government and build a modern standing army. By allying itself with such *âyans* as recognized the need for reform, the Porte endeavoured to deal with its internal enemies, even while fighting external wars. Unfortunately, Selim's new army, the Nizam-el-cedid, was not conspicuously successful in the field, and his apparatus was continually threatened by the implacable hostility of the Janissaries. The fundamental cause of his failure lay however in the inadequacies of the revenues, now largely pre-empted by the *spahijas*. The resulting imbalance between fiscal resources and spending needs led to the debasement of the currency, a short-term expedient which only worsened the situation, because much of the revenue was levied as specific taxes whose real value declined as prices rose. Selim was overthrown by the Janissaries in 1807 and was murdered, but a counter-stroke in 1808 by his ally, Mustafa Pasha the Standard Bearer, saved the regime, and under Selim's cousin Mahmud II (1808–38) the impetus for reform was resumed.[31] Little could

---

[29] Boué, *Turquie*, III, pp. 126–7.

[30] Ibid., p. 245; George Keppel, *Narrative of a Journey across the Balkan by the Two Passes of Selimno and Pravadi* (London, 1831), I, pp. 268–9.

[31] Charles and Barbara Jelavich, *The Establishment of the Balkan National States* (Seattle, 1977), pp. 101–4.

be achieved while the Ottoman Empire was at war with Russia, but the Peace of Bucharest in 1814 released resources which were applied to internal pacification. Little by little, the Porte won back its authority. Pasvanoglu, and later Ali Pasha, were overthrown, and the reconstituted *nizam* began to prove more effective against internal enemies.

Ottoman reform and economic revitalization in Bulgaria 1826–1869

The decisive stroke came in June 1826, when, to forestall a Janissary revolt, the Janissary order and its Dervish allies were suppressed in a well executed bloodbath. This swung the balance of power in favour of the military and bureaucracy.[32] The way was now clear to deal with the *spahijas* and to repossess their revenue raising powers. Suppression of the *spahiluks* was achieved in 1832–4. The *spahijas* lost their fiefs, and their right (in theory at least) to demand labour services. The tithes reverted to the state. The *spahijas* were compensated belatedly and inadequately with government pensions for the loss of their tithes.[33] With this move, the Porte secured itself a revenue base more appropriate to the enforcement of enlightened absolutism, and emancipated itself from its feudal past. By 1840, it was able to collect its tithes in money through its own administrators.

The suppression of the *spahiluks* was a milestone, too, in the process of modernizing the structure of property rights. The *chifliks* remained untouched though their owners had to pay the tithe. They had no legal right to tied labour, since this flowed from the feudal privilege of *spahiluk*, but in practice, many treated their peasants as serfs. By decoupling rights in real estate to the notional service implied by fiefdom, the Porte tacitly acknowledged the existence of heritable private property, and created a need for the codification of civil law.

The centralization of power was strongly associated with the revival of commerce. The hold gained over provincial administration led to a serious effort to suppress banditry. This was not achieved overnight. Even by the time of the Bulgarian liberation, banditry had not been wholly rooted out,[34] but security of commerce markedly improved with the extinction of the *k'rdzhalija* armies, permitting internal trade and transport to expand. Berov's analysis of Balkan land freight costs provides an indicator for this development. Relative to the general index of prices, land freights, which had stood at 100 at the end of the sixteenth century

---

[32] L. S. Stavrianos, *The Balkans since 1453* (New York, 1961), pp. 302–3.
[33] Konstantinov, 'Zemedelieto', p. 30.   [34] Irechek, *B'lgarija*, II, p. 255.

and 110 at the end of the seventeenth, rose as internal security deteriorated, to 201 in 1787 and to 256 in 1813–26.[35] At those levels, they would
have discouraged specialization in all but luxury commodities, and it was
no accident that the success of Ambelakia in foreign trade in the early
nineteenth century was associated with the very high value of its red-dyed
cotton yarn.[36] But the freight index subsequently dropped precipitously
to 87 for the period 1843/76, and this opened up a whole new range of
commercial possibilities.

During the 1830s, Ottoman markets were easily accessible to foreign
trade, though subject to state interference. A further modest stimulus to
trade growth was given by the Anglo-Ottoman Treaty of Balta Liman of
1838, which removed the power of the authorities to impose restrictions
and removed the disincentive to crop production which had been caused
by the right of pre-emption.[37] The embargo on grain exports was lifted in
1840.[38] The effects of opening up trade with Western Europe are frequently misrepresented in the literature. Its earliest manifestation was a
trebling of British exports to the Ottoman Empire between 1835 and
1852. Ottoman imports were mainly of manufactures, while exports were
of raw silk and agricultural produce. Stavrianos argues that the effects on
the Ottoman Empire of opening up her trade were passive, since she ran a
huge bilateral payments gap on her trade with Britain, which only gradually diminished after 1845.[39] However, this trade gap with Britain arose
because Ottoman grain went to Italian and French rather than British
destinations, possibly because hard wheat was sought principally for
making pasta.[40] As a result, the Ottoman trade deficit with Britain was
largely offset by a surplus with France, of about 20 million francs a year
between 1847 and 1856.[41] Subsequently, between 1845 and 1864,
Ottoman exports to Britain rose to 3.8 times their former level.[42] Pamuk
has calculated an annual series for Ottoman exports, which confirms that
export growth broadly kept pace with that of imports, at least till 1853,

---

[35] Recalculated from data in table on p. 81 of Ljuben Berov, 'Transport Costs and Their
Role in Trade in the Balkan Lands in the 16th-19th Centuries', *Bulgarian Historical
Review* (1975).
[36] William M. Leake, *Travels in Northern Greece* (London, 1835), III, p. 387; Henry
Holland, *Travels in the Ionian Islands, Albania, Thessaly, Macedonia etc., during the Years
1812 and 1813* (London, 1815), pp. 324–7.
[37] See discussion in Sevket Pamuk, *The Ottoman Empire and European Capitalism
1820–1913* (Cambridge, 1987), pp. 20, 99.
[38] F. Kanitz, *La Bulgarie danubienne et le Balkan. Etudes de voyage, 1860–1880* (Paris, 1882),
p. 478.
[39] Stavrianos, *Balkans*, p. 320. As Turkey did not publish trade statistics, British statistics on
trade with Turkey were those usually cited by historians.
[40] Henry C. Barkley, *Between the Danube and the Black Sea* (London, 1876), p. 332.
[41] Xavier Heuschling, *L'Empire de Turquie* (Brussels, 1860), pp. 185–6.
[42] Stavrianos, *Balkans*, p. 320 for 1845; *Statesman's Yearbook*, 1869, p. 504 for 1864.

and that a residual small trade deficit was offset by tribute and rent payments from Egypt.[43] This commercial upsurge was heavily concentrated upon the European part of the Ottoman Empire. In per capita terms the European provinces generated 2.7 times as much export trade to Britain as the Asiatic. The relationship is similar for the import trade.[44]

The consequences were felt with especial force in Bulgaria. The export of corn from Bulgaria and Rumelia rose from 296,000 hl in 1840 to 1.6 million hl in 1848.[45] In 1847, 'astonishing progress' was reported in cultivation in Varna sanjak since the liberation of the export trade. 'Only six years ago,' it was claimed, 'the fruitful soil of Varna sanjak was largely deserted; already more than one third of the cultivable land is tilled.'[46] Another source, noting the conversion of 'hitherto sterile terrains' into 'fertile gardens', attributed the 'aura of prosperity' either to the reforms or to the improvement of security.[47] Both influences interacted, and the stimulus was all the stronger for that.

Foreign trade growth and the improvement in political security caused the hitherto problematic value of land to rise sharply. The response of the landlords to this opportunity was similar to that which had occurred during the trade expansion of the previous century. There was renewed speculation in land leases, attended as always by the seizure of free villages, and their transformation into *chifliks*. According to a survey article, there was a particularly intensive wave of new *chiflik* formation between 1839 and 1851.[48] However, there is little solid evidence that the *chifliks* increased as a proportion of the cultivated area in the course of the period 1800–78. According to Dimitrov, around 1800, *chifliks* covered 20 per cent of the cultivated area.[49] A study of nine villages near Plovdiv in 1844, where holdings were generally small, shows that land held by absentees comprised 17 per cent of the arable surface.[50]

For the early 1860s, *chiflik* land varied from 40 per cent of cultivated area in southwest Bulgaria (and Vardar Macedonia) to 22 per cent in

---

[43] Pamuk, *Ottoman Empire*, pp. 23, 149, 208, 214.

[44] Taking A. Ubicini, 'L'Empire ottoman, ses divisions administratives et sa population', *L'Economiste français* (28 July 1877), p. 108 for population, and *Statesman's Yearbook*, 1882, pp. 469–70 for exports from Turkey to Britain, 1871–6.

[45] A. Ubicini, *Letters on Turkey* (tr. Lady Easthope, London, 1856) I, p. 327.

[46] Michoff, II/1 (1943), pp. 116–17.   [47] Michoff, III (1950), p. 188.

[48] Dušan Berić, 'Problemi propadanja ekonomskog sistema osmanskog carstva u periodu 1848–1878', *IČ*, XXIX-XXX (1982–3), pp. 369–70.

[49] John R. Lampe and Marvin R. Jackson, *Balkan Economic History, 1500–1950* (Bloomington, IN, 1982), pp. 36–37.

[50] 'Large agricultural enterprises' however only totalled 8 out of 300 holdings surveyed. Averaging 10.5 hectares, they accounted for 8.2 per cent of the cultivated area. See Tevfik Güran, *Structure économique et sociale d'une région de campagne dans l'Empire ottoman vers le milieu du XIX-e siècle* (Sofia, 1979), p. 38 and Table 3.4, p. 69.

northeast Bulgaria and 10 per cent in the region of Sofia.[51] Berov's estimate of an overall 21–23 per cent for this period is probably reasonable. However, the *chiflik* was probably then at the peak of its significance, for a Russian survey made at the time of the liberation shows that in the 1860s *chifliks* accounted for substantially less than 20 per cent.[52] If Berov is correct in estimating that the area under crops doubled between the 1840s and 1860s,[53] then the *chifliks* too would have been expanding, but not necessarily any faster than agricultural property as a whole.

The *chifliks* were seldom large; for northeast Bulgaria, Berov treats farms which he estimates as of 13.8 hectares and upwards as falling into this category.[54] The main feature distinguishing these estates from the peasant holdings is that their holders did not work the land themselves. Normally they were cultivated entirely by hired labour, but were often leased out, sometimes to tenant farmers, sometimes to sharecroppers.

But a new form of property right, identified as *gospodarl'k* (lordship) now appeared. The erstwhile *spahijas* did not abandon their perquisites without a struggle. They remained powerful local bosses, and a frequent response to the loss of tithing rights was the levying of a double tithe – that is a tithe of one-ninth of what remained after the state tithe had been collected. This common situation is illustrated by a complaint by the peasants of Sharlintse village:[55]

The *spahija* is making our village into a *chiflik*, but it is not a *chiflik*, rather a village, as we can certify how our forefathers themselves broke in the Sultan's land and we built our own houses. The *spahija* has said that he is taking from us a tithe of a ninth part for the Sultan. But since then we have learned that this was a lie, and that the Sultan does not want two tithes.

Although this appeared to the peasants to transform their village into a *chiflik*, Hristov points out that this was an intermediate form of exploitation. Though the area of Bulgaria under *chiflik* land was fairly modest, the spread of *gospodarl'k* meant that large numbers of 'free' peasants were subjected to significant burdens in addition to the imperial tithe, of which the levy of the ninth, which was by no means ephemeral, was among the most important. As this rested on no defined or customary legal right, it was also understandably strongly resented.

The emergence of economic pluralism – a crucial step in the formation

[51] S. Draganova, *Berkovsko selo v navecherieto na Osvobozhdenieto* (Sofia, 1985), p. 30.

[52] Lampe and Jackson, *Balkan Economic History*, p. 135.

[53] Ljuben Berov, 'Ravnishte na ikonomichesko razvitie na b'lgarskite zemi po vreme na osvobozhdenieto', *Trudove na visshija ikonomicheski institut 'Karl Marks'*, I (1979), p. 20.

[54] Ibid., p. 49.

[55] Hristo Hristov, *Agrarnijat v'pros v B'lgarskata natsionalna revoljutsija* (Sofia, 1976), p. 112.

of an enterprise economy – required the creation of a legal code to regulate the property rights so created. This meant that it was also necessary to curtail the inequality in law between Muslim and non-Muslim subjects. The enthusiasm of the *âyans* for annexing cultivated or cultivable land may have been beneficial insofar as it was associated with the growing volume of commerce. However, as it was combined with a rising tithe revenue for the state, it also worsened the lot of the peasants, and diminished their security, resulting in a fresh round of uprisings. These attracted the attention of the Great Powers, who accordingly pressed the Porte for reforms to protect the Christian populations. They were pushing on an open door. The state had a strong interest in providing holdings for the peasants and in protecting their property rights, because peasant property was relatively easy to tax, while the *âyans* were adept at turning their estates into *vak'fs* – nominally religious endowments, in practice, tax shelters. Moreover, when uncultivated and untaxed *mirieh* land was allotted to peasants, it was valorized into tithe-bearing *mülk*. As early as 1830, a Black Sea village was settled by the state with Gabrovo and Trjavna region uplanders,[56] and attempts were also made by the state in 1851 to buy out lordly land for resale to the peasants.[57] However, Christian peasants needed more security in law for this process to be taken very far.

The Ottoman Empire entered the *Tanzimat* – the reform era – in November 1839 with the proclamation of the Imperial Rescript of Gülhane. This loosely worded document offered a broad pledge of equality of treatment between subjects, and a regulated system of taxation.[58] The *Tanzimat* – whose literal translation means perestroika – affirmed a principle of government without detailing a programme of legislation, and the application of *Tanzimat* principles was so gradual and uneven as to support the contention that the reforms were totally without effect. Opinions on this have been modified however. For example, the arbitrary confiscation of property fell into disuetude,[59] and servile tenure, which was theoretically abolished along with the *spahiluks*, disappeared in practice during the 1840s and 1850s. Where it survived, it took the form of debt peonage, which was by no means as harsh as it sounds (see below, pp.157–8).

The legal framework for landholding was only belatedly updated between 1858 and 1869. The new laws never quite accepted that *mülk* land, that is, cultivated land which paid the tithe, could be a fully

---

[56] Herbert Wilhelmy, *Hochbulgarien*, I, *Die ländlichen Siedlungen und die bauerlich Wirtschaft* (Kiel, 1935), p. 151.

[57] Berić, 'Problemi propadanja', p. 370; Stavrianos, *Balkans*, p. 276.

[58] Stavrianos, *Balkans*, p. 316.   [59] Ibid., p. 317.

negotiable asset, but they did at least specify inheritance rights upon it, and curtailed the abusive creation of *vak'fs*.[60] Christians won equal rights in the courts in 1840,[61] and did – over time – find it easier to defend them.

From mid-century onwards, land rights began to flow from Muslim hands, especially those of absentee landlords,[62] into the hands of Christian purchasers.[63] This tendency was encouraged by the authorities. In Danube vilayet (North Bulgaria) under the government of Midhat Pasha between 1864 and 1867 the reforms were put into practice especially energetically, and action was taken under his administration further to promote the resettlement of the lowlands.[64] Not only did the authorities try to resettle peasants on state lands, the peasants themselves entered the land market to buy out fragments of *chiflik* land. At Kazanl'k, high land prices prevailed, as Bulgarians bought out scraps of land in peripheral areas.[65] Similar trends were apparent throughout Thrace[66] and here and there the former pattern of landownership was entirely overturned. In Vranjska Pčinja the *begs* fell into such poverty that they forced their servants to buy them out, but at prices which were so low that they made rich men of the purchasers in the longer run.[67]

So why were the *chiflik* owners increasingly willing to sell up? Lampe and Jackson explain that the attractions of absentee landownership were diminished by the loss of associated labour services and tithing rights, and that studies of *chiflik* properties show that the returns on them were low.[68] By the 1860s, landowners were facing a tightening labour market, and a migrational drain on agricultural labour caused them considerable concern.[69] Judging from the behaviour of harvest wages, labour was becoming increasingly expensive.[70] The reason for this was probably exogeneous to the Bulgarian economic system, for the opening up of the international grain trade in the 1860s diverted migrant labour in large quantities across the Danube to Romania, where it was used highly productively in large-scale cereal agriculture.[71] This development tended to marginalize the returns to owners of less highly capitalized *chifliks*.

An important feature of the agrarian system, as it emerged in the last

---

[60] Hristov, *Agrarnijat v'pros*, p. 36.   [61] Stavrianos, *Balkans*, p. 317.
[62] Konstantinov, 'Zemedelieto', p. 21.   [63] Irechek, *B'lgarija*, II, p. 148.
[64] Wilhelmy, *Hochbulgarien*, I, p. 151.
[65] Aleksand'r Pavlov, 'Ikonomicheskoto razvitie i s'stojanie na gr. Kazanl'k', *Kazanl'k v minaloto i dnes* (Sofia) I (1912), pp. 282 and n. 2, 283.   [66] Irechek, *B'lgarija*, II, p. 148.
[67] Rista T. Nikolić, 'Vranjska Pčinja u slivu južne Morave. Antropogeografska Ispitivanja', *NSZ*, II (1903), p. 117.   [68] Lampe and Jackson, *Balkan Economic History*, p. 135.
[69] Margarita Todorova, 'Za polozhenieto na majstorite stroiteli ot Elensko prez 60–te godini na XIX v', *Muzei i pametnitsi na kulturata*, I (1965), pp. 23–4.
[70] Pet'r Tsonchev, *Iz stopanskoto minalo na Gabrovo* (Sofia, 1929), p. 42.
[71] *B'lgaro Rum'nski vr'zki i otnoshenija prez vekovete. Izsledvanija* I (XII–XIX v.) (Sofia, 1965), pp. 346, 356–7.

two decades of Ottoman rule, was that it placed high, but predictable, fiscal and rent demands upon most cultivators. After experimenting with the direct collection of the tithe by its own servants, the Porte turned to indirect collection, by auctioning the tithing rights out to tax-farmers. From the point of view of the fisc, this turned out to be more efficacious, because keen competition for tithe-leases constrained the costs of collection to 10.3 per cent of the revenue.[72] Consequently, the tithe farmers sought to increase the profitability of the business at the expense of the cultivator, and the literature represents *iltizam*, the tithe farming system, as yet another burden on the backs of the peasantry. This is probably incorrect. Although the new system was by no means free of abuse, the peasants had a fairly clear idea of what was rightfully due from them, and were adept at cheating the fisc even of this. Contrary to the traditional view that tax farming led to gross extortion, the extent of over-taxing was probably slight.[73]

The rate at which the imperial tithe was levied also increased to 12.5 per cent, probably in 1858, though there is some dispute about this.[74] So because of the existence of the *chifliks*, the system of *gospodarl'k* (the double tithe) and the exactions of government, cultivators in Ottoman Bulgaria had to surrender a significant proportion of their produce to non-producer interests. Rent payments on *chiflik* land to Muslim landlords accounted for about 11 per cent of total farm production, as landlords commanded about half the output of the 22 per cent of the cultivated area held as *chifliks*.[75] However, unless he farmed directly through a steward, the landlord would surrender the greater part of his share to the tenant. Güran's research shows that on leased properties, wages absorbed 50 per cent of net crop production, rent 13 per cent, while the remaining 37 per cent provided a return to the enterprise and capital of the tenant.[76] All landholders had to pay the tithe both on crop output (*dan'k*) and on small livestock, as well as certain property taxes. In 1844 taxes in the Plovdiv villages absorbed 18.4 per cent of their

---

[72] Consular figures for the 1867 Adrianople sheep tithe show the amount collected by the tithe farmers exceeded the amount turned over to the treasury by 10.3 per cent, Michoff, III (1950), p. 607.

[73] For the conventional view see Hristov, *Agrarnijat v'pros*, pp. 175–6 and Pamuk, *Ottoman Empire*, p. 89; the contrary view is put by Edmund Spencer, *Travels in European Turkey in 1850* (London, 1851), I, pp. 253–4 and Irwin T. Sanders, *Balkan Village* (Lexington, KY, 1949), pp. 64–5, 69. It receives endorsement from Slavka Draganova, 'De la production agricole, l'imposition fiscale et la différenciation sociale de la population paysanne en Bulgarie du nord-est durant les années 60–70 du XIXe siècle', *Bulgarian Historical Review* (1977), pp. 79–80.

[74] The tithe of one eighth may only have applied to Muslim villages, see Slavka Draganova, *Materiali za Dunavskija Vilaet* (Sofia, 1980), p.5.   [75] Berov, 'Ravnishte', pp. 45–50.

[76] Güran, *Structure économique*, p. 23.

Table 2.1 *Revenues and expenditures in Ottoman Bulgaria (£ Turk)*

Danube vilayet	1863	1864	1865	1866
Revenue	1,127,646	1,173,330	1,315,894	1,357,635
Expenditure	309,454	349,335	n.a.	n.a.
Plovdiv sanjak	1872	1874	1875	
Taxes and duties	466,605	580,820	798,487	
Expenses	n.d.	29,144	26,643	

revenue.[77] Peasants in the Berkovsko region were paying one seventh of their total incomes in taxes of various kinds,[78] though this may have reflected the relative weakness of the Ottomans in this part of Bulgaria. Taken overall, it is likely that 20–30 per cent of total farm output was used other than by the cultivator.

This was not oppressive by European standards of the day, but compared with Serbia and Montenegro it forced a high degree of monetization on the economy. This takes no account of the petty purchases of the peasants themselves. The cultivating peasants probably retained most of what they were left for subsistence consumption,[79] though this was not the case in the industrial villages.

A large proportion of both rents and taxes were remitted outside the territory, mainly to Constantinople. The landowners whose estates in the Burgas region were leased to the Brakalov firm were all residents of the capital.[80] This was commonly the case also in southern Bulgaria.[81] Similarly most of the tax revenues were also syphoned out of the provinces to the centre. Table 2.1 shows the provincial financial accounts (in £ Turk) for the Danube vilayet, according to the official gazette, and those of Plovdiv sanjak according to the vilayet yearbook and to More.[82] The balance, it appears, was remitted to Constantinople.

If, say, half the revenues of the estates and of the tithe farmers, and

[77] Ibid., p. 85.
[78] Slavka Draganova, 'Raspredelenie na pozemlennata sobstvenost v severozapadna B'lgarija v navecherieto na osvobozhdenieto', *Studia balcanica* (Sofia), XVII (1983), p. 164.
[79] M. R. Palairet, 'The Decline of the Old Balkan Woollen Industries, 1870–1914', *Vierteljahrschrift für Sozial- und Wirtschaftsgeschichte*, LXX (1983), p. 344 and sources thereto.   [80] Hristov, *Agrarnijat v'pros*, pp. 146, 148.
[81] More, *Under the Balkans*, p. 19.
[82] *Dunav*, III (1867) supplement to No. 161; *Salname* [Edirne] Defa 3, 1289, pp. 160–1; More, *Under the Balkans*, p. 20.

three-quarters of the tax revenue were remitted out of the provinces, then a sum approaching 20 per cent of farm product was being transferred to external recipients each year.

As part of what remained was self-consumed, these unilateral transfers represented a high proportion of Bulgaria's traded income. The transfers must have been discharged by running a corresponding surplus balance on visible trade. This characteristic of Bulgarian trade was noted by St Clair and Brophy, who reckoned that the territory generated a large export surplus, the positive balance being swallowed by expatriated profits.[83] More, estimating the export of the Philippopolis (Plovdiv) sanjak at £Turk. 1,034,000 in farm products and £436,000 in industrially processed commodities, reckoned imports to amount to only £520,000. If from this favourable balance of about £1,000,000 were deducted 'the tax the people have to pay, and the sums extorted by rapacious tax gatherers, tithe-farmers, zaptiehs etc., the actual sum left for the population will be very small indeed'.[84] To generate this export surplus in the teeth of poor communications, the domestic price level had to be low, as in fact it was.

Imperfect though they undoubtedly remained, Ottoman institutions of mid-century were a huge advance on those which had pertained in the time of the *k'rdzhalijas*. Moreover, the improved stability they created was felt in Bulgaria long before it had penetrated to the outlying provinces. Therefore the Bulgarian lands participated earlier and more fully in the post-1830 economic upswing than the Ottoman provinces in the western Balkans. A report of 1845 still bewailed the decline of agriculture, attributing it to the attraction of the towns, and to an 'apathy' inherited from a less secure era. However, this 'apathy' no longer weighed in Bulgaria and Rumelia, where the *Tanzimat* reforms were first applied.[85] Another observer noted how 'hitherto unfruitful and sterile terrains were converted into fertile gardens, since labour and the rural properties, hitherto oppressed by the abuses of fiscality were revived by just and equitable laws. . .'[86] Still, the process had far to go. According to consular observation, 'in the neighbourhood of the capital and the trading ports, the condition of the countryman is much better and more secure than in the more distant regions where the unbridled official arbitrariness finds a free unsupervised field for extortion and oppression of all kinds'.[87]

[83] S. G. B. St Clair and C. A. Brophy, *A Residence in Bulgaria* (London, 1869), p. 137; see also Michoff, III (1950), p. 347.   [84] More, *Under the Balkans*, pp. 18–19.
[85] Ubicini, *Letters*, I, pp. 326–7.   [86] Michoff, III (1950), p. 188.
[87] Michoff, II/1 (1943), p. 115.

Ottoman institutions and industrial renaissance.

Rural manufactures for long-range trade – that is to say *proto-industries* – usually developed in areas where a relatively dense population outstripped the supply of cultivable land, and turned to manufacturing for the market as a marginal source of income. The development of such industries is argued by protagonists of proto-industry theory to have been a critical step towards the emergence of a modern enterprise economy. The reasoning includes demographic considerations, and the growth of an industry-dependent labour force. Both points are well taken, but in this study, it is the concomitant vigorous expansion of the exchange-based economy and its associated institutions, and the formation of human capital which will receive the main emphasis. A less emphasized, but perhaps critical component of proto-industry theory, however, is its insistence that for proto-industrial income to comprise a significant part of total income, the industrial village needed access to the produce of adjacent areas where large-scale farming created regular and rising surpluses. These would be needed to offset the food deficiency which increasing labour specialization in manufacturing created.[88] This condition was well satisfied in Bulgaria and Macedonia by the migrant harvesting mechanism.

Even so, at first sight, the Bulgarian provinces were unpromising territory for proto-industrialization. Compared with Serbia, they were thinly populated. In 1870, northern Bulgaria had an estimated 30.9 inhabitants per km^2, Eastern Rumelia 26.7, whereas Serbia had 34.2. Were Bulgaria's population to have distributed itself according to the availability of cultivable land, it would, like that of Serbia, have orientated itself mainly to subsistence farming, especially if fiscal pressures to produce for the market had been mild. For despite its more dense population (together with an inferior land endowment, and steady immigration) the Serbian economy had virtually no labour engaged in industry, and abundant free land at the margin of cultivation.[89] By comparison, the even less densely populated Bulgarian lands exported perhaps 50,000 migrant workers each year[90] – despite which, they supported an active proto-industrial economy.

As we have already seen, the peasant population of Ottoman Europe in the early modern period had tended to recede into the hill areas, and this

[88] See 'Protoindustrialization: Theory and Reality. General Report', pp. 11, 12 of Eighth International Economic History Congress (Budapest, 1982), Section A 2.

[89] A. A. Paton, *Researches on the Danube and the Adriatic* (London, 1862), I, pp. 15–16.

[90] France. *Bulletin Consulaire* 1884 Bulgarie. L'agriculture et l'exploitation du sol en Bulgarie (Ruse, 10 Feb. 1884) p. 757.

tendency was strengthened between 1790 and the 1830s by the land annexing activities of the *âyans* and the depredations of the *k'rdzhalijas*. Thus one of the fundamental building blocks for proto-industrial development was put into place – concentrated peasant communities in hill areas with an inadequate supply of farmland. Moreover these communities had already been developing their industries in the eighteenth century, and a corresponding industrial culture, which Bulgarian historians associate with the 'early renaissance'.

During the *k'rdzhalija* period, access to market outlets was made difficult, and this depressed the internal trade in manufactures. The supply of seasonal labour to the estates was probably a more important means than industry of offsetting food deficits. Even so, certain upland townships did maintain a high volume of commerce, not so much within the Ottoman Empire as with Austria. This partly reflected Austria's long-running concern to expand her foreign trade with the southeast, and her resulting dependence on Balkan merchants as intermediaries.[91] The most spectacular fruit borne of this trade was the rise of the cotton processing industries of Ambelakia and Tirnavos in Thessaly, which reached their apogee during the period of the Continental Blockade. On a lower key, similar trades developed between Austria and the townships of the Balkans. For example, Kalofer township supplied Vienna at the beginning of the nineteenth century with Morocco leather ('Cordovans') and rose oil. The proto-industrial economy of Thessaly declined after 1810, partly because of market changes, but mainly because labour became free to take up land.[92] Like the commerce of Thessaly, that of Kalofer declined abruptly from 1814 onwards, partly because of economic instability in Austria, partly because of deteriorating transit conditions. The response of the Kalofer merchants to the breakdown of their trade link with Austria was much the same as that of the merchants of Thessaly – namely to pack up and resettle in some more promising trade centre, in this case Odessa. A similar movement took place from the ironworking town of Gabrovo.[93] The ensuing decline of manufacturing in Thessaly proved terminal or nearly so, but was less severe for Bulgaria. Kalofer's trade with Austria did gradually revive, though the underlying product base was changing. Despite this, its manufactures remained at a depressed level till the late 1830s.[94]

[91] Traian Stoianovich, 'The Conquering Balkan Orthodox Merchant', *JEcH*, XX (1960) pp. 260, 297–300.
[92] Palairet, 'Désindustrialization'; S. Petmezas, 'Patterns of protoindustrialization in the Ottoman Empire – the Case of Eastern Thessaly c.1750–1860', *JEEcH*, XIX (1990), pp. 597–601.   [93] Tsonchev, *Gabrovo*, p. 240.
[94] N. Nachov, *Kalofer v minaloto, 1707–1877* (Sofia, 1927), pp. 33–4.

Until the suppression of the Janissaries in 1826, the upland industrial communities would have found it difficult to penetrate deeply into the Ottoman home market because the Janissaries had protected the prerogatives of the urban guilds, but thereafter, the guilds came to lack the ability to restrict freedom of trade.[95] The opportunity this created for the upland industrial communities seems not to have been exploited immediately, but the 1840s marked a turning point for their manufacturing trades. They already had a population framework which favoured their specializing in industrial activity, and now insecurity was diminishing and commerce was rapidly opening up. The entrepreneurs of the upland townships exploited the potential of this favourable conjuncture. As we shall show, in Chapter 3, the flowering of the upland industries between about 1840 and 1877 was remarkably powerful, and was based primarily on the expanding Ottoman home market. The implications of institutional and commercial reform for the growth of industry in Ottoman Europe have been widely misunderstood, because the opening up of commerce had two mutually conflicting effects on the upland industries. On the one hand, hitherto sheltered trades had to compete with imports paying a low *ad valorem* tariff of 5 per cent, raised in 1861 to 8 per cent. Ottoman industries were also handicapped in competition with imports, save within their home provinces, by internal customs levies of 12 per cent (abolished in 1870) which goods brought in by foreign merchants did not have to pay. The disadvantages suffered under these arrangements were not so severe as they appear. Since domestically produced raw materials had to pay 12 per cent *ad valorem* on export, those industries which used local raw materials which were in surplus (most obviously wool) could obtain them at significantly below world market price. Even so, it is generally assumed that in an age when western Europe was cutting manufacturing costs by moving its textile industries into factories, it would have required highly protectionist tariffs in less developed countries for them to avoid being de-industrialized. So the integration of the Balkan peninsula into the international market as a surplus producer of primary commodities and an importer of manufactures would have tended to divert resources into farming and away from import-competing industries.

To a considerable extent this process did take place, but on the other hand, the *relative* shift towards farming coincided with such a powerful growth of demand for exchange-goods that both domestic manufactures and imports could benefit, as they tended to specialize in different sectors of the market. The extent to which the people of the upland economy

[95] Donald Quataert, *Ottoman Manufacturing in the Age of the Industrial Revolution* (Cambridge, 1993), p. 6.

could (or would want to) shift out of industry and into farming was limited. As security returned, the once abandoned lands became valuable, and returned rapidly to cultivation. Hill dwellers began to flow back into the plains, but the extent to which they could resettle was limited. Despite occasional state assistance, they found it difficult to acquire holdings on valley lands, partly because of the spread of cultivation in the hands of larger resident proprietors,[96] but also because the latter tried to restrict the grant of new cultivation leases.[97] Moreover, leases were often made unattractive, because the notables expected cultivators to pay the double tithe. Though large numbers of Bulgarian peasants emigrated across the Danube into Romania, where better conditions were offered them,[98] the hill country, especially the Stara Planina and the Rhodope, continued to enfold an exaggeratedly large population. Many of these people were still obliged to seek their living from commercial and industrial pursuits. Given the rising buoyancy of the market for their products, this was not too difficult, so upland industry expanded alongside plains agriculture. As much of this industry was efficient and expanding in its demand for labour, its own development held population within the rural manufacturing areas, as for example at Sopot.[99]

As certain industries did decline, the development experience of the Ottoman Empire has been held up as a sombre example of industrial destruction and the creation of dependency at the European periphery. This already well-rehearsed view[100] has been endorsed by Wallerstein (as one might expect)[101] and by Josef Matuz, to whom the decline of Ottoman industries provides the centrepiece of his critique of Ottoman economic 'failure'.[102]

This view has been questioned by Quataert. Despite the fragmentary nature of the available quantitative record, he estimates that for the Ottoman Empire as a whole there was some regression in Ottoman manufacturing during the first half of the nineteenth century, but this gave way to vigorous recovery post-1870.[103] Pamuk has tried to quantify the

---

[96] Hristov, *Agrarnijat v'pros*, pp. 13–14.   [97] Wilhelmy, *Hochbulgarien*, I, p. 151.

[98] D. P. Ivanov, 'Spasenieto na B'lgarskata emigracija v Rum'nija', *Nova B'lgarija*, I, 70 (11 Mar. 1877), p. 271.

[99] I. A. Bogorov, *Osnova zaradi naprava na edna fabrika da prede i t'che pamuk v Plovdiv* (Constantinople, 1863), pp. 8–9.

[100] For example, D. Ergil and R. Rhodes, 'Western Capitalism and the Disintegration of the Ottoman Empire', *Economy & History*, XVIII (1975), pp. 50, 53.

[101] Immanuel Wallerstein, 'The Ottoman Empire and the Capitalist World Economy: Some Questions for Research', in *The Social and Economic History of Turkey 1071–1920*, ed. Osman Okyar and Halil Inalcik (Ankara, 1980).

[102] Josef Matuz, 'Warum es der ottomanischen Türkei keine Industrieentwicklung gab', *Südosteuropa mitteilungen* (1985), III, pp. 43–6.

[103] Quataert, *Ottoman Manufacturing*, pp. 161 ff.

decline of the Ottoman cotton spinning and weaving industries in the territory comprised within the frontiers of 1911. The major area of decline was, of course in hand-spinning, the volume of hand-spun cotton yarn production declining from 12,900 tonnes in 1821 to 1,000 in 1910, with the most rapid loss of employment occurring between 1841 and 1871. Hand weaving probably declined by around 31 per cent between 1821 and 1881, but then nearly doubled by 1910. Machine industry made no offset at all till about 1880.[104] (One would be happier with the estimate if allowance had been made for the use of cotton for wadding rather than spinning.) Pamuk concludes from the experience of the cotton industry that the Ottoman Empire probably did de-industrialize before 1870, but interpretatively, the study is less revealing than it appears to be. His method can not be applied to differentiate between subsistence and unmechanized commercial production, and as the subsistence sector predominated,[105] it does not establish the trends in paid industrial employment. A decline in subsistence production is neither an indication of developmental stagnation (if anything the reverse) nor of welfare loss. Though these studies question the facile assumption that European enterprise created underdevelopment at the (Ottoman) 'periphery', the issue remains indeterminate.

The 'peripheralization' argument is generally applied to the Ottoman Empire as an entirety, with little regard to the different economic structures of the various provinces. Issawi has provided evidence that certain industries in Anatolia and Ottoman Europe declined in the face of European machine produced imports, but being better informed on the Asiatic provinces, he is sceptical on the supposed de-industrialization of this area.[106] He fails to mention the industries which were rising, especially in Bulgaria and southern Macedonia, though the industrial renaissance is well documented in Bulgarian texts. The confusion has arisen because some industries which did decline, as for example, the old established fine-textile industries at Shkodër, Tirnavos, Salonica, Diarbekir, Brusa (Bursa) and Aleppo,[107] were located in cities where their distress was highly visible to Europeans who wrote about them. On the other hand, the expanding sectors of industry were hidden in the small towns and villages, particularly in the Balkan uplands; Ubicini, to whom Issawi sources his affirmation of industrial decline,[108] neither knew nor wrote

---

[104] Sevket Pamuk, 'The Decline and Resistance of the Ottoman Cotton Textiles, 1820–1913', *Explorations in Economic History*, XXIII (1986).   [105] Ibid., p. 208.

[106] Charles Issawi, *Economic History of Turkey 1800–1914* (Chicago, 1980), pp. 275–6, 298–9.   [107] Ubicini, *Letters*, pp. 339–41.

[108] Charles Issawi, *The Economic History of the Middle East, 1800–1914* (Chicago, 1966), pp. 41, 43–5.

anything about them. A process was happening, familiar to economic historians of the early modern period, the ruralization of manufacturing, the creative destruction of moribund, guild-ridden city industries and of rural industrial rebirth.

It is instructive to examine one example of 'de-industrialization' in Ottoman Europe – the decline of the centuries old woollen cloth industry of the Salonica Jews, whose techniques were brought originally by them when they immigrated from Castille.[109] The industry existed primarily to supply the Porte with military clothing for the Janissaries, and therefore enjoyed great privileges. These included the right to pre-empt a quarter of all the wool brought into Salonica at a low fixed price, imposing in effect a levy upon wool exports.[110] As early as 1694, the industry was in trouble since the Janissaries were rejecting the cloth as unsatisfactory.[111] Yet the state continued throughout the eighteenth century to take up the cloth, despite its deteriorating quality and the fact that the Janissaries no longer wore it, and sold it off for what it would fetch. The producers made no effort to seek alternative outlets.[112] Despite this, in the 1780s Salonica was 'the sole town where coarse cloth is worked for Janissary uniforms', while other, Anatolian, centres were of relative insignificance.[113]

Early in the nineteenth century, the debasement of the Ottoman coinage, while immediately affecting its foreign exchange value, led (as is usual with depreciation) to a slower upward adjustment of domestic prices. This made Ottoman produce – including wool – increasingly cheap in foreign currency terms to importers. The Ottoman state, to which the purchase of Salonica woollens had become a burdensome formality, failed to raise the price it paid for them. So the Jews sold the pre-empted wool for export, and in so far as they continued manufacturing, tried to maintain their margins by using unexportable wools of low quality. Even so they found the trade decreasingly rewarding. Unable or disinclined to dispose of their appalling manufactures on the free market, they gradually gave up making them.[114] It may be doubted whether the extinction of the industry occasioned as much regret to the producers as to their historian, because in the 1820s the Porte was back in the market, buying 'almost all the cloth produced in Salonica' as well as that

[109] Nicolas Svoronos, *Le commerce de Salonique au XVIIIe siècle* (Paris, 1956), p. 187.
[110] Edme Mentelle, *Géographie comparée. . . Turquie d'Europe* (Paris, 1785), pp. 232–3; Cousinery, *Voyage dans la Macédoine*, I, p. 49.
[111] I.-S. Emmanuel, *Histoire de l'industrie des tissus des Israélites de Salonique* (Lausanne, 1935), p. 53.
[112] Cousinery, *Voyage dans la Macédoine*, I, p. 49; Emmanuel, *Histoire*, pp. 56–8.
[113] Mouradja d'Ohsson, *Tableau général de l'empire Othoman* (Paris, 1791), IV, p. 228.
[114] Emmanuel, *Histoire*, pp. 55–6.

produced in Plovdiv (also said to have been in industrial decline at the time) despite which it was unable to satisfy its requirements.[115] Perhaps this was because the Salonica Jews were diversifying into carpet making, for which the local wools were better suited, and undercutting the carpets of Smyrna in quality and price. Salonica carpet making is claimed soon to have collapsed, 'probably after the plague of 1838 which carried off half the Jewish population of the town'.[116] However, its death notice was premature, for in 1859 there were 6 carpet factories in Salonica, which exported 400,000 francs worth of merchandise. Business was clearly diversifying, for the manufacture of cotton towels also flourished in Salonica at this time, as did silk reeling, employing 2,000 people in the mid-1840s.[117] A little later, the Salonica Jews successfully introduced machine cotton spinning.[118] These substitutions may have been associated with fluctuations in the city's industrial activity, but they illustrate the danger of associating the demise of specific, weak industries with generalizations on industrial decline.

Though Salonica woollen making declined, no industry flourished more vigorously in the Balkan uplands than the manufacture of woollen cloth. If there was one sector of manufacturing in which Ottoman Europe was becoming vigorously competitive, this was it. The experience of the Salonica woollen industry will not serve as an example of displacement by imports, for when the state could not get its orders filled, it turned for supplies, not to the importers, but to the producers of the Balkan uplands.[119]

So long as fearsome transport conditions separated the cities, which were also the principal centres in which manufactures were consumed, from the upland industries which could undercut their prices, city manufactures could, after a fashion, flourish. However, with the easing of freight costs, they faced fierce rural competition. The booming trade in heavy woollen *aba* cloth at Samokov began in the 1840s, 'when better roads were made, and relatively prosperous conditions of life began, because the depredations of the *k'rdzhalijas* and *delibashas* had been overcome. From then it continued to strengthen increasingly till the Russo-Turkish War, and after it till 1882. . .'[120] Similarly, the crafts began to flourish in Gabrovo around mid-century,[121] for 'when peace was restored from the *k'rdzhalijas*' braiding machines were brought to Karlovo, and

[115] Nikolaj Todorov, *Balkanskijat grad, XV-XIX vek.* (Sofia, 1972), p. 270.
[116] Emmanuel, *Histoire*, p. 59.
[117] B. Nicolaidy, *Les Turcs et la Turquie contemporaine* (Paris, 1859), II, pp. 344–5; Quataert, *Ottoman Manufacturing*, pp. 119–20.   [118] See Chapter 3, below.
[119] See Chapter 3 below.
[120] Hr. Semerdzhiev, *Samokov i okolnost'ta mu* (Sofia, 1913), p. 207.
[121] Tsonchev, *Gabrovo*, p. 78.

were to become the mainstay of its industrial prosperity.[122] Trades such as these were orientated inevitably to Ottoman city markets, where they would have encountered and defeated local competition. At least in part, the manufacture of cotton towels at Brusa was undermined by competition from towels made in Pirdop, in the Stara Planina, when a boom in silk reeling forced wages in Brusa upwards.[123] Contemporary comments about displacement by imports are often prefaced by remarks about 'changes in taste',[124] which means that imports rarely competed directly with home products. Yet one great attraction of the Ottoman market, as perceived by the Bulgarians who traded into it, was that it was the most conservative of markets.[125] It is likely that in so far as manufacturing within the 'core' of the empire declined, especially within the cities, it was displaced mainly by competition from its own Balkan 'periphery'. This even occurred within Bulgaria itself. At Veliko T'rnovo, the weaving industry declined as clothmaking migrated to the upland Balkan townships of Gabrovo and Trjavna.[126]

This process – the growth of rural industry and the decline of some of the weaker urban industries, was developmentally beneficial, even though it resulted in part from the retention within the manufacturing areas of population which at the margin could have been more productively employed in farming. For if the plains had more readily absorbed the outflow of the hill population, the Bulgarian economy would probably have reverted to a subsistence basis, like that of Serbia. With this would have been lost the dynamic efficiency associated with specialization, whether in manufactures, or in agricultural products.

---

[122] Nachov, *Kalofer*, pp. 270–1.
[123] N. Konstantinov, 'Stupanski formi i tehnika na industrijata v B'lgarija predi osvobozhdenieto', *SpBID*, VI (1902), p. 462; Quataert, *Ottoman Manufacturing*, p. 59.
[124] For example, see A. Viquesnel, *Voyage dans la Turquie d'Europe* (Paris, 1868), I, p. 292.
[125] Tsonchev, *Gabrovo*, p. 240.   [126] Kanitz, *Bulgarie*, p. 141.

3 Agriculture and industry in Ottoman Bulgaria in the twilight of Ottoman rule

The farm economy

The dominant sector of the economy of late Ottoman Bulgaria was arable farming, both for subsistence and surplus. Principal agricultural products were cereals and for northern Bulgaria these accounted in 1870 for 59.4 per cent of final farm output. Grapes and wine accounted for a further 12.4 per cent, and the balance (to 78.4 per cent) was drawn from a range of minor crops, including fruit, oilseeds, beans, cabbage and tobacco.[1] The remainder was composed of animal products. In the south (not included in these statistics) rose growing, centred on Kazanl'k, and rice round Tatar Pazardzhik, were also significant crops.

Except in the densely populated hill areas, agricultural methods were extensive, reflecting the favourable ratio of land to labour, and therefore wasteful and negligent in the eyes of observers, who tended to judge efficiency in terms of the intensity of land use. According to St Clair and Brophy:

One of the effects of the misgovernment of the country is that every rayah is the owner of more land than he knows what to do with, and therefore it is not to be expected that he should make the most of every acre. When he has turned over one furrow, he ploughs on the other side of the ridge so that his field is turned with just half the labour which an Englishman would give to the same surface.[2]

Areal yields however were tolerable, because this extensive method of soil preparation was compensated by heavy seeding,[3] a sensible practice where grain was cheap and labour scarce.[4]

The lack of pressure on the supply of arable land meant that two and three course systems of open field agriculture predominated. Smaller holders probably fallowed less of their land than large ones. Even so, in 1844, in the Plovdiv villages, where the average holding was of but 3.44

---

[1] Based on the statistics underlying Table 3.2.
[2] S. G. B. St Clair and C. A. Brophy, *A residence in Bulgaria or Notes on the Provinces and Administration of Turkey* (London, 1869), p. 152.   [3] Ibid., p. 153.
[4] David Urquhart, *Turkey and its Resources* (London, 1833), p. 146.

hectares, fractionally over half the arable was fallow.[5] Two course agriculture was slowly giving way to a type of three course system, in which maize and pumpkins could be integrated within the cropping cycle. The share of fallow was consequently falling, though the process was gradual, since there were offsetting losses in grazing. Fallow was not 'dead land', but land which was grassed over, sometimes for several years at a time, and so provided an important source of communal pasture.[6] The system produced respectable grain yields to seed. A leasehold farmer, writing to his financial backer in 1864 and 1865, reckoned the return he obtained from winter wheat at between 7 and 10 fold in a good year, and between 4.5 and 7 in a bad one.[7] St Clair and Brophy, perhaps extravagantly, estimated the grain yield at 'at least' 10 to 1.[8] Wheat yields for neighbouring Serbia in 1867 were officially calculated at 11 quintals per hectare, and 7.25:1.[9] These lie within a range verifiable from other data. Yet Serbian farming methods were regarded as much inferior to those of Bulgaria, as was the quality of Serbia's land endowment.

The quality of estate agriculture was considered to be superior to that practised on the peasant holdings.[10] If the activities of professional Bulgar land leasers in Bulgaria and Romania are any guide, farms run by them were organized efficiently, well stocked, even partially mechanized.[11]

Livestock husbandry did not normally provide the plains farmer with a large proportion of his final output. Low precipitation made it difficult to feed much livestock, so the common pastures were generally small, the land being held for preference under the plough, albeit intermittently. Combined with the water meadows (which were grazed after the hay-making) the grazing area was equal to but 10 per cent of that of the arable.[12] In Güran's Plovdiv villages, livestock seem only to have provided 5 per cent of farm production (though the figure is artificially depressed by double counting) and this was probably not exceptional.

We have argued that the distribution of population in Bulgaria, affected as it was by the institutional evolution of Ottoman rule, had left the plains

---

[5] Tevfik Güran, *Structure économique et sociale d'une région de campagne dans l'empire ottoman vers le milieu du XIXe siècle* (Sofia, 1979), pp. 67–8, 69.

[6] N. Konstantinov, 'Zemedelieto v B'lgarija predi osvobozhdenieto', *Sbornik na narodni umotvorenija*, XXVI (1912), pp. 37–53.

[7] Hristo Hristov, *Agrarniat v'pros v B'lgarskata natsionalna revoljutsija* (Sofia, 1976), p. 152.

[8] St Clair and Brophy, *Residence in Bulgaria*, p. 249.

[9] Vladimir Jakšić, 'Stanje zemljoradnje u Srbiji', *GSUD*, XLI (Belgrade, 1875), pp. 5–9.

[10] Michoff, II/1 (1943), p. 117. For an opposing view see John R. Lampe and Marvin R. Jackson, *Balkan Economic History 1500–1950* (Bloomington, IN, 1982), p. 137.

[11] Hristov, *Agrarniat v'pros*, pp. 146–8; 'Za polozhenieto i stopanskata dejnost na B'lgarskata emigratsija v'v Vlashko prez XIX v.', in D. Kosev et al., *B'lgaro Rum'nski vr'zki i otnoshenija prez vekovete*, I (Sofia, 1965), esp. pp. 346–56.

[12] GBC Bulgaria 1884, pp. 2–3.

relatively underpopulated, while areas where Ottoman pressure was weak were populated densely. Upland areas of the latter sort were associated more with manufacturing than with commercial farming, but there were also substantial farming areas with high population density. They were characteristically settled almost entirely with Bulgars, and enjoyed a wide measure of self-government. Of these the largest was the district of T'rnovsko, densely populated, with big villages close to one another.[13] The part round Ljaskovets township was 'the most cultivated corner of Bulgaria, the only region in the entire country where each fragment of land is utilized'.[14] Densely populated it may have been, but it was not the less prosperous on that account, for it evolved intensive, commercialized forms of farming, which, like the industries of the uplands, complemented the extensive grain specialization of the more thinly populated plains.

Since the eighteenth century, part of the manpower of T'rnovsko had been migrating periodically for work. In the 1760s much of this labour was employed in the Greek owned market gardens of Constantinople. At that time market gardening was not a skill indigeneous to the area, but the T'rnovsko migrants learned the techniques from the Greeks and applied them for work on their own account in Romania, and later still further afield.[15] Since market garden produce was sold to best advantage in nearby urban markets, there was little to be gained from establishing this form of cultivation in T'rnovsko itself, but the intensive techniques were clearly applicable, and raised the level of husbandry well above that in the rest of Bulgaria. The region therefore began around the mid-nineteenth century to support an active commerce; Ljaskovets carts loaded with premium quality onions, and with peppers were a familiar sight throughout Bulgaria. Seed nurseries also developed to supply the market gardening gangs. Above all, the area moved into viticulture, and exported an annual 15,000 hl of wine and 3,000 of brandy.[16]

Parallel with the cultivating economy of the plains, to which the raising of livestock was but a minor appendage, there existed a transhumant stockraising economy. Summer grazing in the Balkan mountain ranges was alternated with overwintering on lowland pasture. The preferred winter grazing grounds were in the lowlands between Edirne and the Sea of Marmara where winter fattening was possible, because

[13] Konstantin Irechek, *Knjazhestvo B'lgarija* (Plovdiv, 1899), II, pp. 85–6.
[14] Ibid., p. 250.
[15] Tsani Ginchev, 'Nekolko dumi ot istorijata na nasheto gradinarstvo (bahchovandzhil'k) i uredbata na gradinata', *Trud* (v. T'rnovo) I (1887), pp. 1184–9.
[16] M. Moskov, *Ljaskovets, minaloto i b'dninata mu* (v. T'rnovo, 1920), pp. 18, 19, 28.

the mild climate permitted winter grass growth. Livestock brought here were usually consigned to the Constantinople butchery trade, but stock held over winter other than for slaughter migrated to plains regions adjacent to the high summer pastures, where it could at least survive the winter, if not fatten through it. The Sofia, Lukovit and Pleven fields are specifically mentioned as winter pastures, as well as the Dobrudzha and the environs of Burgas on the Black Sea coast.[17] As there was little permanent grassland in the plains, the fallow fields of their villages became essential to the transhumant system, as Wilhelmy indicates:[18]

As long as the two and three field farming systems still gave plenty of fallow land, the Aromunes [a nomadic tribe] were very welcome winter guests to the farmers. The dung of their sheep flocks, which were moved gradually inside movable hurdles over the stubble fields, supplied a valuable supplement to the insufficient quantity of their own stable manure.

Transhumant stockraising had to be conducted on a substantial scale. Besides being the main occupation of certain privileged nomadic tribes (Mokans, Yürüks and Aromunes)[19] it attracted the participation of powerful and well organized Christian capitalist *chorbadzhijas*. The upland pasture rights enjoyed by these various interests were zealously protected by the authorities. The nomads enjoyed exclusive rights on certain crown grazing lands, *yaylaks*, and the *chorbadzhijas* secured privileges of their own. The *chorbadzhijas* of Kotel township owned flocks of up to 10,000 sheep which had been grazed transhumantly till the early nineteenth century, but the authorities provided them with such valuable pasture rights in the Dobrudzha that they subsequently held the flocks there permanently, primarily for the sale of wool and cheese.[20]

Livestock and its products contributed 21.6 per cent to final farm output in 1870, and within this sector the dominant product was milk (26.5 per cent) from cows, goats, ewes and buffaloes. The balance was made up mainly of slaughter animals (33.5 per cent net of fodder cost), wool, horses, honey, cocoons, fish and barnyard produce. As stock-raising was organized for commercial ends rather than subsistence, it gave rise to substantial exports. Slaughter sheep were probably the main product. On the eve of the liberation, 200,000 – 250,000 sheep were sent to Constantinople each year from the sanjak of Plovdiv alone,

[17] G. S. Gunchev, *Vakarel. Antropogeografski prouchvanija* (Sofia, 1933), p. 153; Herbert Wilhelmy, *Hochbulgarien* (Kiel, 1935), I, pp. 274, 277.
[18] Wilhelmy, *Hochbulgarien*, I, pp. 277–8.   [19] Ibid., I, pp. 274–9.
[20] Iv. Ev. Geshov, 'Ovcharite ot Kotlensko i zh'tvarite ot T'rnovsko', *PS*, XXXII-XXXIII (1890), pp. 311–16; Wilhelmy, *Hochbulgarien*, I, p. 275.

Table 3.1 *Farm production indicators for Ottoman Bulgaria 1852–1876*

Year	Varna grain export	Vidin grain output	Agricultural tithe (million piastres)
1852	223.3		
1853	279.1		
1857	175.3		
1858	239.8		
1859	254.1		
1860	138.1		
1861	274.4		
1862	360.7		
1863	296.8		
1864	410.6		
1865	366.0		
1866	539.4		
1867	594.6		22.1
1868	527.6	5,070	38.0
1869	233.2		20.1
1870	149.0	2,640	n.a.
1871		3,990	27.0
1872	401.5	2,479	29.0
1873	370.1		37.6
1874	402.2		33.5
1875	374.3		50.3
1876		5,982	

Sources: Vidin grain output (000 metzen): Michoff, II/2 (1953), pp. 300, 355, 372–3, 492; Varna grain export (000 charges): 1852: Michoff, II/1 (1943), p. 442; 1853– : Michoff, I (1941), pp. 4, 12, 17, 21, 24, 27, 29, 31, 34, 39, 46, 55, 63, 74, 78, 84, 89, 91; Tithe: TsDIA, f. 20 op. 1 a.e.66 f.167.

and 6,000–8,000 oxen.[21] Cheese, wool, and eggs were also sent in large quantity to Constantinople, and sheepskins to France.[22]

Indicators for farming trends before 1878 are very imperfect, but the following three series indicate a broad if uneven upswing up to 1875 or 1876. The first series (in Table 3.1) is of grain exports through Varna, the principal Black Sea port, the second of crop production in Vidin sanjak, and the third is of revenue from the tithe on cultivated produce in the territory which was subsequently to be Eastern Rumelia.

The table indicates that the economic upswing of the 1860s was

---

[21] GBC E. Rumelia 1876, pp. 639–40.
[22] Ibid., GBC Bulgaria 1876, p. 1564. For Vrattsa, see F. Kanitz, *La Bulgarie Danubienne et le Balkan. Études de voyage, 1860–1880* (Paris, 1882), p. 311; Metodi Stojanov, *Grad Pirdop v minaloto i sega* (Sofia, 1941), pp. 236–7.

Table 3.2 *Bulgaria. Sectoral farm output 1865–1873*

	(million leva of constant 1910 value)						leva
Year	Animal products	Animals	Cash crops	Grains	Garden crops	Total	Total per-capita
1865	46	35	29	294	14	418	223
1866	53	39	30	294	12	428	221
1870	44	35	57	218	12	368	228
1873	46	39	55	212	9	360	217

Source: see BALKSTAT

followed between 1869 and 1872 or 1874 by stagnation or recession, with renewed expansion in the mid-1870s. The last two or three years of Ottoman rule were unusually prosperous. This is suggested not only by the tenuous indicators in the table, but also by consular observation. Grain production was estimated in 1876 at 1.5 million tons (metric fous) (the corresponding figure for 1873 can be calculated at 1.4 million) while in 1877, the cereal crop in both Danube and Edirne vilayets was reported to be still better, and of excellent quality.[23] This was not unique to the Balkan provinces: Ottoman exports peaked in 1876.[24]

Quantifying Bulgarian farm production

With some reservations as to the quality of the data, we have attempted to estimate farm production in that part of the Danube vilayet which was subsequently to form the Bulgarian state of 1878–85. Table 3.2 tracks farm production in absolute and per capita terms, though it would place an excessive burden on the data to represent the serial as a time trend. We have had to assume such parameters as fixed output of young animals and milk per cow, cow buffalo, or sheep, according to Popov's estimates, and to assume also that the weight of livestock was constant. Figures are expressed in terms of constant 1910 prices.

The data is drawn from contemporarily published statistics which leave much to be desired, though there is a certain consistency to them.[25] The figures given are gross, including seed requirements, but the intersectoral transfer of grain fodder is deducted from the output of livestock raising.

To set these figures in context, we will demonstrate with Figure 12 (i) below that they indicate a substantially higher productivity in farming

[23] GBC Bulgaria 1876, p. 1565; GBC Constantinople 1877, pp. 871–2.
[24] Sevket Pamuk, *The Ottoman Empire and European Capitalism 1820–1913* (Cambridge, 1987), p. 149.   [25] See BALKSTAT.

than was subsequently to be achieved before World War I, save in a few exceptional years. This conclusion runs contrary to received opinion on the subject, and obviously depends on the validity of our statistics. An alternative estimate for the end of the Ottoman period was calculated by Berov, who applied data researched by Draganova on the tithe records for Silistra *kaza* of Danube vilayet. This produces figures for farm output which are much lower than our own.[26] Berov's calculation was based on the crop output of 412 farms in 1872–4. The tithe records do not provide information on the arable area of these farms, so to estimate their size, Berov applied yield figures calculated from tithe returns of certain villages in Eastern Rumelia in 1880. From these figures, and from contemporary price data, he calculated the value of the yield per *dünüm* of land of the sample farms, and multiplied the result by an estimate of Bulgaria's total arable area. A crude allowance was made for the yield from stockraising by borrowing an estimate of Popov's for the 1890s. Berov's total for Bulgaria's farm output comes to 1,620 million piastres gross, 1,380 million net. On a rural population of 2.41 million this would provide a net income of 572 piastres per head.

Our own calculations are expressed in prices of 1910. To make Berov's figure comparable, we calculated an unweighted average in 1910 of the prices of farm commodities priced by Berov for 1865/77. In 1910 a basket of these commodities costing 100 piastres in the earlier period would have cost 29.34 leva.[27] So in 1910 prices, 572 piastres becomes 167.8 leva. Against this, our figures for 1870 and 1873 were 228 leva, and 217 leva.

A large part of the discrepancy arises from the improbably low cereal yield estimate of 5.4 quintals per hectare assumed by Berov. As we will note when discussing yield trends (p. 186) wheat yields to seed in 1889/92 were 5.48:1 and subsequently declined rather than rose. Now the sowing density for 1906–13 fluctuated between very narrow limits of 2.0–2.2 quintals per hectare, with a median of 2.1, so we infer that wheat yields in 1889/92 were about 11.5 quintals per hectare. In 1903–5 they were 11.4 and in 1911–13, 11.3. If we were to accept Berov's 5.4 quintals/hectare figure as valid for the 1870s, we would also infer that yields, having remained stable till just after the liberation, suddenly more than doubled in nine years, and then remained static for the next twenty. Moreover, his implied wheat yield to seed is 2.5:1. This is improbable on

[26] Ljuben Berov, 'Ravnishte na ikonomichesko razvitie na B'lgarskite zemi po vreme na osvobozhdenieto', *Trudove na visshija ikonomicheski institut 'Karl Marks'*, I (1979), pp. 13–44; Slavka Draganova, 'De la production agricole, l'imposition fiscale et la différenti ation sociale de la population paysanne en Bulgarie du nord-est durant les années 60–70 du XIXe siècle', *Bulgarian Historical Review*, II (1977), pp. 73–9.

[27] The basket comprises wheat, rye, barley, wine, beans, cabbage, tobacco, potatoes, honey, rice, and fish. 1865/77 prices from Berov, 'Ravnishte', pp. 18, 26 (note 26).

two counts. Firstly, yields are unlikely to have grown in so discontinuous a fashion, and secondly, on van Bath's figures for European grain yields 1500–1820, yields never averaged less than 3.5:1 anywhere in Europe.[28] Berov's Eastern Rumelia figures may be correct for certain less fertile areas in a bad year – as 1880 was – but if we were alternatively to assume that in the 1870s yields were the same as in 1889/92 and subsequently, then the 412 holdings in the Silistra region did not have 28,255 *dünüms* under cereals but only 14,030, and fallow is scaled down proportionately. The area of the 412 farms now falls from 53,965 *dünüms* to 32,472, or 79.5 *dünüms* per holding. When the calculation is reworked on this basis, the per capita output rises to 208 or 248.5 leva. (The presentation of alternative figures is explained in the next paragraph.) Eliminating Berov's livestock estimate of 17.36 per cent of total output, which is not derived from data contemporary to the tithe figures, net crop production per head becomes 172–205 leva, which compares more closely with the figure of 166–179 leva which can quickly be calculated from Table 3.2.

Further evidence that Berov's yield assumption is too low derives from his conclusion that the 412 sample farms averaged 131 *dünüms* (12.03 hectares). This is improbably large. A much larger sample of 8,347 farms was compiled by Draganova, which she estimated on a different basis to have averaged 83 *dünüms* per holding, which is close to the 79.5 *dünüms* which our recalculation implies. (Dimitrov estimated Bulgarian pre-liberation farms at a still smaller 56.9 *dünüms*.) To correct for the apparently large size of his farms – which in fact was illusory – Berov applied a per *dünüm* yield 19 per cent greater than that of the sample, to compensate for the higher areal productivity of smaller holdings, which is why our recalculation produces a range rather than a single figure, the upper end incorporating the adjustment, the lower excluding it. Since the 412 farms were so much smaller than Berov supposed, the adjustment becomes superfluous, and the lower recalculated figure of 172 leva per head (excluding livestock) is neatly bracketed by our direct estimates of 166 and 179 leva.[29] (Our calculation is based on contemporary herd statistics and also gives a more substantial livestock yield than Berov's borrowing from Popov.) In short, Berov's calculation, when modified by more probable yield estimates, affirms rather than refutes our own pre-1878 estimates.

[28] Slicher van Bath, 'Agriculture in the Vital Revolution', *Cambridge Economic History of Europe* (1977), V, p. 81.

[29] These figures differ slightly from those presented in Palairet, 'Farm Productivity under Ottoman Rule and Self-Government in Bulgaria c.1860–1890', in *East European History*, ed. Stanislav J. Kirschbaum (Columbus, OH, 1988), pp. 98–103, as I have slightly lowered my estimate of 1870 and 1873 output, and have standardized to 1910 prices rather than 1908 prices.

Industries: the Bulgarian manufacturing centres

Parallel with the quickening pace of farming activity in Ottoman Bulgaria, there was a still more powerful upsurge of commerce and industry in the uplands. We have already shown that population distribution favoured proto-industrialization. The hill areas, particularly those settled overwhelmingly with ethnic Bulgars, were densely populated and short of farmland. Access to farming in the plains was restricted; an iron collar of established arable property kept the labour force of the uplands locked into non-agricultural activity for the greater part of its employment. However, upland surpluses of manufactures could be bartered for the surplus produce of the farming areas, and this gave rise to an animated commerce once the suppression of banditry and the opening of foreign trade liberated the manufactures of the hill population into an expanding market.

The principal foci of proto-industry in the period 1850–78 were the small towns of the Stara Planina and its offshoot the Sredna Gora, of which the best documented are Samokov, Pirdop, Panagjurishte, Karlovo, Kalofer, Sopot, Kazanl'k, Koprivshtitsa, Gabrovo, Trjavna, Zheravna and Sliven. As already noted, they boasted an industrial tradition stretching back into the eighteenth century, but most were commercially moribund during the time of the *k'rdzhalijas* if only because of the penal costs which transport then imposed. Their commercial renaissance began in the 1830s or 1840s, after which their growth was rapid. To give an impression of these towns and their industrial culture we look in detail at the development of two of them, Koprivshtitsa and Trjavna.

The beautiful town of Koprivshtitsa lies at 1,060 metres above sea level on a high pass which separates the Stara Planina from its southern spur, the Sredna Gora. Its fields were scanty and infertile. What little grain they bore after heavy manuring was largely cut as fodder to support the flocks that grazed the mountain meadows, the only substantial natural resource available to people of the town.[30] No village lay within three hours walk of the town so it was isolated even from a local exchange of produce. Almost everything consumed there had to be brought in by packhorse from the plain round Plovdiv over 40 miles away.[31] The flocks had to winter far from home, in the valleys round Edirne, so the very isolation of Koprivshtitsa paradoxically imposed a high degree of commercial contact with the outside world. This was no subsistence community; the sheep,

---

[30] L. Oslekov, 'Koprivshtitsa', *Jubileen sbornik po minaloto na Koprivshtitsa (1876–1926)*, ed. Arhimandrit Evtimii (Sofia, 1926), pp. 452–3.

[31] Konstantin Irechek, 'P'tni belezhki za Sredna Gora i za Rodopskite planini', *PS*, IX (1884), pp. 23, 28.

organized in large flocks and owned by the town *chorbadzhijas*, were held mainly for commerce. The wethers were driven each year for sale to the butchers of Constantinople, which together with Plovdiv took most of the cheese and butter. Part of the wool was retained locally for textile making. Koprivshteni also bought up and drove to Constantinople the surplus sheep of other hill regions, and the richer townsmen contracted to farm the imperial tithe on livestock over a wide region which stretched to the Albanian borders. They seasonally employed several hundred fellow townsfolk in this lucrative if dangerous occupation.[32]

The Koprivshtitsa textile trades date back to the eighteenth century, but they probably did not dominate the town's economic life till around 1850. Koprivshtitsa, though a free Christian community, had lacked a protector during the time of troubles, and was thrice sacked by *k'rdzhali-jas* in 1793, 1800 and 1809.[33] The inhabitants re-established themselves, but the much shrunken community had little need to look beyond the sheep for a livelihood. As late as 1843 most inhabitants were shepherds.[34] But as population recovered, from 150 in 1810 to 8,000 in 1860, the strong commercial upswing in the Ottoman economy favoured an increasing orientation to proto-industrial endeavour. At the height of its prosperity, in the early 1870s, Koprivshtitsa numbered 9,000–10,000 inhabitants.[35] By then, the sheep trades had been displaced in importance by the manufacture, tailoring and embroidery of woollen cloth, the production of hosiery and slippers, and a complex of associated commercial activity.

A similar outline could be presented for the other manufacturing townships of the Stara Planina. Take Trjavna, less a town than a scattered group of fifty-four little settlements 'in the mountainous recesses of the Trjavna Balkan' on the north slope of the Stara Planina.[36] Trjavna was situated in near impenetrable forest, and so remote from the main lines of communication that it was often unmarked on nineteenth-century maps. It was largely undisturbed by the authorities.[37]

Trjavna, despite its physical isolation, had long maintained lively external links. In the eighteenth century, it had been a centre for the silk industry,[38] and in the nineteenth used its silk in making *gajtan* (braid) and clothing. Unlike Koprivshtitsa it seems not to have suffered during the

---

[32] Oslekov, 'Koprivshtitsa', pp. 503–9, 518–20.   [33] Ibid., pp. 487–9, 512.

[34] Fotinov (1843) extract in K. V'zv'zova-Karateodorova (ed.) *Nepres'hvashti izvori* (Plovdiv, 1975), p. 284.

[35] Stojan Pranchov, *Koprivshtitsa ot tochka zrenie istoricheska sotsialna i ikonomicheska* (Plovdiv, 1886), p. 15.   [36] Kanitz, *Bulgarie*, p. 185.

[37] Asen Vasiliev, *B'lgarski v'zrozhdenski majstori* (Sofia, 1965), pp. 16–17, 99.

[38] Iv. Goshev, 'V Trjavna prez vremeto na poslednite t'rnovski g'rchki vladini (1820–1870)', *B'lgarska istoricheska biblioteka*, III (1930), p. 198.

k'rdzhalija period, and it attracted an inflow of refugee settlers from the north Bulgarian plains, who fled 'under pressure from the Turks'.[39] At that time, field agriculture had been limited to the raising of rye and oats, and even stockraising supplied no more produce than was needed locally. However, the growth of population led to deforestation, to make way for more arable plots. Even so, few inhabitants depended totally on farming for their living, and engaged instead in a heterogeneous and changing array of occupations, all geared to external markets,[40] through which the town's food deficit could be filled.[41]

Trjavna became best known for the accomplishments of its migrant gangs of builders, and for the style of architecture which was associated with their work. Above all, Trjavna specialized in church building. This gave rise to a demand for fixtures and fittings, so the gangs sometimes included specialized wood-carvers and decorators. A related skill was ikon painting, a craft cherished and confined to certain families,[42] whose practitioners made the ikons in their studios in winter, and dispersed in summer to distribute them.[43]

As a craft town, and as such was it described in the 1820s,[44] Trjavna and its outliers – like Koprivshtitsa – came alive in winter. In summer only women were encountered.[45] As building was a summer trade, the builders spent the winter engaged in tailoring – some working from house to house in the villages, others working in the township's draperies. Some fifteen to twenty merchants took their products out to the Balkan market places and fairs each summer, along with a range of heterogeneous manufactures, including harness, wooden implements, and, above all, *gajtan*.[46] In the 1860s a road was built up to the town, and this further assisted its development.[47] A visitor to Trjavna in 1871 was struck by the animation of this 'Bulgar Nuremberg', and by its competition for markets with its larger rival, Gabrovo. He commented on the 'great industrial ingenuity' with which the crafts used water power, in the active ironworking trades, tanning and leatherwork, and on the quilts which were made for the market by the women both in Trjavna and in nearby Jeltets.[48] But, as ever, the making and dyeing of woollen, silk and linen *gajtan*, and the making up of that *gajtan* into products such as harness, was probably Trjavna's leading industry.

[39] Asen Vasiliev, 'Materiali za trjavnanskite narodni majstori-stroiteli i rezbari', *Izvestija na instituta po gradoustrojstvo i arhitektura pri B'lgarska akademija na naukite* (1952), p. 218.
[40] NBKM. fond 129 a.e. 166. Hristo Daskalov, 'Istorija na Trjavna', f. 39.
[41] Ivan Bogdanov, *Trjavna prez v'zrazhdaneto* (Sofia, 1977), p. 87.
[42] Daskalov, 'Istorija na Trjavna', ff. 48–9.   [43] Goshev, 'V Trjavna', pp. 201–2.
[44] Bogdanov, *Trjavna*, p. 83.   [45] Kanitz, *Bulgarie*, p. 184.
[46] Daskalov, 'Istorija na Trjavna', f. 57.
[47] Jean Erdic, *En Bulgarie et en Roumélie* (Paris, 1885), p. 82.
[48] Kanitz, *Bulgarie*, pp. 171, 185–9.

The shortage of farmland, common to both Koprivshtitsa and Trjavna, was universal to the upland manufacturing towns. At Kotel, for example, the holdings often amounted to little more than an intensively cultivated garden.[49] At Zheravna, only the high cost of bringing in food from the plains caused the population to farm the meagre soil at all.[50]

What these townships shared, besides their need to exchange manufactures and services for food, was their geographic isolation, which was so vigorously compensated by the activation of trade links with the outside world. The diversity of their manufactures has been emphasized, particularly those of Trjavna, lest the impression be given that the Balkan townships were no more than mass producers of a limited range of textiles. It is impossible to estimate the total industrial labour force of these places before the liberation, but we may be sure that it greatly exceeded that which earned its living from the dominant woollen trades.

Textile manufacturing

It was cottons rather than woollens that began the upsurge in manufacturing in the Bulgarian industrial districts. They became vulnerable to competition from cottons woven from machine yarn when large-scale imports of cotton yarn and manufactures arrived from Britain. This caused the textile centres to concentrate on weaving and printing, in which cheap manual labour competed successfully with the machine for a long time. The cotton towelling trade prospered at Pirdop, and remained active up to 1878, turning over 200,000–300,000 francs a year.[51] Calicos were woven at Karlovo, and were passed on for block printing at neighbouring Sopot. This industry began in about 1820.[52] As late as 1864, 1.5 million piastres of Karlovo prints were traded on Prilep fair in Macedonia.[53] The Pirdop towel makers, who had hitherto used local yarn, brought in Manchester warps and cheap weft spun in Macedonia.[54] By this means they stayed competitive till about 1860, after which cotton manufacturing was slowly run down in favour of the very remunerative manufacture of woollen *gajtan*.[55]

Woollen manufacturing was the largest of the upland proto-industries.

[49] Ibid., p. 395.
[50] Danail Konstantinov, *Zheravna v minalo i do dneshno vreme* (Zheravna, 1948), p. 63.
[51] N. Konstantinov, 'Stupanski formi i tehnika na industrijata v B'lgarija predi osvobozhdenieto', *Sp.BID*, VI (1902), p. 462.
[52] *Rapport na komissiata po izuchvanieto na ikonomichesko polozhenie na naselenieto v gradovete Karlovo i Sopot* (Karlovo, 1883), p. 11.   [53] GBC Macedonia 1864, p. 587.
[54] Konstantinov, 'Stupanski formi', p. 462.
[55] Stojanov, *Pirdop*, p. 219; V. Aleksandrov, 'Iz istorijata na edin zapadnal pomin'k', *Sp.BID*, IX (1905), p. 8.

Its magnitude can be quantified, though the only pre-liberation figures which can be used with confidence relate to around 1870. At about this time the woollen manufactures of the Bulgarian provinces engaged about 73,000 persons, most of them part-time. As Table 3.3 shows, they produced roughly £650,000 worth of woollens from 4,870 tonnes of raw wool. Approximately 74 per cent of this output came from the sanjaks of Plovdiv and Sliven, to the south of the Balkan range, later to become Eastern Rumelia, where commercial woollen production per capita was five times that of northern Bulgaria.

The commercialization of sheep raising contributed to the growth of the woollen industries by yielding a supply of wool whose quality was well suited to their demands. About 60 per cent of the wool which came to the market was soft, curly and white, described as 'metis' or 'demi-merino'. Since the graziers held ewe flocks and made much of their income out of cheese, the wool was not of the finest; for that the industry had to draw upon merino flocks held by the crown, but it was sufficiently good to attract purchasers who exported it to Marseille for the woollen industry of the Midi.[56] Its price was low as well, since it was in surplus and faced a 12 per cent duty on exportation.[57] It was much superior to the coarse grey wool which was produced by the peasant sheep.

The woollen industry was divided into two principal branches, the one making woollen cloth, the other braid (*gajtan*). The main products woven were a heavy (800 grams per m²) fulled woollen cloth from carded yarn called *aba* or *balo*, and a lesser but growing quantity of *shajak*, 42 per cent lighter than *aba*[58] and better suited to manufacturing clothes of European type. *Abas* were manufactured especially at Kotel and Sliven, at Panagjurishte and in the Rhodope, *shajaks* on the north slope of the Balkan at Trojan and Trjavna, at Samokov and in the Sredna Gora. Altogether about 1.6–1.8 million square metres of woollen cloth was made. Because of the limitations of the peasant loom, most was woven to narrow widths of 27–40 cm and when tailored it needed to be seamed with large quantities of woollen *gajtan*.[59] The yarn was spun by the women of the textile towns and some of their outlying villages. They wove much of the cloth as well, especially in the towns. These materials were collected up by local merchants, who had them finished or worked into piece goods and *gajtan* in their workshops, in which a large part of the male population was occupied.

---

[56] Michoff, I (1941), pp. 4, 7, 14, 22; Michoff, III (1950), pp. 517, 607, 608; GBC Edirne 1868, pp. 168–9.

[57] Xavier Heuschling, *L'Empire de Turquie* (Brussels, 1860), p. 143.

[58] For cloth weights see BALKSTAT. Austrian sources refer to these cloths as Halina and Loden.

[59] Ivan Undzhiev, *Karlovo. Istorija na grada do Osvobozhdenieto* (Sofia, 1968), p. 61.

Table 3.3 *Woollen output of Bulgaria c. 1870*

Region	homespun woollen cloth		Factory cloth	Gajtan (braid)	Total	Sources
	Aba	*Shajak*				
(000m²)						
N. Bulgaria	–	153.4–154.6	26.0			(1–4)
Sliven	184.5	253.0	170.2			(5–6)
Plovdiv	384.3–502.7	411.0–548.0	–			(7)
BULGARIA	568.8–687.2	817.4–955.6	196.2		1582–1839	(8)
(tonnes)						
N. Bulgaria	–	66.0–66.5	12.4	460	538.6	(1–4)
Sliven	147.6	108.8	81.4	–	337.8	(5–6)
Plovdiv	307.4–402.2	176.7–235.6	–	670	1,154.1–1,307.8	(7)
BULGARIA	455.0–549.8	351.5–410.9	93.9	1130	2,030.4–2,184.6	(8)
Value – million leva						
N. Bulgaria	–	(– 0.75 –)		3.12	3.87	
E.Rumelia	4.09	(– 3.76 –)		4.55	12.40	
BULGARIA	4.09	(– 4.51 –)		7.67	16.27	(9–10)
Less value of raw wool input 4.87 million kg at 1.481 leva per kg.					7.21	(11)
Value of net woollen industry output					9.06	

Sources: see BALKSTAT.

Though these goods were domestic manufactures, production techniques became increasingly efficient. In spinning, the large wheel, first used at Karlovo and Kalofer, was diffused through the textile towns, giving the spinners an edge over peasant competition, which still used the distaff.[60] Fulling mills were also spreading.[61] *Gajtan* making showed especially strong technical improvement. In the eighteenth century it was plaited without machinery, but around 1800, the task began to be mechanized by the use of manually powered wooden braiding machines (*charks*) which were introduced from Kronstadt (Brasov) in Transylvania, and were copied by Bulgarian craftsmen.[62] By around 1860 these *charks* were being replaced by metal machines, grouped together in small watermills.[63] The productivity gains greatly reduced the price of the product, which fell by 65 per cent between 1857 and the 1870s.[64]

Textile demand

The final products of the Balkan woollen cloth industry were largely consumed by the Ottoman urban population and the army. *Aba* and braided *aba* products were bought throughout the empire, especially by nomadic peoples. *Shajak* was wanted by the more westernized elements. The demand for woollen cloth was largely urban as Balkan peasants lacked purchasing power and contrived to be self-sufficient in clothing materials. This did not inhibit development of the industry for the absorptive capacity of the Ottoman market was increasing, as foreign trade growth provided a motor for the expansion of internal exchanges. There was no question whether native cloth could compete against imports – it was so competitive on the Ottoman market that European goods were largely restricted to the fashion trade. In 1872 Bulgarian woollen cloth was regarded by the Austrians as potentially exportable, because of its cheapness and solidity.[65] There is abundant evidence that the woollen industry expanded in output at least up to 1870; to take but two indicators, the volume of Bulgarian woollens brought to Uzundzhovo fair rose between 1857 and 1869 from 1.03 million piastres to 4.7 million, while the trade capital of a putting out firm at Kotel,

[60] Konstantinov, 'Stupanski formi', pp. 457–8.
[61] Zhcchka Janakieva, *Abadzhijstvoto v slivenskija kraj* (Sliven: Okr'zhen istoricheski muzej, 1978), p. 4, n. 1.
[62] Pet'r Tsonchev, *Iz stopanskoto minalo na Gabrovo* (Sofia, 1929), p. 282; Michoff, II/1 (1943), p. 126.
[63] V. Aleksandrov, 'Istorijata', pp. 4–5; Konstantinov, 'Stupanski formi', p. 458.
[64] A. Pavlov, 'Ikonomicheskoto razvitie i s'stojanie na gr. Kazanl'k', *Kazanl'k v minaloto i dnes*, I (Sofia, 1912), p. 291.   [65] Michoff, II/2 (1953), pp. 337, 396.

Stanchev Bjanov rose from 140,000 piastres in 1862 to 428,000 in 1871.[66]

Gajtan production expanded even more vigorously, because demand was probably price elastic. As Balkan peasants purchased increasing quantities of *gajtan* to make up the cloth which they wove for their own use, demand for *gajtan* rose out of proportion to sales of cloth. Gabrovo and the Sredna Gora towns established something of a monopoly in this industry, aided by the abundant waters which flowed through them. By the late 1860s, 6,000 plaiting machines were operating, taking up the yarn produced by 34,000 spinners.[67] By value, sales of *gajtan* equalled 84 per cent of sales of woollen cloth, and by weight exceeded them (Table 3.3).

The growth of *gajtan* making demanded an expanding labour force, so the burgeoning demand for *gajtan* yarn tended to force out other branches of textile manufacture. As early as 1826, the *kapudzhi bashija* of Plovdiv sought to suppress *gajtan* making in the interest of the local *shajak* industry.[68] By mid-century, *gajtan* making was displacing the cotton cloth manufacture of Karlovo, the block printing trade at Sopot, and the towel weaving trade of Pirdop.[69] The prosperity of the Bulgarian proto-industries depended on their ability to adapt continuously to demand side changes, and therefore on market information and ability to innovate in response. For example, when the importation of calicos damaged the weaving trade at Pirdop, sales plunged, and weavers scattered throughout Anatolia and Macedonia to seek work. Apparently drawing on their experience, the local craft association found out about the techniques used for making towelling bathrobes at Brusa and Constantinople, and assimilated them so successfully that the weavers returned and built up a trade in them worth 400,000 – 500,000 leva. As this trade fell away in turn, Pirdop built up its trade in *gajtan*.[70]

To some extent Bulgarian textiles sold themselves. Merchants from the western Balkans and from Anatolia regularly visited the Bulgarian textile towns and the fairs on which textiles were distributed.[71] However, a large proportion of the cloth these towns produced was also made up into garments either in the towns themselves, or carried out by tailors and made up by them in the centres of consumption. The tailoring trade of Panagjurishte

---

[66] Ibid., pp. 73–4, 303–4; Konstantin Kosev, *Za kapitalisticheskoto razvitie na B'lgarskite zemi prez 60–te i 70–te godini na XIX vek* (Sofia, 1968), p. 43.   [67] See BALKSTAT.

[68] *DBI.* III, doc. 152 of 24 Aug. 1826.

[69] I. Sak'zov, 'Razvitieto na gradskija zhivot i na zanajatite v B'lgarija prez XVIII i XIX vek', *B'lgarija 1000 godini, 927–1927* (Sofia, 1930), p. 692; Aleksandrov, 'Istorijata', p. 8; Stojanov, *Pirdop*, p. 219.   [70] Konstantinov, 'Stupanski formi', pp. 462–4.

[71] For example, see Stefan Zahariev, *Geografiko istoriko statistichesko opisanie na Tatar Pazardzhishk't kaaz'* (Vienna, 1870), p. 47 n. 8.

expanded briskly between 1859 and 1866, when merchants started taking garments to Pirot and Constantinople.[72] At Samokov, tailors cut and sewed garments for sale to merchants from Bosnia and Albania, and this trade sustained a large and highly profitable turnover. These merchants found it convenient to stop over at Samokov en route for Constantinople, which was their principal destination, place and pre-pay for orders, then pick up the goods on the way home. Most of the garments they bought were 'most commonly tailored clothes' of inferior cloth but they also bought semi-finished goods, later to be finished at retail by Bosnian tailors.[73] A similar trade was engaged in by the tailors of Kotel. They conducted so large a volume of business with Greek traders as to claim, with some exaggeration, that 'the whole of Greece wore Kotel *aba*'.[74]

Soon many Ottoman cities were supporting Bulgarian tailors.[75] At Koprivshtitsa and Kalofer, they produced better quality garments. These were partially cut and sewn in the townships, but the bespoke trades for which they were aimed required that they should be finished in the centres of consumption according to customer orders and locally prevailing tastes. Therefore tailors from the Bulgarian textile townships could be found at work throughout the Balkans and beyond. In the 1860s, some of Koprivshtitsa's 1,500 tailors worked the year round in their workshops, but the majority left the town for long periods to tailor and sell garments woven of Koprivshtitsa cloth.[76] They were to be found at work especially at Plovdiv and Edirne, in the Greek islands and in the larger towns of Anatolia.[77]

The biggest concentration of Bulgarian tailors was at Constantinople. About 8,000 of them were resident there in January 1863.[78] Of these, Koprivshtitsa and Kalofer supplied the largest number and the most prominent personalities. Koprivshtitsa tailors first arrived in significant numbers in the 1820s to work in the *Hambarya*, the army tailoring workshop which clothed the nizam, but they subsequently branched out into civil trade. In around 1870, 41 Koprivshtitsa merchant houses dealt in Constantinople in the *aba* trade and at least 800 master journeymen and apprentices from Koprivshtitsa were usually to be found in their employ or working as independent craftsmen.[79]

[72] V. Cholakov, *Opisanie na selo Panagjurishte* (2nd edn Panagjurishte, 1940), p. 11.
[73] Hr. Semerdzhiev, *Samokov i okolnost'ta mu* (Sofia, 1913), p. 210.
[74] M, Arnaudov, *Iz minaloto na Kotel* (Sofia, 1931), p. 58.
[75] Irechek, 'P'tni belezki', p. 28.   [76] Oslekov, *Koprivshtitsa*, pp. 512, 515.
[77] Iv. G. Govedarov, *Koprivshtitsa v sv'rzka s' duhovnoto ni i politichesko v'zrazhdane* (Sofia, 1919), pp. 68–9.
[78] N. Nachov, 'Tsarigrad kao kulturen tsent'r na B'lgarite do 1877 g.', *Sbornik na b'lgarskata akademija na naukite*, XIX (Sofia, 1925), p. 176.
[79] Govedarov, *Koprivshtitsa*, p. 16; Oslekov, 'Koprivshtitsa', p. 516; Pranchov, *Koprivshtitsa*, p. 22.

Nachov leaves a brilliant account of the life and business of these merchant tailors and their assistants. Some worked in Galata and Tophani
but the largest number concentrated at the *Balkapanhan*, an ancient cara-
vanserai in the heart of old Stambul.[80] Each summer, long caravans of
carts loaded with bales of merchandize set out from Koprivshtitsa en
route for the Levant. In 1870, about 300 tonnes of clothing, in semi-manufactured condition, valued at about £160,000 Turk., and 20,000 dozens
of stockings[81] were sent out of the town, mainly for Constantinople, a
journey which took a month. They were accompanied by journeymen
who were set to work with the needle wherever the caravan stopped, and
by youths sent out for the first time to be apprenticed to the trade. On
arrival at the Imperial City, the apprentices would face a hard life, sweated
long hours 'for a *para* a thousand stitches' by masters who stinted on their
food, but this was the normal route to independent status, and often substantial wealth. Therefore 'all the prominent families gave children' to be
trained to the craft.[82]

Merchants from all over the Middle East placed orders at their shops,
and some of the best customers came from Egypt. This led one merchant
from Koprivshtitsa to set up a branch workshop in Constantinople to deal
with the demands of the Egyptian trade, and later to move this enterprise
to Alexandria and Cairo where 100 permanent workers were employed
by it.[83] Tailors from Klisura dispersed annually in search of clients along
the Anatolian coasts and the Aegean islands.[84] Kotel tailors were to be
found at work at the Balkan fairs, in the north and east Bulgarian towns
and the Dobrudzha supplying the inhabitants with clothing, some ready-
made, and some tailored for the customer.[85] At Panagjurishte, much of
the cloth was sold off, but part was packed into carts and taken by the
tailors to other towns, where they rented shops and ran up clothing for
their customers.[86]

Tailoring therefore became inextricably linked with the manufacturing
processes, which were feminized as a result. It was the womenfolk of
Klisura who produced the annual 130,000 arshins of *shajak* which the
tailors of that town distributed so widely.[87] So much of the manpower of
Koprivshtitsa engaged in tailoring that the women had to work full
time spinning and weaving *aba* for them. As they also engaged heavily in

[80] Nachov, 'Tsarigrad', pp. 4–5, 178–80.
[81] Govedarov, *Koprivshtitsa*, pp. 67–8 n. 7; Pranchov, *Koprivshtitsa*, p. 21.
[82] Oslekov, 'Koprivshtitsa', pp. 513–6.
[83] Nikolaj Todorov, *Balkanskijat grad, XV–XIX vek* (Sofia, 1972), pp. 256–60.
[84] Hr. F. Popov, *Grad Klisura v Aprilskoto v'zstanie* (Sofia, 1926), p. 8.
[85] Arnaudov, *Kotel*, p. 56; Sv. Iv. Manev, 'Kotlensko', *Sp.BID*, VII (1903), p. 509.
[86] Marin T. Vlajkov, *Belezhki v'rhu ekonomicheskoto polozhenie na grada Panagjurishte predi i
    sled v'zstanieto* (Plovdiv, 1904), p. 18.   [87] Popov, *Klisura*, p. 8.

stocking knitting, the tailoring trade outran the locally available supply of material, so the merchant tailors bought in cloth on the fairs and the markets of other towns.[88] We know of one large merchant tailor who bought in *aba* made in the Rhodope villages, which he obtained at Tatar Pazardzhik and brought to Koprivshtitsa to be run up into clothing in his own workshop and in those of his trade associates.[89] Kalofer tailors, too, drew on yarn and cloth produced not only in the town and its environs, but also from as far afield as Gabrovo, partly by purchase of goods brought to Kalofer to market, and partly by placing putting-out contracts.[90]

The textile industries of Macedonia

The manufacturing economy of the Ottoman Balkans extended southwards into Hellenic Macedonia and Thrace, where, as we noted in Chapter 2, domestic textile industries were strongly established. The raw material base of these industries continually changed in response to market conditions. Take Veroia, one of several textile centres in Pella. In the late eighteenth and early nineteenth centuries, Veroia and environs were noted for spinning and weaving towelling and shirts of linen from locally grown hemp and flax.[91] The town also dyed cotton yarn with Turkey red,[92] but all this yarn was exported for further processing in central Europe; the towelling and shirts were made for Balkan markets and were never made of cotton,[93] probably because this was a relatively expensive raw material. But as cotton prices eased, the towelling industry began to substitute linen with cotton, as yet on a small scale, because of the pressure of import competition. In the late 1850s, Veroia, Salonica and Edhessa exported 574,000 francs worth of cotton towelling, mainly to Levantine markets.[94] But for the time being, woollens predominated, for the same reasons as in Bulgaria. The immediate environs of Salonica produced 4.2 million francs worth of *aba*, while the textile centres of Pella, including Veroia, produced 1.7 million francs worth of woollen cloth, which were exported throughout the Balkans. Further south, Litochoron and Livadia specialized in the long established manufacture

[88] Stoil Staneff, *Das Gewerbewesen und die Gewerbepolitik in Bulgarien* (Ruse, 1901), p. 13.
[89] Todorov, *Balkanskijat grad*, p. 257.
[90] N. Nachov, *Kalofer v minaloto, 1707–1877* (Sofia, 1927), p. 270.
[91] William M. Leake, *Travels in Northern Greece* (London, 1835), III, p. 287.
[92] Edme Mentelle, *Géographie comparée ou analyse de la géographie ancienne et moderne – Turquie d'Europe* (Paris, 1785), p. 238.
[93] E. M. Cousinery, *Voyage dans la Macédoine* (Paris, 1831), I, p. 70.
[94] B. Nicolaidy, *Les Turcs et la Turquie contemporaine* (Paris, 1859), II, p. 344.

of heavy woollen *skuti*,[95] exporting 1.2 million francs worth into maritime Mediterranean markets.[96] Silk also became a significant local textile product, especially at Edhessa, and a mechanized textile silk reeling enterprise was established there in 1868.[97] The zone of industrial activity extended as far north as Monastir (Bitola), or more exactly to a group of hill villages outside Monastir, rather than to the town itself. Small quantities of woollen cloth and clothing from Monastir region (and from Kruševo) were sold on Prilep fair in 1864,[98] and 1.5 million piastres of woollen stockings left Monastir for the Ottoman provinces in 1867.[99]

The future of textile manufacturing in Hellenic Macedonia was to lie in cotton spinning, but competitiveness in this industry awaited the introduction of machinery. Three cotton mills were set up in or near Salonica between 1866 and 1875, and a fourth at Naousa in 1876.[100] The effect of this development would be to shift outwork labour into cotton weaving, the viability of which would be restored, and (presumably) the woollen and linen trades would be run down to release the necessary labour.

With the exception of the Niš *pašaluk* which formed part of the Bulgarian industrial zone, the lands stretching north and west from Monastir through into Bosnia were devoid of substantial domestic woollen industries, and provided market outlets for the Bulgarian and south Macedonian textile manufacturers. At least in the uplands, poor communications, endemic political instability and brigandage,[101] all of which had so much abated in Bulgaria, created an unfavourable environment for manufacturing and commerce. So rather than depend on handicrafts as a source of cash income, peasants left their villages in droves as periodic migrants (*pečalbars*). Textile work and migrant labouring were not mutually complementary, because the absence of male labour diverted the work of the women into maintaining farm production.

The woollen industry and the Ottoman state

Military contracts formed an important component of demand for woollens. However state influence and intervention was a mixed blessing. Before the reform era, the Ottoman state, when it required a service from its subjects, resorted without hesitation to compulsion. It did not do this because the market mechanism was inoperative, and it never sought

[95] Michael Palairet, 'Désindustrialization à la périphérie. Etudes sur la région des Balkans au XIXe siècle', *Histoire, économie et société*, IV (1985), p. 266.
[96] Nicolaidy, *Les Turcs*, pp. 344–5.
[97] Stanoje Mijatović, 'Grad Voden', *Brastvo*, XVIII (Belgrade, 1924), p. 71.
[98] GBC Macedonia 1864, p. 587.   [99] GBC Macedonia 1867, p. 625.
[100] Dančo Zografski, *Razvitokot na kapitalističkite elementi vo Makedonija za vreme na turskoto vladeenje* (Skopje, 1967), p. 482.   [101] GBC Macedonia 1856, p. 208.

service without reciprocal compensation. Rather it regarded its subjects as vassals who were duty bound to execute its bidding. For its subjects, the execution of the state's commands might not necessarily be a burden, because a duty performed under customary terms could ossify into a privilege, and there are plenty of examples of this. Nevertheless, it could make subjects wary of performing new services for the state, for fear that past service might be seized on by the authorities as a precedent for future demands. For example, in 1822 the state arsenal at Constantinople directed the governor of Varna to send fifty carpenters, since it was short of labour. They were to be paid and fed, but failed to arrive because 'the Varna population fears it, claiming that this duty of supplying workers would become customary'.[102] The Varna peasants probably had good cause for their fears, as the interventions of the state to secure supplies of *shajak* for the army show.

In the 1820s the Ottoman army reforms increased the need for woollen clothing,[103] but the moribund weaving industries of Salonica and Plovdiv were incapable of producing the quantity needed. So from 1827 onwards, alternative sources were sought.[104] Having ascertained that certain textile villages in the Rhodope produced the kind of cloth the army wanted, the military authorized its cloth contractors to force orders upon the producers.[105] This forced supply was only abolished in 1865.[106] The work was contracted at administered prices, and these were unattractive. Either because of the dishonesty of the putting out firms like Gjumjushgerdan, which handled most of this business, or because producers retaliated in the only way open to them, the supplies delivered to the military were insufficient in volume, and frequently rotten in quality.[107] Further heavy-handed attempts were made to overcome the shortfall in the supply of military cloth. In 1832, the state attempted to boost supply from Sliven by sending in a senior tax official 'to put into good order in Sliven district the production of *aba* needed for army clothing and to ensure a useful and respectable life for the *reaya* there'.[108]

The outcome was characteristic of what happened when officials were given special powers for procurement. The weavers were forced to supply cloth at 60 per cent of its market price, and the purchasing agents resold part of it back to the merchants to make a killing. Certain weavers there-

[102] *DBI.* III, doc. 132, pp. 68–9.   [103] Nachov, *Kalofer*, p. 50.
[104] Todorov, *Balkanskijat grad*, p. 270.
[105] Konstantin Kanev, *Minaloto na selo Momchilovtsi, Smoljansko* (Sofia, 1975), p. 512; N. Todorov, 'Svedenija za tehnologijata na Slivenskite tekstilni izdelija ot 30te godini na XIX v', *Sbornik za narodni umotvorenija*, L (1963), p. 408 n.1.
[106] Kanev, *Momchilovtsi*, p. 512.
[107] *B'lgarija* (Constantinople), I (1859) p. 22 col. 1; I, p. 28; I, p. 63; II (1860), p. 59; *DBI.* III, docs. 183, 315, 459.   [108] *DBI.* III, doc. 280, p. 154.

upon smuggled their cloth out of the district preventing the purchasers from filling their orders.[109] In 1837, the state, still unable to secure sufficient supplies, wanted to reimplant the techniques of the Rhodope industry at Erzerum in eastern Anatolia.[110] These efforts of the as yet unreformed Ottoman state to 'promote' industrial activity should caution against the assumption that state orders would necessarily have promoted production. In this case they damaged an already established industry. The great advance associated with the reforms was that they entailed the recognition of economic pluralism, and required the state to operate within the framework of the market economy.

The early woollen mills were established exclusively for state contract work, to supply uniform cloth for cutting and sewing by the Bulgarian tailors at the Hambarya. They were a response to the inability of the state to secure supplies by the coercive means to which it was accustomed.[111] Until the 1860s at the earliest, woollen manufacturing for the free market showed little sign of migrating from cottage and craft shop to the factory, probably because it would have gained little or nothing in efficiency by doing so. Thus the early factories did not compete with the proto-industries; rather, their production was complementary. The state was under no illusion that it would secure its cloth more cheaply by factory methods; it simply wanted to assure itself of supplies.[112] As it turned out, the factory products cost it dear, and the quality problem remained unsolved.[113]

Regarding their partial dependence on imported uniform cloth as strategically insecure, the authorities were open to any proposal, fraudulent[114] or otherwise, which might lead to improvement of the internal supply of military cloth. Their attempts to promote production at Sliven indirectly bore fruit when Dobri Zheljazkov, a Sliven mechanic, who engaged also in the trades of weaver and cloth merchant, learned of the potential for machine production when visiting a textile mill at Ekaterinoslav in Russia. He liquidated his trading stock to buy equipment and smuggled it from Russia to Sliven, to circumvent Russia's prohibition on machine exports. Probably in 1834, he set up a weavery at his wife's house, and quickly expanded into other buildings. As he wanted state orders, he looked for and quickly won state funding and protection. The resulting parastatal enterprise replaced his former workshops and employed a payroll of 500. Zheljazkov brought in new machinery from

[109] *DBI.* III, doc. 315.   [110] *DBI.* III, doc. 408.
[111] Todorov, *Balkanskijat grad,* pp. 204, 251, 270.   [112] *DBI.* III, doc. 377.
[113] *DBI.* III, doc. 551; Todorov, *Balkanskijat grad,* pp. 277, 278; D. Mishajkov, 'Ocherk na fabrichnata v'lnena industrija v B'lgarija', *Sp.BID,* VIII (1904), p. 475.
[114] Ami Boué, *La Turquie d'Europe* (Paris, 1840), III, pp. 100, 102.

Verviers.[115] The factory, still working and employing 400 souls in 1870, never competed for orders on the market, and charged the army more than the going market price. The main thrust of its effort was in carding (to which it devoted its water power) and to (hand driven) mule spinning,[116] rather than weaving, though it had a few flyshuttle looms. Its competition had no effect on the local hand weaving trade, which continued to flourish, at least till the late 1850s.[117]

In 1847 a smaller factory was set up by the putting out firm of Gjumjushgerdan near Plovdiv.[118] They had a curious mixture of motives, one of which was to find an outlet for produce raised on the nearby Gjumjushgerdan estate at Dermendere. But the main aim was to supplement the supply of hand spun yarn. As the founders pointed out to the Ottoman intendant, only by machine spinning could they meet orders of the size the army wanted to place, because their putting out network in the Rhodope lacked the capacity. So the local weavers' guild, instead of fearing for its members' livelihood, welcomed the venture as it promised to ease their supply of semi-manufactured material.[119]

The early factories were used, not to substitute cottage manufacturing, but as high-cost marginal supplements to productive capacity, needed because of the inelasticity of the supply of proto-industrial labour. Not until the 1870s were factories set up to supply outputs in the free market. The inefficiency of the early woollen mills is commonly explained by the difficulty of doing business in the feudal environment of the Ottoman state. To some extent this argument is valid, though not in the intended sense. The experience of these mills shows that conditions had yet to be created which would promote the formation of a productive factory workforce. This was because there was as yet little demand for such employment, so the factories were saddled with high labour costs.

Zheljazkov, apologizing for the shortcomings of the Sliven factory's products, told his imperial employer:

The local workers whom I attracted to work were beginners and I was compelled to instruct each of them from the beginning. Besides this, because of the fear which exists of entering state employment, the fear of state work was only overcome by the payment of very high wages, the provision of their food and payment of their military exemption tax (*cizye*) and other assisting measures. . . By this means I succeeded in attracting the necessary workers, but as these were beginners most of the work we delivered was defective.[120]

---

[115] 'Dobri Zheljazkov fabrikadzhijata', in *100 godini b'lgarska industrija 1834–1937*, ed. V. Nikolchov (Sofia, 1937), pp. 5–7.   [116] Todorov, *Balkanskijat grad*, pp. 277, 278.
[117] Ibid., p. 281.
[118] Nikolai Todorov, 'Za naemnija trud v b'lgarskite zemi k'm sredata na XIX v.', *Istoricheski pregled BAN*, XV (1959), pp. 12–13.   [119] Ibid., pp. 22–3.
[120] Todorov, *Balkanskijat grad*, p. 280.

These workers were not the experienced domestic textile workers of Sliven town. 'The Bulgarian inhabitants' says Staneff, 'stood well economically and consequently did not take up factory work.'[121] Even the payment of the *cizye* for non-Muslim workers attracted few Christians to work in the factory. Rather the employers had recourse to the services of a marginal element, gipsy girls and poor Muslim widows.[122] These became the permanent labour pool on which the factory had to draw. A visitor in the 1860s described the female element of the labour force as 'Turkish gipsies . . . hastening on their entry to their workshops to veil themselves up in their yashmaks.'[123]

In some cases, the factories forced the labour of unfree workers. A woollen mill which was founded in 1867 at Bali Effendi, a suburb of Sofia, attempted in 1867 to solve its labour supply problem by exploiting 200 orphans as weavers under the guise of educating them.[124] This state institution was set up to supply the gendarmerie with uniform cloth.[125] It was more than a mere workhouse, for new Czech machinery was installed in 1869, with further mechanization to follow in 1870.[126] The textile factories were also at various times worked by convict labour[127] and by Ottoman soldiers.[128]

The Plovdiv factory of Gjumjushgerdan employed free male migrant workers,[129] but its performance does not suggest this arrangement was satisfactory. They were probably craft journeymen of Greek origin from the upland textile towns and from Plovdiv. Their pay, at 75 piastres a month in 1847 was not high, but they received their subsistence as well. It was never a very profitable factory.[130] Its labour costs seem to have risen sharply by 1868 to between 0.45 francs and 2.5 francs a day.[131] It may have been for this reason that, a few years later, the Gjumjushgerdans allowed the mill to 'go to ruin'.[132]

Bulgarian industry 1869–1877

Among Bulgarian writers there is a consensus that the proto-industries reached their apogee in the 1860s, then declined rapidly in the face of import penetration. We will show in Chapter 7 that these industries

[121] Staneff, *Gewerbewesen*, p. 131 n. 1.
[122] S. Tabakov, *Istorija na grad Sliven* (Sofia, 1929), III, p. 113; Radka Bradinska, 'Navlizaneto na b'lgarskata zhena v promishlenoto proizvodstvo', *Profs'juzni letopisi* (1968), p. 211.   [123] Tabakov, *Sliven*, III, p. 113.
[124] Aubaret, 1876, in Michoff, III (1950), pp. 696–7.
[125] Wilhelmy, *Hochbulgarien*, II, p. 113.   [126] Michoff, II/1 (1953), pp. 318, 346.
[127] Mishajkov, 'Ocherk', p. 475.   [128] Tabakov, *Sliven*, III, p. 114.
[129] Todorov, 'Naemnija trud', p. 21.
[130] Dimit'r Mladenov, *Pojava na fabrichen proletariat v B'lgarija* (Sofia, 1961), p. 10.
[131] Michoff, III (1950), p. 583.   [132] GBC E. Rumelia 1876, p. 640.

Table 3.4 *Textile industry indicators for Ottoman Bulgaria 1862–1877*

Year	Turnover of Gjumjushgerdan (000 piastres)	Capital of Stanchev, Bjanov associates (£ Turk.)
1862	n.d.	1,400
1863	n.d.	1,830
1864	n.d.	2,100
1865	n.d.	2,700
1866	n.d.	n.d.
1867	n.d.	2,970
1868	n.d.	n.d.
1869	1,769	3,875
1870	1,177	n.a.
1871	1,687	4,280
1872	1,787	4,440
1873	2,168	4,000
1874	2,457	n.a.
1875	2,620	5,000
1876	2,671	5,100
1877	2,853	n.a.

Source:
Kosev, *Kapitalisticheskoto razvitie*, pp. 42, 43.

collapsed after the liberation, but there is little hard evidence of a wide-spread *pre*-liberation decline, and some evidence of further expansion. The period 1869–77 was less expansionary than the preceding decade, but this was probably inevitable given the international trade recession after 1873.

Gajtan making probably expanded right up to the liberation. At Gabrovo, after meteoric growth in the 1860s, production grew a further 19 per cent between 1870 and 1877.[133] The pattern was probably similar at Pirdop.[134] However, the evidence is inconsistent. One writer on Kazanl'k claims that its *gajtan* industry declined between 1850 and 1877;[135] another states that its 'tempo' strengthened right up to the liberation.[136] Again, the Samokov woollen industry was in decline in the 1870s, but enjoyed brisk business during the 1877–8 war itself, executing military orders.[137] The evidence in Table 3.4 above, showing two series

[133] Pet'r Tsonchev, *Iz stopanskoto minalo na Gabrovo* (Gabrovo, 1929), p. 311.
[134] Al. G. Dodov, 'Gajtandzhijstvo na gr. Pirdop', *Sp.BID*, VIII (1904), p. 331.
[135] Pavlov, 'Kazanl'k', pp. 319, 320.
[136] T. B. and M. St[ajnov], 'Industrija v Kazanl'k', *Kazanl'k v minaloto i dnes*, III (1928), p. 544.   [137] Wilhelmy, *Hochbulgarien*, II, pp. 9–10.

which indicate the level of business activity of two major firms in the woollen putting-out trades, indicates that the volume of transactions rose strongly to the very end of the Ottoman period, in sympathy with the strong performance of the farm economy.

There was also a tendency towards factory production which was stimulated by free market influences, rather than by state intervention. In discussing the transition from proto-industrial to factory production, Mendels emphasizes the rising cost of the former system, caused by its very success in diffusing manufacturing tasks to an ever widening circle of workers. In particular, rising wages would provide a spur to mechanization. It seems likely that such a sequence occurred in the Bulgarian provinces in the 1870s. Unfortunately there is little data, but we know that the cotton weaving trade of Sofia had to pay its workers sharply rising wages after 1870, as insatiable peasant demand for its products created shortfalls in supply.[138] As we have already indicated that wages in farming were also rising at this time, it would not be surprising if wage inflation affected the woollen industries. Declines in certain distressed Bulgarian industries may have been induced by rising returns within the more progressive trades, and in farming, squeezing the margins of entrepreneurs and causing them to reduce output.

The growth in the demand for yarn to the end of the period of Ottoman rule in Bulgaria was caused largely by the expansion of *gajtan* making. Gabrovo *gajtan* manufacturer Kalpazanov began making arrangements for providing himself with spinning capacity. His plans were not to be put into action till after 1878,[139] but other mechanized enterprises began to appear during the last years of Ottoman rule. In 1870, a *shajak* factory opened at Panagjurishte, and in 1870 and 1874 two workshops with machinery were opened at Sliven. Again in 1874, a spinnery with carding and combing machines was set up at Asenovo, and another 'textile factory' transiently appeared at Vladaja near Samokov.[140] At Karlovo, Ivan Grozev opened a woollen mill in 1875 mainly as a servicing facility to the trade, and found himself deluged with carding, fulling and spinning contracts.[141] At Gabrovo, Kalpazanov installed a carding engine in 1872, which he built at his own forge, and in 1873 he was using wool sorting machinery.[142] At Pirot (subsequently to pass to Serbia), another small woollen mill was set up in 1872, mainly to card wool, spin yarn for braiding and carpet making, and to make *gajtan*. Uniquely, this enterprise was founded by a Muslim, one Ali Beg, though operated by a Bulgarian

[138] Konstantinov, 'Stupanski formi', pp. 449–50.   [139] See below, p. 245.

[140] Kosev, *Kapitalisticheskoto razvitie*, pp. 64–5, 67.

[141] G. T. D[anailov], 'P'rvata b'lgarska tekstilna fabrika', *Sp.BID*, VI (1902), p. 569.

[142] Tsonchev, *Gabrovo*, p. 616.

master from Samokov. During its short existence it provided useful services to the local woollen trades.[143]

On the basis of the fragmentary evidence presented both for agriculture and textile manufacturing, we conclude that although the most rapid phase of expansion was probably concluded in the late 1860s, the output of the Bulgarian lands, in both sectors, was at or near its peak at the time of the liberation. Ottoman rule in Bulgaria was extinguished at the high tide of its prosperity. We reject the contention that the collapse of Ottoman rule in Bulgaria was the political counterpart to the collapse of its economy.

[143] Milivoje M. Savić, *Naša industrija i zanati* (Sarajevo, 1922), II, pp. 119–20.

4   Serbia 1815–1875: institutions, resources and market forces

The emergent Serbian state

While the core provinces of the Ottoman Empire were well settled with Muslims, the more powerful of whom exercised territorial control, Serbia was a borderland where the Muslim population was too thin for the *âyans* to exercise tight control over the Christian Serbs. In the eighteenth century, the lands comprising the Belgrade *pašaluk*, later to be the core area of Serbia, were contested between the Ottomans and the Habsburgs; between 1789 and 1791 the territory was occupied by Austrian forces. The power vacuum within Serbia had unwelcome attributes for the Serbs – the territory was particularly susceptible to the attention of marauders – but it also meant that they were able to arm themselves, and when faced with overwhelming force, to take refuge across the Danube.[1]

At the Treaty of Svishtov, 1791, Austria withdrew from the *pašaluk*, requiring the Ottomans to respect the rights of the Serbian population. To comply was much in the interests of Sultan Selim who did not want the revenues of the *pašaluk* diverted into the hands of the Janissaries, or those of their ally Pasvanoglu of Vidin, who coveted the province. Selim appointed his supporter Hadži Mustafa Pasha to govern Belgrade. To prevent the interposition of the *âyans* in the tax collection system, the Serbian villages were taxed *en bloc*, and collection was left to the headmen. Threatened by the Janissaries, who were converging on Belgrade, Hadži Mustafa also permitted the Serbs to retain their weapons, and used them as political allies to compensate for the lack of reliable troops of his own.

Consequently, the *âyans* were given no chance to carve out latifundia, the taxes were light, trade was unrestricted, and the thin population largely governed itself. The Austrian frontier stood open to a burgeoning trade in livestock.[2] Disposing natural resources far in excess of their capacity to exploit them, the Serbians enjoyed a period of prosperity and

---

[1] Charles and Barbara Jelavich, *The Establishment of the Balkan National States, 1804–1920* (Seattle, 1977), pp. 26–7.
[2] Ekonomski institut N. R. Srbije, *Proizvodne snage N. R. Srbije* (Belgrade, 1953), p. 6.

even stability,[3] which attracted a strong inflow of settlers from the dinaric zone.[4] Essentially, Serbia was experiencing a system of government whose fundamentals would later be embedded within the autonomous Serbian state.

However, in 1798, the Porte, now at war with France, had to strip Serbia of troops, and allow the Janissaries to return to Belgrade. They were not slow to exploit this opening. Hadži Mustafa was assassinated by them in 1801,[5] and disorders ensued as they seized land,[6] fought off each others' claims, and endeavoured to bring the Serbian villagers to heel. Armed clashes with the Serbs culminated in 1804 in an open Serbian uprising, led by Karadjordje. The insurgents proclaimed themselves to be the Sultan's loyal subjects who sought only the rights they had previously enjoyed, but they looked to Russia for help, and received Russian assistance. This threatened the security of the Porte. From 1806, it was once more at war against Russia, and failure to break the rebellion could cause the *pašaluk* to slip under Russian control. After the failure of a punitive expedition in 1805,[7] the situation was allowed to drift, since the Russian war tied up the Porte's resources. But in 1812, the Russians, faced with Napoleon's invasion, disengaged themselves from the Balkans, and made peace with the Porte at the Treaty of Bucharest. The Ottomans resumed their efforts to reoccupy the province. The Serbs, seldom coherently organized, were crushed in 1813. A horde of Muslims streamed back to reassert their claims,[8] but Ottoman policy towards the territory vacillated between repression and a search for an accommodation with the local chieftains, who could still summon up armed support.

Fresh uprisings broke out in 1814 and 1815, in which the insurgents won several small but decisive battles. By now, Russian threats were again brought to bear on the Porte, so the Ottomans compromised with the new insurgent leader, Miloš Obrenović, rather than reinvade the territory and risk renewed embroilment with the Russians. As Obrenović was prepared to accept limited autonomy, the Porte recognized him as its vassal, and as supreme leader of Serbia. The Serbians were to govern themselves, more or less as they had done under Hadži Mustafa, and would pay the head tax to Miloš. He would in turn pay tribute to the Sultan. Ottoman garrisons would remain in Belgrade and in several other fortresses.

Miloš had to assert himself over rival Serbian factions which disputed

---

[3] Tihomir Djordjević, *Iz Srbije kneza Miloša* (Belgrade, 1924), p. 25.
[4] Jovan Cvijić, 'Metanastazička kretanja, njihovi uzroci i posledice', *NiPS (Belgrade)*, XII (1922), pp. 5–6.   [5] Djordjević, *Iz Srbije*, p. 25.
[6] Jozo Tomasevich, *Peasants, Politics and Economic Change in Yugoslavia* (Stanford, CA, 1955), p. 38.   [7] Jelavich and Jelavich, *Balkan States*, p. 32.
[8] Georges Castellan, *La vie quotidienne en Serbie au seuil de l'indépendance, 1815–1839* (Paris, 1967), p. 32.

his authority. Recognizing that control over land and revenue was the key to power, he resisted the efforts of local chieftains to carve out latifundia. Fearing that regional governors might establish territorial fiefs on the basis of their delegated powers of tax collection, he treated them as salaried officials, holding them responsible for collecting the head-tax, without letting them remunerate themselves from the proceeds.[9] The threat of refeudalization was real; rights of *spahiluk* could not be abolished till the consent of the Porte had been secured in 1833,[10] and some former Janissary *čifliks* had been seized during the revolutionary period by local chieftains.[11] Probably on the basis of these rights of *spahiluk*, Serbian notables began to behave towards their peasants as feudal aristocrats. In 1827, one chieftain compelled them to provide corvée labour on his land.[12] He built up substantial blocks of real estate, and Milić writes of 'massive corvées used by large elders' properties'. Miloš played the same game, since he regarded himself as above the law, and made himself the largest agricultural proprietor of his period.[13] Yet fearing a growing challenge to his power from the embrionic aristocracy, he aligned himself with the peasant aspiration to free landownership.

In 1835 he took a decisive step in stopping the refeudalization of land tenure: the right of territorial administrators to demand corvées was suppressed.[14] This, combined with the earlier suppression of *spahiluk*, reduced the attraction of holding large complexes of land. The wealthy, finding that 'the land is without value for the town inhabitant, who can neither work it nor have it worked on his account',[15] sought (like Miloš himself) to buy real estate abroad, mainly in Romania where the agrarian framework ensured a higher and more reliable return than in Serbia. The best documented of these investors was Major Miša Anastasijević (1803–85) who rose from the peasantry to extreme wealth. He graduated via the salt supply business in 1828 into purchases of salt leases and *spahiluks* in the Romanian Principalities; these investments were linked with loan contracts to Romanian magnates.[16] Such investment behaviour probably made mid-nineteenth-century Serbia a capital exporting country, for want of an institutional framework suitable for deploying

[9] John R. Lampe and Marvin R. Jackson, *Balkan Economic History, 1500–1950* (Bloomington, IN, 1982), p. 112.   [10] Tomasevich, *Peasants*, p. 39.
[11] John R. Lampe, 'Financial Structure and the Economic Development of Serbia, 1878–1912' (unpublished Ph.D. thesis, University of Wisconsin, 1971), p. 27; Nikola Vučo, *Položaj seljaštva. Knj. I, Eksproprijacija od zemlje u XIX veku* (Belgrade, 1955), p. 2.
[12] Djordje Magarašević, 'Putovanje po Srbiji u 1827 god. 1827', in *Biblioteka baština*, I, ed. S. Velmar-Janković (Belgrade, 1983), p. 269.
[13] Danica Milić, *Trgovina Srbije 1815–1839* (Belgrade, 1959), pp. 54, 58–9.
[14] Ibid., p. 58.   [15] AAE CCB tome. 3. Report of 13 July 1863.
[16] Matija Ban, 'Život Majora Miše Anastasijevića', *GSUD* (Belgrade, 1890), pp. 272–6, 285–6.

investment funds at home.[17] In consequence, the smallholding structure of Serbia survived largely undisturbed.

Miloš welcomed immigrants, and to strengthen his support, saw they were provided with land, if need be at the expense of the resident population.[18] To consolidate his peasant power base, he decreed in 1836 the non-seizure of homesteads for repayment of debt;[19] and to provide for security in time of war or famine he emulated the Hungarians in establishing maize granaries in each community.[20] As a contribution to his people's welfare, this was a measure of great significance. The lack of grain production for surplus left communities exposed to famine in years of harvest failure. The scheme was practicable, because maize was easier than wheat to store on a small scale. The communal granaries survived right up to World War I.

At least from 1833, Miloš obtained the bulk of his revenue by levying the head-tax in a shadow currency, the tax piastre, which was fixed at a rate far in excess of the market piastre in which the tribute was reckoned.[21] In 1837 the head-tax brought in £150,000 sterling and the tribute cost £21,900.[22] Being highly acquisitive, Miloš sought additional revenue by bringing foreign trade under his control, selling export licences to favoured businessmen.[23] His manipulation of the export trade weighed upon the more commercially active notables and the urban merchants, who were excluded effectively both from the perquisites of *spahiluk* and from free participation in international trade.

As long as Serbians felt threatened by Ottoman pressure, Miloš could rule as an autocrat. However, from 1829 when autonomy was guaranteed under the Treaty of Adrianople, he was pressed by opposition from the Serbian notables and the business community.[24] They forced him to proclaim a constitution in 1838, and to abdicate the following year. His son soon followed him into exile, and Aleksandar, son of Karadjordje, was made prince. Foremost among the demands of Miloš's opponents, who styled themselves the Constitutional Defenders, was freedom of commerce, so a bonfire of controls on prices, trade and finance followed their assumption of power.[25] The minimum homestead law was also dropped. Its abandonment is dubiously claimed to have resulted in agrarian insolvencies which contributed to increasing disenchantment with the Constitutional Defender government.

[17] V. Stojančević, *Miloš Obrenović i njegovo doba* (Belgrade, 1966), p. 447; AAE CCB. t. 3 dispatch of 8 July 1863.   [18] Djordjević, *Iz Srbije*, pp. 42, 48–50.
[19] Tomasevich, *Peasants*, p. 42.   [20] Ami Boué, *La Turquie d'Europe* (Paris, 1840), III, p. 38.
[21] Lampe, 'Financial Structure', p. 101.   [22] PRO FO 78 312. despatch of 10 June 1837.
[23] Lampe, 'Financial Structure', p. 78.
[24] L. S. Stavrianos, *The Balkans since 1453* (New York, 1958), pp. 252–3.
[25] Lampe, 'Financial Structure', p. 89.

The Constitutional Defenders fell in 1859, and Miloš Obrenović returned to power in his old age. He died in 1860, and was succeeded by his son Mihailo (1860–8). Their restoration cemented the small-scale ownership policy, because the Obrenović princes still regarded the peasantry as their power base, and took paternalistic measures to insulate the peasants from economic pressures. New homestead laws were enacted in 1861 and 1873, the first of which provided for the distribution of state and *opština* land to landless and land-short families,[26] while the second restored the prohibition on the seizure of homesteads by creditors.[27]

Notionally, the Obrenović restoration represented a defeat for economic liberalism. Miloš and Mihailo were to try to bureaucratize their rule, and they set up a standing army. Yet this did not presage a shift towards big government. Free trade continued, and small government was forced on all Serbian rulers regardless of their inclinations. In time the peasants were able to exert formidable political pressures for low taxation, which ensured that Serbian governments fell into penury if they tried too hard to expand the compass of their activity.[28]

Before 1878, economic interventions were conditioned mainly by military preoccupations. The Serbian government built up an arms industry. In particular, funds were lavished on the state arsenal at Kragujevac, and (less successfully) in supplying it with metals from the iron and copper mines at Majdanpek. Between 1848 and 1858, 1.58 million Austrian florins – the equivalent of two years' tax revenues – were swallowed by Majdanpek with no discernable result. The true resource cost was still greater because corvée labour, valued at 800,000 florins, was also used, as well as timber from the state forests of the area, to which no cost was ascribed. The Kragujevac arsenal cost 250,000 dinars a year to run.[29] What the army wanted, on the whole it got, as was noted (approvingly) by a foreign staff officer before the military débâcle of 1876:[30]

In default of luxury industry, [Serbia] has made a war industry. There are no silk factories, only those for military blankets; no jewellery nor marquetry nor goldsmiths' work, but powdermills, cartridge works, cannon foundries and arms factories. No manufacture of novelties nor of fashion goods, but of military equipment and clothing and baggage supplies. No operas but military schools; no palace, but good barracks, hospitals and regimental schools.

---

[26] Vučo, *Položaj*, p. 12.   [27] *Proizvodne snage*, pp. 9–10.
[28] Michael Palairet, 'Fiscal Pressure and Peasant Impoverishment in Serbia before World War I', *JEcH*, XXXIX (1979), pp. 719–40.
[29] GBC Serbia 1895, p. 5; M. Dj. Milićević, *Kneževina Srbija* (Belgrade, 1876), p. 948; Miroslav D. Popović, *Kragujevac i njegovo privredno područje* (Belgrade, 1956), pp. 337–8.
[30] *La Serbie et la Bulgarie en 1876, explorées par un officier d'état major attaché d'ambassade* (Paris, 1876), p. 21.

As a precondition to opening the interior to commerce, transport conditions needed urgent improvement. The road network that Serbia inherited from the Ottomans was better than was sometimes claimed, but over much of the country it could not take wheeled traffic.[31] However the calls of the military on Serbia's modest budgets precluded heavy expenditures on civil infrastructure.[32] Only in 1864 and 1866 was legislation introduced to provide for the main traffic arteries to be macadamized.[33] Though progress was made, these roads did not lower transport costs sufficiently to support the long-range movement of bulk commodities. In the 1870s, some of the most fertile districts along the Morava valley were largely cut off from markets, even though the main north–south trunk road passed through them. Rather than use road transport, the firm of Despinić, trading from Kovin on the Danube opposite Smederevo, tried to tap the valley of the Great Morava by rafting it down river, because of obstructions which prevented steamer traffic. The attempt only attained partial success, as much of the freight was lost.[34] The need for this desperate expedient to monetize the crops of a relatively accessible lowland area is an indication of the extreme fragmentation of the market.

It was only with railways that interior regions would effectively be integrated into the market. Up to 1878, Serbia built none. Vučo explains this failure in terms of great power politics, and of Serbia's lack of capital and engineers,[35] but it was more a matter of choice. From 1851 onward a stream of foreign railway construction proposals were put forward, and all were turned down. If the army had wanted railways it could probably have had them, but it feared that railway projects might divert funds from its own wasteful investment priorities. With monumental lack of foresight, its staff feared a railway to the Ottoman frontier might be a liability in wartime.[36] Railways were also unwanted by the trading community, which disposed strong influence with the administration. Business feared that the monopolistic system of 'exorbitant profits, long credits and slow returns' might be jeopardized by them.[37]

These were the salient institutional characteristics of the Serbian state. In the following section we examine the structure of the farming system in the mid nineteenth century. Because of the paucity of statistical data, it is

---

[31] Danica Milić, 'Ekonomski potencijal ustaničke Srbije', in *Istorijski značaj srpske revolucije 1804 godine* (Belgrade, 1963), pp. 169–70.

[32] PRO FO 78 1377 1858. Despatch of 5 Mar. 1858.

[33] Nikola Vučo, 'Železnički saobraćaj kao faktor privrednog razvoja Srbije u XIX veku', *AHOI*, V (1977), pp. 172–4.

[34] A. Aleksić, 'Morava, njeno sadašnje stanje i mogućnost plovidbe', *GSUD, 2nd section*, XI (Belgrade, 1879), pp. 72–80.   [35] Vučo, 'Saobraćaj', p. 176.

[36] D. Arnaoutovitch, *Histoire des chemins de fer yougoslaves, 1825–1937* (Paris, 1937), pp. 38–54, 52.   [37] PRO FO 78 2237. No. 4 comm. of 16 May 1868.

difficult to bring the structure of the Serbian economy into focus before the 1860s. Only then did detailed economic data become available, thanks to Vladimir Jakšić (1824–99), a German-trained statistician who in 1864 founded a statistical section within the Finance Ministry.[38] It would be convenient to represent conditions in the early 1860s, when the Serbian economy suddenly emerges in quantitative perspective, as those of an undeveloped economic system in a stable state. But Jakšić's work showed that this system was not in equilibrium; it was becoming decreasingly productive. The reasons for this deterioration require analysis, after which we examine the impact made by the trade boom of the 1860s and early 1870s. As an aid to this research, use has been made of the registers of a census taken in 1863 of population, real estate and monthly incomes.[39]

Economic structure 1840s-1860s

In contrast with Bulgaria, Serbia was overwhelmingly rural. Towns of 2,000 or more inhabitants accounted for but 4.1 per cent of population in 1834 and 7.0 per cent in 1863.[40] The economy was based on smallholder subsistence farming. The countryside was politically stable, Christian, illiterate and 'coarse in its appetites without being sober'.[41] Farming was virtually the only rural occupation; there was little cottage industry, and little urban craft industry either. There were no large estates, and hardly any rural properties which were worked primarily for commercial ends. The number of holdings in this period is not known, but in 1863, landlessness was still rare save among urban dwellers.

The farmsteads and their surrounding fields were set in a milieu of open range wasteland. In 1867, the cultivated area (including meadows) accounted for 15 per cent of the land surface of Serbia.[42] A century later, in 1965, some 62 per cent of Serbia's land was being cropped.[43] Therefore only about 24 per cent of Serbia's cultivable surface was cultivated in the 1860s. So population was not as yet pressing at the margin of cultivation. Much of the uncultivated land was rich, and provided the peasants with the grazing resources for a large animal population. Besides

---

[38] Holm Sundhaussen, 'Historische Statistik als neues Arbeitsgebiet der Balkanforschung' (manuscript), p. 5. The statistics were published in Državopis Srbije (20 vol. 1863–89).

[39] For a fuller analysis of this document see Michael Palairet, 'Rural Serbia in the Light of the Census of 1863', JEEcH, XXIV (1995). The census registers for 1863 are manuscripts shelfmarked as Ministarstvo finansija, Popisne knjige, 1862–4. The document is incomplete but surviving records capture about 70 per cent of the population.

[40] See above Table 1.10.   [41] AAE CCB t. 1. despatch of 14 May 1847, fo. 390.

[42] Serbia: Državopis Srbije (Belgrade, 1871), V, pp. 1–115.

[43] See S. Broekhuisen, Atlas of the Cereal Growing Areas of Europe (Amsterdam, 1969).

this it yielded the produce of forestry, hunting and gathering, in the form of timber, barrel staves, game, fish, leeches and fruit. Gathered products provided significant export earnings, particularly sumach for tanning.

Much of the untilled area in Serbia was open pasture which had resulted from deforestation, but there still remained in the Šumadija extensive oak woods whose acorns provided a much prized source of forage for huge numbers of pigs.[44] In other parts of the country the waste was bare limestone rock, whose scrub flora was capable only of supporting goats, but at higher, cooler altitudes, mountain grasslands were exploited systematically for grazing sheep and cattle as a seasonal complement to the meadows in the valleys. The herding sector in 1859 produced an estimated 51 per cent of farm output.[45] Not all of this output can be ascribed to exploitation of waste, because hay and arable by-products contributed an input to stockraising, but even so, the cultivating economy produced little more than did open range pastoralism. Obviously the exploited yield per hectare of the wasteland varied according to accessibility and vegetation, but at least in the choicest areas, the value per unit of area of uncultivated land in private hands in 1863 exceeded that of the cultivated land, a very real consideration in the apportionment of land use.

We estimate from figures retrieved and tabulated by Jakšić that 22 per cent of the surface area of Serbia in 1847 was cultivated; 53 per cent of the cultivated land was under arable crops; vineyards occupied 4.2 per cent and meadows 28 per cent.[46] Orchards and miscellaneous crops (mainly tobacco, vegetables, legumes and fibre plants) were not picked up by the 1847 land survey, but there were 14.9 million fruit trees, which, if planted at 281 per hectare (as in 1897) would have covered 53,000 hectares.[47] The area under miscellaneous crops would have occupied the residual 4.5 per cent of the cultivated area, if their proportion to the area under cereals were the same as in 1867.

The prime purpose of arable farming in Serbia was to provide for familial self-consumption. The staple of daily life was the maize crop, which occupied 55 per cent of the arable in 1847 and 52 per cent in 1867.[48] Maize was not exported, but since the 1820s it had come to supplement acorns and beech mast in the fattening of pigs, and by this

---

[44] GBC Serbia 1872b, pp. 345–6.   [45] See below, Table 4.2.

[46] Vladimir Jakšić, 'Stanje zemljoradnje u Srbiji', *GSUD*, XLI (Belgrade, 1875) pp. 1–103.

[47] The 1847 figures for the number of stands of fruit trees were printed in *Čiče Srečkov list za Srbske zemljedelce* II (1848), issues 7–24, see tabulation in Michael Palairet, 'The Influence of Commerce on the Changing Structure of Serbia's Peasant Economy 1860–1912' (unpublished Ph.D. thesis, University of Edinburgh, 1976), p. 425; number of stands in 1897 is given in *SKS*, XVI, p. 366.

[48] Jakšić, 'Stanje zemljoradnje', pp. 24–44.

means it found its way indirectly onto the export market.[49] Next in extent of cultivation was wheat, with 24 per cent and 29 per cent. Wheat was marketed for the consumption of interior towns which lacked access to imported supplies. The tendency for wheat to occupy a growing proportion of the arable reflects in part its expanding export in the 1860s, in part its increasing use in rural diet. Wheat was sown mainly in the Sava valley, and to a lesser extent in the Danube plain, but hardly at all in the hill country in the south.[50] Within the maize-based system of agriculture, little land was fallowed. The earliest survey of fallows indicates that in 1897 they occupied but 3.3 per cent of the arable surface.[51] In many areas, especially the alluvial river valleys of central Serbia, maize, which was frequently a hoe crop, was sown for many years in continuous monoculture.[52] When the land showed signs of exhaustion, it was sown for one year with a 'hard' crop such as winter wheat, and then put over to grass. This grass does not appear to have been sown, so it was only after a period as thin scrub pasture that it could serve for an extended period as hay meadow. When hay yields in turn fell off, the land was ploughed up and brought back under maize.[53] Thus the lack of fallow, the large extent of meadow and the concentration on animal husbandry were mutually linked. Along much of the wheat growing Sava valley, land in the 1890s moved from three to four years grazing, to one year of maize, then three to four of wheat.[54] Earlier in the century, there was less wheat in the cycle, less enclosed pasture and more meadow grass. In upland areas, something close to a shifting agriculture was practised, but still with the same basic structural cycle, of arable – grazing – meadow.[55] Because meadow and tillage were cyclical phases in the use of land, the compilers of the 1863 census found it difficult to distinguish between the two. For Belica district, in the fertile centre of the country, they identified a small amount of permanent arable and a larger area of 'tillage and meadow' which was no doubt subject to the cycle described. This maize-based cropping system contrasts with two or three field cereal agriculture which predominated in Bulgaria, and left up to half the land in any one year in fallow.

Crop yields were not measured in the 1847 and 1867 censuses of cultivation, so Jakšić estimated production on the basis of areal yields in

---

[49] Slavko Gavrilović, 'Prilog pitanju trgovine svinjama izmedju Austrije i Srbije u prvoj polovini XIX veka', *Zbornik za istoriju* (Novi Sad) XXVII (1983), pp. 141–2.

[50] Palairet, 'The influence of commerce', pp. 141–55.   [51] *SKS*, XVI, p 359.

[52] Vladimir Karić, *Srbija. Opis zemlje, narode i države* (Belgrade, 1887), pp. 341, 342, 344.

[53] Stanoje Mijatović, 'Resava', *NiPS*, XXVI (Belgrade, 1930), p. 173.

[54] Herbert Vivian, *Servia, The Poor Man's Paradise* (London, 1897), p. 162.

[55] Borivoje Milojević, 'Radjevina i Jadar. Antropogeografska ispitivanja', *NSZ*, IX (Belgrade, 1913), pp. 664–5.

Croatia – Slavonia in 1851, generated by a survey which also established yields to seed, whose mean was 7.3 for wheat, for barley 6.3, for maize 39.[56] Jakšić argued that Serbia's yields were similar, which we accept because these seed yields accord with those given in Serbian prefecture reports. In seven districts in 1873, yields to seed were estimated at a mean 6.5 for wheat, 12.1 for barley and 43.2 for maize.[57]

Livestock provided rural Serbia with most of its cash income, mainly through the export trade. For Serbia in 1843–5, livestock amounted to 65 per cent of exports, in 1862–4, 61 per cent. Pigs (which went to Austria) accounted for 49 per cent of exports in 1843–5 and 45 per cent in 1862–4. Cattle accounted for 11 per cent of exports in 1843–5 and 10 per cent in 1862/4. In 1843, Austria took 56 per cent of the cattle export; 44 per cent went to the Ottoman provinces, probably in transit through Bosnia to Dubrovnik. Thanks to trade concessions granted by the Porte in 1833, a flourishing export of sheep and goats went out from eastern Serbia to Constantinople, through Bulgarian intermediaries who supplied it to meet the demand for meat at *bayram*.[58] This trade absorbed 48,000 animals a year in 1843–5. Of the non-livestock residual the largest item was a group of traditionally exported animal products: tallow, lard, wool, sheepskins and goatskins, worth 5.9 million piastres in 1843 (17 per cent of exports) and 13.3 million in 1863 or 15 per cent. Grain exports were negligible in 1843–5 and 2.8 per cent of exports in 1862–4. The balance was made up of retraded commodities not of Serbian origin which passed indirectly between Austria and Turkey, and of the produce of hunting and gathering, such as gall-nuts, leeches (of which 225,000 piastres worth went to Austria in 1863, probably on their way to France), honey and wax, and the hides of wild animals.[59]

This economic system reflected the low population density of the mid nineteenth century, and made Serbia akin in certain respects to the extra-European lands of recent settlement; indeed the prospect of being given land attracted large numbers of homesteading settlers, whose arrival boosted the growth of population. So although life expectation at birth was short at around twenty-five years, population density doubled from 15.1 per km in 1820 to 29.4 in 1860.[60] The growth of population was reabsorbed almost entirely within the farm economy.

[56] Jakšić, 'Stanje zemljoradnje', pp. 3–4, 12, 20, 26.
[57] AS.MF E XII 1/1874 531, 1395, 898, 948, 574, 135, 297.
[58] Kliment Džambazovski, 'Snabdevanje carigradske pijace sredinom XIX veka sitnom stokom iz Kneževine Srbije', *IČ*, XXIX-XXX (1982–3), pp. 316–19.
[59] Export statistics for 1843–5 were tabulated in *SN*, 3 June 1847, pp. 169–70, 6 June 1847, pp. 173–4, and 10 June 1847, pp. 177–8; 1862–4 export statistics from *Državopis*, I, II and III.   [60] See above, Table 1.9.

Gradual impoverishment

For Serbia, population growth should have presented few problems while the wide internal frontier remained unfilled. A British visitor observed in about 1860 that 'if the present production of Servia became insufficient for the subsistence of the population, they have only to take in waste land, and improved processes of agriculture will remain unheeded until the population begins to press on the limits of subsistence'.[61]

This prediction subsumed the monumental assumption that only the cultivated area really mattered, and that per capita output would remain stable till the limits to subsistence were approached. The writer underrated the massive contribution to economic welfare made by the open grazing, and ignored the difficulty of reorientating trade from livestock to cultivated produce. For with rising density of settlement, the contribution made by pastoralism would decline even if the size of the herd could be held stable. The loss could not be fully offset (in the absence of technological change) by a corresponding increase in the cultivation and marketing of arable crops, for if it could, then the peasants would have marketed crops rather than livestock in the first place, as in Bulgaria. So the diminution of pastoral resources could only be offset if connexions could be forged with external markets to make it more advantageous to exploit the arable for exchange purposes.

In the early days of the Serbian principality, comments concerning peasant welfare hint at a crude if unstable abundance. Accounts from the 1840s left an impression of crude affluence,[62] and a high real wage level.[63] But after mid-century, observers believed the country was getting poorer. In 1863, a consular agent expressed the belief 'that the people of Servia were better off and more thriving in the early days of their independence than they have been subsequently'.[64] Two years later (but before the 1866–7 livestock and land surveys had been undertaken) figures were released for 1843–63 on the value of estates of orphans administered by the state. It was argued from these figures, not only that the number of orphans had risen sharply relative to population, but also that the value of their individual estates had diminished, particularly when expressed in terms of the amount of land such funds would buy.[65] It is possible that a rising proportion of small orphan estates came under

[61] Andrew A. Paton, *Researches on the Danube and the Adriatic* (London, 1862), I, pp. 115–16.
[62] Dr M. I. S., 'Neke primedbe o mom putovanju iz Beograda preko Kragujevac u srez Levački', in Petar Ž. Petrović, *Putovanja po južnoslovenskija zemljama u XIX veku* (Belgrade, 1954), pp. 92–3.   [63] PRO FO 78 485. despatch of 31 Dec. 1842.
[64] GBC Serbia 1863, p. 244.   [65] *Državopis*, II, pp. 77, 83.

state management, rather than that orphan estates maintained a constant size relationship with properties as a whole, but the study reflected a concern that the country was getting poorer. Jakšić claimed that poverty and mortality were rising, not only on account of the orphan estates evidence, but also by the intertemporal comparison of farm survey data, to which we shall shortly turn.[66] In due course, the impoverishment thesis was to be picked up by the French consul and by the pamphlet literature, and used to attack the rise of the army and bureaucracy under the Obrenović dynasty.[67] The reasoning behind these attacks was unsatisfactory, but the basic argument that the country had been getting poorer since the 1830s or 1840s ought to be taken seriously; let us look at the statistical evidence.

The expansion of cultivation and of crop consumption failed to keep pace with the growth of population, if the 1847 land survey (retrieved by Jakšić) is compared with that for 1867, and taken in conjunction with the international trade statistics which became available from the 1840s. Jakšić estimated from this data that per capita cereal consumption had declined 22 per cent between the 1840s and 1860s.[68] This assessment was subsequently endorsed by his successor at the Statistical Department, Vladimir Jovanović.[69] If we modify Jakšić's figures to accommodate the area under fruit, population increased by 21 per cent between 1847 and 1867 but the cultivated area only increased by 6 per cent.[70] Contraction in per capita cultivation may have begun as early as the 1830s. A German source of 1840 purports to show that 390,768 days of ploughing (of 0.58 hectares) were under arable, with 413,716 days of pasture and 164,912 days of vineyard.[71] These figures probably relate to 1834, when a tithing survey was carried out.[72] Subsequently, tithes were abolished in favour of a flat rate poll tax, removing the need for subsequent land surveys. On this basis, cultivation expanded 24 per cent between 1834 and 1847, while population rose by 36.6 per cent, implying significant per capita shrinkage. A passing comment by Jakšić[73] also suggests a sharp diminution in meadow area between these dates.

Contraction in the area cultivated per capita between 1847 and 1867 seems to have occurred mainly in the north-west of the country. Jakšić, arguing the case for decline, demonstrated the consistency between

---

[66] Jakšić 'Stanje zemljoradnje', p. 101.

[67] T[aso] S[tojanović], *Naš ekonomski položaj* (Belgrade, 1881), pp. 20–2, 52–3; AAE CCB t. 4. Despatch of 11 Mar. 1869, fo. 360.   [68] Jakšić 'Stanje zemljoradne', p. 48.

[69] Vladimir Jovanović, 'Statističan pregled našeg privrednog i društvenog stanja', *GSUD*, L (1881), pp. 385–92.   [70] Ignoring plums, Jakšić gives 10.4 per cent, 'Stanje zemljoradne'.

[71] Milić, *Trgovina*, p. 54.   [72] Jakšić, 'Stanje zemljoradnje', p. 1.   [73] Ibid., p. 88.

cultivation and livestock trends, and despite criticism, stood on his close association with the data gathering process to defend his figures and conclusions.[74] It seems reasonable to treat comparison between the 1847 and 1867 statistics as a valid exercise, even if a certain agnosticism is in order in using the Milić data and in reviewing Jakšić's conclusions. If the latter were valid, the area cultivated (and by inference the volume of produce won from it) failed over the period from the 1830s to the 1860s to keep pace with the growth of population.

So holdings contracted, and the population became less productive in consequence, despite the massive availability of good uncultivated land. The cause of this contraction is to be found in the performance of the livestock economy. Jakšić did not argue that human consumption of cereals was diminishing, but that stagnation in cultivation was associated with a decline in the demand for arable and meadow produce as fodder, for animals whose numbers were declining for exogeneous reasons. So it is to the livestock sector that we now turn.

Although we lack a complete livestock statistic for the 1840s to compare against that for 1866, the number of horned cattle advanced 19.3 per cent between 1846 and 1859, but then fell away to 1866 so that growth between 1847 and 1866 amounted to only 10.2 per cent.[75] Pigs were not counted in 1847. The first pig census was made in 1859, and between then and 1866 their numbers declined even more sharply than those of cattle, from 1.77 million to 1.29 million.[76] Jakšić suggested that the decline in cultivation was a response to the diminished animal fodder requirement. As it was most evident in hay, maize and barley, which were used wholly or partly as animal fodder, and least in wheat and rye, which were solely for human consumption, he may have been right. The especially sharp diminution in meadow land (down 30 per cent on a per capita basis), certainly appears to be related to the diminution of livestock numbers – provided that they actually diminished. This is a serious point, because it is not known whether the livestock enumerations were conducted in the same season.[77] Even so, the decline in numbers, though not necessarily reflected accurately by the census data, was accepted as a fact by contemporaries. Moreover, later enumerations revealed a decided long-run downtrend in the animal stock. Given the importance of livestock to total output, we need to know why animal numbers declined. The expansion of the crop area was too slow to account for a significant diminution in pastoral resources, especially as this expansion was restrained by lack of demand for fodder crops.

[74] Ibid., p. 98.   [75] Ibid., p. 97.   [76] Državopis, IV, pp. 114–19.
[77] Proizvodne snage, p. 207.

Livestock health

An obvious candidate for consideration was livestock epidemics, but evidence for the period indicates that Serbia was blissfully free of this particular scourge. There was indeed a serious outbreak of 'typhus of horned cattle' in 1854, but the despatch which documents it indicates that the problem was infrequent, and that vigorous and potentially effective measures were used to eradicate it.[78] Painstaking research by Dragoljub Divljanović has shown that frequent and often disastrous epidemics of cattle plague swept the Balkans and the Hungarian plain between 1831 and 1875. However, only minor outbreaks occurred in Serbia, and these were swiftly localized and contained by efficient frontier controls.[79] French consular evidence supports Divljanović's case, for the year after the 1854 outbreak, reports of 'bovine epizootic' caused Serbia to quarantine animals in transit, and it was later discovered that no such outbreaks had occurred in Serbia itself.[80] The temporary downturn in cattle and pig exports in the late 1850s was attributed by Milošević to closures of the Austrian frontier against Serbia after reports of livestock epidemics in the Ottoman Empire, of which Serbia was formally a province. Cattle plague raged in Bosnia, Bulgaria and Wallachia in 1857–9, but not in Serbia.[81] This was true not only for cattle but for pigs as well, for neither Milošević nor the consular reports of the period indicate that serious pig epidemics affected Serbia.[82] Outbreaks of swine fever did occur, but had no serious impact on production (though they did have an impact on Austrian willingness to import). For example, swine fever caused significant mortality among pigs in Smederevo region in 1859. Nevertheless, the animals bred successfully, and sustained a heavy export.[83] In fact, Austrian interference with the pig trade was a reaction to alleged persecution of Austrian traders in Belgrade.[84] A worsening of livestock epidemics must be rejected as causing shrinkage in livestock production. If anything, this problem was easing.

Deforestation and the pastoral economy

In explaining the fall in the pig population, contemporaries placed weight on the effects of forest clearance.[85] The collapse of pig exports in 1857

[78] AAE CCB t. 2. Despatch of 4 Dec. 1854, fo. 303.
[79] Dragoljub Divljanović, *Govedja kuga u Srbiji i njenom susedstvu tokom XIX veka (1800–1882)* (Belgrade, 1969).
[80] AAE CCB t. 2. Despatches of 10 Apr. 1855 (fo. 330) and 23 Apr. 1855 (fo. 331).
[81] Divljanović, *Kuga*, pp. 66–71.
[82] S. Dj. Milošević, *Spoljna trgovina Srbije od 1843–1875 godine* (Belgrade, 1902), p. 14.
[83] AS MF E 1860 II 123. No. 5223 of 31 Dec. 1859.
[84] PRO FO 78 1459 1859. Despatch of 16 Oct. 1859.   [85] Milošević, *Trgovina*, p. 20.

was attributed not only to the slump in Austrian demand, but also to deforestation.[86] The forests which provided the best pig grazing lay in a belt across the Šumadija, the economic heartland of Serbia. These were oak and beech woods, and they provided the principal source of pig fodder. The free availability of acorns and beech mast concentrated the pig population within this wooded belt.[87]

The relationship between the extent of the oak forests and the production of pigs is, however, indirect. The means of raising them varied regionally, but Drobnjaković's account of the traditional pig raising system in Jasenica (Podunavlje) is representative. In summer the pigs foraged on the village pastures, but in autumn, once the acorns had dropped, they were driven into the forests, where they grazed and put on weight at least till mid January. Animals designated for sale were then put on maize.[88] Therefore the number of animals grazed in any particular year did not much depend on the abundance of forest grazing – or indeed of crops, which were only fed to them at the finishing stage. The breeding stock might 'multiply well', even 'excessively', despite a lack of both.[89] The animals offered on the market would however be 'very weak and thin'.[90] However, if acorns abounded (which in the 1850s and 1860s they seldom did) the stock would be 'well fattened',[91] and would command a remunerative price.[92]

As the oak trees covered rich lowland soil, they were rapidly destroyed. As early as 1840, the diminution of forest pig grazings caused acute inter-village strife in the fertile Mačva.[93] To those engaged in herding in the main stockraising areas, the forests were regarded as the ultimate basis of wellbeing. They complained shrilly against those who felled the oaks and undermined the sustenance of their herds,[94] but to little avail.

Quantitative evidence on forest clearance is unavailable for the period, as the first published survey of forests was not carried out till 1897. However, the pace of destruction in the middle third of the nineteenth century was rapid. In 1852 it was claimed that the forest area had shrunk by half over the preceding twenty years.[95] In 1867, forested land was estimated at 25 per cent of surface area, with cultivation occupying

---

[86] AAE CCB t. 2. Despatch of 20 Aug. 1858, fo. 372.   [87] Karić, *Srbija*, p. 364.

[88] Borivoje M. Drobnjaković, 'Jasenica', *NiPS*, XIII (1923), pp. 214–15.

[89] See, for example, the 1864 report from Kosmaj *srez*, AS MF E 1865 VII. 7. No. 4014 of 31 Dec. 1864.   [90] AS MF E 1865 VII 7. No. 6032 of 1865.

[91] AS MF E 1860 II 123. No. 5272 of 31 Dec. 1859.

[92] As in Jasenica, in 1868, when acorns abounded. AS MF E 1869 XIII 1. No. 40 of 3 Jan. 1869.

[93] M. D. Milojević, *Mačva, Šabačka Posavina i Pocerina* (Belgrade, 1962), p. 43.

[94] Danica Milić, 'Šume kao prirodni uslov za neke privredne delatnosti', *AHOI*, X (1983), p. 101.   [95] Slobodan Jovanović, *Ustavobranitelji i njihova vlada* (Belgrade, 1925), p. 80.

16 per cent and waste the residual 69 per cent.[96] Moreover the pace of forest clearance in Serbia did not slacken. In 1897, the forest area had been reduced to 10 per cent. Of this, oak forest accounted for 25 per cent.[97]

Obviously woodland had to be cleared to accommodate the rising density of settlement, but the excessive speed of its disappearance despite its critical importance to stockraising, resulted from the institutional preferences of a mass smallholder society. Firstly, forests stood *in re nullius*. The principle that private ownership should only be recognized in tilled land inhibited the passage of woodland into the hands of private persons who might have an interest in enclosing and preserving it. A law of 1845 explicitly declared that natural forest could not be privatized, and private ownership of forest land was only uneasily admitted in 1861.[98] The woodlands were therefore preyed on by all and sundry since none could protect them, even though the game must end with a negative sum.

Rather than act as an umpire, the Serbian state acquiesced in deforestation, because of the importance the peasant attached to his felling rights. During the revolutionary period, the courts sanctioned the principle that land belonged to the person who cleared it, which could only have encouraged forest clearance.[99] Under Miloš's rule, gestures were made towards forest protection but as a populist gesture the new constitutional government of 1839 permitted Serbian subjects almost unlimited felling rights for a trifling fee of 1 piastre. Only in 1857 was a systematic felling tariff imposed. Even this modest measure was furiously opposed as 'one of the greatest crimes of Aleksandar Karadjordević and his government against the people'. It was promptly repealed by Miloš on his restoration in 1859. As felling rights remained a hot electoral issue, no forestry law was passed till 1891. By that time the oak woods had largely disappeared.[100]

Wooded land gradually passed from public to particular ownership. This tendency has been associated with deforestation on the mistaken assumption that private interests wanted forest only to clear it. During the 1830s, the state held tracts of forest which it made available at low cost to the pig traders for grazing, but villages increasingly appropriated this land (and failed to pay the grazing dues on it). From this intermediate stage, much subsequently passed into private hands.[101] Vučo draws attention to numerous instances where forests were illegally privatized, often by

[96] Jovanović, 'Statističan pregled', p. 229.   [97] *SGKS*, 1900, p. 206.
[98] *Proizvodne snage*, p. 242.   [99] Milić, 'Ekonomski potencijal', p. 166.
[100] S. Jovanović, *Ustavobranitelji*, pp. 81–2; *Proizvodne snage*, pp. 23–4, 241–3.
[101] Miroslav D. Milojević, *Razvoj i osobine stočarstva u istočnoj Srbiji* (Belgrade, 1972), pp. 12, 15.

merchants who enclosed them. To Vučo, this was an aspect of the primitive accumulation of capital at the expense of the peasants, who were thereby deprived of their rights.

Vučo, however, fails to show that privatized forests were destroyed by their *de facto* owners;[102] on the contrary, it is more likely that they enclosed them to protect them, and to this extent inhibited depletion. In Smederevo *okrug*, where pig raising was big business, it was reported in 1859 that all the woodlands of English oak were enclosed, and belonged to private individuals. They yielded well, while the unenclosed Turkey oak yielded little for anybody.[103] Similarly, in Posava (Valjevo) in 1866 it was only in the occasional enclosed forest that the oaks yielded a harvest, the acorns in the communal forests being destroyed by caterpillars.[104] In this region, the oak forests had once been 'as dense as a green sea', but by the 1870s, they survived only as fragments detached and enclosed by individuals and communes to prevent the destruction of their traditional source of pig fodder.[105] However, ownership rights in enclosed forest were less securely defined than in cultivated land. Where villages had privatized forests by division and distribution and communal rights upon them were thereby extinguished, they tended to be protected. But in the Šumadija many villages required owners of woodland enclosures to open them in the grazing season to the pigs of the whole village. This externalized too much of the gain from holding oak and beech woods, and contributed to their disappearance.[106]

The extension of cultivation had a disproportionate effect on the clearance of woodland, because peasants did not rotate crops nor hold land in fallow, but ran maize repeatedly on the same land till its fertility failed. The reversion of this land to pasture and meadow was probably an accommodation to the unavailability of virgin land, and it is likely that much of the 'meadow' land at mid-century was wrecked arable, left by the cultivator who moved on to clear new sections of forest to replace it.[107] This land would not reafforest itself, because it would be grazed by flocks and herds. Besides this, peasants were profligate in their use of felled timber, which they treated as a free good. Their depredations were supplemented by charcoal burners and the distillers of pitch and resin, an activity which was regarded as a quick way for those in distress to earn

---

[102] Nikola Vučo, 'Šume u procesu prvobitne akumulacije kapitala u Srbiji', *AHOI*, X (1983), pp. 89–94.   [103] AS MF E 1860 II 123. No. 5223 of 31 Dec. 1859.

[104] AS MF E 1867 137. No. 83 of 2 Jan. 1867.

[105] Milićević, *Kneževina Srbija* (1876), p. 364.

[106] Sreten Vukosavljević, *Istorija seljačkog društva* III, *Sociologija seljačkih radova* (Belgrade, 1983), pp. 534, 51.

[107] O. Srdanović-Barac, 'Poljoprivreda Srbije pod knez Mihailom prema Feliksu Kanicu', *Ekonomika poljoprivrede*, XXXII (1985), p. 626.

some cash.[108] Moreover, the state, so far from conserving forest, wrecked it on a grand scale to feed the appetites of the Kragujevac ordnance installations, and its concessionaires at Majdanpek illegally embarked on a scheme of mass commercial felling.[109]

A further relationship between forest use and livestock husbandry is argued in a report of 1861 on farm conditions by the sub-prefect of Vračar district (adjacent to Belgrade town). Cultivated fields and meadows both communal and private were usually enclosed with rough fences, because the livestock were grazed without supervision, and would otherwise stray onto the arable and hay. These fences had to be renewed annually, because they were allowed to deteriorate after the harvests, when the animals were free to graze the stubble. They ended up as fire-wood and had to be rebuilt the following spring.

The sub-prefect condemned this system on several grounds. Firstly, the enormous effort of building these enclosures each year curtailed the amount of land which could be cultivated. This effort was intense, since peasants held fragments of land separated from the common fields, each of which required its own enclosure. The quality of the fences was variable, so animals frequently broke through to the standing crops, leading to endless litigation. Finally, the volume of felling needed to maintain this arrangement was enormous. A peasant who only held land in the common field needed to build 95–114 metres of fence each year, and one with separate land, 380.

He therefore recommended that the villages should have their animals shepherded, to keep them off the arable. The enclosures could then be removed. This was the normal practice, he claimed, in the Bulgarian border region of Serbia, round Knjaževac. Moreover, he wanted peasants stinted in the quantity of livestock they held, to improve their quality and reduce wastage, with resultant savings in time, deforestation and crop losses.[110] His account points up a relationship between extensive livestock raising and creeping deforestation.

However, it is unlikely that the diminution in livestock numbers represented a shift towards optimizing the stock and raising livestock output. The individual farmer could not easily maximize livestock output other than by maximizing the number of animals he held; better-off farmers responded by carving out new enclosures in which to hold their animals separate from those of their neighbours, but they did so in the teeth of popular hostility. The state authorities were not unsympathetic to the

---

[108] Radomir M. Ilić, 'Ibar. Antropogeografska proučvanija', *NSZ*, III (Belgrade, 1905), pp. 566–7.   [109] GBC Serbia 1863, pp. 217–18; *The Times*, 12 June 1868.

[110] AS MF E 1862 V 101 no. 3383 of 31 Dec. 1861. The measure of fencing in this quotation is the *fat* (Viennese *klafter*, standardized in 1871 at 1.9 metres).

creation of closes, but the *opštinas* were reluctant to recognize rights in land so created. To judge from the high value attached to these closes, they contrived an artificial scarcity.

The livestock export trade

In mid-nineteenth-century Serbia, despite the pressure of deforestation, pig raising provided the largest single source of cash, mostly from export earnings, as well as a major source of subsistence. So, as the forests receded, peasants were forced gradually to abandon their former grazing practice, and hold the pigs in the villages throughout the year, over-wintering them on their own maize and on the produce of any enclosed forest they might own.[111]

They regretted having to adapt in this way, for the older system of pig management burdened the pig raiser with few costs. As long as the forests provided good natural grazing, the product was heavy (though seldom fat) and provided easy money. They could also afford to let the animals mature slowly, over two or even three years, to reach their maximum weight. Maize feeding imposed a higher cost structure, while failure to in-winter the animals would result in them going to market underweight. On the whole, pig raisers accepted the resultant losses, grudging the maize needed to substitute the acorns foregone.[112] Either way they would want to dispose of the pigs more quickly, for little would be gained by holding them when deferment of sale would not lead to much gain in weight.

The diminution of forest pastures, and the consequent diminution in the returns to holding pigs, resulted in a persistent decline in the size of the breeding stock at least from 1859. In the medium run this did not cause the export of pigs to decline, rather the secular trend between the 1840s and 1870s was unmistakably upward. Firstly, pigs were being exported lighter and younger, and this swelled the number exported. Secondly, pressure for cash earnings caused a rising percentage of the pigs produced to go to market. For example, in 1859 in Smederevo *okrug* the pigs were reported to have multiplied well, but as harvests were poor, 'so every pig went for money'.[113]

Young pigs, in the condition in which they left the farm gate, were unready for consumer markets. The largest part of the export would be bought up by merchants or itinerant commission agents, by whom the pigs would be driven from the Serbian interior to the river ports on the

[111] Drobnjaković, 'Jasenica', pp. 214–15.   [112] GBC Serbia 1863, p. 234.
[113] AS MF E 1860 II 123. No. 5223 of 31 Dec. 1859.

Sava and Danube. The largest number was ferried across the Sava at Sremska Mitrovica in the west and driven on through Srijem and western Hungary to Wiener Neustadt. Most of those originating in the Morava valley passed through Smederevo, where they crossed the Danube (often driven across the ice in winter) to Kovin, whence the trails through Hungary took them to the market at Györ. Here they would be fed on acorns by the Györ merchants,[114] before being passed on for consumption in Austria and Bohemia. The opportunity to establish a fattening trade in Serbia was greatly enhanced in 1856 when the Staatsbahn railway from Budapest via Timisoara reached its Danube terminal at Baziaš. Pigs from eastern Serbia could now be fattened near the Serbian Danube ports, mainly Smederevo, Dubravica, Veliko Gradište and Ram,[115] and hauled down the river, in 'trellissed in pig ships' (probably barges) operated by several small steamer companies[116] to Baziaš for consignment to Steinbruck, the burgeoning livestock market which serviced Budapest.

The response was immediate. Fattened pig exports from Serbia leaped from 22,000 a year in 1854/6 to 67,000 in 1857/9.[117] In Smederevo, Serbia's largest Danube port, firms such as that of Aron Despinić set up stables to hold animals bought by their agents in the interior for fattening prior to shipment.[118] However, the trade was circumscribed by the difficulty of procuring cheap maize in Serbia; thus we find merchant Aničić, in 1857, buying 154 tonnes of maize across the Bulgarian frontier in Vidin, because it was so much cheaper there than in Serbia. He intended to drive a herd there for fattening on this maize the following year.[119] These pigs would subsequently be freighted to Budapest via Baziaš. Like Aničić, the Smederevo merchants drew heavily on external maize supplies, mainly from Kovin on the Hungarian bank of the Danube. This was because insufficient maize was delivered by local peasants to Smederevo, while supplies from the Morava valley were intermittent and uncertain, and transport difficulties discouraged maize purchases in the interior even when supplies were offered.[120] On occasion, when maize supplies proved inadequate, merchants were obliged hastily to terminate fatten-

[114] 'Začetak svinjskog trga u Ugarskoj I', *Trgovinski glasnik*, 1 Oct. 1895, p. 1.
[115] MuS. Sava Stanković papers 507/66, Jovanović- Despinić, 3 Feb. 1876.
[116] Felix Kanitz, *Serbien. Historisch-ethnographische Reisestudien aus den Jahren 1859–1868* (Leipzig, 1868), p. 11.   [117] Milošević, *Trgovina*, pp. 18–19.
[118] For background on this firm see Leontije Pavlović, *Arhiva Arona Despinića o trgovini Srbije i Austrougarske od 1808–1859* (Smederevo, 1968).
[119] Kliment Džambazovski, 'Uticaj hatišerifa od 1830 i 1833 na režim stočarenja i trgovine stokom na istočnoj granici Kneževine Srbije', *Odredbe pozitivnog zakonodavstva i običajnog prava o sezonskim kretanjima stočara u jugoistočnoj Evropi kroz vekove* (Belgrade, 1976), pp. 327–8.
[120] MuS. 326/66 Braće Arandjelović, Jagodina, – Stanković, 21 Oct. 1873.

2. Smederevo, Serbia. The Danube port in 1859

ing.[121] The reason why they fattened the pigs in Smederevo was to avoid the high tariffs for stabling and fodder in the commercial pig pens at Steinbruck,[122] not because maize in Serbia was especially abundant or cheap – since it was neither of those things.

The larger part of the export trade, that of western Serbia, which passed through Mitrovica and the other Sava ports, was not diverted to Bazias and Budapest. It continued to be driven overland to Austria. So too were unfattened pigs from Smederevo, which were still driven to Györ as late as 1875, though the general orientation of Smederevo's fattened pig export was to Bazias railhead. The failure to fatten pigs exported from western Serbia, and only a proportion of those from the Morava valley, reflected the scarcity of maize, especially in the western part of the country where wheat cultivation predominated.

At Smederevo, many animals which had been driven from the interior were regarded as too small, weak and underfed to be worth fattening.

---

[121] MuS. 373/66 Stanković- Despinić, 9 Nov. 1876.
[122] 'Podižimo klanica', *Odjek*, 3 Nov. 1884, p. 2.

This was probably because of the shrinking supplies of acorns, which forced producers to sell them underweight. The fattening trade wanted acorn fed pigs, and was prepared to pay a 50 per cent premium for them over the price of completely lean ones, even though they needed further intensive maize feeding to bring them to exportable weight. Even when short of supplies, the Despinić firm and its agents avoided purchasing underfed pigs.[123] As a result, the trade in fattened pigs, once established, showed little tendency to expand; in 1873/5 the number exported had only reached 74,000 a year, barely more than in 1857/9, and was declining as a proportion of the total pig export. Even in the 1860s the supply of lean pigs threatened to glut the market, and a fall in exports was predicted from Serbia's inability to fatten all the pigs it exported.[124] Till 1875, buoyant markets disguised the problem, but a time would come when Serbia would be allowed to export pigs to Hungary only in fattened condition.

Like the pig trade, the cattle export gradually rose over time. The cattle trade, at least to Hungary, was of animals which had worked some years at the plough and were then sold to upland graziers, while still capable of putting on weight, for resale to the butchery trade. This grazing business was of especial importance in the high plains of northeast Serbia.[125] As with pigs, the ratio of exports to breeding stock was rising, so again it is to be inferred that the age of oxen at export was falling, and that a rising proportion of the country's beef was being exported.

As the pig based economy receded with the woodlands which fed it, the area of low-grade pasture expanded. Much of this was capable only of grazing sheep, so the diminution of pig numbers between 1859 and 1866 was accompanied by a rise in sheep from 2.4 million to 2.7 million.[126] As the sheep pastures of eastern Serbia became overgrazed, peasants were forced to graze sheep on the stubble fields, a common practice in more highly cultivated countries, but one which was regarded in Serbia as a desperate and abhorrent measure.[127]

Because of these tendencies, livestock exports were extraordinarily buoyant despite the diminution in breeding stock. Serbia's international trade figures do not at face value support the notion of a stagnant economic system, least of all in the livestock sector. In 1843–5 exports were valued at 34.6 million piastres, and in 1862–4, at 87.5 million, a rise of

[123] MuS. 518/66 Radojković – Despinić, 22 Nov. 1860; 464/66 Stanković – Despinić, 22 June 1875.   [124] Srdanović-Barac, 'Poljoprivreda', p. 628.

[125] For the organization of grazing in the high *salaśes* of these districts, see Ljubomir Jovanović, 'Mlava. Antropogeografska proučavanja', *NSZ*, II (Belgrade, 1903), pp. 272–4, and Ant. Lazić, 'Ekonomski centri Homolja i Zvižda', *Glasnik geografskog društva*, XIV (Belgrade, 1928), p. 123.   [126] *Državopis*, IV, pp. 114–9.

[127] Kosta Popović, *Put licejskih pitomaca po Srbiji godine 1863* (Belgrade, 1867), p. 87.

153 per cent, or 107.5 per cent allowing for inflation. [128] This far exceeds the probable 24 per cent growth of population for the same period, implying that exports per capita rose by 68 per cent, or at 2.8 per cent per annum, which far exceeded their growth in any subsequent twenty-year period. Summary head count figures given for this period by Milošević suggest the following movements in export volume of animals (in 1862–4 prices).[129]

1843–5	100
1847–9	116
1852–4	187
1857–9	125
1862–4	188

The trend of these exports was erratic, and its deceleration is not surprising, considering the marked fall in numbers between the livestock censuses of 1859 and 1866. In the longer run, the export trade could only expand through the growth of crop production for commercial ends, because of the inelasticity of the extensive stockraising. This process of substitution got under way on a modest scale by the early 1860s. Grain exports were still negligible (and were more or less offset by imports of the same) but 28 per cent of the pigs exported were partially fattened. By 1870 the ratio of fattened to lean pigs fluctuated with the rainfall and thence with the maize harvest.[130]

Let us now take the export and land use figures together and assume that no significant advances were achieved in raising yields per hectare. Since crop yields failed to rise between 1867 and 1900, it is unlikely that they would have risen earlier in the century. Therefore, a sharply rising proportion of a relatively static volume of farm production was delivered to export markets. Moreover, the growth of livestock exports in itself depleted the animal stock. In 1856, when their level was at a temporary peak, animals were being exported increasingly young, and to a considerable extent as breeding stock.[131] This is what we should expect to have

---

[128] All export commodities were reported both in quantity and value terms from 1862 onwards, but only live animals were counted in 1843–5, and other commodities were listed only by value. But given the predominance of animals and animal products, we can assume that the general export price level moved at the same rate as that for live animals. If so, then valuing livestock exports in 1843–5 at 1862–4 prices, export prices rose between 1843–5 and 1862–4 by 18.3 per cent, and 25.4 per cent if a base year valuation is taken; 1843–5 foreign trade data is from *SN*, 3 June, 6 June and 10 June 1847, 1862–4 data from *Državopis*, I–III.   [129] Milošević, *Trgovina*, pp. 13–19.
[130] GBC Serbia 1872a, p. 551 and 1872b, pp. 345–6.
[131] AAE. CCB t.2 despatch of 12 Feb. 1856, ff. 344–5.

happened if peasants were encountering increasing difficulty in finding fodder for them, because of the diminution of the oak forests.

The counterpart of the growth of livestock exports was a decrease in their availability for home consumption. On this point we have to depend on qualitative evidence. In the 1820s and 1830s, travellers in Serbia believed the Serbians to be heavy eaters of meat, mainly pork. The peasants ate meat on over 100 days a year, as well as substantial quantities of lard and dairy products.[132] After mid-century, however, the apparent abundance of meat, which the huge livestock export suggested, did not exist, and a report of 1863 observed that pork consumption was unexpectedly low.[133] By the 1870s 'only very large proprietors' consumed meat in their daily diet,[134] and the traditional rafter hung with hams had become 'the finest jewel in a meat consuming peasant house'; a 'meaty' house was rated rich.[135]

The small size of the holdings

Despite low density of population familial holdings were remarkably small. The 1863 census registers for four selected rural districts (Belica, Zaječar, Podunavlje and Trnava) show an average household size as 5.12; 98 per cent of these households owned land, but mean holding size was but 3.5 hectares, including 2.0 hectares in tillage; 19 per cent of the area of these holdings was composed of uncultivated closes. The small size of these holdings may be gauged from the fact that by 1895 the density of the rural population had increased by 80 per cent, yet 82–92 per cent of householders still held land, on average 6.4 hectares, of which 3.1 hectares were under arable crops.[136]

If people in 1863 had wanted to cultivate more land, they could have done so, but they did not. They were really only interested in acquiring pastoral resources and meadows to cushion the effects of deforestation and communal overgrazing on their capacity to support livestock. Detailed census data for the relatively rich northern district of Podunavlje (environs of Smederevo) in 1863 showed that the richer the household, the less of its real estate assets were held in arable, the more in uncultivated closes. By value of landholdings, the smallest householders (with 0–1,000 dinars of fixed capital) held 49 per cent of their capital in arable land, the richest (with 10,000 dinars and over) 13 per cent, although household wealth correlated strongly with family size. Clearly what poorer householders lacked was enclosed grazing. Poor households held a

---

[132] Castellan, *Serbie*, pp. 147–8.   [133] GBC Serbia 1863, p. 21.
[134] Karić, *Srbija*, p. 109.   [135] Milićević, *Kneževina Srbija*, p. 412.   [136] *SKS*, XVI.

mere 7.9 per cent of their wealth in meadows and 3.4 per cent in closes, the richest households 9.4 per cent and 21.7 per cent respectively. As a percentage of the farmland they held, the difference between the holdings of rich and poor households were still more marked as the richest households held 50 per cent of their assets in built property, including shops and taverns in nearby towns, while the poorest had 17.6 per cent of their property in built assets, that is, their cottages. Land values reflected the strong demand for land associated with livestock raising. In Podunavlje, arable was valued at 306 dinars per hectare, closes at 659 and meadows at 867.[137] So recent clearings for arable were rare, but there had lately been a spate of enclosures of public lands for use as private woodland.[138] Remarking in 1863 on the absence of recent clearings, the Statistical Department observed that 'in general we do not accept this task as willingly as hitherto'.[139]

Peasant culture and economic stagnation

So despite the continual growth of population, the clearing and cultivation of marginal land had come to a halt. Up to the early 1860s, grain prices were too low to attract peasants to raise substantial quantities of it for sale – or even for fattening livestock for the market – though producers across the Sava and Danube in fertile Srijem and the Vojvodina sent grain to Belgrade for human consumption,[140] and to Smederevo as fodder for livestock fattening, despite the fertility of the environs of both these towns.[141] Given the cultural values, technology and organizational arrangements on the Serbian bank, Serbian producers did not compete with them, even though pressures to do so were steadily mounting. As late as 1860, Belgrade imported most of its food, so small were the surpluses marketed by home producers.[142] Yet only the previous year, when there were complaints of high bread prices in the town, fields of corn only a few kilometres distant lay unharvested, and were entirely ruined.[143]

Grain sales had developed originally in response to poverty, not to opportunity. An early reference to grain sales tells of peasants flooding Belgrade market with grain one harsh winter because of their desperate need to buy firewood.[144] So it was the poorer peasants who did not hold

[137] See Palairet, 'Rural Serbia', table 8, p. 90.
[138] AS MF A I 86 1864. no. 3145 of 20 June 1863.   [139] Državopis, II, p. 83.
[140] Vladislav Milenković, Ekonomska istorija Beograda (Belgrade, 1932), pp. 125–6.
[141] For evidence of regular maize consignments from Kovin to Smederevo in the 1850s and 1860s, see Despinić papers cited in Palairet, 'The influence of commerce', p. 180, n. 4.
[142] PRO FO 1527. No. 66 Cons. of 31 Dec. 1860.
[143] AAE CCB t. 2. Despatch of 7 Nov. 1859, fo. 402.
[144] AAE CCB t. 1. Despatch of 7 Mar. 1842, fo. 221.

sufficient livestock to win an income from it who were forced earliest into the grain market. As will be shown below, the peasants of the poor-soil areas of the 'stockraising' south, lacking livestock to sell, came under most pressure to flood the market with grain; while in the fertile north and centre, where grain was easy to raise and relatively easy to export, surpluses remained small because livestock was available to cover most farmers' cash needs.

The more comfortably placed peasant considered the marketing of livestock as the only legitimate means of generating cash, and regarded the raising of grain for sale (or even for fattening pigs) as 'gipsying', a matter for shame, because it robbed the household of its basic food. A Šabac editor (writing in 1906) recollects how, till around 1870, his family's farm sold only unfattened livestock. When one of his forebears returned from Šabac market with gold earned from selling grain, he was accused by his mother of disgraceful behaviour, and the money was flung in his face.[145] Opinion formers inveighed against the trading of agricultural produce as 'speculation'. Mounting agrarian debts and distraints were attributed by them to 'clumsy trading' by peasants for 'desultory and insecure gains'.[146] Peasants in distress would seek advances on their crops, so some would fall into the hands of usurers. 'The Morava has fallen into great debts'; wrote Milićević, 'many peasants were ruined; many had to leave their fine houses and properties . . . as a result of lightly thought out indebtedness . . .'[147] Such moralizing attitudes towards the sale of grain arose because affluent peasant families needed (as yet) neither to sell grain nor to take credit, so by muddled inference, grain sales became identified not as a sign of poverty but as its cause. Social pressures and high minded efforts to distance peasants from the market (by obstructing the opening of shops in the villages, and by preventing homesteads from serving as loan collateral) contributed to the tardiness with which the grain trade developed. Moreover, there was little need for farmers to overproduce to ensure supplies in a bad year, for the communal maize granaries insured against this risk.

Though distress might induce petty sales of grain, strong incentives were needed to persuade the more substantial farmer to market his crops, if only to overcome standing prejudices. There was a practical point, too: to produce grain in quantity in the relatively fertile districts, farmers often needed to hire labour, and this was not readily forthcoming from the local peasantry, most of whom were themselves short handed. However, the

---

[145] Lj. Vulović, 'Jedna misao – Kako da se pomognemo', *Podrinske Novine* (Šabac) 26 Feb. 1906, p. 108.
[146] Aleks S. Jovanović, 'Zadruga po propisima našeg gradjanskog zakonika', *GSUD*, XXXVI (Belgrade, 1872), p. 245.   [147] Milićević, *Kneževina Srbija*, p. 1074.

price of grain was too low to enable farmers to offer wages which would attract migrant workers from longer distances. In Ključ (northeast Serbia) 1865 was an abundant year for maize, but at prevailing prices farmers could not offer wages sufficient to attract workers from the Banat to come and harvest it.[148] The weakness of demand was not confined to cereal agriculture. Serbian vintages enjoyed a large sale in the interior, but the common complaint was that wine prices were unattractively low, for want of export outlets. As a result the commercial vineyards of eastern Serbia were in distress and decline.[149] It was the same with the plum orchards. The fruit could be made marketable by distilling it, but in good years much of the crop was redundant and served as livestock fodder.[150]

Why did mid-nineteenth-century Serbian rural society organize its economic life so unproductively, and accept the creeping immiseration which was the result? In trying to explain peasant economic behaviour, weight must be accorded to cultural obstacles to adaptive strategies. Contemporaries had little doubt why farming was unproductive: the peasants were lazy. Cultivation was disdained, it was argued, when income could more easily be secured by driving pigs into the forests and selling them in the markets, than by breaking and cropping virgin soil. In 1837 state agronomists complained of their frustration in urging the peasants to adopt improved agricultural practices. Rather than getting the jobs attended to on time, they preferred to while away their leisure in the taverns.[151] In emotive terms, a journalist writes in 1848 of families suffering the consequences of the idleness and drunkenness of their men: 'I have myself seen women with children in their arms . . . frequenting the market places and pleading that their husbands be turned back from the taverns.'[152] Government was still trying in 1863 to 'stimulate cultivation of the soil by a choice of seed and by introducing improved agricultural tools'. Its efforts remained unappreciated by the peasants, who found it 'less troublesome and cheaper to rear pigs for the Hungarian market', and to grow no more grain than they needed for their households.[153] This system, 'suited to the lazy habits of the pure Serb population'[154] had served them adequately in the past, so they failed to adapt to changed circumstances.

[148] AS MF E 1866 VIII 2. No. 3665 of 31 Dec. 1865.
[149] Michael Palairet, 'Serbia's Role on International Markets for Silk and Wine 1860–1890', *AHOI*, IV (1977), pp. 168–71.
[150] Ljubica Trajković (ed.) *Valjevo i okolina* (Belgrade, 1956), pp. 47–8; Jakšić, 'Stanje zemljoradnje', p. 96.   [151] Milojević, *Mačva*, p. 32.
[152] *Čiče Srečkov list*, 29 May 1848, p. 170.
[153] PRO FO 78 1882. Cons. no. 18 of 4 May 1865.
[154] PRO FO 198 13. Dalyell's report dated May 1859.

The culture of laziness affected most of the western Balkans. Ethnologists of the school of Jovan Cvijić associated it with the patriarchal 'dinaric' lifestyle. Dinaric man, they argued, esteemed heroic and collectivistic attitudes, and despised their antithesis, the values of the hard-headed petty shopkeeper.[155] In Bosnia – as, indeed in Serbia – the 'warlike people have no predilection for agricultural pursuits', and left the finest arable land for grazing.[156] We shall return to this theme in Chapter 5 on Montenegro, for there the problem assumed its most acute form.

In explaining the small cultivated area per head, Vladimir Jakšić at the Statistical Department argued from a lengthy compilation of internationally comparable statistics that:[157]

European peasants are almost three times as hard working as ours, and Americans at least four times; but even without the numerical evidence we have cited, the well known fact is clear to each of us that our farmers are not so receptive to work as they should be, and in this all Serbs are equal, for wherever they care to live, even the other Slavs sharply exceed them in this aspect.

This statement, and the implied analysis behind it, would no doubt be accepted with little modification by Gregory Clark, who argues that the greatest part of the productivity gap between west and east European farm labour in the first half of the nineteenth century can be explained, not with reference to the amount of land cultivated, nor to farm technology, but by the difference in the intensity of labour. Hungry east European peasants worked less and stayed hungry; their more productive western counterparts ate better, and were able to work harder.[158] Clark suggests that: 'the people in low-productivity areas . . . either worked little or they exerted themselves little when at work . . . or their mental life is otherwise alien to us. They were not merely people like us who happened to be lacking certain pieces of knowledge.' This comes close to saying they were habitually lazy. Clark may be gratified that mid-nineteenth-century administrators in the Balkans would have agreed with him.

Clark's view is that behaviour was culture linked, emanating from a moral economy which thwarted the desire of individuals to better their station by working harder, because their fellows regarded such action as anti-social. Rural Serbia fits this description. Its income distribution at district level was unusually egalitarian, with Gini coefficients of per capita income distribution in 1863 ranging between 0.07 in the poorer districts

[155] Vladimir Dvorniković, *Karakterologija jugoslovena* (Belgrade, 1939), pp. 663ff.
[156] Edmund Spencer, *Travels in European Turkey in 1850* (London, 1851), p. 334.
[157] Jakšić, 'Stanje zemljoradnje', p. 69.
[158] Gregory Clark, 'Productivity Growth without Technical Change in European Agriculture before 1850', *JEcH*, XLVII (1987), pp. 419–32.

to 0.28 in the richer.[159] This evidence, together with the foregoing discussion on dinaric lifestyles, indicates the force of resistance to the departure from a declining pastoralism.

Regional differentiation in incomes in the 1860s

Without disregarding behavioural explanations, we must look more carefully at market conditions, which varied greatly on a regional basis. Although incomes per head were evenly distributed within rural districts, there were wide income differences between districts. Among the fifty-two districts for which we were able to extract data, per capita income ranged between 274 dinars in Tamnava (a figure exceeding the income of most towns) to a lowly 33 dinars in not very distant Azbukovac. This wide divergence did not reflect transient local harvest conditions, but to a large extent was real, because the Finance Ministry tried to eliminate transient income fluctuations in the census, so as to provide a basis for taxation for several years ahead.[160]

Research into the 1863 data suggests there were several reasons for these acute divergences. One significant determinant of regional income variation was the implicit valuation of the labour of adult women.[161] In richer districts, women's labour generated 76–90 per cent of the income generated by men's labour, but in relatively poor districts, the corresponding figures were 35–62 per cent. In richer districts, where the marginal product of farming was high, women were drawn actively into farm tasks, in poorer districts, where marginal product was low, their labour was underutilized.

A clear cut difference also emerged in a test limited to one rich (lowland) and one poor (upland) district in the contribution to income made by the sale of livestock. In 'rich' Belica 66 per cent of families earned income from the sale of livestock, deriving 177.7 dinars per family from these sales, whereas in 'poor' Trnava 31 per cent of families enjoyed such incomes, and these derived but 37.1 dinars per family from them.

Peasants in rich and fertile areas also obtained better prices for grain surpluses than peasants in poor soil uplands. In 1863 the best prices were fetched for maize in the fertile northern lowlands, the natural surplus areas, while prices in the backward upland south were relatively low, even though the meagre upland soil made it more difficult to grow grain at all. Though the volume of internal trade was small because of poor

---

[159] Palairet, 'Rural Serbia', table 5, p. 84.
[160] AS MF A I 118 of 1864. No. 4426 of 27 Aug. 1863.
[161] As the figures in the registers for income from labour did not attribute this income to individual family members, this conclusion was reached through regression analysis.

communications, the infertile south was sending grain northward to meet an urban demand which the richer farmers of the north chose to leave unsatisfied.[162]

Maize prices were relatively high in the fertile north because this market was becoming integrated with that of Hungary (and the international grain market) and because the pig raising in the north drove up maize demand. Conversely, in the poorer south, a lack of outlets for local produce glutted urban grain markets, while the relative lack of livestock (especially of pigs, which needed grain fodder, unlike cows and sheep) minimized on-farm demand for maize.

The contrast therefore stands out between lowland farming regions where peasants found it more lucrative to sell livestock onto the international market than to sell grain, and upland regions where lack of livestock forced peasants to sell grain, despite its low price. It is likely that the tax system further aggravated the problem of the remoter regions. As the direct tax was collected at the same per capita rate from all regions, lowland farmers had few problems in selling enough livestock to meet their tax liabilities, but fiscal pressure in the uplands forced out grain – for want of any alternative cash staple – in quantities which local markets could barely absorb. Therefore lowland peasants husbanded resources to maximize their pastoral capabilities, drawing heavily on the services of their womenfolk to assist, and minimized the area they held under grain, while upland peasants ploughed their land up, despite its infertility, but did not hold sufficient livestock to keep their women productively employed.

This reading of the available data is supported by empirical evidence from Ignjić's study on the remote upland Užice region. He wrote that the low prices of cattle and agricultural produce in the late 1860s were 'not the result of a large production but rather of low consumption and the need of producers to pay taxes and tax surcharges'.[163]

The influence of the market

To summarise, in the lowlands, it was unprofitable to put land under grain which could serve the needs of the livestock economy; in the uplands, farmers sold grain for want of livestock, but the high cost of producing it and the low price it fetched discouraged any orientation to the market greater than was needed to pay the taxes.

At the margin, increasing numbers of peasants, even in the fertile north, would have to find alternatives to the sale of livestock to avoid

---

[162] Palairet, 'Rural Serbia', pp. 96–100.
[163] Stevan Ignjić, *Užice i okolina, 1862–1914* (T. Užice, 1967), p. 75.

being forced into distress or a meatless diet. During the late 1850s and early 1860s, there were numerous complaints concerning peasant indebtedness. Conventionally, indebtedness is explained as inevitably accompanying the breakdown of the subsistence economy. Peasants, it is argued, were drawn increasingly into cash relationships which they had no experience of handling. They could be sucked into debt by selling crops in advance and in excessive quantity, and then be forced to borrow to meet shortfalls in their provision of subsistence. Misjudgements of this nature can certainly be documented. In Šabac *okrug* in 1866, grain prices were so attractive at harvest time that the people, 'wanting to get hold of some money as soon as possible', left themselves with insufficient food to tide them over to the next harvest.[164]

We should, however, be cautious about explaining the growth of debt in terms of the growing facility with which peasants could earn cash. Commercialization also afforded an opportunity to extinguish existing debt, which had piled up as incomes from traditional sources (i.e. livestock) were squeezed. The emergent debt problem *preceded* the growth of the grain export trade, and this trade, so far from aggravating debt distress, alleviated it. The 1861 report from Vračar explained that peasant debt had been growing 'in the years since the monetary crisis began'. This probably refers to the financial crisis of 1857, to which Austria reacted by interfering with livestock imports from Serbia. This caused a rural liquidity crisis in Serbia, which pre-dates any tendency towards crop monetization; it was claimed that 34,000 disputes went to the courts, of which 24,000 concerned unpaid debts.[165] But 'people have responded to their over-indebted condition', wrote the Vračar sub-prefect, 'partly on the advice of the authorities, but rather more of their own inclination, to pay off their debts themselves, so they have for some years been improving their agriculture...' In 1861 maize was sown not only for domestic purposes and livestock feed, but also to produce a surplus for sale. 'This autumn, the people did not relax in the least, but seeking profit from sowing grain this year, they are sowing an increasing amount.'[166] One may doubt whether such efforts could greatly have offset rising debt pressure, because prices were still too low to make grain an attractive market crop – and the surpluses tended to be the unplanned result of abundance. In 1861, again, in Smederevo *okrug* – which enjoyed relatively easy market access – a bad harvest was ascribed partly to drought, but also 'to some extent because the people, richly rewarded by the harvest of 1860, neglected to sow the autumn grain on time'.[167]

---

[164] AS MF E 1867 VIII 137, Pocerina srez, no. 64 of 3 Jan. 1867.
[165] *Proizvodne snage*, p. 5.   [166] AS MF E 1862 V 101. No. 3383 of 31 Dec. 1861.
[167] AS MF E 1862 V 101. No. 934 of 1 Feb. 1862.

In the years following the 1863 census, the hitherto slow tempo of market integration accelerated. In neighbouring Hungary, farm production was being unified with the demands of the European market. This dragged prices upward, and caused merchants to augment supplies with produce from Serbia, raising produce prices in Serbia's more accessible areas closer to world market levels. They had far to move. In 1829, Serbia had been 'probably the cheapest country in Europe. It is even cheaper than southern Hungary, and that's saying a lot.'[168] In both Hungary and Serbia, a transient peak of export activity was attained in 1868/9 when high prices coincided with rich local harvests, but Komlos points out that this exceptional conjuncture only interrupted a more gradual speed-up which began in the mid-1860s and lasted till the mid-1870s, after two stagnant preceding decades.[169] Grain at last flowed out onto export markets in rapidly increasing quantities, and at historically favourable prices. Between 1862/5 and 1872/5, Serbia's export of farm commodities rose by 95 per cent by value; so a general price rise of 42 per cent induced a 37 per cent increase in supplies.[170]

This upsurge in Serbia's commerce owed little to forces endogenous to the Serbian economic, demographic or social systems. The easing of frontier formalities at Belgrade and the improvement in the internal highways facilitated commercial expansion,[171] but such advances were of minor significance. Faced with severe pressures to depart from their previous economic lifestyles, and presented with new, and more attractive commercial possibilities, Serbian peasants, at least in the fertile plains, responded positively, if hesitantly, to a strengthened commercial stimulus.

Yet it remains unclear why this response was not stronger. Supply was not 'pushed' by the rising pressure of settlement, nor by rising taxes. Indeed supply was less than unitarily elastic to price, and those areas which suffered most from demographic pressures and the burden of direct taxation lacked access to the international market. Moreover, revenue from personal taxation fell between the early 1860s and the mid 1870s in per capita terms, especially if the inflation in export prices is taken into account, so tax policy, if anything, diminished the incentive to crop monetization.[172]

Farmers needed better market infrastructure; they remained dependent on access to little urban markets, on which local businessmen purchased produce in petty quantities to pass into wider trade. Isolated

---

[168] Otto Dubislav pl. Pirh [von Pirsch], *Putovanje po Srbiji u godini 1829*, tr. D Mijušković (Belgrade, 1983), p. 56.
[169] John Komlos, *The Habsburg Monarchy as a Customs Union* (Princeton, 1983), pp. 75–8.
[170] See Table 1. 8, of Palairet, 'The influence of commerce', p. 37.
[171] *Jedinstvo* (Belgrade), 10 Sept. 1872, p. 401.   [172] Palairet, 'Fiscal pressure'.

partly by bad communications, and partly by the restrictionist policies of the state, peasants found it difficult to find buyers for produce which could not be driven on the hoof. As early as 1823, Kosmaj villagers petitioned the prince to let a merchant conduct trade in their villages, enabling them to turn their surpluses into money.[173] Most grain markets were local and easily glutted, so huge inter-town disparities existed in grain prices. 'Speculators' began to exploit export opportunities, but it needed in-coming businessmen to exploit the arbitrage potential of pulling Serbia into the European trading system; Serbian businessmen showed little initiative, and were content to participate as agents *(kalauze)* for importer interests.[174] But few large-scale grain traders were active in Serbian markets in the 1860s and 1870s,[175] and far more grain – and other products – could have been produced for export if farmers had been brought into better contact with the trade.

This dynamic role of the intermediary could be critical to the monetization of rural produce. The integration of Serbia into the international produce market was not confined to grain. The 1860s and 1870s witnessed also the development of trades based on the plum crop. The value of plum based exports rose from virtually nothing in the early 1860s to exceed the value of grain exports by the end of our period. To monetize the crop, it had to be smoke-dried to prunes, a technique not native to Serbia. The commercial acumen, financial skills and technical know-how which animated the burgeoning export of prunes were provided not by local merchants, but by immigrant businessmen from Bosnia, where the trade had been established earlier. In particular, the prune trade was pioneered by the firm of Krsmanović-Paranos, and most other names which were active in the early years of the trade were connected closely with the pioneering firm.

The plum growing areas were less accessible to the export market than those capable of bearing grain surpluses. So, without the enterprise and organization provided by Paranos and Krsmanović, it is doubtful whether the superabundance of Serbia's plum orchards would have been exploited so energetically. The export of plum jam *(pekmez)* began soon after the trade in dried plums, and was again the result of external interest in Serbia as a supply source. The teams of jam makers that toured the Serbian villages during the picking season were mostly composed of foreign workers and were financed and controlled by the Budapest produce firms.[176] The point emphasized here is that commercial

[173] Borivoje M. Drobnjaković, 'Kosmaj', *Srpski etnografski zbornik*, XLVI (Belgrade, 1930), p. 49.   [174] Milenković, *Ekonomska istorija*, pp. 97–8.   [175] Ibid., p. 97.
[176] Michael Palairet, 'Merchant Enterprise and the Development of the Plum-Based Trades in Serbia, 1847–1911', *Economic History Review*, XXX (1977), pp. 590–9.

enterprise did not arise indigenously; it was associated in its early stages with in-coming enterprise, whose dynamism contrasted with the passivity of the settled merchant class.

Similarly, the silk boom, which ephemerally gripped Serbian producers during the same period, owed nothing to domestic enterprise, and was wholly the result of a feverish search by importers for uncontaminated silkworm eggs. The later wine boom of the 1880s was analogous, though in both these cases, when importer interests lost interest in Serbia as a marginal supply source, the internal networks which they had created collapsed, and the trades quickly dwindled for want of locally based enterprise.[177]

The upsurge of produce exports did not put an end to the debt problem, for as peasants increasingly depended on earnings from cereals, a bad harvest could drive whole villages into the hands of usurers.[178] Yet the hopes reported by the Vračar sub-prefect in 1861 – that grain sales might alleviate indebtedness – now had a reasonable chance of fulfilment. For example, an excellent maize crop in Jasenica district of Kragujevac okrug in 1868 enabled peasants significantly to reduce the debts they had contracted in previous years,[179] though this prosperity was partly the windfall result of an improvement in prices coupled with an abundant crop. In Jasenica, that most profitable maize crop had been harvested despite reduced sowings, while in Jadar district, the autumn sowings of 1868 (for harvesting in 1869) had been reduced 'because the year was very fertile with all things and they could not easily put their summer crops in order on time, and when they had done so, they were then engaged in distilling plum-spirit and other jobs'.[180]

Here and there, peasants responded more actively to the new conditions. In Rasina district of Požarevac okrug in 1863, implements remained unmodernized, but 'the people, having seen from year to year that hard work and careful cultivation enrich and reward them, work harder and put more seed on the land, as indeed they have this year'. These improvements had been consistently pursued over the previous five years, and the arable was being carefully manured (which was rare in Serbia) 'so that even the weaker fields can bear a crop'.[181] In Negotinska, in 1866, the peasants 'bought light iron ploughs brought in from Austria, and ploughed with them, and with good seed'.[182] In Kragujevac okrug the

[177] Palairet, 'Serbia's Role', pp. 177, 181.
[178] Svetozar Marković, *Celokupna dela* (Belgrade, 1912), II, p. 50.
[179] AS MF E 1869 XIII-1. No. 40 of 3 Jan. 1869.
[180] AS MF E 1869 XIII-1. No. 7111 of 31 Dec. 1868.
[181] AS MF E 1864 VI-7. No. 676 of 4 Feb. 1864.
[182] AS MF E 1867 VIII-137. 119 No. 3737 of 31 Dec. 1866.

people were 'working at agriculture much better than in previous years and sow more wheat and cereals than before'.[183] Interestingly, the brisk demand for maize in neighbouring Gruža also caused the peasants to feed their pigs as much as possible on acorns; as a result, 'it is observed among the people that it is much more rational to keep and set up woodlands than was done up to a few years ago'.[184] In the passage from Milićević (dated 1876) quoted above on indebtedness and distress in the Morava valley, the debt problem was discussed in the *past* tense. He continued: 'but they [the peasants] affirm that they are now cured of the sickness'. To Milićević, rural indebtedness was a moral issue, so he left the impression that the 'cure' signified a return to the austere consumption patterns of the past, which had been financed solely by the sale of livestock – and not by 'speculation' in grain. But given the production trends of the time, it seems likely that the the Morava peasants were dis-indebting themselves by selling more grain (and at higher prices) and not by withdrawing into subsistence.

Indeed, Milićević was witnessing a structural shift in economic behaviour, the Serbian counterpart of the economic renaissance of pre-liberation Bulgaria. In Serbia, however, it was a purely farm based phenomenon without a manufacturing component. Old attitudes concerning the immorality of selling grain or fattening livestock with it gradually gave way in the lowlands to the values of a less heroic, more commercially aware culture. The Šabac peasants, who had previously regarded such activities as disgraceful, learned better than any to accommodate to the changing commercial realities of the period.[185]

The growth of the plum based trades diffused the commercial upswing geographically, because plum cultivation was most dense in areas of lower grade arable, characteristically in rolling country. If the crop was successfully monetized it produced a return per hectare higher than first-class arable. Besides this, once dried, the prune was much more transportable than grain, because its value per unit of weight was about 2.5 times as high. Thus plum growing provided a surrogate for arable intensification. The main beneficiaries of the plum boom tended to be 'middle income' areas in the centre and west of the country, where it diffused prosperity more widely than if monetization had depended on grain and livestock alone.[186]

The commercial upswing reached the poorer and remoter parts of Serbia, but with less force. Užice okrug, for example, lay at the southern fringe of the plum growing belt, and suffered serious transport problems,

---

[183] AS MF E 1869 XIII-1. No. 5098 of 31 Dec. 1868.
[184] AS MF E 1869 XIII-1. No. 23 of Jan. 1869.   [185] Vulović, 'Kako da se pomognemo'.
[186] Palairet, 'Plum-based trades', pp. 586–90.

while the dry east and southeast of the country were unsuitable for plum raising. The conjuncture of 1863–75 penetrated the south, as well as the north. Even Užice enjoyed something of a 'golden age', based on the export of cattle,[187] but the earliest surviving data on export outlets, in 1880, show that exports of grain, cattle and pigs were still heavily concentrated on the Danube basin area of Serbia and the lower Morava valley. So the export boom probably widened the economic gap between the poorer and richer parts of the country; as a peasant of Užice informed Milan Milićević: 'It is not the Šumadija here, where the householder's cellar is filled with barrels – rather a few nomads' tents, camps and thatched cabins, with nothing much around them. One could move a whole village by midday.'[188] It is related that, during the 1876–8 campaigns, soldiers from Šabac, stationed in the hill country round Ivanjica near the Ottoman border, mistook the hovels of local peasants for haystacks, and tore them down for bedding. To their amazement, 'tearful children' came out to plead with them not to destroy their homes.[189] The representative for Užice district in the parliament of 1878 hardly exaggerated when claiming that 'there is no poorer district except that of Rača in Užice okrug'.[190]

The import trade

During the boom years, the import volume should have risen more rapidly than the volume of exports, because the forces which caused domestic produce prices to converge upwards towards those pertaining in the international market should conversely have caused the prices at which manufactures were sold domestically to converge downwards towards the world market level. There is evidence that this improvement in the barter terms of trade in fact occurred. Changing customs classifications and units make it difficult to establish a definitive series for import prices, but the sample commodities tabulated in Table 4.1 do behave more or less in the way predicted.

The sample is too small to establish a precise trend in import prices, but even the most inflationary of these commodities, sugar, rose in price by much less than the overall 41.6 per cent increase in export valuation prices, while metal prices were clearly falling. So the essence of the economic revolution of 1862/5–1872/5 was a sharp improvement in the terms at which farmers traded, which induced them to monetize produce which had hitherto not been worth marketing.

---

[187] Ignjić, *Užice*, p. 74.   [188] Milićević, *Kneževina Srbija*, pp. 626–7.
[189] Sreta A. Popović, *Na mirisnome Zlatiboru*, 3rd. edn (Belgrade, 1908), p. 57.
[190] Ignjić, *Užice*, p. 74.

Table 4.1 *Serbia. Import prices of sample commodities 1863–1875*

	1863	1864	1865	1872	1873	1874	1875
Iron	2.80	3.43	n.d.	3.26	2.46	2.40	2.50
Copper	25.96	27.89	21.75	18.71	20.02	21.40	20.42
Lead	3.38	5.19	n.d.	4.27	4.13	4.10	4.12
Sugar	6.55	6.99	6.00	8.17	7.39	6.50	6.78
Shawls	25.37	51.74	25.75	28.13	28.44	28.39	28.39

Sources: International trade, annual statistic published in *Državopis Srbije*. Figures for 1863 appear in vol. II, pp. 93–115; for 1864 and 1865 in vol. III, pp. 1–46; for 1872–5 as vol. X. (Units: piastres per oka, shawls per box.)

The benefits of this improvement in the terms of trade needed to filter through to the producer, if he were to respond to them. Peasants encountered almost as much difficulty in exchanging their money for consumer goods as in finding a buyer for their surpluses. Rural shops were badly needed, but the state, prompted both by its fear of rural debt, and by the interest of the urban shopkeepers and craftsmen, restricted their spread. Under Miloš's rule, village shops were grudgingly licensed to trade, but only in necessities, and were taxed so heavily that few were opened.[191] But suddenly the villages came to be seen by businessmen for their potential as consumers. Their distance, both physically and psychologically from the towns, meant that good business was to be enjoyed in ministering to the demands of an underserviced countryside. The villages, even in rich Belica and Podunavlje, were at the time of the 1863 census almost without shops, and even taverns were few and far between. But a table based on replies to a survey of 1883, which asked about the location of village shops and the date of their opening, disclosed the following incomplete information on village shops existing in 1883, according to date of opening:[192]

1853	1
1864–7	5
1868–70	24
1871–4	17
1875–9	8
1880–3	18

[191] Tihomir Djordjević, *Srbija pre sto godina* (Belgrade, 1946), p. 150; Vučo, *Raspadanje*, I, pp. 323ff.   [192] Adapted from Vučo, *Raspadanje*, I, table facing p. 330.

Considering the probable transience of such businesses, the fact that two-thirds of the shops surviving in 1883 had been set up during the 1864–74 upswing is evidence of mounting rural prosperity during the trade boom. (The subsequent decline also suggests its transience.) The table is incomplete, for the opening of some shops is undated, and many regions failed to file returns. It is noticeable that nearly half these shops were in the *okrug* of Požarevac, one of the most fertile and best-connected regions in the country. Rural commerce was slower in penetrating the interior, and the few shops in the southern provinces were of more recent date than most of those near Požarevac. These shops ministered to the burgeoning demands of the newly affluent Požarevac villagers. In the immediate district of the town, it was claimed that every village had acquired a shop of some sort (in which case the figures presented above understate). Moreover, these shops were tapping discretionary demands – which naturally invited disapproval. The peasants of Homolje district complained that the village shops led young people 'to steal food from their homes to procure useless cheap goods at the shop'.[193] The sub-prefect of the Morava district wrote:[194]

I came to the conclusion that the peasants are in favour of the village shops, on condition that they only sell goods essential for the peasantry, like salt, iron, colonial goods [i.e. sugar, spices, rice etc.] agricultural equipment, but that [the sale by them] should be prohibited of all other wares such as textiles in general, rings, ear-rings, and similar trifles which are corrupting, especially of the women, as these buy them even though they have no real need of them, but only so that they can show them off to the others.

Naturally these sentiments, put into the mouths of the peasants, would have been influenced by strident representations made by urban businesses that these shops were costing them trade, and by the craftsmen, who feared that most of what the village shops sold, especially the 'trifles', would be imported goods.

The new peasant affluence was expended on far more than the adornment of women's ears; from the early 1860s till the early 1870s, Serbia was invaded peaceably by a growing inflow of migrant workers. They came mainly from Macedonia, western Bosnia and Bulgaria, and engaged in rural house building in the relatively affluent northern villages. These workers, of whom Svetozar Marković complained that they denuded the country of 'money' and deprived local workers of wages,[195] were estimated in number at 5,000 in 1863, their repatriated earnings at £50,000 sterling. By 1872, their number may have quadrupled, as their earnings had risen reportedly to £200,000. (A French report of the same

---

[193] Ibid., p. 332.   [194] Ibid.   [195] Marković, *Celokupna dela*, II, pp. 50, 70, 74.

Table 4.2 *Serbia. Sectoral farm output 1859–1875*

	(million dinars of constant 1910 value)						dinars
Year	Animal products	Animals	Cash crops	Grains	Garden crops	Total	Total per-capita
1859–60	33	59	49	34	7	181	186
1861–5	33	55	52	35	8	183	177
1866–70	35	56	58	41	9	199	175
1871–5	37	60	61	45	9	212	176

Source: see BALKSTAT.

year estimates their numbers at an improbable 80,000.)[196] This influx reflects the animation of rural markets during this period.

Trends in farm output, 1859–1875

Table 4.2 above sectoralizes the contribution of farm output to Serbia's GDP between 1859 and 1875, and estimates the overall trend in its value per capita. There was a tendency for output to shift away from stockraising, as the contribution of animals and animal products declined from 50 per cent in 1859/60 to 46 per cent in 1874/5. Given severe supply side pressures on livestock raising, the extent of this shift was insufficient to raise per capita output at the end of the period to the level of 1859–60, despite the recovery following the trough of 1864–6. The prosperity of the late 1860s and early 1870s was therefore due less to the productive progress achieved in these years than to the improvement in the barter terms of trade, which enabled consumption to rise relative to output. This explains why the prosperity of the period turned out to be transient.

The urban economy

Towns in Serbia accounted for but 7 per cent of the population in 1863. The level of urbanization was even less than might be predicted from the volume of commercial activity in the villages, modest though this was. The principal reason was that the largest sector of export activity, the pig trade, barely touched the Serbian towns. It was organized mainly by traders from Hungary, who bought their supplies directly from the

[196] GBC Serbia 1863, p. 239 and 1872b, p. 343; AAE CCB t. 5 despatch dated 30 Dec. 1872.

producers, usually through Serbians working on commission. Other types of livestock were traded at fairs, rather than at urban markets, and these fairs conducted a large part of the exchange trade with the villages. Urban artisans complained incessantly at this, for it gave itinerant bagmen and unlicensed artisans opportunities to divert trade from their shops.

Notwithstanding the large volume of trade which bypassed them altogether, Serbia's towns were numerous, though for the most part very small. Their large number was encouraged by the authorities, as a means of exercising political control over the rural areas.[197]

The townspeople were on average richer than the villagers, with incomes averaging 182 dinars against 112. However, modal urban incomes tended to be below those in the adjacent rural areas, and the urban average was pushed up by the presence of the literate classes, officials and merchants. In one case, Gornji Milanovac (founded in the 1850s),[198] 36 per cent of the town's income resided in the hands of people on the state payroll, so much of the business transacted by its craftsmen and shopkeepers was generated by the demands of its official class.

However, Gornji Milanovac is an extreme example of urban dependence on state spending. In four other towns of relative substance whose registers were analysed, salary incomes did not exceed 15 per cent of the total, so the greater part of their business must have depended on the supply of goods to the villages, and to a lesser extent the purchase of farm produce, part of which was then exported. The two functions were often combined, after the familiar trading-store model, whereby peasants took merchandise on credit and paid it off with settlement in kind. Trade tended to be seasonal and intermittent, and the towns only came to life at the Sunday markets.

The urban elite consisted of the salariat and the more substantial merchants, and it was the merchant families who supplied the educated personnel which the state recruited into its administrative and judicial appointments. In trade, distinctions between wholesale and retail business were blurred, except in Belgrade, where much of the stock of the provincial trader was procured. Elsewhere the shops were little differentiated, though there was a notional distinction between the storekeeper who sold 'manufactures' such as drapery and metalwares, and the spicer (*bakalin*), who specialized in 'colonial' products, such as rice, sugar, coffee and other non-perishable foodstuffs.

As a relatively well-to-do group, merchants held much of the land within the administrative area of their towns. For example, in Jagodina,

[197] Branislav D. Kojić, *Varošice u Srbiji. XIX veka* (Belgrade, 1970), pp. 4–6.
[198] Živadin M. Stevanović, *Postanak i razvitak Gornjeg Milanovca* (Čačak, 1968), p. 14.

the average merchant held 3.5 hectares of land, compared with the average urban head of family with 0.96. Merchants as a result held 38.5 per cent of the town's land, though they comprised but 10.6 per cent of its households. Merchant-owned land was mainly held in arable, as an adjunct to trading, particularly livestock fattening. In the smaller towns, where turnover of merchandise was particularly slow, shopkeeping was often an extension to the business of commercial farming.[199]

In all towns, much of the population was composed of craftsmen, their families and employees. Characteristic trades were tailor, cobbler, smith and joiner. Artisans tended to be poorer than the merchants. Few, except for tailors, who tended also to trade as drapers, owned much property, or employed more than one journeyman. They were seldom highly skilled, and they floated between different occupations. This generalization excludes the towns of the Niš *pašaluk*, as yet in Ottoman hands, where the commercial and manufacturing environment was similar to that of Bulgaria. This is why, after its annexation into Serbia, the region was more urban and commercially specialized than the older provinces.

The towns as a whole grew more rapidly than total population. Although much of the fast rising volume of international trade bypassed them, at least it offered the townspeople a rising volume of exchange business, while the growing tax take had a similar effect as the official class expanded. As craft manufacturing entities, however, they would become vulnerable to the growth of external competition. In 1863, poor communications still sheltered town artisans against import competition, which is why they produced a wide range of inefficiently made goods in small quantities. They were further protected by the high mark-ups on imported manufactures which compensated for their slow turnover.[200]

The trade upswing of the 1860s and early 1870s put pressure on craft manufacturing. Craft incomes were squeezed as rural produce was bid up in price by export demand, while their capacity to force through compensating price rises was restrained by the price stability of imported goods. As imports rose in response to the growth of rural demand, it seemed from the craftsmen's standpoint that foreign competitors were trying to ruin them by seducing their peasant customers with underpriced trash. Boom conditions probably deferred adjustment, but this made the ensuing recession all the more acute. Distress symptoms were apparent in a return of guild membership for 1879; in town after town the returns include marginalia such as that for Belgrade, where seventy-five master quilters were listed, but of these only thirty-seven were working. In

[199] K. V., 'Iz istorije trgovine. Zemljoradnici i trgovci', *Nova trgovina* (Belgrade) Apr. 1952, p. 307.   [200] 'Naša trgovina', *Šumadinka*, 1856, no. 20, p. 156.

Smederevo four out of twenty master tailors were still in practice, in Užice half the cobblers and a quarter of the sandal-makers had ceased to work and nine out of thirty saddlers had given up business. Some no doubt had retired, but others were trying to find alternative means of winning a living, like eight out of the twenty-four cobblers of Aleksinac who 'because of slack trade engage in other businesses'. Reports from Gornji Milanovac, Kruševac, Kladovo and Veliko Gradište carried marginalia telling the same tale of decline, so the distress in urban crafts was probably felt generally throughout the country.[201]

Textile manufacturing

Prosperity between 1863 and 1875 provided no stimulus for commercial textile manufacturing. The institutional framework and factor endowment of the economy offered little incentive to produce textiles save for household self-consumption. So the country was virtually devoid of the proto-industrial foundations for the rise of large-scale manufacturing. Some partially mechanized textile factory projects won state approval and assistance, but were uniformly unsuccessful.

Serbia's first 'factory' was set up in 1852 on state property at Topčider, just outside Belgrade. A Serbian civil servant, Atanasije Nikolić, persuaded his government to lend him 19,000 Austrian florins to convert a watermill into a factory for blankets and broadcloth. Working mainly to government order, it used convict labour and a mixture of manual and power driven spinning equipment. The factory wove with handlooms. The enterprise was given state orders, but was incapable of meeting them efficiently. A perennial shortage of water power led to its supplementation with an ox-powered treadmill. Skilled workers were brought from Austria but, as they were too costly to maintain, the mill suffered from inadequate technical supervision. Delivery dates were missed, the firm ran up losses, and could not service its debts. From 1859 to 1862, production ceased, and such equipment as was not stolen, deteriorated. The state renewed its interest in securing military supplies after the Belgrade bombardment of 1862, so the mill was recommissioned, but the shortage of power still caused production to be intermittent. Declining to throw good money after bad, the government refused to buy the factory a steam engine, and the remaining equipment was sold off for 100 ducats to one Stefan Popović, who took it to Užice (southwest Serbia) where he opened a weavery in 1868.[202]

[201] AS MNP S Kut. 5 XXII-1.
[202] Leposava Cvijetić, 'Fabrika čohe u Topčideru – Prva beogradska fabrika', *Ekonomski Anali*, XXXI-XXXII (1970), pp. 63–82.

Popović, a Belgrader who had settled in Užice in 1863, expected to succeed because of the cheapness of wool there, and because the flow of the Detinje river would drive the machinery without interruption. Naturally, he also expected (and received) state help. There existed in Užice and environs a cottage industry which made cotton cloth for the market,[203] which Ignjić suggests provided the mill with cheap weaving labour. But Užice was not a proto-industrial town, though it had a few handloom craft shops. Like the Topčider venture, Popović's mill depended on soft loans from the state and on army orders for blankets, because on the open market its products were undercut by imports from Bosnia. In 1880, Popović won a monopoly concession for (large-scale) blanket making, but (as an indication that the mill was probably uncompetitive even against local handicraft production) the concession did not allow him to demand the closure of craft blanket making shops.[204] So the business remained unprofitable, and the concession was sold in 1885 to a firm which had recently erected a mill at Paraćin.[205] The Užice factory was closed, and Popović became office manager in Belgrade for the Paraćin mill.[206]

Conclusion: half a commercial revolution

Despite the low density of settlement in mid-nineteenth-century Serbia, the country suffered creeping impoverishment, especially during the trade depression of the late 1850s. The 1830s and 1840s were looked back upon as a golden age, for thereafter neither the cultivated area nor the herds of cattle kept pace with the growth of agricultural population.

The sluggishness with which waste was taken into cultivation reflected the low marginal utility of cereal products. This resulted from the low market price of grain and the relatively high returns from livestock, which encouraged peasants to hold their land in pasture. Yet they were under pressure to cut back their herds because of deforestation. Lack of secure rights in grazing woodland forced peasants into competitive despoliation. Diminution of oak and beech deprived them of pig fodder over winter, forcing them either to sell underweight pigs to the export trade or to devote maize to feeding them, in the first case sacrificing unit value, in the second raising unit costs. Despite this, strong demand conditions stimulated a rising volume of exports, supply being enhanced by the delivery of lighter, thinner animals. However, the rising export of livestock encroached on subsistence consumption of animal products.

---

[203] Karić, *Srbija*, p. 696.   [204] Ignjić, *Užice*, pp. 99–102.   [205] See below pp. 258–60.
[206] M. M. Savić, *NiZ*, I (Sarajevo, 1922), p. 218; Kanitz, *Srbija*, I, p. 511.

In the long run, this process was unsustainable, so peasants had to raise grain for commerce as well as for subsistence. But it was mainly in the poorer areas of the country, where farmers lacked livestock to sell, that grain was produced for the market. Lowland farmers were only drawn into the grain market between 1863 and 1875 as integration with external markets tilted the terms of trade in their favour. Increased rural monetization, at least in the north, was reflected in the multiplication of village shops, which supplied incentive goods which served to bind farmers more closely into market production.

These stirrings in the farm economy damaged the urban craftsmen, for the inflow of imported manufactures undermined domestic manufacturing competition. Economic transition in Serbia was less impressive than that which was taking place in Bulgaria, since the growth of domestic demand failed to stimulate an analogous proto-industrial sector. Attempts with mechanized production did not result in cost savings.

5   Bosnia and Montenegro before 1878

The western Balkans lay before 1878 at the periphery of Ottoman power. Their remoteness from the Ottoman mainstream was not offset by the relative propinquity of Mediterranean civilization in the Austrian controlled coastal strip of Dalmatia. Seen from the coast, the dark and menacing hills of the interior were less a hinterland than a frontier. The dinaric zone – from northern Bosnia to the Pindus – remained largely tribal, a mozaic of patriarchal cultures. Its greater part, Bosnia-Hercegovina, was an Ottoman vilayet, but it was ruled by a native Muslim elite whose power till mid-century was little constrained by Ottoman centralization. Authority in the unmapped Arnautluk – the Albanian lands – was still more fragmented. Squeezed between Bosnia and Arnautluk, and cut off from the Adriatic by fortified Austrian territory, lay Montenegro, tribal, Orthodox Christian and Serb speaking – whose cohesion in wartime enabled its people to rule themselves according to their own dispensation. Economic life in the dinaric lands focused mainly on upland pastoralism, the dark area of the Balkan chiaroscuro. Given the paucity of contemporary sources, the best insights perhaps lie, as is argued by Karl Kaser, in using the tools of the historical anthropologist,[1] and ethnographic work on the area provides a vital, if biased, source of historical information.

Pre-reform Bosnia to 1851

Until the Ottomans lost control to Austria-Hungary in 1878, Bosnia-Hercegovina was an imperial borderland, over which central government had relatively weak control. As elsewhere, a Muslim elite ruled over subordinated Serb-Orthodox and Catholic peasants. Unlike the majority of Muslims in Bulgaria, Serbia and Greece, who were ethnic Turks or Albanians, most Bosnian Muslims were descendants of the Christianized people of medieval Bosnia, and preserved much of their south Slavic

---

[1] Karl Kaser, 'The Origins of Balkan Patriarchy', *Modern Greek Studies*, VIII (1992), pp. 1–37.

3. Muslim women in Sarajevo

culture, including the language. According to Noel Malcolm, the majority population of pre-Ottoman Bosnia adhered only nominally to the
semi-defunct Bosnian Church, and adopted Islam without much resistance during the sixteenth and seventeenth centuries. A resistant,
Franciscan-led minority remained true to their faith. Except in
Hercegovina, Serbs – Christians of the Orthodox faith – were a negligible
presence. The growing Bosnian Orthodox community, argues Malcolm,
was mainly created by immigrations by Serbs and Vlachs from Serbia
proper and Old Serbia during the early modern period. These migrations
were encouraged by the Ottomans so as to repopulate thinly settled lands,
and, by providing labour, to valorize them as sources of taxation and rent.
Muslims formed the largest population group in the province. By the
(optimistic) reckoning of the vilayet authorities in about 1870, they composed some 49.8 per cent of the population.[2] A Serbian source (which
conversely sought to emphasize the numerical weight of the Serb-
Orthodox population) showed the Muslims at 33.7 per cent in 1865,[3]
while the first Austrian census, carried out in 1879 (prior to which there
had been heavy Muslim emigration) recorded Muslims at 38.7 per cent.[4]

[2] Bosnia. *Salname*, 1288 (1871), pp. 134–5.
[3] 'Statistični podatci o Bosni, Hercegovini i jednom kraju Stare Srbije', *GSUD*, III (O.S.
XX) (Belgrade, 1866), pp. 226–7.
[4] *Ortschafts und Bevölkerungs-Statistik von Bosnien und Herzegovina* (Sarajevo, 1880), p. 4.

It is probable they had formerly comprised around 40 per cent of the population.

Political and agrarian power was concentrated upon perhaps 6–7 per cent of Muslim families,[5] but the Muslims as a whole formed a cohesive political group. The mass of Muslim petty proprietors supported or acquiesced in the leadership of their co-religionists. As the power of central government declined during the eighteenth century, the Bosnian Muslims increasingly governed themselves, and viewed themselves as defenders of the last remaining Ottoman frontier to face the threat of Habsburg expansionism.[6] This heightened their self-perception as a military caste, which accorded with the system of Ottoman government before the reforms. Aware of their distinctness from the Muslims of the Ottoman heartlands, they aspired as the Ottoman state decayed to an autonomy like that which had been wrested from the Porte by Egypt and Serbia.[7]

In discussing the sources for structural economic change in the heartlands of Ottoman Europe, we have stressed the significance of the recentralization and reform of Ottoman government. In Bosnia, where the centralizers had to confront the cohesive Muslim elite, the new Ottoman order only began to be imposed after the mid nineteenth century. However, Bosnia's political arrangements were not the sole factor in the non-emergence of a Bulgarian-style economic revolution. Geography endowed it neither with natural trade routes, nor with potential surpluses of foodstuffs. Bosnia's potential lay neither in farming nor in small industries, rather in the industrial exploitation of its subsoil and forest wealth, which had to await the Habsburg occupation.

Control over landed estate and unfree cultivators was the basis of Muslim power in Bosnia-Hercegovina. A few non-Muslim businessmen held land rights but 'in the whole vilayet there is barely a Christian peasant who owns his land and house'.[8] These people, and more than a few Muslims, were regarded by their masters as a productive underclass which existed to sustain their own needs.

The native elite held sway in Bosnia up to 1851. They strongly resisted the attempts of the Porte to establish an effective administration. The Ottoman reforms were designed to undermine the old feudal order of society, and, at least in the short term, such a transition would work to their obvious disadvantage, without holding out any clear attractions to

---

[5] See below, p. 136.
[6] Stanford J. Shaw and Ezel Kural Shaw, *History of the Ottoman Empire and Modern Turkey*, II, *Reform, Revolution and the Republic* (Cambridge, 1985), p. 149.
[7] Ahmed S. Aličić, *Uredjenje bosanskog elayeta od 1789 do 1878 godine* (Sarajevo, 1983), p. 19.   [8] Gustav Thömmel, *Beschreibung des Vilajet Bosnien* (Vienna, 1867), p. 147.

the rest of the population. In particular, the Bosnian Muslims were reluctant to tolerate interference with their dispositions towards the *reaya*, whom they ruled firmly, but on the basis of custom, which made for a measure of domestic stability. The extent to which the peasantry was alienated from its rulers is easy to exaggerate. The principal authority on the administration of Ottoman Bosnia, Ahmed Aličić, claims that in their desire to maintain home rule, the Muslim leaders enjoyed the probable support of the majority of the population.[9]

The Porte was unwilling to concede the autonomy the Bosnians sought; on the contrary, it sought to regain control of the province, its administration, its revenues and its armed forces. Consequently, it wanted the Janissary order, which effectively controlled Sarajevo, suppressed in Bosnia as elsewhere, and it also tried to abolish the feudal administration to enable its own appointees to rule. As the Bosnian *spahijas* and military administrators (the *kapetans*) had converted the imperial tithes into their own private revenues, Bosnia, relative to its population, remitted less revenue to the centre than any other province.[10] This gave the Porte a powerful incentive to abolish feudal privilege.

The Bosnian *âyans* disposed armed force, and it proved less easy to turn them against each other than it did with the *âyans* of the other provinces. So the Porte had an uphill task in reasserting its authority. The Bosnian *bashi-bozuka* militias were not particularly effective when faced with expeditionary forces from the centre, but it was one thing to march into the territory, another to sustain the writ of central government. For example, a successful expedition in about 1819 established the incorruptible Jelaludin Pasha as governor in Travnik. It subdued the whole territory, but within a short time Jelaludin was recalled and poisoned.[11] Further successful expeditions followed, including that of Abdurahman Pasha in 1827, but his troops mutinied and he was replaced by an appointee who was more complaisant to Bosnian interests. Between 1831 and 1833, under the rule of Husein Kapetan Gradaščević, Bosnia-Hercegovina was for most practical purposes an independent state.[12] Even with the resumption of central control in 1833 by Kara Mahmud Pasha, the power of the Bosnian elites was little diminished, and a 'barbarous independence still prevailed'.[13]

Elsewhere in the Ottoman Empire, the *spahiluks* were abolished with relative ease once the Janissaries had been crushed, but in Bosnia the ordinance which was supposed to convert the *spahijas* into a regular

---

[9] Aličić, *Uredjenje*, p. 21.   [10] Shaw and Shaw, *Ottoman Empire*, p. 149.
[11] G. Arbuthnot, *Herzegovina, or Omer Pacha and the Christian Rebels* (London, 1862), pp. 102–3.   [12] Aličić, *Uredjenje*, p. 19.   [13] Arbuthnot, *Herzegovina*, p. 118.

gendarmerie (with compensation for the dissolution of feudal rights) was largely ignored. Right up to 1851, most holders of feudal privileges in the land and in the collection of tithes hung onto their rights though technically they had been abolished.[14] In fairness, however, many former *spahijas* did not receive the compensation which they had been promised,[15] so they were unlikely to relinquish their customary claims.

Up to 1839, the struggle between central and provincial power had been concerned with the control of revenue and armed force, but with proclamation of the Rescript of Gülhane the current of reform shifted to the wider issue of Christian rights. This only heightened the resistance of the Bosnian Muslims. In 1848 a reforming governor, Tahir Pasha (1846–50) tried seriously to implement the principles of the Tanzimat, but the *âyans* formed an unholy alliance with the Serbian and Montenegrin leaders, who saw an opportunity of detaching Bosnia from the Empire. The Bosnian *âyans* rose successfully against the government, to reassert their own prerogatives. Once more the Porte cobbled together an expedition against them, under the leadership of Omer Pasha Latas. Omer's forces swept through Bosnia and then Hercegovina, punishing and pacifying. So effectively did Omer cow the opposition that effective central government measures could now be implemented.

The period before 1851 in Bosnia is therefore regarded as antecedent to reform. This does not mean that institutions were unchanging during this period. Most cultivable land was held in fief by the *spahijas* and *kapetans*. As elsewhere, these men increasingly tried to transform their fiefs into landed estates, *čitluks*, while retaining control of the peasant populations entrusted to their administration. As long as they held the traditional rights associated with *spahiluk* – and this means up to the 1830s – it was customary for masters to concede life leases to the *kmets* or cultivators. These imposed the obligation to pay tithe, and a rent of one-twelfth to one-ninth of the harvest, depending on local custom, as well as certain customary dues, and a small amount of labour service to cultivate such land as they held in domain.[16] Till the 1830s, the cultivator rarely had to concede more than one-fifth of his crop. However, the erosion of the perquisites of *spahiluk* by a government eager to claw back the revenues it had previously relinquished to the *spahijas* caused them not only to convert fief as far as they could into *čitluk* but also to seek compensation at the expense of the *kmets*, through heavier labour services and larger shares of the produce.[17] This period, especially the years 1840–3

---

[14] Aličić, *Uredjenje*, p. 21.
[15] J. de Asboth, *An Official Tour through Bosnia and Herzegovina* (London, 1890), p. 160.
[16] Ferdinand Schmid, *Bosnien und die Hercegovina unter der Verwaltung Österreich-Ungarns* (Leipzig, 1914), p. 301.   [17] Schmid, *Bosnien*, p. 301.

and 1847–50 is associated in the literature with the intensive raising of the burdens on the *kmets*.[18]

Since peasant rights were founded on custom which had been disturbed profoundly by the pressures of reform, and since the Tanzimat provided an outlet for dissent, the Ottoman authorities tried to deal with the consequences of their fiscal reforms for the Christian communities. They wanted to limit the extent to which the landowners could pass on the incidence of higher taxation to their cultivators. As a result, a commission was established in 1848 by Tahir Pasha to outline the principal systems of agrarian relations which then pertained, and to codify prescribed practice on the basis of its findings.

There were four characteristic types of arrangement. First there were free peasants, nearly all Muslims, who held their own petty *čitluks*. They (like most other landed proprietors) payed tithe to the state, and cultivated with the labour of their own families or with hired labour. More substantial proprietors had their land sharecropped. The customary rights of their tenants had been eroded so much that this second group were paying the landowners (*čitluk sahibijas*) between one-quarter and one-third of the gross crop which remained after surrender of the tithe. Yet these were relatively well-to-do peasants, who held their own draft animals and seed, and probably amounted to 40 per cent of all cultivators; farms such as these predominated in the fertile Posavina.[19] Thirdly, there were also *kmets* who sharecropped with the landlord's equipment and seed, and were left with half of what remained after tithe grain and seed had been withdrawn.

Fourthly, and least satisfactorily placed, in Tahir's view, were cultivators whose landlords farmed substantial complexes of their lands directly. These *kmets* payed a labour rent for their rights to allotments and this unremunerated labour amounted to the full-time services of one adult male per household, which on a household size of about ten constituted half its able-bodied male labour force.[20] Even then, the *kmet* household still had to pay tithe on its own produce, return the landlord his seed, and, depending on the quality of the land, give him between one-ninth and one-fifth part of the residual crop.

These systems of division were not the result of any particular code of practice. The commission's findings provided only an approximate and incomplete model of agrarian relations in the previous decades, with modifications to the disadvantage of the *kmets*,[21] but other descriptions

---

[18] Dušan Berić, 'Problemi propadanja ekonomskog sistema osmanskog carstva u periodu 1848–1878', *IČ*, XXIX-XXX (1982–3), p. 370.

[19] Eastern Bosnia adjacent to the river Sava. Thömmel, *Beschreibung*, p. 148.

[20] *Državopis Srbije*, III (Belgrade, 1869), p. 101.   [21] Schmid, *Bosnien*, p. 301.

do not differ greatly. Thömmel reported that a *kmet* who gave three to five days labour in a week to his landlord had also to surrender in tithe and share-rent between one-third and half of his crop.[22]

The findings of Tahir's commission led to the formal codification of the second arrangement described by the commission, as a fixed basis for future contracts. It was ordered that the direct farming of *čitluks* with labour given in lieu of rent should cease, and be substituted by share-cropping. After deduction of tithe, a third or quarter share of the residual would go to the landowner.[23] From the point of view of many landlords, this reform threatened a considerable loss of revenue. Coming on the eve of the Muslim rebellion of 1848, it seems to have ranked among the causes of Muslim unrest.

Bosnia in the reform era 1851–1877

Once the territory had been subjugated by Omer, the authorities began a sustained programme of administrative change. The first concern was to extract more revenue from the province, and definitively to suppress the remaining rights of *spahiluk*, which were auctioned off. In the economic field, the most powerful effect of the reconquest was probably in establishing order and security of property. In neither respect was there any overnight improvement, and repeated Christian disturbances broke out in the Hercegovina. Yet by the 1860s it could be claimed for many years in succession that 'the most perfect tranquillity' prevailed, despite the attempts of the Slavic press to depict and incite revolution. Security of life and property, and 'freedom from injustice and oppression' were compared favourably with Serbia or Austria – though neither of these countries were particularly good exemplars.[24]

The principles of the *Tanzimat* were acknowledged insofar as the rights of Christians in the purchase of land were acknowledged, and heirs to holdings no longer had to pay entry fines.[25] Nevertheless, Tahir's reform was not implemented, so burdens on tenants continued to rise, and the state, by raising its demands on the province as a whole, alienated both the Muslim and *kmet* factions. Minor expeditions were continually ordered to deal with both Muslim and Christian dissidence. Measures against Catholics awakened the interest of the Austrians, who abetted Catholic demonstrations in the Hercegovina. The new impetus given to Christian rights was revived by Hatt-i-Humayun (1856) and led in Bosnia to the passage in 1859 of a special land law, the *Safer* law. This

---

[22] Thömmel, *Beschreibung*, p. 146.   [23] Aličić, *Uredjenje*, p. 78.
[24] GBC Bosnia 1867, p. 574.   [25] Aličić, *Uredjenje*, p. 67.

sought to implement the 1848 decree of Tahir Pasha, more or less in its entirety. This time it was effectively enforced. Its effects were far-reaching, were other than anticipated, and of questionable benefit.

The *čitluk sahibijas* were a fairly small group. Their descendants in 1895 amounted to 5,833 heads of family, or 2.6 per cent of the agricultural population,[26] though their proportion would have been higher than this at mid-century. As nearly all were Muslims, however, they probably amounted at that time to around 6–7 per cent of the agriculture-dependent Muslim population. There were certain great estates, particularly in the Posavina, but most *čitluks* were small, sometimes extending to a call on the services of a single peasant household, or even sharing these with another petty *aga*. In 1879, the landlords controlled some 84,942 families of *kmets*,[27] probably about 15–20 tenant families each. As a rule, the former *begs* and *agas*, however poor, did not labour, but subsisted after a fashion on the labour of the *kmets*.

The *čitluk sahibijas* could not treat with the labouring classes as if the latter were superabundant, for the province was not densely populated, nor was population growing rapidly. At 19.9 persons per km^2 in 1860, Bosnia-Hercegovina may well have been the most thinly populated territory in Ottoman Europe.[28] Much of the land was mountain and forest, but with so thin a population, and with a substantial class needing labour services from others to support them, there was an inbuilt shortage of cultivators. In the Hercegovina, free market wages were sufficiently high to induce a seasonal inflow of labour from Dalmatia, and at least between 1850 and 1860 wages rose sufficiently to discourage the growing of cotton.[29] In a free labour market, labour would have enjoyed a high proportion of the fruits of its toil, so the control of *čitluks*, rather than control of their cultivators, would have yielded little profit to their owners. Rights of *spahiluk*, which were equivalent to the levy of a tax, would have been more valuable. So the magnates who were obliged, in effect, to swap their jurisdictional revenues for incomes stemming from the ownership of real estate would lose income unless they raised their demands upon the *kmets* who cultivated their land above the market equilibrium rate. Consequently the loss of *spahiluk* revenues prompted them to coerce labour more energetically than hitherto. In theory labour was not bound to the service of any particular landowner, and had practice equated with theory, the peasants would not have submitted to the burdens of service and crop surrender disclosed by the 1848 commission. In practice, however, landowners exercised the effective informal power to coerce.

---

[26] *Glavni rezultati popisa žiteljstva u Bosni i Hercegovini ot Aprila 1895 . . .* (Sarajevo, 1896), p. lix.   [27] *Ortschafts und Bevölkerungs-Statistik*, appendix gatefold.
[28] See above, Table 1.9.   [29] Arbuthnot, *Herzegovina*, p. 68.

Regulation of the burdens on the cultivator under the *Safer* law therefore institutionalized the imposition of a controlled economic rent to the landowner, over and above the market rent.

Still, the reform was put in place to diminish that economic rent to a level below what the unrestrained political clout of the landowners could have exacted. Landlords in the richer plains areas, who had hitherto farmed their domain lands using labour services, were presumably worst hit, since it was this system which the *Safer* law explicitly suppressed. Domain had to be converted to tenanted smallholdings, which in itself would have entailed losses (otherwise landlords would have converted domain voluntarily). The regulation of these tenancies would have increased the losses suffered by them, because they could not evict unsatisfactory tenants, however little they chose to produce, nor vary the terms of their leases. The low price of land in the late 1860s would not suggest that investment in *čitluks* was particularly profitable.[30]

After the reform, the burden borne by the *kmets* was still heavy; allowing for a state tithe of 12.5 per cent, the *beg*'s share, and provision for seed, the *kmet* would keep only 35 per cent of his produce for consumption if division of the crop were scrupulously carried out. To compensate for this burden, the *kmet* tenancy was usually applied to substantial holdings, of around 20 hectares per family.[31] Compare this with the familial holding pertaining in Serbia in the 1860s of around 3–4 hectares. Thus holding size should have been large enough to eliminate underemployment as a constraint on labour productivity. Despite this the system created underemployment. The signs of agricultural progress which were so notable in Ottoman Bulgaria found little echo in Bosnia. All writers emphasize the extremity of rural apathy, because the institutionally regulated sharecropping arrangement accorded little incentive for initiative either by landlords, who could not subdivide, nor farm in domain, or by the tenants, whose obligations were always proportionate to their output.[32] As the Austrians were later to discover in administering the agrarian institutions bequeathed them by the Ottomans, the abundance of land at the *kmet*'s disposal meant he could cultivate it in an extensive fashion but still obtain a sufficiency from his share in the crop. Thus, his tenancy agreement operated as a form of highly progressive taxation; at a low level of labour input per hectare, the landlord captured no more than a return to land itself, but any increase in output per hectare won by raising the input of labour would be shared with the landlord, together with the fisc, who between them would extract the greater part of the marginal labour

---

[30] Jahresbericht des Konsulates des norddeutsches Bundes zu Sarajevo für das Jahr 1869, *Preussische Handelsarchiv*, XI (1870), p. 260.　　[31] Asboth, *Official Tour*, p. 166.

[32] Johann Roskiewicz, *Studien über Bosnien und die Herzegovina* (Leipzig, 1868), p. 84.

product. As the landlord could not compel the tenant to provide this additional input, it was not worth the tenant's while to trade leisure for material output.

Austrian sources claimed that the peasants remained subject to extortionate and illegal agrarian burdens, but they concede that the abolition of labour-rent was effective. Asboth claimed that there were still too few constraints on arbitrary behaviour towards the peasants by those who had a lien on their produce, for the administration still depended on the authority of the *âyans*. 'If the lot of the rayah was insufferable', he wrote, 'the cause lay not so much in the institutions themselves, but in the manner they were carried out, and in the abuses and outrages which had arisen.'[33] On the other hand, instances where tenants had to pay 10 or 20 per cent over the legal rent were diminishing, and 'much less frequent than the depreciators of Turkey would have us to believe'.[34]

Aličić, who has combed the archives, claims there were few complaints from tenants on improper treatment by the landlords. They were, however, shrill in complaining against the administration of the tax system.[35] A Russian source in 1869 alleged that the prisons of Bosnia were filled with thousands of tax-debtors,[36] and it was, in fact, a tax grievance which sparked the Hercegovinian revolt of 1874 which led to the Ottomans' loss of the province. Even so, the basis of complaint was fundamentally about the rising but legitimate level at which taxation was levied, rather than about malpractice in collecting it. Consequently the Porte considered most complaints to be unjustified.[37] Anyway, as this was an inflationary period, it does not necessarily follow that tax burdens were rising in real terms. In fact the burden on the *kmets* of taxation was much lighter than the burden of rent, but caused unrest because it was rising, while the now controlled rent burdens, though onerous, were stable.

The process of reform did not terminate with the passage of the Bosnian land law. Especially under Topal Osman Pasha (1861-9) the administration launched a major programme for the building of carriageable roads. In pre-1851 Bosnia, wheeled traffic was virtually unknown. Road-building had been initiated by Omer after the reconquest with an eye as much to 'public tranquillity' as to commerce.[38] His immediate successors failed to sustain the effort, but, largely on Osman Pasha's initiative, a tolerable network of arteries was constructed. Osman's roads were not well maintained, but despite their shortcomings, they were reckoned in 1868 to be the best in the empire.[39] In 1872, 320 hours (about 1,500

[33] Asboth, *Official Tour*, p. 166.   [34] Arbuthnot, *Herzegovina*, p. 60.
[35] Aličić, *Uredjenje*, p. 174.   [36] Berić, 'Problemi', pp. 373–4.
[37] Aličić, *Uredjenje*, pp. 174–5.   [38] GBC Bosnia 1859, p. 462.
[39] GBC Bosnia 1868, p. 326.

km) of these roads had been completed, none of which had existed ten years earlier.[40] Osman's administration also promoted secular education, health and sanitation, and in 1869 contracted with the Austrian *Sudbahn* for the construction of a railway, guaranteeing a 5 per cent return on the cost of construction.[41] The section between Banja Luka and Novi was opened in 1872.[42]

Taken as a whole, the reforms probably made a positive impact on the economy. Even from critics of the administration, disparagement was tinctured with grudging praise. Despite the slothfulness of the authorities, and a system described as misgovernment which fell short of actual oppression,[43] the condition of Bosnia on the eve of occupation by Austria was less ruinous than was commonly alleged. Despite periodic outbreaks of peasant violence, especially in Hercegovina, it remained tranquil. Aličić emphasizes the improved security of property rights as the most positive stimulus given by the reforms. Although they did not diminish dissatisfaction they 'had a more progressive character and more positive results than has been shown up to now in our [Yugoslav] historical literature'.[44]

According to Serbia's leading statistician,[45] Bosnia's trade expanded between 1835/8 and 1864/5 more rapidly than did the trade of neighbouring Serbia. No figures were published to support this claim, which was advanced to draw attention to the sluggishness of Serbia's own trade growth, but from such fragmentary data as we possess, it seems that in the mid-1860s, Bosnia's trade volume stood at a slightly higher per capita level than Serbia's.[46] Jakšić also considered that the condition of Bosnia's Serb population had improved since Omer Pasha's 1851 campaign. In 1869 he claimed (without furnishing evidence) that after years of moribundity the Serb population, despite wars and uprisings, was growing even more rapidly than in Serbia. He ascribed this growth to the material betterment of the common people which resulted from the pasha's 'wise measures' and to the introduction of the *Tanzimat* into the territory.[47]

The productive structure of Ottoman Bosnia

Much of Bosnia is hill and mountain country, so in its farming, Bosnia (like Serbia and Montenegro) was more dependent than Bulgaria on extensive stockraising, and much less orientated to arable. In 1865

---

[40] GBC Bosnia 1872, pp. 593, 596.   [41] *Sarajevski Cvijetnik*, 29 May 1869.
[42] Shaw and Shaw, *Ottoman Empire*, p. 150.   [43] Arbuthnot, *Herzegovina*, pp. 209–13.
[44] Aličić, *Uredjenje*, p. 170.   [45] *Državopis Srbije*, III, p. 48; *Srbija*, 28 Sept. 1869, p. 372.
[46] Bosnia's exports were valued at 9.76 million florins in 1864, in which year Serbia's were 15.43 million dinars. These figures represent 16.1 dinars per capita and 13.3 dinars respectively. Thömmel, *Beschreibung*, pp. 77, 156; *Državopis*, VII.
[47] *Državopis*, III, p. 110.

stockraising accounted for 50.5 per cent of gross output, and in 1873 (which was probably a bad harvest year) for 62.4 per cent. But despite the predominance of stockraising, Bosnia's export trade was surprisingly diversified. In 1858, cattle, sheep and pig exports accounted for not more than £104,985 or 22.9 per cent of total exports, and in 1864 for 32.9 per cent.[48]

There are fertile lowlands in northwest Bosnia, the Bosanska Krajina, and in the northeast, the Posavina. During the latter years of Ottoman rule, the farms of these regions generated a rising surplus of grain which was exported to food deficient Dalmatia and into central Europe. This attained 44 per cent of total exports by 1864.[49] The surplus was mainly of wheat, rather than of maize, which was the principal crop, for as in Serbia maize was mainly raised for subsistence, and for animal fodder. The northern towns of the province therefore maintained a highly active commerce in farm products right up to the occupation by the Habsburgs in 1878.[50] These exports disappeared after the Austrian occupation of 1878, partly because of the rapidly increased demand of the Bosnian cities for wheaten flour. Northern Bosnia, the Posavina in particular, also exported prunes on a large scale especially through the Sava port of Brčko. These amounted in 1858 to £82,400 of export earnings (17.5 per cent of exports). In Hercegovina, conditions also favoured crop production, and its major export was tobacco. Other substantial export items included timber and iron.

At mid-century small industries made Bosnia almost self-sufficient in the petty artisan manufactures for which demand was heaviest. Although cottons and woollens were significant items of import, the import trade was dominated by 'colonial goods', which could not easily be produced in Bosnia itself, coffee (£57,300 or 13.3 per cent of imports), sugar, and rice, imported mainly through Trieste.

The (dubious) quantitative data that survive show that Bosnia-Hercegovina during the late Ottoman era was only 42.6 per cent as productive in farming as Bulgaria in 1865, and 33.4 per cent in 1873. Our estimates for gross farm product are set out as Table 5.1.

Later and more reliable figures for Bosnia under Austrian rule may be compared with those for the Bulgarian state. They confirm that Bosnia was significantly the less productive of the two economies, and there is reason to suppose that the gap would have been wider in the Ottoman era; but it is to be doubted whether Bosnia was really so unproductive under Ottoman rule. Contemporaries stressed in particular the serious underes-

---

[48] GBC Bosnia 1858, pp. 455–8.   [49] Thömmel, *Beschreibung*, pp. 156–7.
[50] Otto Blau, *Reisen in Bosnien und der Herzegovina* (Berlin, 1877), esp. pp. 112, 120–1, 181.

Table 5.1 *Bosnia. Sectoral farm output in 1865, 1869 and 1873*

| | (million crowns, 1910 value) | | | | | | |
Year	Animal products	Animals	Truck crops	Grains	Garden crops	Total	Total per-capita
1865	26	21	3	40	2	93	95
1869	25	16	2	18	2	64	67
1873	25	17	3	21	2	67	73

Sources: see BALKSTAT.

timation of the herd figures. According to Hašim Šerif, official statistics recorded the pig population at 196,763 in 1873 and 161,484 in 1875. Yet in 1874 and 1875 Bosnia managed to export 82,636 and 84,630 pigs to Austria-Hungary, a volume impossible to reconcile with so modest a stock.[51]

How the figures in Table 5.1 compare with output in the pre-reform era (before 1851) we simply do not know. We cannot exclude the possibility that Bosnia had been more affluent before the reforms than after them. The reforms were different in nature to those which functioned in Bulgaria, and would have diminished incentives in farm production, causing per capita output to fall. Before the reforms, the *kmets* acquiesced more readily in Muslim rule than they did subsequently, despite the supposed benefits the reforms conferred on them. Could it be that the deterioration in political conditions reflected a sharpening of group tensions, as the cake to be shared dwindled in size?

The question has to remain unanswered, but Ottoman rule in Bosnia was not precipitated by economic collapse, any more than it was in Bulgaria where the ending of Ottoman rule coincided with best-ever levels of farm output. The literature on Bosnia insists that the economy declined after about 1870 (but it also does for Bulgaria). The reasoning given for the decline in Bosnia is that the Porte retrenched on provincial expenditures and raised taxes to improve its international credit standing. Whether retrenchment affected the underlying Bosnian farm economy is doubtful. Our statistics show output in 1869 and 1873 contracting sharply from the level of 1865, but a consular report for 1871 speaks of a recent run of crop failures.[52] The subsequent deterioration in political conditions cannot have been helpful, but the effects of the insurgencies

---

[51] Hašim Šerif, *Istoriski osvrt na razvoj stočarstva u Bosni i Hercegovini* (Sarajevo, 1963), pp. 29–33.   [52] GBC Bosnia 1871, p. 1334.

may be exaggerated. Consular reports on Bosnia for 1876–8 emphasize both the localization of the insurrections, and the abundance of the crops enjoyed in the last two years. The harvest of 1877 was 'one of the richest that has been known in this country for many years', and the cattle trade was flourishing. The crops in 1878 were still better, though much of the harvest was to be lost because of the occupation.[53] The Austrians did not take over a collapsed economic system – though the turmoil that accompanied their occupation inflicted serious short-term loss.

Montenegro: history and institutions

Until 1852 Montenegro was a confederation of tribes over which the *vladikas* lacked even an effective taxing power. The age-old conflict with the Ottomans was caused by struggles over grazing rights, banditry, and support given from Montenegro to insurrectionary movements in the Hercegovina. Before 1851 the Ottoman Empire had been too weak to pose a sustained threat to the Montenegrins. However, after his successful campaign in Hercegovina in 1851, Omer Pasha invaded Montenegro. The expedition ended inconclusively, thanks to Russian and Austrian pressures on the Porte, but it exposed Montenegro's military inadequacies. This resurgence of Ottoman power forced the Montenegrin rulers to unify the tribes into a modern fighting machine, capable of withstanding it. The next ruler, Danilo I (1852–60) took ruthless measures to force the tribes to submit to his power and his taxes.[54] A fresh uprising in Hercegovina led to another Ottoman invasion in 1858, but the Montenegrins ambushed and destroyed a superior Ottoman force at Grahovo. This led to renewed border instability, heightened banditry, and renewal of the Hercegovinian uprising in 1861. Danilo's successor Nikola (1860–1916) faced Omer again, but saw his army shattered at Rijeka Crnojevica and was made to sign the humiliating Convention of Scutari (1862). Forced by superior power to keep the peace with the Ottomans, Montenegro then enjoyed a thirteen-year period of tranquillity, economic stabilization and institutional development.

Economic structure

In April 1868, 13,565 persons in Montenegro were assessed for direct tax, *dacija*, which was levied on cultivated land and livestock. Their mean holdings amounted to 1.02 hectares of arable, 0.98 hectares of meadow and about 0.15 hectares of vineyard. These holdings were small by

---

[53] GBC Bosnia 1876, p. 973; 1877, pp. 810–11; 1878, p. 995.
[54] Mirčeta Djurović, *Trgovački kapital u Crnoj gori u drugoj polovini XIX i početkom XX vijeka* (Cetinje, 1958), pp. 41–2.

comparison with those in other parts of the Balkans. They are about 70 per cent of the size of those in central Serbia in 1863 and 26 per cent the size of those in northeast Bulgaria in 1866/7.[55] Moreover crop yields per hectare were low even by Balkan standards. Apart from grains and potatoes, wine was the only significant product of cultivation.

Livestock holdings compensated. These averaged 21 sheep, 10 goats, 3.8 head of cattle, half a pig and 1.7 beehives per family.[56] These figures are much in excess of the Balkan average. Between 1855 and 1912, value added by livestock raising accounted for a mean 60 per cent of farm production. Of this the largest single output was milk. In 1910 it accounted for 37 per cent of animal production and 19 per cent of total farm production. Meat animals and poultry accounted for a further 21 per cent.[57] Together with products of the gathering economy, pyrethrum, sumach and medicinal herbs, and of freshwater fishing on Lake Skadar (Shkodër) the export of livestock and dried meat onto the coastal market at Cattaro (Kotor) provided the basis of the export trade.

Most stockraising was transhumant, to make maximal use of the mountain pastures and minimize the need for cultivated fodder. Patterns evolved of some complexity, according to local conditions. The 'reverse migration' system was probably representative. In this variant of transhumance, hill hay would be mown in summer on intermediate level pastures, while livestock grazed the *suvats*, the waterless high level pastures above the tree line. In autumn when the rains began, the animals would be brought down to the villages, and when snow made further grazing difficult, they would be driven *upwards* to feed on the hill hay, stored where it had been mown. When the new grass appeared at village level they would be brought down again but as spring advanced to summer they would graze progressively higher levels, as heat and drought burned off the lowland grass.[58] Systems such as this, designed to extract the maximum of available grazing, are indicative of a perennial fodder shortage, particularly in winter. As the pastures were owned communally or by the state, rules were enforced as to when any particular hillside was open and closed.[59]

---

[55] Calculated from ACG, Senat 10, Protokoli dacije 1867–8. Comparable figures for Bulgaria are taken from Slavka Draganova, *Materiali za dunavskija vilaet* (Sofia, 1980), p. 470.

[56] ACG, Senat 10, Protokoli dacije 1867–68. The vineyard figure is inexact as some areas were taxed by wine production instead; this is allowed for, but only approximately. The original figures excluded animals (except pigs) less than a year old (ACG MF II/A – 15 no. 201, Cetinje, 8 Mar. 1894, para. 15) but this has been corrected for.

[57] Valuations at mean market price of Feb., Apr., June, Aug., Oct., Dec. 1911, *Glas Crnogorca*, issues for 26 Nov. 1911 and 5 Jan., 25 Feb., 7 Apr., 28 Apr., and 12 May 1912.

[58] Borivoje Ž. Milojević, *Visoke planine u našoj kraljevini* (Belgrade, 1937), p. 196; a good survey of transhumance is Jevto Dedijer, 'La transhumance dans les pays dinariques', *Annales de géographie*, XXV (1916), pp. 347–65.

[59] R. Wyon and G. Prance, *The Land of the Black Mountain* (London, 1903), p. 173.

The central activity connected with summer grazing was the *bačija*, the milking of sheep and goats and the making of cheese and other milk products. Since the *bačija* was normally conducted far from the villages, usually on the *suvats*, the peasants erected cabins and sheds (*katuns*) at the *bačija* for temporary accommodation and storage.[60] Snow would also be stored there in winter in ditches covered with straw, for such was the porosity of the soil on the *suvats* that the *bačija* would otherwise be waterless.[61] *Katuns* would also be needed in places where hill hay was mown. The *katun* system enabled the grazing economy to accommodate limited population growth, since in locations where this was feasable, the workers at the *katuns* would attempt to cultivate a little land around them. Expanding families could then let some of their members use the *katuns* for year-round settlement, and as the *katuns* of different families tended to be grouped together, they would gradually evolve into 'daughter' villages. Their inhabitants would in turn seek out locations for new, higher level *katuns* of their own.[62] This process of upward colonization was a common feature of dinaric pastoralism. It took precedence over making more intensive use of the lower valley lands, primarily because it entailed no fundamental change of lifestyle.

The higher the line of settlement was driven the less secure became its subsistence, particularly in winter. So high-level villages would be obliged to seek winter grazings for their flocks at low levels, often perforce a long distance from home.[63] This led Montenegrin stockraisers to draw upon the resources of adjacent territories, especially those on the lower *karst* of the Adriatic coast. In the 1860s, animals from Katunska *nahija* (district) were regularly driven down in winter to Austrian territory to exploit its climate which was mild enough for grass growth to be sustained through winter. In hard winters they were especially dependent on this arrangement. But inland locations in the Hercegovina were also used by the mountain people of Pješivci, though the grazing of Ottoman territory was not always attended with happy results. Some tribes took their flocks to overwinter as far away as the Sava valley.[64]

[60] The *bačija* system is brilliantly described in Wayne S. Vucinich, *A Study in Social Survival. Katun in the Bileća Rudine* (Denver, CO, 1975), pp. 105–45.
[61] Dedijer, 'La transhumance', pp. 350–1.
[62] Petar Šobajić, 'Bjelopavlići i Pješivci. Plemena u Crnogorskim Brdima', *NiPS*, XV (Belgrade, 1923), p. 255.
[63] Jovan Cvijić, 'Metanastazička kretanja, njihovi uzroci i posledice', *NiPS*, XII (Belgrade, 1922), p. 35.
[64] Andrija Jovičević, 'Crnogorsko Primorje i Krajina', *NiPS* (Belgrade, 1922), p. 125; Šobajić, 'Bjelopavlići', p. 324; R. J. Dragićević, 'Prilozi ekonomskoj istoriji Crne Gore (1861–1870)', *Istoriski Zapisi*, 1954, pp. 429, 441–2; Borivoje Ž Milojević, *Dinarsko primorje i ostrva u našoj kraljevini. Geografska ispitivanja* (Belgrade, 1933), p. 398.

Consumption and poverty

Montenegrin diet reflected the resources available, so it was sparing in farinaceous foods and in alcoholic drink, but more generous in milk products. Dietary frugality was a general rule even when not imposed by force of circumstances.[65] Montenegrin peasants ate but twice a day. A meal at daybreak or at noon consisted of a piece of bread baked from maize flour or from some coarse grain, described as 'a black gritty compound about as palatable as a lump of Newcastle coal'. In the evening, the same or a broth of maize and beans was consumed. This was accompanied at least in summer with milk, usually soured.[66] Potatoes had been introduced between 1780 and 1786, and in the *karst* uplands, especially Katunska *nahija*, they substituted bread to an increasing extent. Between 1839 and 1848 there was even a small potato surplus for export to Cattaro (Kotor).[67] In hard times when there was little or no grain, 'a baked or boiled potato had to suffice for a day'.[68] Meat was eaten, fresh and dried, but few households partook of it in their daily diet. Since few parts of the country supported the vine or the plum tree, alcoholic beverages had to be imported and were therefore expensive.[69] As a result, drunkenness was rarer than in Serbia or Bulgaria.[70] On feast days, however, meat was eaten to excess, accompanied by wine or *šljivovic*.[71] Up in the *katuns* where cheese was made during the *bačija*, the regular diet was much richer in milk, cream and cottage cheese than it was in the valleys, so that those who sojourned there normally gained weight.[72]

In terms of its value, both in a market and in a nutritional sense, the diet of the Montenegrins was no worse than that of Serbia, and they lived reasonably healthily on it. Access to milk products was the key to prosperity, with the result that the people of the higher villages 'ate better and more', and were regarded as healthier than those of the valleys, even though the latter might have grain to spare.[73]

[65] Jovičević, 'Crnogorsko primorje', p. 133.
[66] Bernhard Schwarz, *Montenegro. Schilderung einer Reise durch das Innere* (Leipzig, 1883), p. 457; GBC Montenegro 1887, p. 10; Wyon and Prance, *Black Mountain*, p. 3; Nikifor Dučić, *Književni radovi*, III (Belgrade, 1893), p. 126; Gabriel Frilley and Jovan Wlahovitj, *Le Monténégro contemporain* (Paris, 1876), p. 121.
[67] Sime Peričić, 'Prilog poznavanju trgovine izmedju Kotora i Crne Gore od 1815 do 1850 godine', *AHOI*, III (1976), p. 71.
[68] Djordjije Pejović, *Iseljavanja crnogoraca u XIX vijeku* (Titograd, 1962), p. 12; Dučić, *Književni radovi*, III, pp. 126, 313.
[69] Frilley and Wlahovitj, *Monténégro*, pp. 117, 121.   [70] Dučić, *Književni radovi*, III, p. 126.
[71] Wyon and Prance, *Black Mountain*, pp. 3, 170; Frilley and Wlahovitj, *Monténégro*, p. 121; Dučić, *Književni radovi*, III, p. 126.   [72] Vucinich, *Social Survival*, p. 130.
[73] Šobajić, 'Bjelopavlići', p. 256; Vucinich, *Social Survival*, p. 116.

High altitude and isolation contributed to protect much of the population from malaria, endemic in the nearby marshy lowlands of Hercegovina, and from tuberculosis, to which they were none the less susceptible. Then as now the Montenegrins were remarked for their good physique and high stature, claimed in 1902 to be an average of 1.80 metres for males. Even the people of Mirkovići, despite their extreme frugality, were claimed to be healthy and strong, and little troubled by diseases. Child mortality was thought to be high, and was attributed 'mainly to parental neglect'. (However, Montenegro probably stood relatively well on this count, as, in 1948–52, infant mortality there was the lowest in Yugoslavia.)[74]

Consumption of clothing, 'the sole luxury of the Montenegrin', pre-empted a large slice of cash income. As elsewhere in the Balkans, the houses might be bare of comfort, but 'inordinate vanity in appearance' caused the people 'to impoverish themselves for the sake of gorgeous clothes'.[75]

Our information on food consumption, health and clothing indicates that in normal years Montenegro was not especially disadvantaged by Balkan standards. Nevertheless, the country was a by-word even among Balkan observers for its poverty. 'I can guarantee', wrote Dučić, 'that there is not a nation in Europe which lives more poorly than the Montenegrin nation. Neither the Irish nor the Scots can be compared with them in this.'[76] If poverty be construed as life on the razor's edge between satisfaction and destitution, then Montenegrins lived perennially in that condition. The crops seldom sufficed to meet the exiguous levels of grain consumption to which the population was accustomed, and they were subject to serious year to year fluctuations because the porosity of the *karst* rock made the harvest acutely vulnerable to drought. Grain was usually imported but communications inhibited its commercial circulation in rural areas. Even in the relatively abundant 1880s, not a year went by without reports of starvation and famine mortality reaching the government in Cetinje.[77] The supply of livestock products was also at the mercy of a hard winter, since the output of hay usually fell far short of the minimal winter fodder needs of the animals. Deep snow could result in huge losses, and a single adverse winter could reduce the animal stock by a fifth or more.[78]

[74] GBC Montenegro 1887, p. 14; Wyon and Prance, *Black Mountain*, p. 5; Jovičević, 'Crnogorsko primorje', p. 134; Miloš Macura, *Stanovništvo i radna snaga kao činioci privrednog razvoja Jugoslavije* (Belgrade, 1958), pp. 30–1.

[75] Frilley and Wlahovitj, *Monténégro*, p. 117; Wyon and Prance, *Black Mountain*, p. 7.

[76] Dučić, *Književni radovi*, III, pp. 125–6.

[77] Žarko Bulajić, *Agrarni odnosi u Crnoj gori (1878–1912)* (Titograd, 1959), pp. 157–60.

[78] GBC Montenegro, 1887 p. 3; P. A. Rovinski, *Chernogoriya v eya proshlom i nastoyashtem*, (St Petersburg, 1897), II/1, p. 691.

Patriarchal culture and banditry

Farming, especially in the mountainous Katunska district and the Brda, did not demand an intense input of labour, because the arable plots were so small and unproductive, and because stockraising depended on unimproved grazing. Crop tending could therefore be assigned largely to the women. Because armed conflict or the threat of force was a constant feature of this society, Montenegrin culture accorded to the male the exclusive role of warrior and shepherd, burdening the women with the drudgery. The intensity of sexual subordination was extreme even by Balkan standards. With manual labour held to be 'derogatory to a man', there was substance in the stereotype which emerged of a lazy, arrogant and bellicose nation. Of course the stereotype reflected male attitudes and behaviour, but the obverse of this coin, the exploitation of women as beasts of burden was readily remarked on.[79] Even the import trade, in salt, liquor and manufactures, was brought in mainly on the backs of women carrying 45 lb packs.[80]

Since the output from the grazing economy could not be increased substantially by applying more labour to it, population growth elsewhere in the Balkans was normally accompanied by a shift towards arable cultivation.[81] Little of the sort occurred in Montenegro. Physical conditions were undoubtedly unfavourable to such a structural shift, but the cultivation potential was far from exhausted. Contemporary writers considered the peasants to be highly resistant or inadaptable to anything other than a pastoral existence. Their inadaptability is understandable, since the adoption of more intensive farming systems would call for heavy inputs of the labour of men who under the pastoral regime were accustomed to doing little work of any kind.

The problem was a very real one. Nineteenth-century pastoral life did permit men a lazy lifestyle, while departure from it called for a greater work commitment. Reflecting in 1936 on 'the traditional Bosnian laziness' characteristic of the dinaric regions of that province, Bičanić argued that it had become a thing of the past, and claimed frequently to have been told by villagers, 'If we worked only as much as our old people used to work, everyone would die of hunger.'[82] Montenegro was probably slower to make this transition.

[79] 'Montenegrin Economics', p. 8; Frilley and Wlahovitj, *Monténégro*, p. 120; Vladimir Dvorniković, *Karakterologija jugoslovena* (Belgrade, 1939), pp. 656–7; Wyon and Prance, *Black Mountain*, p. 5; Schwarz, *Montenegro*, p. 447; GBC Montenegro 1895, p. 14.

[80] Ami Boué, *La Turquie d'Europe* (Paris, 1840), III, p. 170.

[81] See M. R. Palairet, 'The Influence of Commerce on the Changing Structure of Serbia's Peasant Economy 1860–1912' (unpublished Ph.D. thesis, University of Edinburgh, 1976), esp. Chapters 1 and 3.

[82] Rudolf Bičanić, *Kako živi narod. Život u pasivnim krajevima* (Zagreb, 1936), p. 111.

In such a society, where agricultural work was left to the women, male distaste for any work save that of a pastoral or military nature would be rationalized by regarding it as 'derogatory'. Trades, as well as agriculture, were held to be demeaning. In Ami Boué's words: 'In Montenegro they are so infatuated with the estate of arms that all other crafts are despised; thus all their tailoring is a feminine occupation [and] all blacksmiths are called gipsies.'[83] Housebuilding, carpentry, ironwork, tailoring, even shopkeeping, were low status occupations, 'repugnant to the national notion of honour and freedom', and were practised mainly by immigrants, who earned high wages from them because of the lack of labour market competition.[84] As late as 1910, trade and commerce were largely monopolized by Muslims and Albanian Catholics.[85] Those few peasants, mainly from Riječka *nahija*, who worked as masons or carpenters commanded reasonable wages and seldom lacked work, but elsewhere, 'only the weaker brotherhoods enter into crafts'.[86] Not surprisingly, there was hardly a trace of cottage industry, though ostensibly underemployment in farming should have promoted its development. One of the puzzles concerning the regional structure of the Balkan economy is why some hill areas developed proto-industries, and others similarly placed did not. The question defies a definitive answer, but in the dinaric provinces, male attitudes to farm work caused female labour time to be committed to farm tasks. Therefore, female labour, which normally provided the basis for proto-industrial manufacturing, simply became unavailable for this purpose.

Such attitudes inhibited development in Montenegro not only of cottage industry, but also of periodic building labour migration or (as was notable in neighbouring Hercegovina) itinerant trading. These were constructive responses to the shortage of exchange incomes from which most Balkan mountain areas suffered, and in the absence of such a response the only alternative was parasitism.

Among the Montenegrins, this usually took the form of cattle raiding and armed attacks on highway traffic. As women did the farm work, the men had time on their hands, and neither the opportunity nor inclination to put it to productive use. They also found it difficult to convert produce into cash, so the attractions of banditry were heightened. Those, more or less, were the grounds on which Prince Nikola defended the system to a visitor, Viscountess Strangford, in 1863. She saw the problem as 'occa-

[83] Boué, *Turquie*, III, p. 117.
[84] GBC Montenegro 1858, p. 138; 1887, p. 13; 1895, p. 14; Dučić, *Književni radovi*, III, p. 131.   [85] 'Montenegrin Economics', p. 9.
[86] Andro Jovičević, 'Narodni život (Riječka nahija u Crnoj Gori)', *Zbornik za narodni život i običaje južnih slavena*, XV (Zagreb, 1910), p. 85; Šobajić, 'Bjelopavlići', p. 56.

sioned by poverty and sheer habitual wildness rather than any deep-rooted ill will'.[87] By representing these activities as armed struggle against an external enemy, the value system of this pastoral society could not only tolerate banditry but glory in it. The preferred target was cattle, because of its easy marketability. It could therefore be claimed in all seriousness that, at least in years when grain prices were high, banditry was an essential branch of economic life.

Banditry seems to have reached a peak of intensity after the battle of Grahovo (1858) when Ottoman civil power beyond the Montenegrin borders was temporarily weakened. Heavy sales of booty followed on the coast, 'materially improving the condition of families who had it to sell'. The need to sell booty and purchase grain sharpened Montenegrin aspirations for improved access to markets.[88] None were more celebrated as bandits than the Kuči tribe, who, in hard times, 'lived almost solely from rapine and war booty'. The Kuči did not, however, wait for a famine. To them banditry was a well-organized business. It even provided a primitive social security, because part of the loot was earmarked for the relief of widows and orphans.[89] This tribe had no monopoly on banditry, since the Ceklinjani of Lake Skadar were 'acclaimed as heroes of the first rank on water', where they plundered the commerce of the lake, 'and by this means were enormously enriched'.[90]

Till 1855 the right to plunder in Ottoman territory was sanctioned by Montenegrin law, and only then was forbidden by the Prince, who was anxious to achieve international recognition of Montenegrin statehood. His loyal subjects appreciated that the law was cosmetic in design, and redoubled their efforts to abuse it.[91] As a Montenegrin 'artlessly' confessed to a visitor: 'If it were not for the Turks, I don't know how we should live.'[92] In any case, they had never been particularly selective as to their targets. In the eighteenth century, Dubrovnik rather than the Ottoman provinces had been the prime target, because the pickings were richer, and Montenegrins were alleged to carry off Dubrovnik girls to sell to the Turks.[93] In the nineteenth, Kuči gangs preyed on all and sundry, including fellow Montenegrins.[94]

Active warfare against the Ottomans offered exceptional opportunities for looting and provided a strong incentive to the tribes to take part. After 1878, opportunities for organized banditry diminished, but old

[87] Viscountess Strangford, *The Eastern Shores of the Adriatic in 1863* (London, 1864), pp. 162, 187–8.   [88] Pejović, *Iseljavanja*, pp. 167–9.

[89] Jovan Erdeljanović, 'Kuči, pleme u Crnoj Gori', *NSZ*, IV (Belgrade, 1907), p. 245.

[90] Jovićević, 'Riječka nahija', p. 100.   [91] Pejović, *Iseljavanja*, p. 168.

[92] Strangford, *Eastern Shores*, p. 188.   [93] Pejović, *Iseljavanja*, pp. 31–2.

[94] Erdeljanović, 'Kuči', p. 245.

habits died hard. Behind the soldiers in the Balkan Wars followed the women, to return from the front bent double under burdens of looted household goods.[95] Capture of territory (as late as 1918) was followed by a frenzy of looting, which drew in even those who opposed it, for fear of being left out.[96] In 1991, when the first news filtered out that Montenegrin troops were shelling Dubrovnik, I wrote to the press, speculating that this attack presaged a new wave of organized plundering. I hardly believed my own argument, but it was balefully affirmed by Misha Glenny's account of the campaign. Serbia had 'given' the Montenegrins Dalmatia as a soft and profitable target. The high point of the invasion was the sacking of the duty-free shop at Dubrovnik airport, and in the rear of the army's scorched earth procession through southern Dalmatia, lorry loads of plunder returned to flood Montenegrin markets.[97]

Overwintering and emigration

The inherent unviability of economic life in Montenegro conditioned its people to draw on external resources, not only through banditry but by colonistic emigration. Montenegrins 'did not accept hunger either as fate or as God's punishment, but as a natural phenomenon which frequently beset them and for which they found a cure. . . In the regions where hunger so frequently afflicted, and in which people were in normal circumstances hungry rather than replete, proportionately little did they die of hunger.'[98] If in autumn it was clear that food and forage could not last out till spring, households would split up. As many people would be left at home as could be maintained on the available food, while the rest, mainly the able-bodied, would leave the villages, commonly driving their animals with them in search of subsistence.

They often set out in desperate condition, and with few scruples as to how they might achieve their aim. A party from Nikšić and Piva arrived on the Serbian frontier in 1835 without papers, but armed to the teeth. To the worried officials they seemed more capable of armed robbery than of any useful service. Originally an occasional phenomenon, overwintering migration had become by the mid-nineteenth century an established pattern, the numbers involved fluctuating according to food conditions. Thus long-range winter migration came to coexist alongside the routine

---

[95] Mary E. Durham, *The Struggle for Scutari* (London, 1914), p. 198.
[96] Milovan Djilas, *Land Without Justice* (London, 1958), p. 89.
[97] Misha Glenny, *The Fall of Yugoslavia* (London: Penguin, 1992), pp. 130–3.
[98] Milenko Filipović, 'Odlaženje na Prehranu', *Glasnik Geografskog društva*, XXVII (Belgrade, 1947), p. 77.

upward migration of the summer months. Some migrants would seek work in the towns, in labouring, vine-tending or market gardening, while the women would launder, clean, carry or grind.[99] Overwintering migrants had to seek work when the labour market was at its weakest, and they were consequently poorly paid. Overwinterers who worked in the Hercegovinian towns received little or nothing in addition to their keep, but those who took their livestock with them were enabled to keep their flocks intact. The circumstances surrounding these migrations were sufficiently bleak for the migrants to consider severing their links with home if they could find free lands for resettlement.

Overwintering led migrants not only to the towns and coasts, but also down towards the interior lowlands of the Balkan peninsula. These migrations led to permanent emigration. In 1839, a bad harvest in Montenegro resulted in the arrival in Serbia of some 280 Montenegrin families 'to seek bread for themselves by labouring this winter'.[100] This group, or a similar party of 110 families who arrived in September had not eaten for four days, and a letter they brought with them indicated that the majority would settle permanently while the rest would overwinter and return.[101] In this way, overwintering became a channel for emigration. Movements of population like this generated a chain reaction since later migrants would converge on settlements of previously departed kin and fellow villagers. Overwinterers could be encountered on the roads asking after the whereabouts of earlier departed relatives.[102]

Serbia was an especially attractive destination for immigrants of dinaric origin. In the 1790s, the province, then under the benevolent rule of Hadži Mustafa Pasha, attracted an immigration wave, and from the time of Karadjordje onward the new Serbian state maintained a vigorous immigration policy. In 1815, Prince Miloš initiated what was to become a standing arrangement with the rulers of Montenegro concerning the immigration of Montenegrins. In the 1830s, the *nahija* of Kruševac, recently recovered from the Ottomans, was earmarked for Montenegrin resettlement.[103] The generous assistance usually extended to immigrants facilitated their transition from overwinterers to settlers. Liberal doles of cash were provided them and their interests were usually defended by the prince when the inevitable disputes arose between them and the resident population.[104] A tentatively estimated 11,600 immigrants a year, mainly

[99] Ibid., pp. 76–90, esp. p. 85.   [100] *Serbske Narodne Novine*, II (1839), no. 102, p. 406.
[101] Pejović, *Iseljavanja*, p. 143.   [102] Filipović, 'Odlaženje', p. 89.
[103] Tihomir R. Djordjević, *Iz Srbije Kneza Miloša. Stanovništvo, naselja* (Belgrade, 1924), pp. 23, 42, 48; Vladimir Stojančević, *Miloš Obrenović i njegovo doba* (Belgrade, 1966), pp. 193–5; V. Sekulović et al., *Kruševački kraj juče i danas* (Kruševac, 1961), p. 48; Pejović, *Iseljavanja*, p. 133.   [104] Pejović, *Iseljavanja*, p. 134.

from the dinaric regions, responded to this opportunity during the 1830s.[105]

Labour migration

Young male Montenegrins migrated in search of work throughout the nineteenth century, in particular to Constantinople and its environs. The authoritative work of Djoka Pejović provides detailed information on these migrants. Their earnings provided a means by which they could pay their taxes and support their families, so the state intervened to ensure that the migrants fulfilled these obligations. In 1856, 452 workers went to Constantinople, in 1858, 241, in 1869, 442 and in 1874, 239.[106] Most worked as servants and labourers, members of the 75,000 strong *bekiar* colony of transients who provided the city with much of its labour force.[107] Rich men and embassies sought the services of Montenegrins especially as bodyguards, watchmen and stableboys. Later they were to be found as bank guards and doormen who 'graced the entrances to the most distinguished buildings in Constantinople, in fine clothing with sidearms'. Links and protection helped them secure these favoured jobs, but larger numbers had to engage in port and construction work, which was less to their taste.[108] The pay was usually good, but was all too easily dissipated through drink and gambling. So the Montenegrin senate placed these workers under the control of captains, whose duty was to collect a head-tax from them, to press them to remit funds for the support of their families, and forcibly to repatriate wastrels and unauthorized emigrants.[109]

Industry in Ottoman Bosnia

The industries of Bosnia-Hercegovina were mainly of the urban guild type, some making high grade wares for the urban elites, others making coarse goods for local markets.[110] Perhaps there was a systemic weakness in Bosnia's failure to develop at the proto-industrial level, caused by the stultifying political influence of the Muslim landowners. But it is unlikely that industry in Bosnia, even under favourable circumstances, could have evolved similarly to the way it did in Bulgaria. Remote from the Levantine

---

[105] Ekonomski institut N. R. Srbije, *Proizvodne snage N.R. Srbije* (Belgrade, 1953), p. 67 col. 2.   [106] Pejović, *Iseljavanja*, pp. 181, 184, 185.

[107] A Ubicini, *Letters on Turkey* (tr. Easthope) (London, 1856), I, p. 24.

[108] Adolfo Weber, *Put u Carigrad* (Zagreb, 1886), p. 169; Pejović, *Iseljavanja*, p. 344; Jovičević, 'Riječka nahija', p. 94.   [109] Pejović, *Iseljavanja*, pp. 350, 363–4, 186, 97.

[110] The standard source is Hamdija Krešeljaković, *Esnafi i obrti u Bosni i Hercegovini* (Sarajevo, 1961).

market on which so much Bulgarian manufactured produce was sold, Bosnia was close to Austria-Hungary, and this raised the price of agrarian surplus goods relative to that of manufactures.

Because of the dominance of the Muslims in Bosnia, the Christian population could not seek sanctuary in isolated uplands as in Bulgaria during the period of the *k'rdzhalijas*, so localized population pressures which pushed peasants into manufacturing activity in Bulgaria seem not to have been present in Bosnia. In the Hercegovinian borderlands, where much of the woollen industry was located, its scale may have been restrained by the high local wage level we earlier noted.[111]

Low population pressure was to some extent offset, as in Bulgaria, by the existence, characteristic of the Ottoman dominions, of sizeable upland townships that provided pools of proto-industrial labour. So here and there small textile industries could be found in the townships of the mountainous southwest. A workshop carpet making industry was active at Zenica, and environs,[112] and coarse blankets were made at Visoko, Foča and Prozor.[113] Bosnian blankets (probably made mainly at Foča) were exported to Serbia, and undercut those produced by the state assisted factories at Topčider and Užice.[114] But few woollens other than blankets and carpets were produced for the market, so the territory provided a substantial outlet for Bulgarian textiles.

The dinaric environment and culture of Bosnia did not favour the development of labour intensive, female orientated industry. In searching for a partial explanation for the weakness of commercial textile manufacturing in this area, we cannot rule out negative cultural influences, since locational, factor endowment, and institutional considerations provide an inadequate explanation. As in Montenegro, orientation to stockraising may have pre-empted female labour time for farm tasks, because of male unwillingness to engage in manual labour.

However, in Ottoman Bosnia, a few attempts were made to introduce mechanized textile production. A profitable joint-stock woollen factory flourished in Sarajevo between about 1860 and 1868, but, for reasons unknown, it was sold off and closed down.[115] In about 1870, the vilayet administration promoted a company to manufacture woollen cloth for the garrisons, but it failed, allegedly because the products and the cost of sewing them were undercut by Rumelian *sukno*. Irritated at the absence of

---

[111] Arbuthnot, *Herzegovina*, pp. 68–9.   [112] Krešeljaković, *Esnafi*, p. 104.
[113] Thömmel, *Beschreibung*, p. 176.
[114] Leposava Cvijetić, 'Fabrika čohe u Topčideru', *Ekonomski Anali*, 31–32 (1970), p. 79; Stevan Ignjić, *Užice i okolina 1862–1914 (Titovo Užice, 1967)*, p. 100.
[115] Kemal Hrelja, *Industrija Bosne i Hercegovine do kraja prvog svetskog rata* (Belgrade, 1961), p. 24.

large-scale woollen manufacturing, despite the exported abundance of wool and the ready availability of water power, the administration tried again in 1873 to establish a woollen mill in Sarajevo to manufacture 80,000–100,000 arshins of *sukno* for the military. Its plans, it proclaimed, would not be left unexecuted 'like some of those up to . . . now';[116] 378 investors were induced to put up 94,000 piastres.[117] That was probably the last they heard of the project.

On the other hand, no Balkan territory was better favoured by its natural resources for the growth of heavy industry. During the Ottoman period the leading artizan industries of Visoko, Fojnica, Bihać, Stari and Bronzeni Majdan, Gornji Vakuf and Banja Luka were in metalwares,[118] especially in gun barrels, sabres and horseshoes. Some of this industry was internationally competitive; horseshoes were a significant export commodity, and knives manufactured at Foča from 'country made steel' were exported in quantity to Egypt.[119]

The basic raw materials underpinning these industries were very high quality iron ores, and the still abundant supply of timber. The charcoal iron industry of Bosnia lingered on into the late nineteenth century despite its technological backwardness. Its output was estimated in 1864 at 8,000 – 9,000 tonnes, produced from 127 furnaces.[120] The industry competed on the quality of its output, described in 1858 as equal to the best Swedish iron, and the manufacturers of Graz in Austria imported it for specialist purposes.[121] The trend of exports seems to have risen at least to 1869. In 1858, 1,650 tonnes were exported, and in 1864, exports were valued at 130,000 Austrian florins. At the local price of 8–9 florins a centner, the implied export was of 1,529 tonnes.[122] However, a report of about 1864 suggests the export of iron was worth 4 million piastres, about three times the above export valuation.[123] In 1869 exports attained 3,500 tonnes.[124] There is no sign up to that date of any loss in export competitiveness.

By the beginning of the Austrian Occupation period, the industry had contracted by about half since 1864, for it produced 4,300 tonnes, probably in 1881, from about 100 furnaces.[125] A propagandist for the occupation regime attributed the decline of the industry to technological obsolescence, but the Austrian regime itself damaged it by imposing trade restrictions and heavy taxes on the industry's fuel.[126]

[116] *Bosna*, 7 Jan. 1873, p. 1.   [117] *Bosna*, 15 Apr. 1873, p. 2.
[118] Bosnia. *Salname* 1291 (=1874), pp. 149–50.   [119] Arbuthnot, *Hercegovina*, p. 73.
[120] Thömmel, *Beschreibung*, p. 153.   [121] GBC Bosnia 1858, p. 460.
[122] Thömmel, *Beschreibung*, pp. 153, 156.   [123] Roskiewicz, *Studien*, pp. 312–13.
[124] 'Turkei. Jahresbericht des Konsulats des norddeutschen Bund zu Sarajevo für das Jahr 1869', *Preussisches Handelsarchiv*, XL (7 Oct. 1870), p. 383.
[125] Asboth, *Official Tour*, p. 403.   [126] GBC Bosnia 1881, p. 680.

This was a diffused industry with at least five active mining areas – Visoko (Vareš), Fojnica, Prijedor, the Majdans and Banja Luka. The best data relate to the Vareš iron furnaces, but they accounted only for 20–30 per cent of capacity, and their average output in 1876–8 was a mere 184 tonnes per annum.[127] The numerous small metalworking centres probably depended on locally smelted ores. It is therefore possible that this industry expanded after the reforms, opening up new ore beds. Boué, writing before the reforms, thought metal smelting to have been artificially restricted because the peasants knew of many mineral deposits but feared that if the masters learned of them, they would force them to labour on them.[128] After the reforms, this influence should have diminished, facilitating the expansion of the iron industry. On balance it appears that iron smelting expanded and prospered throughout the years of Ottoman rule, despite its technological obsolescence.

Besides iron ore, the existence was well established of abundant coal, salt and other minerals, some of which had been exploited at a petty level for centuries. The two salt pits of Tuzla produced 406 tonnes of salt per year.[129] However, subsoil wealth could not be exploited as a basis for large-scale industry by gradual evolution from an artizan scale of production. Its valorization required imported investment, mineralogical and engineering skills. Above all, it needed a transport network. For example, the coal mines of Bihać were intermittently exploited, but in 1874 were idle because of transport difficulties.[130] Foreigners were not ignorant of the possibilities, and the authorities displayed a fitful interest in promoting mining enterprises. However, serious interest was deterred during the first half of the nineteenth century, because the weak and corrupt administration encouraged fraudulent speculation.[131] Badly administered concessions then led to disputes, and saddled the state with heavy awards of damages. This caused a revulsion in administrative circles towards awarding concessions to foreigners, and several major contracts were arbitrarily terminated after Omer's reconquest. Mining laws were now made excessively restrictive.[132]

Despite the forest wealth of Bosnia, only one small sawmill was established, in 1860. Austro-Hungarian business in timber products confined itself to an intermediary role.[133] Lack of transport was an obvious barrier to expansion; in 1858 most of the oak exported from the interior was sold as barrel staves because the need to haul it on packhorses limited the

---

[127] *Bosna i Hercegovina na Milenskoj izložbi u Budimpešti godine 1896* (Budapest, n.d.), p. 9.
[128] Boué, *Turquie*, III, p. 67.   [129] Bosnia. *Salname* 1291, p. 146.   [130] Ibid.
[131] See, for example, the career of Hadži Ali Pasha, recounted in Arbuthnot, *Herzegovina*, pp. 36–8.   [132] Arbuthnot, *Herzegovina*, p. 223; GBC Bosnia 1867, p. 574.
[133] Hrelja, *Industrija Bosne*, pp. 21–2.

length of the logs.[134] The timber trade was also inhibited by the institutional environment. Ignorant of the worth of Bosnia's natural resources, and obsessed by the fear that foreigners would make a killing at its expense, the state demanded unrealistic prices for concessions, causing negotiations to fall through.[135] Its aim to develop these resources without foreign participation was futile, in view of its financial and organizational incapacities.

[134] GBC Bosnia 1858, p. 460.   [135] GBC Bosnia 1872, p. 594.

Ottoman Bulgaria

Though the institutional structure of Ottoman Europe before the reforms was inimical to enterprise, the material conditions of life were not necessarily poor. Bulgarian writers refer to the Ottoman period as one of national slavery, but foreign visitors to the Bulgarian provinces considered the peasant population to be comfortably provided for. As early as 1829 when, by most standards, institutions were still highly abusive, Keppel was 'exceedingly struck with the condition of the Bulgarian peasantry', which was comfortably and cleanly housed, well dressed, and manifested a certain affluence in the coins and rings with which the women ornamented themselves.[1] Urquhart extended a similar generalization to Ottoman Europe as a whole, noting that 'the price of labour in Turkey in proportion to the price of corn is higher than in any country in Europe', and gave as his reason, that labour 'is so exceedingly productive'.[2]

The ability of labour to capture a return commensurate with its high productivity depended on the constraints placed upon its freedom to sell its services, and the extent to which its marginal income could be taxed away. Its legal status was both ambiguous and subject to local variation. Relatively few peasants could be described as unequivocally free, but a matrix of obligation and privilege was as likely to create economic rent as to create submarket factor returns. The case of the Samokov iron industry illustrates the point. As late as the 1840s the ironmasters controlled a theoretically servile labour force, but this did not make it cheap. These workers formed something of a hereditary caste. Though tied to their jobs, they enjoyed heritable land rights, till 1839 they payed no head tax to the state,[3] they maintained a guild which acted as a closed shop, and

[1] George Keppel, *Narrative of a Journey across the Balkan by the Two Passes of Selimno and Pravadi* (London, 1831), I, pp. 309–10.
[2] David Urquhart, *Turkey and its Resources* (London, 1833), pp. 146–7.
[3] Ibid.; *Hochbulgarien*, I, p. 162.

they received special privileges from their employers, from whom they stole systematically.[4] In their case study of a supposedly representative ironworker family of Samokov, in the 1840s, Daux and Le Play observed that, though bound to the employer by hereditary debt, the family enjoyed food doles and grazing rights, and lived fairly well from its multiple sources of income. The hereditary debt was less than the family's disposable assets, and carried a modest 5 per cent interest charge.[5]

Nevertheless, there was no lack of popular dissatisfaction. The period of the Bulgarian 'renaissance' was marked by repeated minor insurrections, in 1835, 1836, 1837, 1841, 1842, 1850, 1862, 1867, 1868, 1872, 1875 and 1876. None were serious from the point of view of the Ottoman administration, to which disorders were routinely to be expected and harshly punished. However they and their instigators loom large in Bulgarian historiography, because they document the growth of national consciousness, and certify to the intolerability of Ottoman rule. The prime focus of the last revolt, in April 1876, was the upland manufacturing townships and their hinterlands. The agricultural villages took little part in it. According to Hristov:[6]

The April Uprising could not embrace the valleys and plains of . . . Bulgaria, where millions of Bulgarian peasants lived, worked and perished, beaten down, pillaged and terrorized by alien rule, by the Ottoman ruling class and by the robbers, murderers and thieves they tolerated . . . The peasants whose property was seized by the Muslim estate owners, and who were compelled to work unpaid on the *chifliks* could not be raised to revolt. Nor could the *chiflik* workers (sharecroppers and labourers) who, in the largest number and most directly experienced upon their own backs the violence, arbitrariness, and exploitation by the masters, be enlisted into the struggle.

This rhetoric fits ill with research by Slavka Draganova on the tax registers of the 1860s and 1870s for Ruse, Shumen and Silistra in northeast Bulgaria and Berkovsko in the northwest.[7] Draganova's careful analyses disclose a different picture, in which landless and near-landless peasants were an insignificant minority, mainly of migrant shepherds, and in which the 'middle peasant' predominated numerically. Of these four territories, it was only in Silistra that the average Muslim family held more land than its non-Muslim counterpart. In the other territories, non-Muslim hold-

[4] Hr. Semerdžhiev, *Samokov i okolnost'ta mu* (Sofia, 1913), pp. 202–3.
[5] Nikolaj Todorov, *Balkanskijat grad, XV-XIX vek.* (Sofia, 1972), pp. 386–8.
[6] Hristo Hristov, *Agrarniat v'pros v B'lgarskata natsionalna revoljutsija* (Sofia, 1976), p. 54.
[7] Slavka Draganova, 'Raspredelenie na pozemnata sobstvenost v severozapadna B'lgarija v navecherieto na Osvobozhdenieto', *Studia balcanica*, XVII (1983), esp. pp. 164–71; Draganova, 'Différentiation de fortune dans les villages de la Bulgarie du nord-est durant les années 60 et 70 du XIXe siècle', *Bulgarian Historical Review*, 1980, esp. pp. 74–6, 85–6.

ings were 18 per cent, 10 per cent and 57 per cent larger than Muslim holdings. (Tatar holdings, the establishment of which had been a source of grievance to the Bulgarians, were significantly smaller than those of either of the major groups, and made no significant inroads into Bulgarian property.) Moreover, a 'numerous middle class stratum was in the process of formation' in these villages, which was 'fully conscious of its economic power', and its 'spirit of enterprise' permitted the 'Bulgarian nation to raise itself economically', as 'the thin Turkish upper crust wasted away'.

It was, however, the manufacturing towns which were renowned as the most prosperous settlements in the Ottoman Balkans. Because of the tightness of the labour market, there was little lack of employment, and wage rates were firm. The going return to hand spinning was a fairly steady 4–5 piastres (about 1 franc) for a full day's work, equal to the pay of a journeyman and not low by Balkan standards. Moreover the representative textile family received income from a multiplicity of sources. Its manpower might be engaged in the tailoring shops, *gajtan* mills, dyeworks and general trades of the town, away at work with transhumant flocks, or in migrant tailoring, while the women and children span and wove. The land too provided a supplementary resource, and for many a family, 'manufacturing gave work . . . to female labour which was otherwise weakly represented in the main economy. Engaged only a few months in agriculture . . . the women were for the rest of the time confined to attending to their housework.'[8] At Elena, a hill town whose crafts included pottery, silk raising and reeling, and the weaving of woollen cummerbunds, nearly all the families held vineyards and arable, in a quantity almost sufficient for their support. Pottery flourished, while the woollen craft 'gave satisfactory incomes to the houses that engaged in it', probably, we may infer, because it did not have to feed them.[9]

For these reasons, the prosperity derived from manufacturing, especially in the woollen trades, was not confined to the entrepreneurs. Rather, as at Samokov, it 'brought the bosses opulence, and the workers, if no other, at least a tolerable life'.[10] The beautiful town houses of Koprivshtitsa stand as a memorial to an age of proto-industrial prosperity in contrast to the miserable dugouts of many villages. Towns such as Kotel, Trjavna and Kalofer all received the tag of 'golden' in contemporary parlance.[11] It is claimed that this wealth was highly concentrated

[8] Metodi Stojanov, *Grad Pirdop v minaloto i sega* (Sofia, 1941), p. 224.
[9] S. S. Bobchev, *Elena i Elensko prez vreme na osmanskoto vladichestvo* (Sofia, 1937), pp. 15–17. [10] Semerdzhiev, *Samokov*, p. 216.
[11] A. Jochmus, 'Notes on a Journey into the Balkan, or Mount Haemus, in 1847', *Journal of the Royal Geographic Society*, XXIV (1854), p. 74; Ivan Bogdanov, *Trjavna prez v'zrazdaneto* (Sofia, 1977), pp. 86–7; N. Nachov, *Kalofer v minaloto, 1707–1877* (Sofia, 1927), p 270.

(though the evidence on this is ambiguous) but it does not follow from this that the producers themselves faced grinding poverty.[12] It is notable that the best evidence to rebut the 'myth' of proto-industrial prosperity that could be mustered by the rigidly orthodox historian Gandev was an aphorism from Marx.[13] There is ample evidence that well-being was fairly widespread. Richer women as well as poorer ones wove for the market,[14] which they would not have done if the wage were a pittance. At Pirdop, where *gajtan* making gave rise to thirty years of high prosperity,[15] 'every woman had money of her own and rare was the woman who did not carry on her neck and ears rubles, jermiluks and mahmudias'.[16] Of course for a woman to acquire those coveted coins, she and her family had to toil far into the night, and to suppress discretionary consumption. Nevertheless, the prevailing work ethic of the proto-industrial community made this the norm of behaviour.[17] As visitors to the textile towns remarked, all leisure, and even the normal household tasks were sacrificed to the manufacture of textiles.[18]

The period from about 1830 to the liberation in 1878 is seen by Bulgaria's historians as the culminating phase of their national 'renaissance'. This Bulgarian 'renaissance' was not, in essence, a local response to the imported ideas of the French Enlightenment, though it created an environment which was receptive to the sloganizing of Enlightenment ideas. Peter Sugar, from his reading of Bulgarian authors, suggests that the 'renaissance' was *sui generis,* 'and an interesting local development that permits a set of western ideas . . . to find a fruitful soil in Bulgaria'.[19] This argument does not pretend that the 'renaissance' emerged within an environmental vacuum, for Bulgarian authors recognized that the cultural and political components of the 'renaissance' could not be divorced from the economic. In other words, the development of enterprise culture generated the material means to sustain the broader cultural advance.

Commerce and educational attainment advanced together. From the 1830s onward, Bulgarian-language schools and reading rooms prolife-

[12] See Ju. Nestorov, *Grad Kotel* (Kotel, 1933), p. 10; Ivan Undzhiev, *Karlovo. Istorija na grada do Osvobozhdenieto* (Sofia, 1968), p. 67.
[13] Hristo Gandev, *Problemi na B'lgarskoto v'zrazhdanie* (Sofia, 1976), p. 453.
[14] M. Arnaudov, *Iz minaloto na Kotel* (Sofia, 1931), p. 55.
[15] Al. G. Dodov, 'Gajtandzhijstvo na gr. Pirdop', *Sp.BID,* VIII (1904), p. 336.
[16] Stojanov, *Pirdop,* p. 224.
[17] Marin T. Vlajkov, *Belezhki v'rhu ekonomicheskoto polozhenie na grada Panagjurishte predi i sled v'zstanieto* (Plovdiv, 1904), p. 20; Arnaudov, *Kotel,* p. 62.
[18] *Uchilishte,* II (1872), p. 123, col. 2; D. Bogorov 'Njakolko dena rashodka v Kalofer', *Turtsija,* II, p. 42 col. 3.
[19] Peter F. Sugar, 'The Enlightenment in the Balkans: Some Basic Considerations', *East European Quarterly,* IX (1975), pp. 499–507.

rated, especially in the commercial-industrial townships and in many of their outlying villages, and these were supported mainly by the local business communities. At Koprivshtitsa, the tithe farmers had to be literate and numerate, and were well noted for the endowments they made to schools, including in 1858, the gift of extensive tracts of pasture to provide funds for the upkeep of these institutions.[20] The merchant tailors also attached a high importance to the education of their children, and founded and maintained schools in Constantinople, with the result that the Koprivshteni and Kalofertsi made up the majority of the Bulgarian intelligentsia in the city.[21] In time the well-to-do sent their sons to Constantinople, not to learn the craft but to finish their education there.[22]

We stressed earlier that communities such as Koprivshtitsa were far more than mere industrial villages; they were commercial communities which depended for their prosperity on their ability to open up external links. This made the business class highly mobile, spatially as well as occupationally. At the height of its prosperity the town's far flung commerce caused the greater part of its manpower to work abroad. In winter it became 'a womens' town'.[23] Although many of the tailors and others migrated only 'temporarily', a cycle of thirty years' permanent residence abroad (the *gurbet*) was not unusual since there was little work to detain them at home. So the annual summer visits of the merchants, tithe collectors, tailors, schoolmasters and the rest amounted primarily to the celebration of reunion, at lavish banquets held on the meadows beyond the town.[24] Behind the magnificent facades, many of the houses were empty shells, for 'as soon as any of the inhabitants . . . starts to get rich, he leaves his ancestral hearth and goes to Plovdiv'.[25]

The emigration of 'distinguished, prominent, and rich' Koprivshteni to that city and to Edirne was of long standing, dating back to the troubles of the early nineteenth century.[26] Plovdiv was full of them. Though many chose to Hellenize,[27] they progressively Bulgarized the city, besides providing the core of the Bulgarian communities at Edirne and elsewhere in Thrace.[28] By the 1840s the Koprivshtitsa tithe gatherers and their

---

[20] Luka N. Oslekov, 'Koprivshtica', *Jubileen sbornik po minaloto na Koprivshtitsa (1876–1926)*, ed. Arhimandrit Evtimii (Sofia, 1926), pp. 453, 519–21.
[21] Ibid., p. 516; Iv. G. Govedarov, *Koprivshtitsa v sv'rzka s duhovnoto ni i politichesko v'zrazhdane* (Sofia, 1919), pp. 15, 40.　[22] N. Nachov, *Hristo P T'pchileshtov* (Sofia, 1935), p. 164.
[23] Konstantin Irechek, 'P'tni belezhki za Sredna Gora i za Rodopskite planini', *PS*, IX (1884), p. 28.　[24] Govedarov, *Koprivshtitsa*, p. 79 n. 8.
[25] Irechek 'P'tni belezhki', p. 28; Karavelov (1874) extract in K. V'zv'zova-Karateodorova (ed.), *Nepres'hvashti izvori* (Plovdiv, 1975), p. 338.
[26] Govedarov, *Koprivshtitsa*, p. 68; Bobchev (1873) extract in V'zv'zova-Karateodorova, *Neprezh'vashti izvori*, p. 427.
[27] Karavelov (1874) in V'zv'zova-Karateodorova, *Neprezh'vashti izvori*, p. 338.
[28] Irechek, 'P'tni belezki', p. 28.

descendants formed the elite of Plovdiv society, a mandarin class active in the support and service of the Porte.[29] Further afield, Koprivshteni entered the circle of the Galata bankers;[30] in Egypt former sheep traders evolved into dairy merchants of Alexandria[31] while one Hadzhi Nencho became a powerful landowner and banker in Cairo. In 1851, a commercial house was established by the brothers Pranchov in Vienna, which survived at least till 1919, and it is to one of its scions that Bulgaria owes its first native work of political economy.[32] In a word, Koprivshtitsa generated through its trades far more than its fair share of the educated, mobile and rich: and it tended to export them all. This had certain important consequences: the prosperity of the town depended on the convenience to its migrant businessmen of using it as a manufacturing base, a dependence which was to have serious results for it, and for similar towns after the liberation. More immediately it also meant that Koprivshtitsa, Panagjurishte and similar towns acted as points of diffusion of the culture of the 'renaissance'.

Koprivshtitsa and its sister towns in the Sredna Gora earned a reputation for the exceptional intelligence of their people (which means they were predominantly literate) and for providing Bulgaria with the schoolteachers, pamphleteers and politicians who assiduously fanned the flames of national consciousness.[33] The drive for education created a large class of literates whose numbers and salary aspirations outran the capacity of the Bulgarian communities to employ them. As there were few opportunities for Bulgarians in official service, the 'renaissance' created a frustrated intelligentsia.[34] This intelligentsia obsessed itself with nationalist ideology, using a rhetoric so paranoid as to alienate it as much from the values of the Church and the business leadership, as from those of the Ottoman government. Meininger instances a protracted struggle at Gabrovo between 'reformist' schoolmasters and the town elders, in which one issue, revealingly enough, was the wish of the 'reformists' to remove 'commercial languages' from the school curriculum;[35] in other words, the struggle was about whether nationalist values should prevail over the aim for which the schools were founded, which was to sustain the material culture which supported them. It was because Ottoman institutional change favoured the Bulgarian economic 'renaissance', that the political

[29] Konstantin Irechek, *Knjazhestvo B'lgarija* (Plovdiv, 1899), II, p. 146.
[30] Oslekov, 'Koprivshtitsa', p. 516; Govedarov, *Koprivshtitsa*, p. 55.
[31] Stojan Pranchov, *Koprivshtitsa ot tochka zrenie istoricheska, sotsialna i ikonomicheska* (Plovdiv, 1886), p. 32.   [32] Govedarov, *Koprivshtitsa*, pp. 70–1.
[33] F. Kanitz, *La Bulgarie danubienne et le Balkan* (Paris, 1882), p. 263.
[34] Mercia Macdermott, *A History of Bulgaria 1393–1885* (London, 1962), pp. 237–8.
[35] Thomas Meininger, 'Teachers and School Boards in the Late Bulgarian Renaissance', in *Bulgaria Past and Present*, ed. Thomas Butler (Columbus, OH, 1976), esp. pp. 34, 39.

grievances of the new intelligentsia – itself a product of that 'renaissance' – failed to unify the Bulgarians against the Ottoman regime.

Historiographically, the 'renaissance' has served not only as a vehicle for examining the evolution of a distinctive Bulgarian national culture (which is legitimate), but also to explain the emergence of Bulgarian statehood; national self-esteem is flattered by de-emphasising the great power diplomatic manoeuvring which brought the new state into existence. However, the spuriousness of this exercise should not invalidate the reality which lay behind the economic aspect of the 'renaissance'. Yet, here again, historical analysis is distorted to discredit the contribution of the former 'colonial' power. The Bulgarians argue that their economic 'renaissance' took place in the teeth of a corrupt, decadent and predatory Ottoman administrative environment. It is however more congenial to logic to suggest that the strengthening of Ottoman institutions made it possible for Bulgarian, Hellenic, Jewish and even Muslim enterprise to flourish during the latter decades of Ottoman rule in Bulgaria.

Ultimately the cultural and economic forces acting upon any given territory will depend to a large extent on the capacities and attitudes of its peoples, independent of the institutions under which they are governed. In those Asiatic provinces of the Ottoman Empire where the indigenous culture was overwhelmingly Islamic, it is hard to detect a similarly powerful economic renaissance before 1878. It has been variously argued that this was because of the want of economically rational institutions and the lack of an enterprise mentality[36] – or because of an institutional package described as 'the Asiatic mode of production'.[37] Quataert's book on Ottoman industry will force some modification of this view, and we reiterate that in the Bulgarian provinces in particular, the combination of Bulgarian, Greek and Jewish enterprise with Ottoman institutional change induced impressive economic advance.[38]

Bosnia

What of Bosnia-Hercegovina? By comparison with Bulgaria, the pre-1878 literature strongly communicates the image of a sleepy, squalid environment, lacking in dynamic qualities, especially before 1851. Yet it was not particularly poor. Spencer, travelling on the eve of Omer Pasha's

[36] Josef Matuz, 'Warum es in ottomanischen Türkei keine Industrieentwicklung gab', *Südosteuropa mitteilungen* (1985), III, pp. 43–6.

[37] Caglar Keyder, 'Protoindustrialization and the Periphery, a Conceptual Enquiry', pp. 17–19, Papers of Section A2: 'La Protoindustrialization: theorie et realité', of VIII International Economic History Congress, Budapest 1982.

[38] Donald Quataert, *Ottoman Manufacturing in the Age of the Industrial Revolution* (Cambridge, 1993).

reconquest, and much aware of the anarchy then pertaining, conceded none the less that 'wherever we roam, we find abundance of provisions, and rarely ever an individual who may be said to be in actual want'.[39]

In Bosnia, the dominant cultural forces were Muslim and Ottoman associated, whereas the 'renaissance' in Bulgaria was essentially an Orthodox Christian affair. The emergence of a broadly based Orthodox or Catholic material culture in Bosnia is less easy to discern. However, Muslim writers have stressed that appraisals of Muslim rule have been tainted by the open bias of non-Muslim writing against Ottoman associations, and require reappraisal. (Again,the former imperial power receives heavy handling from historians of the former subject nation.) But while we must caution against assuming the undynamic character of Bosnian economic life was associated with the overly long survival of feudal Muslim rule, the culture of the 'lazy' patriarchal society persisted stubbornly. According to the British consul in Sarajevo in 1869: 'Half the evils attributed to the Turkish government arise from the ignorance, indolence and superstition of the populations themselves, and they must very much change their nature before a great and general advance in civilization took place, do what the government may to promote it.'[40]

Only in a limited sense did the reforms after Omer's reconquest make the territory less backward than it had been hitherto. Indeed, it is likely that after the reforms, Bosnia was marginally poorer than it had been under feudalism. All classes were being pressed increasingly severely by the rising demands of the state. Even if this had not been the case, it is probable that, as in Serbia, the baleful effects of forest clearance on the prosperity of the livestock economy contributed to a shrinkage of resources. We do not claim that Ottoman rule, either before or after the reforms, conferred much benefit to the territory, but it should also be remembered that Austrian sources had a bias towards denigrating it, in order to justify the prospective or actual Austrian 'civilizing mission' there, just as most Slavic sources had an interest in upsetting the status quo.

The belated Ottoman renaissance in Bosnia probably stimulated the development of commerce. By the 1850s a flourishing colony of wealthy Serb-Orthodox merchants had established itself in Sarajevo, and handled a rising volume of trade with Austria.[41] In reply to attacks emanating from the Serbian press, the semi-official *Sarajevski Cvjetnik* retorted in 1869 that 'for these nine years since [Topal] Osman Pasha became *valija* of

---

[39] Edmund Spencer, *Travels in European Turkey in 1850* (London 1851), I, p. 363.
[40] GBC Bosnia 1868, p. 327.
[41] Aleksandar Giljferding, *Putovanje po Hercegovini Bosni i Staroj Srbiji* (Sarajevo, 1972 from Russian original of 1859, tr. B. Ćulić), p. 83.

Bosnia, the Bosnian Christians have advanced morally and materially. Trade flourishes day by day, and among the merchants there are plenty of capitalists.'[42] Osman was nevertheless removed from office, despite his considerable achievements, not least of which was the acquiescence of the Bosnian Christians in his rule. His efforts were not confined to infra-structure programmes; the administration (it was claimed) 'had always shown itself ready to aid the establishment of schools'. If the 'richer Christian merchants' were quick to denounce the educational backwardness of the province as stemming from Turkish oppression, the lack of demand for education had also to be taken into account.[43] According to official statistics of 1871 and 1874 respectively, 35,996 and 39,161 children were enrolled in schools; they were overwhelmingly Muslim: 87.6 per cent in the 1871 statistic, and 88.5 per cent in that for 1874.[44] However, a sympathetic observer could find little positive to report of the Muslim schools, and even the Christian schools were of 'inferior description'.[45]

Free Serbia

With low taxation and mass peasant freehold landownership, it is easier to see Serbia as a reasonably prosperous land before 1878, because of the favourable balance between land and labour. As economic endeavour was orientated to unrestricted comparative advantage on the basis of a cheap resource endowment, it could be observed for Serbia that 'as a consequence of the ease with which the Servian agriculturalists make money – by merely sending herds of swine into the oak forests . . . labour is highly paid'.[46]

We have however noted that this equilibrium was unstable. As early as the 1830s, environmental degradation was making inroads into its prosperity, undermining the old pig-raising economy whose essence was described above. The *Grunderzeit* years brought a flush of prosperity to farmers, and a limited amount of modernization, but had little positive effect upon the already archaic business structure of the towns.

Even so, the resource base of Serbia was no barrier to the flowering of a Bulgarian-type 'renaissance', though distribution and structure undoubtedly were. With so much of its income locked within peasant subsistence farming, and with little domestic commerce to aliment the material

---

[42] *Sarajevski Cvjetnik*, I, 13 (27 Mar. 1869), p. 1.   [43] GBC Bosnia 1868, p. 327.
[44] Bosnia. *Salname* 1288 [1871], pp. 140–4; *Salname* 1291 [1874], pp. 130–6. I have excluded the *sandžak* of Novi Pazar from both figures. In neither case are they dated to any specific year.   [45] GBC Bosnia 1872, p. 594.
[46] PRO FO 78 485. Cons. 31 Dec. 1842.

culture of its towns, the Serbian 'enlightenment' could only sink shallow roots. This is not to belittle the immense intellectual achievement of Serbia's literary men in shaping a modern national culture. Nor should we disregard the support that intellectual endeavour received from the philanthropic efforts of rich men such as Miša Anastasijević. Anastasijević 'believed in education as the way to national wealth', and among other large philanthropic benefactions founded the Belgrade High School in 1863.[47] He was not alone in his endeavours; mention may also be made of Ilija Milosavljević Kolarac (1800–78) who also made his pile in salt speculation, enabling him to found a literary fund and leave money for the university.[48] However, there were too few such swallows to add up to an enlightenment summer, and the recipients of their largesse were few and unrepresentative of Serbian society. It was no accident that the Serbian national renaissance remained focused upon Novi Sad in southern Hungary, where the material basis for civilization was far more advanced.

In Serbia itself, the cultural renaissance was diffused by a small political elite, largely through the instruments of government, upon a peasant population which was apathetic towards it, whereas in Bulgaria, material culture was polycentric and carried forward by multifarious agencies which commanded little political power. Consequently, what was new in Serbia was imported rather than autochthonous, *mimikeia* as Dimitrije Djordjević has put it, the culture of crinoline and whalebone, redingote, top hat and billiard room, accessible only to a self-conscious and partly *déraciné* elite.[49]

The Serbian economy lacked the institutional dynamism of Ottoman Bulgaria. Most obviously it lacked the basis for proto-industrial development such as occurred in the Balkan towns (including the towns Serbia was to annexe in 1878). Its own provincial towns served only the local needs of the rural hinterland that they administered. There are occasional references to towns in Serbia producing local specialty goods for inter-urban commerce, such as knives from Jagodina,[50] 'red' *sandals* from Užice,[51] and carpets from Knjaževac,[52] but at mid-century, such trades were petty in scale and declining. One trade which was notable by its rarity was that of weaver, for cloth was either imported, or else fabricated by the peasants for their own use and sent to the tailor for finishing. There

[47] Matija Ban, 'Život Majora Miše Anastasijevića', *GSUD*, LXXI, p. 288.

[48] *Spomenica Beogradske trgovačke omladine 1880–1930* (Belgrade, 1931), p. 60.

[49] Dimitrije Djordjević, 'Balkan Versus European Enlightenment: Parallelisms and Dissonances', *East European Quarterly*, IX (1975), pp. 487–97.

[50] Emile de Borchgrave, *La Serbie administrative, economique et commerciale* (Brussels, 1883), p. 177.   [51] Milivoje M. Savić, *Naša industrija i zanati* [*NiZ*] III (Sarajevo, 1923), p. 401.

was no equivalent in Serbia of the Bulgarian hill towns, where large numbers of workers plied similar trades, for businessmen who distributed their products into the markets of three continents. Where an urban weaving trade existed, as at Ćuprija, its technology was archaic even by Balkan standards. According to Spencer (1850) 'the principal occupation of the inhabitants both men and women seemed to be weaving. The loom being placed in a hole in the ground, nothing but the head and shoulders of the operator remained visible.'[53] However, the 1866 census showed that there were only 21 blanket makers in this town of 2,439 inhabitants,[54] and this was the only trade which could correspond with Spencer's description. To Kanitz, Ćuprija was the sort of 'sad', dirty and neglected place in which the Balkans abounded, whose population spent most of its day squatting idly at its doors. The image is as far as possible removed from that of the Balkan proto-industrial township.[55]

The archaic urban craftsman survived because of the high costs of importing manufactures into the interior. As a high cost producer he did not seek to sell into wider markets. Rather, he struggled tirelessly to stop the emergence of a wider market which would threaten his own interests.

As Serbia was an embryonic nation-state in an era of rising national consciousness we might expect its governments to have promoted popular education. To some extent they did; but despite this, Serbia was probably less literate and less educated than Ottoman Bulgaria. A sketchy, church-based network of schools had existed in Serbia in the eighteenth century, but the turmoil of two revolutions largely swept it away. Prince Miloš was himself illiterate, and perhaps on that account slow to concern himself with public education. In fact, some 72 schools had been established in Serbia by 1835–6, but they counted but 2,514 pupils, and these mainly urban. They could scarcely have provided an intensive education, since teachers were so difficult to recruit. Many of them were immigrants from Austria who had to be attracted with high remuneration, and from the examples we have it appears that the pupil-teacher ratio was in the order of 60–70:1.[56] Miloš's son Mihailo, when he ascended the throne in 1860, tried to refocus Serbian culture from Novi Sad to his own country. He therefore set up cultural institutions and attempted to make inroads into illiteracy;[57] but in 1866, the Serbian

---

[52] See Chapter 9.
[53] Spencer, *Travels*, p. 61.   [54] *Državopis*, XII.
[55] Feliks Kanitz, *Srbija. Zemlja i stanovništvo od rimskog doba do kraja XIX veka* (Belgrade, 1987), I, p. 239.
[56] Georges Castellan, *La vie quotidienne en Serbie au seuil de l'indépendance, 1815–1839* (Paris, 1967), p. 275.
[57] Charles and Barbara Jelavich, *The Establishment of the Balkan National States, 1804–1920* (Seattle, 1977), p. 67.

countryside was still 98.4 per cent illiterate.[58]. As late as 1883, when the number of schools had risen to 618, with 821 teachers and 36,314 pupils, there were still many large villages with no schools; education remained essentially an urban middle-class affair.[59]

These figures compare poorly even with those cited above for Ottoman Bosnia, and reasons for the still greater contrast with Bulgaria cannot be difficult to seek. There was little or no demand for education outside the towns. Few peasant families, save those more substantial *zadrugas* with significant urban and market based business to transact, had any real use for education. For them, education was an apparently needless luxury – and one whose establishment threatened the imposition of taxes to pay for it.

The hunger for learning which one encounters in the literature on the Bulgarian and Greek populated lands under Ottoman rule found little echo in Serbia. When Mackenzie and Irby arrived in Veles (Slavic Macedonia) in about 1863, the Bulgarian schools of this small town were allegedly educating 500 pupils. Their *dragoman* had thoughtfully laid in a stock of books in Salonica, mainly on religious subjects, and quickly disposed of the lot at a hefty 2s 6d a copy.[60] In Serbia, on the other hand, nurses Pearson and McLaughlin 'never saw any books in any language, except a few magazines in German'.[61] Serbia's early start as a self-governing state resulted in no substantial advance of material culture, compared with Bulgaria; rather the reverse.

The nineteenth-century Ottoman revival was beginning to provide a political environment, at least in Bulgaria, in which economic life could diversify and develop. As the Bulgarians were largely excluded from the military and political cultures of the Ottoman state, their preoccupations tended to orientate towards business success. In Bosnia, we have detected only the earliest glimmerings of an analogous movement. Christian culture remained far more heavily subordinated to Muslim hegemony, and the Muslims remained too heavily committed to the perquisites of landownership and the exercise of political authority to support a lively enterprise culture of their own. In Serbia and (especially) Montenegro, enterprise culture was submerged under a dead-weight of mass subsistence smallholding. As in Bosnia, patriarchal dinaric culture reinforced collectivistic and 'heroic' values to the detriment of economic individualism.

---

[58] T[aso] S[tojanović], *Naš ekonomski položaj* (Belgrade, 1881), p. 77.
[59] Emile de Laveleye, *The Balkan Peninsula* (London, 1887), p. 173.
[60] Miss G. G. M. Mackenzie and Miss Irby, *Travels in the Slavonic Provinces of Turkey in Europe* (London, 1867), p. 141.
[61] E. M. Pearson and G. McLaughlin, *Service in Servia under the Red Cross* (London, 1877), p. 92.

The Bulgarian 'renaissance' was therefore replicated neither in Bosnia nor in Serbia. The remaining problem was whether the dynamism of its 'renaissance' enterprise culture would be sustained once the Bulgarian economy 'Serbianized': that is to say, when Ottoman political and agrarian institutions had been shed, as they were abruptly in 1878.

Part II

Economic decline and political freedom 1878–1914

We have argued that the institutional structures of Ottoman rule had contributed in Bulgaria to the formation by the 1870s of a fairly highly monetized agrarian economy with a large export sector, and a developed upland proto-industrial economy which was complementary in its product mix to the import trade, rather than competitive with it. Neither Serbia nor Bosnia derived a comparable stimulus from their own institutional arrangements. Their potential, so far revealed, was still exclusively agrarian. In Serbia, destruction of woodland eroded the basis of the country's prosperity, though this was obscured by favourable international market conditions in the 1860s and early 1870s. It was not at that stage predictable whether the creeping damage to the resource base might be offset in the long run by gains from international market integration.

Stripping Bulgaria from the Ottoman system entailed the simultaneous dissolution of the institutions which had supported economic progress up to that date. The main effect of this political upheaval would be to 'Serbianize' the Bulgarian economy, to turn Bulgaria into a mass small-holder society with a large subsistence sector and a shrunken urban and non-agricultural economy. In particular it would imply the shrinkage of proto-industry, which we have identified as a principal source of dynamism. Such a tendency would be counter-developmental, and we will show in Chapter 7 how the Bulgarian economy converged on the Serbian model in the 1880s.

Chapter 8 reviews the economic performance to 1914 of the two dinaric economies of Bosnia-Hercegovina and Montenegro. Upon Bosnia the events of 1875–8 conferred not self-government but occupation by Austria-Hungary. Bosnia's new masters opened up its natural resources of timber, fuels and ores. If Bosnia was exceptional in its economic progress before 1914 this was solely due to the exogenous force of quasi-colonial intervention. However, the Habsburg administration did not attempt to reform the agrarian system, a delicate (and unstable) compromise of interests which provided neither for the capitalistic dynamic of large estate farming, nor for the weaker dynamic of peasant freeholding.

Bosnia's southern neighbour, independent Montenegro, lacked the dynamic supplied by the bootstraps administration of the Habsburg *Landesregierung*. Its social structure was similar to Serbia's, but its productive orientation akin to that of Bosnia. The economy and society of Montenegro provide a paradigm of the retarding influences on human endeavour to which all the Balkan economies were exposed to varying degrees.

The development of textile manufacturing in Bulgaria and Serbia is explored in Chapter 9. In Bulgaria in the 1880s domestic textile work largely disappeared as its function was taken over by mechanized textile manufacturing. The experience of the textile industries is examined in depth in order to throw light on the industrial retardation of the Balkans up to 1914. In Chapter 10 we explore further reasons why the economies of Serbia and Bulgaria failed to respond positively to the opportunities created by the new technologies of the era and the increasing integration of the Balkan states within the European trading system.

Macedonia is treated separately in Chapter 11. Up to 1878, it was integral to the economic region of which Bulgaria formed part, and its southern, Hellenic, area enjoyed similar industrial progress. As it remained under Ottoman rule till 1912, the experience of Macedonia offers insights as to the development path of Bulgaria had it not been 'liberated'.

In the final chapter, I summarise my principal arguments, and bring together quantitative evidence on Balkan economic performance before World War I to justify the conclusion carried in the title: evolution *without* development.

Bulgaria after 1878: origins of productive decline

The era of Ottoman rule and economic progress in Bulgaria was brought to a summary close in 1878. In April 1876 an insurrection broke out in the region of Panagjurishte, which cost the Ottomans considerable effort to suppress. About 1,000 Muslims had been murdered, and this led to brutal reprisals, whose severity was then exaggerated beyond proportion,[1] and reported at length in the press, particularly in Britain. As intended by the Russians, these stories of 'Bulgarian atrocities' inflamed west European political passions against the Ottomans, and proved the undoing of their regime in Bulgaria and Bosnia. The Disraeli government was forced to abandon its diplomatic support for the Ottoman Empire, by which it had counter-balanced Russian ambitions for conquest. The Russians, already heavily involved in the Balkans, saw their way clear to attack Turkey unmolested by Anglo-French intervention, and in 1877 invaded Bulgaria. By the spring of 1878 the Porte had to sue for peace, and, under the Treaty of San Stefano, it surrendered the entire Balkan peninsula, most of which the Russians converted into a Bulgarian satellite state. This was intolerable to the western powers, and Russia was forced at the Congress of Berlin to return half the conquered area to Ottoman control. A slimmed down Bulgarian principality was created, which comprised most of the former Danube vilayet. (Most of the Dobrudzha was awarded to Romania, and the Niš region to Serbia.) Bulgaria was tacitly recognized to be a Russian area of influence. In order to limit Russian expansionism, the sanjaks of Plovdiv and Sliven, south of the Balkan range, were welded into an autonomous province of Eastern Rumelia, which was placed under an international administration.[2] In theory, both Bulgaria

---

[1] Figures circulated alleging the murder of 12,000 and more Bulgarians by Turkish irregulars. According to Richard Millman, 'The Bulgarian Massacres reconsidered', *Slavonic and East European Review*, LVIII (1980), pp. 218–31, a less well publicised contemporary estimate of 3,700 was probably more realistic.

[2] The definitive study of this administration is Elena Statelova, *Iztochna Rumelija (1879/1885): Ikonomika, politika, kultura* (Sofia, 1983).

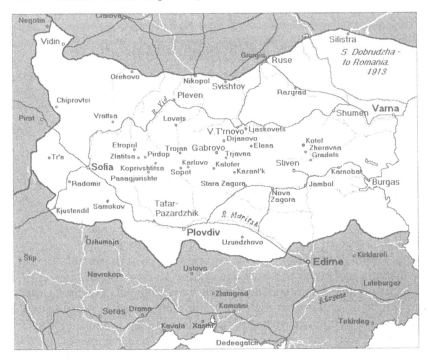

Map 2 Bulgaria, frontiers of 1885–1912

and Eastern Rumelia remained under Ottoman sovereignty, but in practice, the Porte lost any semblance of control in these territories; even the land rights of Muslim residents, though guaranteed by the powers, were largely disregarded. In 1885, a successful putsch was mounted in Eastern Rumelia to unify it with Bulgaria. Serbia, fearful of the potential strength of her enlarged neighbour, immediately invaded, but her army was badly beaten by the Bulgarians at Slivnitsa. After that, the union of the provinces was left unrecognized externally, but *de facto* undisturbed.

In this chapter we examine the impact of de-Ottomanization on the economic life of the Bulgarian provinces. This topic is neglected by the literature, which tends to treat the new Bulgarian state as a *tabula rasa*, a new country which had freed itself of the dead hand of Ottoman rule, to embark on a slow transition towards capitalism. We have already showed that such an approach misrepresents the achievements of the Bulgarian economy at the close of the Ottoman period, and it will be argued that decolonization ushered in a protracted phase of economic decline.

Retrogression in Bulgarian farming after the liberation

The liberation entailed an agrarian upheaval. A source of Bulgarian discontent under Ottoman rule had been the supposed inequality in land ownership between Christian and Muslim. Actually, the Christian holdings had probably been on average somewhat larger than those of the Muslims, but it was nonetheless the case that most of the large estates had been in Muslim hands.[3] The seizure of Muslim lands began as soon as the fortunes of war permitted. In the wake of the advancing Russian army, many Muslim farms were sacked, and their owners, if they had not fled in time, were murdered.[4] Many who had fled, leaving their estates in the stewardship of Bulgars, were to find that their property had been sold off in their absence. Hordes of hill villagers descended to the plains to take up vacated farms.[5] The provisional Russian administration in northern Bulgaria encouraged this process by prohibiting 'foreigners' (i.e. expatriate Muslim landowners) from holding more than 2.2 hectares of land. The intention was to force the pace of land sales. To re-people the vacant land, the door was thrown open to expatriate Bulgars – from Thrace, Macedonia and the Banat – who were given 3–6 hectares a family, and pasture rights, from the land reserves of the state.[6] The Berlin treaty of 1878 prevented the two Bulgarian governments from openly expropriating their Muslim populations, and the limitation on expatriate holdings had to be countermanded.[7] Seizures and compulsory sequestrations were supposed to be compensated but seldom were. Further large quantities of land passed from the hands of emigrating Muslims via the market. In Eastern Rumelia land sales worth 102.1 million piastres took place between 1879 and 1883.[8] This land was usually sold cheaply since it glutted the market. In 1888 land was changing hands at a third of the price it commanded under Ottoman rule.[9] In Stara Zagora province, land prices in 1895 were reported to be about two-thirds of their pre-1877 level.[10] In the southwest of Bulgaria a further 2,316 hectares of land were compulsorily transferred by the courts to peasant ownership.[11] Many rural communes bought up *chifliks* collectively, and divided the holdings

[3] See Slavka Draganova, 'Différentiation de fortune dans les villages de la Bulgarie du nord-est durant les années 60 et 70 du XIXe siècle', *Bulgarian Historical Review*, II (1980), pp. 68–86.

[4] Hristo Hristov, *Agrarnijat v'pros v B'lgarskata natsionalna revoljutsija* (Sofia, 1976), pp. 267–72.   [5] Konstantin Irechek, *Knjazhestvo B'lgarija* (Plovdiv, 1899), II, pp. 220–1.

[6] B. Minces, 'Preselencheskijat v'pros v B'lgarija', *B'lgarski pregled*, IV, 8 (1897), p. 89.

[7] 'L'agriculture et l'exploitation du sol en Bulgarie', France. *Bulletin Consulaire [BC]*, 1884, p. 756.   [8] Irechek, *B'lgarija*, II, p. 178.   [9] GBC E. Rumelia 1887b, p. 4.

[10] *Izlozhenie: Stara zagora* (1895), p. 19.

[11] Ljuben Berov, 'Ravnishte na ekonomichesko razvitie na b'lgarskite zemi po vreme na Osvobozhdenieto', *Trudove na visshija ikonomicheski institut 'Karl Marks'*, I (1979), p. 48.

among their members.[12] Not only were the prices generally low, but in many cases they were never paid in full. In the case of lands taken over by the peasants who tilled them, the Bulgarian government stood as intermediary between the emigrants and the purchaser, who was required to repay the state over ten years. Most of the debtors managed to pay 'quite insignificant instalments and long in arrears'. Outstanding nominal sums were finally paid off in inflation money after World War I.[13]

By one means and another, many former labourers became landowners for the first time, 90 per cent of them in one district of Stara Zagora province, 20 per cent in another.[14] These purchases, mostly from prospective emigrants or expatriated Muslims, imposed a significant burden upon the gold reserves,[15] but for all that, the transfer was highly advantageous to the Bulgarians, though it was one of several factors which caused the state to drift into mounting foreign indebtedness.

The tax burden on Bulgarian farming was also much alleviated by the ending of Ottoman rule. In Eastern Rumelia, the tithe, which had averaged 40.4 million piastres in 1873–5, yielded 32.2 million in 1879, 28.0 million in 1880 and 30.0 million in 1881,[16] though the price level had increased significantly. The tax on buildings fell dramatically from 6.66 million piastres in 1876 and 6.45 million in 1877 to 643,000 in 1880/1 and 973,000 in 1881/2, partly because the peasants were exempted from paying it, while the tax on incomes, levied upon urban trades and rural earnings from stockraising and carting, fell from 6.50 million in 1876 and 6.22 million in 1877 to 3.63 million in 1880/1 and 4.34 million in 1881/2. The authorities were especially solicitous towards the peasant. The budget for 1883–4 provided for tax adjustments which would further lower the burden on rural incomes by about 1.1 million piastres, compensated by an equivalent increase on urban incomes,[17] and in 1884, the rate of the sheep tax was reduced by 11 per cent.[18] The governor of the province, Aleko Pasha, found it politically expedient to favour the peasants in this way, and also to allow them to fall into arrears on their tax commitments. His successor Hr'stovich endeavoured to ingratiate himself through a similar policy, and it was claimed that peasants used the money instead to buy out departing Muslims.[19] Arrears on the tithe

[12] Irechek, *B'lgarija*, II, p. 179.
[13] Mihail Andreev, *Istorija na b'lgarskata burzhoazna d'rzhava i pravo, 1878–1917* (Sofia, 1980), p. 73.   [14] Irechek, *B'lgarija*, II, p. 179.
[15] John R. Lampe and Marvin R. Jackson, *Balkan Economic History, 1550–1950* (Bloomington, 1982), p. 215; Irechek, *B'lgarija*, II, p. 178.
[16] TsDIA. f. 20 op.1 a.e.66 f. 167.
[17] E. Rumelia. *Zakono-proekt za dan'chite v'rhu nedvizhimostite i v'rhu prihoda predstaven na Oblastnoto S'branie v obiknovenata mu sesija ot 1883 g.*
[18] Statelova, *Iztochna Rumelija*, p. 136.   [19] GBC E. Rumelia 1887b, p. 4.

accumulated rapidly, especially between 1881/2 and 1883/4 when they advanced from 297,000 piastres to 16.4 million.[20] The latter sum represented about 50 per cent of the tax yield. Matters were much the same in northern Bulgaria where:[21]

Under the Turkish administration [the peasant] had to pay the tithe and other more or less vexatious taxes; to acquit himself and render the masters favourable he had to work hard and to demand of the land that it produce sufficient to satisfy the demands of the conquerors. Today on the contrary, the peasant pays virtually nothing and is astonished when some tax is claimed of him, regarding the abolition of tithes and taxes as an ineluctable consequence of independence and liberty.

It was not only the peasant farmer who benefited; so did the labourer. The era of the liberation saw a massive rise in wages. In an inquiry on conditions in Zlatitsa district in 1884 it was estimated that agricultural wages there had doubled since the liberation.[22] Harvest wages at Stara Zagora, which had averaged 10 piastres a day before the liberation fluctuated between 15 and 17 piastres between 1880 and 1883.[23] The *Rumanki*, girl reapers from Gabrovo, who had been paid 5–12 piastres for each dünüm of land reaped in 1877, received up to 40 piastres in 1885.[24] Since prices were also rising, the rise in real wages was less than in money terms, but still substantial. These wages were also sustained by the continuing heavy demand for farm labour in Romania and Bessarabia, which sucked in an annual migration of about 50,000 workers from Bulgaria,[25] while at the same time Bulgaria was drawing heavily on migrant labour from Macedonia.[26] At least in the mid-1880s, labourers on the large farms were reckoned to be at least as well off as the peasants.[27]

In short, the liberation reduced the burdens on the peasantry, and gave it greater access to land. The former returns to commercial landowners were partly redistributed to labour. So the resources disposed by the peasants rose. A significant proportion of the countervailing loss was borne by non-resident interests. After the liberation, Ottoman taxes were compounded for a small tribute, and Muslim rentiers lost most of the value of their real estate. The former transfer of tax, rent, and farm profit to non-resident recipients, mainly in Constantinople, had required the Bulgarian provinces to run a large surplus on merchandise trade to offset it.[28] So the massive reduction of these outward transfers released a great deal of

[20] TsDIA. f. 20 op. 1 ae. 66 f. 28.   [21] *RC*, XXXII (1880) in Michoff, I (1941), p. 119.

[22] *Sbornik ot statisticheski svedenija za stopanskoto polozhenie na Zlatishkata okolija (Sofijsko okr'zhije)* (Sofia, 1888), p. 48.

[23] A. T. Iliev, *Staro-zagorski okr'g v narodo-ikonomichesko otnoshenie* (Stara Zagora, 1885), p. 41.   [24] Pet'r Tsonchev, *Iz stopanskoto minalo na Gabrovo* (Gabrovo, 1929), p. 42.

[25] *RC*, 1884, p. 757.   [26] GBC Bulgaria 1889, p. 32.   [27] GBC Bulgaria 1884, p. 3.

[28] Robert J. More, *Under the Balkans* (London, 1877), pp. 18–20.

liquidity into the economy of the former Bulgarian provinces.

Freed from the burdens laid upon them by the Ottomans, the peasants enjoyed an unaccustomed affluence. By historic standards, an unusual amount of money circulated in the Bulgarian villages after the liberation,[29] attracting the mushroom growth of rural shops and taverns.[30] Despite the 'deplorable' 1879 harvest, a sudden boom in building began in Plovdiv.[31] 'Everywhere', wrote one foreign observer, 'reigns a certain abundance even though the devastations of the recent war have still not been effaced.'[32]

However, these gains were taken out partly in subsistence consumption. This was only to be expected. The deliveries the peasant had formerly made to the market had borne high transactions costs because of the poorly developed transport network and the leaky construction of peasant carts.[33] For a time after the liberation, transport conditions, if anything, deteriorated. In the short run, security worsened, as in 1880 bands of brigands were 'multiplying'.[34] Movement of grains in winter was virtually impossible because of the state of the roads, and the distance of most villages to export points.[35] So, as the peasant now enjoyed discretion as to whether to market or to self-consume his produce, he responded to the incentive to do the latter.[36] This led to the observation 'that these people are very well off, although they have not much money to spend'.[37]

The material gain to the peasant was smaller than the loss to those who lost by the redistribution, because the supply of labour into the economy diminished. This occurred because the peasants elected to take part of their gains in increased leisure. In 1879–80, about 150 feast days were being celebrated each year, 'during which all works are idle'.[38] The Russian 'anniversaries' had added themselves to the Bulgarian ones, so that 'the most minor saint closes the shops', and efforts of the government to 'react against the emancipatory tendencies of the religious authority' had not (at least in 1884) had much effect.[39] The writer of the following vivid account in the press of Eastern Rumelia soon after the overthrow of Ottoman rule regrets that the opportunities created by the new freedom were being dissipated in idleness. He writes of:[40]

the undisciplined life, the negligence towards personal work that astonishes us. Many have abandoned the plough and devoted themselves to drinking, and others, if they have not altogether abandoned it, very seldom go out to the fields

[29] Michoff, I (1941), p. 119.   [30] GBC E. Rumelia 1887b, p. 3; *Doklad: Sliven 1883*, p. 14.
[31] *Maritsa* (Plovdiv) II 136 (20 Nov. 1879), p. 1.   [32] Michoff, III (1950), p. 740.
[33] Michoff, I (1941), p. 118.   [34] Ibid., p. 97.
[35] *Izlozhenie: Stara zagora* (1895), pp. 83–4.   [36] *RC*, 1884, p. 756.
[37] GBC Bulgaria 1884, p. 3.   [38] Michoff, I (1941), p. 148.
[39] Jean Erdic, *En Bulgarie et en Roumélie* (Paris, 1885), pp. 166–7.
[40] 'Kak nekoi seleni proumervat novij zhivot na nasheto otechestvo?' *Maritsa*, 25 July 1878, p. 3.

with it. No more is seen in them that hard working spirit which formerly was common to all peasants. Too many people think that now we are free of the Turks, they do not have to work nearly so much, but this is false.

We have seen with our own eyes in certain places in Plovdiv province many of our peasants hanging around the taverns and spending whole working days there without thinking of work. Similar reports have reached us from many other places in our fatherland. In some places the taverns become more and more numerous, and on weekdays we find them full of people, who drink the entire day even though an *oka* of wine sells at 5 piastres or more.

One of our friends, who visited several villages in Plovdiv province a few days ago tells us that one working day he found several peasants lying under a haystack at the edge of a village. He asked them if it was a holiday, as they were not going out to work, they replied that now it was 'freedom' and it was not necessary to do much work. Another friend tells us that when he travelled from a place twelve hours away he never saw a single plough in the fields although it was time for ploughing. But in several places he saw new taverns being built. . .

Much the same happened in Bulgaria. 'Not believing himself any more an obligant towards the state [the peasant] has diminished proportionately the work he imposed on himself', reducing his effort to that needed for the procurement of subsistence.[41]

Though the rising level of wages was good news for the labourer, it contributed to undermining the farming system. Acute labour shortages held up the harvests especially in the Rumelian plains and led to spoilage of grain.[42] Complaint was heard that it was no longer possible to obtain conscientious farm workers, so buyers of estates were frequently compelled to abandon them or lease them out.[43] Contemporaries wrote of vast tracts of fertile land which lay uncultivated for want of the hands for working them and rendering them productive, attributing this to the reduction of work effort on the part of the peasants.[44] At Kat'r chair, 2,460 *uvrats* of state pasture, the leases on which had formerly earned the treasury 19,100 piastres a year, had to be leased between 1879 and 1882 at an average of 2,725 piastres. The loss of revenue was attributed to the 'invidious economic condition which, as everyone knows well, lasts even to today'.[45] As late as 1892, it was reported that Bulgarian peasants were unable to take up land as fast as it was being abandoned by emigrating Muslims.[46] This was particularly the case along the fertile Black Sea coastline, where the Muslims had predominated in the population. Around Varna a third of the fields were said to be uncultivated,[47] and

[41] Michoff, I (1941), p. 119.

[42] *Izlozhenie: Vrattsa 1891–1892*, p. 11; Irechek, *B'lgarija*, II, p. 182.

[43] *Izlozhenie: Stara Zagora* (1895), p. 34.

[44] Michoff, *cl*, p. 119; L. Pajakov, 'Ekonomicheski pogled v'rhu B'lgarija', *Promishlenost*, I (1888), p. 83.   [45] TsDIA. f. 20 op. 1 ae. 66 fo. 9.   [46] GBC Bulgaria 1892, p. 27.

[47] *RC*, LXXVII (1892), p. 89.

those which were still being cropped were choked with weeds.[48] It was estimated in 1886 that if only the arable could be exploited to its former extent, the grain export would double.[49]

Although Muslim land was bought up at historically low prices, it was to become a burden on many of those who bought it. By the later 1880s, the prices paid began to seem low only in retrospective terms, not in terms of prospective yields. Tax pressures were beginning to bite deeper into earnings. A few years after the war, the old tithe was replaced by a cadastral land tax, both in Bulgaria and Eastern Rumelia. The intention behind this measure was to press farmers to utilize lands which had fallen out of cultivation, since the tax was payable whether the land were cropped or not. In Eastern Rumelia, where the basis for assessment was more onerous than in Bulgaria, the expectation was so unrealistic that the law had later to be amended to allow tax concessions to owners of land which had remained permanently uncultivated during the postwar era.[50] Even so, cadastral taxation, together with an effort to deal with the arrears problem, resulted in rising taxation pressures, particularly on the larger farm which was most likely to face difficulties in getting its land fully cropped. Moreover, while wheat prices, reflecting world market trends, were sliding, from 16.07 leva per quintal in 1882 to 11.29 in 1889 and, after a brief recovery, to a nadir of 10.79 in 1894,[51] the pressure of the land and livestock taxes was rising sharply, even in money terms, bringing an abrupt end to the period of light taxation enjoyed by farmers in the immediate post-liberation years. A wave of liquidations followed. Marxist historians see this as the expropriation of the peasantry, but it is more likely to have had the opposite effect. The employing farmer was most at risk, caught in a vice between much increased wages and falling product prices.[52] Particularly vulnerable were those who had borrowed heavily to make their land purchases, and then found they could not cultivate all the land on which they were paying interest and land tax.[53]

In order to offset the rise in wage costs, larger proprietors tried to mechanize. In 1885, sixty reaping machines were imported into southeast Bulgaria, but the attempt to apply them was none too successful. The infrastructure was lacking in machine maintenance, the holdings had

---

[48] France. *BC*, XX, 2nd semester 1890 p. 485.

[49] France. *BC*, XV, 1st semester 1888, p. 61.

[50] TsDIA. f. 20 op. 1 ae. 65 fo. 4; Konstantin Irechek, *Putovanja po B'lgarija* (1974 edn), p. 845.

[51] J. S. Mollov and Ju. Totev, *Tseni na zemedelskite proizvedenija u nas prez poslednite 54 godini, 1881–1934* (Sofia, 1935), p. 90.

[52] T. Vasil'ov, 'Belezhki v'rhu v'treshnoto s'stojanie na B'lgarija prez 1888 god.', *PS*, XXVIII–XXX (Sofia, 1889), p. 574; *Izlozhenie: Stara Zagora*, 1895, p.34.

[53] *Izlozhenie: Sevlievo 1890–1891*, p. 7; GBC Bulgaria 1889, p. 21.

become too fragmented, and the labourers, defending their new-found bargaining power, 'refused to bind the sheaves because they thought the machine reapers would take away their livelihood, so the owners had to abandon them and reap with labourers. Today [the machines] are gathering rust in the barns.'[54] A few large *chifliks* could survive by deploying labour-saving technology; in 1892, one large Muslim *chiflik* in northeast Bulgaria, extending over thirty villages, was in business, using traction engines and steam powered flour and timber milling machinery.[55] Its subsequent performance we do not know, but even those agricultural estates which survived the liberation, or were built up at that time, were reportedly in moribund condition by the beginning of the twentieth century. Around Burgas, the *chifliks* were all in decline and decay:[56]

Where they survive, they work by primitive means, without a serious attempt at modernization. All are liquidating themselves by selling their property to peasants in large or small pieces. There are no agricultural properties with modern equipment. Several *chifliks* whose owners have attempted to modernize them by introducing ploughs and machines have only piled up debts and lead a miserable existence, which makes progress impossible.

Market trends during the first post-liberation decade therefore seem fatally to have undermined any form of agricultural enterprise other than that of the peasant who worked largely for subsistence. The country was therefore saddled with a less flexible, and potentially less progressive agriculture than had previously existed. The consequences were felt immediately and they persisted. Though the yield of the 1879 harvest was considered 'deplorable',[57] it was nearly a decade before there was much improvement, and even that, as we shall see, was partly ephemeral.

The agrarian upheaval led not only to contraction in the area cultivated, but also to a short-term collapse in stockraising. In 1867, the Plovdiv and Sliven sanjaks had supported 2,862,000 sheep and goats.[58] In 1879/80 however, only 1,426,000 were counted in Eastern Rumelia. There was then a sharp recovery. In 1881/2, the figure improved to 1,745,000,[59] and in 1883 to 2.28 million.[60] The pattern for Bulgaria is similar, if less abrupt. In 1870 there were 5.01 million sheep, and in 1883, 4.27 million.

Besides the overall shrinkage in livestock numbers, structural changes occurred which probably reduced the yield per unit of livestock. The

---

[54] *Izlozhenie: Stara Zagora*, 1895, p. 39; D. Usta-Genchov, 'Zhetvarskite zadrugi niz T'rnovsko', *Sbornik za narodni umotvorenija nauka i knizhnina*, 7 (1892), p. 495.

[55] *RC*, LXXVII (1892), p. 80.

[56] Burgazka t'rgovsko-indust. Kamara. *S'krateni protokoli za sasedeniata na I i II redovni sesii* (Burgas, 1909), p. 43. [57] *Maritsa*, 20 Nov. 1879, p. 1. [58] GBC Edirne 1868, p. 167.

[59] TsDIA. f. 158 op. 1 ae. 17 f. 28 gives sheep and goat statistics for 1879/80–1881/2.

[60] *Godishna statistika za Iztochna Rumelija*, 1883, pp. 146–7.

shrinkage in livestock numbers was variously attributed to the emigration of the Muslims, to deforestation, and to an epizootic brought in by the Russian invasion.[61] The large-scale and transhumant sectors took the brunt of the decline, while the revival probably reflected the building up of herds and flocks in peasant hands. From Tatar Pazardzhik the decline was attributed to a want of finance, and this was expressly related to the disappearance of the big graziers.[62] The Kotel flocks in the Dobrudzha similarly declined, partly because of frontier changes, but partly because the common pastures were becoming overstocked because of intakes into arable cultivation. Sheep raising in the Dobrudzha passed into the hands of petty proprietors, and the big *chorbadzhija* flocks gradually disappeared.[63] Much the same was reported from the Rhodope, whose shepherds found themselves excluded from, or subjected to double taxation in, their overwintering pastures on the Aegean coast. It is claimed that sheep numbers at Chepelare collapsed between the liberation and 1912 from 30,000 to 2,500.[64] The large-scale export of 30,000 fattened rams from Panagjurishte to Constantinople also declined abruptly after the liberation, to a mere 4,000 – 8,000 by the end of the nineteenth century: here as elsewhere, sheep raising became the preserve of the petty proprietor.[65]

The decline of large-scale stockraising was associated with the breakdown of transhumance. The literature gives emphasis to the political barriers which hampered cross-frontier migratory movements after 1878, but their effect is probably exaggerated. Transhumant stockraisers also had to contend with a sharp diminution of the area under pasture in Bulgaria itself. The alienation or ploughing up of communal pasture had hitherto been prevented by the Ottoman authorities. By restricting the amount of land under cultivation in the interest of the stockraising economy, an adequacy of natural fertilizer had been ensured. After the liberation, communal pastures were invaded and ploughed up by land hungry peasants.[66] Pasture declined especially in lowland areas where Muslim property was abandoned. Here peasants tended to break up and cultivate land which had presumably been private pasture, for the sake of the high yields such land would give under crops, leaving behind a trail of wrecked arable which was of relatively little pastoral value.[67] The illegal

[61] France. *BC*, XXI, 1891, 2nd semester, p. 442.
[62] *Izlozhenie: Tatar pazardzhik 1890–1891*, p. 54.   [63] Geshov, 'Ovcharite', p. 312.
[64] Georgi Chichovski, *Srednorodopski problemi* (Asenovgrad, 1935), pp. 13–14; Hr. P. K[onstantinov], 'Nekolki dumi za iselvanieto na pomatsite iz rodopskite pokrajnini', *B'lgarska sbirka*, II (1895), p. (1) 24.
[65] Marin T. Vlajkov, *Belezhki v'rhu ekonomicheskoto polozhenie na grada Panagjurishte predi i sled v'zstanieto* (Plovdiv, 1904), pp. 16–17.
[66] Irechek, *B'lgarija*, II, p. 88.   [67] *Izlozhenie: Vrattsa 1889–90*, p. 18.

depletion of state and communal woodland became widespread, and was ineffectively controlled till 1907.[68] It was just such lands that had been used by transhumant flocks. As the peasants themselves had few animals, intakes from this pastoral reserve would put more (and better) arable land at their disposal, but for lack of manure they would be unable to maintain its fertility. Such a sequence occurred round Zlatitsa.[69] The reduction of (or exclusion from) lowland grazing forced flocks to be reduced in the uplands. The decline of transhumant husbandry in the Rhodope forced the conversion of mountain pasture to tillage, though the simultaneous decrease in the supply of sheep manure imposed declining crop yields on the arable, despite generous fallows.[70]

Other sources claim that the loss of grazing arose from the diminution of fallowing. In Stara Zagora province, the arable had formerly only been cropped every second year, alternating with longish fallows. The latter had been an important source of grazing for the livestock, and its manure kept the soil in heart. After the war, the fallows were reduced, putting an excessive burden on the common pasture.[71] Certainly, the innovation of cadastral taxation provided an incentive to see that as much land as possible earned a yield in the short term. Yet this explanation seems too simple. In 1889, about one-third of the arable surface was fallow, probably no less than under the Ottomans.[72] On the other hand, the farmer who had hitherto operated long fallows, which had been enriched by the manure supplied by transhumant flocks, might well have to speed the rotation with annual fallowing if the manure were no longer forthcoming, and in so doing would make his fallow land less useful as a pastoral reserve. Certainly the long two to three-year fallow was disappearing.[73] The exact mechanism by which the transhumant system was undermined is not altogether clear, but it is evident that the former upland – lowland symbiosis was being undermined to the detriment of both. The hill stockraiser lost his flocks, the plains dweller part of the manure which had enhanced the fertility of his soil. The authorities became concerned that the excessive amount of wheat cropping was causing soil erosion[74] and it was claimed that in Stara Zagora, areal crop yields had been halved in consequence.[75]

---

[68] Richard J. Crampton, *Bulgaria 1878–1918. A History* (Boulder, CO., 1983), p. 189.
[69] *Sbornik ot statisticheski svedenija za stopanskoto polozhenie na Zlatishkata okolija (Sofijsko okr'zhie)* (Sofia, 1888), p. 98 (reference to Chelopek village).
[70] Chichovski, *Srednorodopski problemi*, p. 8.   [71] Iliev, *Staro-zagorski okr'g*, pp. 53–4.
[72] 'Doklad do g.-na Ministra na Narod. Prosveshtenie ot industrijalnata komissija pri Ministerstvoto na Narodnoto Prosveshtenie', *Promishlenost*, III, 1890, p. 784.
[73] GBC E. Rumelia 1887b, p. 2.
[74] *Doklad do g-na Ministra na Narodnoto prosveshtenie ot industrijalna komissija pri Ministerstvo na Narodnoto prosveshtenie za s'stojanieto na zemedelieto i skotov'dstvoto* (Sofia, 1891), p. 8.   [75] Irechek, *B'lgarija*, II, p. 185.

The undermining of the fodder basis of large-scale stockraising led to qualitative deterioration in the herds and flocks. From Vrattsa it was reported that 'in place of our former fine cows and heifers, we maintain and feed thin livestock suitable for nothing'.[76] What had once been superior breeds of cattle had been allowed to degenerate till they were indistinguishable from the unimproved stock.[77] It was suggested that deterioration of the breed had been caused by reckless overslaughtering to meet the demand of the Russian occupation forces in 1878–9.[78] It was the same with sheep: in the region of Stara Zagora, the superior Karnobat breed was giving way to sheep of the local breed.[79]

As a result of the reversion of sheep raising into the hands of subsistence farmers, and the associated deterioration in breed, both the quality and quantity of wool available to manufacturers on Balkan markets deteriorated after the liberation.[80] In 1881 farmers in Eastern Rumelia were curtailing their output of wool because of rising production costs.[81] The peasants were raising sheep of an inferior (wool) breed which made more efficient use of the meagre resources on which they maintained them. They also diverted their wool to self-consumption.[82] As only about a third of Bulgarian wool output ever reached the market,[83] Eastern Rumelia, and subsequently Bulgaria as a whole, were forced into importing wool. Even in 1887, wool was being imported from Odessa,[84] and the need to import wool grew steadily thereafter.[85]

Considerable losses, both in the quantity and quality of farm production were caused by the harassment of the Muslim population. The Muslims are treated in the literature as a consuming element, rather than as producers, but this was only true of a wealthy minority of urban Muslims. An observer with long experience of Eastern Rumelia wrote that, 'as practical farmers, the Turks were more laborious, painstaking, and assiduous, even more progressive, after their manner, than any of the subject races, and their farms were distinguished by neatness and the produce by a marked superiority which the others never cared to attain'. The loss of 'a large proportion of its best agriculturalists' he considered to have 'much crippled' the province.[86] In Zlatitsa district, where the former

[76] *Izlozhenie: Vrattsa 1889–1890*, p. 18.   [77] *Doklad . . . ot industrijalnata komissija*, p. 49.
[78] GBC E. Rumelia 1886, p. 5.   [79] Iliev, *Staro-zagorski okr'g*, p. 67.
[80] St. Popović, 'Ekonomni izveštaj o putu u Knjaževac', *Glasnik Ministarstva Finansija* (Belgrade) II (1883), p. 589; Plovdivsko t'rgovsko-industrialna kamara, *Izvlechenie ot stenografskite protokoli. . . 1897*, pp. 12–13.   [81] TsDIA. f 158 op. 1 ae. 16 fo. 42 & vo.
[82] G. Zannetoff, *Die haus-und fabrikmässige entwicklung der bulgarischen textilindustrie* (Berlin, 1927), pp. 13–14.
[83] D. Mishajkov, 'Ocherk na fabrichnata v'lnena industrija v B'lgarija', *Sp.BID*, VIII (1904), p. 491.   [84] GBC E. Rumelia 1887a, p. 5.
[85] BAE Dossier 2807 X No. 2161. Bulgarie: rapports commerciaux. fo. 88.
[86] GBC E. Rumelia 1887b, pp. 3, 4.

Muslim population was largely displaced by Bulgarian in-comers, an official report found that 'although the economic deterioration of Zlatitsa *okolija* began long ago, it is generally admitted that before the liberation it looked like a very fine garden compared with its present condition'.[87]

An example of the losses that could be entailed through the displacement of the Muslims may be seen in the matter of rice growing in the province of Plovdiv. Before the liberation, this crop had yielded 500,000 to 600,000 kilés worth at least 13–14 million piastres a year, mostly in exports. Moreover, as it was grown in alternation with grains, it doubled the return to seed obtained from the latter.[88] Rice growing was suspended after the war ostensibly for sanitary reasons, but 'in all probability' to force out the Muslim proprietors of the rice-fields. Although restarted in 1884 under restrictive conditions, rice growing was subsequently abandoned over half the area, allegedly because of excessive wages and the high rents demanded by the administration, which seems to have acquired control over it. At no time before 1923 did output exceed a quarter of what had been produced under the old regime. This was no mean loss to a territory whose export trade had been running at about 50 million piastres.[89]

Sericulture and tobacco growing were also damaged. At Lovech, 50,000 oka of cocoons had 'formerly' been raised each year, but in 1879/80 production was down to 15,000 *oka*.[90] The prime reason was that Bulgarian production was being damaged, as elsewhere, by the disease *pébrine*, probably caused by the import of contaminated seed. Production was also affected by Muslim emigration, for under Ottoman rule, silk had been raised largely by Muslim women.[91] So when the state wanted to restore the industry, it tried illicitly to recruit skilled female operatives from Edirne to instruct its own workpeople.[92] Tobacco growing in the region of Vidin was largely in the hands of Tatars, a Muslim minority well regarded for their laboriousness and painstaking farm work. The Tatar immigration in the 1860s had been noted at the time to 'have given an impulse to agriculture', and by 1870 to have 'greatly improved the cultivation of the soil'.[93] As a relatively under-privileged group, the Tatars held wretchedly small holdings, a limitation which probably impelled them to seek intensive types of cultivation. Even so, they were hated by the Bulgarians because the Ottoman regime had implanted them on allegedly Bulgarian farmland; these too were forced to emigrate, and an abrupt decline in tobacco growing resulted.[94]

---

[87] *Zlatishka okolija*, p. 22.   [88] TsDIA. f. 20 op.1 ae.66 fo. 198.

[89] *Salname* (Edirne) 1289 (=1873), p. 187; GBC E. Rumelia 1887a, p. 1; *RC*, LXXVII (1892), pp. 113–14.   [90] Michoff, I (1941), p. 130.

[91] AN F12 7191, Varna, 25 Aug. 1890. f. 31.   [92] GBC Bulgaria 1892, p. 24.

[93] Michoff, I (1941), pp. 26, 57.   [94] *RC*, LXXVII (1892), p. 58.

Viticulture was also – at best – an undynamic sector in liberated Bulgaria, though its difficulties were not related to post-Ottoman institutional change. The serious shortage of wine on the international market in the 1880s caused by the spread of phylloxera in France created extremely favourable market conditions for Mediterranean producers. It raised wine prices in Bulgaria as well, but little was exported because the product was thin and unsuitable for the blending needs of purchasers.[95] Then in about 1891, phylloxera entered Bulgaria, and by the late 1890s production was in sharp decline.[96] Among the minor crops, the production of rose oil – of which some 518,000 muskals were produced in 1871[97] – also sank temporarily into decline, partly because of physical destruction suffered in the rose-growing areas, but to some extent also because the labour was lacking.[98]

Aggregate farm performance

The retardation of the farm economy associated with the liberation is quantified in Table 7.1, which also indicates that the fall in farm productivity turned out to be irreversable in the longer run. After the decade-long depression which followed the liberation a good harvest in 1889 ended a run of dismal ones.[99] The completion of the railway trunk line in 1888, and a 30 per cent reduction in freight tariffs[100] probably assisted. The upswing was not long sustained. From 1896 onward, production per rural dweller subsided and entered a period of ragged stabilization, at a level which in per capita terms fell well short of that which had been achieved in the latter years of Ottoman rule. Even after the recovery in the late 1880s, the behaviour of the seed ratio suggests that grain agriculture never reattained the productivity of the late Ottoman period. In Chapter 3, it was estimated that seed ratios before the liberation had probably averaged 7 to 1 or better but the average for Bulgaria in later years shows no advance. In 1889–92 it was 5.48,[101] for 1906–9, 4.29 and for 1910–13, 5.15.[102]

Commerce and industry

The diminution in the Bulgarian farm economy after the liberation led to a sharp depression in commerce and in the formerly flourishing

[95] GBC E. Rumelia 1888b, p. 7.   [96] *Izlozhenie: Vrattsa 1891*, p. 26 and *1898/9*, pp. 12–14.
[97] *Salname* (Edirne) 1289, p. 189.
[98] L. Oslekov, 'Koprivshtitsa. . .', *Jubileen sbornik po minaloto na Koprivshtitsa (1876–1926)* (Sofia, 1926), pp. 460–1; Michoff, I (1941), p.105.   [99] GBC Bulgaria 1889, p. 9.
[100] GBC E. Rumelia 1888a, p. 2.
[101] Calculated from data in I. Atanasov, *Statisticheski sbornik za Knjazhestvo B'lgarija* (Sofia, 1897), pp. 260–1.   [102] *SGBTs*, 1913–22, pp. 44–5.

Table 7.1 *Bulgaria. Sectoral farm output 1865/73–1914*

Year	million leva annual average at 1910 prices:						leva
	Animal products	Animals	Cash crops	Grain	Garden crops	Total	Total per capita
1865–73	47	37	43	255	12	394	222
1879–80	34	30	33	170	13	279	170
1881–85	38	34	34	152	13	272	159
1886–90	63	52	53	259	20	447	174
1891–95	68	56	62	341	21	546	203
1896–1900	77	58	69	308	22	534	184
1901–5	85	61	83	326	17	571	181
1906–10	98	70	75	329	24	595	175
1911–14	103	74	54	384	31	645	137
1923	84	61	120	286	23	574	146

Source: BALKSTAT.

industrial sector. We noted above that the reduction in transfer payments out of the territory created a surge in liquidity within it. A strong inflation of prices promptly ensued. An unweighted index of Bulgarian commodity prices rises 70 per cent between 1870–4 and 1887.[103] In Stara Zagora province of Eastern Rumelia, whose economy was relatively well integrated into international trade in primary products, the price of dairy produce rose by 65 per cent, wine, wool and livestock rose by 18–34 per cent, and wheat by 16 per cent.[104] Prices rose most strongly in areas distant from international market exchanges, and especially affected goods which did not enter international trade. In the city of Niš, annexed from the Ottoman Empire in 1878 by Serbia, the price of seventeen staple commodities rose by an average of 68 per cent between the pre-liberation period and 1883.[105]

This inflation did not affect the rate of exchange of the currency, since it was no more than the means by which international payments were re-equilibrated on the cessation of outward transfer payments. The sharp price rises in the areas annexed by Serbia seem only to have brought those prices into line with prices pertaining in the rest of that country, for in

[103] Lj. Berov, *Dvizhenieto na tsenite na Balkanite prez XVI-XIX v i Evropejskata revoljutsija na tsenite* (Sofia, 1976), pp. 289, 291.   [104] Iliev, *Staro-zagorski okr'g*, pp. 67, 97, 105.
[105] Milan Dj. Milićević, *Kraljevina Srbija* (Belgrade, 1884), III, p. 133.

Serbia itself food prices followed the deflationary world market trend by falling 13.4 per cent over the same period.[106]

As a result of the reversion to subsistence farming, which left most farm products in relatively short supply on the domestic market, the export trade collapsed. The port of Silistra, which had handled some 3 million francs worth of exports in 1876, exported goods valued at but 604,000 francs in the first ten months of 1879.[107] The port of Varna was reported in about 1880 to be in a much worse state than under the Ottomans because of the inexorable diminution of its export trade.[108]

While the volume of exports as a whole diminished, its structure changed as exports in which the territory enjoyed a lesser comparative advantage disappeared, leaving the export trade to a small range of commodities in which comparative advantage was greater. This meant that exports became dominated by cereals. Exports of grain through Varna rose by 60 per cent between the average of 1862–74 and the mid-1880s.[109] Nevertheless, the overall growth of cereal exports was almost certainly less favourable than this because Varna, lacking a deep-water harbour, had not been the main outlet for cereals before the liberation. Bulgarian surpluses were probably exported as Romanian, as they were picked up by the merchants of Galatz and Braila.[110] Cereals became the dominant export commodity, because, of all major farm products, they were least suitable for diversion into self-consumption. Livestock and animal product exports, on the other hand, fell sharply as self-consumption increased. Leather, iron bars, sheep and cattle, wool and dairy products virtually ceased to be exported. Similarly, the range of textile exports became more specialized. *Aba* cloth, tailored clothing, hosiery, towels and printed cottons were no longer exported in significant amounts, while the export of *gajtan* (braid), *shajak* and carpets survived.

Since the rate of exchange remained unaltered, the price of imported goods did not rise nearly as much as that of Bulgarian products. In Stara Zagora province, imports rose in price 10–20 per cent, presumably reflecting increased transactions costs and easy selling conditions, but this was far less than the price rise in domestically produced goods.[111] The price of 'colonial' goods actually fell, despite the sharp rise in domestic prices.[112] Importers were therefore presented with a sudden shift in relative prices, which was to their advantage when competing

---

[106] Dragiša Lapčević, *Položaj radničke klase i sindikalni pokret u Srbiji* (Belgrade, 1928), p. 56.   [107] *Maritsa*, 23 Nov. 1879, p. 7.

[108] F. Kanitz, *La Bulgarie danubienne et le Balkan* (Paris, 1882), p. 471.

[109] Michoff, I (1941), pp. 27, 29, 31, 34, 39, 46, 55, 63, 74, 78, 84; France. *BC*, XV (1888, Jan. – June) Commerce et navigation de Varna en 1886, p. 61.

[110] GBC Bulgaria 1876, p. 1565.   [111] Iliev, *Staro-zagorski okr'g*, pp. 97, 105.

[112] Irechek, *B'lgarija*, II, p. 179.

against domestic products. As domestic manufacturing went into a sharp decline, so it is claimed that it was being destroyed by a wave of imports.

It is probable, however, that no such import invasion occurred. Take the woollen trade, potentially the most vulnerable to import displacement. There was no upsurge in the import of woollens. Indeed it is likely that the Bulgarian provinces had been a much better market for cloth imports during the Ottoman period than they were subsequently. The losers from the agrarian upheaval, in particular the urban Muslims, had long been the heaviest spenders on manufactured goods. It was reckoned that the 'Turkish' women would annually spend five times as much money with the clothing trade as their Bulgarian counterparts.[113] Many of these Muslims now emigrated, hitting the market for English cotton prints.[114] Those who remained were impoverished, and the curtailment of their spending also reduced the size of the domestic market.[115] Importers bewailed the emigration or impoverishment of the Muslims as the prime cause of their declining sales.[116] Their demand was not compensated by the increased purchasing power of Bulgarian peasants. Peasants who took advantage of the increased amount of land at their disposal to increase their cash incomes through an increased sale of grain seem mainly to have turned the receipts into specie hoards and jewellery.[117] Possessing their own wool, they spent little on woollen goods.[118] It was not only the peasants who supplied their own textiles. A third of the urban population did the same.[119] As Table 7.2 shows, imports of woollens were static between 1880/1 and 1899/1901.

There was no boom in imports because the farm sector both diverted its produce out of the market, and reduced its effort, so the losses borne by the former rent recipients were not offset by increased purchases by the gainers. Thus imports and domestic manufactures were left to struggle for a shrunken home market. In this respect, as we have seen, imports had a decided price advantage, because their supply cost had not been affected by the increase in the general price level. This explains a paradox which emerges from contemporary comment. 'Money', it was said, 'became more abundant: people who had before been content to wear native homespuns now elected to dress *à la franca.*'[120] Or, as a Bulgarian

---

[113] Janssen's report on Bulgaria in Michoff, I (1941), p. 126.
[114] GBC Bulgaria 1885, p. 4 and 1883, p. 2.   [115] Michoff, II/2 (1953), p. 614.
[116] *RC*, LIII. Philippopoli, 25 Feb. 1886, p. 344.
[117] *RC*, LXXVII, Voyage en Bulgarie, 22 Oct. 1892, p. 139.
[118] G. E. D-va, 'Znachenieto na v'tr'shnija pazar za nashata v'lnena industrija', *SpBID*, XIV (1910)I (1941), p. 586.   [119] Kiril G. Popov, *Stopanska B'lgarija* (Sofia, 1916), p. 302.
[120] GBC Bulgaria 1889, p. 31.

Table 7.2 *Woollen cloth imports into Bulgaria 1880–1881 to 1899–1901*[a]
(million leva)

	N. Bulgaria	E. Rumelia	Bulgaria
1880–1[a]	1.37	n.d.	n.d.
1882–3[a]	0.91	0.25	1.16
1886–8	–	–	1.55
1889–91	–	–	1.51
1894–6	–	–	1.56
1899–1901	–	–	1.16

[a] corrected for mutual Bulgaro-Rumelian trade.

source saw it, the large amount of gold which had entered the country had led 'a significant part of the population [to] throw themselves at European manufactures', to the detriment of the domestic crafts.[121] Clearly, what was happening, was not so much a change in tastes, as an alteration in the relative prices of domestic and imported goods, the cross-elasticity of demand for which was quite high, at a time when total demand for manufactures was declining.

The consequent damage to domestic manufacturing was severe, and the decline of urban small-scale manufacturing especially striking. Pre-liberation Samokov had supported 426 craftsmen, and in 1888, 58.[122] In Stara Zagora district, there had been in the Ottoman period 488 crafts-men, on the eve of war 493, and after the wars only 186.[123] At Karlovo, of 60 tanneries before the liberation, 16 survived in 1883.[124] At Gabrovo and environs, the number of ironworking shops declined from 360 before the liberation, to 60 in 1882 and 49 in 1910.[125] At Vidin, the former ribbon and silk manufactures, once exported throughout the Middle East, were said in 1891 to be 'almost abandoned'.[126] Plovdiv too was reported to be in decline at the same time, at least as a manufacturing centre, its lace and cloth manufactures 'in full decay' supposedly because of the emigration of the richer Muslims, and the decline of its fairs.[127] The output of the candlemaking trade of Sofia declined 90 per cent between 1875 and 1898.[128] The decline in the home market was so severe, even for trades which were not much affected by import competition, as to force a

[121] *Kratko izlozhenie po zemledelieto i zanajatite v B'lgarija* (Sofia, 1889), p. 19.
[122] Zhak Natan, *Ikonomicheska istorija na B'lgarija sled osvobozhdenieto* (Sofia, 1938), p. 49.
[123] Iliev, *Staro-zagorski okr'g*, pp. 88–9.
[124] Stoil Staneff, *Das Gewerbewesen und die Gewerbepolitik in Bulgarien* (Ruse, 1901), p. 27.
[125] Tsonchev, *Gabrovo*, pp. 205, 250.   [126] *RC*, LXXVII (1892), p. 55.
[127] France. *BC*, XIX 1890 1st semester, p. 225; *RC*, LXXVII (1892), p. 117.
[128] Crampton, *Bulgaria*, p. 215.

4. Artisan Quarter, Samokov, Bulgaria – a protoindustrial town in decline

Table 7.3 *Woollen output of Eastern Rumelia 1883*

Okrug	*Aba*	*Shajak*	Factory cloth	*Gajtan* (a)	Total	Source
(000m²)						
Sliven	96.9	132.8	113.4			(1–2)
Plovdiv	24.5	28.0	–			(3)
T. Pazardzhik	29.3	–	–			(4)
TOTAL	150.7	160.8	113.4			
(tonnes)						
TOTAL	120.6	69.1	54.3	369.7	613.7	
value – million leva						
	0.86	0.96	0.56	3.06	5.44	(5–6)
less value of 1,414.8 tonnes raw wool						
input at 1881–4 mean price of 1.617 leva/kg					2.29	(7)
Net output of woollen industry					3.15	

Sources: BALKSTAT statistics

diversion of output from the home to the export market. This happened with the carpet industry of Chiprovtsi. Muslim emigration reduced domestic demand, as a result of which surplus production had to be diverted to the Constantinople market.[129]

Most domestic industries were in no position to compete. Even though their prices had risen, they could not easily absorb their increased costs. Their raw materials were more expensive – wool price inflation is an obvious example of this. Moreover, the general level of wages had risen much more than that of prices. Both in Niš and Stara Zagora, wages far outpaced commodity prices, rising 187 per cent and 60 per cent respectively.[130] Naturally, entrepreneurs endeavoured to hold the inflation in their wage costs down to a figure less than the general level of inflation, but this could only be done by imposing a real wage cut on their workforce (or on themselves, if self-employed) at a time when real wages outside the manufacturing sector were rising steeply. The result was that most of their labour melted away.

As the largest of the domestic industries, the experience of the woollen industry fully accords with this hypothesis. From the liberation onwards, the woollen industries went into an abrupt decline. Table 7.3 shows *gajtan* and cloth output for Eastern Rumelia in 1883; comparison with Table 3.3 (p.

[129] Adolf Strauss, 'Bulgarische Industrie', *Österreichische Monatschrift für der Orient* (Vienna) XI (1885), p. 209.
[130] Milićević, *Kraljevina Srbija*, p. 133; Iliev, *Staro-zagorski okr'g*, pp. 41, 42.

71) indicates that in this territory total woollen output by weight had fallen 61 per cent since the Ottoman period. The fall for cloth was 73 per cent and for *gajtan* 45 per cent. Comparable data are lacking for northern Bulgaria.

Despite the severe decline in output, value per unit of output rose – with the result that in value terms the extent to which output contracted was 56 per cent or 5 percentage points less than in physical terms. Value added in manufacturing fell by 55.2 per cent. At this time total output was probably around its nadir, though as the industry moved to the factory, a further massive shrinkage of employment was yet to occur. Two points are at once apparent, first that much of the post-liberation diminution in hand-worked woollen output had occurred before the industry mechanized, and second that money returns to factor inputs had increased since the Ottoman period.

The increase in value added reflected inflation in wool prices, and a money wage increase for labour. We have already noted the way in which the diminution of large-scale sheep raising had both reduced the supply of wool and lowered its quality. In Eastern Rumelia, with its relatively high commitment to the woollen industry, this led to immediate wool shortages and the need to import. The manufacturers were complaining soon after the liberation of the import duty on wool, which had been set at 6 per cent, and lobbied for the suppression of the tariff on wool from Bulgaria, if only, as they explained, because it handicapped them *vis-à-vis* Bulgarian producers.[131] The governor of the province was sufficiently impressed by their representations temporarily to suppress this tariff to afford the industry badly needed assistance.[132] But the former cost advantage, which had arisen from manufacturing from a net export commodity (and one which had hitherto needed to pay 12 per cent *ad valorem* on export) had been lost forever.[133]

The worsening of wool supply conditions hastened a shift in production from wool intensive *aba* cloth towards that of the lighter *shajak*, a higher proportion of whose price was composed of value added in manufacturing, as shown in Table 7.4 below. An example of this occurred at Koprivshtitsa, which before 1878 had produced exclusively *aba*.[134] Soon the returns to making *aba* were completely wiped out, after which it continued to be made only in a few remote areas where it was difficult to monetize the raw wool.[135]

---

[131] TsDIA. f. 151 op. 1 ae. 16 f. 51.   [132] TsDIA. f 158 op. 1 ae. 16 f. 42 and verso.

[133] Mishajkov, 'Ocherk', p. 494.

[134] Stojan Pranchov, *Koprivshtitsa ot tochka zrenie istoricheska sotsialna i ikonomicheska* (Plovdiv, 1886), p. 22.

[135] Sv. Iv. Manev, 'Kotlensko', *Sp.BID*, VII (1903), p. 512; D. Mishajkov, 'Belezhki v'rhu domashnata shaechna industrija v B'lgarija', *Sp.BID*, VII (1903), p. 534.

Table 7.4 *Cloth production in the Kotel region:*
output prices and productivity 1852–1870 to 1903

	Market price for woollen cloth (leva per m²)		Value added per day's hand manufacturing labour (leva)		
	aba	fulled *shajak*	*aba*	fulled *shajak*	source
1852–70	7.34	n.d.	1.28	n.d.	(1)
1865–75	6.52	4.17	1.00	0.66	(2)
1871–7	6.48	n.d.	0.70	n.d.	(1)
1875–80	n.d.	6.34	n.d.	1.34	(2)
1878–82	5.98	6.28	0.66	1.33	(1)
1883–7	5.08	5.46	0.07	0.84	(1)
1888–92	3.98	4.13	nil	0.40	(1)
1893–7	3.40	3.39	nil	0.31	(1)
1898–1902	3.13	2.77	nil	0.24	(1)
1903	4.04	3.35	nil	0.19	(3)

Sources: Based on data from (1) Manev, 'Kotlensko, pp. 509–10; (2) Berov, *Dvizhenieto*, p. 258; (3) D. Mishajkov, 'Belezhki', p. 534. Converting with the parameters applied in BALKSTAT.

An even more pressing problem for the merchants was the diminution in the supply of labour. Concern over this problem was usually expressed indirectly, with reference to the shortage of yarn, but scattered comments about rising labour costs also exist. For example, the price of textile labour rose sharply at Gabrovo,[136] and at Pirdop and environs the reward to spinning was claimed to have trebled.[137] However, the general rise in textile wages was probably much smaller than that claimed for Pirdop. Table 7.4 illustrates the movement of value added per kg of woollen cloth output. This rose from 4.59 leva in around 1870 to 5.61 leva in 1883. So 22 per cent was the maximum wage rise which the merchant could concede the worker without eroding his own margin; and even this rise was transient. This was because the woollen manufacturer could not pass his cost increases on to the consumer, as open international competition caused demand to be price elastic. It is likely that profit margins were indeed eroded,[138] but a huge wage adjustment would have been required to re-establish the labour force at its pre-liberation level. As already noted, the gain in wages at Niš and Stara Zagora far exceeded 22 per cent, to say nothing of the 117 per cent rise in harvest wages during the same period.[139]

[136] Staneff, *Gewerbewesen*, p. 118.   [137] *Zlatiskata okolija*, p. 17.   [138] Ibid., p. 17.
[139] Irechek, *B'lgarija*, II, p. 183 n. 49.

In fact 22 per cent would have fallen short of compensating for the increased cost of living.

So those who remained to spin for the *gajtan* makers were obliged to work for a wage which had risen in money terms, but had fallen in real ones. Knowing that their services were in short supply, they compensated themselves by adulterating their yarn, to which the manufacturers responded by trying to import their raw material. This sequence occurred both in Kalofer and Sopot in the Sredna Gora, and at Gabrovo.[140] It led to an outbreak of violence in the Sredna Gora *gajtan* towns when mobs of women attacked the property and persons of yarn importers. The gendarmerie were called out and the authorities, after punishing the ringleaders, prohibited the import of yarn.[141] The *gajtan* manufacturers petitioned desperately for the restoration of yarn imports. They argued that they had no long-term intention of importing yarn, but needed the threat of yarn imports as a sanction against the spinners. 'If permission to import European yarn is given, the local *gajtan*-yarn workers will begin to turn out better quality yarn and will hand it over more cheaply and that in itself will end the import of European yarn.' Otherwise, they warned, their businesses, already in steep decline, would close with large stocks of bad unsaleable *gajtan* on their hands, and 'then will begin a critical time because so many poor women will lose their livelihood'.[142] At Gabrovo, the anger of the spinners was targeted more at the new machine spinning mills which were beginning to appear, and the spinners there petitioned the Tsar of Russia for their closure.[143]

The loss of resources to the woollen industry was also in part the result of Muslim emigration. Bulgarian writers assert that these industries were purely based on Bulgarian enterprise and labour, but this was not entirely true. At Pirdop and environs, yarn production before 1878 had depended on the work of 5,000 Muslim women, and after their displacement wool was only spun 'here and there in the villages' despite the much increased level of remuneration.[144]

The post-liberation regime of labour shortage and inflationary product prices also affected the carpet trades of Chiprovtsi and its neighbouring villages. Prices rose strongly after the liberation, despite loss of markets, reaching a peak in 1885.[145]

Demand side difficulties also afflicted the woollen industries. Import competition was undoubtedly a problem, but its main effect for Bulgarian

---

[140] For Gabrovo see Tsonchev, *Gabrovo*, p. 312.
[141] Hristo Gandev, 'V'lnenieto na sopotskite i karlovskite predachki prez 1883 god.', *Profesionalna mis'l*, II (1941), pp. 20–7.   [142] TsDIA. f 158 op. 1 ae. 35 ff. 5–6.
[143] Tsonchev, *Gabrovo*, pp. 71, 621.   [144] *Zlatishkata okolija*, p. 17.
[145] TsDIA. f 173 op. 2 ae. 674 fo. 259 vo- 260.

producers was to confine their products to the mass-market (such as it was) since imports were really only effective at the 'fashion' end, which they had in any case commanded before 1878. The artisan and petty bourgeois market remained the preserve of the Bulgarian manufacturer.[146] British manufacturers indeed made forays into the market for *shajak,* underselling it with woollens made from shoddy,[147] but importers bewailed their own lack of success, attributing it in part to competition from cloth 'made at Sliven, Kazanl'k, and Kalofer', which was 'of a really good quality, and so cheap as to defy all competition'.[148]

Indeed the industry was more concerned about the closure of export markets to its products than about the threat of import competition. The worst losses in this respect were in Bosnia (closed for the benefit of Czech woollen producers) and Serbia, which was trying to foster its own woollen industries. Samokov *gajtan* production was particularly severely hit by Bosnian tariffs. The Ottoman market was not lost; between 1879 and 1885, and again between 1900 and 1910, Bulgarian textiles came in duty free.[149] Even during the intervening period the only tariff was of 8 per cent *ad valorem.* Here, Bulgarian cloth enjoyed a niche which was fairly secure against western European competition.[150] But even the Ottoman market was for a time difficult to sell into, because of the reported distress in Anatolia after the 1877–8 war, which forced consumers to curtail their consumption of *gajtan.*[151] Still, the shrinkage in Ottoman demand for Bulgarian textile products was more regional than general. Soon after 1878, a group of tailors from Derekoi (Momchilovtsi) learned that their colleagues working in Smyrna were 'deluged with work' (possibly because of the withdrawal of many of the Bulgarian tailors to the new Bulgarian state). On this news, more departed for Smyrna, where their expectations were largely satisfied.[152] Complaints about trade barriers might carry more weight, were it not that the establishment of a competing *gajtan* industry in Serbia was promoted by the difficulty encountered there in securing *gajtan* from Bulgaria.[153] On the whole, supply side problems weighed far more heavily in the diminution of the Bulgarian textile proto-industries than demand limitations.

[146] G.E. D-va, 'Znachenieto', pp. 586–7.   [147] BAE. 2807 X 2161. fo 17.

[148] France. *BC,* XXI (1891 2nd semester) Turquie d'Europe-Commerce de la Roumélie orientale en 1890, p. 442.

[149] As a result of a trade treaty, with Bulgaria according Turkey similar treatment for cotton yarns, Mishajkov, 'Ocherk', p. 562.

[150] V. Atanasov, 'Kakvo trebva na nashata tekstilna industrija', *Sp.BID,* I (1896), p. 188; Burgazka T'rgovsko-Indust. Kamara, *S'krateni protokoli . . . na I i II redovni sesii . . .* (Burgas, 1909), pp. 47–8, 172.   [151] Michoff, I (1941), p. 102.

[152] Konstantin Kanev, *Minaloto na selo Momchilovtsi, Smoljansko. Prinos k'm istorijata na srednite Rodopi* (Sofia, 1975), p. 503.   [153] See below, p. 262.

Table 7.5 *Output of factory woollen cloth, Bulgaria 1870–1903*

	(m²)	Percentage of total output	Sources
1870	196,200	11.5	(1)
1889–90	566,400	n.d.	(2)
1903	1,484,000	81.9	(3)

Sources: BALKSTAT statistics.

Conversion to large-scale enterprise

For the woollen textile industry in Bulgaria, the principal trend from 1870 to the early twentieth century was the displacement of proto-industrial by mechanized production, factory produced cloth rising from 11.5 per cent to 81.9 per cent of total output (see Table 7.5). The initial effect of the events of 1876–8 was to retard progress in mechanization. Existing factories were destroyed or fell into ruin, and their severe losses of circulating capital made it difficult for businessmen to set up new ones. Despite this, between 1885 and 1892 the number of woollen factories rose from six to twenty-five,[154] and between 1894 and 1911 the value of the textile industry's capital assets rose by 7.2 per cent per annum.[155] Woollen textiles accounted in 1907 for about 24 per cent of net large-scale output.[156]

The origins of the large-scale woollen industry lay in the post-liberation yarn supply shortage which attracted entrepreneurs throughout the Balkans to build spinneries,[157] onto which they later grafted weaving capacity. The wage rises and yarn shortage reported at Gabrovo were definitely among the stimuli to the establishment of factory spinning. The mechanization of spinning at Trjavna was said to have resulted from the same causes.[158] In Bulgaria, the factories were set up mainly at two former centres of woollen cottage industry, Gabrovo and Sliven, which in 1903 accounted for 81 per cent of all factory woollen cloth output.[159] The shortage of fixed capital and the urgency of the need by the drapers and *gajtan* makers to control spinning capacity is reflected by the fact that the factories were launched mainly by consortia of such merchants, who took shares in order to entitle them to take their own materials to the factories for servicing.[160]

---

[154] Dimit'r Mladenov, *Pojava na fabrichen proletariat v B'lgarija* (Sofia, 1961), p. 65.
[155] K. G. Popoff, *La Bulgarie économique 1879–1911 – études statistiques* (Sofia, 1920), p. 351.
[156] *SGBTs*, I, 1909, pp. 234–5.   [157] Mishajkov, 'Ocherk', pp. 476–8.
[158] Staneff, *Gewerbewesen*, pp. 118, 121.   [159] Mishajkov, 'Ocherk', p. 557.
[160] See S. Tabakov, *Istorija na grad Sliven* (Sofia, 1929), III, pp. 114–15 n. 1.

Table 7.6 *Population of some Bulgarian towns before and after the liberation*

Town	pre-1877	1880
Plovdiv	52,000	40,000
Svishtov	25,000	7,000
Stara Zagora	20,000	10,000
Pleven	15,000	10,000
Lovech	15,000	5,000
Kalofer	8,000	3,000
Nova Zagora	5,000	2,000

Sources: Michoff, I (1941), pp. 101, 103, 107–8, 117, 130, 131.

Structural change and occupational mobility

As a result of the agrarian upheaval, heavy losses of income were sustained by numerous urban Muslim rentiers, and many of these emigrated. As the economy also reverted significantly towards subsistence farming, so the volume of commerce it sustained contracted sharply; and the loss of cost advantages for domestic craft manufacturing, coupled with the diminution of spending by the rentier element, resulted in an even sharper contraction in this sector and its associated commercial infrastructure. All these influences acted in the same direction – towards the deurbanization of the new Bulgarian states. There were a few offsets – firstly, the emergence of a domestically based civil service, though its spending power was constrained by the much shrunken tax base, and secondly, the somewhat increased purchasing power of the peasantry. But the end result was strongly negative, and from the moment of the liberation, many towns rapidly lost population, as indicated by the estimates in Table 7.6.

After the initial urban decline, recovery was slow and faltering. The urban population in 1880 amounted to 19.3 per cent of population, in 1892 to 20.0 per cent, but fell at each census thereafter to 19.1 per cent in 1910.[161] The decline was most notable in the Balkan hill towns, where so much of the industry had been concentrated: the population of fourteen of these fell from 2 per cent of total population in 1880–4 to 1.2 per cent in 1910.[162] An interesting picture emerges when we look at the structural changes in economic life which lay behind their decline.

The 61 per cent diminution of employment in the woollen industry in

[161] Popoff, *Bulgarie économique*, p. 11.   [162] Ibid., p. 12.

the teeth of a 22 per cent wage rise, indicates that textile labour was fairly mobile. The most obvious outlet was into farming. Population migrated from the mountain areas to the fertile lands of northern and southern Bulgaria.[163] Even among those who did not move to the villages, a loss of textile labour resulted from an occupational shift within the manufacturing towns towards agriculture, as for example in the Kotel region.[164] Former pasture land now became available for smallholdings, and for unrestricted forest exploitation.[165] After 1878, Klisura, which suffered a heavy population fall, was to derive its principal support from rose growing and animal husbandry.[166] Even larger towns like Panagjurishte (pop. 9731 in 1905) and Kazanl'k[167] with relatively stable populations turned increasingly to the land for their support. The former town was still 50 per cent self-sufficient in grain as late as 1903, and this was considered to denote a dangerously heavy dependence on external sources.[168] This does not mean that some families turned to farming while others continued to engage in crafts as before, rather that former full-time craftsmen now combined their craft with agriculture, sometimes putting their employees to work part time on vine or rose culture.[169] At Pirdop during the Ottoman period, the land had been in Turkish hands, and the Bulgar townsfolk worked full time at their crafts. After the liberation, craft and commercial employment no longer engaged the tradesmen full time, and their smallholdings were so important to them that all the shops closed down during the harvest season.[170]

The urban textile labour force did not simply revert to agriculture. The new order created openings in commerce, education and administration, which were far more attractive to urban dwellers, and those of the textile towns enjoyed advantages in exploiting them.[171] The teachers of the upland towns seem to have departed *en masse* for jobs in the state bureaucracies.[172] It was notable that in the post-1878 property grab the Sliven people bought urban rather than rural property, and with the late 1880s recession, 'many craftsmen . . . many of them almost without education, abandoned the apron and became officials'.[173] The textile districts also

[163] For examples, see Hr. F. Popov, *Grad Klisura v Aprilskoto v'zstanie* (Sofia, 1926), p. 136; Irechek, *B'lgarija*, II, p. 176.   [164] Manev, 'Kotlensko', p. 514.
[165] Irechek, *B'lgarija*, II, p. 88.   [166] Popov, *Klisura*, p. 138.
[167] Aleksand'r Pavlov, 'Ikonomichesko razvitie i s'stojanie na gr. Kazanl'k', *Kazanl'k v minaloto i dnes* I (Sofia 1912), pp. 324–5.   [168] Mishajkov, 'Belezhki', p. 529.
[169] Irechek, *B'lgarija*, II, p. 197.
[170] Metodi Stojanov, *Grad Pirdop v minaloto i sega* (Sofia, 1941), p. 259.
[171] M. R. Palairet, 'Désindustrialisation à la périphérie. Études sur la région des Balkans au XIXe siècle', *Histoire, économie et société*, IV (1985), pp. 271–4.
[172] Thomas Meininger, 'Teachers and School Boards in the Late Bulgarian Renaissance', *Bulgaria Past and Present*, ed. Thomas Butler (Columbus, OH, 1976), p. 39.
[173] Tabakov, *Sliven*, III, pp. 77, 141.

lost population to the cities. Their longstanding concern for education had created a large literate class, to whom well paid civil service opportunities beckoned strongly.[174] Others, lacking minimal qualifications, gravitated to the cities to seek work, 'however subordinate or ill paid, which releases them from agricultural drudgery'.[175] Thus in the textile districts, the period between 1870 and 1880 was marked by a sharp shrinkage of population, which was to continue for the rest of the century. My own calculations suggest that the twelve mountain towns of Bulgaria most strongly associated with textile manufacturing probably lost about 21 per cent of their population between 1870 and 1880. The extreme case was Klisura with 15,000 inhabitants in 1876 and 1,550 in 1884. Kalofer and Koprivshtitsa probably lost half their population.

The diminution of the textile labour force did not arise only through permanent outward migration. For example, many of the young people began to go out as migrant workers and send remittances back to their families,[176] relieving many of them from the need to earn money by textile work. In 1884, the number of male absentees from Koprivshtitsa was in excess of half the number of households.[177] By 1903, only one of the Kotel textile villages, Gradets, continued to produce *aba* cloth for the market 'in order to sell its wool a few centimes dearer', because its population, uniquely among these villages, had not yet begun to emigrate.[178]

Naturally, not all the former domestic textile workers could substitute textile earnings with other sources of income. There remained a residue of textile labour prepared to work for starvation wages. A few entrepreneurs were able to draw upon this pool, diverting its work into fractionally less unremunerative textile processes. At Tatar Pazardzhik, formerly a tailoring centre, Jewish businessmen established the hand weaving of cotton cloth, re-employing 100–150 women,[179] and at Panagjurishte, Kotel and Pirdop, substantial numbers of girls and women were recruited into sweatshops which paid them starvation wages to turn out imitation Persian carpets.[180] At Trjavna a similar trade was organized on a putting out basis.[181] So not many women continued spinning wool for the market. By 1903 employment in domestic *shajak* manufacturing (including outwork weaving for the woollen mills) had fallen by an estimated 90 per cent, and only a few wretched women remained to offer homespun

[174] Man'o Stojanov, *Kogato Plovdiv beshe stolitsa* (Sofia, 1973), pp. 67–8.

[175] GBC E. Rumelia 1887b, p. 3.

[176] R. Kirov, 'Stopansko povdigane na seloto', *Jubilejna kniga na zheravnenskoto chitalishte 'Edinstvo' 1870–1920* (Sofia, 1921), p. 123.   [177] Oslekov, 'Koprivshtitsa', p. 490.

[178] Manev, 'Kotlensko', p. 512.   [179] Mishajkov, 'Belezhki', p. 540.

[180] Il Janulov, 'Kilimenata industrija v Panagjurishte i nejnite uslovija na truda', *Sp.BID*, IX (1905), pp. 434–7.   [181] BOUCA Rustchuk 1901 II 3, p. 8.

yarn to the merchants, who continued to buy from them as a marginal supply source.[182]

Conclusions

The liberation of 1878 led to profound economic adjustments for Bulgaria over the course of the decade which followed it. Agriculture was peasantized, and as the burdens on the peasants were lifted, it reverted to a considerable degree to subsistence farming. Output fell, partly because peasants took more leisure, partly because farm organization deteriorated. Though the peasants were left somewhat better off, the liberation brought about a forced decline in most sectors of the economy which depended on commerce, destroying many of the proto-industries, but partially substituting their output with factory production.

Developmentally, therefore, the liberation resulted in retardation rather than progress. For all but the subsistence farmer, the years before the liberation looked like a lost golden age. Despite their understandable satisfaction at the expulsion of the Ottomans after the bloodbath of 1876, there were not a few who regretted the more active commercial life of a lost era. In the words of the historian of Panagjurishte, the town 'sacrificed its prosperity and its future on the altar of the freedom of the fatherland'.[183] It had certainly not intended to: its citizens – peasants and supposedly ruined craftsmen – unleashed the April uprising in the heat of anger, we are informed, at Turkish peculation.[184] The old days came to be recalled with nostalgia: 'In truth, times were hard, our property was girdled with robbery, extortion by the Turks was the customary thing, but we nevertheless had something both for them and for ourselves. . . . Turkey was indeed bad, but we had money'.[185] Arnaudov (1931) relates dialogue of 'the old folk': 'You ask me how it was at that time in Turkey? When I came back from the Dobrudzha, my purse was full of money and in the house there was cheese, butter and dried meat – everything. Now there's nothing at all.' Another agrees – but reminds him of 'how we were plundered, and now we are free'. To which came the dry response: 'What's the use of your freedom when your pocket is empty?. . . Eh, *hadzhi*, there will come a time when we will lament for the green banner.'[186]

Liberated from Ottoman institutions, the Bulgarian economy converged structurally on the Serbian. Most obviously this took place

---

[182] V. Aleksandrov, 'Iz istorijata na edin zapadnal pomin'k (Gajtanzhijstvoto v Karlovsko)', *Sp.BID*, IX (1905), p. 14.   [183] Vlajkov, *Panagjurishte*, p. 32.

[184] Mercia Macdermott, *A History of Bulgaria, 1393–1885* (London, 1962), pp. 237, 247.

[185] Manev, 'Kotlensko', p. 511.

[186] M. Arnaudov, *Iz minaloto na Kotel* (Sofia, 1931), p. 57.

through the peasantization of farming, which tended to lower land productivity, reduce the importance of the urban sector, and destroy rural industry. This was a 'one-off' process, but convergence was upon an economic system which itself was declining, because the shift away from stockraising was inadequately compensated by the expansion of cultivation. Both countries now had overwhelmingly peasant economies, heavily subsistence orientated. The decline of large-scale farming discouraged the growth of the market. Bulgarian proto-industry did, it is true, leave a residue of factory manufacturing to replace it, but the sector was as yet of slight significance.

8 Bosnia and Montenegro: political change and economic development 1878–1914

In 1878 the Habsburgs secured treaty rights at Berlin over Bosnia-Hercegovina, which they long had coveted, and quickly established a new administration. As neither Austria nor Hungary would assent to the province being governed by the other, it was placed under the control of the Common Austro-Hungarian Finance Ministry. To its officials, Bosnia was a backward and benighted territory which awaited Austria-Hungary's civilizing mission. Between 1878 and their expulsion in 1918, the Habsburg authorities attempted to weld their new province into the Austro-Hungarian polity and economy, treating the Bosnian economy as clay to be worked according to their prescriptions. Moral justification was lent by the (mendacious) claim that the Ottoman administration had been unable to maintain the rule of law and honest government, and had kept the Christian population in a state of near slavery.

To focus discussion on the economic impact of Habsburg rule on the Bosnian economy, we have constructed serials for farm production and the value added by large-scale industry. These figures invite a favourable appraisal of the Habsburg achievement in this territory.

Bosnian farming under the Austrian occupation

Bosnia's agrarian arrangements were a matter of extreme political sensitivity. Agrarian dissatisfaction had underlain the long-festering Christian revolt in Nevesinje which led to the toppling of Ottoman rule. The Austrians had connived at this, but violent Muslim opposition to the occupation speedily reminded them of the need to walk a tightrope between the factions. To win goodwill, the administration reacted to the tax grievance which had caused such trouble under the Ottomans, by cutting the state tithe back from 12.5 to 10 per cent. In practice this may not have lightened the burdens of farmers proportionately, because payment had to be made in cash according to tariff prices which are argued to have over-valued produce; besides this, the farmer was obliged to meet substantial transactions costs in getting his crops to

Map 3 Bosnia-Hercegovina under Austro-Hungarian rule 1878–1918

market.[1] On the other hand a consular observer of 1888, conceding that the tithes were burdensome, thought nevertheless that valuations were 'generally moderate both in regard to quantity and price'.[2]

The administration promoted technical improvement in farming through extension programmes, but it did not envisage an agrarian revolution. Formally, until 1908, the province remained un-annexed, because the Hungarians feared lest annexation might cause the province to slip under Croatian control. So it remained technically under Ottoman sovereignty. For this reason (ostensibly) and because the monarchy was not in the business of expropriating landed property, the occupation

[1] Božidar Nikaschinovitsch, *Bosnien und die Herzegovina unter der Verwaltung der österreichisch-ungarischen Monarchie ... Bd 1* (Berlin, 1901), pp. 62–3.
[2] GBC Bosnia 1888, p. 2.

authorities were content to administer Ottoman agrarian institutions more expensively and more energetically than their predecessors.[3] Relations between landlord and *kmet* continued to be based on the 1859 Bosnian *Safer* law,[4] which left the overwhelmingly Muslim propertied class in theoretical possession of their land, but fixed the proportion of the crops to be surrendered by tenants. The provincial authority, the *Landesregierung*, recognized the shortcomings of this arrangement, but claimed that under its aegis the condition of the tenants was much alleviated by scrupulous respect for rights in tenure. This was no great gain, since these rights had been protected adequately under the vilayet administration, and it is far from clear that the Austrian regime was any less corrupt, at least in the early 'carpet-bagger' years.

The Austrians anticipated that, in the longer term, tenants would elevate themselves to the status of 'free farmers' by buying out their landowners. The administration was convinced that to permit the *kmets* to sequester the land they tilled would be extremely costly, since the landowners would have to be compensated. Besides this, any such agrarian upheaval would retard the commercial and industrial development of the territory.[5]

In developmental terms, this argument would have had more to commend it had the abolition of labour services in 1859 resulted (as in Hungary in 1848) in the formation of a labour-hiring *Gutswirtschaft* economy. But there remained little *beglik* land, that is to say land owned by the *agas* but untenanted and available for direct farming. On most estates this amounted to a few gardens and paddocks, a shadow of the domain on which the peasants had once provided labour services.[6] The Bosnian system of regulated sharecropping with protected tenancies left landowners no control over the way the land was cropped, and prevented them from subdividing tenancies without agreement by the tenants. As the usufruct of the land was entirely apportioned by sharing (between landlord, *kmet* and the state) the landlord had little incentive to invest in yield-raising investments, and the tenant had a negative incentive to intensify his labour.

It is likely that in 1859, when the *Safer* law was put into effect, it distributed a higher share of the crop to the landowner than he could have secured within a free labour market. The *kmets* were even then free to leave their landlords,[7] but the system had worked because of the practical

[3] The Ottomans governed the province with 120 officials, but the new regime already had 600 in place as early as 1881. Peter F. Sugar, *Industrialization of Bosnia-Hercegovina 1878–1918* (Seattle, 1963), p. 29.   [4] See Chapter 5, pp. 134–7

[5] J. de Asboth, *An Official Tour through Bosnia and Herzegovina* (London, 1890), p. 167.

[6] Guillaume Capus, *A travers la Bosnie et l'Herzégovine* (Paris, 1896), p. 208.

[7] Jozo Tomasevich, *Peasants, Politics and Economic Change in Yugoslavia* (Stanford, CA, 1955), p. 106.

difficulties placed in the way of any tenant who desired to leave the holding, and the lack of alternative opportunities. Under Austro-Hungarian rule, however, the right to leave an employer became effective. The authorities repeatedly emphasized that the *kmet* was not bound to his master, to counter allegations equating *kmet* tenure with servile status.[8] The *kmet* could leave his holding only after the crops had been gathered and the landlord's share (*hak*) had been paid; but this was not unreasonable since he was paying rent in arrears. He also had the right to compensation for improvements.[9] But of more importance than the legal right to mobility was the strong demand for labour created by the occupation, and the weakening of local political control by the *agas*. The attractions of the labour market stripped the *čitluks* of much of their workforce,[10] and meant that *kmet* tenancies would only be retained if the returns enjoyed by the tenants equalled or exceeded those which they could earn in the market.

As a result, returns to land are claimed to have fallen, and as interest rates were high, the price of land fell to very low levels. Asboth, writing in the 1880s, provides figures which suggest that the great estates of the Posavina generated incomes which were trivial in relation to the area of land disposed. The *kmet* holdings into which the estates were divided were very substantial – Asboth claims they normally amounted to about 20 hectares. It seems probable, therefore, that tenants had to be attracted by holdings so large that they could secure relatively generous net returns (after the division of the crop) for the most minimal input of labour. Many *kmet* families had to hire in day labour 'for all field tasks'.[11] The result for the landlord would be low crop yields and hence a low rental per unit of land. So far from being oppressive, the terms offered to tenants attracted 'many European settlers' to 'accept the position of *kmets* under the Muslim *agas*'.[12]

The same source conceded that the system weakened incentives to improvement, and that the area under crops was exploited negligently.[13] Much arable remained 'fallow' (which probably means it served as grazing) and Asboth held that the 'natural indolence' of the peasants was combined with 'a certain amount of mischievous joy that they will thereby lessen their landlords' income'.[14]

The yields from animal husbandry, unlike the crops, were not shared with the landlords. Only very substantial flocks and herds were subject to taxation. In the 1880s, peasants enjoyed almost unlimited pasture rights in

[8] *Der Landwirthschaft in Bosnien und der Hercegovina* (Sarajevo,1899), p. 73.
[9] *IUBH*, 1906, p. 47.   [10] GBC Bosnia 1878, pp. 995, 997.
[11] Pop. Stjepo and V. Trifković, 'Sarajevska okolina (1) Sarajevsko polje', *NSZ*, V (Belgrade, 1908), p. 86.   [12] GBC Bosnia 1888, p. 2.   [13] Ibid.   [14] Asboth, *Official Tour*, p. 282.

the forests, which were now mainly state property, so it was to grazing that they devoted much of their effort.[15] The extensive techniques employed meant that the animals returned relatively low yields, but the favourable conditions for stockraising during the early years of the occupation led to an impressive expansion of herds and flocks. The bias of effort towards stockraising meant that the burdens imposed on *kmets* in respect of their arable crops captured a much smaller proportion of their total output.

Population growth over the ensuing decades made land increasingly scarce and therefore increased the attraction of *kmet* tenure, conferring on it the character of protected rent-controlled tenancy in which the *kmet* enjoyed a rising equity stake. For the *kmet*, this brought no satisfaction, for it meant only that his holding made him better off than if he had none, and did nothing to lighten his burdens, but for the landlord, the tenant became an encumbrance of which it was in his interest to be rid. So landlords tried to break *kmet* tenures. At least by 1902, and probably long before that, untenanted arable was worth more in the landlord's hands than land with *kmets* on it. Among the reasons why peasants were emigrating to Serbia at this time, it was alleged that landlords were encouraging their departure, in order to repossess the tenancies.[16]

The authorities promoted the gradual dissolution of the *čitluks* by encouraging peasants to buy their landlords out but they underestimated the determination of the Muslims to hold onto their land. When the Bosnian assembly at Sarajevo was established in 1910, the Muslim deputies formed a cohesive bloc to promote landlord interests. Their demands included ending the fixed crop division principle, in favour of dividing it according to local conditions and custom. This formula encoded the aim by landlords to increase their share of the crop wherever local market conditions would bear it. They also wanted the right to limit the extent of familial holdings, so as to split them and settle more families on them. Tenants would then be obliged to farm smaller holdings more intensively, and the value of the share-rent would therefore rise. The sponsors of this bill particularly sought the right to repossess land from unsatisfactory tenants.[17] The bill had no chance of becoming law, but it was at about this time that the Krajina was convulsed by a *kmet* uprising, caused, allegedly, by the illegal mass eviction of tenants by local authorities during an attempted strike against tax and rent.[18]

---

[15] GBC Bosnia 1888, p. 4.
[16] Hamdija Kapidžić, *Bosna i Hercegovina u vrijeme austro-ugarske vladavine* (Sarajevo, 1968), p. 28.
[17] *Ferdinand Schmid, Bosnien und die Hercegovina unter der Verwaltung Österreich-Ungarns* (Leipzig, 1914), p. 337.
[18] Vladimir Dedijer, *The Road to Sarajevo* (London, 1967), p. 203.

Table 8.1 *Bosnia-Hercegovina. Sectoral farm output 1879–1914*

	(in million crowns, 1910 prices)						crowns
Year	Animal	Animal products	Cash crops	Grain	Garden crops	Total	Total per capita
1879	29	25	4	17	2	77	76
1882–5	43	32	8	28	5	116	105
1886–90	53	37	12	39	9	150	124
1891–5	53	36	15	52	13	168	126
1896–1900	61	40	15	49	16	181	126
1901–5	59	38	14	47	15	174	114
1906–10	59	37	15	45	19	175	107
1911–14	61	37	17	60	20	194	113

For sources and method see BALKSTAT.

To have acceded to the demands of the landlords might have made the agrarian system more productive but it would have been politically disastrous to expropriate the *kmets* of their equity in the land they farmed. As neither landlord nor tenant could be expropriated, the authorities sidestepped the *kmet* problem, and confined themselves to making more credit available for speeding up redemptions.

Table 8.1 surveys long-run trends in aggregate farm production. Identification of these trends must necessarily be approximate, for the annual farming statistics from 1882 onwards do not include information on prices, which compels us to substitute Serbian prices of 1910 for those of Bosnia. Moreover, animal reproduction rates, carcass weights and milk yields have had to be assumed as constant for want of data.

Ostensibly, Table 8.1 signals that farm production rose sharply in the early years of the occupation, from the very low levels of 1879, which were, if anything slightly above those of 1869 and 1873 (see Table 5.1). But, from 1885, it levelled off. After an eleven-year plateau, per capita production fell away between 1896 and 1902, and then stabilized at the lower level until World War I. Per capita output in farming was lower by 11.5 per cent in 1911/13 than it had been in 1890/2. The initial rise in output was derived mainly from the expansion in cattle (whose numbers trebled between 1873 and 1895) while cereals, having fallen to a trough in 1879, did not surpass their 1865 output till 1890 (when in per capita terms cereal output was still well below that estimated for 1865).

This tendency for farm output per capita to rise during the first post-occupation years and subsequently to decline has also been inferred by Gonsalves and Table 8.1 provides affirmative evidence for her claim.[19] She argues that the improvement of personal security after the occupation, the use of money taxation and the access of peasants to more consumer goods permitted a sharp initial rise in output, but that the productive structure of farming stagnated; consequently, a rapidly rising rural population encountered supply side barriers to output growth, causing farm production to lag the growth of population. In particular, the *Landesregierung* converted the forests formerly held as Ottoman *mirieh* into state property. Though it continued to allow peasants controlled cutting rights,[20] it applied tough forestry laws, to prevent the attrition caused by grazing, and this created a shortage of pasture, forcing farmers to reduce their herds.[21]

Gonsalves concedes that although it declined in the latter years of Austro-Hungarian rule, farm income stood at a significantly higher level than under the Ottomans. Ostensibly the Table 8.1 figures uphold this argument. However (as Gonsalves also notes) Ottoman statistics, particularly on livestock, seriously understated, while the more comprehensive Austro-Hungarian figures did not. Reporting on the livestock census conducted under Austrian rule in 1879, the British consul in Sarajevo reckoned the increase over the figures collected from the Ottoman authorities in 1874 probably arose from the improved collection of data, and that, if anything, a real decline had occurred.[22] In his opinion, too, the 1879 crop was but one-third of the average. This implies that the 1865 crop estimates made by Thömmel reflect the norm for the Ottoman period better than the official figures for 1869 and 1873.[23] So the rise during the 1880s may include a large recovery element.[24]

Besides, the figures appear to show that Bosnian farm production leaped at the outset of the occupation period then stagnated, despite the growth of the labour force. As farm output does not advance in jumps followed by periods of stagnation, a rise followed by a flattening out seems to indicate recovery rather than a leap in efficiency. It is possible that the Austro-Hungarian period saw no net gain to farm output per head of the rural population over 1860s levels. However, this interpretation is probably excessively pessimistic. The veterinary services should have made an impact on livestock yields (treated in Table 8.1. as static) so the true trend

[19] Priscilla T. Gonsalves, 'A Study of the Habsburg Agricultural Programmes in Bosanska Krajina, 1878–1914', *Slavonic and East European Review*, LXIII (1985).
[20] Branislav Begović, *Razvojni put šumske privrede u Bosni i Hercegovini u periodu austrougarske uprave (1878–1918) sa posebnim osvrtom na eksploaticju šuma i industrijsku preradu drveta* (Sarajevo, 1978), p. 173.   [21] Gonsalves, 'Bosanska Krajina', p. 370.
[22] GBC Bosnia 1880, p. 437.   [23] GBC Bosnia 1879, p. 293.
[24] Sugar, *Industrialization*, p. 106.

in animal output was probably more favourable than represented in the table.

Doubtless, there was an efficiency cost in leaving the *kmet* issue in limbo. Yet the institutional framework did not prevent farmers from increasing the productivity of land use. They would have preferred, as the pressures of settlement rose, to clear more forest for grazing. But there was not much good cultivable land at the margin. Between 1886 and 1904 the arable area rose by 12.1 per cent, rural population by 32.4 per cent. The arable area in 1904, at 1.16 million hectares fell short by only 4.5 per cent of its extent in 1955–64.[25] Therefore farmers had to farm more intensively, and to some extent they succeeded. Yields per hectare rose by 65 per cent between 1886 and 1904 letting crop production rise by 85 per cent. Arable output per head rose by a respectable 40 per cent.

But it is the stagnation in stockraising after the mid-1890s which Gonsalves identified as the source of the weakness in farm production. Having peaked in 1896, both livestock and cultivation fell away together. Working from our estimate of the size of the animal stock in any given year, and of that proportion estimated to be breeding stock, livestock production rose only 2 per cent between 1885/7 and 1894/6 and by a further 13 per cent to its peak in 1911/13. Over this period as a whole, annual growth in livestock output, at 0.5 per cent per annum, lagged the 1.5 per cent annual growth of the rural population, which is why the growth of cereal output did not materialize into an overall productivity gain. Even so, the modest performance of the livestock sector indicates intensification since the amount of pasture and meadow declined by 5 per cent between 1886 and 1904. Whether livestock output was unnecessarily constrained by the forestry laws is unclear. In view of what happened in Serbia, the authorities were probably justified in keeping the peasants and their flocks out of them. Begović's view is that the policy should have been more rigorously applied, as peasant access to forest land inhibited farm rationalization.[26]

Though supply side influences – in particular, the increasing lack of grazing – were of critical importance in Bosnia, graziers also faced export difficulties. Like those of Serbia, Bosnian livestock surpluses had to be consigned almost exclusively to Austria-Hungary. Dalmatia absorbed part of this supply, but the principal consumer markets of the monarchy were only accessible through Hungarian controlled Croatia-Slavonia. Bosnian supplies enjoyed (in theory) duty free access, but, in practice, they were subject to interference in the Hungarian interest. Bosnia suf-

---

[25] Table, Schmid, *Bosnien*, p. 413; Broekhuisen, *Atlas*, p. 106.
[26] Begović, *Razvojni put*, p. 172.

fered intermittent market closures in the early 1880s (always on veterinary grounds) but the profitable central European market for pigs encouraged a fast growing export trade. From around 83,000 pigs a year taken by Austria-Hungary before the occupation, the export had advanced to 139,000 head in 1888 and peaked at 345,000 in 1894. Herd size rose correspondingly, as tax was paid on 126,000 pigs in 1888 and 234,000 in 1895.[27]

The relationship between the stock of pigs and the volume exported was close for Bosnia because pigs were raised mainly for the external market, and there was little subsistence demand. In 1895, on complaint of swine fever, the Hungarians closed the frontier to Bosnian pigs (as also to those of Serbia) and required future exports to be slaughtered before admission. Bosnia had virtually no meat packing capacity, and the volume of trade plunged by 90 per cent.[28] It never recovered, even to exploit the shortages created by Austria's commercial war with Serbia in 1906–11, and the number of pigs sagged. The tax yield from the pig stock plunged from 141,000 kr. in 1896 to 78,000 in 1902 though the rate at which it was levied was unchanged.[29]

The disruption of cross-border trade extended also to cattle. They were the object of intermittent closures between 1895 and 1898, though exports subsequently returned to normal levels. In the Serbian case, it was doubtful whether there were any livestock epidemics to justify border closures, but there is no question that Bosnia (like Hungary) was gripped both by swine-fever and foot-and-mouth disease at least till 1898.[30] This provided the Hungarians with unimpeachable sanitary justification for what they were doing, but that was not their reason for doing it. Livestock disease was no barrier to the import of livestock from the Balkans in the absence of political pressure to exploit it.[31]

Hungarian manipulation of Bosnia's export trade bears some responsibility for the poor out-turn of the farming sector. However, demand difficulties were superimposed upon a weakening supply structure, and accelerated a decline which would have occurred anyway. Though a more efficient agrarian system might have strengthened farm production, the negative trend in Bosnian farm output in the 1890s was also experienced in Bulgaria, Montenegro and Serbia within totally different institutional frameworks. We cannot ignore their common

[27] *Statistische Tabellen für Bosnien und die Hercegovina*, I, *Landwirthschaft* (Sarajevo, 1896), pp. 286–91.

[28] Hašim Šerić, *Istoriski osvrt na razvoj stočarstva u Bosni i Hercegovini* (Sarajevo, 1953), pp. 65–7.   [29] *IUBH*, 1906, p. 401.

[30] GBC Bosnia 1896, pp. 2, 9; 1897, p. 3; 1899, p. 2.

[31] See M. Palairet, 'The Influence of Commerce on the Changing Structure of Serbia's Peasant Economy 1860–1912' (Ph.D. Edinburgh, 1976), p. 111.

underlying problems – in particular the failure to adapt to intensive live-stock farming.

Montenegro after 1878

During the relatively tranquil period between 1862 and 1875, Prince Nikola re-equipped his army with Russian assistance,[32] and the Russians encouraged his expansionist appetites. In 1875 the Montenegrins again fostered insurrection in the Hercegovina, despite Nikola's misgivings in view of the risks involved.[33] The events of 1875–8 embroiled the Ottomans in more general warfare, which worked to Montenegro's advantage, and Nikola's army acheived notable successes in the field. So in the aftermath of the Berlin conference Montenegro emerged with 87 per cent more territory, and enhanced national prestige.[34]

The territories Montenegro acquired were more fertile than the mountain heartland, and the Muslim (mainly Albanian) presence was significant. The agrarian regime was highly expropriative. In 1869, the people of Kolašin complained that they had to surrender an eighth of their crop in imperial tithe, and half of it to their *aga*, as well as giving him one day a week of labour, and certain other dues.[35] Though such complaints were exaggerated, they indicate that peasants had to surrender a large proportion of their production in rent and tax.

These revenues sustained the correspondingly substantial urban population of officials and landowning families and those who supplied them with goods and services. As we showed in Chapter 1, the annexation of Ottoman territory in 1876–80 brought four substantial towns (Bar, Ulcinj, Podgorica and Nikšić) into a country which hitherto had no urban economy worth speaking of.

By acquiring this territory, the state was able to reward some of its soldiers at the expense of former Muslim estates in the Podgorica plain. But the principal gainers were the settled peasantry of the area who mostly became proprietors of land they had hitherto sharecropped. Despite their treaty obligations, the Montenegrins swindled the Muslim landowners, large and small, out of most of the value of their assets.[36] The former

---

[32] Gabriel Frilley and Jovan Wlahovitj, *Le Monténégro contemporain* (Paris, 1876), pp. 64–76, 91, 301–11, 320.

[33] David Harris, *Diplomatic History of the Balkan Crisis of 1875–1878. The First Year* (Stanford, CA, 1936), p. 129.

[34] Territory expanded by 4,400 sq km to 9,475 according to Žarko Bulajić, *Agrarni odnosi u Crnoj Gori* (Titograd, 1959), p. 13. However, this commonly used figure overstated according to Austrian military maps, which indicated only 8,629 sq km See J. Cvetić, 'Površina i granična linija Crne Gore', *Delo*, XX (Belgrade, 1898), pp. 483–5.

[35] Bulajić, *Agrarni odnosi*, p. 63.   [36] Ibid., pp. 141–2.

Map 4 Montenegro within its frontiers of 1881–1912 (1859 frontier
is marked //////////)
Source: Radusinović, *Stanovništvo Crne Gore*

urban economy was therefore made redundant. Its income base diminished correspondingly and urban population still more, because the
Muslims departed not only because of economic distress but also through
fear of maltreatment. Indeed urban population overadjusted, leaving the
country undersupplied with urban services, which the Slav population
was neither qualified nor inclined to fill.

Economically, annexation solved few problems. The acquisition of former Muslim property did not long satisfy Montenegrin land hunger, since the balance between land and population worsened as a result of the annexations. Resumed population growth caused the balance further to deteriorate, though it was masked in the 1880s by a run of good harvests. Opportunities for banditry had diminished, and external grazing grounds became increasingly hard to find.

The ineradicable problem of poverty, and the belief among Montenegrins that a living could not be won from within the existing frontiers of the state, impelled Nikola's government towards continued expansionism. Blocked from expanding into Hercegovina and Sanjak by the Austrian army, and lacking ethnically based irredenta beyond his other frontiers, his aims became imperialistic. He wanted to carve a greater Montenegrin state from the Ottoman Albanian territories, which he would rule from Prizren. An opportunity presented itself when, goaded by the Turanizing activities pursued by the Young Turk regime, some of the Albanian tribes rose to assert their own national claims in 1910. The Montenegrins, seeking an opportunity and excuse for invading northern Albania and taking Shkodër, backed the insurgent Catholic Malisori. Turkish reprisals against the Albanian insurgents and border incidents provided the immediate background to the Montenegrin theatre in the First Balkan War, which broke out once the Balkan states had found a way of co-operating militarily despite their mutual jealousies.[37]

If Montenegrin military expansionism had taken place in an earlier era, then, as the Montenegrins brought more and more resources under their own control, they would have evolved into a warrior caste (similar to the Turks themselves) and would have secured the resources they needed by exercising a feudal hegemony over a servile and ethnically differentiated peasantry. The big land accessions in Albania arising from the Balkan War of 1912/13 provided precisely this opportunity, as they brought within the state large non-Montenegrin populations. In the view of Mary E. Durham: 'Judging by their talk, they proposed to live in future as a marauding army. Never fond of work, they declared that they had conquered enough people to do the work for them, and looked forward to a life of something like slave-driving.'[38]

Farm performance in Montenegro

Neither arable nor animal production kept pace with population in the long run, and between 1905 and 1910 the arable area fell steadily from

---

[37] Mary E. Durham, *The Struggle for Scutari* (London, 1914), pp. 7–8, 13–18, 21, 25–6, 127, 161.   [38] Ibid., pp. 293, 252.

33,500 hectares to 29,100. More important to the decline in total farm output was the gradual breakdown of transhumant stockraising. The worst bottleneck developed in the winter fodder supply, of which acute shortages were apparent by 1890.[39] The increasing difficulties of the pastoral economy caused its output to peak as early as 1885, from which level it fell by about 13 per cent to 1909/12. To compensate the fodder shortage, the area of meadow rose by 19.6 per cent. Comparison of 1889 and 1900 data by Bulajić shows a rise from 64 per cent to 66 per cent in the proportion of taxpayers holding meadows, and growth of 26 per cent in the number holding fragments of less than 36 ares.[40] This tallies with the description of peasants struggling to feed diminishing flocks by converting communal grazing into fragments of private meadow.[41]

The division of communal pasture was itself one cause of the developing long-run crisis of transhumance, yet it was also a symptom of more fundamental difficulty. Expanding pastoral production had entailed 'borrowing' lowland resources. The progressive colonization of the higher levels by converting *katuns* into villages with still higher *katuns* of their own increased the proportion of stockraisers with insufficient winter fodder. Moreover, as the density of lowland settlement rose, overwintering migrations by upland graziers became increasingly unwelcome, and conflicts broke out between upland and lowland peasants over grazing rights. Especially after the redrawing of boundaries in 1878, overwintering migrations with livestock were increasingly curtailed.[42] The stock of land also deteriorated in quality. Slash-burn methods were used to clear the woodlands.[43] Deforestation caused soil erosion, and intensified droughts.

Table 8.2 estimates the farm product of Montenegro between 1855 and 1912, at 1911 prices. As crop yields were only available for 1910,[44] we have taken as a proxy in earlier years the yields per hectare achieved in neighbouring Dalmatia. The Montenegrin crop area, as recorded annually in the *dacija* registers and summaries, was assumed to be allocated between crops in the same proportion as in 1910, and the area for each crop was multiplied by the Dalmatian yield figures. Constant yields to livestock numbers over time have also been assumed. As 97.4 per cent of the cattle of Montenegro were still of the unimproved *Buša* type in the

[39] F. Jergović, 'Stočarstvo u Crnoj Gori', *Glas Crnogorca*, 2 Sept. 1891, p. 3.
[40] Bulajić, *Agrarni odnosi*, pp. 154–6.
[41] See Petar Šobajić, 'Bjelopavlići i Pješivci. Plemena u Crnogorskim Brdima', *NiPS*, XV (Belgrade, 1923), pp. 255–6.
[42] Milenko Filipović, 'Odlaženje na Prehranu', *Glasnik Geografskog društva*, XXVII (Belgrade, 1947), p. 89.
[43] Jovan Erdeljanović, 'Kuči, pleme u Crnoj Gori', *NSZ*, IV (Belgrade, 1907), p. 242.
[44] In Bulajić, *Agrarni odnosi*, pp. 19–20.

Table 8.2 *Montenegro. Sectoral farm output 1855–1912
(000 kr of 1911)*

Year	Animal products	Cash crops	Field crops	Total	Per capita output
1855	5,535	1,100	2,414	9,050	–
1863	5,513	1,050	2,423	8,985	141
1868	6,439	2,241	2,556	11,235	168
1869	6,464	702	2,538	9,704	143
1873	7,764	986	1,816	10,567	150
1880	8,955	3,083	7,794	19,832	143
1883–5	14,435	1,807	9,009	25,251	173
1889–90	12,290	1,688	8,309	22,286	145
1893	11,380	1,492	7,636	20,508	129
1895	13,140	8,153	8,153	23,482	145
1897	14,393	2,557	4,997	21,947	133
1900	13,443	1,698	6,893	22,035	130
1903	14,306	3,158	5,822	23,286	132
1905	12,463	1,399	6,049	19,910	111
1906–10	13,139	3,111	8,558	24,808	133
1911–12	13,051	2,192	8,825	24,069	124

For sources and calculation see BALKSTAT.

1930s, this is probably not unreasonable.[45] However, the procedure will understate year to year livestock yield fluctuations.

These statistics indicate that the Montenegrin farm economy was subjected to strong Malthusian pressures. Output (when corrected for territorial changes) remained obstinately static despite population growth of 1 per cent per annum, so between 1863 and 1912 the linear trend in per capita output declined by 20 per cent. By the mid-1880s, the rural economy had reached its productive limits, with a zero marginal return to population increase. Underlying this stagnation was a decline in livestock output between 1883/5 and 1910/12 of 9.1 per cent, with no growth in crop output to compensate. (Arable output declined in absolute terms by 1.7 per cent, if Montenegrin yields followed those of Dalmatia – an optimistic assumption).

[45] Tomasevich, *Peasants*, p. 523.

The only slight gain was in cash crops. Their output rose between 1883/5 and 1910/12 by 29 per cent because of growth in wine production. No growth was achieved in other cash crops. A key activity within this sector was the gathering of wild plant produce. In 1895, sumach (for the tanning trade) chrysanthemum (for pyridine) and laurel leaves (for wreaths) earned 146,000 crowns.[46] But demand for sumach and chrysanthemum declined as surrogates displaced them and by 1905–10 earnings from these commodities had shrunk to 28,000 crowns a year.[47] Tobacco had shown promise as a cash crop up to 1903, but in 1904 the state imposed monopsony purchase prices which were so unattractive that, by 1910, cultivation had fallen by 70 per cent.[48] Olive cultivation, having peaked in 1897, declined because attempts to spread it beyond the confines of Bar and Ulcinj failed for climatic reasons.[49] Stagnation in income from these products meant that export earnings continued to come mainly from livestock, hides and wool. As their supply was falling, growth in export volume meant the diversion of these resources from subsistence consumption.

Bosnia: industrialization from above

In justifying their administration of Bosnia-Hercegovina, the Habsburg authorities laid emphasis on the development of large-scale industry. Performance is measurable in indicator form for the period 1881–1914, and can be compared with that of industry in Serbia and Bulgaria.

Because Bosnia's mineral wealth had been surveyed during the Ottoman period, but had not been opened up, the Habsburgs' newly acquired territory offered a promising field for resource based development, though heavy investment was needed for transport infrastructure and processing capacity. The *Landesregierung* wanted to open up its resources as rapidly as financial and political constraints would allow. The lack of existing infrastructure, markets and industrial labour skills limited the attractions of the province to private investors.[50] So the *Landesregierung*'s industrial policy was far more interventionist than any pursued either in Austria or in Hungary. Till the mid-1890s its primary

---

[46] GBC Montenegro 1895, pp. 8–9.
[47] P. A. Rovinski, *Chernogoriya v eya proshlom i nastoyashtem. Geografiya – Istoriya – Etnografiya – Arheologiya – Sovremenie polozhenie*, II/1 (St Petersburg, 1897), p. 625; Mirčeta Djurović, *Trgovački kapital u Crnoj gori u drugoj polovini XIX i početkom XX vijeka* (Cetinje, 1958), gatefold Table A between pp. 244 and 245.
[48] 'Montenegrin Economics – I', *Montenegrin Bulletin*, 4–6 (1 Sept. 1918), pp. 11–12.
[49] Rovinski, *Chernogoriya*, II/1, pp. 610–16, 618.
[50] Dževad Juzbašić, 'Some features of the economic development of Bosnia and Herzegovina between 1878 and 1914', *Survey* (Sarajevo, 1984), p. 148.

effort took the form of railway building. Because of Hungarian political pressures, the Bosnian railway net bound Bosnia primarily to Hungary, through its port at Fiume (Rijeka). The opening of railways then permitted large-scale coal production at Kreka and, around the turn of the century, the establishment of export-generating metals, chemicals and timber enterprises. Indeed the development of these industries became necessary if only to create traffic revenues for the railways.

The *Landesregierung* established and operated a substantial proportion of the province's industrial capacity, and was not averse to nationalising existing private firms. In 1907, the state sector accounted for 32.7 per cent of large-scale industry, in terms of pay-roll volume.[51] Among its first actions had been the monopolization of tobacco and salt. The installation of two large state run tobacco factories in Sarajevo and Mostar in 1880 provided the initial industrial boost, though the subsequent growth of this industry was slow.[52] The role conceded to private enterprise was strictly controlled by concession procedures, and the acquisition by the authorities of large equity stakes gave much of the private sector in mining and industry a parastatal character. For example, the *Landesregierung* conceded all significant mineral deposits to a company, Gewerkschaft Bosnia, in which it took 20 per cent of the shares, and bought out the outside stockholders in 1886. Only in a judicial sense can the firm be regarded as 'private'. In 1885, the Bosnia company transferred its iron mining concession to the newly formed Vareser Eisenindustrie A. G., in which 53 per cent of the equity was held by the administration, the rest by a Viennese bank. This company monopolized iron mining at Vareš, displacing several small-scale operators, and subsequently established a very profitable ironworks there. A company formed in 1892 to build a factory at Zenica to refine pig iron from Vareš also had a state participation of 25 per cent, and the administration and its officials held substantial interests in most other major industrial firms.[53]

As farming tended to be subsistence orientated, and its output static, it is unlikely to have generated much growth in market consumption. There is a consensus in the literature that resources for state activity were wrung out of agriculture by the exertion of downward pressures on rural consumption. Hauptmann emphasizes the social costs of industrialization, which he claims was sustained by the forced export of agrarian produce with the consequent depression of mass living standards.[54]

[51] Calculated from table in Schmid, *Bosnien*, p. 545.
[52] Ambroz Kapor, *Prerada duvana u Bosni i Hercegovini od prvih početaka do 1923 godine* (Sarajevo, 1954), pp. 20, 71–2.   [53] Sugar, *Industrialization*, pp. 52–3, 104–12.
[54] Juzbašić, review of Ferdinand Hauptmann, *Die Osterreichish-ungarische Herrschaft in Bosnien und der Hercegovina 1878–1918* (Graz, 1983), in *Godišnjak društva istoričara Bosne i Hercegovine*, XXXV (Sarajevo,1984), p. 153.

Regardless of whether this analysis is correct, little large-scale enterprise developed to exploit domestic demand. Most capacity created during the Austro-Hungarian period was orientated to external markets. Its primary function was to export the province's coal, minerals and timber either in raw or semi-manufactured form. According to Hrelja, export based industries employed 85.79 per cent of the industrial labour force.[55]

A case can be made for describing timber as a leading sector. While mining and metals production were largely confined to state enterprise, the *Landesregierung* operated a generous long-term concession policy towards private forestry and timber enterprises, because it urgently needed the timber royalties they paid. The opportunities so created engendered a lively response.

Bosnia's oak forests had been exploited during the Ottoman period for barrel staves, which were sold mainly to the French vintners. At the time of the occupation, the industry was producing at a very depressed level because of a slump in demand which lasted till 1881, and because supply was inhibited by the political disturbances of the mid-1870s.[56] Machine technology was not used. Even the largest firm, Morpurgo and Parente, organized its 2,300 workers on the domestic system. The administration accorded priority to the expansion of the stave trade, because its recovery would not have to wait upon the completion of expensive investments in infrastructure and modern plant. The export of staves grew at a remarkable pace once prices started to revive – from 2.5 million in 1883/4 to 25 million in 1890,[57] though in the late 1890s it went into decline partly because of depletion.

By this time the structure of the timber industry was changing rapidly because of concessions awarded for the large-scale saw-milling of coniferous softwoods. This industry required heavy investment outlays on sawmills and access infrastructure. Therefore concessions were awarded to enable their operators to achieve economies of very large-scale production. Consequently,the industry came to be dominated by two firms (out of eighteen) which accounted between them for 68.6 per cent of all cutting.[58]

Of these, the largest was the firm of Otto Steinbeis, a Bavarian industrialist, who established his first Bosnian saw-mill at Dobrljin in 1893, and a second larger one at Drvar in 1901. The Steinbeis firm expanded to

[55] Kemal Hrelja, 'Razvoj industrije u Bosni i Hercegovini do drugog svjetskog rata', *AHOI*, I (Zagreb, 1974) p. 29.
[56] Branislav Begović, 'Kretanje proizvodnje i eksporta hrastove duge u periodu austro-ugarske uprave u Bosni i Hercegovini', *AHOI*, VI (Zagreb, 1979), pp. 45–6.
[57] Ibid., pp. 51, 56.   [58] Begović, *Razvojni put*, p. 88.

employ 10,000 workers. A second large saw-milling business, the Austro-German partnership of Eisler & Ortlieb was established at Zavidovići, in 1899. Both firms constructed networks of forest railways, Steinbeis building 425.4 kilometres and Eisler 159km. These lines were for the most part solidly built engineering works which were later integrated into the Yugoslav railway system. The industrial installations of both firms were technically advanced, and their production costs were low. Begović describes the Eisler – Ortlieb plant as among the largest and most up to date in Europe at that time.[59] So rapid was the growth of the Bosnian timber industry between about 1893 and 1904 that its exports came to be viewed by the international market as a threat to its stability.[60]

The claim of the timber industry to a leading sector role rests not only on its impressive expansion and its significance as an industrial aggregate, but also on the linkages it created with other industries. From 1907 onwards, it provided the basis for cellulose pulp manufacture (also for export) when the Steinbeis firm built a pulp mill in partnership with a Swiss paper manufacturer. Its aim was to utilize the waste timber which could not be sawn profitably, and which had hitherto been burned off.[61] Though most timber was exported as sawn planks and barrel staves, it also provided raw material for several substantial joinery firms.

Timber also provided a key input into the metals and chemicals industries. Despite the large scale on which the Vareš ironworks operated, it smelted with beech charcoal, which it obtained from the state forests on privileged terms.[62] The alternative would have been to import coke since the brown coal of Kreka was unsuitable for smelting. Charcoal smelting was not inefficient considering the circumstances, and the very pure metal it produced made the Zenica rolling mill a viable proposition. But, because of the high cost of charcoal won by traditional methods, the administration wanted the Vareš ironworks supplied with charcoal produced by industrial dry distillation. So, in 1897, with the backing of a German manufacturer and the Leipziger Bank, it established a parastatal enterprise at Teslić for the dry distillation of beech timber. The supply of this enterprise accounted for a further 7.5 per cent of all timber cutting. The attraction to the German partners lay in concessions which enabled them cheaply to secure and process the distillates and transport the products. Initially they concentrated on producing methyl alcohol, which was sold to the aniline industry, but the development of smokeless explosive

[59] Ibid., p. 70.
[60] Kemal Hrelja, *Industrija Bosne i Hercegovine do kraja prvog svjetskog rata* (Belgrade, 1961), pp. 64–5.   [61] Begović, *Razvojni put*, p. 67.
[62] *Die Österreichisch-ungarische Monarchie in Wort und Bild. Bosnien und Hercegovina* (Vienna, 1901), p. 483.

caused them to shift to producing acetone.[63] Though never very successful financially, the Teslić plant was in 1914 the largest acetone producer in
Austria-Hungary. The state forestry enterprise also furnished raw
material for a match factory which was established in 1900 outside
Sarajevo by a Jewish firm. This was one of the few significant enterprises
set up by local businessmen.[64]

Timber, iron and coal were not the only elements in a resource-based
programme of industrialization. Bosnia's resources of chalk, water power
and rock salt were also exploited for the production of industrial chemicals. The province acquired several large chemical works, including an
ammonia-soda plant at Lukavac which drew on brine supplied from the
Tuzla wells, and a hydro powered electro-chemical factory at Jajce.
Outputs of the latter included caustic soda and calcium carbide. On a
smaller scale, the chemical industry produced for home demands which
were met by a small oil refinery and a soap-works.

Under Austro-Hungarian rule, Bosnia's large-scale industrial production advanced to a level which far surpassed that formed either in
Bulgaria or Serbia. The comparison is displayed in Table 8.3. The figures
for Bosnia in 1907 are taken from the sole census of businesses undertaken in the province. It distinguished between large and small establishments and provided data on employment and pay-rolls, but not on
production quantities or values.[65]

The comparative information assembled in Table 8.3 is therefore based
on these employment statistics for large-scale establishments. Immediately evident is the relatively large size of production unit in Bosnia,
characteristic of Gerschenkron type 'industrialization from above'.
Insofar as the figures are comparable (and the comparison does not
favour Bosnia because of its more restrictive definition of large scale)
Bosnia in 1907 was three times as industrialized as Serbia in 1910 and
five times as industrialized as Bulgaria in 1910/11; and by 1910/11,
Bosnian industrial production had expanded by a further 13 per cent.[66]

To give a rough figure for net large-scale industrial output in Bosnia-
Hercegovina in 1907, we note that Bulgarian net output in 1910/11 was
3.6 times the wage and salary roll, implying a net output for Bosnia in

[63] Begović, *Razvojni put*, pp. 38–40.
[64] Branislav Begović, 'Sedam decenija razvojnog puta industrije šibica u Bosni i
Hercegovini u svjetlu arhivske gradje', *Narodni šumar*, XXVI (1972), pp. 211–15, 371.
[65] These were published in *IUBH*, 1908, pp. 119–202, and are synopsized in Schmid,
Bosnien, p. 545.
[66] Industrial employment and horsepower figures for other years were derived from statistics in the *Landesregierung*'s annual reports, which aggregated values for firms visited by
the factory inspectorate. They show much smaller employment totals than the 1907
census because of their lack of comprehensiveness.

Table 8.3 *Large-scale industry indicators in Bosnia, 1907, Bulgaria and Serbia (1910)*

	Population (millions)	Establishments	Employees per establishment	Employees per 000 inhabitants	Pay-roll (kr) per establishment	Pay-roll (kr) per inhabitant
Bosnia	1.81	187	166.9	17.2	20,538	11.3
Bulgaria	4.34	333	45.2	3.5	9,614	2.2
Serbia	2.92	465	34.6	5.5	10,144	3.5

Source:
Palairet, 'Habsburg Industrial Achievement in Bosnia-Hercegovina, 1878–1914', p. 149.

1907 of around 74 million crowns. On the eve of the Balkan Wars, Bosnia's net large-scale industrial output was probably substantially greater than the combined net large-scale output of Bulgaria and Serbia.

At the time of the occupation there had been little large-scale industry in Bosnia-Hercegovina, so the structure which existed in 1907 resulted from sustained high rates of production growth. To reconstruct Bosnia's industrial performance from 1881 to 1915, in Table 8.4, we identified thirty-three industrial outputs from which it was possible to construct production serials for mining, metals, engineering, timber, paper and pulp, chemicals, and food, drink and tobacco. This left a small (4 per cent) residual for which data is lacking, including stone and glass, leather, textiles, clothing, printing and power. The fulcrum of the serial was, as in Table 8.3, the 1907 business census. To generate composite serials representing all-industry value added, it was assumed that pay-roll share in 1907 accorded with sectoral share of value added, since no data was available for industrial capital stock or profits. The output of each sector in 1907 was weighted by its share of the total large-scale industrial pay-roll in that year, and the branches of industry for which information was lacking were assumed to constitute a constant 4 per cent proportion of total industrial value added. The general index presented in Table 8.4 below is standardized by setting total large-scale industrial value-added in 1907 at 1,000. Its ambit extends to the same activities and definition of scale used for the Bosnian data in Table 8.3.

The all-industry index displayed in the final column of Table 8.4. indicates very high annual growth of 12.4 per cent over the period 1881–1913. This index gives the misleading impression that industrialization started virtually from scratch after the occupation. However, some activities picked up by the index (in particular metals and salt-making) had already been established during the Ottoman period,[67] but these enterprises were not concessioned by the *Landesregierung*; At Prijedor, ten 'small' firms extracted 15,000 tonnes of iron ore and smelted 1,600 tonnes of pig in 1882.[68] Similarly the salt-works established in 1885 at Tuzla took over supplies of brine which had been exploited under Ottoman rule, and which were probably still producing salt up to that year.

Though it therefore flatters the Austro-Hungarian achievement for the very early years, the index is reasonably rugged from the early 1890s, and reflects the reality of very rapid growth in the 1890s and a pronounced deceleration after 1906. The heyday of Bosnian industrialization was the period in office of Count Benjamin Kállay, who directed the

[67] See above Chapter 5, pp. 154–5.   [68] Sugar, *Industrialization*, p. 106.

Table 8.4. *Bosnia-Hercegovina 1881–1915: Index of large-scale industrial value-added (all industries 1907=1,000)*

Year	Coal	Minerals	Metals	Engineering	Timber	Paper + Pulp	Tobacco + Food	Chemical	All-Industries
1881	2	—	—	6	2	—	18	—	29
1882	3	15	—	7	2	—	28	—	58
1883	5	26	—	7	2	—	28	—	70
1884	6	37	—	6	4	—	30	—	87
1885	8	32	—	7	7	—	31	1	89
1886	10	31	—	7	7	—	35	1	95
1887	12	28	—	8	11	2	37	2	105
1888	15	12	—	8	7	2	43	2	93
1889	17	15	—	9	7	2	39	3	110
1890	20	19	—	9	21	2	46	2	146
1891	25	22	—	10	37	2	50	3	155
1892	36	28	—	11	29	2	53	4	170
1893	46	24	—	13	44	2	57	4	198
1894	56	32	—	15	58	2	61	5	239
1895	67	40	6	21	35	2	64	28	273
1896	75	50	10	26	37	2	61	36	308
1897	77	50	22	28	33	2	66	32	324
1898	92	58	25	33	38	2	64	40	368
1899	103	63	27	36	100	2	71	59	482
1900	132	95	40	44	140	2	69	48	595
1901	149	96	49	47	152	2	68	68	659
1902	142	100	74	48	153	2	70	81	698
1903	157	81	75	57	196	2	75	73	746
1904	162	87	68	61	253	2	84	88	839
1905	181	99	61	62	256	2	84	114	895
1906	199	105	67	68	292	2	85	109	966
1907	208	103	67	76	278	23	87	118	1000
1908	221	107	71	79	285	56	85	109	1055
1909	233	87	63	84	303	69	93	125	1102
1910	237	80	71	86	280	73	92	124	1087
1911	258	85	77	91	279	83	100	113	1131
1912	286	98	83	102	288	83	108	122	1219
1913	282	126	74	103	279	82	104	115	1215
1914	270	102	62	98	173	57	118	90	1009
1915	268	87	38	93	73	20	121	65	795

Landesregierung from 1882 and died in tenure of his post in 1903. Kállay was an extremely energetic administrator, who maintained throughout his term a passionate commitment to what he construed as Austria-Hungary's mission to civilize the province. Over the period of his administration, large-scale industrial production grew at a mean 12.9 per cent per annum. Even if we disregard the problematic earlier figures, his last decade witnessed expansion of 14.2 per cent per year, from a base which was no longer of negligible size. Kállay's achievements did not come cheaply. He was, theoretically, required to run a bootstraps administration which would not burden the Austro-Hungarian Finance Ministry with the cost of his developmental programmes. However, his innovative use of the financial resources of his ministry and his willingness to build up a large public debt indirectly required subsidization from common Austro-Hungarian funds. Building the railways entailed raising large external credits, saddling the provincial treasury with rapidly rising debts to the Viennese banks. As these railways generated little profit, this placed severe strains on the revenue. The industrial enterprises also burdened the provincial finances. Many private ventures were carried only by heavy state subsidy, alongside a crop of prestige projects of dubious economic value. In Kállay's words: 'I at least would have had the courage' to make 'material sacrifices ... in order to get these industries established'.[69] (The material sacrifices were not of course borne by Kállay himself: he had few qualms about profiting personally from them.)

The extremely high rate of industrial growth sustained in the 1890s (15 per cent per annum) inevitably decelerated, though it continued at 8.4 per cent per annum between 1900 and 1906, and a faltering 3.3 per cent per annum during the last seven pre-war years (1906–13). Sugar associates the deceleration of growth with the change of leadership after Kállay's death in 1903 as his successor, Count Istvan Burián (1903–12), was less well disposed towards the programme, and more restrictive in awarding concessions. To some extent this was a necessary fiscal retrenchment. At the time of Kállay's death, the Bosnian treasury was under serious pressure. Provincial expenditure had soared from 13.6 million crowns (equivalent) in 1882 to 48.8 million in 1903. The costs were being passed on to the population in the form of sharply rising taxation.

Yugoslav writers argue that the development of Bosnia-Hercegovina was retarded by its colonial status, and that the interests of the province were sacrificed to those of Hungary and Austria. We have already noted the negative effects of Hungarian interference with the Bosnian livestock

---

[69] Ibid., p. 57.

trades; analogous interference in the industrial field became apparent in the years following Kállay's death. Kállay himself had largely ignored these pressures but Burián could not. The conflict of interest was not a straightforward one of industrial Austria restricting its colony to the supply of raw materials and semi-manufactures rather than letting it produce finished goods which might compete with its own outputs. The problem was complicated by powerful political pressures which emanated from Hungary, itself a primary producing territory. The Hungarians wanted the Bosnian administration to run budget surpluses to meet occupation costs and lighten the burden on their own finances. This burden had grown through Kállay's financial manipulations. Although Kállay had rebuffed the Hungarians on this issue, his successor did not. Fiscal rectitude meant easing up on industrialization,[70] so Hungarian demands were motivated by the competitive threat that industrialization in Bosnia posed to their own interests. Burián's less supportive regime of subsidies affected certain hot-house enterprises, for example a paper mill which eventually closed, and probably also the inefficient sugar industry. Milling, too, was severely restricted in the Hungarian interest. The match enterprise was another victim of Hungarian pressures. The Hungarians had tried to prevent its ever being concessioned, and although Kállay's administration overrode their objections, the firm was compelled to produce safety matches, though Hungarian producers faced no similar restriction. Burián's administration did nothing to compensate the firm when approached in 1905.[71]

Iron ore mining and iron smelting, after rapid expansion in the 1890s, ceased to expand much after the turn of the century. The Hungarians (and to a lesser extent, the Austrians) wanted Bosnian iron ore for their own smelters, and restricted the development of smelting capacity on Bosnian soil. This caused protracted disputes over the allocation of iron ore mined in Bosnia, checking the expansion of smelting, and leading to the otherwise inexplicable failure of the authorities to open up the rich ore-field of Prijedor, at a time when the inferior Vareš beds were beginning to suffer depletion.[72]

It was the cessation of growth in timber exports from 1904–6 onward which brought about most of the deceleration in industrial growth. Decline in the export of barrel staves and stagnation in the export of sawn timber can both be attributed to political interference. The decline of the barrel stave industry in Bosnia owed much to pressures by producers in Croatia-Slavonia which caused Burián in 1904 not to renew existing

[70] Juzbašić, 'Features', p. 153.　　[71] Begović, 'Sedam decenija', pp. 215–16, 371–3.

[72] Ferdo Hauptman, 'Borba za bosansko željezo pred prvi svjetski rat', *Godišnjak istorijskog društva Bosne i Hercegovine*, X (1959), pp. 168–92.

contracts in Bosnia.[73] Weak, relatively undercapitalized timber interests – in Austria as well as in Hungary – also wanted Bosnian timber production forced within the timber cartel, because Germany had raised its timber tariff in 1900, and prices in the Habsburg monarchy remained weak from then onwards.[74]

The administration agreed not to release new concessions, and to adopt a restrictive stance towards existing contracts. Above all, the Hungarians exercised massive political influence to prevent the Bosnian railway network from sending exports into Austrian Dalmatia and the Mediterranean ports, and to force Bosnia's exports through Hungarian territory. These pressures prevented the forest railways not only from acting as common carriers but even from being linked with the railways of Dalmatia.

There were other possible contributory causes for industrial deceleration besides those attributable to trade policy. Ore depletion has already been mentioned; it is also likely that the energetic tapping of new wells caused the brine source for the salt industry to diminish as the water table fell. This problem became acute by the beginning of World War I.[75] Similarly, in timber, although commercial cutting was carefully administered, the inexorable inroads of forest depredation by the peasants offset the replanting programmes.[76]

Slow industrial expansion during Burián's administration was sustained as existing enterprises (especially in coal mining and carbide production) expanded and modernized. It was also on the point of yielding to a new expansionary phase. The slow-down caused resentment in Bosnia against Austrian and Hungarian restrictionism. Bosnian business interests agitated for a countervailing voice. Formal annexation in 1908 led in 1910 to the opening of the assembly at Sarajevo. This provided a mouthpiece for domestic interests, and led in 1912 to industrial improvement and public works legislation.[77] Assembly members called for local interests to be encouraged to participate in the timber industry. The output quota policy and the refusal to award new concessions had caused production to remain concentrated in the hands of the established foreign saw-milling firms. So a new round of forest concessions was auctioned off, specifically to open the industry to native business. It had no such effect, because the companies formed to operate the concessions quickly sold out to foreign firms. However, these firms committed themselves to

[73] Begović, *Razvojni put*, p. 165.
[74] John R. Lampe and Marvin R. Jackson, *Balkan Economic History, 1500–1950: from Imperial Borderlands to Developing Nations* (Bloomington, IN, 1982), pp. 315–6.
[75] Hrelja, *Industrija Bosne*, p. 57.   [76] Begović, *Razvojni put*, pp. 180–1.
[77] Hrelja, *Industrija Bosne*, p. 180.

large investments, though they did not succeed in bringing new capacity on stream by the time that World War I broke out.

During this period the Hungarians were at last forced to agree to the linking of the Bosnian railways with those of Austria and Serbia, and to the development of the Prijedor ore-field. These political changes did not have time to work through to the industrial economy by the outbreak of World War I, so Table 8.4 does not indicate a resurgence of industrialization in the last few years which preceded its outbreak. But there were sufficient new projects in the pipeline to surmise that industrial progress would have accelerated if war conditions had not supervened. Large railway building programmes were in hand, as well as the iron ore, smelting and timber industry projects alluded to above. Six cities were to get power stations, and large hydroelectric projects were announced for further chemical industry expansion.[78]

There were other signs too, of an upturn in economic activity and of new sources of domestic momentum. During the heyday of Kállay's industrialization drive, Bosnia remained almost un-banked, so domestic financial institutions took virtually no part in industrial finance. In 1910–11 Bosnia disposed 37 francs in bank assets per capita, compared with 263 for Serbia and 167 for Bulgaria. In this respect the province was less progressive even than Ottoman Macedonia with 42.[79] But the paid-up capital of limited liability banks belatedly shot up by 89 per cent between 1910 and 1912, while the number of Raffaisen type rural banking co-operatives rose from 73 to 228.[80]

Rail-freight volume, a parameter closely associated with National Product, similarly indicates a strong upturn. Between 1905 and 1910, it expanded at 5.3 per cent per annum, but there was then a pronounced acceleration in 1910–13 to 8.3 per cent. Such figures indicate that the Bosnian economy was far from stagnant, even in the Burián years, and that a renewed acceleration was developing on the eve of World War I.

Local enterprise and small-scale industries

The above discussion has focused on large-scale industry. Most of it was foreign or state owned, and orientated to the export of semi-manufactures. It has been argued that industrialization policy inhibited the development of domestically based industries to serve local markets, and frustrated the creation of linkages into final manufacturing which would have fostered a more broadly based industrialization. However, in Bosnia,

---

[78] GBC Bosnia 1911, p. 8; 1912, p. 11.
[79] Lampe and Jackson, *Balkan Economic History*, p. 304.
[80] GBC Bosnia 1911, p. 8 and 1912, p. 11.

as in the Balkans in general, small-scale artizan industry continued up to World War I to account for a high proportion of industrial output. At first sight, the statistics create a contrary impression. The 1907 business census extended to all enterprises (except farms) regardless of size, and identified 29,243 industrial establishments, all but 187 of which were small in scale. Of these smaller establishments, 3,671 employed 8,012 workers, while 25,385 establishments used only the labour of their proprietors. The wage roll of the smaller firms was therefore small, 2.058 million crowns, or 9.1 per cent of total industrial pay-roll. (Their employment was larger than this, but employees of small-scale establishments earned but 257 kr. a year compared with 658 paid in larger ones.) However, the 1907 census does not value the labour of proprietors. It seems reasonable to ascribe to the labour of artizan masters a reward equivalent to that earned by workers in large-scale industry, rather than the rate paid to their assistants. On this basis, proprietorial labour would have been worth 19.1 million crowns, and the notional pay-roll of small industry should be adjusted accordingly to 21.7 million, i.e. 51 per cent of a total industrial pay-roll thereby enlarged to 42.2 million. Its contribution to output certainly cannot be dismissed as insignificant.

Small industry accounted in Bosnia-Hercegovina for a smaller fraction of industrial output than was the case in Bulgaria or Serbia, but Bosnia had a larger proportion of its population engaged in artizan industry than Serbia but a smaller proportion than Bulgaria. Small-scale industry was made to look relatively insignificant in Bosnia-Hercegovina because of the rapid build-up of the large-scale sector, and not because the territory was, by Balkan standards, underendowed with artizan level industrial enterprise.

Small industry complemented the export-orientated large-scale sector by supplying local markets with consumer goods. The two largest branches were clothing and food-processing. Including the contribution made by entrepreneurs as workers, their combined pay-roll amounted to 5.44 million crowns, or 75 per cent of the total 'effective' pay-roll of these industries. If the state-monopoly tobacco factories are excluded from the food sector, the small-scale proportion rises to 91 per cent.

However, small-scale business did not give rise to larger enterprise. The only substantial firms created by Bosnian businessmen lay within the mainstream of timber and mining, and domestic wealth holders were more attracted to investment in quoted securities than in active industrial entrepreneurship.[81] Reasons for this apparent failure of native enterprise are elusive. It was not directly associated with the predominance of Muslim culture. In fact, the Muslims were more enterprise orientated

---

[81] Hrelja, *Industrija Bosne*, p. 120.

than the Christians. Owners of industrial firms included 198 persons per 10,000 of the Muslim faith, while the corresponding figures for Catholics and Orthodox Christians were 166 and 111.[82]

One industry which should have developed from local grass-roots, the manufacture of textiles, was an area of conspicuous failure. Its negative experience may offer insights into the more general problem. The Bosnian experience contrasts with that of Bulgaria and Serbia, where domestic enterprises, rooted in proto-industrial origins, showed themselves capable of establishing viable textile factory production.

Under Ottoman rule, Bosnia had drawn substantially on southern Bulgaria for its woollens. This region alone had furnished Bosnia with 5 million piastres annually of ready-made clothing in the 1860s.[83] Imports from the Balkans were drastically curtailed when the Austro-Hungarian tariff was applied. This should have opened opportunities for import substitution, but the growing market for woollens continued to be satisfied largely from outside the territory. The textile tariffs were not applied to encourage local industry, rather to provide a captive market for Czech textiles, and right up to World War I, these virtually monopolized the lower end of the Bosnian market. It should not have been difficult for Bosnian manufacturers to compete against them on the mass market for coarse woollens. It is true that Serbian and Bulgarian woollens were protected on their own home markets from Austrian competition, but we will argue (Chapter 9) this had little significance for the development of these industries, because they were low cost producers of the coarse woollens the Balkan mass market sought.

As it was, Czech manufacturers failed to match their exports well with the idiosyncracies of Bosnian demand. At the upper end of the market, Bosnia brought little profit to the Czechs as British and French cloths, woven to Bosnian patterns, were difficult to challenge.[84] In the mass market, Czech products, though cheap, were of poorer quality than the Rumelian, and ill adapted to Bosnian tastes, even though they imitated the Bulgarian style of manufacture.[85] The insecure hold enjoyed by Czech woollen textiles encouraged Bulgarian and Serbian woollen manufacturers to try to break back into the Bosnian market, despite the formidable tariffs. In 1899, Sliven manufacturers aimed at Bosnia as a market area for their cloth, while the Bosnian market for *gajtan* was targeted by the leading Serbian manufacturer.[86]

[82] Schmid, *Bosnien*, p. 543.
[83] Johann Roskiewicz, *Studien über Bosnien und die Herzegovina* (Leipzig, 1868), p. 315.
[84] *Narodni glasnik* (Temišvar) 10/22 June 1879, p. 2.
[85] Sugar, *Industrialization*, p. 145; GBC Bosnia 1885, pp. 421–2; *Sp.BID*, I, p. 511.
[86] AS. MNP(T) 1906 41 7: Münch – MNP 4 Feb. 1904, no. 771; BOUCA 1899 bd. 1, Plovdiv, p. 8.

Bulgarian and Serbian exporters never really broke through on this market; it was too well protected. The consequent gap in supply should have provided a niche for local manufacturers, but the niche remained untenanted. The administration received several applications for textile manufacturing concessions, but up till 1911, only one enterprise was enabled to start up. This was a cloth and blanket factory at Sarajevo established in 1889 by a Muslim landowner, Muhamed Aga Užičanin. It was undercapitalized and incompetently managed, surviving only by dint of government handouts.[87] In 1908 it was taken over by a blanket makers' co-operative with the help of a substantial bank loan.[88]

Sugar surmises that Bosnia would probably have acquired a woollen industry had not proposals from Czech interests to establish mills in the province been resolutely blocked by the *Landesregierung*. The administration may have had its own plans for textile development.[89] Nevertheless, the attitude of the administration towards the Užičanin mill does not suggest hostility to local textile manufacturing initiative. So the lack of local competition on this market still needs explaining.

It is possible that the industrial wage level in Bosnia inhibited the gradual transition to machine woollen production observed elsewhere in the Balkans. The boom in employment conditions which followed the Austrian occupation drove wages up to levels which made textile enterprise unprofitable. 'Under Austrian auspices, no doubt new industries can spring up,' wrote the British consul in Sarajevo in 1879. 'But in the meantime, many artizans find it more profitable to abandon their trades and work as day-labourers, as they can thus earn at the present moment 2s 6d to 3s per diem.'[90] When the administration tried to revive the dwindling artizan industries, it achieved little, possibly because relatively high pay was needed to attract labour. Wages were higher than in Serbia or Bulgaria.[91] Nevertheless, the argument that consumer goods industries failed to develop because wages were too high is unsatisfactory. As noted in Chapter 5, Bosnia had failed to establish a strong textile proto-industry under Ottoman rule, and the wage argument is unpromising for that period. In the Balkans, proto-industrialization furnished the key building block for textile enterprise, and the absence of this building block in Bosnia may explain its absence there. Of course, industries of the proto-industrial type declined sharply during the 1870s and 1880s throughout the Balkans, and Bosnia was no exception. Unlike Sliven, Gabrovo or Leskovac, the pre-industrial textile centres in the

---

[87] Sugar, *Industrialization*, pp. 147–8.
[88] Milivoje M. Savić, *Naša industrija i zanati* (Sarajevo, 1922–3), I, p. 219.
[89] Sugar, *Industrialisation*, p. 212.   [90] GBC Bosnia 1878.
[91] Sugar, *Industrialisation*, p. 246.

Hercegovinian borderlands faded away after the occupation without leaving any residue of large-scale enterprise. They had never amounted to much anyway, which was why the territory had provided so large a market up to 1878 for the Bulgarians. So the businesses that controlled them had little opportunity to develop either the financial capacities or the marketing skills of their Bulgarian counterparts.

The Bosnian administration's interest in promoting small industries was concentrated on resuscitating and preserving traditional craft skills, such as metal chasing and tapestry, for aesthetic rather than commercial reasons.[92] However, it is the spontaneous forces of commercialization in manufacturing and the formation of enterprise which give significance to the proto-industrialization process, not the activities of the state. Ultimately, failure in woollen manufactures probably indicates a lack of the appropriate business skills in the Bosnian commercial community.

It seems that the Bosnian business environment was less conducive to industrial endeavour than that of Bulgaria or Serbia; underlying the earlier failure to create a proto-industrial structure lay a culture which resisted commercial enterprise. This brings us back as a line of enquiry to the negative developmental influence of patriarchal dinaric society in Bosnia as in Montenegro. Given the lack of a domestic enterprise culture, the intervention of the state to industrialize on the basis of resources and imported capital seems rational and probably cost little in discouraging spontaneously based industrialization.

Bosnian economic development in comparative perspective

The unsatisfactory performance of the Bosnian farm economy and of domestically based enterprise indicates that the linkages from the large-scale sector which would sustain autochthonous growth were still weak at the outbreak of World War I. However, the determined push by the state for industrialization, its railway and large-scale heavy industry orientation, and its relative neglect of agriculture, are reminiscent of the Gerschenkron account of Russian industrialization before 1914. If the Russian economy 'took-off' it did so on the basis of a large-scale industrial sector which was (relatively) about the same size as Bosnia's. In 1900 the Russian mining and manufacturing labour force in large-scale industry amounted to about 13.9 persons per 1,000, in 1913 to 18.1. The figure we calculated for Bosnia in 1907 was 17.2.[93]

---

[92] *La Bosnie-Herzégovine à l'exposition internationale universelle de 1900 à Paris* (Vienna, 1900), pp. 29–34.

[93] For estimates on the Russian labour force see P. Gattrell, *The Tsarist Economy 1850–1917* (London, 1986), p. 85.

Table 8.5 *1910 national product per capita of various territories in US$ of 1970 value*

Germany		958	Czech lands	*819*	–
Austria	*810*	802	Hungary	*616*	684
Dalmatia	*650*		Italy		546
BOSNIA		546	Greece		455
Croatia	*542*	–	Transylvania	*542*	–
Serbia		462	Russia		398

Sources: Palairet, 'Habsburg Industrial Achievement', Table 3. For methodology see Crafts, 'Gross National Product in Europe 1870–1910', pp. 387–401. The Austro-Hungarian regional estimates (italicized) come from Good, 'Austria-Hungary'.

On most other economic indicators, Bosnia had progressed to a higher level than Bulgaria or Serbia by World War I, and compared favourably with Russia. For example, the Bosnian railways in 1909 provided 51 kilometres of passenger travel per head of the population. This was low by Russian standards (about 130 kilometres) but compared favourably with Bulgaria at 45 and Serbia at 30 kilometres.[94] In 1910, moreover, the Bosnian postal service handled 16.7 letters per head, whereas Serbia's mail amounted to 8.9, and Bulgaria's to 6.4.[95] These differences are significant because the volume of letters per capita was a sensitive correlate of the level of per capita GNP in pre-1914 Europe.[96] The Russian level was also below Bosnia's in this respect, with 12 mail items per head in 1909.[97] Again, in foreign trade, Bosnia was far more committed than its Balkan neighbours. In 1910, exports were valued at 71.4 crowns per head,[98] that is to say 2.1 times the per capita export of Serbia, and 2.4 times that of Bulgaria.[99]

Work by Crafts has suggested an indirect means of estimating Bosnia-Hercegovina's per capita income with proxy variables, in terms relative to

[94] Passenger-km. on the State Railway (85.56m) from *Bericht über die Ergebnisse der bos. herceg. Landesbahnen für das Jahr 1909* (Sarajevo, 1910), pp. 92–3 and on the Dobrlin line, in 1910 (10.49m), *Geschäftsbericht der k. u. k. Militärbahn Banja Luka-Doberlin für das Jahr 1910* (Banja Luka, 1911), p. 16. Figures for this line are not available for 1909, so are prorated to the proportion of 10.7 per cent of State Railway traffic carried in 1910; *SGBTs*,1910, p. 394; *SGKS*, 1909–10, pp. 494–5 (standard and narrow gauge lines).

[95] For Bosnia see Schmid, *Bosnien*, p. 615; for Serbia, *SGKS*, 1909/10, p. 479, and Bulgaria, *SGBTs*, 1911 p. 378.

[96] N. F. R. Crafts, 'Gross National Product in Europe 1870–1910: Some New Estimates', *Explorations in Economic History*, XX (1983), pp. 391–2.

[97] With 1944m. mail items according to B. R. Mitchell, *European Historical Statistics 1750–1970*, p. 656.

[98] *Glasnik srpskog geografskog društva*, II (Belgrade, 1913), p. 321.

[99] Russia's export trade in 1910 amounted to about 9.0 roubles per capita, or 23 crowns.

that of other European countries, while David Good, working on similar lines with different proxies has calculated estimates for the regions of Austria-Hungary. By applying Crafts' method and variables to our Bosnian data, the league-table as of 1910 (Table 8.5) may provide an interesting, if insecure perspective.

These national product proxies place Bosnia at a level of development by 1910 intermediate between Hungary and the Balkan states. Despite Bosnia's structural economic weaknesses, it was as productive as Italy and far more so than Russia. Lack of data for earlier years prevents us from tracking the growth rate during the Austrian period, and the sources of growth (other than large-scale industry) remain uncertain. Bosnian farm output per head did advance by 29 per cent between 1879/82 and 1909/11 or by 0.8 per cent per annum and this would be compatible with a much higher rate for the economy as a whole. Yet in 1909/11, Bosnia's farm output per capita was probably only 80 per cent of Serbia's. Nevertheless, it is probable the *Landesregierung* induced far more rapid development than would have occurred if it had been left to its own devices like the Balkan states.

The 'civilizing mission' in its Balkan context

The *Landesregierung* (especially under Kállay) aimed to inspire in Bosnia's people 'a feeling that they belong to a great and powerful nation'.[100] Through social and economic progress, the territory was to serve as 'a model and example for the other Balkan countries'.[101] Kállay, mindful of the capacity of the conflicting nationalisms and centrifugal political instincts to tear the territory apart, fostered the concept of *Bošnjaštvo* – a territorial loyalty over-riding religious and nationality distinctions. Economic success was essential to *Bošnjaštvo*, for the population had to be made conscious that its material interests were better served within the economic system of *Mitteleuropa* than within the culturally backward Balkan milieu. Sugar expresses a guarded optimism in appraising the Habsburg achievement in these terms, and Banac pays Kállay the compliment of describing his government as being 'as efficient and progressive a colonial administration as any that Britain could boast of...'[102]

Most (former) Yugoslav writers, to whom condemnation of 'non-national' rule was an unquestioned tenet were pessimistic in evaluating the Habsburg administration of Bosnia. Hrelja claimed that the imbal-

---

[100] Sugar, *Industrialisation*, p. 201.   [101] Juzbašić, 'Features', p. 146.
[102] Ivo Banac, *The National Question in Yugoslavia. Origins, History, Politics* (Ithaca, 1984), p. 360.

5. At the market place, Sarajevo.

ances in the industrial development of the province burdened it with a heavy legacy of colonial exploitation.[103] This stance was not, however, universal. Branislav Begović, author of an important study on the timber industry, advanced a vigorous revisionist view. Emphasizing the technically rational and enlightened programmes pursued in connexion with forestry and forest conservation, he argued that this sector contributed strongly to the well-being and economic advance of the province. He then broadened his argument into an attack on Yugoslav historiography for its 'degradation of science and practice', and its penchant for 'designating everything which is revealed [by historical research] as negative with the intentional suppression of all that could be accepted and treated as good and positive. . .' in order to undervalue 'success in the field of Bosnian-Hercegovinian forestry and industry in the period of Austro-Hungarian rule'.[104]

Yugoslav critics of the Austro-Hungarian regime in Bosnia-Hercegovina were on firmer ground when reviewing its social policies. Nevertheless, this is a field within which one must be particularly wary of the 'degradation of science and practice'. The most glaring failure was in the field of education. Bosnian literacy rates were low even by undemanding Balkan standards.[105] The 1910 Bosnian census disclosed (for

[103] Hrelja, *Industrija Bosne*, p. 181.   [104] Begović, *Razvojni put*, p. 183.
[105] Bosnia and Bulgaria, over age 7, Serbia, over age 5.

the first time) a literacy rate of 12.2 per cent, compared with Bulgaria in 1910, at 42 per cent, and Serbia in 1900 at 20.3.[106] Illiteracy was associated with a woeful neglect of education: as late as the 1911/12 school year, only 48,425 children, 17 per cent of the eligible age group, received elementary schooling.[107] As Ottoman statistics indicate that 39,161 children were enrolled in schools in about 1874,[108] the rate of school enrollment had declined from around 22 per cent since the beginning of the Austro-Hungarian period. The first education statistic of this period (for 1879) indicates that enrollment numbers had declined by 19 per cent since 1874,[109] and this implies that there was no subsequent advance at all. Public health was another area of relative weakness, as it was throughout the Habsburg monarchy; the most accessible indicator, mortality in the first year of life, was for Bosnia in 1910, 162 per 1,000, compared with 140 for Serbia and 159 for Bulgaria.[110]

Living standards in a mainly non-wage economy are notoriously difficult to determine. However, the wages paid in large-scale industry were higher than in the Balkan states. The average for Bosnia-Hercegovina in 1907 was 658 crowns, for Serbia in 1910, 630.5 dinars, for Bulgaria in 1910/11, 547 leva. (All these currencies approximated in value to the French franc.) As the day-wage disbursed in Bosnian mining and metals production rose by 13.0 per cent (from 2.46 to 2.78 crowns) between 1907 and 1910,[111] it is likely that industrial labour in Bosnia-Hercegovina cost around 744 crowns in the latter year, that is to say 18 per cent more than in Serbia and 36 per cent more than in Bulgaria.

The fact of the Sarajevo assassination inevitably obstructs an optimistic appraisal of Habsburg rule in Bosnia. Gonsalves has tentatively suggested linkage between economic deceleration in farming and the shot which killed the archduke.[112] Contemporaries complained that rural living standards had been deteriorating for many years up to 1910, so she suggests that economic weakness – as charted by the decline from the mid-1890s of per capita farm output – contributed to the rural unrest which preceded the Sarajevo assassination. The linkage is interesting, but the use of long-run economic variables to throw light on political events is always

[106] *Rezultati popisa žiteljstva u Bosni i Hercegovini od 10 Okt 1910*, pp. 23, 33; for Bulgaria, Kiril G. Popov, *Stopanska B'lgarija* (Sofia, 1916), p. 29 and Serbia, *SKS*, XVI, pp. cxxvii, xciii.

[107] *Bericht über die Verwaltung von Bosnien und der Hercegovina, 1913* (Vienna, 1914), p. 22.

[108] In Ottoman Bosnia, excluding the sanjak of Novi Pazar. See data in *Salname-i vilayet-i Bosna*. Defa IX, sene 1291 (=1874/5), pp. 130–6.

[109] H. Brachelli, *Statistische Skizze der Österreichische-Ungarische Monarchie* (8th edn, Leipzig, 1881), p. 53.

[110] Schmid, *Bosnien*, p. 206 (for infant deaths); *IUBH*, 1911, p. 2 (for live births); *SGBTs*, 1912, p. 100; *SGKS* 1909/10, p. 103.   [111] *IUBH*, 1908, p. 229; 1911, pp. 232–3.

[112] Gonsalves, 'Bosanska krajina'.

dubious. It does not signal that Austria-Hungary's 'civilizing mission' in Bosnia-Hercegovina failed in socio-economic – or even in political – terms. In an age when the assassin's bullet had become an instrument of ideological dissatisfaction, the activities of Gavrilo Princip and his student friends are scarcely proof that the peoples of Bosnia were particularly dissatisfied with their lot. The grievances of 'Young Bosnia' were not economic; rather they fused republican, anti-clerical, and anarchist gut feelings into a utopian crusade. If anything, the conspirators deplored the economic achievements of the regime because they kept the business community satisfied with the status quo and the masses apathetic to the revolutionary clarion. The uprising which 'Young Bosnia' hoped to spark failed utterly to materialize. Instead, the attentat led to anti-Serb riots in Sarajevo, and expressions of disgust among the leading Serbs of Bosnia that such an action had been committed in their name.[113]

How much did the 'civilizing mission' achieve? Most visibly it initiated the development of modern industry. Bosnia-Hercegovina, with 21 per cent of the combined population of Bosnia, Serbia and Bulgaria, contained about 54 per cent of the region's large-scale industry, almost all of which was built up during the Austrian period. Though progress decelerated after Kállay's death, signs of renewed and broad-based growth emerged on the eve of World War I. The agrarian system of regulated tenures was sub-optimal in efficiency, because it discouraged landowners from investing in improving their holdings, and prevented them from exercising managerial control over the cultivators. But it was more equitable than the latifundial alternative, while being more market orientated than the Serbian or Bulgarian systems of peasant freehold. Bosnia-Hercegovina remained illiterate and under-banked under Habsburg rule, but by Balkan standards its population availed itself of a high level of transport and communications, and its economic life was deeply penetrated by exchange relationships. Large-scale industry paid better wages than it did elsewhere in the Balkans. Per capita income was dragged up from characteristically Balkan levels to levels approaching those of central Europe. True, the idea of *Bošnjaštvo* made little headway save among the Muslims, but economic success did act to a degree as a solvent of political tensions, though the Yugoslav myth insists on having it otherwise.

The achievement was as yet unbalanced and fragile, as is characteristic of dualistic economic development. The linkages which would have sustained economic development under a changed set of institutions failed to emerge. So growth was not resumed after the war; dismantled and damaged industrial equipment was not subsequently replaced. Between

[113] Dedijer, *Road to Sarajevo*, p. 328.

the world wars, under Yugoslav rule, the Bosnian economy underperformed the sluggish Yugoslav economy as a whole.[114] This retrogression has obscured Bosnia's performance before 1914 as a successful variant of Gerschenkron's 'extreme backwardness' typology.

Montenegro after 1900: commerce and industry

Because of the unviability of their farms, Montenegrins remained under pressure to seek alternative sources of subsistence. While the state sought outlets in territorial expansionism, the people continued as previously to seek emigration outlets. However, after 1878, Serbia became increasingly unwilling to receive them. The Montenegrins there did not adapt easily to the discipline of settled agriculture – or indeed to any discipline at all – and this created political resistance to further immigration. Allegedly, the Montenegrin authorities continued to 'dish out passports for Serbia, as if Serbia were free butter',[115] but from December 1906, Serbia refused to admit new settlers.[116] An attempt at settling Montenegrins in Bulgaria had been equally unfruitful.[117] So, as opportunities for resettlement in the Balkans dried up, *Gastarbeiter* migrations to the Ottoman capital, and to construction projects in Greece, intensified.

Work in Constantinople made Montenegrins aware of the existence of a world-wide labour market, and they began to migrate in significant numbers to the USA around the turn of the century, many having come from Constantinople.[118] The closure of Serbia to immigration added to the transatlantic flow. Nearly all were young men who departed unaccompanied. They were expected to remit their earnings home, and return quickly. By 1911, much the greater part of the labour migration had converged on the USA, where were to be found 8,584 out of 10,109 reservists – i.e. Montenegrin men of military age – absent abroad.[119]

Politically, emigration to the USA sharpened Cetinje's drive for *Lebensraum*. Exaggerated reports circulated as to the scale of the movement, convincing Nikola that it was undermining his military strength, and that only by the seizure of new lands could his peasants – his soldiers – be enabled to remain within the country. Fears that half the army had melted away were exaggerated but the figure did reach 19.7 per cent of reservists by 1911.[120] So land grants in territories to be liberated were

[114] Hrelja, 'Razvoj industrije', p. 34.
[115] 'Bratstvo za bratstva. Jedna neprijatna ali iskrena reč', *Videlo*, VIII (1887), 165, p. 2.
[116] Djordjije Pejović, *Iseljavanja crnogoraca u XIX vijeku* (Titograd, 1962), pp. 441–2.
[117] B. Mintses, 'Preselencheskijat v'pros v B'lgarija', *B'lgarski Pregled*, IV (1897), pp. 8, 87–8; *RC*, LXXVII (1892), p. 137.   [118] Pejović, *Iseljavanja*, p. 376.
[119] Pavle S. Radusinović, *Stanovništvo Crne Gore do 1945 godine* (Belgrade, 1978), p. 133.
[120] Ibid., p. 133.

Table 8.6 *Indicators of urban economic activity in Montenegro 1904–1911 (000 crowns/perpers)*[a]

| Year | Incomes from | | |
	Trade & crafts	Wage labour	House rents
1904	6,170	254	371
1905	5,270	241	374
1906	5,640	276	393
1909	9,690	409	598
1911	14,150	754	959

Note:
[a] 1 perper = 1 Austrian crown, at 23 to the £ sterling.
Sources:
ACG MF II/A-21 fs. 5–6; II/A-39 d summary sheet; II/A-39 e (aggregate for returns of individual towns).

promised to returning emigrants. Lest that incentive be insufficient, the Americans were requested to repatriate all Montenegrins in the event of war, whether they wanted to return or not.[121]

Although endogenous forces for structural change remained weak, the economy gradually monetized and urbanized, and even acquired a few factories. The much shrunken urban population re-expanded, though never proportionately to its size before 1878. Towards the end of the period, in 1905–11, there were signs of a powerful upswing in urban commerce, even though the rural economy was in absolute decline. This can be seen in Table 8.6, constructed from tax records, which embraced urban incomes from 1904 onwards.

This expansion was probably connected closely with the growth of the import trade. Import volume rose from 4.6 million perpers in 1905 to 8.2 million in 1910. Agricultural imports rose modestly from 874,000 perpers to 1.13 million, and despite the decline of the farm economy, this reflected only the rising price of grain. The big growth areas were in textiles and clothing, dyestuffs, metals, leather, wooden and spicers' goods.[122]

Since commodity exports remained flat, invisible exports and capital imports must have risen fast. The most likely source of invisible earnings was the growth of emigrant remittances, and these must overwhelmingly have originated from the USA. It was thus the export of manpower to the United States that probably sustained the growth of urban activity.

[121] Pejović, *Iseljavanja*, pp. 449, 380, 381.
[122] Djurović, *Trgovački kapital*, pp. 242 and 'table B' gatefold between pp. 244 and 245.

The second source of urban expansion was capital imports. Given the lack of any proto-industrial tradition, and the negligible size of the internal market, economic progress would have to depend as in Bosnia on the provision by external financiers of modern infrastructure – for the perennially indigent government of Prince Nikola had no means of financing such works. It seemed at the beginning of the twentieth century that Montenegro might find in Italy a foreign patron willing to build infrastructure and exploit its resources in a manner analogous to Austria-Hungary's investment in Bosnia. The initiative came from a Venetian syndicate led by Giuseppe Volpi. Its long-term aim was to develop Adriatic trade connexions between Venice and the Balkans and the Ottoman Empire, to challenge Austria's bid for commercial hegemony. In the longer term Volpi's group hoped to build a railway through Montenegro's port of Bar (Antivari), through Serbia to link the Adriatic with the Black Sea. Italian initiative was warmly encouraged both by Serbia and Montenegro. The syndicate's first operation, in 1903, was to provide Nikola with a 2.5 million lira loan against security of a tobacco monopoly.[123] The company built a tobacco factory employing 340 workers, but as noted above, the low purchase price paid to growers caused tobacco growing to decline.

With a foot in the door, the Italians planned next to develop the port at Bar, and to construct a short narrow-gauge railway linking it with Virpazar on Lake Skadar (Shkodër). The railway and port works, backed by Banca Commerciale Italiana, were completed in 1909. This modest project was intended to spearhead the proposed Adriatic to Danube railway, but the immediate aim was probably to provide a link into the commerce of Albania, via a shipping service established on the lake. As subsequent plans for the railway system envisaged a terminal on the Albanian coast, rather than at Bar, the line was not extended into the interior of Montenegro, and the initial Italian impetus to the country's development was maintained mainly through commerce and local authority loans which financed the construction of utilities at Cetinje.[124]

Italian ambitions also extended to colonization. Between 5,000 and 8,000 hectares of potentially fertile marshland near Ulcinj were to be drained under concession to the 'Dr. Theodoric Company', and settled by Italian colonists, but the project was cut short by the outbreak of World War I.[125]

Domestic banking was non-existent till 1901, but thereafter

---

[123] Angelo Tamborra, 'The Rise of Italian Industry and the Balkans (1900–1914)', *JEEcH*, III (1974), pp. 87–120.   [124] Djurović, *Trgovački kapital*, p. 239.

[125] Jagoš Jovanović, *Stvaranje crnogorske države i razvoj crnogorske nacionalnosti* (Cetinje, 1947), p. 348.

Table 8.7 *Capital lent under interest in Montenegro 1904–1911 (000 crowns/perpers)*

Year	Lent privately	Deposited with banks	Total
1904	2,922	23	2,935
1905	2,700	37	2,737
1906	2,823	26	2,850
1909	2,734	239	2,972
1911	550	2,469	3,019

Sources as for Table 8.6 and Djurović, *Trgovački kapital u Crnoj gori*, p. 215.

expanded rapidly, mainly by diverting interpersonal debt into bank deposits. Despite the powerful growth of import-connected urban business activity, the volume of financial claims held by the private sector stagnated (Table 8.7).

Nevertheless, the concentration of capital into the fledgling Montenegro banks provided resources which found their way into the formation of industrial enterprise. As in Bosnia, the first industrial enterprises in Montenegro exploited natural resources, in this case, timber. Rapid growth of banking after 1900 induced the re-equipment of a timber mill at Nikšić, which had originally been erected from state funds. A second was set up, also using bank funding, at Kolašin.[126] For a time these sustained an export trade in timber, of which 1,286 tonnes were exported in 1905. Timber exports subsequently dwindled to insignificance,[127] but this was probably because supply was diverted by expansion in domestic construction. Though the government built roads, mainly by paying for the labour out of grain subsidies sent by Russia, serious forestry development required rail connexions into the interior, and these were never built.

Though there was no proto-industrial basis for the emergence of modern manufacturing, the prospect of military orders led to the opening of a small woollen mill at Danilovgrad in 1908.[128] Apart from the above ventures, an olive oil mill at Ulcinj, and two joint-stock breweries at Nikšić comprised more or less the sum total of modern industry. The first of these breweries, 'Onogošt', founded in 1896, was such 'a ramshackle place, producing very poor beer',[129] that it was soon displaced by the second 'Trebješa', whose beverages were at least palatable.[130]

[126] Ibid., p. 346; Djurović, *Trgovački kapital*, pp. 218–19.
[127] Djurović, *Trgovački kapital*, table A opp. p. 244.   [128] J. Jovanović, *Stvaranje*, p. 346.
[129] Wyon and Prance, *Black Mountain*, p. 261.
[130] J. Jovanović, *Stvaranje*, p. 346.

Table 8.8 *Montenegro. Taxable urban incomes 1911 (000 Austrian kr.)*

Interest from persons	549.7
Interest from banks	2,469.3
Wages and salaries	754.1
Mills	22.0
Fulling mills	2.1
House Rent	989.7
Trade and crafts	13,706.7
Total	18,493.6

Source: ACG MFiG II/A-39 e. Kr. crnogorski ministarstvo finansija i gradjevina. Glavno državno računovodstvo. Razrez poreza u oblastima . . . 1911 god.

Montenegro's national income 1911

With the help of the figures on urban taxation, it is possible roughly to estimate Montenegro's National Income in 1911, when taxable urban incomes were recorded (in 000 Austrian kr.) as shown in Table 8.8.

Our estimate for gross farm product for that year is of 22.67 million perpers (at current price), or 19.95 million after a 12 per cent allowance for depreciation. If we assume this to equal the net income of the rural population, and add this sum to the total earnings of the urban population, NNI becomes 38.45 million perpers. On a population of 211,909 this amounted to 181 perpers ($37) per head. This is only a rough measure, overstating in so far as interest payments were transferred from the rural to the urban sector, and understating on account of non-farm rural outputs. It does however indicate that the small urban sector generated a remarkable 48 per cent of net income, a level of activity which must reflect the growing impact of remittances and Italian financed public works.

In the dinaric territories, home grown sources of economic dynamism were still minimal in 1914, and economic progress apparently depended overwhelmingly on externally driven initiatives.

9 The textile industries in Bulgaria and Serbia 1878–1914

The period 1878–1914 saw the gradual emergence of large-scale textile manufacturing in the Balkan states. In relatively backward economies, textile manufacturing was usually among the first industries to use machine technology, because the products enjoyed a sufficiently broad consumer demand to reap economies of scale. On the supply side, textile manufacture was seldom a 'new' industry, for machine manufacturing largely replaced pre-industrial handwork. It could therefore draw upon the declining domestic system for enterprise, labour and capital. Moreover, mechanized textile technology was relatively simple and scale economies could be achieved with modest capital outlays. Textile technology was also slow to change in the late nineteenth century, so Balkan producers could use old equipment and sub-optimal systems, yet compete against best-practice firms through their access to cheap labour and material inputs.

In examining demand and supply side influences on the development of the Balkan textile industries, particular reference will be made to their proto-industrial inheritance, and the advantages derived from this. The rise of machine textile manufacturing was a significant strand in economic modernization in the Balkans, but cannot be ascribed a leading-sector role. The study analyses the constraints on the scope for textile based industrialization.

Restructuring the Bulgarian woollen industry

Until 1878 Balkan textile manufacturing was concentrated within the uplands of Bulgaria and Hellenic Macedonia, where the institutional environment favoured enterprise formation and held down the cost of labour. Bulgarian textile producers and merchants serviced a large and expanding Ottoman home market. For Bulgarian textile sales, mainly of woollens but also of cotton kerchiefs, the Anatolian and Levantine markets predominated, but the more westerly centres sent much of their output to the western Balkans. At the time of the liberation, the *gajtan* (braid) manufacturers of Karlovo and Sopot sent Bosnia, Macedonia and Serbia 400, 550 and 300 tovars (of 128 kg) a year of *gajtan*, out of an estimated 1,900 produced,[1] while Macedonia and Bosnia were also major consumers of their printed cotton kerchiefs.[2] Similarly, the woollen clothing trade of Samokov was massively dependent on Bosnian demand, besides selling smaller quantities in Serbia and the south west Balkans.[3] So, looking at the other side of the coin, Bulgarian hegemony over the Balkan market inhibited the growth of woollen manufacturing in the other Balkan territories.

As shown in Chapter 7, the upheaval of 1878 radically altered the spatial conditions for woollen industry development. For Bulgaria's woollen industries, supply conditions worsened as the country's economic structure converged upon that of Serbia, after the breakdown of Ottoman institutions which had formerly differentiated it. As the proto-industrial labour force melted away, and as wool was diverted from the market towards self-consumption, the textile supply curve shifted sharply to the left, eroding the competitive advantage that Bulgarian manufacturers had hitherto enjoyed. Their resulting failure to supply their export customers efficiently after the liberation created openings for competing industries elsewhere in the Balkans. Woollen entrepreneurs in Bulgaria rose to the challenge in the 1880s and 1890s by mechanizing their operations, and their business skills served them in good stead. They therefore retained a strong position in their home market and in exporting to the Ottoman Empire, where their coarse heavy woollens and *gajtan* could withstand European competition.

Nevertheless, their sales were curtailed by new tariff barriers. The Austrians drew Bosnia into their own protectionist tariff zone, applying a duty of 45 per cent on Bulgarian cloth,[4] and 100 per cent on ready made clothes.[5] The Ottoman Empire applied its own modest external tariff against the new Bulgarian state, and against Eastern Rumelia after annexation by Bulgaria in 1885. The same event provided Serbia with an excuse not only for the war of 1885, but also for slapping punitive tariffs on Bulgarian imports, though their effectiveness was reduced by smuggling.[6] In 1897, the ultra-high Serbian autonomous tariff, which had charged Bulgarian *gajtan* at 300 dinars per kg was dropped to 26 dinars,[7] but still afforded significant protection.

Woollen production was mechanized in the former proto-industrial

---

[1] *Raport na komissiata po izuchvanieto na ikonomicheskoto polozhenie na naselenieto v gradovete Karlovo i Sopot* (Karlovo, 1883), pp. 19–20.   [2] Ibid., pp. 10–11.
[3] Hr. Semerdzhiev, *Samokov i okolnost'ta mu* (Sofia, 1913), p. 210.
[4] 'Po iznos't na nashite shajetsi i gajtani', *Sp. BID*, I, p. 511.
[5] Semerdzhiev, *Samokov*, p. 207.
[6] AS MNP (T) 1898 VI 2. Braće Minh–MNP, 29 Aug. 1895, no. 4660 of 1895.
[7] AS MNP (T) 1905 XV 9. Janković–MNP, 15 Mar. 1898, no. 1751 of 23 Mar. 1898.

areas of the Balkans by local enterprises, and appeared in entirely new locations where plant was located by trans-national firms. This distinction is clear cut. Bulgarian woollen factories were established solely by local firms at Gabrovo, Sliven, Trjavna, Samokov, Karlovo and Kazanl'k, all centres of woollen proto-industry. Factory woollen production progressed earlier in Bulgaria than elsewhere in the Balkans, thanks to its proto-industrial base, but its expansion was restricted largely to displacing the output of the proto-industry. In Serbia, Leskovac developed as a woollen manufacturing town as a result of local enterprise applied to an existing commercial and proto-industrial structure. However, non-indigenous woollen factories were established in Paraćin, a town with no former industrial tradition, and subsequently in the capital, Belgrade. As there was little proto-industry to replace, growth was secured through import substitution. So far from declining, as in Bulgaria, woollen proto-industry in Serbia expanded alongside factory production.

We now examine how entrepreneurial decisions and market environments affected the growth of woollen manufacturing in Bulgaria and Serbia. Of the Bulgarian woollen industry centres in 1903, Gabrovo, which produced around 3 million leva of woollen cloth[8] and about 800,000 leva of *gajtan*, was regarded as the country's premier woollen centre. The first Gabrovo woollen mill was established in 1881 by Ivan Kalpazanov (1835–89) his brother Pencho and P. Tsokev. Ivan Kalpazanov was a *gajtan* manufacturer and woollen cloth putter-out. Before the liberation, this innovative entrepreneur planned to open a spinning mill because his business was threatened by an incipient shortage of yarn.[9] War interrupted his plans, but subsequently, rising wages and deterioration of yarn supply made it urgent to implement them. In particular, the decline of the tanning trade robbed the woollen industry of its supply of tanner's wool, which had served best for making hand-spun *gajtan* yarn.[10] Kalpazanov could not enlist much local financial support, so his factory, at Bichkinja, 2 kilometres outside Gabrovo, was built on a shoestring outlay of 30,000 francs, mainly from a legacy from his father-in-law. The original equipment was of 240 German made machine spindles and two power-looms. The business earned a profit of 67,056 piastres in 1882/3, the first full year of operation. This represented about 45 per cent on the original investment, and encouraged Kalpazanov to treble his spinning capacity in 1883.[11]

[8] D. Mishajkov, 'Ocherk na fabrichnata v'lnena industrija v B'lgarija', *Sp.BID*, VIII (1904), p. 557.
[9] Pet'r Tsonchev, *Iz stopanskoto minalo na Gabrovo* (Sofia, 1929), pp. 617–18.
[10] Stoil Staneff, *Das Gewerbewesen und die Gewerbepolitik in Bulgarien* (Ruse, 1901), p. 118.
[11] Mishajkov, 'Ocherk', p. 477; Tsonchev, *Gabrovo*, pp. 618, 622; Staneff, *Gewerbewesen*, p. 118.

Kalpazanov's success encouraged emulation by another group of *gajtan* manufacturers led by Hristo Bobchev. In 1884 they opened a partnership mill, the 'Aleksand'r', in Gabrovo town, with 576 spindles and 2 power-looms. The 'Aleksand'r' mill also expanded briskly.[12] Again the original object was to obtain yarn for the *gajtan* mills, but by 1888 half their yarn was being woven inside their factory into *shajak* cloth. The enterprise traded in cloth on its own account, but its primary function was to process raw materials brought to it by its members for a fee.[13] This *ishljem* system, in which factories were used as servicing facilities for shareholders, predominated among the early mills.[14] While the shareholders wanted their mills to profit, their motive for investing in them was to gain better access to yarn (or cloth) than they could by putting materials out to hand-workers.

This too was Kalpazanov's original motive, but unlike most early factory founders, for whom the investment was essentially defensive, Kalpazanov regarded machine manufacturing as a means of expanding his business. In 1887, he built a second mill alongside the first. This was equipped with English woolcombing machinery and 720 spindles to spin combed yarn for *gajtan* of better quality, and to weave worsteds. This time, he had no trouble in securing financial backing, so the mill was owned by a wider circle of *gajtan* manufacturers. The following year he built a third mill from his own resources, to provide additional carding and weaving capacity to win contracts for military broadcloth. He also opened a coal mine to ensure a supply of fuel.[15]

By this time (1888) the remaining Gabrovo *gajtan* manufacturers and cloth merchants realized that access to machine produced yarn had become a prerequisite to survival, and 49 of them formed a company, 'Uspeh', which raised 298,000 leva[16] to open the 'Ferdinand I' mill in Gabrovo, with 632 spindles and 2 power-looms.[17] Shareholders were given the right to bring their materials to the mill for spinning at a fixed fee – again the hallmark of a defensive investment.[18] The Ferdinand mill burned down the year after it opened, but was soon reconstructed with a low-interest loan from the Bulgarian central bank; it was profitable enough for the loan to be paid off without difficulty.[19]

Not till 1903 was any further factory of this type built in Gabrovo, for having displaced the output of the former hand-work sector, the factories had to operate within a growth-less market. Expansion of the turnover of

[12] *Izlozhenie: Sevlievo 1888*, p. 24; Staneff, *Gewerbewesen*, p. 118; Tsonchev, *Gabrovo*, p. 526.
[13] Dimit'r Mladenov, *Pojava na fabrichen proletariat v B'lgarija* (Sofia, 1961), p. 29.
[14] Staneff, *Gewerbewesen*, p. 123.   [15] Tsonchev, *Gabrovo*, pp. 624–5.
[16] *Izlozhenie: Sevlievo 1889–1890*, pp. 16–17.   [17] Mishajkov, 'Ocherk', p. 478.
[18] *Doklad: Sevlievo 1892–93*, p. 52.   [19] Mishajkov, 'Ocherk', p. 478.

the original factories was therefore gradual rather than spectacular. In 1889/90 they used 786,600 leva of raw materials, in 1897/8 1.27 million, and in 1899/1900, 1.36 million.[20] Therefore, the new factory enterprises that were set up in the 1890s tried to penetrate areas of the market which the bulk woollen producers failed to reach. In 1892 the firm of Hadzhi-Berov and Momerin set up a factory with eight power-looms to produce fine cloth from British woollen yarn,[21] while in 1891 and 1898, two small knitting mills were opened,[22] and in 1902, a hemp cloth factory.[23]

At nearby Trjavna, whose woollen merchants regarded themselves as being in competition with their larger neighbour,[24] the formation of factory enterprises was similarly impelled by shortages of yarn for the *gajtan* and cloth trades.[25] A factory which span and wove *shajak* was built in 1883 or 1884 by Tihol Bonchev & Co.[26] Its early success encouraged the establishment of a second in 1890, and later a third.[27] Characteristically, of these small town factories, the second raised its capital from 17 shareholders, none of whom owned more than 2 of the company's 22 shares of 4,000 francs; unusually, however, all production was for corporate account[28] rather than on *ishljem*. At the end of 1893, the Trjavna factories counted 960 spindles, 8 power-looms and 31 hand-looms. Only one used steam power. Their production overloaded the market, however, and incompetent management led to the closure of two of them in 1896 and 1897. They were refinanced by a local bank in 1898, but the bank failed[29] and by 1899 all three had closed.[30] In 1911 one of the mills was operating in the hands of the Ruse Commercial Bank. By this time it had been re-equipped with modern machinery.[31]

Vigorous growth of woollen manufacturing also occurred in Sliven, whose woollen output in 1903 was estimated at about 2.25 million leva.[32] After 1878, the industry, facing the difficulties in yarn supply that afflicted all woollen industry centres, nucleated around the old state factory, which, archaic in its equipment as it was by now, at least possessed 4,520 spindles.[33] When the Russians occupied the town in 1877, the factory closed, and its stocks were sold off to the cloth merchants; but

---

[20] *Izlozhenie: Sevlievo 1889–90*, p. 15; *1897/98*, p. 32; *1899/1900*, table 2 between pp. 22 and 23.   [21] *Izlozhenie: Sevlievo 1898/99*, p. 22.   [22] *Izlozhenie: Sevlievo 1899/1900*, table 2.

[23] Tsonchev, *Gabrovo*, p. 536.

[24] Jean Erdic, *En Bulgarie et en Roumélie* (Paris, 1885), p. 82.

[25] Staneff, *Gewerbewesen*, p. 121.   [26] *RC*, LXXVII (1892), p. 136.

[27] Staneff, *Gewerbewesen*, p. 121.

[28] NBKM. Daskalov papers. Fond 129 a.e. 186 fs. 25–25vo.

[29] Staneff, *Gewerbewesen*, pp. 121–2; Mishajkov, 'Ocherk', p. 478.

[30] *Izlozhenie: T'rnovo 1898–99*, p. 19.   [31] *Izlozhenie: T'rnovo 1910–1911*, p. 50.

[32] Mishajkov, 'Ocherk', p. 557.   [33] TsDIA. fond 159 opis 1. a.e. 191 ff. 9vo-12.

when the Russians withdrew, the Sliven cloth merchants hastened to bring it back into service.[34]

They formed a company, 'Napred'k', with 600,000 piastres of capital to lease the mill (which was valued with its machines in 1884 at 330,000 francs),[35] and were accorded an advantageous deal in February 1880 by the provincial Director of Finances (Schmidt). This gave the company the right to produce all uniforms for the province[36] at favourable contract prices,[37] paying no rent for the factory, but allowing the provincial treasury 15 per cent of the profits. The factory sold only woollen cloth, and in 1883/4, 32 per cent of output was supplied to the government, the rest being disposed of on the market.[38] This arrangement yielded handsome returns: after deducting 15 per cent, shareholders' profits (in piastres) ran at:

1880/1	382,283
1881/2	363,401
1882/3	285,152
1883/4	298,964

TsDIA. f. 158 op. 1 ae. 33. Direktsija na finantsiite na Istochna Rumelija, fs. 61–8.

These represented a return to capital invested by the company of between 48 and 64 per cent, besides which the mill provided its members with supplies for their own businesses. In 1885 a new contract with the state imposed a rent on the factory of 43,000 piastres, but the tax on profits was substituted by a 5 per cent levy on dividends.[39] However, the factory, which had served as a stop-gap for the Sliven *abadzhijas* (merchant tailors) during the post-liberation supply crisis, gradually became redundant to their needs. About 1,200 spindles and some carding machinery were destroyed in a fire in 1888.[40] Although the company won remission of rent to make good the damage,[41] its mill fell into decay, probably for want of investment.[42] A new company, 'B'lgarija', with 144,000 leva capital,[43] was formed to lease the mill from the state in 1892[44] and produced 45,000–60,000 metres of cloth per year in the mid-1890s,[45] but

[34] S. Tabakov, *Istorija na grad Sliven* (Sofia, 1929), III, pp. 114–15 note 1.
[35] TsDIA. f.159 op. 1 a.e. 191 f. 9vo.   [36] TsDIA. f.158 op. 1 a.e. 33 f. 50vo.
[37] TsDIA. f.20 op. 1 a.e. 229 fs. 34–6.   [38] TsDIA. f.158 op. 1 a.e. 33 f. 31.
[39] TsDIA. f.159 op. 1 a.e. 191 f. 5.
[40] TsDIA. f.159 op. 1 a.e. 191 ff. 72–72vo and 9vo-12 (pencil entries).
[41] Ibid., ff. 72–72vo and 93.   [42] Tabakov, *Sliven*, III, p. 115.
[43] *Izlozhenie: Sliven 1895–1896*, p. 79.
[44] *Doklad: Sliven 1894–95*, table 4 between pp. 34 and 5, and note.
[45] *Izlozhenie: Sliven 1896–7*, p. 33; *1895–6*, p. 80; *Doklad: Sliven, 1894–5*, table 4.

was defunct by 1901/2, and the factory idle.[46] Some of its buildings then served at times as a textile school,[47] at others from 1904 as a gaol.[48]

The town produced around 650,000 arshins of cloth in 1883,[49] but 'Napred'k's' contribution (in 1883/4) was a mere 84,700 arshins.[50] As the mill did not supply yarn to the weaving trade, the cloth merchants, including many of 'Napred'k's' shareholders,[51] still concerned by the high cost and bad quality of yarn and cloth supplied through their domestic networks, began building scratch capacity of their own. The profitability of Napred'k encouraged them to go ahead, but their finances barely sufficed to enter factory production. Unlike their counterparts in Gabrovo who pooled funds to gain access to machine production, each Sliven firm tried to acquire its own. Two small spinneries with handloom weaving sheds were established during the Rumelian period, but as conditions became more competitive from 1885 onward, putting-out was displaced by a rash of little factories: sixteen had appeared by 1892 alongside the 'Napred'k' factory, twelve in Sliven town, and four at a nearby village.[52] Despite their undercapitalization, they managed by 1889 to improve the quality and competitiveness of their products.[53] The small size of these factories can be seen from their employment, averaging 35 workers in 1904, with 357 spindles,[54] and a mean fixed asset value of 65,200 leva (£2,600) in 1896.[55] In aggregate (including the 'B'lgarija' factory) they turned out 308,000 metres of cloth in 1896/7. By then they had largely eliminated the use of domestic workers, to whose livelihood factory competition had become 'ruinous' by 1892.[56] A number of outworkers continued to weave with yarn supplied by the factories,[57] but their number declined from 1,500 in 1892 to 500 in 1896.[58]

Technically, the Sliven factories clung, except for spinning, to artizan methods. As coal was dear,[59] water and manual power prevailed. Though workers with power-looms could produce two or three times the amount of cloth produced by those working with handlooms, power weaving was uneconomic.[60] In 1895, the factories held 17 power-looms and 233 flyshuttle looms, but while 94 per cent of the handlooms were being worked,

[46] *Izlozhenie: Burgaz 1901/2*, p. 45.   [47] *Izlozhenie: Burgaz 1907/8*, p. 39.

[48] Mishajkov, 'Ocherk', p. 475; Tabakov, *Sliven*, III, p. 115.

[49] *Doklad: Sliven Sep. 1883*, p. 11.   [50] TsDIA. f. 158 op. 1 a.e. 33 f. 68.

[51] Compare the names of Napred'k's founders (see Tabakov, *Sliven*, III, p. 115) with those of the factory owners listed in *Doklad: Sliven 1894–95*, table 4.

[52] Staneff, *Gewerbewesen*, p. 120; *Doklad: Sliven 1894–5*, table 4.

[53] GBC Bulgaria 1889, p. 30.

[54] Mishajkov, 'Ocherk', p. 480 (spindlage) and p. 499 (spindles per worker).

[55] *Izlozhenie: Sliven 1896–97*, p. 33.   [56] *RC*, LXXVII (1892), p. 101.

[57] D. Mishajkov, 'Belezhki v'rhu domashnata shaechna industrija v B'lgarija', *Sp.BID*, VII (1903), pp. 538–9.   [58] Staneff, *Gewerbewesen*, p. 70.

[59] Tabakov, *Sliven*, III, pp. 137–8.   [60] Mishajkov, 'Belezhki', p. 539.

10 power-looms stood idle.[61] However, the government complained of the quality of the cloth it was receiving, and threatened withdrawal of military contracts if weaving remained unmechanized, so the factories installed more power-looms in 1898.[62] Even so, five years later they still retained 151 handlooms (along with 43 power-looms) which they used to meet their export orders.[63] Only after protection in Turkey put paid to their export trade, did Sliven convert completely to power weaving.[64]

The 'Rozova dolina' joint stock woollen mill at Kazanl'k was built in 1890 to spin wool for *gajtan* making.[65] The 230,000 leva needed for the business[66] was raised from a syndicate of *gajtan* merchants led by the Stajnov brothers, while outside capital was furnished by at least four local businesses, led by rose oil merchants D. & B. Papazoglu.[67] The *gajtan* traders wanted the mill as an *ishljem* facility, to spin wool for them for a fee, so the mill was modelled on the 'Aleksand'r' mill at Gabrovo.[68] As soon as it opened, it dispensed with the services of domestic hand spinners.[69] Like most other Bulgarian mills, Rozova dolina was equipped to weave, and was installed with power-looms, but as at Sliven, power weaving was uncompetitive with hand-loom work,[70] so weaving was abandoned in 1894. Even then, the business lost money, and the spinnery was leased to a Gabrovo firm the same year. Subsequently Papazoglu bought the factory outright, and leased it to the Stajnovs.[71] The Stajnovs gradually bought out the smaller *gajtan* firms, but realizing that this ailing trade could only be restored by scrapping the old *gajtan* machines, they built a factory with thirty modern braiding machines in 1908 and integrated it with the spinning enterprise. A lace-making facility was also added.[72] Each move indicates an effort by the *gajtan* trade to retain business in a declining market, by lowering the production costs of its traditional products, but the *gajtan* market was declining too fast to be profitable. In 1909, the factory generated the lowest return to capital of any branch of the Bulgarian textile industry.[73]

[61] Staneff, *Gewerbewesen*, p. 126.
[62] Mishajkov, 'Ocherk', p. 566; Staneff, *Gewerbewesen*, p. 125.
[63] Mishajkov, 'Ocherk', pp. 480, 566.
[64] Kiril G. Popov, *Stopanska B'lgarija* (Sofia, 1916), p. 327.
[65] Aleksand'r Pavlov, 'Ikonomicheskoto razvitie i s'stojanie na gr. Kazanl'k', *Kazanl'k v minaloto i dnes*, I (Sofia, 1912), p. 321.   [66] Mishajkov, 'Ocherk', p. 479.
[67] T. B. and M. St[ajnov], 'Industrija v Kazanl'k', *Kazanl'k v minaloto i dnes*, III (1928), pp. 540–1; GBC Bulgaria 1890, p. 19.
[68] Pavlov, 'Ikonomicheskoto razvitie', p. 321; St(ajnov), 'Industrija v Kazanl'k', p. 540; Mladenov, *Pojava*, p. 29.   [69] Pavlov, 'Ikonomicheskoto razvitie', p. 324.
[70] St(ajnov), 'Industrija v Kazanl'k', p. 540.
[71] *Doklad ot bjuroto na plovdivskata t'rgovsko-industrialna kamara . . . prez 1895 i 1896 godini* (Plovdiv, 1897), p. 175; Pavlov, 'Ikonomicheskoto razvitie', p. 328.
[72] St(ajnov), 'Industrija v Kazanl'k', pp. 546–7.   [73] Popov, *Stopanska B'lgarija*, p. 330.

The Karlovo woollen mill was built in 1891 by Evlogi Georgiev, a Bucharest banker,[74] at a cost of 360,000 leva, as a benefaction to his native town.[75] The object was to provide yarn for the ailing *gajtan* trade.[76] Georgiev intended the mill's profits to support local education and a hospital,[77] and in 1892, he bequeathed it to the town to apply the profits as he had intended.[78] The local council leased the mill to Ivan Astardzhiev & Co. who were probably former putters-out in the cloth trade.[79] The mill's 1,244 spindles provided more capacity than was needed to supply the local *gajtan* industry, which the mill itself soon absorbed.[80] Its 15 power-looms partially displaced domestic weaving, though it retained 60 outwork weavers, whom it supplied with yarn.[81]

At Samokov in 1885 a company, 'B'dashtnost', composed of seventeen investors, probably merchant tailors, opened a woollen mill as a service facility for their business of supplying gendarmerie uniforms to the Bulgarian government.[82] A second mill was opened in around 1894 by a group of investors who constituted themselves in 1900 as the Samokov Company. Their motive was likewise to use the mill as a servicing facility to lower the cost of yarn.[83] Both mills also manufactured on their own account. However, they were not profitable, and their example did not invite emulation.[84]

All woollen mills erected in the old proto-industrial towns were established by local enterprises. Only two woollen mills with foreign participation were erected in Bulgaria before World War I. Neither was constructed in an established area of textile manufacturing, and neither was of much importance. The only woollen textile enterprise to be established in Sofia was founded in 1906. This mill, set up by a Bulgarian – Czech partnership, Berov and Horenik, specialized in fine cloth. It probably aimed to sell European type products to city dwellers. This is indicated both by its location, and by the fact that it sent substantial consignments to Plovdiv.[85] The other was a cloth factory opened in Kjustendil (southeast Bulgaria) just before World War I, by a French

---

[74] GBC Bulgaria 1890, p. 19.   [75] *BOUCA*. 1906 part 1. Plovdiv 1906, p. 5.
[76] *Doklad: Plovdiv 1888–89*, p. 34.   [77] *Izlozhenie: Plovdiv 1889–90*, p. 24.
[78] Vasil Aleksandrov, *Iz istorijata na grad Karlovo* (Sofia,1938), p. 58.
[79] *Izlozhenie: Plovdiv 1899–1900*, p. 56; Staneff, *Gewerbewesen*, p. 122.
[80] Ivan Undzhiev, *Karlovo. Istorija na grada do Osvobozhdenieto* (2nd edn, Sofia, 1968), p. 80 note 2.   [81] *Doklad ot bjuroto na plovdivskata industrialna kamara*, p. 99.
[82] Semerdzhiev, *Samokov*, p. 212; Mishajkov, 'Ocherk', pp. 472–3.
[83] Mishajkov, 'Ocherk', pp. 472–3, 478; Staneff, *Gewerbewesen*, pp. 122–3.
[84] Semerdzhiev, *Samokov*, pp. 212–13.
[85] AN F12 7280 Mouvement commercial de la Roumélie orientale . . . 1906.; RC CLVI (1912) p. 67; John R. Lampe and Marvin R. Jackson, *Balkan Economic History, 1500–1950* (Bloomington, IN, 1982), p. 246.

businessman, Camille Simone, who invested 620,000 francs in it. Kjustendil had no woollen industry background.[86]

Table 9.1 reviews the growth of factory woollen production in Bulgaria and its markets. The early growth of the industry (predominantly at Sliven) had been primarily concerned with substituting hand spinning to compete in the export trade to the Ottoman Empire. But between 1887 and 1896 exporting became progressively more difficult. Attention (assisted by privileges and tariffs) switched to import substitution, and to displacing proto-industrial woollens from the home market. During this phase, factory production expanded at Gabrovo and capacity was established at Karlovo and Kazanl'k. In the 1880s it had been easy for machine woollen manufacturing to expand by displacing handicraft producers, but by the mid-1890s, expansion by displacement of proto-industry and imports had run its course. Future sales would depend on domestic military and civil demand, and on conditions on the Ottoman market, the sole significant export outlet.

In 1896 excess capacity began to appear.[87] Most Sliven factories could 'hardly cover their expenses because of the big depression of trade'.[88] The Trjavna and Kazanl'k mills fell into distress, while the operators of the old state mill at Sliven gave up the struggle. From then onwards, although the home market was far from stagnant, the industry preoccupied itself with winning shelter and privileges to maintain its profits. We shall argue, however, that protection had little effect on the volume of production, because the industry's share of the home market stagnated, and because, as an exporter of products similar to those it sold in the home market, it scarcely needed protection to hold its market share.

State orders for military cloth were an area where growth was possible through import substitution. In 1886, Austrian factories supplied Bulgaria with 75,000 metres of cloth and 5,000 army greatcoats, while Russian factories won orders for 40,000 metres of cloth (which they failed to meet). Even then, domestic suppliers to the military market were heavily protected. Allowing for transport costs and tariffs, the true extent of preference to home producers was estimated by their Austrian competitors in 1886 at 30 per cent.[89] As yet, the Bulgarian factories could afford to neglect the military market, despite government premia of 6.5 – 15 per cent over the lowest (duty paid) public tender.[90] In 1892, far from wanting

---

[86] Simeon Damjanov, *Frenskoto ikonomichesko pronikvane v B'lgarija 1878–1914* (Sofia, 1971), p. 206.
[87] V. Atanasov, 'Kakvo trebva na nashata tekstilna industrija', *Sp. BID*, I (1896), pp. 186–7.
[88] *Izlozhenie: Sliven 1895–96*, p. 80.
[89] 'Zur wirthschaftslichen Lage Bulgariens III', *Handelsmuseum*, II (1887), p. 397.
[90] *RC*, LXXVII (1892), p. 101.

Table 9.1 *Bulgarian woollen factory cloth and yarn, sales 1887/8–1912 (in 000 leva)*

Year	Current prices	Factory output or sales (i)	Outwork value added (ii)	Total sales (iii)	Export sales (iv)	Home market sales (v)	Home sales as % of home market (vi)
				Constant prices of 1900			
1887/8	1,916	1,949	314	2,263	1,466	797	35.2
1889/90	2,079	2,272	314	2,586	1,415	1,171	44.1
1891/2	2,674	2,974	314	3,288	1,169	2,119	65.2
1895	5,634	5,527	(100)	5,627	1,003	4,624	76.1
1896	5,094	4,734	89	4,823	861	3,962	69.5
1900	6,300	6,300	76	6,376	1,377	4,999	86.9
1903	7,250	6,005	(76)	6,081	1,449	4,632	72.1
1907	8,902	6,746	(72)	6,818	2,338	4,480	66.1
1909	10,867	7,577	72	7,649	2,277	5,372	66.2
1911	11,406	9,447	(72)	9,519	2,457	7,062	62.2
1912	11,439	9,196	(72)	9,268	908	8,360	64.8

For sources and calculation, see BALKSTAT. Estimates in parentheses.

to support prices, the Ministry of Commerce warned manufacturers to cut back on price rises.[91] But the growth of capacity forced the factories to compete more actively for military orders, and by 1896, 'any merchant in the trade will tell you that cloth for the army is being overproduced'.[92] Even so, this was a smaller privileged market than Bulgarian suppliers had enjoyed under Ottoman rule, for army orders in about 1903 amounted to 150,000 metres,[93] no great advance on the 131,000 metres attained by the Sliven mill in 1872.[94] By this time, moreover, the orders were being shared between ten factories.[95] They represented about 23 per cent of home demand. Supranormal profits from supplying state orders therefore assumed critical importance for the industry, as they allowed the mills to stay afloat despite low usage of capacity. Only on the eve of the Balkan wars did military orders boost production.[96] They probably pushed the mills to their capacity, despite the collapse of exports, for in 1913, big orders for military khaki were placed abroad.[97]

With army orders an undynamic element till 1911 or 1912, growth in home sales had to come through the expansion of the civil market and through substituting imports. The industry lobbied for and won protectionist measures. The tariff, which had been set by treaty at 8 per cent in 1878, was raised to 10.5 per cent in 1894, and again to 18 per cent in 1897.[98] In 1896 government employees were forced to wear Bulgarian cloth at work. Little expansion of sales could have been expected from this irritating restriction. Lower ranking officials usually bought Bulgarian cloth anyway while senior officials were exempted from the regulation.[99] The industry exploited this regulation to widen its margins on a static volume of sales by hoisting prices to its captive consumers.[100] The external tariff was raised again in 1906 and in 1913 afforded protection to the textile industries of 19.2–22.2 per cent.[101]

As there was little scope for import substitution in coarse cloth, in which Bulgarian manufacturers were efficient, expansion involved trading up, into worsteds, mixed cloths, patterns and 'novelties'. This was also the sector in which domestic demand was growing most strongly. In 1906 it was reported that:

A decade ago the Bulgarian, rather than pay a high price, would have gone without; but at the present time, there is a noticeable tendency, more especially

[91] *Sp.BID*, I, p. 524.   [92] Atanasov, 'Kakvo trebva', p. 187.
[93] Mishajkov, 'Ocherk', p. 560.   [94] Tabakov, *Sliven*, III, p. 114.
[95] Mishajkov, 'Ocherk', p. 560.   [96] GBC Bulgaria 1913, p. 6.
[97] PRO FO 368 800. Anglo-Syrian Trading Company-FO, 23 May 1913.
[98] Mishajkov, 'Ocherk', p. 574.   [99] Staneff, *Gewerbewesen*, pp. 113–14.
[100] *Izlozhenie: Plovdiv 1901–2*, p. 48.
[101] Lampe and Jackson, *Balkan Economic History*, pp. 265, 267.

among the townsfolk, to buy goods of a better quality and even articles which a few years ago would have been reckoned as luxuries.[102]

But this was a tough market to break into. Resources had to be shifted into an area of persistent comparative disadvantage. The products offered were neither cheap nor elegant;[103] as late as 1910, affluent consumers would not be seen dead in locally made cloth.[104] Products of this type required a wider range of equipment and of skills than were needed to produce *shajak*, and diseconomies arose from the small scale on which they were produced.[105] Quality cloth had to be made entirely from imported yarn. The Sofia mill, which specialized in this market, imported all its raw materials from Belgium.[106] There was much talk about improving quality to take advantage of the rising tariff, but the statistical picture is clear: import substitution could only add about a third to the size of the home market, and the endeavour to make significant inroads here was unsuccessful.[107] As Table 9.1 showed, the proportion of cloth sales taken by imports rose from 28 per cent in 1903 to 34 per cent in 1907 and 38 per cent in 1911. The expansion of the industry was carried by the 4.5 per cent annual growth of home market demand, and this was faster than the growth of the industry itself.

The figures displayed in Table 9.1 took no account of the import of ready-made clothing. This expanded in the early years after the liberation, because the few masters in Bulgaria capable of 'French' tailoring made ill-fitting clothes and frequently damaged the cloth.[108] So consumers who aspired to a dash of gentility bought off-the-peg clothing mostly of Austrian provenance, while the smart set bought clothes through the catalogues of the Paris and Vienna fashion houses.[109] Imports of ready-made woollen clothing reached a peak of 2.31 million leva in 1891/5 – a turnover greater than that of imported woollen cloth. But they fell away to 1.36 million in 1896–1900 and to 967,000 in 1901/5. During the same period, the import of woollen cloth rose by about the same amount. This was caused by growth in Bulgarian dressmaking and tailoring, making up imported cloth, since the duty on imported clothing was four times as high as that on cloth, and this provided a high protective duty on the value added in the clothing trade.

---

[102] GBC Bulgaria 1906, p. 7.   [103] *RC*, LXXVII (1892), p. 101.
[104] G. E. D.-Va., 'Znachenieto na v'tr'shnija pazar za nashata v'lnena industrija', *Sp.BID*, XIV (1910), p. 586.   [105] Mishajkov, 'Ocherk', p. 481.   [106] *RC*, CLVI (1912), p. 67.
[107] D. Mishajkov, 'V'lnenite tekstilni fabriki v B'lgarija i tehnite pazari', *Sp.BID*, XII (1908) p. 70; 'Bulgarie et Roumélie orientale: mouvement commercial pendant l'année 1894', p. 11; *RCADCF*, no. 304.
[108] *Izlozhenie: Tatar-pazardzhik 1890–1891*, p. 118; *1894–95*, pp. 15–16.
[109] AN F12 7280. Bourgas. Mouvement commercial et maritime de Bourgas en 1908; GBC Bulgaria 1897, p. 30.

Many Sofia drapers now attached clothing *ateliers* to their stores. This should have given the Bulgarian factories a chance to win orders from the drapers for cloth which would otherwise have been of foreign provenance.[110] However, the extent of this substitution was probably insignificant. Although the tailoring trade may have been expanding in the major cities, it was probably declining in the country as a whole.[111]

Bulgarian woollen mill products enjoyed easy market conditions from 1906 onwards thanks to peasant prosperity, aided by a swing in the terms of trade towards agriculture.[112] The high tariff let them ride the boom in country sales of traditional cloth, marking up their prices. They made no further effort to substitute imports, and accepted a diminishing share of the domestic woollen market, because of the unprofitability of competing at the top end.

With the loss of former markets in Bosnia and Serbia, Bulgarian woollen exports were confined largely to the Ottoman Empire. 'Almost the whole' of these exports originated from Sliven.[113] This market was circumscribed, since the range of cloths within which Sliven competed was narrow, and its competitive edge was fine. Even the small tariff over which Sliven cloth had to compete in the Ottoman Empire after the unification of Eastern Rumelia with Bulgaria restrained growth in sales. Bulgarian cloth exports, which ran at 312 tonnes in 1886/8, only advanced to 331 tonnes by 1896/8. But in 1900 they were given duty free treatment on the the Ottoman border, and advanced to 446 tonnes in 1906/8.[114]

Although exports to the Ottoman Empire accounted for more than half of Sliven's output,[115] its entrepreneurs seldom bestirred themselves to promote their sales on the Ottoman market. Up to 1878, they had sold the cloth which their outworkers had manufactured to Ottoman military and civil buyers who arrived each year to obtain supplies.[116] Up to the Balkan Wars, this trade continued on the same 'very primitive' lines, saving only that the work had been transferred to factories.[117] Sliven manufacturers made few efforts to court their clientele, and were not

---

[110] Mishajkov, 'V'lnenite tekstilni', p. 69.

[111] P. Tsonchev, 'Shivaskijat zanajat v Gabrovo', *Sp.BID*, XIV (1910), pp. 352–6.

[112] M. R. Palairet, 'Land, Labour and Industrial Progress in Bulgaria and Serbia before 1914', *JEEcH*, XII (1983), pp. 176–7.   [113] Tabakov, *Sliven*, III, p. 116.

[114] *Desetogodishna statistika za v'nshnata t'rgovija na B'lgarija 1886–1895* (Sofia, 1906), pp. 480–3; *1896–1905* (Sofia, 1912), pp. 646–9; *Statistika za t'rgovijata na Knjazhestvo B'lgarija s chuzhdite d'rzhavi . . . prez 1906 godina . . . prez 1907*, p. 224; *. . . prez 1908*; Tabakov, *Grad Sliven*, III, p. 116.

[115] In 1894/5, 56.4 per cent, and in 1896/7, 58.2 per cent. *Doklad: Sliven 1894–95*, table 4; *Izlozhenie: Sliven 1896–97*, p. 33.   [116] Tabakov, *Sliven*, III, pp. 53–4.

[117] *S'krateni protokoli za sasedeniata na I i II redovni sesii na Burgazkata t'rg.-industrialna kamara* (Burgaz, 1909), p. 48.

scrupulous in the manner in which they executed their orders.[118] They knew their business however, and were justified in regarding the Ottoman market as safe. Bulgarian *shajak* enjoyed much greater prestige in Constantinople than competing imported cloths,[119] and as competition from Ottoman manufacturers was weak, the Sliven mills continued to win military as well as civil orders.[120]

Yet the Ottoman market was changing, and what Sliven supplied changed with it. Despite frequent reference to the durability of Bulgarian export cloth, the Sliven manufacturers knew their advantage rested on price as much as on quality, and on their ability to simulate an unchanging and antiquated product. This made their wares increasingly difficult to sell in the more Europeanized Bulgarian home market.[121] They came to terms with the loss of cheap wool by adulterating their cloth with recycled wool, wool waste and shoddy. In 1909, lower grade Sliven export cloth was said to contain 25 per cent of recycled wool (imported from England), and allowing also for the use of shoddy, the proportion of adulterants in these goods may have risen to 30–40 per cent; some of the produce was 'of such low quality that you could pull it apart in your hands'. The manufacturers claimed they knew their business better than their critics, and urged that adulteration made their cloth more elastic and gave it a better sheen, and that the days were past when Bulgarian cloth was bought for its durability.[122] This was probably true, for British imitation *shajak* made from shoddy was selling at 1.50 francs per metre compared with the Bulgarian at 4.50–6.00 francs.[123] However Sliven was precariously dependent on a single export market, and it was only a matter of time before Turkey would turn to protection. Sliven cloth offered little but cheapness in relation to weight, an advantage which could be wiped out at a stroke, and its simple technology could speedily be replicated. This consideration prompted one manufacturer (Stefanov) to test market his cloth in free-trade Britain, but without success.[124] At the end of 1910, Bulgaria's cloth began to pay an 11 per cent duty in Turkey. Even this mild tariff created 'extremely unpleasant conditions on the Turkish market', especially as competing capacity was being built at Smyrna.[125] It was the beginning of the end. Exports of *shajak* tumbled from 3.96 million leva in 1910 to 2.21 million in 1911. In 1912 they were down to 1.17 million, and with the disruption of trade following the Balkan wars, they shrank yet again to 243,642 leva in

[118] Mishajkov, 'Ocherk', p. 570.   [119] Atanasov, 'Kakvo trebva', p. 188.
[120] Mishajkov, 'V'lnenite tekstilni', pp. 72–3.   [121] Ibid., p. 76.
[122] *Burgazka ... kamara*, pp. 117, 170–2.
[123] BAE Dossier 2807 no. 2161, 10 Feb. 1904, fo. 17.   [124] Tabakov, *Sliven*, III, p. 118.
[125] 'Nashiti tekstilni fabriki i turskija pazar', *Sp. BID*, XV (1911), p. 188.

1913.[126] From then on, Bulgaria's textile industry worked for the home market alone. But although these factories had geared their production to the Ottoman market, a wave of rationalization, concentration and investment left them able to adapt. At the end of 1911, the Sliven industry, though it reckoned it still 'ruled the Turkish markets' was confident that if these were lost, it could accomodate itself to new conditions.[127] This led to further reduction in the number of firms, and the re-equipment of the industry, but its postwar record in some measure fulfilled its self-confident prediction.[128]

Woollen industry mechanization in Serbia

In Bulgaria, local entrepreneurship was so solidly entrenched in the manufacture of woollens that outsider participation was insignificant. But in the old territories of Serbia, large-scale woollen industry initiatives up to 1878 had been ineffectual. As no significant domestic industry occupied the ground, opportunities existed for outsider penetration, with government encouragement.

Serbia was indeed becoming an increasingly attractive territory in which to manufacture Bulgarian type woollens. In 1878, it was more densely populated than Bulgaria, and a growing labour force was becoming available for rural manufacturing. For example, at Knjaževac a decaying household carpet manufacture was making way for commercial *šajak* weaving,[129] and this small industry produced a 'surplus' of 3,000 metres a year by 1891.[130] But by the late nineteenth century, new proto-industrial concentrations could no longer expand as easily as they had done earlier in Bulgaria. The pressure of competition from factories which were simultaneously being built in the same country held returns to handicraft producers at levels too low to attract large numbers of participants, so these industries themselves needed to mechanize to survive. So the rising textile industries in Serbia were associated from the start with at least partial mechanization.

The first major woollen enterprise in Serbia was set up at Paraćin in 1882 at the invitation of the Serbian government.[131] It was owned by the firm of Münch and Schumpeter, whose factory at Brno in Moravia had

---

[126] Customs entry 590 in *Statistika za t'rgovijata na Tsarstvo B'lgarija s chuzhdite d'rzhavi . . . prez 1910 g; . . . prez 1912 g; . . . prez 1913, 1914 i 1915 godini* (Sofia, 1921).

[127] Tabakov, *Sliven*, III, p. 166.   [128] Ibid., pp. 166–84.

[129] *Put licejskih pitomaca . . . po Srbiji godine 1863*, ed. Kosta Popović (Belgrade, 1867), p. 124; St. Popović, 'Ekonomni izveštaj o putu u Knjaževac, Pirot, Vranju, Leskovac i Niš' (Part 2) *Glasnik Ministarstva Finansija*, II (no. 38, 8 Oct. 1883), pp. 605–6.

[130] GBC Serbia 1891, p. 24.

[131] Milivoje M. Savić, *Naša industrija i zanati*, I (Sarajevo, 1922), p. 218.

handled Serbian military contracts since 1874.[132] By Balkan standards this was a big mill, with experienced management and superior equipment.[133] In 1891 it was 'one of the best cloth factories in central Europe', equipped with 3,400 mule spindles and 96 power-looms.[134] It began as a high-cost enterprise which depended on military orders,[135] but, in a few years, it drove the hand-made woollens of Panagjurishte (Bulgaria) out of the Serbian market.[136] Soon the firm was trying to export. In 1890, Münch enlisted the support of the Serbian consul in Skoplje for a project to open a warehouse there, and in 1893 a test marketing in Salonica gave good promise.[137] The firm began to compete vigorously in the Ottoman market against the Bulgarians, offering (allegedly) imitations of Bulgarian export cloth.[138] In 1894, its cloth was being imported in a small way by the tailors of Monastir (Bitola in Macedonia) because of its reputation for solidity and strength.[139] Its exports rose every year from 1897 to 1903 when they attained 315,000 dinars.[140] By then, foreign customers had overcome their initial mistrust of the mill's products, and were coming to Paraćin to place orders.[141] Even Bosnia became a target market. Despite the huge tariff that Austria imposed in the interest of the Czech manufacturers, their outputs were less well matched to local tastes than those of the Balkan states. Once the Paraćin mill had been equipped for *gajtan* production, its management set up a branch office at Sarajevo for distribution, and was initially encouraged by its success.[142] Despite these efforts, the Paraćin mill was not profitable and when it was destroyed by fire in 1904, rumour circulated that the fire was started to defraud the insurers. Whether this was true or not, the Münch family did not rebuild, and diverted their resources into mining.[143]

We can learn much about the problems of woollen manufacturing in Serbia from the difficulties of the Paraćin mill. Profitability was affected by Münch's original assumption that he would 'have at his disposal all the wool in Serbia',[144] which up to 1878 had indeed been cheap, in surplus,

---

[132] AS MNP (T) 1906 41 7. Münch. & Schumpeter – Min. Fin. 7 Nov. 1879.

[133] M. M. Kostić, *Pisma s puta Beograd – Paraćin – Zaječar* (Belgrade, 1896), pp. 40–54.

[134] *Službeni vojni list*, XI (1891), pp. 573–4, 579.   [135] GBC Serbia 1888, p. 17.

[136] Marin T. Vlajkov, *Belezhki v'rhu ekonomicheskoto polozhenie na grada Panagjurishte predi i sled v'zstanieto* (Plovdiv, 1904), p. 22.

[137] AS MNP (T) 1906 41 7. Consulate general, Skoplje-MNP, 3 May 1890 and no. 620 of 1893.   [138] Tabakov, *Sliven*, III, p. 116.

[139] 'Izveštaj bitoljskog konsulata o privredi, trgovini i saobraćaju u bitoljskom vilajetu za 1894–tu godinu', *SN*, LXII (1895), 214 col. 4.

[140] *SGKS*, 1897, p. 320; 1898–9, p. 334; 1900, p. 286; 1901, p. 326; 1902, pp. 325–6; 1903, pp. 349–50.   [141] AS MNP (T) 1906 41 7. Minh – MNP, 4 Mar. 1902, no. 1504.

[142] AS MNP (T) 1906 41 7. Münch – MNP, 4 Feb. 1904, no. 771.

[143] 'Razvoj Paraćina i njegove fabrike stakla', *Komuna* (Belgrade) XIII (1966) no. 3, pp. 36–7; Ekonomski institut N. R. Srbije, *Proizvodne snage N R Srbije* (Belgrade, 1953), p. 470, col. 2.   [144] *RC*, LXXV, 1892, p. 11.

and of good quality.[145] Under his concession he committed himself only to import wool that could not be bought locally.[146] He studied the location problem at some length, and rejected the proto-industrial south as lacking the conditions for modern textile factory enterprise. He decided on Paraćin for the sake of its water power, which he harnessed by taking over a state watermill.[147] Apart from that, Paraćin was a wool market, whose wool and wool washing trades were the mainstay of the town's prosperity.[148]

But Paraćin had no industrial background. Its communications were far from ideal, and Münch later regarded his factory's location as a handicap. Domestic wool supplies proved unsatisfactory, because the entire inventory for a year had to be bought at shearing time, otherwise the merchants would promptly export it.[149] Moreover, the available wool was coarse and shaggy, because it was shorn but once a year,[150] and its shortcomings adversely affected the texture of the cloth.[151] Moreover, the wool market was so narrow that Münch's purchasing drove prices up sharply.[152] So by 1891 the factory imported 57 per cent of its wool[153] despite heavy transport costs. This exposed its proprietors to press attacks for failing to buy Serbian wool.[154] So long as the mill was protected by its fifteen-year monopoly concession, the problem was more of political embarrassment than of business viability, but when a rival firm opened a woollen mill in Belgrade in 1897, the transport cost disadvantage borne by the Paraćin mill caused profits to fall. Münch also complained that labour cost him more than his competitors in Leskovac in the south, but the location advantage enjoyed by his competitor in Belgrade was the greater. On these grounds he opposed the Belgrade concession.[155]

The Belgrade rival was Eugen Michel, who went to Serbia in 1889 as Münch's weaving master. A man of substance who disposed capital from the sale of a factory in Germany, Michel worked for Münch for two years then settled in Belgrade to engage in business.[156] He desperately wanted

---

[145] For wool supply trends, see Michael Palairet, 'The Influence of Commerce on the Changing Structure of Serbia's Peasant Economy 1860–1912' (Ph.D. thesis, University of Edinburgh, 1976), pp. 276–81.

[146] Concession dated 16 Apr. 1880 in AS MNP (T) 1895 XII 79.

[147] AS MNP (T) 1906 41 7. Münch and Schumpeter – Min. Fin. 7 Nov. 1879; ibid., no. 7819 of 21 July 1880.   [148] *RC*, LXXV (1892), p. 11; Kostić, *Pisma s puta*, pp. 35–7.

[149] AS MNP (T) 1906 41 7. Münch and Schumpeter – Min. Fin. 25 June 1882.

[150] AS MNP (T) 1906 41 7. Münch and Schumpeter – MNP, 29 June 1883.

[151] E. de Borchgrave, *La Serbie administrative, économique et commerciale* (Brussels, 1883), p. 182.   [152] AS MNP (T) 1906 41 7. Minh – MNP, 11 Dec. 1890, no. 7765.

[153] *Službeni vojni list*, XI (1891) p. 523.   [154] Kostić, *Pisma s puta*, pp. 49–50.

[155] AS MNP (T) 1902 1 107. No. 1880 of 26 Mar. 1899; MNP (T) 1906 41 7. No. 5067 of 2 Aug. 1897.

[156] AS MNP (T) 1895 XII 79. No. 2380 of 1895; ibid., no. 1375 of 1894.

to set up a woollen mill in Belgrade in competition with his former employer, whose prices he offered to undercut by 20–25 per cent.[157] To get round the Paraćin mill's monopoly which expired in April 1895, Michel proposed to set up a centralized spinning and finishing factory to service an outwork network of hand weavers.[158] Long after the Paraćin mill's monopoly expired Münch struggled to prevent Michel from starting up,[159] and Michel did not secure his concession till March 1897. He brought in Karl Wolf (who also invested in building a hemp processing mill in Vranje) as a partner,[160] and erected his factory on the outskirts of Belgrade at Karaburma, where it employed 200 hands. The business was rapidly built up. According to Michel's estimates, his investment rose from 350,000 dinars in 1897 to 1.43 million in 1906. This probably reflected successful trading, and in 1906 the mill was running at capacity.[161] Michel sought a further ten year concession that year, for which he was prepared to sink a further 2 million dinars in the mill, but fell seriously ill. His partner Wolf then agreed to transfer the mill to Ilić brothers, the sons of Kosta Ilić of Leskovac.[162] In their hands, the mill was expanded further, and in 1914 was reckoned the largest textile mill in Serbia.[163]

Indigenous woollen enterprises were formed only in the former Niš *pašaluk* (annexed from the Ottomans in 1878) where there were long-standing proto-industries centred on three larger towns, Leskovac, Pirot and Vranje. Leskovac and Vranje engaged in the domestic manufacture of hempen cordage, and Pirot in carpet weaving. These districts were poorly endowed with fertile land, and were settled with a largely non-dinaric population, so there was abundant rural labour on which the woollen industries could and did draw. At the time of the liberation, domestic woollen manufacturing was 'much in repute' in Leskovac and environs,[164] to which it had recently spread (probably from Pirot).[165] As in Bulgaria, household woollen manufacturing declined during the following decade, and for similar reasons.[166]

Despite the presence of woollen and ropemaking proto-industries, the new woollen enterprises originated not from putting-out but from the

[157] AS MNP (T) 1895 XII 79. No. 2514 of 11 June 1893.
[158] AS MNP (T) 1895 XII 79. No. 4910 of 15 Aug. 1893.
[159] AS MNP (T) 1906 41 7. Münch – MNP, 2 Aug. 1897, no. 5067.
[160] AS MNP (T) 1907 38 10. No. 130 of 1907.
[161] AS MNP (T) 1906 45 6. E. Mihel and Komp. Beograd – MNP, 20 Oct. 1906, no. 6405.
[162] AS MNP (T) 1907 38 10. MNP – Ministarski savet, 3 Jan. 1907.
[163] Jaša Grgašević, *Industrija Srbije i Crne gore* (Zagreb, 1924), p. 193.
[164] AS MNP (T) 1898 VI 2. Popović-Ilić – MNP, 2 Sept. 1895, no. 5002.
[165] Sergije Dimitrijević, *Gradska privreda starog Leskovca* (Leskovac, 1952), p. 13.
[166] AS MNP (T) 1898 VI 2. Popović-Ilić – MNP 2 Sept. 1895, no. 5002.

wholesale distribution of textiles, especially *gajtan* imported from Bulgaria through Leskovac. Leskovac merchants re-exported this *gajtan* throughout the western Balkans. As these supplies became difficult to secure after the liberation of Bulgaria, Leskovac merchants had a powerful incentive to establish *gajtan* mills of their own to safeguard their businesses, and they acted energetically.[167] The early industrial ventures started on a petty scale with minimal equipment, reflecting the limited resources of their founders. It was a characteristic of fledgling factory businesses established in a proto-industrial milieu, that the early *gajtan* mills were set up not in the town itself, but in nearby villages, selected for access to water power. Right up to 1896, the yarn needed was collected mainly from the local peasant women. The businesses were, however, run from Leskovac town.

The development of woollen manufacturing in Leskovac owed much to its enterprise culture, a feature it shared with Gabrovo in Bulgaria. Not for nothing was Leskovac (optimistically) dubbed 'the Serbian Manchester'. It was strongly orientated to craft manufacturing; whereas in 1884 Belgrade counted one craft business per 63.5 inhabitants, Leskovac counted one for 21.0.[168] The woollen firms started from the smallest possible beginnings, but most were expanded and updated repeatedly, mainly by the ruthless plough-back of profits. Trajković stresses the entrepreneurial cult of the early Leskovac industrialists, with their emphasis on frugality and hard work.[169] Their doctrine ('we eat paprikas and build factories') made excellent sense in an environment where the marginal efficiency of capital was high but external sources of finance were meagre. In this respect the precocious industrialization of Leskovac may be compared with the slow progress of its larger neighbour, Niš, for all that the latter enjoyed much superior communications. Niš, observed a consul, 'is notorious among Servians for the want of business aptitude and energy of its inhabitants'.[170]

Why Leskovac, not Pirot? Before the liberation Pirot had enjoyed far greater industrial repute than Leskovac. It had also been the commercial focus for an industrial hinterland which extended to Chiprovtsi, and several nearby villages.[171] The 'enormous' trade of Pirot and its annual fairs testified to the industrial character of the town and its environs, and to its importance in Balkan commerce.[172] Besides producing woollen and

[167] Dragoljub Trajković, *Istorija leskovačke industrije* (Belgrade, 1961), pp. 16–18.
[168] Dimitrijević, *Gradska privreda*, p. 8.   [169] Trajković, *Leskovačke industrije*, pp. 24–5.
[170] PRO FO 105 97. Confidential, 9 Aug. 1892.
[171] Adolf Strauss, 'Bulgarische Industrie', *Österreichische Monatschrift für den Orient* (1885), XI, p. 208.
[172] Konstantin Kosev, *Za kapitalisticheskoto razvitie na B'lgarskite zemi prez 60–te i 70–te godini na XIX vek* (Sofia, 1965), p. 76; K. N. Kostić, 'Pirot', *Glasnik srpskog geografskog društva* (Belgrade, 1912), I, pp. 86–8.

cotton cloth, the district manufactured and traded in woven carpets, on a scale which made Pirot carpets an article of mass consumption in the Balkans.[173] As early as 1873, one Ali Beg had set up a woolcombing and spinning establishment at Pirot, which was elsewhere described as a 'municipally owned woolcombing factory'.[174]

Despite this promising background, the subsequent industrial history of Pirot has to be written in largely negative terms. The factory was destroyed during the liberation and was not replaced. A number of carding machines were set up from the 1890s onward, but till World War I, most of the wool continued to be hand spun.[175] Pirot lost part of its carpet supply because the new Serbo-Bulgarian frontier separated the town from the Chiprovtsi villages. But unlike Leskovac, which in the 1880s made good its production base by local large-scale manufacturing, Pirot made no analogous response. Carpet manufacturing continued as a domestic industry, and still employed 1,000 workwomen in the town as late as 1890.[176] Yet this staple industry was in obvious distress, and the town itself 'of poor and sad enough aspect', in 1891.[177] To revive the trade, a 'state carpet factory' was set up by a society in about 1888 and was granted 10,000 dinars of government assistance, plus the patronage of Queen Natalia.[178] This was a well-intentioned co-operative, designed to advance wool to its members at 5 per cent interest, and to uphold the price of the product. It failed because the merchants found outside labour to undercut the society's products, and because the members who were 'all poor women carpet makers' treated it as a dispenser of cheap consumer credit.[179] A joint stock company 'to improve the manufactory of carpets' was then promoted (probably in 1891) but the flotation failed for lack of subscribers.[180] Yet there was nothing implausible about the venture; successful carpet factories were established in Bulgaria with exiguous resources both at Panagjurishte,[181] and at Kotel (though not at Chiprovtsi).

The desultory history of industrial initiatives at Pirot seems to be associated with co-operative and philanthropic rather than commercial aims; in this respect high-mindedness was a poor substitute for the single-minded pursuit of gain at Leskovac. Nor was it only the Pirot carpet trade

---

[173] Kostić, 'Pirot', p. 90.

[174] Vladimir Karić, Srbija. Opis zemlje, narode i države (Belgrade, 1887), p. 407; M. M. Savić, Naša Industrija i Zanati (Sarajevo, 1922), II, p. 118.   [175] Savić, Industrija, II, p. 119.

[176] Serbia. Ministarstvo Vojno, Statistika država balkanskog poluostrva. I Kr. Srbija (Belgrade, 1890), p. 79.   [177] RC, LXXV (1892), p. 16.

[178] AS MNP (T) 1889 X 21. Čilim a.d.-MNP 26 May 1889; RC, LXXV (1892), p. 16; GBC Serbia 1888, p. 24.   [179] AS MNP (T) 1902. I 88. Izveštaj 20 Jan. 1890, no. 377.

[180] GBC Serbia 1891, p. 23.

[181] G. T. Danailov, 'Kilimenata industrija v B'lgarija', Sp. BID, IV (1900), pp. 692–4.

which stood in want of mechanization. Pirot was the one region in Serbia which maintained a substantial domestic *šajak* manufacture. This industry expanded until World War I, and sold beyond the confines of the local market. In 1911, a Šabac merchant advertised clothing 'made from the famous Pirot *sukno* [worsted] and *šajak* at reasonable prices'.[182] But nobody thought to mechanize the industry.

The first Leskovac *gajtan* mill was set up at Strojkovac village in 1884 by four Leskovac *gajtan* merchants, including Antonije Popović, Gligorije Jovanović and Mita Teokarević, for an investment of 72,844 dinars.[183] Lacking skills in *gajtan* production, they brought in Stevan Bojadzhiev, a *gajtan* specialist from Karlovo. His job was to smuggle *charks* – braiding machines – out of Bulgaria, and to set them up in a rented watermill. The partners bought their wool on the market, supervised its washing and combing, then put it out to 700–1,200 domestic spinners according to season. Between 5 and 6 tonnes of the yarn was also imported, against 35 tons of wool spun locally, but this was reserved for up-market work, since it cost 40 per cent more than locally spun yarn.[184] In 1889, Teokarević, now in partnership with one Trajko Djordjević, shifted some of his machinery to Vučje village, because of the unreliability of water power at Strojkovac, and by 1890 the firm had thirty-four machines at the latter village, forty-eight at the former.[185] But the firm's output was still limited by water supplies, and the entrepreneurs chafed at the administrative burden imposed by putting-out.[186] Imported yarn was too expensive, while local hand-spun yarn was in short supply in summer because of the seasonal diversion of women's labour to the fields.[187] The firm was sitting pretty despite its problems, because competitors had to forage for such supplies as they could obtain from Bulgaria, usually by devious means.[188] So to consolidate its advantage, the Vučje firm tried to get emulators barred from competing with it. It had friends in administrative circles, who blocked two applications to manufacture *gajtan* in 1891,[189] and it secured concessionary privileges in 1890, though the other Leskovac merchants stopped it securing monopoly rights.[190]

182 *Trgovinski-zanatlijski šematizam za 1911.* Advertisement no. 40.
183 Trajković, *Leskovačke industrije*, pp. 24–5.
184 AS MNP (T) 1898 VI 2. Sreski načelnik, Leskovac – MNP, 1 July 1890, no. 3677; Popović-Ilić – MNP, 11 Feb. 1898, f. 3vo; Popović et al. – Načelnik sreza Leskovca, 9 Aug. 1885.
185 AS MNP (T) 1898 VI 2. Popović–MNP, 12 May 1889, no. 2024; Sreski načelnik, Leskovac–MNP, 1 July 1890, no. 3677.   186 *RC*, LXXV (1892), p. 19.
187 AS MNP (T) 1898 VI 2. Sreski načelnik, Leskovac – MNP, 1 July 1890, no. 3677 fo.2 vo.   188 Trajković, *Leskovačke industrije*, p. 17.
189 AS MNP (T) 1898 VI 2. Kostić – MNP, 5 Mar. 1891, no. 1526; MNP – Načelnik, srez Leskovca, 28 Aug. 1891; Braće Koste Osman-Begović – MNP, 12 Mar. 1891, no. 1711.
190 AS MNP (T) 1898 VI 2. Concession to Antonije Popović, dated 8 Sept. 1885.

So in 1890 or 1891 two more Leskovac *gajtan* merchants, Gligorije Petrović and Mihailo Janković, won the backing of Kosta Ilić Mumdžija, a self-made Leskovac chandler, usurer and money changer, and invested 72,000 dinars in manufacturing *gajtan* at a mill at Kozari village.[191] Another Bulgarian specialist, Manuilo Iliev of Kalofer, was brought into the syndicate to run the mill.[192] As at Vučje, the enterprise depended both on skilled Bulgarian workers, and on 'their old implements from ruined Bulgarian factories'.[193] In 1895, Janković broke with his partners, and with a Bulgarian collaborator, set up a fourth *gajtan* factory in a watermill at Grdelica village.[194]

At this time, the Paraćin mill, which (unlike the Leskovac mills) owned its own spinning capacity, acquired equipment to make *gajtan*, and invaded the market hitherto controlled by Leskovac.[195] A price war ensued, to the gratification of the Serbian *abadžija* trade, which was the main purchaser.[196] For the Leskovac *gajtan* manufacturers, the long deferred decision to enter into machine spinning was now inescapable. The Vučje and Kozari firms sank their differences, and scraped up the cash to set up a small mule spinnery in Leskovac town. It was concessioned to spin for *gajtan* making,[197] but was also equipped with a few looms.[198] In February 1897, it started work with ninety-two employees to make *gajtan* and woollen cloth.[199] This installation did not end the yarn shortage, but further cut-throat competition ensued between Leskovac and Paraćin to secure official orders.[200] Leskovac had the better of it, for it made heavy inroads into the profits of Münch's enterprise.

In 1904, the destruction of the Paraćin mill caused a shortage of *gajtan* and cloth. So three top employees at Paraćin, headed by Josip Jovanović, bought salvaged equipment and yarn stocks from their erstwhile employer, and set up a second small spinnery at Kozari, a location which attracted them for its water supply. Their enterprise span and plaited *gajtan*, knitted hosiery, and manufactured and sold knitting wool to the peasants in the Šumadija.[201] Acting on the same stimulus, Popović and

---

191 Dimitrijević, *Gradska privreda*, pp. 18–19; Trajković, *Leskovačke industrije*, p. 20.
192 *Proizvodne snage*, p. 471, col. 1.
193 AS MNP (T) 1898 VI 2. Popović–MNP, 25 Aug. 1890, no. 5120.
194 AS MNP (T) 1905 XV 9. Janković–MNP, 3 May 1895, no. 2707; Janković–MNP, 30 May 1895, no. 3089; Trajković, *Leskovačke industrije*, p. 21.
195 AS MNP (T) 1898 VI 2. Popović–Ilić – MNP, 11 Feb. 1898, fo. 1.
196 AS MNP (T) 1906 41 7. Belgrade abadžija esnaf – MNP, 12 Jan. 1904.
197 AS MNP (T) 1898 VI 2. Concession to Popović-Ilić i komp. dated 31 May 1895.
198 Trajković, *Leskovačke industrije*, pp. 20–1.
199 AS MNP (T) 1898 VI 2. Commission of inspection, 17 July 1897, no. 3774.
200 AS MNP (T) 1898 VI 2. Popović–Ilić i komp.-MNP, 11 Feb. 1898, pp. 3–3vo.
201 'Fabrika gajtana, vunenog pletiva i vunice u Kozari', *Trgovinski glasnik*, XXII (1912), no. 75, p. 4.

Table 9.2 *Serbia 1889–1912: woollen industry gross output*
(000 dinars, current prices)

| | Woollen cloth | | | | | | | |
	Paraćin	Belgrade	Leskovac	Total	*Gajtan*	Cloth and *gajtan*	Exports	Home sales
1889	1,146	–	–	1,146	145	1,291	–	1,291
1893	740	–	–	740	357	1,097	–	1,097
1896	1,602	–	–	1,602	(231)	1,833	–	1,833
1897	2,203	–	189	2,391	231	2,622	44	2,582
1898	663	25	310	999	651	1,650	50	1,600
1899	894	(300)	257	1,451	483	1,934	92	1,842
1900	1,567	600	472	2,639	416	3,055	155	2,900
1901	1,001	700	478	2,179	343	2,522	172	2,350
1902	855	334	385	1,574	568	2,142	310	1,832
1903	788	500	462	1,751	651	2,402	316	2,086
1904	(394)	486	475	1,355	202	1,557	–	1,557
1905	–	540	536	1,076	331	1,407	39	1,368
1906	–	650	732	1,382	305	1,687	29	1,658
1907	–	600	723	1,323	530	1,853	13	1,840
1908	–	1,500	1,874	3,375	484	3,859	–	3,859
1909	–	1,350	3,554	4,904	–	4,904	–	4,904
1910	–	(1,180)	(1,320)	2,500	(500)	3,000	–	3,000
1911	–	(1,230)	(2,270)	3,500	(500	4,000	–	4,000
1912	–	1,980	3,520	5,500	275	5,775	–	5,775

Note: Leskovac includes factory at Grdelica.
Sources and calculation: see BALKSTAT.
Figures in parentheses are estimates.

Jovanović (of the original Strojkovac partnership) bought up Janković's Grdelica *gajtan* mill the same year, and by widening the partnership in 1906, refurbished the weaving side. In 1911 they embarked on a major expansion programme.[202]

For the woollen industry in Serbia, figures broadly comparable to those in Table 9.1 for Bulgaria are given in Table 9.2 above. They are, however, given only in current prices, as we lack a satisfactory index of price movements such as the Bulgarian export statistics provide. (Serbia's cloth exports were negligible as a proportion of output.) The trend shown does however conceal significant price inflation, as an ambiguously defined index of prices of 'wool, cloth' rises 32 per cent between 1901/2 and 1910/11.[203] To put sales of woollens by Serbia's factories in comparative

[202] Trajković, *Leskovačke industrije*, p. 21; Grgašević, *Industrija Srbije*, pp. 211–12.
[203] John R. Lampe, 'Financial Structure and the Economic Development of Serbia, 1878–1912' (Ph.D. Thesis, University of Wisconsin 1971), p. 405.

perspective with those of Bulgaria, we note that over the period 1889–1911, Serbian woollen production expanded (at current prices) by 5.3 per cent per annum, significantly less rapidly than that of Bulgaria at 8.0 per cent per annum, even though in 1889 Bulgaria's output was already 61 per cent larger than that of Serbia. Of course, Bulgaria had an established export market presence which Serbia lacked, but Serbian manufacturers never won as large a home market as the Bulgarians. In 1911, Serbia sold on the home market (including military cloth and *gajtan*) about 1.37 dinars of goods per capita of the population, Bulgaria 1.97 dinars. Expressed in terms of cloth sales to the urban population, the comparison is of 8.3 dinars to 10.3. This relatively poor performance merits explanation.

As an 'infant' industry in the 1880s, without an established export business, and with little home market protection, the early growth of woollen manufacturing in Serbia depended heavily on military orders. In the 1880s the Paraćin mill was almost wholly dependent on them. As in Bulgaria, such orders carried a premium, in this case 10 per cent over the price offered by importers.[204] In 1891 Paraćin (then the only domestic supplier) was annually manufacturing 250,000 metres of army cloth.[205] But from then on, military orders declined. In the shorter term, this was because the state could not sustain payment for the volume of military orders that it had hitherto placed while funding current deficits with new foreign borrowings;[206] and in 1895 Münch (like most other creditors of the government) complained of his difficulties in extracting settlement for military supplies.[207] In 1896, the mill supplied the military with about 169,700 metres of military cloth. This is consistent with the observation published in 1897 that Münch held an army contract for 150,000 metres per annum.[208] Subsequently, the Paraćin mill had to share its state orders with its newly founded Leskovac and Belgrade competitors. Between 1899 and 1903, it executed sharply fluctuating orders for an average of 29,600 metres a year,[209] while Popović – Ilić at Leskovac manufactured an annual 24,300 metres and about 300 army blankets.[210] By this time Michel's Belgrade factory was also in the market for military cloth, which accounted for a substantial part of his annual output,[211] but it seems unlikely that military orders provided the industry with more than 100,000 metres of business. Such a throughput would have been worth

[204] GBC Serbia 1899, p. 6; de Borchgrave, *Serbie*, p. 182.
[205] *Službeni vojni list*, XI (1891), p. 581.   [206] See Lampe, 'Financial Structure', pp. 138 ff.
[207] AS MNP (T) 1906 41 7. Braće Minh–MNP, 20 June 1895, no. 3624.
[208] Herbert Vivian, *Servia, the Poor Man's Paradise* (London, 1897), p. 116.
[209] *SGKS*, 1898–9, p. 334; 1900, p. 286; 1901, p. 326; 1902, pp. 325–6; 1903, pp. 349–50.
[210] AS MNP (T) 1906 46 37. MNP–Državni savet, 28 Apr. 1905.
[211] AS MNP (T) 1906 45 6. No. 6405 of 1906.

Table 9.3 *Civil and military turnover of the Paraćin woollen mill 1896–1899 (000 dinars)*

Year	Civil	Military	Total
1896	494[a]	1108	1603[a]
1897	575[a]	1627	2207[c]
1898	642[a]	338	980[c]
1899	715	327[b]	1043[b]

Sources:
[a] AS MNP(T) 1902 I 107 report on the factory for 1898;
[b] Same document, report for 1899;
[c] *SGKS*, III, 1896–7, and IV, 1898–9.

around 800,000 dinars. The trend in military orders continued to fall. In 1911, they amounted to only 650,000 dinars.[212] As this diminishing demand was now shared round an increasing number of firms, it had ceased to provide a sizeable prop for an industry whose output was then running at about 4 million dinars. Moreover, the fierce mutual competition between manufacturers extinguished the element of monopoly profit which military orders had provided the Paraćin mill in its heyday.[213]

The irregular pattern of military orders caused sales fluctuations by the woollen factories in Serbia to overlay the growth trend much more markedly than in Bulgaria, as is evident from the experience of the Paraćin mill (Table 9.3).

For the industry as a whole, growth in sales to the civilian home market was rapid, at least from the mid-1890s, though from small beginnings, as shown in Table 9.4.

The fourfold growth in cloth sales from the late 1890s to 1911 is an indication that the civil home market was the main basis for production growth. As in Bulgaria, woollen manufacturing in Serbia was at its most efficient in producing coarse *šajak*. But unlike the Bulgarian woollen mills, those of Serbia had no domestic production to substitute, only imports which came in over an 8 per cent tariff. In the 1880s virtually all cloth on the Serbian market came from industrial Europe, except for *šajak* imported from Bulgaria. Even at this time Münch had always tried to sell some of his output to civil consumers. In 1895, he claimed that 'our factory meets all the domestic needs of the lower class in *sukno* and

[212] IKKS, *Izveštaj o radu i stanju industrije u 1911 godini* (Belgrade, 1912), p. 23.
[213] IAB. Minute book of Koste Ilića Sinovi a.d. 1910–1914, fo. 19 (Board minute of 18/31 Aug. 1911).

Table 9.4 *Civil home market sales of the Serbian woollen industry 1896–1911 (000 dinars)*

Year	Total	*Gajtan*	Cloth
1896	720		
1897	980	231 ⎫	about 7–800
1898	1,580	651 ⎭	
1899–1903	1,400	500	about 900
1911	3,350	500	2,850

Note:
If the estimate for military demand in 1891 (of 250,000 metres noted above) is roughly correct, there would have been no woollen cloth production that year for civil use at all.

šajak.[214] But civil home demand for coarse cloth would have fallen well short of 1 million dinars, of which imports in 1900 took 211,000 dinars. Far wider scope for potential import substitution was in worsteds and light woollen fashion cloth, of which imports were worth 1.6 million.[215]

So any substantial expansion of domestic sales required manufacturers to compete in the market for finer cloth. From the early 1890s, Münch endeavoured to sell cloth of superior quality.[216] But in this area of the market, the competition of the Czech woollen mills was formidable. Belgrade itself – by far the most important internal market – lay but the width of a railway bridge from Austro-Hungarian territory. Culturally this proximity also meant that the Serbian capital and its wealthier consumers were even less isolated than those of Sofia. In the 1880s the women of Belgrade were said to be assiduous followers of the Paris and Vienna fashions.[217] 'There is hardly a bourgeois family', wrote the French consul, 'who does not know of the catalogues of our big stores and which does not use them. "Au Printemps" particularly is assured of an important Belgrade clientele.' Moreover, the high mark-ups on goods sold in the Belgrade shops encouraged people to shop abroad, 'wherever possible'. This only meant crossing the Sava bridge to Semlin (Zemun) whose wares enjoyed the customs privilege of frontier zone status.[218]

Given the competitive pressure at the finer end of the market, Serbian manufacturers would not have tried to compete in it had the market in coarse cloth been as large as they had expected. To succeed up-market

[214] AS MNP (T) 1906 41 7. Braće Minh–MNP, 20 June 1895, no. 3624.
[215] *Statistika spoljašne trgovine kr. Srbije za 1900 g*, import list nos. 78 and 79 (coarse cloth), and 84, 85 (fine).   [216] AS MNP (T) 1906 41 7. No. 3624.
[217] F. Bianconi, *Cartes commerciales, nr. 4. Royaume de Serbie* (Paris, 1885), pp. 31–2.
[218] Rene Millet, *La Serbie économique et commerciale* (Paris, 1889), pp. 181–2.

required vigorous sales promotion. Thus Münch found it necessary to maintain a Belgrade warehouse for the produce of his Paraćin mill, and to forge a close relationship with the tailoring trade. In 1889, he proposed to organize a tailoring co-operative in Belgrade, which he would subsidize on condition that it only worked with Paraćin cloth.[219] The proposal was well received, and may have been adopted, as in 1895 the Münch enterprise owned 'a factory for tailoring mens' clothes' alongside its Belgrade warehouse.[220] To spearhead his assault on the upper end of the market, particularly worsteds, he installed his own combed yarn spinnery, a facility then regarded in central Europe as advanced technology.[221] Yet this venture into worsted production was not successful. Having peaked at 12,447 metres in 1900, valued at 99,576 dinars, or 5.8 per cent of turnover, worsted production fell away to 588 metres in 1901.[222]

Facing declining military demand, a saturated market for coarse cloth, and crushing import competition in the home market for fine cloth, the industry had only one further option – to emulate the Bulgarians and break into the export market in *šajak* and *gajtan*. As we have seen, Münch devoted huge efforts to pressing up his sales abroad, but these efforts were apparently unprofitable, and insufficient to employ his mill near capacity. The newer firms also wanted to build up export sales; in 1904 one Leskovac mill was hopeful of increasing its sales to Bosnia, Macedonia and, later, Anatolia,[223] while Michel of Belgrade in 1906 claimed to have 'carved out a road for our manufactures in the Orient'.[224] But little came of this; after the destruction of the Paraćin mill, we may infer from Table 9.2 that few further efforts were made by the industry to hold its export market.

This was probably because profits became easier to earn at home, when conditions changed with the protective tariff of 1904, which quintupled the duty on textiles to 40 per cent.[225] There was no immediate response. After the Paraćin mill burned down, its smaller competitors were unable to take over its market share, so sales of Serbian factory cloth remained for four years at depressed levels despite favourable market conditions (see above, Table 9.2). Heavy investment was going to be needed to update and improve equipment. Unable to make headway against imports, the Michel firm proposed to expand its capital, labour and machinery in 1906 so as 'to manufacture that which till recently was manufactured by Mr Münch'. The firm admitted that neither it nor the

---

[219] Mihailo M. Živančević, *Naše zanatstvo i Zanatlijski pokret* (Belgrade, 1938), p. 48.
[220] Kostić, *Pisma s puta*, p. 49.   [221] Ibid., p. 47.
[222] *SGKS*, 1900, p. 286; 1901, p. 326.   [223] AS MNP(T) 1906 46 37. No. 5384 of 1904.
[224] AS MNP (T) 1906 45 6. No. 6405 of 1906.
[225] Lampe, 'Financial Structure', pp. 220–1.

Leskovac factory could displace the import of fine cloth, because its manufacture demanded greater labour skill and improved machinery.[226] From 1908, the two factories, having expanded their installations, were in a position to try. Both decided to build combed yarn spinneries.[227] Having reattained the scale of operations formerly enjoyed only by the Paraćin mill, the industry enjoyed several prosperous years. Even so, it admitted in 1911 that it was still uncompetitive (even behind tariff walls) in 'the superior qualities', and owed its existence to its advantages in making common cloth.[228]

Tariff protection and cotton manufacturing

The period 1878–1912 also witnessed the development of machine cotton spinning. Well before 1878 locally made cotton products had been squeezed out of Balkan markets by imported cottons because of the high cost of hand spinning, and cotton textiles bulked large in the import totals of all the Balkan countries. However, yarn imports also expanded, because as the price of cotton yarn fell, it was used increasingly for warps to substitute home-produced yarn, especially of linen in domestic mixed cloth weaving; this eliminated the laborious growing, retting, scutching and spinning of flax and hemp by which peasants obtained their non-woollen subsistence textile needs.[229] 'The peasants of Serbia', it was reported in 1892, 'are represented as a non-consuming element whereas in my belief they form the chief consumers of British cotton yarns which the women spend the winter weaving into cloth.'[230] This was equally the case in Bulgaria, where cotton yarn was mainly bought by country people who 'weave it into their own diverse cloths'.[231] The Balkan rural market sought cheap, coarse count cotton yarn, in which the high wage industries of western Europe could potentially be undercut by machines served by cheap Balkan labour.

The growth of mechanized cotton weaving in the Balkan states was, however, dependent on high tariffs and military supply concessions. Several ventures were established by British cotton spinners to facilitate the export of their yarn. In coarse cloth, power-loom weaving was barely competitive with the handloom, so the industry wove mainly from fine imported yarn, for urban and military markets. Therefore connexions between the cotton spinning and weaving enterprises were weak, despite

[226] AS MNP (T) 1906 45 6. No. 6405 of 1906.
[227] Ibid., MNP (T) 1906 46 37. Ilić–MNP, 8 Sept. 1904, no. 5384.
[228] *La Serbie à l'Exposition universelle de 1911 à Turin* (Belgrade, 1911), p. 254.
[229] Savić, *Industrija*, I, p. 281.   [230] PRO FO 105 96. Consular no. 6 of 10 Sept. 1892.
[231] *RCADCF*, no. 176, Bulgarie: Bourgas. Mouvement du port de Bourgas en 1893, p. 6.

the desire of governments to foster the simultaneous development of the two branches of the industry. In 1906, a Serbian merchant who was seeking a cotton weaving concession explained that, 'Unqualified persons are of the opinion that it is necessary first to erect a spinning mill, and then a weaving factory. This is an entirely erroneous view.' Having noted how much the cotton industry in western Europe still depended on English yarn, he added, 'even if there were spinning mills in the country they would nevertheless not satisfy our need because they would only spin coarse counts to no. 24 and we need finer yarn from no. 36 upward'.[232] The advice, which was valid, was ignored, for a report of 1910 says that spinning concessions were being awarded so that the Serbian weaveries would not have to import their raw material.[233] It was probably only to appease the state that the Ilić firm (which came to dominate the industry) undertook in 1910 to spin as well as to weave, for it took no action to install the appropriate spinning capacity.[234]

In Bulgaria and Serbia cotton spinning and weaving were new industries, implanted mainly by outside agencies. The largest factory in Bulgaria (at the time of its opening) was a cotton spinning mill built in 1897 by Manchester interests, incorporated as the National Cotton Spinning Company of Bulgaria Ltd with nominal capital of £60,000.[235] Originally the promoters considered building their mill at the Danube port of Ruse,[236] but finally opted for the seaport of Varna. Locational considerations were dominated by ease of importing American cotton, and obtaining seaborne supplies of coal. Varna had no proto-industrial background. The company's 'Prince Boris' mill was equipped with 8,000 spindles and space for more.[237] The factory was built 'of a plan allowing of gradual extension',[238] and expanded its spindlage to 11,400 in 1902 and 15,000 in 1913.[239] The enterprise faced teething troubles in its first years, and only got into profit in 1901/2, when it managed to pay a maiden dividend of 5 per cent.[240] But, by 1905, it was doing well enough to pay out a three times covered 10 per cent.[241] The improvement in its fortunes was unconnected with any increase in output; in 1901 its output was 2.5 million lbs, in 1905, 2.36 million lbs, and in 1910 2.5 million lbs.[242]

[232] AS MNP (T) 1907 XXXVIII 12. No. 6356 of 24 Oct. 1906.
[233] IKKS, *Izveštaj o radu i stanju industrije u 1910 godini* (Belgrade, 1911), p. 11.
[234] AS MNP (T) 1914. No. 4876 unfasciculated of 27 Mar. 1914.
[235] PRO FO 368 (1909) 278. Farrar-Grey, 8 Mar. 1909.   [236] PRO FO 78 4953.
[237] GBC Bulgaria 1898, p. 54; *BOUCA*, 1900 bd. 1 Varna 1900, A II 5, p. 17.
[238] GBC Bulgaria 1906, p. 5.
[239] *BOUCA*, 1902 bd. 1 (1) Sofia 1902, A II 1, p. 20; GBC Bulgaria 1913, p. 6.
[240] PRO FO 78 5298. Brophy-Elliot, 26 June 1903.
[241] BAE Dossier 2807 X. No. 2161, f. 27.
[242] *BOUCA*, 1901 bd. 1 Sofia 1901, A II 1, p. 17; 1905 bd. 1 (1) Varna, A II 4, p. 5; GBC Bulgaria 1910, p. 14.

There were no serious foreign proposals for cotton spinning in Serbia, probably because of the lack of a seaport, so the industry was late in appearing despite the strong domestic market for yarn. In 1903, the town savings bank at Niš assisted one of its directors, Kosta Kacika, to open a small cotton mill with fifty or sixty workers. Its site opposite the railway station at this main-line junction indicates its preferred location.[243] In 1910, the savings bank invested 610,000 dinars to secure 80 per cent of the stock,[244] and imported 'up to date and advanced machinery of the American system, procured in England', in order to match Crompton yarn in quality and undersell it.[245] This suggests that ring spindles were being substituted for mules; 3,200 spindles were installed,[246] and as the mill did good business, their number was increased to 6,000 by 1914. Like Varna, the Niš mill concentrated on the intermediate coarse counts of 8–24. It produced about 500,000 lbs of yarn a year.[247] The output, of course, went mainly to the peasant handlooms.[248]

A number of small workshop cotton weaveries were set up in Bulgaria, mostly producing 'indigeneous cloths' for local consumption,[249] and a few larger ones, like Kalchev's towel and cloth factory at Plovdiv.[250] But more substantial development took place in the environs of Varna. A small establishment was set up at Devna village in 1903. Enjoying stiff protection, it was so successful that the owners erected a second, larger factory there in 1906 and both worked very profitably. The Devna firm had no connexion with the Varna spinning mill, and the local businessman who set it up was associated with a rival Manchester cotton export firm (possibly Cromptons). It drew all its yarn from England.[251]

A larger cotton weaving enterprise with 800 power-looms[252] was established at Jambol by the consortium that owned the Varna spinnery. It obtained a concession in 1907, but by dubious means which were designed to obscure common ownership with the spinning mill. The need for subterfuge arose because both factories claimed wide regional monopoly rights. It was therefore alleged that the company had no interest in using the concession, save to block anybody else from competing in

[243] Sevdelin Andrejević, *Ekonomski razvoj Niša od 1830 do 1946 godine* (Niš, 1970), p. 53.
[244] Lampe, 'Financial Structure', pp. 307, 311.
[245] Oldham Local Studies Library, Crompton Papers. Uncatalogued series box 3, 'Miscellaneous items' – advertisement of Niška aksionarska štedionica.
[246] IKKS, *Izveštaj ... u 1911*, p. 23.   [247] Grgašević, *Industrija Srbije*, p. 214.
[248] Andrejević, *Ekonomski razvoj Niša*, p. 58; GBC Salonica 1892, p. 22.
[249] *RCADCF*, 1904 Jan.–June, No. 339. Commerce et navigation de Roustchouk en 1902, p. 15.   [250] *Izlozhenie: Plovdiv 1906–1907*, p. 36.
[251] *BOUCA*, 1905 bd. 1 (1) Varna 1905 A II 4, p. 6; 1906 bd. 1 Varna 1906, p. 3; 1907 bd. 1 Varna 1907 A II 4, pp. 3–4.
[252] PRO FO 368 942. Report for 1912–13 on the Trade of Bulgaria, p. 6.

the field.[253] By 1909, the factory had still not been erected, the company 'deem[ing] it wiser to defer erection of the mill till [political] affairs had settled down'.[254] Only in 1911 did it build the factory,[255] and not till 1913 did it begin production.

In Serbia, several mechanical cotton weaving enterprises were established by domestic interests, but none would have fared well in the absence of protection. There was a tenuous connexion between the older domestic weaving trade at Užice and the establishment there of Serbia's largest cotton weaving factory. The Užice cottage industry of cotton weaving enjoyed commercial success at a minor exhibition in 1897, an event which is claimed to have encouraged the establishment of the cotton weaving factory.[256] This factory grew out of the old Stojan Popović woollen mill which was turned in 1890 into a cotton weaving 'school'. It recruited local and village girls, paid them a pittance of 0.20–0.60 dinars a day and justified its claim to being a school by offering (but not providing) two hours a week of instruction. It was supported locally as a source of cloth for the Užice merchants, who had been cut off from Bosnian supplies, but was inadequate as a substitute; it could not attract sufficient pupils, and ran at a loss.

In 1900 it was closed, but three years earlier, the town textile interest decided to erect a factory linked to a hydro-electric generator, in which the alumnae of the weaving school would be employed. A company was floated, issuing low denomination shares, so as to reach as many investors as possible. The issue flopped, but soft state loans enabled the factory to open on a small scale with fourteen looms. At first its output was too coarse to sell successfully, but by May 1901, ninety girls were at work, former 'scholars', whose experience encouraged the management to enter the market for better quality cloth. With government assistance the enterprise struggled by, but profit performance was poor till the tariff was raised in 1904; thereafter, as an established sheltered producer, it could hardly go wrong.[257] In 1906, turnover advanced 47 per cent on 1905, assisted by protracted closures at Cromptons' Belgrade weavery (see below, p. 277) which eased what was still an oversupplied market.[258] The firm's main problem from then on was its utter incapacity to satisfy its clientele. It was barely able to meet local orders at Užice, and had no depot in Belgrade through which to service the national market.[259] To

[253] PRO FO 368 394. Memo in 40161/10 (political).
[254] PRO FO 368 278. Farrar-Grey, 8 Mar. 1909.
[255] PRO FO 368 518. No. 49593 of 1911; no. 38279 of 30 Sept. 1911.
[256] Grgašević, *Industrija Srbije*, p. 209.
[257] Stevan Ignjić, *Užice i okolina 1862–1914* (Titovo Užice, 1967), pp. 103–14; Grgašević, *Industrija Srbije*, pp. 209–10.   [258] *BOUCA*, 1905 bd. 5. Belgrad 1906, A XIX 3, p. 26.
[259] AS MNP (T) 1907 38 1. Izveštaj . . . I Povl. Užičke aks. tkačka radionica, 18 Feb. 1907.

rectify this, shareholders decided greatly to enlarge its capacity,[260] for the firm had become profitable thanks to the tariff, and in 1909 paid a 12 per cent dividend on the first issue of its shares.[261] By 1911 it had 130 power-looms and was still paying 12 per cent.[262]

Another weavery was built as a joint stock venture in Niš in 1908, together with dyeworks and printing shop, through the initiative of Mita Ristić, a local cloth merchant who envisaged it explicitly as an import substituting operation. The factory was to produce scarves and shawls, and started with modest equipment.[263] Like the Užice mill, it prospered under protection and expanded to house 150 power-looms by 1911.[264] Finally, a cotton weaving establishment with 220 power-looms was erected in 1911 by the Kosta Ilić firm at Leskovac, as a branch factory to its enterprise in Belgrade.[265]

Foreign interest in weaving cotton in Serbia was stimulated by the attraction of military contracts, offered at 10 per cent over market price.[266] This encouraged two Berliners, Albert Boas and Willi Eser, to open a power weavery in Belgrade at the end of 1896, in partnership with Aleksa Obradović, a Belgrade merchant who had secured the concession in 1895. The firm won substantial War Ministry orders for cotton or linen cloth, but by May 1899 it was put into liquidation by the Berlin partners and the factory was sold up. The Germans were disenchanted by heavy losses caused by managerial incompetence, which led to the mill producing an unprofitably small quantity of bad quality cloth.[267] A tangled legal dispute between the German and Serbian partners ensued.[268]

Also interested in promoting cotton weaving in Serbia were A. & A. Crompton & Co Ltd, cotton spinners of Oldham. Cromptons' dealings with Belgrade dated back to about 1860. Their exports through merchants F. Sternberg & Co, whom they took over in 1895, made 'Crompton' a household word throughout southeastern Europe.[269] Cromptons wanted to increase their sale of yarn in Serbia by weaving it there into cloth for military contracts. Unusually for a foreign venture,

[260] Ibid.
[261] K. K. Österr. Handelsmuseum, *Serbien. Wirtschaftliche Verhaltnisse, 1909* (Vienna, 1910), p. 23.   [262] Ignjić, *Užice*, p. 112.
[263] Nikola Vučo, *Razvoj industrije u Srbiji u XIX veku* (Belgrade, 1981), p. 241; Andrejević, *Ekonomski razvoj Niša*, pp. 54–5; Grgašević, *Industrija Srbije*, pp. 214–15.
[264] IKKS, *Izveštaj*, 1911, p. 23.   [265] Ibid., p. 23; *Proizvodne snage*, p. 479.
[266] PRO FO 105 129. No. 10 comm. of 4 Aug. 1898.
[267] AS MNP (T) 1900 XI 42. Mihel-Eser, 2 Aug. 1899, under cover of no. 3887 of 1899; Min. Vojno, ekonomsko odeljenje-MNP, 23 Feb. 1900, no. 971; Živković-MNP, 31 Mar. 1900, no. 1639, fo. 2.
[268] PRO FO 105 130. Crompton – Foreign Office, 3 Nov. 1899; AS MNP (T) 1900 XI 42. MNP-Min. Vojno, 21 Dec. 1899; MNP-M Stojanović, 10 Jan. 1900.
[269] Elsie Ballard, *A Chronicle of Crompton* (Crompton, 1967), pp. 101, 104.

they planned to use intermediate technology, to mobilize the domestic labour of the peasant households. Observing that the peasant loom was 'huge, clumsy and laborious' they calculated that peasant outwork weaving could only be enlisted if productivity could be raised.[270] A small treadle-driven warp loom designed for Balkan needs was patented by George Hattersley and Sons of Keighley. Cromptons obtained a concession to supply these looms on easy terms to peasant households.[271] They established a central workshop with fifty looms in which the outworkers would receive free instruction.[272] Large productivity gains were claimed for the new looms, and the idea appealed to the Serbian authorities who espoused it as their own.[273]

In May 1895, a Belgrade merchant, Božidar Živković, obtained a concession for the weaving of cotton hemp and linen. Živković was probably fronting for Cromptons. His concession required him to build a technically modern factory employing at least twenty-five workers,[274] but it was coupled with a commitment to establish an outwork network of handloom weavers.[275] Cromptons put up the funds for him to open a hand weaving shed in Kneza Miloša street, in Belgrade.[276] In 1896, they floated the First Royal Servian Privileged Weaving Co Ltd, to take over Živković's concession and shed, Živković becoming their junior partner and manager in Belgrade.[277] Živković secured government contracts which appeared to offer a fair rate of return, but by May 1897 Cromptons were having to meet his debts, because start-up costs outran his budget.[278] At this time, the firm was running six workshops,[279] but only three existed in 1899, at Belgrade, Ćuprija and Leskovac, in which eighty-five people were employed.[280] Into these workshops they introduced the modified hand-looms, hoping they would become the nuclei of a substantial home weaving industry.[281] But they ran into difficulties in securing army orders. In 1899, the firm, now styled as Crompton & Živković,[282] tried to to sign up 100 households, the minimum number

---

[270] GBC Serbia 1892, pp. 23–4.
[271] LRO Crompton family of High Crompton. (DDCp) Box 730, Crompton – Cheetham, 16 Dec. 1895.   [272] Vučo, *Razvoj Industrije*, pp. 219–20.
[273] 'Hebung der Textilindustrie in Serbien', *Handelsmuseum*, IX (1), 1894, p. 172.
[274] AS MNP (T) 1907 38 32. Concession of 31 May 1895.
[275] AS MNP (T) 1900 XI 42. Živković–MNP, 4 Dec. 1895, no. 6644.
[276] AS MNP (T) 1900 XI 42. Company–MNP, 27 July 1899, no. 3887.
[277] London. Defunct Companies Register. No. 15630 of 1896, PRO box 48413, agreement between Živković and Cromptons dated 8 June 1896.
[278] LRO. DDCp box 737, M. Cheetham–Joshua Crompton, 17 May 1897.
[279] Vučo, *Razvoj Industrije*, p. 221.
[280] AS MNP (T) 1900 XI 42. Živković–MNP, 31 Mar. 1900, no. 1639, fo. 1.
[281] AS MNP (T) 1900 XI 42. No. 1639 of 1900.
[282] AS MNP (T) 1900 XI 42. No. 6644 of 1895.

needed to convince the Serbian war minister that the project would become a dependable supply source. They failed.[283] Cromptons therefore decided to establish a power weaving mill instead, and bought a new site in Belgrade on which to build. But when the Boas and Eser mill appeared on the market, they snapped it up for £14,500 sterling, closed the factory on Kneza Miloša, and moved their business into it, incautiously neglecting to wait for official clearance. They applied immediately for army orders, since the factory was 'installed exclusively with the aim of meeting military needs'.[284]

Like other foreign enterprises, they soon discovered that Balkan officialdom could be both corrupt and xenophobic. Buying the Boas and Eser mill was a bad mistake. Not only had it supplied the army with rotten cloth and in less than contracted quantity, but it had tried to invoice a consignment of imported fly-sheets as domestically made.[285] The War Ministry affected to regard the new owners as heirs to the derelictions of the predecessor firm, adopted a hostile attitude to them,[286] and stubbornly and disingenuously found excuses for not placing military contracts with them. It seems that Cromptons failed to spread round the right douceurs, which British companies did not like doing. The firm then tried to win orders by subcontract, but negotiations again foundered, and the Ministry placed them abroad. Živković 'being of a very irascible disposition ... imprudently conducted his negotiations with the Ministry of War with an amount of heat which gave great offence'.[287] The denial of military orders closed the factory from July 1901 till the beginning of 1903.[288] The dispute was never cleared up. Although Cromptons continued weaving in Belgrade till 1906, with 125 looms, they kept running foul of the War Ministry, losing their orders again in 1905. In 1904 and 1905, the firm was racked by 'endless labour strikes' which stopped the factory for long periods.[289] It managed to reopen, but in 1906 its privileges were revoked, and fearful of incurring renewed losses, Cromptons closed the factory.[290] They subsequently sold it to the Ungarische Textil Industrie a.g.,[291] a hemp spinning business in Szeged, and in 1910 the factory was sold again to the fast expanding Vlada Ilić

---

[283] AS MNP (T) 1900 XI 42 Vučković–Min. Vojno, 30 Dec. 1899.

[284] AS MNP (T) 1900 XI 42. Živković–MNP, 31 Mar. 1900; Mihel-Eser, 2 Aug. 1899.

[285] AS MNP (T) 1900 XI 42. No. 971 of 1900.

[286] AS MNP (T) 1900 XI 42. No. 1639 of 1900, f. 1 vo.

[287] PRO. FO 105 129. No. 18 comm. 24 Nov. 1899; FO 105 130. Crompton–FO, 2 Nov. 1899.   [288] AS MNP (T) 1907 38 32. No. 6009 of 1903.

[289] BOUCA, 1904 bd. 2 (2) Belgrad A XVIII 5, p. 18; 1906, bd. 5 Belgrad 1906 A XIX 3, p. 25.   [290] AS MNP (T) 1907 38 32. No. 6719 of 1906.

[291] Nikola Vučo, 'Razvoj industrije u Beogradu do 1914 godine', in Istorija Beograda, II (Beograd, 1974), p. 461.

textile interest, which expanded it and in 1913 installed 100 Northrop looms.[292]

Textile markets, protection and self-consumption

At this point, we can draw certain conclusions regarding the market environment facing the Balkan textile industries. The woollen industry, the key sector in Bulgaria and Serbia, was efficient and internationally competitive in producing coarse woollens and *gajtan*, precisely those activities in which the predecessor proto-industrial manufactures of Bulgaria had excelled. The main thrust of the industry's expansion was therefore to displace the earlier form of manufacture. It could not substitute up-market imports from western and central Europe, for even with protection it was uncompetitive. It is possible that protection retarded rather than accelerated the development of the industry by redirecting resources into areas of serious comparative disadvantage. In a freer market, manufacturers would not have diminished the interest they had earlier displayed in pursuing export orders.

But given the market environment they faced, could it be expected that manufacturers would continue their pursuit of export based expansion in the coarse cloth market? The experience of the Paraćin mill does not suggest that the option, though it generated significant sales, was particularly profitable. It was unprofitable because the firm's drive for exports was mounted from a home market base which was insufficient to work the mill close to capacity. This brings us to an underlying problem about which the manufacturer could do little. Just as the new woollen industries had taken over the markets of their unmechanized predecessors, these in their time had evolved from the household manufacture of substantially the same articles which most Balkan families had made for their own consumption. They had aimed these products at a mainly urban market of consumers who did not produce them for themselves. The distress of the old woollen industries after 1878 had been caused partly by the shrinkage of that urban market.

As a result, the manufacturer of coarse woollen cloth might be efficient in terms of international production costs, but faced that most elusive of competitors, the peasant who manufactured for subsistence. Subsistence producers would purchase manufactures if provided with really large cost advantages in doing so. The expansion of the *gajtan* industry had been made possible by the retreat of the subsistence sector in this product, and cotton spinning was sustained by the willingness of subsistence producers

---

[292] Grgašević, *Industrija Srbije*, p. 197.

to substitute cheap strong factory cotton yarn for hempen and flaxen yarns which had been made by laborious manual methods. But the subsistence producer of woollen cloth was more difficult to shift. In 1903, according to our own estimates, the population of Bulgaria consumed the equivalent in weight of 2.2m of *shajak* per head. Of this quantity the subsistence sector accounted for 73 per cent.[293] Much the same was the case elsewhere in the Balkans.

The production of textiles for subsistence involved a massive mobilization of effort. According to Popov, 200 days of female labour time were applied on average in Bulgarian peasant households on the eve of World War I to the provision of textile items for their own use.[294] Had this activity been in decline, then large-scale industry would have been assured of a rapidly growing market. But, at least for woollens, this failed to happen. In 1883, in Eastern Rumelia, non-market woollen consumption per capita had amounted to 1.51 m equivalent. In Bulgaria in 1903, it had, if anything, risen to 1.61. In Serbia, trends were more favourable to the large-scale producer, because subsistence production was indeed falling, from 2,243 gm per head in 1867 to 2,183 in 1883 and 1,162 in 1903 (for Bulgaria the 1903 figure was 1,628 gm).[295]

A strong determinant of the amount of woollen cloth that a household would provide for itself was the quantity of wool it disposed. Where sheep raising was being squeezed by arable farming, as in the fertile but densely populated north of Serbia, growth was created in the market for coarse cloth, but not necessarily for factory coarse cloth, for the principal supplier to this market was the domestic woollen industry of the Pirot region. In Serbia as a whole, the sheep population per head declined from 1.61 to 1.31, but in Bulgaria it was remarkably stable, declining from 2.1 to 2.0.[296] These sheep were fairly evenly distributed among the Balkan peasants, and were no longer held, as they had been before 1878, in large flocks for commercial purposes. They were in fact the subsistence providers – of milk, meat, hides and manure, as well as of wool – of the Balkan farmer, and his family's ability to maintain a stable level of self-provision kept it firmly out of the market for woollens. We may also surmise that protection, by driving up the price of woollen manufactures relative to that of farmers' cash crops, increased the incentive of the peasant family to remain self-sufficient in woollen textiles.

Thus the one area of the woollen market in which the Balkan factory was competitive was demand by poorer and more conservative townsfolk and a small fraction of the peasant market. This meant that by far the

[293] Palairet, 'Woollen Industries', p. 353.   [294] Popov, *Stopanska B'lgarija*, p. 301.
[295] Palairet, 'Woollen Industries', p. 339.   [296] Popov, *Stopanska B'lgarija*, p. 246.

greater part of the woollen market – and its most dynamic part – was for woollens of a type which could not easily be produced for self-consumption, and equally could not be produced efficiently by the factories.

Because of complementarity between the commercial production of coarse cotton yarn and subsistence sector weaving, spinning seemed to offer more promising expansion potential. This potential was heightened by the capacity of cotton spinning to make unmechanized cotton weaving more competitive in the market. The main beneficiary within the Balkans of this development was however Hellenic Macedonia, where the industry developed relatively early from proto-industrial origins. The industry was late in reaching Bulgaria (and still later in Serbia) and it is difficult to assess the extent to which the factories in these countries were dependent on protection. But at least in product market terms their environment was favourable. Other areas of Balkan textile manufacturing were, however, more or less protection dependent. This was most obviously so with finer woollen cloths, but equally the success of the cotton weaving industries in the last few, highly protected years before the Balkan Wars implies that they depended heavily on protection. Analysis of product markets provides only half an explanation of performance, though it goes far towards explaining why the textile industry tended to diversify away from strength into weakness. The following section deals with key supply side issues.

New technology and the Balkan textile factories

Stage theories of development, from which proto-industrialization theory borrows too generously, maintain a sharp discontinuity between cottage and craft shop manufacturing, and its successor, factory industry with powered machinery. Proto-industry could achieve productivity gains only through extending the division of labour, but factory production provided both an immediate lift in labour productivity through mechanization, and the promise of self-sustained growth through continual updating of technology. Just such a discontinuity was apparent when immigrant or trans-national enterprise started up in the Balkans, equipped with relatively modern machines and techniques. There were two reasons for the trans-national's choice of up-to-date technology; on the one hand, it produced goods which had hitherto been imported rather than produced locally and needed the corresponding techniques for making them; on the other, it introduced systems of manufacturing which were technically similar to those applied in the firm's home country, usually irrespective of whether such technology was attuned to the factor and product markets it faced in the Balkans.

However, the trans-national enterprise played only a minor role in displacing proto-industrial production, and the discontinuity between old and new breaks down when we examine the factory enterprises in the Balkans which grew from proto-industrial origins. Technology in the textile proto-industries had not been static. Increasingly productive techniques had been applied, most notably in the production of *gajtan*. The *gajtan* mill itself was a technological hybrid, as it plaited homespun yarn with water-powered machines in small units which can be described as craft shops or factories according to taste; one of these, at Kalofer, had enjoyed factory status when founded in 1864, but its technology could not have differed from that of the other *gajtan* mills.[297] There were many transitional features in factories such as those of Sliven which had grown out of the proto-industrial system. Both powered and manual manufacturing processes were applied in them, and the powered machinery was (at least in the early years) technically obsolete; conversely the factory fly-shuttle handlooms were far more productive than the primitive looms used in the cottages; besides this, only part of the manufacturing process was performed in the factory, the rest being done through the outwork system. The articles produced by such factories were similar to those made by handicraft techniques, as they were aimed at the established markets which the domestic manufactures had served. If the machine made product differed, the producer would falsify it to make it appear like handicraft work. Even among trans-national ventures there were attempts to introduce transitional systems of work, as illustrated by the unsuccessful plans of Cromptons and of Michel in Belgrade to introduce intermediate weaving technology into Serbia.

The package of machinery applied in the early factories which had grown from the proto-industries was not selected from any fine calculation of optimality by the entrepreneurs, because they were isolated from the main currents of European practice, and had only a hazy knowledge of what was available. In Chapter 3, we discussed how the technology of *gajtan* making reached Bulgaria, not from the industrial west, but from Transylvania, and how the primitive treadle machines were improved by experiment in Bulgaria itself. We saw, too, how Zheljazkov smuggled his machines from such an improbable source as Russia, then replicated them, even though better machinery must have been available in western Europe, had he known how to get access to it. Forty years later, communications had not greatly improved. Kalpazanov, probably the most energetic Bulgarian businessman of his day, never saw a carding engine till 1871; he thereupon built one at his own forge.[298]

So the pioneering industrial entrepreneur in the Balkans was faced

[297] Ibid., p. 327.   [298] Tsonchev, *Gabrovo*, p. 616.

with informational barriers which introduced a randomness in the technology he adopted. Take the introduction of *gajtan* manufacturing at Leskovac, which up till then had been confined to the Bulgarian woollen centres. Plaiting machinery was no monopoly of the Bulgarians, and could have been obtained in Vienna, but the Leskovac merchants knew only that Bulgaria was the source of the technology they wanted to adopt, and therefore went there to obtain it. Not surprisingly, Bulgaria prohibited the export of braiding *charks*, so Leskovac manufacturers had to smuggle them out, and this was risky. Mihailo Janković claimed that after bringing secondhand *charks* out of Bulgaria, he was kidnapped on the border by Bulgarian gendarmes, locked up and shaken down for 5,000 dinars.[299] In bringing woollen spinning to Gabrovo, Kalpazanov obtained his original, unsatisfactory machinery from Germany, but later, when more advanced equipment was needed, the Gabrovo mill owners travelled to England to buy machines, which arrived with English fitters to install them and instruct the workforce.[300]

When the *gajtan* manufacturers at Leskovac decided to spin their own yarn, they had little idea how to go about it. One of the proprietors of the *gajtan* mill at Vučje took advantage of a visit by the Belgian consular agent to question him closely about the spinning equipment he would need, and asked to be put in touch with Belgian makers of textile machinery. The agent duly noted the request, but commented that the enterprise lacked the resources and technical abilities to undertake such an investment.[301] In 1895 or 1896, faced with the competition of Münch's Paraćin mill, which was invading their market for *gajtan*, the two merged Leskovac *gajtan* manufacturing partnerships knew only that their erstwhile Bulgarian suppliers owned spinning and weaving machines. So under pretext of visiting a Bulgarian mill to order goods, they surreptitiously noted details from the makers' nameplates on the machinery they saw. Then, as Turkish was their only foreign language, they sent the young son of one of them, who spoke German, to buy the machines in Germany.[302] On this hit and miss basis the Leskovac woollen spinning industry was equipped.

But communications improved. The diffusion of machinery into the Balkans was facilitated by western European business activity in eastern markets, and by the commercial contacts it fostered. After Zheljazkov had

[299] AS MNP (T) 1905 XV 9. Janković–MNP, 14 Mar. 1900, no. 1579.
[300] L. Pajakov, 'Ekonomicheskoto dvizhenie v Gabrovo', *Promishlenost* (Svishtov) I (1888), p. 70.　[301] *RC*, LXXV (1892), pp. 18–19.
[302] Trajković, *Leskovačke industrije*, p. 19. This son may have been Vlada Ilić, who would have been 13 or 14 at the time, and who was afterwards educated in Vienna, Grgašević, *Industrija Srbije*, pp. 36–7.

set up his factory at Sliven in 1834, he expanded his inventory by copying what he had acquired. But when the enterprise was enlarged with state assistance, new machinery was drawn from Verviers, the woollen manufacturing town in eastern Belgium; it is claimed Zheljazkov rode horseback to Verviers to buy these machines.[303]

Why Verviers? Verviers' houses had been exporting heavy woollen cloth to Bulgaria and the Levant at least from 1811, when they were supplying Janissary uniforms. The trade suffered vicissitudes, but in 1838 the Verviers' house of Lemoine won new contracts to supply the Ottoman government with uniform cloth, and maintained a high volume of sales.[304] From woollen manufacturing, Verviers diversified into textile engineering, and the long standing trade connexion identified Verviers in the minds of Bulgarian businessmen as the source for supply of textile machinery. In 1865 the Sliven factory was modernized, with over 100 new pieces of machinery. These were also brought probably from the factory of Houyet et Feston in Verviers.[305] Subsequently all the factories founded at Sliven in the 1880s turned to the 'S. A. Vervietoise pour la construction des machines' for their machinery.[306] The connexion was fostered strongly by the Belgian minister in Sofia.[307] Almost every year technicians from Verviers came to Bulgaria to service and repair machinery, and to deliver and fit new machines ordered by the enterprises.[308] At Gabrovo too, Verviers supplied engines, boilers and machines for at least two new woollen factories.[309] The industrial links between Bulgaria and Belgium were to broaden further; several Gabrovo factories installed electric lighting equipment that had been built in Liège, and by 1914, Belgium was foremost among the providers of direct industrial investment in Bulgaria.

Labour supply and textile mechanization

In Bulgaria's woollen manufacturing towns, factory industry inherited the labour supply of its proto-industrial past, but this did not fit closely with its own labour requirements. Domestic manufacturing had employed large numbers of townswomen and peasant women, all working at home, as well as a cadre of skilled manpower for the specialised workshop finishing trades. Superficially, the correspondence between the

[303] 'Dobri Zheljazhkov, fabrikadzhijata', *100 godini b'lgarska industrija 1834–1937*, ed. V. Nikolchov et al. (Sofia, 1937), p. 7.
[304] BAE. 4117 V. Cuelebraeck–MAE, 12 Aug. 1851.
[305] Mladenov, *Pojava*, p. 18; Tabakov, *Sliven*, III, p. 113.
[306] BAE. Film B 24 – Df. 144. Boursiers du gouvernement, f. 10.
[307] Tabakov, *Grad Sliven*, III, p. 115.   [308] *RC*, LXXVII (1892), p. 100.
[309] *RC*, CLVI (1912), p. 70.

proto-industrial and factory-based labour forces was closest at Gabrovo. In 1903 the woollen factories employed 657 workers, of whom 530 were female.[310] A survey of 624 workers (out of 820) showed that 39 per cent were residents of the town, while nearly all the rest came from the surrounding villages, especially Zlataritsa with 45 per cent. Of the males 72 per cent were adult, but 85 per cent of the females were of 10–18 years, 12 per cent were 18–25 and 3 per cent were over 25. Only nine female workers were married.[311] So the characteristic Gabrovo textile worker was a girl from the town or a nearby village (but not the main mill village of Bichkinja) who worked a few years at the mill but withdrew from employment on marriage.

The availability of such labour was associated with the poor-land farm economy of the Gabrovo region, but this labour was dissimilar to that which had engaged in domestic manufacturing, which was composed of married women working within their homes. A high proportion of domestic workers were local townswomen, and, because of their family obligations, they would not leave their homes to work in factories. Disturbances occurred when they saw their livelihood being taken away from them, and somebody got up a petition to the tsar of Russia to close Kalpazanov's factory. Some townswomen were able to continue as outworkers for the factories, but the demand for their services diminished steadily.[312] So the factories drafted their labour predominantly from the villages because workers could not be supplied in sufficient quantity from the town itself.[313] Indeed the only married women who worked at the mills had sick husbands or were widowed or divorced, and were therefore forced to maintain themselves and their dependents.[314] Since Gabrovo was surrounded by hill villages, in which the labour of young females tended to be redundant to farming except at seasonal peaks, country girls who would formerly have sought work in the town in domestic service entered the factories. As a result, 'in the town is felt from year to year an increasing shortage of servants'.[315] Moreover, in summer when the girls were wanted on the farms, the factories had difficulty in holding onto labour.[316] Thus factory industry at Gabrovo, despite its proto-industrial roots, created a largely new workforce, which displaced the old.

The Gabrovo factories enjoyed at least that advantage associated with a proto-industrial past of being able to draw on labour from an overpopulated rural hinterland. However, rural dwellers in most regions of

---

[310] Mishajkov, 'Ocherk', p. 496.   [311] Tsonchev, *Gabrovo*, pp. 537–9.
[312] Mishajkov, 'Ocherk', p. 496.
[313] Staneff, *Gewerbewesen*, p. 70; Tsonchev, *Gabrovo*, p. 621.
[314] Pajakov, 'Ekonomicheskoto dvizhenie', p. 71.   [315] Tsonchev, *Gabrovo*, p. 541.
[316] Mishajkov, 'Ocherk', p. 497.

Bulgaria tended after the liberation to acquire more land and to need less income from domestic industry, so the mechanization of industry was accompanied by the loss of the proto-industrial labour force which the villages had supplied. This loss of domestic industry labour was, after all, the principal incentive for the textile entrepreneurs to mechanize. So conditions at Gabrovo were not necessarily representative of those elsewhere. Crucial to the ability of Gabrovo to attract rural labour was that most of the labour supplying villages lay within walking distance of the town. But the proto-industrial hinterlands of the textile towns extended to a much wider radius, and the outer proto-industrial periphery could not supply labour for urban factories.

Take the case of Sliven. Its immediate environs were of fertile lowland, but historically its networks for the supply of domestically manufactured cloth had extended deep into the Stara planina, to Kotel, Zheravna and other outlyers. As elsewhere, the real remuneration for domestic textile work declined after the liberation, and the volume of trade diminished rapidly. To the people of the Stara planina, it seemed as if the Sliven factories were robbing them of their livelihood, and this led to outward migration in search of work. But as long distances (and therefore extended periods away from home) were involved, it was the men who migrated, not the women. Their remittances and the produce of the soil provided a living for the families, but as the women were underemployed, they did not wholly abandon textile work; in 1903, 4,000–5,000 pieces of homespun woollen cloth were made in Kotel and its villages for external sale.[317] They also diversified from making woollen cloth in competition with the factories into making carpets, an industry yet to be mechanized in Bulgaria.[318] But the effect of transferring work from the household to the mill was to sever Sliven from its former proto-industrial hinterland.

So the labour force structure at Sliven differed from that at Gabrovo. Here 75 per cent of the labour force was male, and 80 per cent was over 16. Almost all the workers were Sliven town residents, even in the four factories at nearby Sotirja village, indicating that this location was used solely for its water power. The Sliven factory labour force was described as (relatively) old and experienced, and almost totally dependent on factory wages. It was also largely literate and became influenced by Menshevic thought.[319] The minority of female workers were (as they had been during the Ottoman era) gipsy girls and widows, characteristically marginal labour force elements, for there was no abundant pool to be

---

[317] *Izlozhenie: Burgaz 1903/04*, p. 47.
[318] Sv. Iv. Manev, 'Kotlensko', *Sp.BID*, VII (1903), pp. 512–43; *Jubilejna kniga na zheravnenskoto chitalishte 'Edinstvo' 1870–1920* (Sofia, 1921), pp. 123, 127–8, 287, 289.
[319] Mishajkov, 'Ocherk', pp. 496, 497, 507, 550.

drawn on, as at Gabrovo, of rural female and child labour; the land round Sliven was richer and agriculture provided adequate employment and income.[320]

Sliven's male textile factory workers were neither docile nor (apparently) cheap. They were aware of their indispensability, because at a pinch they could find work and wages in farming. They also learned to organize effectively. As early as 1884, workers at the 'Napred'k' and Sar'ivanov woollen factories came out on strike.[321] They struck again, for higher wages, in 1896. Although this strike collapsed, they were out for a third time in 1902. The employers brought in Macedonian refugee labour to break the strike, but this failed and they had to concede higher wages and shorter hours to their employees.

Our principal authorities, Mishajkov and Staneff, make much of the contrast between labour force structures at Gabrovo and Sliven, representing this to have been to the advantage of Gabrovo, whose cheap female labour created the supernormal profits necessary to build up a relatively high level of mechanization, while dear labour at Sliven constrained profitability and consequently the application of machinery.[322] In 1903, Gabrovo factories applied 2,569 leva of machinery per worker, to Sliven's 1,742 leva.[323] However, it would be inaccurate to represent Sliven as a high-wage and Gabrovo as a low-wage town. Table 9.5 presents data for labourers' day wages in a number of textile centres in Bulgaria and Serbia. Although the present discussion is limited to the Gabrovo – Sliven comparison, the table will be used with reference to other centres as well.

As Table 9.5 shows, Gabrovo was indeed a lower-wage town than Sliven in the mid-1890s, the earliest years for which we have relevant comparative data, but the gap had almost closed by 1899–1902, and was unequivocally reversed by 1906–9. By then Gabrovo was a high-wage town, not because of agricultural advantages, but because its population and that of its hinterland were unusually fully committed in industrial employment. The town itself had the highest proportion of its population of any town in Bulgaria in industrial pursuits (54.6 per cent) and the environing district was second among the sixty-seven rural areas in the same respect, with 22.5 per cent. Sliven ranked much lower on both counts, at fifteenth with 32.5 per cent and eleventh with 7.0 per cent respectively.[324]

It was usually claimed that the Sliven factories had predominantly

---

[320] Staneff, *Gewerbewesen*, pp. 130–1, 132.
[321] Man'o Stojanov, *Kogato Plovdiv beshe stolitsa* (Sofia, 1973), p. 66.
[322] Mishajkov, 'Ocherk', pp. 499, 551–2.
[323] Calculated from Mishajkov, 'Ocherk', p. 479.
[324] Popov, *Stopanska B'lgarija*, pp. 281–2.

Table 9.5 *Labourers' day wages in Bulgarian and Serbian towns 1893–1909 (in leva or dinars)*

	1893–96	1899–1902	1906–9
Sofia	1.95	1.67	2.17
Gabrovo	1.46	1.53	2.63
Sliven	2.47	1.65	1.93
Samokov	1.43	1.04	1.72
Varna	2.24	2.27	2.56
BULGARIA	1.83	1.46	1.82
Leskovac	1.27	0.91	1.68
Belgrade	1.92	2.18	2.59
SERBIA	1.36	1.19	1.33

Note:
The dinar and lev were usually close to parity with each other.
Sources: Statistika za srednite pazarni tseni na domashnite zhivotni, po-vazhnite predmeti za zhiveene i nadnitsite v B'lgarija prez desetiletieto 1893–1902 (Sofia, 1906), p. 118; *Statistika za t'rgovijata na knjazhestvo B'lgarija i srednite godishni pazarni tseni ... prez 1906*, p. 507; same serial for 1907, p. 517; 1908, p. 517; 1909, p. 545; *SGKS*, 1893, pp. 134–5; 1894–5 pp. 212–13 and 220–1; *Statistika cena poljoprivrednih proizvoda u Kr. Srbiji, 1896–1900* (Belgrade, 1902), pp. 52–3, 226–7; *SGKS*, 1900, pp. 232–3; 1901, pp. 272–3; 1902, pp. 274–5; 1906, p. 317; 1907–8, p. 367; 1909–10, pp. 361, 376.

employed male labour because fly-shuttle handlooms needed men to work them. However, employment of a skilled male workforce, whose wage level was tending to fall, discouraged the adoption of the power-looms which Gabrovo had installed from the beginning, because its dependence on female labour left it little option. In the late 1890s, power-looms were introduced at Sliven, but largely as a result of pressure by the state, and not by the inclination of the employers. Even then the sex-composition of the workforce did not change. Although the Sliven factories were undercapitalized compared with those of Gabrovo, their labour was more productive, and their export orientation indicates that they were highly competitive.[325] As Sliven was becoming an increasingly low-wage market for adult male labour – at least relative to Gabrovo – so it clung tenaciously to the handloom. This does not mean that the Sliven mills failed to update the means with which specific tasks were performed; when the Austrian consul reported on Sliven in 1908, he was favourably impressed with the modern machine technology which he saw.[326] On the

[325] Mishajkov, 'Ocherk', pp. 496, 499.
[326] *BOUCA*, 1909 bd. 1. Bourgas Jahresbericht 1908, p. 3.

eve of World War I, Popov was still making invidious comparisons between the textile technologies of Sliven and Gabrovo,[327] but the techniques used at Sliven corresponded well to the local markets for power and labour, and to the product markets in which Sliven competed. In this case, the proto-industrial inheritance of labour skills was a powerful factor which worked to Sliven's advantage; it may also explain why it did not recruit more female labour.

At Samokov, labour force structure was similar to that at Sliven. Males comprised 71 per cent of the woollen industry workforce, and 96 per cent was over 16 years old.[328] Similarly the industry was allegedly slow to innovate. It is claimed that wage costs were too high for Samokov woollens to be fully competitive with imports from Austria, or for the factories to make much profit.[329] Now Samokov fell on hard times after the liberation, and vegetated economically up to World War I. A glance at Table 9.5 will affirm that it was, and remained, a low-wage town. So, if the industry suffered from the relatively high cost of employing male labour (in a way in which Sliven did not) it was not using its labour force efficiently. In terms of wool used per worker, and gross output per worker it lagged far behind Sliven or Gabrovo. A clue to its inefficiency is that it was set up for power weaving rather than handloom work in 1903,[330] implying that it lacked the reservoir of skilled weavers which sustained Sliven's competitive success, or access to cheap female labour as an adequate substitute.

Leskovac was also a strong craft town, and after 1878 its district became increasingly committed to domestic industry. The dominant cottage industry was rope-making. In 1879, there were 300 master rope-makers in the town.[331] At that time, the trade was beginning to extend into the countryside. In 1883 about 1,000 workers made a living from hemp processing in the Leskovac district,[332] but by 1912, the the number of rope-makers in Vranje okrug (in which Leskovac was located) had risen to 7,000.[333] This growth was accompanied, however, with a persistent and serious fall in the earnings which could be made from the craft. Taking 1884/7 as 100, earnings fell to 51.7 in 1890/4, to 33.5 in 1900/4 and 29.2 in 1905/8.[334] Acceptance by a rapidly growing labour force of a declining level of remuneration indicates a growing surplus of labour, which enabled the factories to recruit at low wages. The diffusion of rope-making into the villages was in part the work of the rope

---

[327] Popov, *Stopanska B'lgarija*, p. 327.   [328] Mishajkov, 'Ocherk', p. 496.
[329] GBC Bulgaria 1895, p. 4.   [330] Mishajkov, 'Ocherk', p. 480, 499.
[331] AS MNP (S) k.5 XXIII. Podaci o radnjama za 1879 – Leskovac.
[332] M. Dj. Miličević, *Kraljevina Srbija. Novi krajevi* (Belgrade, 1884), p. 132.
[333] 'Izvoz kudelje i užarije', *Ekonomist*, I (1912), p. 113.
[334] See Palairet, 'The Influence of Commerce', p. 415.

merchants, who sought cheaper supplies than had been provided by the urban guildsmen. For the villagers, the wage offered by rope-making was acceptable since it provided only a supplementary income source, but it reduced the urban rope-makers to near starvation.[335] So, after rising to 1891, the number of urban rope-makers began to fall, as more and more abandoned the trade. Trajković claims that rope-makers provided a valuable recruiting base for the hemp cloth factory which was built there.[336]

The Leskovac factories hired their labour exceptionally cheaply.[337] Of all the textile towns listed in Table 9.5, wages in Leskovac were the lowest; until 1904, when they began to rise somewhat, they were well below the average for Serbia. Much use was made of cheap unskilled seasonal workers.[338] Leskovac labour was used for strike-breaking in Bulgaria, and in Salonica the Leskovac area was known as a reservoir of cheap industrial labour.[339]

However, the craft environment of Leskovac did not provide industry with appropriate industrial skills. When the *gajtan* mills started up, they all needed to import skilled Bulgarians. Later, the town factories placed heavy reliance on skilled Czech labour, and difficulties after 1900 in retaining these workers held back the expansion of their business.[340] The non-substitutability between proto-industrial and factory labour is suggested by a complaint of 1890, concerning the effect of the Strojkovac and Vučje mills on the local labour market:[341]

Because of the concession given for the exclusive production of *gajtan* at least ten masters of this craft and over 1,000 workers of both sexes have lost their livelihood and earnings and have consequently fallen with their families into distress. The Serbs who were originally in the factory were replaced by foreigners. Instead of training our people in this craft, they were used in this factory as coachmen, common labourers and carriers of goods so that if the foreigners left the factory it would collapse. . . The further existence of this factory kills domestic production and deprives workers, former craftsmen and producers of wool of the essentials of life.

The firm denied that it had put anybody out of work, and pointed to the volume of spinning employment it had created. (The Leskovac sub-prefect endorsed this denial.) Moreover, the factory's initial dependence on Bulgarian skills was ended by apprenticing and training Leskovac boys in the craft.[342] However, this also shows that Leskovac had no pool of

---

[335] Nikola Vučo, *Raspadanja esnafa u Srbiji* (Belgrade, 1954), I, p. 413.
[336] Trajković, *Leskovačke industrije*, p. 50.   [337] Ibid., pp. 51–2.
[338] Aristomen Ristić and Svetomir Stojanović, *Leskovac juče i danas* (Leskovac, 1935), p. 69.
[339] Velimir Vasić, 'Pečalbarstvo istočne Srbije' (Doctoral thesis, University of Belgrade, Faculty of Law, 1950), pp. 191, 183.   [340] Lampe, 'Financial Structure', p. 259.
[341] AS MNP (T) 1898 VI 2. Mitić–MNP, 18 Mar. 1890, no. 1762.
[342] AS MNP (T) 1898 VI 2. Popović–Načelnik sreza Leskovca, 19 June 1890, no. 8167; Sreski Načelnik, Leskovac–MNP, 1 July 1890, no. 3677.

labour skills to draw on in advance. Most of its labour was totally unskilled. It was also unorganized till 1914. When strikes broke out in the Leskovac factories in March that year, the Socialist movement tried to unionize the workforce; the employers locked the workers out and brought a trainload of Albanians up from Gnjilane in Kosovo to break the strike.[343] Leskovac had the advantage characteristic of an area of rural industry of disposing virtually unlimited supplies of cheap labour, but this did not give it favourable access to industrial skills.

What of the capital cities and seaports as a source of labour supply? This was not an important consideration in choosing these locations. The advantage which attracted textile industries to Belgrade and Varna was the low cost of importing raw materials. A further but lesser advantage was access to local consumer markets. This consideration accounted for the location in Sofia of its sole woollen enterprise. If wage rates had been a significant determinant of location we should have expected Sofia rather than Belgrade to have exerted the greater pull on the textile industry, whereas the reverse was the case. As may be seen from Table 9.5, Belgrade and Varna were relatively high priced labour markets, though Sofia was not.

The relatively high cost and increasing militance of labour in Belgrade slightly discouraged textile factory development there. By 1902, Belgrade was the centre of the strike movement in Serbia, where 70 per cent of all strikes up to that date had occurred.[344] They had not yet touched the textile industry, but this was not long delayed, and the strike-proneness of its workforce played a part in causing the Crompton firm to withdraw. There was also the case, in 1905, of a Hungarian bank which tried to divest itself of its weaving interests in Belgrade, because of the high wages being paid to its workers, 'all of whom were reported to be socialists'. The wage paid was 2.5–3.0 dinars a day for men and 2 dinars for women.[345] This corresponds with that paid in Belgrade by the Ilić firm in 1908 of 2–4 dinars for men and 1.8–2.5 for women.[346] These wage rates were much higher than at Leskovac where going rates in 1910 were 0.8–1.2 dinars and 0.6–1.0 dinars respectively.[347] Although city wages were higher than those in the small towns, they afforded the employer an elastic labour supply. The factories tended to be located on the outskirts, so that

[343] AS MUD (P) 1914 XVIII 98. No. 9313; 1914 19 80. Radnička komora–MUD, 23 May 1914, no. 11640.

[344] Mladen Vukomanović, *Radnička klasa Srbije u drugoj polovini XIX veka* (Belgrade, 1972), p. 299.

[345] Andrija Radenić, 'Izveštaji madjarskih privrednih izaslanika o prilikama u Srbiji 1901–1914', *IČ*, XIV-XV (1963–5), p. 413.

[346] AS MNP (T) 1907 38 10. Questionnaire to Ilić firm for 1908/9.

[347] Trajković, *Leskovačke industrije*, p. 51.

the predominantly urban residents they employed[348] could be supplemented by male peasant migrants from the countryside;[349] and as the city dwellers lacked access to alternative incomes from farming, poorer city women worked at hosiery knitting and the sewing of clothing in growing numbers.[350] As discussed above, both Michel and the Cromptons envisaged using Belgrade household labour for outwork weaving.

Varna, location of the British cotton mill in Bulgaria, was less than ideal for labour supply since it was set in a rich agricultural hinterland. In planning the enterprise, the founders were little concerned by this, since pay levels were 'infinitesimal' compared with those in Oldham,[351] ranging from 0.50 to 2 leva a day.[352] Nevertheless, they reckoned without serious productivity problems which curtailed output.

Initially the firm recruited mostly male labour, and worked an 8–9 hour day. Productivity was low, and the firm replaced many of its men with girls, put them on piece rates, and lengthened the factory's hours. This shifted the burden of low productivity onto the workforce, whose earnings fell and only gradually recovered.[353] In 1902, most workers were drawn from Varna itself.[354] The next year, the business suffered from a strike, which forced expensive concessions on it,[355] and 'from a short supply of labour owing to an abundant local harvest'.[356] Harassment by the local socialists continued.[357] So the management decided to recruit labour from the deep interior. The following winter,[358] town-criers in Shumen, Ruse, T'rnovo, Razgrad and elsewhere proclaimed 'The Varna factory needs a lot of workers, offers most attractive conditions, with 40–80 leva a month pay, pleasant accommodation, cheap food and return travelling costs paid.' Reportedly, 'hundreds' of young females were signed up.

This was not a one-off recruiting drive, but a long-term policy. It was temporarily effective, for employment rose between 1904 and 1906 from 500 to 650.[359] However, supply difficulties remained unsolved. In 1907, the labour force stood at 377 workers, of whom 59 per cent were male.[360] Factory legislation in 1910 acted as a brake on output by ending the night-shifting of women and children,[361] and the following year despite 'high activity', the labour force was down to 300.[362]

---

[348] Ilić 1908/9 questionnaire.   [349] *Trgovinski glasnik*, 4 Feb. 1911, p. 1.
[350] Savić, *Industrija*, I, p. 294.   [351] GBC Bulgaria 1900, p. 4.
[352] Staneff, *Gewerbewesen*, p. 137.
[353] Radka Bradinska, 'Navlizaneto na B'lgarskata zhena v promishlenoto proizvodstvo', *Profs'juzni letopisi*, 1968, p. 219; Mladenov, *Pojava*, p. 51.
[354] *BOUCA*, 1902 bd. 1 Sofia 1902, A II 1, p. 20.
[355] *BOUCA*, 1903 bd. 1. Varna A II 5, p. 30.   [356] GBC Bulgaria 1904, p. 5.
[357] *BOUCA*, 1904 bd. 1 (1) Varna, p. 4.
[358] A. Rakovska, 'Zhenskijat naemno-rabotnishki trud v B'lgarija i negovoto razvitie', *Novo Vreme*, IX (1905), p. 717.   [359] GBC Bulgaria 1903, p. 5 and 1905, p. 8.
[360] *SGBTs*, 1909, p. 234.   [361] GBC Bulgaria 1910, p. 14.   [362] GBC Bulgaria 1913, p. 6.

Skilled factory labour

Neither the old proto-industrial area nor the new textile factory location could easily supply engineers and machine specialists. Recruitment of foreign labour for these posts imposed significant cost disadvantages on Balkan textile firms. The early Bulgarian factories skimped on specialists to an extreme degree. Initially, western European technical skills were employed in the Gabrovo factories, and probably at Karlovo and Samokov as well,[363] but only sparingly. In his first mill, Kalpazanov employed but a single German master.[364] Berov's weavery made do with a Czech manager and no other foreign employee.[365] The small scale of production made hiring specialists impracticable,[366] and the mill owners tried to dispense with the services of foreigners the moment they had imparted a modicum of operating skill to the native employees. A Gabrovo observer noted:[367]

It is interesting how the intricate machines which were brought into these factories are being managed today by the owners themselves, by the men of Gabrovo. We had reason to be present at the opening of one of these factories which was fitted by two Englishmen; how astonished these Englishmen were a few days after the machines had started work, when they were told there was no further need of them, that they themselves could manage them, and today indeed, the complex English machines are managed by the skilled men of Gabrovo.

Presumably they simply hoped there would be no serious breakdowns. For in 1893 Gabrovo manufacturers accepted that:[368]

if one machine, a single screw or other part of some factory machine is damaged, there is not a master in Gabrovo to repair it. The manufacturer is forced either to have a large reserve of spare parts or to send it for repair to the factory where the machine was made. Either way, difficulties and expense are caused for the manufacturers.

Yet Gabrovo was the best established ironworking town in the Balkans, in which in 1872–3 Kalpazanov had been able to build a carding engine and a wool tearing machine at his own forge.[369]

At Sliven, as we have seen, the problem was ameliorated by the periodic visits of Belgian engineers. Eschewing the adoption of dispensable modern machines, the Sliven factory owners clung to their intermediate technology, using water wheels rather than steam power, fly-shuttles rather than power-looms, and fulling mills instead of bale breakers.[370]

---

[363] Staneff, *Gewerbewesen*, p. 124.   [364] Tsonchev, *Gabrovo*, p. 622.
[365] *Doklad: Sevlievo 1892–93*, p. 53.   [366] Mishajkov, 'Ocherk', p. 481.
[367] Pajakov, 'Ekonomicheskoto dvizhenie', p. 70, col. 2.
[368] *Doklad: Sevlievo 1892–93*, p. 50.   [369] Tsonchev, *Gabrovo*, pp. 204–12, 616.
[370] Staneff, *Gewerbewesen*, p. 124.

Gabrovo in 1899 managed with three foreign specialists on a workforce of 753 native workers,[371] while in 1892, Sliven hired no foreign specialists at all.[372]

Even with the minimal use of complex techniques, locally recruited specialists would still be needed to run the factories in the absence of foreign technicians. In 1903 there were ten to twelve skilled workers in Sliven (all dyers) six technicians in Karlovo, and three or four in Gabrovo, as well as a few dyers and specialist weavers.[373] In the early years, most key workers were probably self-taught artisans. Just before the liberation, when Ivan Grozev set up his ill-fated mill at Karlovo, he bought equipment in Brno. To install it, he found a self-taught engineer in Karlovo and sent him to Brno to get experience, then return, fit and maintain the machinery. The factory building was constructed by another Karlovo craftsman.[374] As late as 1910, Bulgarian textile masters were 'uncultured people of low literacy and very basic work knowledge', who 'acquired their specialism by stealth in learning from the German specialists whose place they took'.[375] The turnover of labour was high and firms poached skilled manpower from each other. The founders of the second woollen factory at Trjavna, for example, obtained both their mill manager and their engineer from factories at Gabrovo.[376]

There was in Bulgaria, however, one significant institutional source of textile training: the old Sliven textile mill and the instruction it provided. This mill acted as a point for the diffusion of the new technology. In 1875, when Kalpazanov first considered building his spinning mill, it was to the Sliven mill he went, and what he saw convinced him he should build his own.[377] During the operation of this factory by the 'Napred'k' company in the early 1880s, a school of weaving and dyeing was established in its buildings, which survived, with interruption, into the twentieth century.[378] In 1899 it had only twenty-nine students,[379] but its alumni had a critical role to play in the industry's development. One Sliven factory was established by an ex-pupil in 1889.[380] The head weaver at the Aleksandrov mill at Gabrovo was also a graduate.[381] A student of the school claimed in 1898 that 'almost all of our factories have masters either from the school or from abroad'.[382] Most alumni were dyers, and local manufacturers frequently turned to its instructors for advice on

---

[371] *Izlozhenie: Sevlievo 1898–99*, p. 22; Staneff, *Gewerbewesen*, p. 134.
[372] *RC*, LXXVII (1892), p. 100.   [373] Mishajkov, 'Ocherk', p. 497.
[374] G. T. D[anailov], 'P'rvata b'lgarska tekstilna fabrika', *Sp.BID*, VI (1902), pp. 568–9.
[375] D-va, 'Znachenieto na v'tr'shnija pazar', p. 584.
[376] NBKM. Daskalov papers. Fond 129 a.e. 112, Popov–Daskalov, 20 Feb. 1891, fo. 1–2.
[377] Tsonchev, *Gabrovo*, p. 617.   [378] *Izlozhenie: Burgaz 1907/08*, p. 39.
[379] *Doklad: Sliven 1899–1900*, p. 61.   [380] *Doklad: Sliven 1889*, p. 16.
[381] Mishajkov, 'Ocherk', p. 498.   [382] TsDIA. f. 173 op. 2 ae. 674 fo. 303.

dyeing problems.[383] Among the school's graduates we find master dyer Ivan Peshov of Chiprovtsi, who sought government backing for a plan to update the dyeing of carpets in his native township.[384] What the school offered was unadvanced by European standards. As the Sliven factories relied upon the school for their skilled labour, and for technical improvements from the school's instructors, this may have been a reason for the relatively unadvanced techniques they applied.[385] However, the Austrian consul attributed the good running of the Sliven factories to the 'first rate service rendered by the well run textile school'.[386]

The pattern of skilled labour recruitment was strikingly different in Serbia. Here the textile industries depended heavily on foreign specialists. Compared with Bulgaria, Serbia had easy access to immigrant industrial skills from central Europe.[387] But was this truly an advantage? Higher dependence on foreign textile labour in Serbia also reflected the lack of the locally formed skills which the Bulgarian textile towns inherited from their proto-industrial past or created through training. Had the Serbian factories developed similarly, they would not have needed to import so many highly paid workers and technicians.

In part the use in Serbia of imported labour reflected the preferences of foreign entrepreneurs, who operated on a larger scale than the Bulgarian firms, and were familiar with higher technical standards. When Münch established his Paraćin mill, he brought in a nucleus of Czech workers from his mill in Moravia. He expected them initially to make up 'the greater part' of the workforce, till local people had been trained.[388] The original group was small – 9 German and Czech foremen to supervise 130 Serbians, mainly women.[389] As the enterprise expanded and used more complex equipment, the balance changed. In 1895, 100 out of 400 employees were foreign, and included a 'well known' English engineer, a man of enterprise, 'a great rarity in the true Englishman'.[390] However, by then most foreign employees were probably Serbs from Hungary. This enabled Münch evasively to claim in 1899 that 97 per cent of his workers were Serbs.[391] Probably their labour was cheaper and more readily obtainable than that of Czechs and Germans. Münch's preference for imported skills was paralleled by the Crompton firm. When they took over the former Boas and Eser mill, it lacked skilled masters, and they

---

[383] *Doklad: Sliven 1899–1900*, p. 62.   [384] TsDIA. f. 173 op. 2 a.e. 674. fo. 259–61.

[385] Staneff, *Gewerbewesen*, pp. 124–5.

[386] *BOUCA*, 1909 bd. 1. Bourgas. Jahresbericht 1908, p. 3.

[387] John R. Lampe, 'Varieties of Unsuccessful Industrialization. The Balkan States before 1914', *JEcH*, XXXV (1975), pp. 68–9.

[388] AS MNP (T) 1906 41 7. Münch and Schumpeter–Min. Fin. 7 Nov. 1879.

[389] de Borchgrave, *Serbie*, pp. 181–2.   [390] Kostić, *Pisma s puta*, pp. 47, 52.

[391] AS MNP (T) 1902 I 107. Report on the Münch factory in 1899.

concerned themselves to rectify this deficiency. In 1900, 20 per cent of their workers were Czech, German and non-citizen Serbs.[392] Yet similar preferences were also displayed by the indigeneous Ilić enterprises. Their Leskovac woollen mill employed Austrian and Swiss foremen in 1902,[393] and all the Leskovac firms were heavily dependent on Czech specialists. Lampe points to the high inter-industry correlation for 1910 between the number of foreigners employed and the number of skilled workers in these industries. Although not all foreigners in the textile labour force were skilled, they accounted for 19.3 per cent of it, even though textile manufacturing was by then a relatively mature industry, with long established firms.[394]

Foreign employees were also engaged by Serbia's textile firms for office work. Because of the country's low educational attainment, administration presented a problem which was probably not encountered in Bulgaria with its higher rate of literacy. Firms in Serbia either conducted their book-keeping abroad, or imported foreign book-keepers to do the job on the spot.[395] The Paraćin mill was no exception. In 1895, the office was staffed mainly by Serbs from Hungary.[396] The relatively heavier dependance of the Serbian textile industry on the services of foreign workers was not simply because access to their skills was easier than for Bulgaria, but also because Serbia was even more poorly endowed with skilled and educated personnel.

The basic reasons for this relative deficiency were that Serbia's craft sector had always been much smaller, the country was less urbanized, and literacy was lower. There was an additional factor; if mobility inward was easier than for Bulgaria, so also was outward mobility for skilled labour, especially from Belgrade. Firms were obliged to pay a stiff premium over local rates for foreign personnel, but were reluctant to pay so much for equally skilled Serbians. Consequently, a strong tendency developed, at least from 1907, for Serbian skilled workers to emigrate to central Europe, where their services were better remunerated.[397] Employers underpaid skilled native-born personnel, and paid dearly for foreigners to do the same work because they feared that if they conceded premium wage rates to key domestic labour, the differential would be seized on as leverage by an organized labour movement; however the differential enjoyed by foreigners proved a contentious issue.

---

[392] AS MNP (T) 1900 XI 42. Živković–MNP, 31 Mar. 1900, no. 1639, f. 2–2vo.
[393] *BOUCA*, 1902 bd. 2 (2) Niš 1902, A XVI 2, p. 11.
[394] Lampe, 'Financial Structure', p. 257–61.   [395] Ibid., p. 258.
[396] Kostić, *Pisma s puta*, p. 50.
[397] See articles on emigration in *Radničke novine*, VII (1907), no. 101, XI (1911), no. 20 and no. 264.

Table 9.6 *Commercial woollen output, Bulgaria 1867–1903 (in tonnes, 000 leva of value added)*

	E. Rumelia		N. Bulgaria		Bulgaria	
	weight	value	weight	value	weight	value
1867	1,492–1,646	7,030	538.6	2,030	2,030–2,185	9,060
1883	613.7	3,150	n.d.	n.d.	n.d.	n.d.
1903	713–742	2,030	502–521	2,650	1,216–1,264	4,670

Source: Palairet, 'Woollen Industries', p. 351.

Comparative progress in Balkan textile manufacturing

The growth of mechanized textile manufacturing was significant in the gradual industrialization of the Balkans before 1914. For Bulgaria, textile manufacturing was the most important factory industry, accounting in 1907 for 36.5 per cent of net large-scale manufacturing production.[398] For Serbia, whose industrial production was oriented to food processing, in milling, brewing, meat packing, sugarbeet, jam making, distilling and plum drying, the industry was of less importance, but the basis of its development was broadly similar. In neither case was the industry a leading sector; indeed, in Bulgaria, it was a far smaller sector of the economy in the early twentieth century than its proto-industrial predecessor at the end of the Ottoman era, four decades earlier, both in relative and in absolute terms. Table 9.6 shows how great a contraction had occurred.

The 48 per cent shrinkage of value added resulted partly from diffusion of the industry after 1878 into Serbia and Macedonia and the loss of the Bosnian market, but the biggest loss was probably of domestic urban demand in the post-liberation upheaval. The unchanging preponderance of the subsistence sector limited mass demand for factory products, and prompted the factories to diversify up-market to compete for urban purchasers, who increasingly favoured imported cloths. As Bulgarian industry was uncompetitive in this market despite rising tariff protection, the effort was ineffectual.

Examining the industry on the supply side, we focused on the putative advantages to firms which had developed from a proto-industrial environment, for the external economies it might be expected to have yielded. There is a strong case for the proto-industry argument since the main factories were established at the old proto-industrial towns of Gabrovo,

[398] *SGBTs*, 1909 p. 236. Net production equals gross production minus material inputs.

Sliven and Leskovac. However, the only clear linkage for these towns was historical. In all of them, there were businesses which engaged in the woollen trades (though at Leskovac there was no prior connexion with woollen manufacturing). In the 1880s machine manufacturing had become necessary to the survival of their businesses, and they built local woollen mills as a defensive investment in their supply chains. No incoming or trans-national firm favoured them as a manufacturing location.

These local firms had no especial advantage in terms of access to capital, and they lacked technical information, so, when they started up, they built sketchy factories which applied obsolescent technology. Nevertheless, the ventures were sufficiently profitable for such shortcomings to be remedied by reinvestment, which gave rise to a culture of accumulation and personal frugality.

Proto-industry theory however gives pride of place to labour endowment, so we would expect entrepreneurs to have been advantaged by cheap industrially orientated labour. However, most proto-industrial workers were women who worked at home and could not be transferred into the mills, so the factories had to create their labour forces from scratch. At Gabrovo, they tapped the labour of village girls. They were low paid, but to utilize their labour, the Gabrovo firms had to apply power machinery in all major textile operations. At Sliven, no similar labour was available, and the industry employed mainly urban adult males, and wove with fly-shuttles. Sliven employers had to pay higher wages than those of Gabrovo, but their experienced labour was used efficiently, though this encouraged retention of obsolete production methods. At Leskovac cheap labour was clearly of advantage to the industry. Though proto-industry made an entirely different commodity, rope, diffusion of this trade into the villages forced down urban wages. Labour was cheaper than average only at Leskovac and Samokov, and most towns could have provided unskilled labour at similar pay. Besides this, none of the towns except Sliven provided the skills needed for factory industry, and all suffered a shortage of skilled personnel. They either had to recruit expensive foreign skills, or accept the inefficiency which flowed from doing without them.

Obviously the concentration of factory industry on the old proto-industrial centres was no accident, but there was no pressing reason for trans-national firms to site their enterprises alongside their indigenous competitors. In-coming firms, Münch at Paraćin, Crompton and Michel at Belgrade and the British cotton mill at Varna, located their plant for access to raw material. In the longer run, city and port locations proved at least as advantageous as the former proto-industrial towns.

10 Serbia and Bulgaria 1878–1914: modernization and productive decline

We now review the economic problems and progress of the two major Balkan states, Bulgaria and Serbia, in the pre-World War I era. Taking the experience of Habsburg Bosnia as the paradigm for a reasonably successful advance from underdevelopment, we ask why both states not only failed to join the European developmental mainstream, but experienced what we will show to have been a significant decline in per capita output during this period. As the economies of both countries continued to be overwhelmingly rural it is to the farming sector that we turn first. In dealing with Bulgaria's post-liberation farm problems we demonstrated in Chapter 7 that farm productivity was in long-run secular decline. Our first task is to trace the performance of the farm economy in Serbia. The buoyancy of international markets had masked the declining trend before 1876, but the deceleration of world trade growth and the accompanying rise in tariff and non-tariff obstacles to Serbia's exports exposed the farm economy's underlying weaknesses. The period 1878–93 was attended by a pronounced structural shift away from dependence on livestock towards the bulk production of cereals for export, but at the cost of a marked downward trend in output per worker in farming. There were, however, trend divergences between Serbian and Bulgarian farming, which arose through differences in relative factor endowments. These led in the early years of the twentieth century to crop yield improvements in Serbia, which were not echoed in Bulgaria. They did little, however, to improve aggregate performance, and this chapter examines possible reasons for the long-run stagnation of both these agrarian economies.

Farming accounted however for slightly less than half the total output of Bulgaria and Serbia at the end of our period. We therefore examine the modernizing sectors of the economy, and the role of the state in particular in retarding the development process, to show why the contribution made by the modernizing sectors was constrained to minimal proportions.

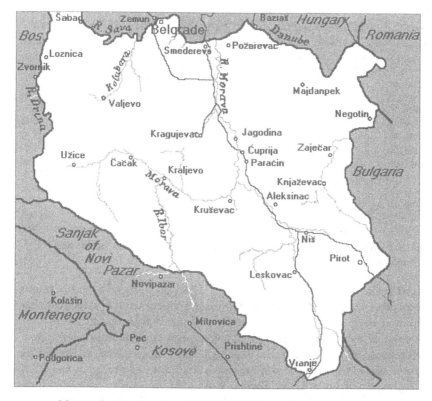

Map 5 Serbia, frontiers of 1878–1912

Economic change in Serbia 1878–1900

We showed in Chapter 4 that commercial activity in Serbia increased up to 1875 as the market became increasingly integrated with the world economy. Nevertheless, peasants still resisted trading arable crops. Although crop exports began to contribute to trade expansion, as did the burgeoning export of prunes, the favourable price of livestock, especially pigs, enabled most farmers to cling to their traditional export specialization, and this continued to provide most of the growth in the export trade. However, the diminution of the pastoral resource base meant that this dependence was not sustainable.

After 1878, farmers depended increasingly for cash income on the marketing of grain and plums. From being the distress export of the smaller peasant, grain fast became the staple cash crop of the lowland farmer. The advance in grain exports is shown in Table 10.1. Their growth was assisted by the opening of railways, but their effect (in the

Table 10.1 *Net annual grain exports from Serbia, 1862–1912 (000 tonnes)*

Year	Maize	Wheat	Barley, rye, oats	Total
1862–65	0.0	0.1	0.5	0.7
1865–70	2.2	21.7	3.7	27.5
1871–75	−0.6	7.2	3.5	10.1
1879–80	−2.8	18.8	4.0	20.0
1881–85	3.7	31.6	7.2	42.5
1886–90	5.3	43.9	8.8	57.9
1891–95	28.8	73.2	26.5	128.4
1896–1900	18.4	72.9	29.6	120.9
1901–05	9.8	68.5	24.0	102.4
1906–10	92.3	98.0	52.9	243.2
1911–12	82.6	102.4	24.9	209.9

Source: Palairet, 'Influence of Commerce', pp. 129–30. Wheat exports include flour, grossed up to allow for milling waste of 20 per cent.

short term) should not be overstated. The postwar grain export boom took place between 1879 and 1884, and it was only in the latter year that the first section from Belgrade to Niš of the Balkan trunk railway was opened. During the next three years, grain exports were rather depressed. Moreover, most of the grain exported was wheat raised in the fertile hinterland of the Danube and Sava ports and was not shifted by rail. This area, especially northwest Serbia, expanded its export of grain more rapidly than the catchment area of the railway. So the opening of the railway lines within Serbia, though it assisted the growth of the trade, was not its primary cause.

As their dependence on grain sales increased, farmers expanded the area of land they put under arable. If we were to take at face value the government survey figures for cultivation in 1889, 1893 and 1897, there was a one-off structural shift in Serbian farming, concentrated in the period 1889–93. After stagnation between 1847 and 1867, the cultivated area within the pre-1878 territory of Serbia advanced from 395,194 hectares in 1867 to 551,445 hectares in 1889, that is to say by 39.5 per cent.[1] But as rural population rose by 42.8 per cent in density during the same period, there was as yet no increase in the cultivated area per capita. Then between 1889 and 1893 (if the land surveys can be trusted) the crop area (excluding fallow) rose by 82.8 per cent from 648,400 hectares to 1.19 million hectares,[2] while population rose by 6.7 per cent. As the

[1] *SKS*, III (Belgrade, 1894), p. lxi.
[2] *SKS*, III, p. vi; *SKS*, IX (Belgrade, 1897), pp. x, 94–5.

number of proprietors of cultivated land also rose, from 257,280 in 1889 to 322,505 in 1893,[3] the area of arable per holding would have jumped from 2.94 hectares to 4.28. However, from 1893 onward, the cropped area abruptly stopped expanding. The 1897 survey shows a retreat from 1893 to 1.02 million hectares,[4] and there was virtually no change in 1905 when it stood at 1.05 million.[5]

Any correction we might impose upon these surveys would be arbitrary, but it is not likely that the area cultivated per head of the rural population advanced in so discontinuous a fashion. The 1889 survey was executed 'rather superficially'.[6] It was claimed that there was significant under-recording, because local administrative organs failed to inform respondents that there was no fiscal motive behind the survey. This problem was rectified in 1893.[7] Indeed the statistical office stated that under-recording accounted for the entire difference between the two surveys. Introducing the 1897 census it reckoned that the 1893 survey had been 'fairly accurate in respect of cultivated area',[8] and that in 1897 it was better still, though in 1900, it was considered that areas in 1893 and 1897 had been overestimated.[9] So if the 1889 survey understates, while those of 1893 and 1897 overstate, the progression of cultivation was more continuous than the raw statistics indicate. Nevertheless, expansion must have been more or less halted by the mid-1890s, even if there were no actual decline. It seems unlikely that there was no growth between 1889 and 1893; this would appear to be an overstatement, probably made by one team of officials to rubbish the work of their predecessors. Trends in grain exports suggest that the area cultivated per head rose more rapidly in the late 1880s and early 1890s than in the preceding or subsequent periods. The figures in Table 10.1 indicate that crop exports surged from 30,400 tonnes in 1885/7 to 77,400 in 1888/90 and 153,600 tonnes in 1891/3. From 1893 to 1905 there was no further quantitative advance though the hardening of prices helped enhance their value. As yields per hectare seem not to have risen, this is consistent with the evidence that the area cultivated stabilized.

Despite expansion in the area cultivated, the overall trend in farm output per member of the farm population fell decisively from 1878 to the end of the nineteenth century. This is displayed in Table 10.2. The relative stability shown in the 1880s reflects a transient boom in wine production. This was a response to the international wine shortage, and in Serbia (unlike Bulgaria) growers responded strongly to export opportunities. The rise in wine output is included within the cash crops column.

[3] *SKS*, III, p. iv; *SKS*, IX, p. vii.   [4] *SKS*, XVI (Belgrade, 1900), p. xxiv.
[5] *SGKS*, 1906, p. 238.   [6] *SKS*, III, p. i.   [7] *SKS*, IX, p. i.   [8] *SKS*, XVI, p. i.
[9] *SKS*, XVIII (Belgrade, 1903), p. i.

Table 10.2 *Serbia. Sectoral farm output 1873–1912*

	(million dinars, 1910 prices)						
Year	Animal products	Animals	Cash crops	Grain	Garden crops	Total	Total per-capita
1873–5	38	61	62	47	9	217	178
1879–80	45	64	84	63	12	268	177
1881–5	46	56	92	75	13	281	173
1886–90	45	51	118	89	14	316	175
1891–5	46	53	84	92	14	289	149
1896–1900	49	51	74	127	15	317	153
1901–5	52	56	53	102	14	276	123
1906–10	60	54	66	134	18	331	137
1911–12	67	57	48	148	20	340	129

Source: see BALKSTAT.

Like those of Bulgaria, Serbia's vineyards were devastated in the 1890s by phylloxera, production slumped, and exports disappeared.[10] Stripping out the transient effects of the wine boom, the 1880s, like the 1890s, were a period of productive decline. Its cause was stagnation in stockraising output insufficiently offset by the expansion of cultivation, in the face of ferociously rapid growth in rural population.

The decline in per capita animal based outputs reflects above all a rapid diminution of the stock of pigs. Their number in the census of 1866 had been recorded at 1.3 million, and despite the accession of territory in 1878, shrank to an estimated 1.1 million by 1883, and 909,000 in the census of 1890. Pig raising, formerly the key contributor to popular well-being, suffered both from demand problems and supply side pressures. Supply had already been squeezed in the 1860s and early 1870s, but the strength of demand from Austria-Hungary had made it worthwhile to maintain production, and to accept the costs of maize feeding, even though the woodland base of the trade was shrinking. But once demand weakened, the difficulties of the pig raisers became acute.

The most visible cause of the diminution of pig raising was increasing

[10] The high figure for 1889 is probably genuine, as it represents a splendid vintage, but the exceptionally high figure for crop production in 1897 was almost certainly the product of ill-advised tampering by the statistical office with the crop returns of that year; in 1893, yields were gathered successfully enough, and fit well with the long-term trend, but in 1897, the Statistical Office, dissatisfied by the local returns, asked the Serbian Agricultural Society to modify them – with absurd results. Contemporary evidence suggests that the harvest of 1897 was poor, and this was reflected in poor export figures. The 1893 harvest is estimated in *SKS*, IX, p. ii; that for 1897 appears in *SKS*, XVI, pp. i–ii.

interference with Serbia's pig exports at the Hungarian border. This began immediately after the Berlin Treaty (1878) and was to culminate during the commercial war of Serbia and Austria-Hungary in 1906–10. Until 1878, Serbian pigs had been accorded easy access to Austria-Hungary and low tariffs. Austria was free to pass on pig exports to Germany, so there was little friction of interest between Hungarian and Serbian producers. Even so the Hungarians periodically threatened to obstruct the trade, especially as the great landowners had a major stake in Hungarian pig production. In 1880, Austria-Hungary interfered with Serbian pig exports to put pressure on Serbia to build her section of the projected railway from Budapest to Constantinople and the Aegean. As capricious closures of the German market were depressing pig prices in Hungary, interference with imports from Serbia would enhance the price of pigs on the Budapest market, so the Hungarians were happy to oblige Vienna in this respect.

Reasonable treatment was conceded by Austria-Hungary to Serbian pig exports in the trade treaty of 6 June 1881, though the tariff was nearly doubled to 1 florin 50 kreutzer per pig.[11] This specific tariff favoured the export of larger animals, and discriminated against the light unfattened animals which provided the bulk of Serbia's export. This was intentional, for it protected the Hungarian pig raiser, characteristically the larger landowner who controlled tracts of woodland, rather than the peasant farmer who took these lean pigs to fatten them for the market. The bias of policy in favour of the large breeder was later to be replaced by outright prohibition against the import of light animals.

Serbia was refused a veterinary convention covering pigs, so as to give the Hungarians a free hand to open or close their market according to demand conditions, on the allegation of disease among imported pigs – without having to provide evidence. Frontier closures which damaged the export trade in 1884 coincided with a glut of pigs on the international market. Only by passive acceptance of political dependence was Serbia able to avoid further closures in the 1880s, for Germany raised its pig tariff against Austria in 1885, and the Hungarians took compensatory action against Romania, which, unlike Serbia, insisted on a mutually acceptable sanitary convention. Despite the unsatisfactory political arrangements concerning the Serbian pig exports, the outcome, as noted in 1887, was 'the growing prosperity of the commerce in livestock with Hungary where each day Serbia finds a more advantageous outlet'.[12]

In the late 1880s, central Europe was ravaged by foot and mouth

---

[11] Equivalent to 3.67 dinars. Correspondence respecting the Commercial Relations between Great Britain and Servia, Commercial no. 24 of 1881, p. 12. *Parl. Papers* 1881 XCIX.   [12] AAE CCB t.7 despatch of 26 Oct. 1887 f. 120.

disease. This led to a further round of frontier restrictions in 1890. Hungary closed its frontier with Serbia soon after Germany had closed its own frontier against Austria. The crisis was eased by Caprivi's liberalization of the German tariff. Caprivi's concern for rapprochement with Austria secured the latter favourable trade treaty conditions. As a result, the Hungarians conceded Serbia a veterinary convention in 1892, and a minor pig export boom ensued. However, the Caprivi government lasted only till 1894, and as produce markets were depressed, the Germans applied a fresh round of prohibitions against Austrian livestock at the end of 1895. As ever, Austria-Hungary sought to insulate itself against losses on the German market at the expense of its Balkan neighbours. Trade with Serbia was disrupted, and an even more ferocious squeeze was applied to exports from its own quasi-colony of Bosnia Hercegovina.[13] In September 1896, Austria-Hungary introduced two new regulations concerning pig imports from Serbia. The first required the pigs to be of a minimum 120 kg weight – which excluded the unfattened export completely. The second ordered that not more than 7,000 Serbian pigs be held at the main Steinbruck market (at Budapest) at any one time; nominally in the interest of hygiene, this regulation encapsulated Hungary's right to treat Serbia as a marginal supplier, without need for recourse to veterinary manipulation.

For the next ten years, fattened Serbian pigs crossed the frontier into Hungary without hindrance, though their numbers were greatly reduced. Prices were buoyant, and as the Hungarians had complete control over the volume of imports, they regarded any further extension of trade barriers as counter-productive, especially as they were also interested in Serbia's potential as a market for exports.[14]

Serbia's 1892 trade treaty with Austria-Hungary expired at the end of 1902, after which either party was free to renounce it on one year's notice. Until the Austrians knew what terms Germany would offer them on expiry of the Caprivi treaty in 1906, they declined to make any new long-term commitment to Serbia. By the time they were in a position to negotiate, Austro-Serbian political relations had cooled to such an extent that Austria used the lack of a trade treaty with Serbia as a political weapon. The main casualty was Serbia's pig trade, much to the satisfaction of her Hungarian competitors. The commercial war remained deadlocked till the end of 1910, after which a quota arrangement was agreed.

The cumulative effect of the uncertainty with which Serbian producers faced the pig export business must in itself have discouraged pig raising,

[13] See p. 211.
[14] Andrija Radenić, 'Izveštaji madžarskih privrednih izaslanika o prilikama u Srbiji 1901–1914', *IČ*, XIV-XV (1963–5), p. 408.

Table 10.3 *Area under forest: Serbia 1884–1905 (000 ha.)*

	'Private'	State	Total
1884	582	700	1,280
1889	n.d.	n.d.	1,041
1893	484	n.d.	n.d.
1897	481	n.d.	n.d.
1905	316	529	845

Sources: 1884: AAE CCB t.7 despatch of 7 July 1888, f. 301; 1889: *SKS*, III, p. vi; 1893: *SKS*, IX, p. x; 1897: *SGKS*, XI, 1906, p. 238; 1905: *SGKS*, X, 1905, p. 277.

and even during periods untroubled by new trade restrictions, pig exports showed little tendency to recover towards previous levels. The number of pigs taken for fattening diminished, despite the restrictions and eventual prohibition on lean pig exports, which should have caused more pigs, not fewer, to be passed on to the fattening trade. The outflow of lean pigs vanished without compensation, which makes it likely that Hungarian interference with the trade merely accelerated decline in this sector.

This decline can be traced to the further erosion of the woodlands, on which the raising of lean pigs had depended. The diminution of woodland (which had already exerted significant pressures on Serbian pig supply before 1876) continued apace after 1878. As Table 10.3 shows, the area under 'private' forest – that is to say forest in individual, *opština* (municipal) or ecclesiastical hands – diminished till around 1905. So too did state forest area, which – if the Bulgarian experience may be used as a guide – was far thinner and less valuable than that in private hands.[15]

The chain of causality seems roughly to have been as follows. In the 1880s population increase accelerated to 2.3 per cent per annum. Farming absorbed most of this growth. Initially peasants responded by extending clearance, broadly pro-rata to population. This continued to erode the balance of population and livestock, so dependence on grain marketings increased. This pressure was heightened by rising taxation demands. Between 1879/81 and 1887/91 the real burden of taxation per capita of the farm population rose by 76 per cent.[16] Enlargement of the crop area was at the expense of woodland and grazing. Even peasants who were relatively highly committed to livestock farming lost woodland

[15] Kiril G. Popov, *Stopanska B'lgarija* (Sofia, 1916), p. 216.
[16] M. Palairet, 'Fiscal Pressure and Peasant Impoverishment in Serbia before World War I', *JEcH*, XXXIX (1979), p. 733.

because of pressure by the rest of the villagers on their enclosed woods. By 1891, the forests were in a miserable state – most of the mountains (in the more accessible regions) were 'stripped from foot to summit', and in the opinion of the Belgian consul, the impending forestry law was now unlikely to meet with great resistance.[17] Clearing woodland opened up arable land, but this meant peasants needed to retain as many draft animals as possible, and use their pasture to graze them. Between 1879 and 1895 draft stock was relatively well maintained (decline in cattle and buffaloes being limited to 4.3 per cent while the horse population rose by 6.3 per cent).[18] Pigs had to make way, their numbers falling by 46 per cent. The effect on total farm production was marked, for whereas cattle provided mainly an input into agriculture plus milk products for subsistence, the entire output of pig raising was delivered in the form of final products, much of which were marketed. The shift into arable therefore acquired a cumulative element; deforestation to extend arable and replace pasture which had been ploughed up eroded income from livestock, and that required compensation by the clearing of still more arable, and the further diminution of pigraising.

Pig producers were therefore caught within a market which squeezed them at both ends. Tariffs, and later prohibitions, reduced the profitability of lean pig production, while the loss of woodland fodder and the pre-emption of pasture for cattle increased the cost of raising young pigs; market conditions favoured the pig fattening trade which flourished at small fattening centres near the main railway line,[19] but the raising of pigs was curbed drastically.[20] As Table 10.4 shows, pig output for home consumption contracted more severely than output for export, at least till the 1890s, when home demand stabilized. So it is likely that supply problems had a more significant effect on pig production than Austro-Hungarian trade pressures, though the latter, by discouraging the activity, hastened its decline.

The Serbian state and agricultural monetization

As it failed to expand its output proportionately to its labour force, progress in Serbian farming must have been thwarted by structural rigidities. Peasant economy continued to be orientated primarily to

---

[17] *RC*, 1892, LXXV, p. 72.
[18] Livestock population in 1879 was estimated in GBC Serbia 1879, p. 904; 1895 figures are from the livestock census of that year.
[19] Stanoje Mijatović, 'Resava', *NiPS*, XXVI (Belgrade, 1930), p. 172.
[20] Dušan M. Pantić, *Spoljna trgovina i trgovinska politika nezavisne Srbije 1878–1892* (Belgrade, 1910), p. 173.

Table 10.4 *Pigraising in Serbia 1859–1912*
(annual averages at constant price, in million dinars)

	Exports	Output	Residual
1859–60	10.1	79.2	69.1
1861–65	15.1	70.3	55.2
1866–70	17.6	66.1	48.5
1871–75	17.4	72.2	54.8
1879–80	12.0	74.6	62.5
1881–85	15.0	55.8	40.7
1886–90	13.6	47.6	34.1
1891–95	14.6	48.2	33.6
1896–1900	8.3	46.2	38.0
1901–05	12.8	48.7	35.9
1906–10	6.9	43.0	36.1
1911–12	8.5	42.7	34.2

Source: BALKSTAT.

subsistence production. Statistics were published for the volume of agricultural produce crossing the market scales of each town and of the volume of business transacted at the country fairs. These figures specifically exclude a number of items, the more obvious of which we have added back in Table 10.5 below. Even so, the total probably mildly understates.

The 126 million dinar total of marketed farm produce may be compared with the total output of the sector, which amounted to 328 million.[21] Therefore farmers monetized 38.4 per cent of their output, possibly a little more. In other words, most peasants had yet to move beyond cultivating for subsistence plus a marketable surplus, particularly as animal products still accounted for around one-third of marketings.[22] The 38.4 per cent monetization of farm output was probably the product of a leisurely rate of monetization. In 1863, exports were equal to about 14.9 per cent of net national income (NNI), but had only advanced to 17.5 per cent by 1910.[23] Adherence to subsistence production must have inhibited the adoption of more intensive systems, for the most powerful agent of structural change in agriculture is the process of market integration; whatever retarded that process would have inhibited the growth (or even the maintenance) of output per worker. We have observed the effects

[21] See lines 1–5 and 20 of Table 10.7, p. 322 below.
[22] See calculation in Table 10.5.
[23] Taking exports in 1863 at 98.13m piastres (*Državopis Srbije*, II, p. 102), net of re-exports, and at 129.1 million in 1910, with NNI in 1863 at 131.9 million dinars, allowing for an addition of 13.6 per cent to gross this to GDP.

Table 10.5 *Monetized farm output, Serbia 1910*
(000 dinars)

Produce sold through urban markets	67,676
Produce sold through fairs	9,544
Animal products sold through urban markets	10,803
Livestock traded at fairs	28,151
Sugar beet	1,143
Tobacco	1,440
Cocoons	621
Milk for urban sale	4,411
Eggs exported	2,217
Total	126,015

Source: Produce weighed on market scales in Serbia in 1910, *SGKS*, 1909–10, pp. 582–5. To this we have applied mean prices in 1910 as in *SGKS*, 1909–10, pp. 376–8. We have also taken fattened pigs at 120 kg live weight (*Izveštaj o radu odeljenja za poljsku privredu i veterinarstvo* [1906] p. 293), oxen and cows at 185.6 kg live weight (ibid., pp. 155–6) and poultry and sheepskins at 1 kg. The fairs statistic is on pp. 570, 572, 574 of *SGKS*, 1909–10. Sugar beet, cocoons, tobacco and eggs are taken directly from our 1910 output statistics.

in Bulgaria of the liberation and its consequences in this respect; we now examine the actions that governments in Serbia applied to the peasantry, inhibiting rural market integration. Most farmers remained only weakly in touch with market forces, and the state, intentionally, maintained their isolation.

Agrarian policies originated to protect the institution of universal peasant landownership, and were applied to minimize the risk that peasants might lose their land as a result of excessive debt. In Chapter 4, we encountered their basic elements together with insights as to official thinking. They date back to the early years of the modern Serbian state – the administration of communal maize granaries to protect the villages from famine; the obligation imposed upon the *opštinas* to allot land from their reserves to immigrants and indigent families; and, above all, the homestead laws which protected a minimum of peasant property from distraint by creditors. These institutions shielded the peasantry from extreme misfortune, but designedly inhibited structural change.

The authorities feared that rural social structure might be threatened by debt, which they saw as an unavoidable consequence of the development of market relationships; their ideal was of a peasantry which sold only pastoral surpluses, and used the proceeds mainly to discharge tax obligations. For the rest, the peasant family should provide its own subsistence needs. It was only a short step from this to try to minimize contact between the peasant and the market for exchange goods. This policy was then hijacked by urban craft and shopkeeper interests, and was implemented to block peasant access to competing sources of merchandise supply, especially of imported goods. Targets for suppression included village shops, pedlars and stallholders at cattle fairs, so as to force the peasants to do their business in the towns with guild-regulated suppliers.

As early as 1839, village shops were restricted by law from selling imported goods, but the law fell into desuetude. Urban interests secured legislation in 1870 which restricted the opening of village shops to locations further than 15–18 kilometres from the nearest town. This law failed to satisfy the *čaršija* (the business community) and it continued to urge the outright closure of village shops. As most local officials recognized the need for rural trade in necessities, the law was not repealed, but was amended in 1891 to restrict rural retailing to a specified list of products. These were in the main agricultural tools and supplies and simple household implements. Anything resembling an incentive good was sternly struck from the list – even the sale of sugar at village shops was strictly forbidden. The law was enforced right up to World War I,[24] though only by dint of continuous war against enterprising rural infractors.[25]

The attack on rural commerce was extended to the country fairs. As these were the point at which peasants would receive money from the sale of cattle, they were also a promising milieu for selling exchange goods. This intensely annoyed the urban craftsmen who regarded the fairs as syphoning peasant purchasing power from their shops into the hands of unlicensed rural competitors. As early as 1859, the duration of existing cattle fairs was curtailed under a law whose ambiguous wording was subsequently interpreted to curtail the sale of manufactures – especially the imported variety. The law was tightened further in 1879 and 1889 in response to artizan agitation, and led to the decline of the fairs, despite the lack of efficient alternatives.[26]

Incentive goods also reached the villagers in the backpacks and horse packs of itinerant traders. They were mostly foreigners, and an easy target politically – though it was in practice difficult to restrict their activity. Their trade was prohibited as early as 1850, and the law was repeated and toughened in 1859, 1860 and 1865. One reason why (tightly regulated)

[24] Nikola Vučo, *Raspadanje esnafa u Srbiji* (Belgrade, 1954), pp. 335–6, 337.
[25] Joel M. Halpern and Barbara K. Halpern, *A Serbian Village in Historical Perspective* (Prospect Heights, 1986), p. 61.   [26] Vučo, *Raspadanje*, pp. 294–300.

village shops were tolerated was in the hope of driving out the pedlar. Though of variable effectiveness, the laws against itinerant trade provided an excuse for guildsmen to drive away potential competitors and for officials to harass them at will.[27]

None of these restrictions could prevent peasants from acquiring discretionary and imported goods if they were prepared to travel to town to buy them, and to pay the inflated margins with which town shopkeepers compensated themselves for the slowness of their turnover. But by making incentive goods artificially difficult and expensive to obtain, the authorities removed a powerful motivation for peasants to trade idleness for work, or to specialize production upon cash staples. Loudly though vested interests might complain at the purchase by peasant women of foreign made cotton piece-goods and trinkets, the rising tempo of rural monetization which we observed for the late 1860s and early 1870s subsequently decelerated and eventually ceased altogether. The growth in volume of farm based exports per capita of the farm population decelerated between the 1860s and 1900s, and by the 1900s it had turned negative.[28] So too did the rate of growth of the urban population, and presumably also of the domestic market.

The legacy of Balkan peasant farming

The farm economies of the Balkan states underperformed relative to those of most other European economies, including those of nearby and relatively backward countries. What shared characteristics differentiated them? One above all: the unassailed dominance of peasant subsistence farming. In most of Europe, large-scale farming maintained a strong presence within the rural economy, and the political framework of government accommodated the latifundial interest. The evidence we have presented has pointed to intrinsic counter-developmental weaknesses in the peasant economic systems which prevailed in Serbia and Montenegro throughout the period, and in Bulgaria after the liberation. There was a strong propensity to cling to self-consumption, and when tax pressures slackened, to revert to it. This propensity was underpinned in Bulgaria by policies designed to force the surviving *chifliks* into dissolution, and in Serbia, by the efforts of the authorities to distance the

---

[27] Ibid., pp. 278, 279–82.

[28] Export volume per capita of the farm population 1862/4–72/4 rose 15.1 per cent, in 1872/4–82/4 by 11.8 per cent, in 1882/4–92/4 by 15.6 per cent, and in 1892/4–1902/4, by 0.4 per cent, after which the trend was negative. See Palairet, 'The Influence of Commerce on the Changing Structure of Serbia's Peasant Economy 1860–1912', (Ph.D. thesis, University of Edinburgh, 1976), p. 37. For urban and rural populations see Table 1.10.

peasants from consumers' markets. In both countries, governments also found it expedient to tax peasants lightly, which minimized their need to market their produce.

A well rehearsed argument in favour of peasant farming (*vis-à-vis* larger-scale farming) is that peasants behaved as self-exploiters, working at the margin for returns markedly lower than the going wage rate.[29] But in the Balkan experience (as demonstrated for Serbian farmers in the 1860s and 1870s, and Bulgarian farmers following the liberation of 1878), peasant capacity to self-exploit was offset by a stronger willingness to trade material income against leisure. Foreign visitors and government officials called it laziness; ethnographers associated this behaviour with the 'heroic' values of pastoral society, and intellectuals sidestepped the issue by referring to the 'pre-capitalistic' attitudes of the Balkan peasantry.

This behaviour was enforced by an environment in which marginal commodity production was tradeable only with difficulty, for want of efficient transport and communications. As late as 1910, there were villages in the rich agricultural hinterland of the Black Sea port of Burgas which lay 30 kilometres from a railway station. Even in dry weather, their inhabitants needed two days work to bring a single cartload of grain to the railway. Some villages were totally unapproachable at certain times of the year.[30] In Serbia, too, especially in the interior uplands such as in the Pirot region, grain could be moved only by packhorse.[31] So reports of surplus crops being burned off or simply abandoned were not uncommon. The marginal value of untradeable produce was too low to encourage peasants to maximize output.

Incremental supplies of livestock produce were, of course, a different matter. But given the structure of stockraising, the elasticity of livestock supply to labour input must have been low, and was more than offset by cutting into the reserves of woodland, which resulted in the absolute decline of this sector. As a result, most peasants shared the near-equality of near poverty.

Expectations were low, and consequently so was output. We have already remarked how in Bosnia terms of tenure which inclined native cultivators to apathetic and poverty stricken indolence were welcomed by immigrants for the opportunities they promised.[32] After the liberation,

---

[29] N. Georgescu-Roegen, 'Economic Theory and Agrarian Economics', *Oxford Economic Papers* (1960).

[30] *S'krateni protokoli za zasedenijata na III redovnija sesija na Burgazkata Trg.-industr. kamara prez Dekemvrij 1909* (Burgaz, 1910), p. 109.

[31] Velimir Vasić, 'Pečalbarstvo istočne Srbije' (Ph. D., Belgrade, 1950), pp. 90–1.

[32] Above Ch.7 p. 206.

Bulgaria hosted immigrants from Hungary, ethnic Bulgarians who were attracted to settle by the lure of cheap land. Coming from a higher material culture, their relatively intense labour and high consumption contrasted with the low-input low-output culture of their neighbours.[33]

Discussions of the slow diffusion of technical change in Serbian farming stress the lack of efficient channels for the communication of improved technologies. Its performance is sometimes contrasted with that of Slovenia, whose farming systems were far more progressive, despite a meagre natural endowment in relation to population, and a mainly Alpine geography. Even in the late eighteenth century crop rotation was practised, along with relatively intensive techniques of livestock management. Between 1869 and 1880, when livestock holdings per capita in Serbia were declining, three out of the four Slovene populated provinces significantly raised livestock holdings per capita, and improved their quality as well.[34] Ashworth, discussing the progress of agriculture in Slovenia, suggests that the relative success of Slovene farmers can be explained in part by their proximity to a substantial German minority, whose progressive techniques invited emulation.[35] But there was more to it than that.

As we noted of Serbia at least from the mid nineteenth century, and of Bulgaria after the liberation, Balkan peasants, seeking short-term returns, would wreck and abandon crop-bearing land, cutting unnecessarily into the reserve of woodland. This was consistent with a pattern of economic behaviour in which land was treated as a mobile asset, and not as the finite resource it was rapidly becoming.

Cvetko Kostić explained that in Serbia 'most villages are young and immigrant'. In an age not long bygone, the Serbian peasant, settled in a milieu with a substantial uncultivated margin, created property on the principle that 'he who brings life to dead land becomes its owner', an attitude reinforced by the adoption of Roman Law and the practice of equal partitive inheritance. This framework presumes that the supply of land is elastic. By contrast, in Slovenia (and Civil Croatia) the stable long settled population was aware of the finite character of the landed resources it owned. It farmed holdings, many of which 'remained unchanged for countless generations'. There was no conception of marginal land as a free good. Inheritance practice reflected Germanic customary law. Land was bequeathed to a single heir, and his siblings were dowered. Kostić

---

[33] N. Daskalova, *Zhivota na Banatchanite B'lgari s. Dragomirovo, Svishtovsko* (Ruse, 1930), pp. 6, 10–11; 'Banatski Bugari', *Male Novine* (Belgrade), 19 Mar. 1902, p. 2.

[34] John A. Arnez, *Slovenian Lands and their Economies, 1848–1873* (New York, 1983), p. 47.

[35] William Ashworth, 'Typologies and Evidence: Has Nineteenth Century Europe a Guide to Economic Growth?', *Economic History Review*, XXX (1977), p. 153.

remarks that the Serbian practice of dividing the land between all the heirs struck Slovenian peasants as absurd, for it would bottle up surplus labour in villages which had only a finite area of land to farm. Rather, the Slovenian farmer took care to ensure a continuity of good, and innovative, technique. He often selected as his residual legatee that child who promised to be the most able farmer (rather than apply primogeniture) and arranged for him to be trained in farm management, not only at home, but also through farm service in another village, where he would be brought into contact with different practices.[36]

Kostić was primarily interested in this system because it created among the collateral heirs the expectation of a non-agricultural career. As a Marxist, he saw economic development as a mechanistic process of shifting resources out of agriculture and into industry, and the Serbian agrarian system inhibited this process by holding excessive numbers of families on the land. In one passage he welcomed the environmental pollution caused by the appearance of industry, since it forced the local population out of farming.[37] However, his analysis of the contrast between the Slovenian and Serbian agrarian systems offers a partial explanation of Serbian (and more generally Balkan) shortcomings in farm management.

The low productivity of Balkan agriculture was associated with the 'ignorance, traditionalism and superstition' of the peasants, and the lack of human capital formation remained an enduring barrier to rational rural economic behaviour, and thus to agricultural intensification. Since the state in all the countries assumed the main burden of educational provision, it bore some responsibility for the educational retardation of the villages. According to Sundhaussen, the educational system favoured in Serbia was geared to its own need to recruit officials, and its content accorded weight to nationalistic values at the expense of vocational training.[38]

Training initiatives are more likely to create economic returns when efforts to expand supply are matched with the growth of educational demand, and in the Balkan village, this was usually absent. In Vukosavljević's vast work on the history of Serbian peasant society, only four lines were devoted to 'work education' – to the effect that the peasants were totally uninterested in it.[39] To the mass of peasants, literacy was of little use in their everyday lives and work. The authorities pushed schools

---

[36] Cvetko Kostić, *Seljaci industriski radnici* (Belgrade, 1955), pp. 33–4.

[37] Ibid., pp. 147–8.

[38] Holm Sundhaussen, 'Von der traditionellen zur modernen Rückständigkeit', Bad Homburg conference on Rückständigkeit und Modernizierung in Sudosteuropa 1830–1940, 1989.

[39] Sreten Vukosavljević, *Istorija seljačkog društva III. Sociologija seljačkih radova* (Belgrade, 1983), p. 374.

and vocational institutions upon an increasing number of villages, but the amenities they offered were poorly esteemed by their recipients. Many peasants, though nominally educated, remained functionally illiterate, and those who benefited from educational provision regarded it explicitly as a means of escaping from farming. This was a negative attribute in peasant eyes for they feared that educated children would be lost to their farms.

Take the experience of the Serbian government's agricultural school at Kraljevo: 'In setting it up it was hoped the peasants would place their sons there, as much as possible at their own expense, and that these young people, on completion of their studies, would return to their villages, and improve not only the lands of their parents, but also those of all the inhabitants of the district.' The intention was unrealistic. The more substantial peasants took no interest in the school and the government filled it with 'persons of diverse origins', all of whom had to be supported. On completion of their studies, 'many of them are seen not to return to agricultural work, but to clutter up the towns in search of jobs as clerks in the administration or in ministerial offices'.[40] This observer was too dismissive of the education provided, but he was right in identifying resistance to education among the farm community, except by those who treated it as a device for escaping the village.

The resistance we noted among the Serbian peasantry to education was also present in Bulgaria, where the main (though unintentional) function of agricultural schools was to qualify their graduates for civil service careers.[41] Take the request of 'a peasant son' for state funding to further his education: he worked on his father's farm in summer and studied in winter. 'My father, a poor farmer does not assist me . . . but at least he did not stop me going to school.' He wanted to be sent abroad for a high-school education – or at least to be sent to an agricultural school in Bulgaria. Why? So that he could get a job as a schoolteacher.[42] The idea that agricultural school training would serve as a prelude to farming seemed absurd, given the small scale on which most of its alumni would be farming. What might be useful to the son of a landed gentleman or a substantial commercial farmer was not appropriate to peasant needs. But there were few large farmers. So little regard did peasant deputies in Serbia have for education, that in 1905 the *skupština* (parliament) agreed to tax schoolbooks in preference to taxing home distillation.[43]

Ultimately rural education programmes were only likely to be of use in farming when the commercialization of the farm sector created a demand for numeracy. In discussing the Bulgarian 'renaissance', we showed that it

[40] *RC*, 1892, LXXV, p. 25.
[41] Richard J. Crampton, *Bulgaria 1878–1918. A Survey* (Boulder, CO, 1983), p. 191.
[42] CDIA. f. 173 opis 2. ae. 674. ff. 117–8.   [43] *Samouprava* (Belgrade), 28 Nov. 1905.

was associated not with the efforts of government but with the organic development of commerce and manufacturing, which created a market for cultural products. This cultural demand-pull was always geographically concentrated and was weakly diffused from its heartlands in the central hill slope areas of the country. It was also weakened by the consequences of the liberation, but it was not obliterated. It was, for example, well established in the market gardening villages of T'rnovo okrug (north-central Bulgaria) where both agricultural and material standards far surpassed those elsewhere in the country.[44] The region had been powerfully affected by the late Ottoman 'renaissance'. It was also the focus of Bulgaria's market gardening trade, whose origins extended back to 1754, and expanded strongly after the liberation. Allegedly, '*all*' gardeners and their wives insisted that their children should be made literate. The literacy achieved was an active one, 'for gardening is unthinkable without pencils and notebooks'; this contrasted with the non-functional literacy of the majority of educated peasants. As a result in T'rnovo okrug 43.3 per cent of the rural population over age 6 was literate in 1905, compared with 28.4 per cent of the rural population of Bulgaria as a whole.[45] According to this study, literacy rates correlated strongly with gardening activity by district within the province.[46]

The example from T'rnovo shows that education had to follow the development of the market economy (which was why urbanites tended to be literate) and the creation of communication links to draw peasants into the market nexus. Even then, its main function would be to facilitate the outflow of labour from farming, rather than assist in the improvement of agricultural technique. This tendency developed in extreme form in Montenegro, where the government became exceptionally energetic in promoting education. The Montenegrin experience suggests that having drawn the literate sons of the more powerful rural families out of farming, it turned them into bureaucrats and officers and enforcers rather than into businessmen, into predators rather than wealth-creators.[47]

Contrasts in the Bulgarian and Serbian farm economies

Though the Serbian and Bulgarian farm economies shared common characteristics, they also displayed significant contrasts. Firstly, Bulgarian

---

[44] M. Palairet, 'The Migrant Workers of the Balkans and their Villages', in *Handwerk in Mittel- und Südosteuropa*, ed. Klaus Roth (Munich, 1987), pp. 41–2.

[45] *SGBTs*, 1909, p. 57.

[46] Marin St. Sirakov, *Gradinarite ot T'rnovsko v stranstvo* (T'rnovo, 1922), pp. 37–8.

[47] M. Palairet, 'The Culture of Economic Stagnation in Montenegro', *Maryland Historian*, XVII (1986), pp. 36–8.

farmers enjoyed a more favourable ratio of land to labour than their Serbian counterparts. This was apparent in the larger amount of grain bearing land that the Bulgarians sowed per head,[48] and their consequent greater output of cereals. Despite this they were left with significantly more grazing resources, and this enabled them also to hold significantly more livestock per capita.[49] This advantage extended to the availability of woodland, with which despite heavy depletion Bulgaria was still relatively well endowed. Most Bulgarian woodland was in *obshtina* and private hands, and this woodland was far more productive than state forest. According to Popov, state forest yielded but 0.4 cubic metres per hectare, *obshtina* forest 0.74 and private forest, 2.90.[50] In Bulgaria in 1908 private forest extended over 439,000 hectares, *obshtina* forest over 1.67 million, and state forest over 645,000 million. In Serbia in 1910, there were 215,000 hectares of private woodland, and 246,000 in *opština* hands. State forest amounted to 570,000.[51] The higher yields from local and privately owned forests, presumably because they were more accessible and better protected, gave Bulgaria an advantage in timber output that was far larger than a simple comparison of forested area (2.83 million hectares against 1.07 million) would indicate.

Moreover, the relative contribution of the livestock and grain sectors in Serbia and Bulgaria was affected by differing market conditions. Despite Serbia's dispute with Austria-Hungary, the price of livestock in Serbia was significantly higher than in Bulgaria. But Bulgaria's advantage in getting cereals out to market via the lower Danube and the Black Sea gave cereals a higher market price than in Serbia. Price signals prompted Bulgarian farmers to specialize towards grain cultivation, while inhibiting Serbia's orientation away from livestock. In dynamic terms, this should have been advantageous to Serbia, because it provided a stronger incentive to adopt mixed farming techniques in the knowledge that enhancements in livestock production would be rewarded by relatively favourable output prices, but Serbian farming was still at too low a technical level to exploit this opportunity.

Bulgarian farmers continued, right up to the Balkan Wars, to expand the arable surface more or less according to need. Pressure of settlement was lower and the state distributed land from its reserves at nominal prices. In Serbia, however, little good potential arable remained uncultivated. By 1899, Serbia had 1.22 million hectares under the five principal grain crops, which occupied 1.23 million hectares in 1912. Bulgaria, by

---

[48] 0.57 ha per head of the population under five main grains, compared with 0.42 ha; see M. Palairet, 'Land, Labour, and Industrial Progress in Bulgaria and Serbia before 1914', *JEEcH*, XII (1983), p. 183.   [49] Ibid., appendix table B, p. 184.

[50] Popov, *B'lgarija*, p. 216.   [51] Ibid., p. 213; *SGKS*, 1909–10, p. 309.

contrast, cultivated 1.84 million hectares in 1899 and 2.54 million in 1912, an increase of 38.4 per cent.[52] The Bulgarians were able to expand grain farming not only because there was more cultivable land at the margin, but also because they were better able to support the requisite draft animals. Whereas Serbia had 356,000 oxen in 1910, Bulgaria had 723,000. Bulgaria moreover had 134,000 draft buffaloes, Serbia around 4,000, Bulgaria 149,541 draft horses, Serbia 63,964. Counting one draft horse as the equivalent of two oxen, Bulgaria had 0.47 draft-ox equivalents per hectare under cereals in 1910, Serbia 0.40.[53]

The ability of Bulgaria's farmers to bring new land under crops discouraged more efficient land use. The three-field systems which predominated incorporated a large amount of fallow. If the figures can be trusted, fallows in 1896/7 occupied 1.094 million hectares (39 per cent of the total area under fallow and the five main grain crops in 1897).[54] Between then and 1904, the fallowed area diminished by 47.7 per cent, but after 1904 the fallowed area ceased to diminish, even proportionately to the rising area sown. In 1904, fallow occupied 21.5 per cent of the land under the five main grains, and fallow in 1912, 21.4 per cent.[55]

In Serbia, however, where land passed directly from maize to grass and back again, any increase in the area cropped cut directly into the supply of hay and grazing, which had been squeezed fine to the detriment of fodder resources. In more advanced areas, peasants responded by sacrificing crop land to create pasture.[56] Belatedly, after about 1901, Serbian farmers, constrained by a static area of cultivation, reacted by raising areal productivity. Wheat yields were recorded at 8.66 quintals/hectare in 1893, and 8.14 in the triennium 1898/1900. More reliable figures show yields of 8.43 in 1901/3, which edged upwards to 8.85 in 1904/6, 8.70 in 1907/9 and 11.09 in 1910/12. The export statistics affirm this buoyancy of yields, for grain exports leaped from 92,300 tonnes in 1903/5 to 197,900 in 1906/8 and 290,900 in 1909/11.[57]

Yield increases may have been associated with improvements in farm equipment. Improvement was admittedly patchy, but in 1909 the peasants of Dobrić (and to some extent Prokuplje) districts had largely ceased

---

[52] Palairet, 'Land, Labour', appendix table A, p. 183.
[53] On the basis of 1910 areas under the five principal grains.
[54] *Rezultati ot posevite i rekoltata v knjazhestvo B'lgarija prez zemledelcheskata 1896/7 godina* (Sofia, 1901), p. 5.   [55] *SGBTs*, 1909, p. 191; 1925, p. 127.
[56] Rista T. Nikolić, 'Okolina Beograda. Antropogeografsko ispitivanje', *NSZ*, II (Belgrade, 1903), p. 921.
[57] See Table 10.1. This boom was also associated with the closure of the Hungarian frontier to exports of pigs; the trade declined sufficiently to release an estimated 34,000 tons of maize a year from the fattening trade to direct export. Palairet, 'Influence of Commerce', p. 319.

to use the wooden plough and the scratch plough (*ralica*) though iron ploughs had yet to appear in an adjacent district. In Niš district the number of modern ploughs advanced from 171 in 1907 to 355 in 1909, threshing machines from 2 to 10. In Smederevo, threshing was nearly all done by steam, and the number of iron ploughs was advancing rapidly.[58]

Bulgarian wheat yields were historically higher than those in Serbia, but they failed to advance and grain exports remained flat.[59] In 1897–9, wheat yields were 9.30 q/h, in 1904/6, 10.94. In 1907–9 they fell back to 8.36, and recovered in 1910–12 to 10.91.[60] Yet Bulgaria, like Serbia, was also building up better farm inventories. The import of farm equipment rose tenfold in weight between 1890 and 1910.[61] Between 1900 and 1910, the number of modern ploughs rose from 48,958 to 114,245, but wooden ploughs also rose from 387,000 to 420,000.[62] Here the main reason for building equipment inventories was to substitute a dwindling supply of traction animals. Between 1904 and 1911 (counting a horse as two ox-equivalents) the traction stock dwindled by 6.4 per cent,[63] despite the 19.3 per cent expansion in the crop area. This equipment was not to raise outputs per hectare, but to save draft capital while expanding the area cultivated.

The more pressing need of Serbia's farmers to intensify cultivation shows up in comparative performance in sugar-beet growing. The advantage to farmers of sowing sugar-beet lay in the intensity with which it enabled – and required – agricultural land to be used, providing a high money yield per unit of land in return for the intense application of labour to it. Only if cheap land were unavailable at the margin of cultivation would farmers be attracted to the crop; otherwise they would seek an equivalent gain in income from enlarging the area they cultivated.

Elsewhere in Europe, large landowners took the initiative in beet growing, establishing mills on their estates. The lack of persons capable financially and technically of such initiatives in the Balkans meant that both Bulgaria and Serbia were latecomers to the industry. The opening of railways made sugar projects possible, however, and in both countries governments contacted European capitalists and induced them to establish sugar mills, offering privileges and home market protection. Governmental interest focused on import saving, since the fiscal consequences would be negative – all prospective investors required subsidies.

---

[58] *Izveštaji podneseni Ministru narodne privrede o dosadašnjem radu za 1908 i 1909 godinu* (Belgrade, 1911), pp. 1007, 1077, 1112.
[59] 776,000 tonnes in 1903/5, 528,000 in 1906/8 and 555,000 in 1909/11, *SGBTs*, 1911, pp. 182–3.   [60] *SGBTs*, 1909, p. 200; *SGBTs*, 1912, p. 132.
[61] To 3,139 tonnes, *SGBTs*, 1911 p. 190.   [62] *SGBTs*, 1911, p. 191.
[63] Popov, *Stopanska B'lgarija*, p. 138.

For the companies which took up the challenge – the Belgian Solvay group who received a concession for a factory in Sofia in 1897, and the German Turn und Taxis group whose Belgrade concession dated from 1898 – an attraction may have been the opportunity to redeploy in the sheltered Balkan markets equipment which had become obsolescent because of rapid technical change.[64] In neither case was the investment remunerative. This was partly because international sugar prices fell so low that the Balkan tariffs provided less than the expected protection, partly also because the mills received less beet to process than anticipated.

In the 1890s, Serbian farmers were only just pressing against the limits of cultivation, while those in Bulgaria had yet to reach this point. Consequently there were grave doubts as to whether beet cultivation could be introduced with profit. In Serbia, a trial planting in the 1880s failed, allegedly because farmers were disinclined to dig the seed in deeply.[65] Ten years later it was forecast that 'as there are no large landowners there will be problems in getting the peasants to grow beet'.[66] A failed experiment in Thessaly seems to verify this apprehension,[67] as does experience in Bosnia where the gendarmerie were needed to force the crop upon the peasants.[68] In 1901, large-scale dumping by Austrian and Romanian exporters caused heavy losses and obliged both the Sofia and Belgrade mills to close.

However, conditions were rapidly changing. Neither factory was to reopen until granted high protection (Bulgaria in 1904, Serbia in 1906) but their efforts had accustomed a widening circle of farmers to the attractions of beet cultivation. In Serbia cultivators were convinced that beet had been more remunerative than any alternative crop, and in Bulgaria numerous peasant deputations demonstrated and demanded the reopening of the factory. When the factories eventually reopened, the area cultivated with beet quickly surpassed the level which had been attained by 1901.

The beet crop statistics tabulated in Table 10.6 show that peasants in Serbia were more strongly attracted to beet growing than their Bulgarian counterparts. From 1907 onward, the Serbian crop comfortably exceeded the Bulgarian even though the price paid for it was 10 per cent lower. It is reasonable to infer that Serbia's higher rural population

[64] Danica Milić, 'Nemački kapital u Srbiji do 1918', *IČ*, XII-XIII (1961–2), p. 329; F. Dorze (Dorzée), *Zaharnata industrija v B'lgarija* (Sofia, 1904), p. 5. This author is denying unattributed allegations that this was what his firm was doing.

[65] GBC Serbia 1888, p. 19.   [66] GBC Serbia 1898, p. 7.

[67] Baron Guillaume, *Grèce. Situation économique* (Brussels, 1900), p. 120.

[68] Peter F. Sugar, *Industrialization of Bosnia-Hercegovina* (Seattle, 1963), p. 156.

Table 10.6 *Sugar-beet production in Bulgaria and Serbia 1898–1913*

Year	hectares		000 tonnes		francs per tonne	
	Bulgaria (1)	Serbia (2)	Bulgaria (3)	Serbia (4)	Bulgaria (5)	Serbia (6)
1898	492	–	6.3	–	15	–
1899	512	–	9.6	–	20	–
1900	1,561	235	27.6	6.2	20	–
1901	2,006	1,160	43.4	24.5	20	–
1902	–	–	–	–	–	–
1903	31	–	0.4	–	–	–
1904	1,339	–	23.0	–	–	–
1905	1,631	–	22.1	–	20	–
1906	2,186	1,100	43.5	13.5	20	16–20
1907	2,285	2,169	25.2	36.7	20	–
1908	2,011	2,230	23.4	35.0	20	18.1
1909	1,707	2,957	20.9	74.8	20	18.0
1910	1,504	3,004	31.7	63.5	20	18.0
1911	2,967	5,035	65.2	91.5	22.8	–
1912	3,300	8,776	61.3	192.6	24	–
1913	4,740	4,408	80.3	49.3	22.5	19.0

Source: Palairet, 'Beet Sugar', p. 50.

density made farmers more receptive to an intensive cash crop than in Bulgaria. If we assume that beet growing properties in Serbia and Bulgaria equalled the average size of farm in these countries, then beet growers in Serbia (in 1908/9) held 24.7 per cent of their land under beet, while those in Bulgaria used 8.6 per cent of theirs.[69] When a second Serbian factory was built at Ćuprija in 1910, it had no problem in finding peasants willing to take advances. Most were small proprietors, who intended to devote a high proportion of their land to the crop, while larger farmers were less interested.[70]

It is likely, therefore, that after 1900 Serbia's farmers were trying to farm more rationally for want of new land to break in, whereas the Bulgarians faced less pressure to change their cultivation practices. However, the period 1905–12 is too short to be certain. Besides, Bulgarian farming, buoyed up by a more favourable resource endowment, and enjoying attractive grain prices, continued to be more productive than that of Serbia. We should not lose sight of the fact that for

[69] Also see Michael Palairet, 'Beet Sugar and Peasant Economy in the Balkans before 1914', *Crisis and Change in the International Sugar Economy*, ed. Bill Albert and Adrian Graves (Norwich: ISC Press, 1984), pp. 47–57.

[70] M. Todorović, 'Jedna privredna pogreška', *Trgovinski glasnik*, 16 Dec. 1911.

both countries rural population density had to attain extraordinarily high levels before farmers tried to raise the low productivity with which they used their land. This of course was the result of the many retarding influences on farming practice.

The weakness of the farm sector not only depressed total output. Both on the supply and demand sides, it hindered industrial expansion. In Serbia modern industry depended heavily on processing farm outputs. Though international trade difficulties interfered with this development, especially for the meat packing and processing industries, the limiting factor was the capacity of farmers to increase the supply of raw material.

Similarly, the weakness of peasant demand constrained the domestic market for consumer products to petty proportions. This limited the expansion of the textile industries. As these were unable to meet 'modern' consumers' tastes, the largest component of their potential market was country demand, but this was largely met by subsistence production, from which it showed little tendency to depart. Likewise, other expanding industries were confined to the small urban market; neither beer nor power-milled grain reached the peasantry. And after 1900, the towns had ceased to grow.

Bulgaria and Serbia: trends in total output

To view the evolution and structure of the Bulgarian and Serbian economies in broader perspective, we provide estimates of their national products reached by aggregating data for each sector. The exercise is only viable for 1910, by which time statistical reporting had improved sufficiently to achieve tolerable accuracy. The abiding principle applied throughout the calculation was to build each sectoral estimate as far as possible on a common procedure and assumptions. The results are presented as Table 10.7.

In 1910, both economies were still dominated by farming which accounted for 47.9 per cent of GDP in Serbia, 50.3 per cent in Bulgaria. As already shown (Tables 7.1 and 10.2) farm productivity was in long-run decline in both countries but growth in the non-farm economy should still have sufficed more than to offset this decline, as it seems to have done in Habsburg Bosnia. We cannot directly reconstruct aggregated estimates of national product for earlier periods, but there is evidence that national product per capita in both countries was declining severely in the medium and long run.

Our NNP figure for Serbia of 193.1 dinars per head can usefully be compared with national income in 1863. This I calculated from the 1863 census at around 132 million francs (dinars) or 115.7–119.3 dinars per

Table 10.7 *National product of Serbia and Bulgaria 1910, by sector of origin (at factor cost in current francs)*

Sector	Serbia		Bulgaria		
	Total 000fcs	Per capita	Total 000fcs	Per capita	Source notes
Cereals	142,469	48.93	407,222	93.88	(1)
Vegetables	20,435	7.02	28,920	6.67	(2)
Other crops	33,800	11.61	60,573	13.96	(3)
Animals	55,025	18.90	71,675	16.52	(4)
Animal products	63,582	21.84	102,108	23.54	(5)
Forestry	7,716	2.65	42,967	9.91	(6)
Mining	1,336	0.46	3,004	0.69	(7)
Food & drink	14,712	5.05	11,555	2.66	(8)
Tobacco	1,177	0.40	8,340	1.92	(9)
Chemicals	98	0.03	1,158	0.27	(10)
Metals	5,516	1.89	449	0.10	(11)
Engineering	681	0.23	2,114	0.49	(12)
Textiles	3,243	1.11	7,038	1.62	(13)
Leather	272	0.09	978	0.23	(14)
Timber	796	0.27	1126	0.26	(15)
Paper	281	0.10	309	0.07	(16)
Stone & glass	1,419	0.49	1,956	0.45	(17)
Small industry	46,025	15.81	102,445	23.62	(18)
Proto-industry	822	0.28	1,205	0.28	(19)
Farm processing	12,487	4.29	27,239	6.28	(20)
Home industry	6,266	2.15	13,082	3.02	(21)
Electricity	3,061	1.05	1,017	0.23	(22)
Cart transport	29,291	10.06	69,091	15.93	(23)
Packhorse transport	4,857	1.67	8,263	1.91	(24)
Railways	8,928	3.07	16,194	3.73	(25)
Tramways	403	0.14	389	0.09	(26)
Shipping & ports	1,438	0.49	1,751	0.40	(27)
Communications	1,937	0.67	4,094	0.94	(28)
Distribution	59,469	20.42	109,499	25.24	(29)
Financial	10,811	3.71	15,554	3.59	(30)
Central govt.	36,442	12.52	53,552	12.35	(31)
Local govt.	6,244	2.14	8,146	1.88	(32)
Education	8,341	2.86	21,241	4.90	(33)
Health	1,495	0.51	3,047	0.70	(34)
Domestic service	522	0.18	5,166	1.19	(35)
Other service	9,216	3.17	13,792	3.18	(36)
Dwellings	37,773	12.97	66,360	15.30	(37)
Construction	19,744	6.78	39,978	9.22	(38)
GDP	658,130	226.03	1,332,596	307.23	(39)
Depreciation	78,976	27.12	159,912	36.87	(40)
NDP	579,154	198.91	1,172,684	270.36	(41)
Interest	−22,258	−7.64	−29,421	−6.78	(42)
Remittances	5,376	1.85	10,791	2.49	(43)
NNP	562,272	193.11	1,154,054	266.06	(44)

Source notes are listed in BALKSTAT.

head.[71] The figure was even then low by western European standards but it was probably similar to that of Hungary in 1867, whose GDMP per head, according to Katus, was 115 francs. Between 1863 and 1910, the price of Serbia's exports rose by 82.8 per cent and an index of consumers' food prices rose by 83.2 per cent.[72] The close agreement between these two indexes suggests they may be used to standardize 1863 per capita income with that of 1910. In 1910 prices therefore 1863 per capita income was 211.5–218.6 dinars. This indicates that per capita income fell between 1863 and 1910 by 9–12 per cent. In reality the fall was probably significantly greater than this, for the 1910 figure picks up non-market house construction, production of household goods, and transport, which would not enter the 1863 statistic. Taking these roughly into account, per capita income could have fallen by 15–20 per cent.

Long-run economic decline was not confined to Serbia. Kiril Popov, at the state statistical office, presented official estimates for Bulgaria's national income of 1,109 million leva in 1892 and 1,647 million leva in 1911. The figures were presented to advertise Bulgaria's economic progress and imply an advance from 335 leva a head to 374.2. However, Popov did not correct for inflation and the omission was deliberate; his own cost of living index rose by 41.3 per cent between 1892 and 1911,[73] so his calculation implied a real per capita income shrinkage of 20.9 per cent. This takes no account of per capita farm output shrinkage between the liberation and 1892 (a good year) of around 10 per cent, over a period during which non-farm output was probably also declining. As Popov's national product calculation was not consistent with modern procedures, the shrinkage it shows should be taken only as indicative.

Trends in real wages confirm this long-term pattern of economic decline. In Bulgaria, builders' real wages in 1887/96 were 10.1 per cent higher than in 1904–13. Similar evidence supports our argument for Serbia, for which we have a longer run of statistics. Builders' real wages were 12.3 per cent higher in 1862–71 than in 1901–10. Both the Bulgarian and Serbian economies were in severe aggregate per capita decline from the mid-1870s to the Balkan Wars (1912/13) and in Serbia's case, quite probably since the 1830s.

This conclusion runs counter to consensual opinion concerning Balkan output trends. The inductive application of growth theory prompts the implicit assumption that there must have been *some* growth

---

[71] See calculation in Palairet, 'Rural Serbia in the light of the census of 1863', *JEEcH*, XXIV (1995) pp. 77–8.

[72] Export prices are tabulated in Palairet, 'Influence of Commerce', p. 37; see cost of living index in *Labour's Reward. Real Wages and Economic Change in Nineteenth and Twentieth Century Europe*, ed. P. Scholliers and V. Zamagni (Aldershot, 1995), Table A17.

[73] Popov, *Stopanska B'lgarija*, p. 324.

in the system, since the range of alternatives it offers is restricted between stagnation (zero growth) and fast growth. Economic stagnation – or retardation – in pre-1914 Europe therefore meant the failure of an economy to sustain near average rates of economic growth. The possibility of outright economic decline is disregarded. Indicator driven estimates of national income tend to track the progress of westernization. Where this was superficial and the subsistence sector large, indicators could signal growth while per capita output was falling. Bairoch's league table of European economic growth performance suffers from this defect. According to Bairoch, Serbia's national income per capita grew by 28 per cent between 1860 and 1910, and Bulgaria's by 29 per cent.[74] Though Bairoch's GDP calculations should never be accepted unreservedly,[75] they support the consensus that the Balkan economies exhibited positive if slow growth. Lampe writes of 'arrested modernization, along an ascending path open to all',[76] and treats Bairoch as excessively pessimistic. Berend and Ránki, while also pessimistic in qualitative terms, draw for their quantitative statements uncritically from Bairoch.[77] These generalizations are endorsed by Preshlenova who identifies Bulgaria and Serbia as having performed relatively – though 'insufficiently' – well.[78] It was never altogether clear whence this growth had emanated, but the conviction that growth must have occurred is illustrated by Jackson's comment on the decline indicated by Popov's output estimates for Bulgaria. Unable to accept 'this surprising result' at face value, he deduced 'a retardation of per capita output, or at most, its very slow growth from 1892 to 1911'.[79]

One of few empirical bases for this consensus was Lampe's work in assembling large-scale industry aggregates for the Balkan states, whose findings we condense as Table 10.8.

Though large-scale industry expanded rapidly, Lampe pointed out that this sector was not of aggregative significance, and that his industrial 'mini-spurts' could not have represented a successful bid (in the Gerschenkronian sense) at industrialization. This we can affirm by reference to Table 10.7, showing value added for large-scale industry (includ-

[74] Paul Bairoch, 'Europe's Gross National Product: 1800–1975', *JEEcH*, V (1976), p. 286.
[75] See comments of John R. Lampe, 'Imperial Borderlands or Capitalist Periphery? Redefining Balkan Backwardness, 1520–1914' in *The Origins of Backwardness in Eastern Europe*, ed. Daniel Chirot (Berkeley, 1989), pp. 195–6.   [76] Ibid., p. 177.
[77] I. T. Berend and G. Ránki, *The European Periphery and Industrialization, 1780–1914* (Cambridge, 1982), pp. 155–7.
[78] Roumyana Preshlenova, 'Austro-Hungarian Trade and the Economic Development of Southeastern Europe before World War 1', in David F. Good, ed., *Economic Transformations in East and Central Europe* (London, 1994), p. 232.
[79] M. R. Jackson, 'Quantitative Economic History in the Balkans: Observation of the Period before 1914', Arizona State University Dept. of Economics EC 74–39, p. 5.

Table 10.8 *Nominal and real output of Serbian and Bulgarian large-scale industry 1898–1911 (million dinars/leva)*

	Serbia		Bulgaria
	real	nominal	nominal
1898	25	n.d.	n.d.
1900	34	n.d.	n.d.
1902	39	n.d.	n.d.
1904	37	28	33 (32.78)
1905	n.d	31	n.d.
1906	45	45	n.d.
1907	n.d.	60	42 (41.55)
1908	60	72	n.d.
1909	n.d.	n.d.	78 (78.32)
1910	61	83	n.d.
1911	n.d.	115	123 (122.51)

Note:
'Real' data are expressed in 1898 prices, 'nominal' in current prices. The nominal figures are footnoted with an estimate of 'about 30 per cent' inflation between 1904 and 1911.
Sources: Lampe and Jackson, *Balkan Economic History, 1550–1950,* p. 250; Lampe, 'Finance', pp. 27–8. Although Lampe's source for Bulgaria is not stated explicitly, his figures agree, after rounding, with those provided in Natan, *Ikonomicheska istorija na B'lgarija sled osvobozhdenieto,* p. 71. The Natan figures are those in parentheses following Lampe's.

ing mining) in 1910 to have accounted despite rapid growth for a mere 2.8 per cent of the GDP of Bulgaria, and 4.5 per cent of that of Serbia. Its contribution even fell far short of that made by artisan industry, at 7.7 and 7.0 per cent respectively, though the sector seems to have been declining in the face of large-scale competition.

For Bulgaria, the 1904–11 'mini-spurt' in large-scale industry has however been treated as a symptom of acceleration in the development of capitalism in industry, foreign trade and finance.[80] Because of the small absolute size of the large-scale manufacturing sector, Bulgarian writers were dismissive of the industrial spurt of 1900–12. Berov argued that earlier historical literature had evaluated industrial progress 'rather too optimistically' in the light of the small aggregates involved.[81] However, this approach may underestimate the indirect impact of large-scale industrial growth between 1900 and 1912 on other sectors of the economy. Cvetana Todorova has argued that the growth of large-scale industry

[80] *Ikonomika na B'lgarija do sotsialisticheskata revoljutsija* (2nd edn Sofia, 1989), p. 323.
[81] Ljuben Berov, *Ikonomičeskoto razvitie na B'lgarija prez vekovete* (n.p.: Profizdat, 1974), pp. 91–3.

diffused change over a broad range of activities, and argued for a specifically Bulgarian style industrial revolution.[82] As Bulgaria lacked subsoil wealth, capitalists were not greatly attracted to investing in Bulgarian industry. In 1909 foreign and co-partnership enterprises disposed of but 14.7 million leva of capital out of a total 66 million leva.[83] Nevertheless, she argues, this measure fails to capture the significance of foreign business investment in the Bulgarian economy, because of large capital inflows into the Bulgarian banking system, and high foreign business activity within the trade sector.[84] She does not argue that this transformation penetrated throughout the economy – the aggregative evidence permits no such interpretation – rather that it initiated a diffusion process.

Most authorities accept that the pace of development in the Balkan states was conditioned by the rate these economies could integrate with the European mainstream, through trade expansion and (critically) through the import of capital. Preshlenova, like Todorova, acknowledges the importance to the Balkan states of trade integration and commercial penetration, by the very dynamic Austro-Hungarian economy. Austria-Hungary was not an ideal trading partner, because of Hungarian jealousies over potential Balkan raw material competition in the Austrian market, but it did nonetheless furnish the Balkan states with a supply of cheap industrial imports. In her view, however, the relationship failed because of the allegedly meagre flow of capital investment which Austria-Hungary provided. Trade was not enough.[85]

We agree that the potential for development by attracting inward industrial investment was probably greater in the short term than that which could be secured by reliance on indigenous enterprise. What was lacking before the beginning of the twentieth century was any counterpart to Kàllay's sustained programme of industrialization in Bosnia on the basis of imported capital and management. Let us recall that achievement: cumulative 12.4 per cent growth in large-scale industry between 1881 and 1913 created an industrial sector which was about 13 per cent larger than that of Serbia and Bulgaria combined, with an industrial payroll (in value per inhabitant) 5.5 times that of Bulgaria, 3.5 times that of Serbia.[86] It was carried entirely by non-indigenous enterprise. The role of domestic firms was minimal, even though the small business sector

---

[82] Cvetana Todorova, 'Kapitalisticheskata industrializatsija na B'lgarija do Balkanskite vojni (1912–1913)', *Izvestija na instituta po istorija*, XXVII (1984).

[83] *Doklad do negovoto velichestvo Ferdinand I Tsar na b'lgarite po sluchaj 25-godishnata od v'zshestvieto mu na b'lgarskija prestol 1887–1912 ot ministerskija s'vet* (Sofia, n.d.), pp. 437–8.   [84] Todorova, 'Kapitalisticheskata industrializatsija', pp. 199–200.

[85] The flow may have been meagre, but Preshlenova's argument is founded on false logic; see Preshlenova, 'Austro-Hungarian Trade', pp. 243–5.   [86] See above, p. 222.

in Bosnia was intermediate in size between that of Serbia and that of Bulgaria.

Bulgaria's relatively strong proto-industrial inheritance created a more powerful, but still inadequate basis for domestic enterprise expansion, and it was largely confined to woollens. Serbia likewise owed much to its Leskovac industrialists, whose background was similar. However, the first generation of industrial entrepreneurs in Serbia to enter into businesses which introduced new products or processes was largely immigrant and non-Serb. The most significant – and enduring – industrial initiatives before 1900 were taken by immigrant businessmen of German and Czech origins, who soon dominated in milling, brewing and meat packing. However, the number of these immigrants was small, and smaller still in Bulgaria, which was more remote than Serbia from Austria-Hungary. In neither country did their business success stimulate much native emulation.

The question then arises, as to what impeded the greater participation of external interests in the industrialization of the Balkan states. Among the decisive factors to consider, the role of the state was probably crucial. This role will be examined in two aspects, railway development and the creation of other externalities attractive to the inflow of investment.

The state and transportation

In an underdeveloped economy, state policy can play a critical role in the creation of transport infrastructure. In both Serbia and Bulgaria, railway issues commanded high political priority. Governments regarded railways as a strategic area of state concern closely analogous to the armed forces and their equipment; in both countries the state sector was centred on transport, munitions and coal mining, the last activity being directed to fuelling the state railways and arsenals. However, their high political profile did not result in railways receiving more investment than the free market would have allocated; the evidence is to the contrary, and it leads to the conclusion that state ownership and management of the railways retarded structural economic change. Table 10.7 indicated that rail transportation in 1910 remained insignificant. It produced 8.9 million dinars value added in Serbia, 16.2 million in Bulgaria, compared to the contribution made by cart and packhorse transportation, 34 million dinars in Serbia and 77 million in Bulgaria.

In Bosnia, the Habsburg administration had attended immediately after annexation to the development of a rail network. The decisions were loaded towards political and strategic rather than economic considerations, so Bosnia obtained a suboptimal railway layout. Even so, the railways (and the extensions built by the forestry enterprises) proved an indispensable foundation for the type of export-orientated industrialization which followed their construction.

In Serbia, however, and to some extent in Bulgaria, governments inhibited railway development. Numerous foreign backed railway schemes were put forward for Serbia between 1851 and 1878,[87] but as noted in Chapter 4, the military and the merchant class between them prevented railways being built. Ottoman Europe was more progressive in this respect, since the Porte could be induced to award concessions. Even so, in 1876, its lines were still mutually isolated, and a network had yet to be created. As early as 1867, the British built line was opened to traffic, while various other railways were completed, and some were still building, at the time of Bulgaria's liberation. Serbia could have had a British financed, British built railway in 1877, but Harry Slade, who represented the engineering firm, was forced to kick his heels in Belgrade for months, while dilatory Serbian officialdom handled the firm's proposal, only to reject it in the end.[88] The reason, of course, was fear of foreign control over a strategic asset.

The railway links built after the treaty of Berlin were forced upon the Balkan states by Austria-Hungary. Only after long-sustained Austrian pressure, were construction works in Serbia commenced in 1881 (on the basis of a disastrous contract with the insolvent French Union Général). Railway building in Bulgaria was no less dilatory. The Sofia–Tatar–Pazardzhik line had been under construction on account of the Ottoman railway administration since 1873, but works were abandoned during the Russo-Turkish war. As late as 1884, all that remained of the railway was the spectacular ruin of an embankment and a mouldering construction camp, side by side with the still newer ruin of an unfinished section of highway which had been started by the Bulgarian government and abandoned when funds ran out.[89] The establishment of the Bulgarian State Railway in 1884 provided a grand plan for future development, but it was undertaken mainly 'to ward off uncomfortable Russian pressure'.[90]

After the main lines had been completed (1888) it was expected that the Balkan states would build branch networks. They did little of the kind. A more pressing priority was to remove the railways from foreign ownership, and in 1888 both countries nationalized the operating compa-

[87] D. Arnautovitch, *Histoire des chemins de fer yougoslaves, 1825–1937* (Paris, 1937), pp. 38–54.   [88] Dorothy Anderson, *The Balkan Volunteers* (London, 1968), p. 65.
[89] Konstantin Irechek, *Knjazhestvo B'lgarija* (Plovdiv, 1899), II, pp. 28–9, 99, 108.
[90] R. Crampton, 'Political Factors in the Modernization of Bulgaria before the First World War' (Bad Homburg conference on Backwardness and Modernization in Southeastern Europe, July 1989), p. 2.

nies. This merely burdened them with compensation payments which damaged their finances, and made it even more difficult to raise funds to build extension lines.[91]

In Serbia, railway policy was directed to fending off other people's proposals for extension. For example, a branch line linked the main line at Velika Plana with the port of Smederevo on the Danube. It had been built by the contractors to give their equipment access to interior sections before mainline tunnelling works between Belgrade and the junction had been completed. But Belgrade interests, fearing that the city might be bypassed by exporters using the shorter Smederevo branch, tried to get the works line pulled up once the main line had been completed. They eventually compromised by leaving the branch line in place, but burdened freight using it with a tariff so high that it proved cheaper to continue consigning goods by road.[92] Similarly ill-advised freight policies were implemented in Bulgaria, particularly on the Jambol – Burgas section.[93] Until 1908 the only new track laid in Serbia and integrated with the public system was built to link various state establishments (the Kragujevac arsenal, the State Coal Mine at Ćuprija, and the parastatal Belgrade meat factory) with the main line.

Balkan governments regarded the railway as a facility of the administration rather than as a provider of economic services. In Serbia, several plans were floated for narrow gauge lines to link the interior towns with the main line and the Danube – Sava river system. They were urgently needed. A firm that promoted a light railway project in 1900 claimed that 'so greatly are railway facilities desired that certain towns and districts are proposing to offer material assistance in order that they may obtain priority'.[94] Similarly in 1881 a group of merchants of Valjevo town associated to seek a concession to link the town with Obrenovac on the Sava, by 'a steam tramway on narrow gauge', for which they surveyed the route. A heavy cart traffic in primary products used the Valjevo – Obrenovac road, and the project looked financially promising.[95] The town was prepared to guarantee a 6 per cent return on the investment. A little later, Požarevac municipality built a light railway to its port at Dubravica to bring in materials for a construction project. Local interests wanted to open the track to passengers and to extend it southward to link with the state railway

[91] John R. Lampe and Marvin R. Jackson, *Balkan Economic History, 1550–1950* (Bloomington, IN, 1982), p. 209.
[92] Milivoje M. Kostić, *Srpska izvozna trgovina od 1893–1903 godine* (Belgrade, 1905), pp. 43–4.   [93] GBC Bulgaria 1890, p. 24.
[94] Prospectus of Royal Servian Railways and Exploration Company Ltd., in PRO FO 105 136.
[95] Emile de Borchgrave, *La Serbie administrative, économique et commerciale* (Brussels, 1883), p. 97.

system.[96] All these initiatives were blocked by the government, which feared that competition might divert freights from the State Railway. The State Railway insisted that standard gauge must be applied throughout the system, but this excuse for blocking private initiatives was invalid because the state lacked the finances to carry its own plans through.[97] Even an existing private mine railway was forbidden a licence to act as common carrier.[98]

Rather more track was built in Bulgaria in the 1890s, all controlled by the state, but realization of railway plans was painfully slow, and in 1896/7 (and still more by 1914) the network was of even lower density than that of Serbia.[99] The timing of construction was also influenced by budgetary conditions, which should have been irrelevant.[100] The railways in which the Balkan states took the keenest interest were strategic projects, of dubious commercial promise. So the Bulgarians wasted vast sums on the Trans-Balkan scheme, and Serbia involved itself in the even less promising Danube–Adriatic project. When, eventually, the Serbian state raised the finance to build extension railways (on narrow gauge, after all) the pace of construction was leisurely. The key line to Užice was not opened till 1912. The impact of these railways was barely felt before World War I, but the loss of commerce which arose from delay in building them may be gauged from a report of the mid-1920s. It speaks of former hamlets and villages on the new line of rail emerging as bustling commercial townships, generating large amounts of rail-borne commerce.[101] These gains could have been reaped twenty or thirty years earlier, but for state obstruction.

Xenophobia, corruption, and industrialization

Neither in Serbia nor Bulgaria, nor even in Bosnia, was the state a central actor in the industrialization process. The Bulgarian state largely confined itself to ownership of the mutually linked complex of coal, railways, armaments and railway workshops. Serbian governments added to the same basic complex enterprises which they nationalized to create revenue monopolies, and one large meat packing factory that local investors declined to finance. Marxist authors claim that before the Balkan Wars the principal function of the state was to develop infrastructure in sectors whose return could not attract private investment, but which were nevertheless indispensable for capitalistic development.[102] This was generally

---

[96] *RC*, LXXV, 1892, p. 37.   [97] *RC*, LXXV, 1892, p. 61.   [98] GBC Serbia 1895, p. 3.
[99] I. T. Berend and Gy. Ranki, *Economic Development in East Central Europe in the 19th and 20th Centuries* (London, 1974), p. 78.   [100] Crampton, *Bulgaria*, pp. 384–5.
[101] D. Jovanović, 'U carstvu šljiva i rakije', *Privredni pregled*, III, 46 (1925), p. 3.
[102] Stefan Tsonev, *D'rzhavno-monopolistichnijat kapitaliz'm v B'lgarija* (Varna, 1968), pp. 21–2, 25, 31.

the case. Even the Bosnian *Landesregierung*, though significant as an industrial investor, was not particularly successful in its enterprises; its key role therefore was its capacity to create a favourable investment environment. The pace of development therefore would turn largely on the performance of the private sector, and for want of native enterprise, on the ability of Balkan governments to attract foreign investment. The relative absence of foreign private sector investment in the Balkans was a significant obstacle to development,[103] but it was not the consequence of a lack of investor interest. Only a small number of foreign backed schemes reached fruition. We must take account of the far larger number of projects which failed, and why they failed.

For Bulgaria and Serbia, the argument we will put forward is that these countries failed to attract inward industrial investment, less because of a lack of interest by foreign promoters, more through the creation of an environment which deterred foreign participation. Though Bosnia's raw material endowment was more attractive to foreign enterprise than that of either Serbia or Bulgaria, a significant deterrent to investment in these countries was the combination of xenophobia, official corruption and undeveloped local business ethics which trans-national firms encountered.

The activity and policies of the state were significant in attracting or deterring investment. In both countries, the state formally encouraged large-scale industry, through successive rounds of concession legislation. In Serbia, the government legislated in 1873 to offer promoters of mechanized industries various privileges, which could not, for treaty reasons, include protection. The 1873 law was extended and updated in 1898.[104] In 1884, about seventy enterprises, predominantly mills, sawmills and brickfields, had registered under the 1873 law.[105] This legislation did little more than remove administratively created impediments to enterprise. In part concessions compensated entrepreneurs for the low level of external protection, but the principal benefits offered took the form of discounts on goods and services (coal, salt, transport) which were provided by the state to unprivileged users at extortionate cost, and of rebates on import duties on inputs. That is to say, these measures simulated conditions for privileged firms which a free market would have provided. Some concessions also granted monopoly privileges. Their effect on industrial expansion was net negative, since the markets monopolized were small and exposed to import competition, and incumbent firms naturally obstructed the entry of new enterprises. On the whole, the concessions

---

[103] Lampe, 'Imperial Borderlands', pp. 198–200.
[104] Nikola Vučo, *Razvoj industrije u Srbiji u XIX veku* (Belgrade, 1891), pp. 9–10.
[105] AN F12 7179. Despatch of 26 Aug. 1884.

systems had little pulling power on foreign firms, though to attempt to trade without a concession would have been foolhardy.

Although the state lacked the ability to create, foster or promote effectively, its institutions could interfere with market forces, raising the risk to enterprise and reducing the returns. In east-central Europe, large-scale industrial investment was closely linked with the decision making of the larger commercial banks. Referring to 'the Reluctant Imperialism of the Foreign Banks',[106] Lampe argued that the European banks regarded long-term industrial investment in Serbia as excessively risky. This risk had both commercial and political parameters. The earliest of the central European banks to build up a significant position on the Serbian market, the Austrian Länderbank, had acquired Serbian railway stock and a large interest in the Serbian tobacco monopoly in 1886. By nationalizing these assets in 1889 and 1890, the Serbian government contrived to discourage financing during the critical decade of the 1890s when so much Austrian investment was pouring into Bosnia. Direct industrial participations by the Länderbank after 1900 in the loss making German sugar factory in Belgrade and in a failed meat packing project can only have impressed upon its directors the inadvisability of committing funds in Serbia. Although it controlled a Serbian affiliate (Srpska kreditna banka) which received first refusal on participation in financing the Paraćin glassworks (1908) it passed it up. So too did the Belgrade Andrejević bank, itself controlled since 1888 by the Hungarian Kommmercialbank. Under Hungarian control, the Andrejević bank confined its operations to short-term advances on first-class paper, and backed out of a potentially lucrative public works project in 1908/9, judging it a bad risk. It was so nervous during the Bosnian Annexation Crisis of that year that it temporarily pulled its reserves out of Serbia, regardless of the loss of sound business and the enmity of the Serbian government. The subsequent decline of the Andrejević bank created openings within the Serbian market for other foreign banks to exploit, but they judged the commercial risks to be excessive.

They also had to contend with the entrenched xenophobia and jealousy of established Serbian institutions. An attempt to found an Italo-Serbian bank to channel Italian industrial investment in Serbia foundered on the vested opposition of the politically influential Izvozna Banka, while a big project for a Banque Franco-Serbe (backed by the Ottoman Bank of Paris) stalled on objections in the Serbian cabinet in 1909 to *any* large foreign dominated banking venture. The project was eventually taken up

---

[106] The evidence for the following discussion on banks is drawn from John R. Lampe, 'Financial Structure and the Economic Development of Serbia 1878–1912' (Ph.D. Thesis, University of Wisconsin, 1971), pp. 331–70.

in 1910, after the Serbian government discovered that domestic interests would not finance a 30 million franc loan to the city of Belgrade. But the Franco-Serbe (despite a subsidy from the French government) proved as cautious in its dealings with Serbia as any central European bank, especially as regards industrial commitments. It would only extend industrial credit at 3–4 per cent over its commercial rate, and despite its declared objectives, it waited till 1913 to make its first industrial investment. A British bank promotion was also deferred through fear of investment risks in Serbia until the commercial war of Serbia and Austria-Hungary had been ended.

The only significant external bank participations in Serbian industry emanated from the secondary centres of Prague and Zagreb, in financing the Ćuprija sugar factory (1911) by the Prague Uveréna banka, and in various railway projects on the eve of the Balkan Wars. But even these banks were cautious in their policies toward Serbian industrial borrowers.

The caution of the foreign banks was entirely rational. A nagging fear shared by foreign firms was that their domestic debtors would not honour their debts, and that no satisfactory sanctions existed to enforce them. As a French consul reported in 1875, Belgrade merchants considered bankruptcy as a means of getting rich quickly. At this time of commercial difficulty, they were looking to the *skupština*, with every prospect of success, to be allowed remission of payment. The Hungarian and German consuls advised their nationals to stop doing business.[107] Belgrade was full of insubstantial traders who were happy to think big, but there were 'relatively few houses with established honorability and solvency'.[108] Even the merchants of Vienna and Budapest, with far better knowledge of business conditions in Belgrade than their British or French counterparts 'sometimes discover to [their] sorrow that [they] have misplaced [their] confidence'.[109]

Dubious commercial ethics extended to the various layers of government and became intertwined with xenophobia. Advising British firms not to participate in a construction scheme of 1895 (which would require the offer of a 10 million franc loan to the city of Belgrade) the consul observed that even the Serbian government had 'no confidence whatever in the capacity of the municipal authorities to carry out such a scheme'. He warned of 'the unfortunate absence of public morality in Serbia', and 'the strong temptation to sharp practice'. 'An outcry is easily raised against foreigners', he noted. 'There is already strong opposition to the present contract being given other than to natives. The slightest hitch or

[107] AAE CC Belgrade t. 5 (1872–80) despatches of 21 May 1875 f. 228 and 27 Sept. 1875.
[108] *RC*, LXI, Report dated 3 Oct. 1887, p. 447.
[109] PRO FO 105 42. Report on the Servian Railways. No 8 commercial of 27 Apr. 1883.

interruption to the works might be made to serve as a plausible excuse for cancelling the contract, and confiscating the security.' As administrations were in continual flux, there was the added danger 'of facing political opponents of the outgoing administration when the works are half completed'.[110] This problem would not go away. In 1903, when a tender was issued by the Serbian State Railways for rolling stock, the British consul advised firms not to bid, fearing that they would not be paid.[111]

Bulgaria attracted even less investment interest than Serbia. Only in 1905 did the first foreign bank establish itself in Sofia. Though backed by the German universal banks, it was extremely cautious in its commercial activities.[112] Gerschenkron, who argues that the failure of the Bulgarian economy to industrialize from 'extreme backwardness' represented a missed opportunity for state intervention, also criticizes the German banks for lack of 'vigour' in identifying investment opportunities.[113]

Though investment opportunities in processing raw materials for export (the favoured target of foreign corporate enterprise) were not favourable in Bulgaria, the authorities could have attracted more corporate capital, at least until around 1906, were it not for their fear of foreign influence. Despite the ostensible attractions offered by concession legislation, the law up to March 1905 'insisted on the administration of such companies being Bulgarian'. Given conditions then pertaining, the requirement was unrealistic, and the law was 'of no avail'.[114] Xenophobic sensitivities baulked the development of the 'Prince Boris' coal mine near Trjavna, which was backed by Paribas. True, the personal backing of the prince overrode the objections of the politicians in the award of the concession in 1897, but until 1910 production was constrained to meagre levels (despite Bulgaria's urgent need for good coal) for want of a link between the mine and the mainline railway. The promoter, Auguste de Serre, wanted to build an extension line as soon as the mine was open, but was refused permission on the grounds that foreign firms should not own railways. The government told the company that if it wanted a line it should lend the state the funds to build it, and underwrite any losses the state incurred in operating it, a proposition which the company sensibly refused. In 1902, transport costs became so burdensome that the mine was temporarily closed. Eventually in 1905, Paribas told the Bulgarians that unless the railway concession was granted it would sanction no more

---

[110] PRO FO 105 111. No. 9 Commercial of 1 July 1895.
[111] PRO FO 105 151. No. 6 Commercial of 11 Feb. 1903.
[112] Lampe and Jackson, *Balkan Economic History*, p. 227.
[113] Alexander Gerschenkron, 'Some Aspects of Industrialization in Bulgaria, 1878–1939', in his *Economic Backwardness in Historical Perspective* (New York, 1965), p. 232.
[114] GBC Bulgaria 1905, p. 8.

loans to Bulgaria. The upshot was a line built on state account, but over suboptimal routing: 'thus compelled by dire financial need, governing circles found themselves obliged to lay out enormous sums for the building of a line, which was not the most convenient either in economic or in strategic terms, and whose operation even today causes the state great difficulties'.[115]

Behind the broad lines of state policy lies the mass of detail which can be uncovered from the official correspondence to which the foreign projects gave rise. Why did so few of these approaches in Bulgaria or Serbia in pursuit of concessions eventually bear fruit, and why were the projects which were undertaken seldom profitable? Many were undercapitalized, poorly planned, or plain fraudulent. Most projects, especially British ones, were launched by free-standing companies which suffered from an 'inherently weak managerial structure, at origin, causing [them] to depend on outside providers of services'.[116] Not one of the many British flotations for business in Serbia fulfilled the aspirations of its promoters.

Allowing for the inadequacies of these companies – and of most of their French and Belgian counterparts – their experience shows the frustrations of doing business in the Balkans. It was not only a question of high level politics; often the worst frustrations arose from relatively humble levels of the bureaucracies. Businessmen encountered xenophobic officials, who not only tried to skim off bribes (this was to be expected) but, if they were not paid off, connived at the ruination of the firms concerned.

Take the experience of the unsuccessful Société d'exploitations minières du Serbie, constituted in France in March 1906 to buy out and operate a mineral dredging project which had been set up by a British firm. The *Société*, operating in the valley of the Pek, spent heavily on local labour and haulage services, but encountered implacable local hostility. This was instigated by the priests, whose authority it threatened. At first sight, the priests were merely indulging in mild extortion. Knowing the dredger had to operate over a continuous line, the priests secured control of fragments of land which lay in its path. By forcing the company to buy them out at an extortionate price, they acquired the capital for further speculations in land over which the dredger would need to move. The company then discovered that they were uninterested in settling at any price, because it had antagonized them by working the men on Sundays, and the priests were in a vindictive mood. In a threatening letter to the

---

[115] Simeon Damjanov, *Frenskoto ikonomichesko pronikvane v B'lgarija 1876–1914* (Sofia, 1971), pp. 1907–200; BAE 2807X no. 2161 (Economic report for Bulgaria in 1902, dated 10 Feb. 1904).

[116] Mira Wilkins, 'The Free Standing Company, 1870–1914: an Important Type of British Foreign Investment', *Economic History Review*, XLI (1988), p. 279.

company, one Pope Jaćić allegedly wrote: 'I warn you that if you get authorization by the minister and even by the Metropolitan, I will force you to stop work. I'll trip you up by all possible means, I will get your workers to rise against you.' He was not bluffing. Cable poles were dynamited. When the priests seized a pile of coal on the spurious claim that it had been deposited on priestly property, they were upheld by a corrupt local official, who had previously been refused a 'loan' he had solicited from the company.[117] The company soon failed.

At about the same time, the French-owned Bor copper mine was paralysed by a succession of strikes. Agitators, reportedly including local government officials, whipped up peasant unrest against the company on account of smoke nuisance caused by the smelter. The company objected that it had never refused to indemnify 'neighbouring properties' for damage caused them, but had not received any properly drawn up claims. In this instance, the firm did receive central government support, and the removal of the officials involved in harassing it.[118]

Xenophobia could lead to ludicrous paradoxes in decision making. Take the meat packing industry. Serbia desperately needed meat packing enterprises to reduce her dependence on the Hungarian market. Because of the politicized character of the meat issue, the concessioning of such enterprises was a matter of political sensitivity. One after another, foreign meat packers were either sent away, or their businesses in Serbia harassed, to minimize foreign influence in the industry.

The meat issue was a long-running affair which recurred intermittently. During the first crisis (1890) Serbia had been assisted in packing meat by a British enterprise which set up temporary facilities at Niš. The firm was admittedly not adequately financed, but its concession was abruptly cancelled by Taušanović, the minister responsible. His opponents 'ascribe[d] the sudden forfeiture of the pork concession to the well known fact that in spite of strong advice to conform to the customs of the country, Marshall [the promoter] persistently refused to bribe in any way'.[119] Further closures of the frontier to Serbian pigs by the Hungarians in 1895–6 returned meat packing to the political agenda. A project was launched to establish a purely Serbian export slaughterhouse. As private capital proved unresponsive to this problematic investment, the Serbian government had to take up most of the shares and to finance the company's short-term financial requirements. However, temporary slaughtering capacity was urgently needed and the new Serbian meat packing society had to co-operate with a German firm, Kolberg & Weber,

---

[117] AAE CC Serbie. N.S. 18 Mines I, 1902–10, fs. 128–159.
[118] Report of the Mines of Bor to the Assembly of 28 Nov. 1908, in AAE CC Serbie N.S. 18 Mines.   [119] PRO FO 105 90, no. 146 of 6 Nov 1891.

which was already operating in Belgrade. The German firm, rather than the new Serbian company, did most of the export slaughtering in 1895/6, but once the crisis had passed, the Serbian company forced Kolberg & Weber out of business and appropriated their site. Kolberg & Weber abandoned the struggle and sold their installations to another German in 1897, whereupon the Serbian company proceeded against him. The new owner warned the Minister of the National Economy that 'Kolberg & Weber were driven out by bullying, but it will not be easy to drive me out'. He was proven wrong, for the Serbian company used compulsory purchase powers to secure the land at half the offer price.[120]

Once the Serbian company was established and in production, all applications for private meat packing concessions were referred to its board for its opinion, which carried political weight. The company's attitude to the proposals of prospective competitors was predictably negative. Its usual response was to agree that additional capacity was needed, but to rubbish all specific proposals. Repeatedly it urged that concessions should not be given to foreigners. When M. Vasseur of Paris asked for a concession in 1899, his application was referred to the Serbian company. The reply he received led him to 'thank the minister for . . . telling him there exists in Belgrade a factory for manufacturing alimentary conserves and salami' (which was not even true). He regretted that he had 'unknowingly threatened to compete with a purely national enterprise'. Though he persevered in trying to obtain his concession, the outcome was negative.[121]

The Serbian company also tried to drive out a smaller established competitor, Kleefisch, who wanted to extend his plant at Jagodina. It claimed he was inadequately equipped, and unable to maintain quality control standards, though other contemporary reports show that he worked, admittedly with little machinery, to far higher standards than the Belgrade factory. It enlisted local support from merchant Dušan Janković who inveighed against 'foreign plunder in the meat trade', and from an old antagonist of Kleefisch, Mika Jevtić, who became mayor of the town, and used his position to fine Kleefisch heavily for illegal work. The fine was however quashed by the district sub-prefect.[122] The familiar cry that meat packing concessions should not go to foreigners was also taken up by the Association of Serbian Industrialists[123] and led to the blocking of a

---

[120] AS MNP (T) 1906 37 8 no. 6142 of 8 Dec. 1896 and no. 6470 of 21 Dec. 1896 and no. 7841 of 3 Oct. 1897; also annual report of the Serbian Meat Packing Company for 1896, under the same cover.

[121] AS MNP (T) 1900 IV 63 Nos. 868 of 16 Feb. 1900; 1396 of 14 Mar. 1900; 6350 of 28 Oct. 1899.

[122] AS MNP (T) 1905 XIV 9 Nos. 2523 of 20 Nov. 1902; 6451 of 8 Nov. 1902; 1905 II 1, no. 6123 of 8 Dec. 1903; 1903 15 19, No 574 of 24 Jan. 1903.

[123] AS MNP (T) 1904 13 12 no. 5901 of 26 Nov. 1903.

string of similar proposals before and during the tariff war. When negotiations with Austria-Hungary developed from 1908 onward, the Serbian side was primarily interested in securing for the Belgrade company monopoly control over all meat packed for Hungary, leaving private meat packers to compete for supplies to export to less profitable alternative destinations.[124]

Similar vexations lay in the path of textile enterprises, both in Serbia and Bulgaria. The Manchester financed cotton spinning mill at Varna became ensnared in the toils of a determined anti-foreign campaign at the outset of its career. One of the managers established an eighteen-year-old millhand as his mistress, and the local press inflamed feeling against 'the English'. The police (who 'may have been trying a little blackmail, their salaries being in arrears') wanted to prosecute him for rape. Demands by officials for bribes were coupled with threats 'that in the event of non-compliance the business of the company would not be allowed to proceed smoothly'. The company spirited the manager out of harm's way, but other officials were also threatened and strikes broke out. The local newspaper howled for expulsion of the English and seizure of their assets. The directors seriously considered closure of the mill.[125] A second cotton mill erected at Jambol was also to meet 'with considerable difficulties at the hands of the authorities'.[126] A government minister tried to gouge £12,000 from the promoters in return for a concession.[127]

The Varna mill survived its vicissitudes, but we noted in Chapter 9 one instance where official harassment caused a foreign firm to pull out altogether. The misadventures of the highly reputable Crompton firm arose through its dealings with predatory officials at the War Ministry. These led to unjustified losses of military orders and officially inspired work stoppages which caused the firm to withdraw from manufacturing in Serbia, and to meet Serbian orders with materials imported over the tariff.

Anti-foreign attitudes were not limited to government officials and domestic trade rivals. They were highly developed in the consciousness of the precocious organized labour movements, whose interventions were on occasion officially connived at. Organized labour in Serbia harassed foreign firms mainly from resentment at the high pay with which they attracted expatriate skills.[128] French official sources in Bulgaria also

---

124　Dimitrije Djordjević, *Carinski rat Austro-Ugarske i Srbije 1906–1911* (Belgrade, 1962), p. 485; IKKS, *Izveštaj . u 1911 g.*, pp. 24–5; Vienna. k.k. Oesterr. Handelsmuseum, *Serbien. Wirtschaftliche Verhaltnisse, 1911*, p. 29.
125　PRO FO 78 5083 Brophy-Freeman 2 Jan. 1900; FO 78 5020 Lees–Salisbury 20 Dec. 1899.　126　GBC Bulgaria 1910, p. 14.　127　Crampton, *Bulgaria*, p. 389.
128　Lampe, 'Financial Structure', p. 261.

warned businessmen of 'the annoyances of all sorts to the entrepreneur in his relations with workers full of pretentions, already organized, syndicated and who have this superiority over their comrades in Europe in the struggle they engage with the *patronat* that they have no needs and can comfortably stop work for a long time'.[129]

The above instances are drawn from documents relating to a narrow range of enterprises. They could easily be multiplied. Xenophobia and official corruption deterred foreign industrial investment in the Balkan states, by offsetting the ostensible attractions extended by the concession laws. Governments might (formally) welcome foreign firms, but the pinpricks which their xenophobic officials and political friends were capable of inflicting could ruin otherwise profitable enterprises. The Balkan states partially stifled the only means available of building up industrial capacity sufficiently rapidly to reverse the inbuilt tendencies of these economies to productive decline.

It may be objected that xenophobia, corruption and dishonesty were not peculiar to the Balkans. They are a symptom of backwardness as well as a constraint on development. Russia, for example, was just as corruptly administered and quite as xenophobic, but this did not prevent a huge contribution to its growth being made by foreign corporate investors. But it must have diminished its effectiveness. One reason why Gerschenkron dismissed Russia's potential for bank-driven growth and argued for the indispensability of state action was because business ethics were too disastrously low for financial institutions to enjoy public confidence. Though standards had improved by the early twentieth century, as they also did in the Balkans, 'some degree of animosity against foreign entrepreneurs and technicians was in clear evidence'. Gerschenkron claims this did not exceed 'moderate limits' – but concedes that such attitudes could discourage investment in countries – like the Balkan states – which lacked the magnetism for entrepreneurs of Russia's apparently inexhaustible subsoil wealth and enormous (potential) domestic market.[130]

Conclusion

Per capita output in farming fell between the early 1870s and 1910/12, by 14.3 per cent in Bulgaria and 27.5 per cent in Serbia. In Serbia, decline was attended by a pronounced shift from the pastoral economy towards the cultivation of cereals for export. The decline of pig raising acted

---

[129] AN F12 7280 (Philippopolis 1907–12, report of Plovdiv consulate for 7 Apr. 1907).
[130] Gerschenkron, *Economic Backwardness*, pp. 19–20, 70.

negatively on performance. This resulted partly from Hungarian interference with Serbia's trade in unfattened pigs, but export difficulties aggravated a supply side decline, in particular the continual erosion of the woodland base for pig raising, and the pre-emption of pasture to support the draft needs of the arable.

Despite the absence of specific export problems for Bulgaria, its productive experience in farming was similar to that of Serbia. Cereal yields failed to recover to levels attained in the 1860s and early 1870s. The poor performance of both countries therefore invited a broader discussion of retardative supply side influences common to Balkan agricultures.

The most obvious was the universality of peasant farming, and its adherence to a subsistence base. In Serbia in 1910 peasants only delivered about 39 per cent of their produce to market. The pattern in Bulgaria was probably similar. In Serbia, the authorities tried to constrict peasant access to incentive goods, so despite the building of railways, their policies retarded the commercialization of farming by the high transactions costs involved.

These were economies into which the techniques for rationalizing farm production, even for the maintenance of soil fertility, were slow to filter. Knowledge needed to be made accessible, but the peasants also had to be motivated to acquire it. They were not. Human capital was not being formed in the village. The penetration of market agriculture was too weak for peasants to see advantages in education. The legacy of the 'renaissance' caused a stronger response in Bulgaria than in Serbia, but it remained geographically restricted.

Despite the similarities between rural arrangements in Serbia and 'Serbianized' post-liberation Bulgaria, the pressure of settlement in Serbia was higher and the shortage of potential arable more acute. Up to World War I, Bulgarian farmers continued to take in new arable land at the margin. After about 1893, their Serbian counterparts could not. So Serbian farmers belatedly responded by adopting more intensive cropping systems. The results showed through in rising crop yields while yields in Bulgaria remained flat. However this positive response in Serbia did no more than to flatten out the hitherto negative trend in farm productivity.

The environment of a declining rural economy was clearly inimical to non-agricultural change, since as late as 1910 farming accounted for about half of total output in each country. Estimating from our own figures on Serbia and from Popov's national income calculation for Bulgaria, growth in the non-farm economy fell far short of offsetting this decline. Neither country exploited the full potential of railways in marketizing production, largely because of resistance by governments to private sector initiatives.

Large-scale industry began to grow rapidly in the last pre Balkan war decade, but as an aggregate it remained insignificant, incapable of inducing the kind of transformation achieved in Bosnia. Domestic enterprise was too weak outside of textiles to provide industrial impetus. Concession laws were designed to attract trans-national enterprises, but few such ventures flourished. It is suggested that the political environment was hostile to such initiatives, and that this hostility was driven by xenophobia.

During the first decade of the twentieth century, the secular downswing in Bulgarian and Serbian per capita output may have been arrested, since farm productivity had ceased to fall, and the non-farm sector probably expanded. Such growth as may have occurred during this decade was from the basis of a very low trough. However, the Balkan states' economies were at last passing through a slow structural transition towards economic growth, though this had been made all the more difficult because of the shrinkage of farm productivity. Todorova's arguments for a 'Bulgarian style industrial revolution', though they press the evidence too far, cannot be dismissed out of hand. Industry continued to expand briskly between the two world wars, and so too, if the Chakalov figures may be relied on, did the Bulgarian economy as a whole, including farming.[131]

---

[131] Asen Chakalov, *Natsionalen dohod i razhod na B'lgarija, 1924–1945* (Sofia, 1946).

11 Economic change in Macedonia and Thrace 1878–1914

Farming and economic life 1878–1912

The agrarian order in Ottoman Europe between 1878 and 1914 remained as it had emerged in the Tanzimat era. However, by the turn of the century, expectations grew of the imminent collapse of Ottoman rule. There was a slow descent into anarchy, particularly in Macedonia. Without apology, we will adopt the evergreen definition of 'Macedonia' provided by a contemporary journalist, as 'a conveniently elastic term which is made to include all the territory anyone wishes to annex'.[1] Murderous rivalries were incited between ethnic groups by partizans of their irredentist patrons in the Balkan states, especially Bulgaria.

In Macedonia's plains and valleys, much of the land was held as *čifliks* allegedly of 100–500 hectares. Their proprietors were customarily described as Turks,[2] in practice they were frequently Albanian. As many were absentees (at least in the 1900s) the larger estates were managed by stewards (*subaše*).[3] Normally there would be a sizeable home farm, cultivated by ten or twelve Slav agricultural labourers (*momci*) who were hired on a six-monthly or yearly basis. The labourers and their families dwelt in cabins around the big house, in a fortified settlement on the home farm.[4] In summer these workers would be supplemented by gangs of migrant reapers, usually young women from the hill villages. The rest of the estate would be tenanted by peasant *čifčijas*, either on (unregulated) sharecropping terms, or sometimes paying a labour rent. Where labour was very scarce the landowners would grant *čifčijas* land against a rent payable in grain according to the number of oxen used for ploughing it, a system which provided the cultivator with a very strong incentive to maximize the crop.[5] The estate would raise arable crops, but

---

[1] M. E. Durham, *The Burden of the Balkans* (London, 1905), p. 76.
[2] Berrisav Arsitch, *La vie économique de la Serbie du sud au XIXe siècle* (Paris, 1936), p 70.
[3] Leonhard Schultze-Jena, *Makedonien. Landschafts- und Kulturbilder* (Jena, 1927), p. 51.
[4] Jovan Hadži-Vasiljević, *Skoplje i njegova okolina. Istorijska, etnografska i kulturno politička izlaganja* (Belgrade, 1930), pp. 224.
[5] Ivan Ivanić, *Maćedonija i Maćedonci*, II (Novi Sad, 1908), p. 562.

much of its land was leased out as winter pasture to semi-nomadic stockraisers.[6]

By the end of the nineteenth century, the *čifliks* were feeling the impact of the rural anarchy (which is why they were fortified, and probably also explains the preference of the *beg*s for absentee status). A steady trickle of estate land came on the market, usually to be bought by collectives of local peasants, but there were no mass disposals of land before the Balkan Wars.[7] The land sales are represented in the literature as responses to declining profitability, bankruptcies, and the difficulty of obtaining sufficient labour.[8] However, authors of most accounts assumed that economic conditions were deteriorating in parallel with the political dissolution of the territory, and there is contrary evidence that estate farming was both profitable and productive right up to 1912. The estates were better equipped than the peasant farms, and reportedly achieved double the yield per cultivated acre, thanks to intensive and mechanized cultivation.[9] Figures collected at the time of Serbia's annexation of Kosovo vilayet estimated that a dünüm of arable (919 square metres) farmed with hired labour yielded 385 kilos of grain, worth 54.5 dinars, of which state tithe and all expenses consumed 30.1 dinars, giving a profit margin of 81 per cent, and a 27.5 per cent return on capital invested. The yield obtained on wheat in the vilayet was 15.9 hectolitres per hectare (similar to yields in the Balkan states).[10] In view of the low market capitalization of land in relation to yield, sales of *chifliks* were probably motivated more by political risk than by distress.

Farming in Macedonia was moderately prosperous on the eve of dissolution. In addition to grain cultivation, the planting of high quality tobacco was booming, and cash cropping also extended to market gardening, rice cultivation, opium, cotton and sesame. In Ottoman Europe on the eve of the Balkan Wars, tobacco was planted over 25,300 hectares, and yielded 22.3 million kilos.[11] Cultivation was expanding rapidly, to some extent displacing wheat and cotton. The industrial crops, among which tobacco predominated, were claimed greatly to have enriched the rural population. Most tobacco was exported to Germany and Austria.[12] In 1910–12, Skopje province raised about 2.6 million kilos of tobacco a year, utilizing seed from Xanthi and Kavalla. Its cultivation was a full-time occupation for the Turks and Albanians who grew it.[13] Opium, another highly profitable crop, was concentrated on the Vardar valley.

[6] Schultze-Jena, *Makedonien*, p. 51.
[7] D. Iaranoff, *La Macédoine économique* (Sofia, 1931), p.42
[8] Schultze-Jena, *Makedonien*, p. 51.　　[9] Iaranoff, *Macédoine économique*, p. 43.
[10] Mita Dimitrijević, *Privreda i trgovina u novoj Srbiji* (Belgrade, 1913), I, pp. 25, 27, 29.
[11] Ibid., p 38.　　[12] Arsitch, *Vie économique*, p. 83.
[13] Hadži-Vasiljević, *Skoplje*, pp. 214–15.

Map 6 Macedonia on the eve of the Balkan Wars of 1912–1913

The high morphine content ensured a brisk sale to the pharmaceuticals industry. The eve of war harvest was about 250 tonnes.[14]

In the whole of Macedonia, only about 11.3 per cent of the soil was cropped. Although much of the territory is mountainous, contemporaries agreed that there was a significant margin of good uncultivated land. In part, this reflected the need of the upland sheep raisers for winter pasture in the lowlands, but there was also an acute shortage of cultivators.

The traditional basis of the upland economy had been transhumant sheep raising combined where practicable with scratch agriculture. After 1878, the iron collar of *čiflik* land continued to make lowland resettlement difficult, so in Macedonia the hills remained relatively overpopulated right up to the Balkan Wars. In the Hellenic region some hill towns attracted manufacturing industry on a substantial scale, but this development was relatively weak in the north and west and in Kosovo. There is an obvious analogy here with conditions in Hellenic Macedonia and Bulgaria during the period of the *k'rdzhalijas*: large-scale agriculture in fertile but underpopulated plains constrained in its expansion by want of labour, and nascent industrial townships in the hills.

There were also differences. In northern Macedonia there were few upland townships of refuge, capable of metamorphosing into centres of proto-industry. Conditions in the mountain zone remained too insecure

---

[14] Iaranoff, *Macédoine économique*, pp. 71–2.

for the development of upland commercial and manufacturing communities. A major source of insecurity was acute friction between Albanians and Slavs. The struggle was essentially over control of grazing, and, on the whole, the Albanians had the better of it. As a result, few Slavic upland communities evolved like the Bulgarian hill towns.

For example, take the environs of Debar, a stronghold of the Albanian *begs*. The large hill villages had maintained themselves through transhumant sheep raising. However, murderous attacks on the shepherds by the Debar Albanians, and seizure of their stock, caused increased dependence on itinerant work, *pečalbarstvo*, while the hill settlements became nothing more than dormitories.[15] The semi-nomadic former shepherds adapted easily to alternative occupations, and acquired experience as packhorse carriers, trading mainly in salt. They diversified into itinerant construction and commerce. These *pečalbars* of the Debar villagers notably traded as innkeepers, and many re-established themselves in this trade in the villages near Belgrade.[16] The many local ethnographic studies of upland Macedonia reveal a great diversity of occupation, especially in construction and associated jobs, but it almost invariably involved migrating from home. Developmentally this had a rather different impact to textile proto-industrialization. More successful migrant communities accumulated capital, but lack of local outlets meant that the developmental impact of their activities was felt rather in the localities to which they migrated, above all Salonica, Constantinople and Sofia. Economic life in overpopulated upland Macedonia merely vegetated.

Macedonia's urban population was exceptionally large by Balkan standards, 24–28 per cent around 1890.[17] This was probably larger than the equilibrium level created by the agrarian and administrative systems, and the population inflows the cities received were too large to be absorbed into the local labour markets. The sources of excess urban population were threefold. Firstly, the migrant economy of the hills created its own urban inflow. Many *pečalbars* resettled in the lowland towns. So too did lowland peasants escaping rural insecurity, whose absence contributed to the agricultural labour shortage. A third important group included an inflow of *muhadžirs*, Muslims who had been displaced from the successor states. Salonica and Monastir attracted large numbers of them.[18] None of these groups were pulled into the towns by the opportunities which

---

[15] M. M. Velj, 'Debar i njegova okolina', *Brastvo*, VIII (1899), pp. 27–36; R. Ognjanović, 'Galičnik', *Južna Srbija*, II (1922), pp. 362–8.

[16] Jovan Cvijić, *Osnove za geografiju i geologiju Makedonije i stare Srbije* (Belgrade, 1911), III, pp. 1012–3.   [17] See above Table 1.10.

[18] Ivan Ivanić, *Maćedonija i Maćedonci. Putopisne beleške* (Belgrade, 1906), p. 198; Cvijić, *Osnove*, III, p. 1032.

beckoned in them. Rather, all three were pushed. The shortage of rural labour was attributed to desertion of the villages in favour of urban settlement, because personal security in the towns was better, and urban incomes were less highly taxed.[19]

The amount of trade these towns generated was too small to support the demand for urban residence. The *pečalbar* migrants from the hills therefore continued to seek their living as migrants. In contrast with Serbia and Bulgaria, where migrant employment was largely a rural side-activity, a high proportion of Macedonia's itinerant masons, dairymen, woodworkers and merchants, who spread out in search of work throughout the Balkans and beyond were themselves urban dwellers. *Muhadžirs* from the former Niš *pašaluk* and from Bosnia are said to have animated the commerce of these towns, but having lost their lands and the incomes from them, they had no option but to engage in trade or enter the labour market, and most lived in more or less genteel poverty.[20]

Contempories viewed the overblown populations of the cities as a source of an abundant labour force for future industrialization, but only in the Hellenic regions did development of this nature take place. Better and less insecure communications were needed, and although the Ottoman authorities undertook fitful road-building programmes, many substantial towns, especially in Albania, were only reachable over hazardous mule tracks.[21]

It is indeed difficult to see how most of the people of these towns made any kind of a living other than as outward migrants or beggars. Take Prilep with a population of about 18,000 in 1897. Local trade was minimal, and there was little craft or domestic industry. Richer Prilep businessmen 'insofar as there any today', depended on their trade establishments in Monastir and Salonica, and invested their profits in local agricultural land. 'Enormous numbers' of Prilep men went out to the Balkan states and as far afield as Vienna and Leipzig, peddling sweetmeats on the streets. For the rest 'the unemployed accumulate, which once instructed in idleness, cannot take up any work' – save perhaps participation in the political gangs. Yet 'the fertile Prilep fields weep for work-hands'.[22] Prilep was typical.

Post-1878 progress in the woollen and cotton industries

Bulgaria's post-liberation difficulties permitted the remaining Ottoman territories in Europe to displace it as a woollen supplier to the imperial

[19] Ivan Ivanić, *Maćedonija i Maćedonci. II Opis zemlje i naroda* (Novi Sad, 1908), pp. 562, 563.   [20] Cvijić, *Osnove*, III, p. 1264–5.

[21] See, for example, the travel account of Mary Durham, *Burden*.

[22] J. Hadži-Vasiljević, *Prilep i njegova okolina* (Belgrade, 1902), pp. 42–4.

market. In Macedonia and Thrace, relatively weak woollen industries were given a new lease of life – and a chance for entrepreneurs to attempt the mechanization of production. At Magarevo and Trnovo, two hill villages near Monastir [Bitola], domestic textile production survived at least till 1914.[23] In 1883, these and two neighbouring villages, Diovo [Dihovo] and Majadag, boomed in supplying the Ottoman army with 340,000 metres of *šajak* and a substantial quantity of *aba*, orders which stimulated a partial transition to factory production. At Diovo in 1885, three merchants set up a mill to provide additional capacity for military orders which had been diverted from Bulgaria.[24] Heading the group was one Bogo Anesti, merchant of Monastir, with financial assistance from Skopje and Salonica interests.[25] The 120–250 Diovo factory workers, mainly women and children,[26] were not Diovo peasants, but were mostly Vlachs from other villages whom the Diovo people considered as foreigners.[27] The locals engaged mainly in migrant work. In 1888, 'minor' exports were sent as far as Syria,[28] and by the 1890s Macedonian cloth production is claimed to have driven Bulgarian cloth from the local market.[29] The Diovo mill also brought in braiding machines from Samokov in Bulgaria,[30] with which it produced 50,000 kilos of *gajtan* (braid) each year.[31] This amount equalled the entire consumption of Serbia, to which by the early 1890s some 12,000–15,000 kg. a year were being sent, through a warehouse established for that purpose in Niš.[32] In 1903 there was a steam-driven factory at Diovo, employing 150, and several smaller water-powered enterprises at nearby Magarevo, producing a similar range of goods.[33] By about 1910, there are claimed to have been four such 'factories' at Diovo, with 250–300 workers each.[34]

Some substantial woollen enterprises were established in the Salonica textile region, but the retarded development there of woollen manufacturing may reflect the relative sophistication of the local consumer market. More than in Bulgaria, local manufacturers had to compete in a market which increasingly preferred imported cloth, since 'all wear European dress and many value fashions',[35] and the low 8 per cent Ottoman tariff afforded little protection. The country market for coarse

---

[23] Milivoje M. Savić, *Zanati i industrija u prisajedinjenim oblastima* (Belgrade, 1914), p. 37.
[24] Dančo Zografski, *Razvitokot na kapitalističeskite elementi vo Makedonija za vreme na turskoto vladeenje* (Skopje, 1967), p. 482–4.
[25] J. Hadži-Vasiljević, 'Grad Bitolj', *Brastvo*, XIV (1911), p. 253.
[26] *SN*, 2 Feb. 1895, p. 118, col. 4 ('Izveštaj Bitoljskog konsulata').
[27] Hadži-Vasiljević, 'Bitolj', p. 253.   [28] GBC Salonica 1888, p. 5.
[29] *SN*, 2 Feb. 1895, p. 118 col. 4
[30] Hr. Semerdzhiev, *Samokov i okolnost'ta mu* (Sofia, 1913), p. 214.
[31] *SN*, 2 Feb. 1895, p. 118 col 4.   [32] AS MNP (T) 1894 I 47. Report of 15 Sept. 1891.
[33] *BOUCA*, 1903 bd. 2 Monastir 1903 A XX 7, pp. 8–9.
[34] Hadži-Vasijlević, 'Bitolj', pp. 252–3.   [35] *Sp.BID*, I, p. 297.

cloths, made up in the home to winter garments, was held by the Bulgarian factories,[36] and between 1900 and 1910 these products entered duty free.[37] First efforts at mechanization took place in 1904, when Seres industrialists asked permission to acquire fulling and carding equipment from the old state factory at Sliven.[38] A *šajak* factory was probably built there as a result, but only in 1906 was a substantial woollen factory set up in Salonica, with spinning equipment, nineteen power-looms and a dyeworks, to produce *šajak* for the Ottoman army.[39] A similar mill with nineteen powerlooms followed at Naousa in 1907, and in 1911 another army cloth factory with thirty powerlooms was built in Salonica.[40]

North of Monastir, there was little textile industry mechanization, although the trade expanded at the cottage industry level. At Tetovo in 1914, about 100,000 arshins of woollen cloth were woven in the households for commerce, and part was exported to Asia Minor. At Veles 200 women produced linen or cotton clothing for the market.[41] The prin-cipal commodity produced with machinery was *gajtan*, whose manufac-ture was established in much the same way as in Serbia. Two small *gajtan* mills functioned at Veles in 1890, with machines brought in by a master from Karlovo in Bulgaria. They continued to use local hand spun wool. Two mechanized textile enterprises were also noted at Tetovo.[42] One was a *gajtan* mill founded by Petar Lekić and Son in 1882.[43] In Skopje another small *gajtan* mill used old Bulgarian braiding *charks* till 1901; these were then replaced with newer machines because they kept breaking down.[44] The *gajtan* mills were still working successfully in 1910,[45] but all were enterprises of trivial size. The producers of Monastir kept their prices low, to discourage local competition.[46] Even though Veles and Skopje were now linked by the main line railway, much of northern Macedonia and the Albanian lands remained 'practically closed to commerce' because of insecurity and lack of roads,[47] and like Bosnia and Monte-negro, removed from the mainstream of Balkan textile development.

[36] *RCADCF,* 1911 (Jan. – June) no. 927, 'Turquie. Mouvement commercial de Salonique en 1909', p. 18.
[37] D. Mishajkov, 'Ocherk na fabrichnata v'lnena industrija v B'lgarija', *Sp.BID,* XV (1911), p. 188.
[38] S. Tabakov, *Istorija na grad Sliven,* III. *Ikonomichen razvoj, naroden bit* (Sofia, 1929), p. 115.
[39] *BOUCA,* 1909 (2) Salonich 1908, pp. 10–11.
[40] 'Tkačka industrija u europskoj Turskoj', *Ekonomist,* II (1913), pp. 189–90.
[41] Savić, *Zanati i industrija,* pp. 30, 35.
[42] Zografski, *Kapitalističkite elementi,* pp. 228–9, 486.
[43] Jaša Grgašević, *Industrija Srbije i Crne gore* (Zagreb, 1924), p. 222.
[44] *BOUCA,* 1902 bd. 2. Üskub XVIII 5, p. 4.   [45] GBC Salonica 1910, p. 29.
[46] *BOUCA,* 1903 bd. 2 (2) Üskub, 1903, A XX 3, p. 5.
[47] GBC Salonica 1897, pp. 12–13.

The textile districts in the southern Rhodope also remained under Ottoman control. Till 1865, their people had been compelled to produce woollens for export, but when the reforms came into effect here, compulsion was removed and (although our source does not relate the two observations) woollen production declined.[48] There was an occupational shift towards building labouring.[49] After 1878, the industry was affected by the loss of the Bosnian market, for which it had hitherto supplied specialty goods, including hosiery.[50] But on balance, the shortage of supplies which followed the liberation of Bulgaria gave the industry in the Rhodope a new lease of life. In 1886, woollen cloth making supported half the population of the textile districts.[51] Wool remained cheap, and in Edirne cost but half the price prevailing in Bulgaria.[52] So the industry concentrated on producing and tailoring material intensive *aba*, which was being abandoned in favour of the lighter *šajak* in Bulgaria. Production of *aba* ran in 1898 at 210,000 metres, with 58,000 metres of *šajak*,[53] and between 1902 and 1905 output was estimated repeatedly as 250,000 metres.[54] Perhaps because of the 'unusual cheapness of manual labour' the manufacture remained unmechanized.[55] Consequently it had difficulty in competing with Bulgarian production from Sliven, mostly of factory cloth[56] which was tricked out to pass as handloom work.[57]

After 1878 machine cotton spinning continued to expand. Mills were established at Salonica, Edhessa, Veroia and Naousa, drawing on locally raised cotton from the area round Seres. As in Serbia and Bulgaria, the industry developed to supply the handloom weavers, both subsistence producers and commercial. Demand for cotton yarn was rising, because, as its price fell, it displaced woollen and linen warps in domestic mixed cloth weaving. We noted earlier the importance of the peasant market for cotton yarn in Bulgaria and Serbia. Similarly, demand for yarn for handloom cotton weaving in the Ottoman lands nearly doubled between 1880 and 1910.[58]

The Macedonian spinning mills enjoyed competitive advantage over British imports in coarse count yarn through their advantageous access to

[48] S. N. Shishkov, *Ustovo. Ah Chelebijski okr'g* (Plovdiv, 1885), p. 42.
[49] Konstantin Kanev, *Minaloto na selo Momchilovtsi, Smoljansko. Prinos k'm istorijata na srednite Rodopi* (Sofia, 1975), p. 523.   [50] Hadži-Vasiljević, *Skoplje*, p. 120.
[51] S. N. Shishkov, *Zhivot't na B'lgarite v Srednja Rodopa* (Plovdiv, 1886), pp. 25–6.
[52] *Doklad . . . na plovdivskata t'rgovsko-industrialna kamara*, p. 77.
[53] *BOUCA*, 1900 bd. 2 Adrianopel 1900, A XX 5.6, pp. 5–6.
[54] *BOUCA*, 1905 bd. 2 (2) Adrianopel 1905 A XX 2, p. 6.
[55] *BOUCA*, Adrianopel 1900, p. 6.
[56] *BOUCA*, 1903, bd. 2 (2) Adrianopel 1903, A XX 1, p. 6.
[57] AN F12 7280. Industrie en Roumélie orientale, 13 Feb. 1908.
[58] Sevket Pamuk, 'The Decline and Resistance of Ottoman Cotton Textiles 1820–1913', *Explorations in Economic History,* XXIII (1986), p. 210.

cheap raw materials and labour. As this perfectly matched the growing demand of the rural market, they delivered most of their output to the peasant handlooms.[59] There was little incentive for these spinning mills to integrate into weaving. However, the growth of peasant cotton weaving created a market for dyed cotton yarn, encouraging the formation of yarn dyeworks to process the output of the mills.[60]

The growth of cotton spinning benefited from the strong local commercial and proto-industrial background, if only for the entrepreneurial talents it fostered. All the mills were founded by locally based Greek and Jewish partnerships, with minimal capital investments. The industry had to fight for survival. The home market was only lightly protected, and the mills had anyway to export much of their output to Bulgaria and Serbia. The industry came under pressure from 1890, when mills such as that at Yeni Kule (Constantinople) opened to spin the coarsest counts (4–8), in which they drove Salonica producers from the Bulgarian market.[61] Between 1901 and 1906, one of the Salonica mills, whose machinery had become obsolete, was closed down in the face of competition from Anatolia,[62] but as Table 11.1 shows, the industry as a whole continued to expand, probably by moving slightly up-market, spinning yarn of counts 8–14, in which imports from Britain were not overwhelmingly competitive.

Early development focused on Salonica. Here wages were higher than in the interior, but capital and enterprise were relatively abundant. Two largish cotton mills were built in 1878 and 1884. Their founders brought machinery from Accrington and employed competent British managers.[63] Initially they made returns of 20–25 per cent on capital,[64] though these were subsequently squeezed. By keeping its technology up to date,[65] the leading mill was able to prosper when easier market conditions returned after 1905, but cost pressures diverted the industry towards the inland industrial towns, where labour was cheap[66] and lower cost machines could be applied to water power. The inland mills probably acquired their machinery second hand to minimize capital costs, and the formula worked. As shown in Table 11.1, the output of the Salonica mills declined between 1891 and 1907 from 3 million to 1.5 million lbs, while that of the inland mills rose from 800,000 to 2.9 million lbs.

By 1912, Salonica and environs had become the cotton spinning focus

[59] GBC Salonica 1892, p. 22.
[60] *BOUCA*, 1903 bd. 2 (2) Salonich 1903, p. 17; 1904 bd. 2 (2) Salonich 1904, p. 8.
[61] GBC Bulgaria 1890, p. 20.
[62] *BOUCA*, 1901 bd. 2 Salonich 1901 A XIX 2, p. 18; 1902 bd. 2 (2) Salonich A XVIII 2, p. 17; GBC Salonica 1906, p. 3.   [63] GBC Salonica 1892, p. 21.
[64] GBC Salonica 1888, p. 9.   [65] *BOUCA*, 1902 Salonich 1902 p. 17.   [66] Ibid.

Table 11.1 *Machine cotton spinning in Hellenic Macedonia 1876–1912*

Year	Salonica			Provinces			Total			Source, page
	Factories	Spindles	Output (m lbs)	Factories	Spindles	Output (m lbs)	Factories	Spindles	Output (m lbs)	
1876	–	–	–	(1)	1,500	n.d.	(1)	1,500	n.d.	(1,482)
1879	(1)	12,000	-0.7	(1)	1,500	n.d.	(2)	13,500	n.d.	(1,482)
1881	(1)	7,952	n.d.	(1)	1,500	n.d.	(2)	9,452	n.d.	(2)
1884	(2)	n.d.	-1.2	(1)	n.d.	-0.2	(3)	n.d.	-1.4	(3)
1886	(2)	n.d.	-2.2	(1)	n.d.	n.d	(3)	n.d.	n.d.	(4, 335)
1891	(2)	18,800	-3.0	(2)	4,200	-0.8	(4)	23,000	-3.8	(5–6)
1903	(1)	n.d.	-1.6					n.d.	n.d.	(7)
1906	(1)	n.d.	-1.5	(5)	n.d.	-2.8	(6)	42,900	-6.4	(1,491–2)
								n.d.	-4.3	(8)
1907	(1)	n.d.	-1.5	(6)	n.d.	-2.9	(7)	46,220	-5.3	(1,492–3)
								n.d.	-4.4	(9)
1908	(2)	18,000	n.d.	(7)	33,000		(9)	51,000	6.5	(10)
1909	(3)	20,200	n.d.	(7)	40,000		(10)	60,200	-8.0(b)	(11)
1910	(3)	n.d.	n.d.	(7)	44,200	-6.4(c)	(10)	n.d.	n.d.	(12,) (7)
1912	(3)	22,800	n.d.	(7)	47,200		(10)	70,000	-5.1	(1,495)

Notes:

a at Veroia, Naousa and Edhessa

b given as 'capacity' rather than 'output'

c given in original as 2.9 million kilos possibly in error for lbs

Sources:

1 Zografski, *Kapitalističeskie elementi*.

2, 3 GBC Salonica 1881 p. 97; 1884 pp. 4, 7.

4 'Salonichs wirtschaftliche Lage', *Handelsmuseum*, II (1887, July–Dec.).

5 Spindlage and provincial output from: GBC Salonica 1892, p. 21.

6 Salonica output from *Rapports Consulaire Français*, 1892 Nr. 22 Turquie. Importance commerciale de Salonique, p. 67.

7,8,9,10,11: GBC Salonica 1903, p. 5; 1906, p. 3; 1907, p. 5; 1908, p. 7; 1909, p. 5.

12. *BOUCA*, 1911, bd. 3, Salonich. Handelsbericht 1910.

of the Ottoman Empire. With a workforce of 1,900 in the provincial mills in 1910,[67] and of about 2,800 including the mills of Salonica, the industry probably exceeded the entire Bulgarian woollen industry in size. It accounted for nearly half of the cotton spinning capacity of the Ottoman Empire, which was left in 1914 with 82,000 spindles (68,500 active) and a labour force of 3,000.[68] By annexing the territory, Greece nearly doubled its own cotton spinning capacity of 73,898 spindles, of which 74 per cent had been concentrated in Piraeus, with minor mills in Livadia and Syros island.[69]

The rise of cotton spinning in Hellenic Macedonia probably had a demonstration effect, encouraging the establishment of a widening range of textile enterprises, including the woollen and hosiery mills referred to above. Additionally, a jute weavery was set up at Salonica in 1905,[70] followed by a factory for cotton wadding in 1908,[71] while in 1911 a rope-works was opened at Edhessa.[72] If we were to take into account industrial developments in olive oil crushing, soapmaking, tobacco and food processing then, by the Balkan wars, Salonica and its hinterland had become a diversified industrial complex, a striking example of proto-industrial transition into what was probably the strongest industrial concentration in the Balkans apart from that of Athens.[73]

The spread of handloom weaving which sustained the market for coarse cotton yarn was not confined to the subsistence sector. The local market for coarse cotton cloth sustained a commercial domestic industry in the teeth of import competition. In Salonica vilayet, there were 350 weaving workshops in the town of Giannitsa,[74] and more in the villages round Zihni (district of Halkis).[75] By 1908, however, some of the spinning mills added weaving sheds for *cabots*, plain white cotton cloth.[76]

Technical obsolescence and the 1905–1914 boom in Ottoman Europe

Competing on comparative advantage endowed by a combination of low wages, low equipment costs and cheap fibres, the textile industries in

[67] Zografski, *Kapitalističkite elementi*, p. 494.
[68] Charles Issawi, *The Economic History of Turkey, 1800–1914* (Chicago, 1980), p. 310.
[69] GBC Greece 1913, p. 12.   [70] *BOUCA*, 1905 bd. 2 (2) Salonich A XX 6, p. 15.
[71] *BOUCA*, 1909 bd. 2. Salonich. Handelsbericht 1908, p. 11.
[72] 'Fabrična industrija u europskoj Turskoj', *Ekonomist*, II (1913), p. 164.
[73] E.-J. Tsouderos, *Le relèvement économique de la Grèce* (Paris, 1919), pp. 173–5.
[74] *BOUCA*, 1910 bd. 2 Salonich. Handelsbericht 1909, p. 8.
[75] Zografski, *Kapitalističkite elementi*, p. 231.
[76] *BOUCA*, 1909 bd. 2 Salonich. Handelsbericht 1908, p. 10.

Ottoman Europe tended to let their technology stagnate. This was dangerous. Relatively low wages might justify the initial adoption of obsolescent machines, but the technology gap could not be allowed to widen. If labour and raw material costs were to rise, the textile firms would be perilously exposed to competition. This happened in Macedonia and Thrace in the last decade before World War I.

Wages started to rise in about 1905–6, as boom conditions developed in the economy.[77] Strong inflationary pressures were generated. The matter is in dispute as to whether this inflation was cost-driven, and as to its effects on real (as opposed to money) wages. Quataert has argued that Ottoman money wage rates lagged inflation and that real wages were consequently depressed,[78] but a collection of wage and price data suggests the contrary.[79] Whatever the case in Anatolia, Salonica experienced strong and persistent wage-pushed inflation. By 1908, wages there, 'though still lower than the European', had risen 60 per cent since 1905,[80] partly as a result of a strike wave, in which employees usually succeeded in winning shorter hours and higher pay.[81] Underpinning the success of strike action was a shortage of labour throughout the economy; sharply rising wage rates were being paid in estate agriculture, despite which farmers were left short handed.[82] Rising emigration contributed, but one industrialist argued that labour was becoming scarce because of the expansion of tobacco growing and processing. 'Where tobacco is processed, there cannot exist a single other factory enterprise.'[83]

Till about 1907, demand stimuli favoured industrial expansion but, from then onward, rising costs began to force closures in the weaker sectors of the textile industries in Ottoman Europe. Consular reporting on the long-established domestic textile industries in the Rhodope ceases to be informative after 1906, other than to acknowledge its existence, and it is to be inferred that it was in decline. The strength of the labour market, particularly in the hill districts of the textile region, and a claimed trebling of wage rates in Edirne vilayet between 1906 and 1911 must have contributed, particularly as the increased cost of living only partially accounted for this rise.[84] The unmechanized woollen industry of Kruševo

[77] BOUCA, 1905 Monastir, p. 5; 1906 Monastir, pp. 6–7.
[78] Donald Quataert, 'The Economic Climate of the "Young Turk Revolution" in 1908', Journal of Modern History, LI (1979), Order no. IJ-00049, pp. D1147–61.
[79] Charles Issawi, 'Wages in Turkey, 1850–1914', in Social and Economic History of Turkey 1071–1920, ed. O. Okyar and Inalcik (Ankara, 1980), pp. 263–70.
[80] BOUCA, 1909 bd. 2, Salonich. Handelsbericht 1908, p. 10.
[81] GBC Salonica 1908, p. 5.
[82] RCADCF, 1908 Jan.–June, no. 686. Turquie. Mouvement commercial du Vilayet de Kossovo pendant l'année 1906, pp. 3–4.   [83] Ekonomist, II (1913), pp. 161–4.
[84] GBC Edirne 1911, pp. 6, 13.

went into steep decline.[85] Soon the domestic industries of Macedonia were 'vegetating' and thought likely to disappear.[86] It was therefore not surprising that the Monastir woollen mills invaded the market of the struggling household industries.[87]

However, mechanization alone was insufficient. In 1907 both of the larger cloth factories near Monastir were obliged to close,[88] and only one subsequently reopened.[89] It was reported of these mill closures that 'the reduction in the local production of wool and the increased difficulty in finding workers . . . have also contributed to this result'.[90] In 1910 the strike movement continued, with employers 'forced in most cases to agree unreservedly to the workers' demands'.[91] The factory building boom faltered because of labour shortages. Wages, it was claimed were 'as high as in Europe' despite the minimal productivity of many industries.[92] The next year, it was again claimed that the escalation of wages threatened the profitability of handicraft industry in inland Macedonia.[93]

Along with rising wage costs and labour militancy, 'soaring' cotton prices forced the closure of a recently built cotton wadding factory in Salonica, and drove one of the spinning mills at Veroia into bankruptcy. The advantage of a cheap local cotton supply diminished after 1900. Again the tobacco boom was the cause of difficulty, because it was a much more profitable crop, and cotton production dropped precipitously to make way for it. So cotton had increasingly to be brought in at high cost from Anatolia.[94] The spinning mills consequently experienced 'unsatisfactory' business,[95] and yarn output fell from 8 million lbs in 1909 to 5.1 million in 1912 (Table 11.1).

Following the redrawing of the political map in the wake of the Balkan Wars of 1912–13, the former Ottoman provinces experienced a sharp financial adjustment crisis, whose effects were felt both in agriculture and in industry.[96] In the newly liberated southern provinces of Serbia, there was a re-run of the agricultural and industrial collapse which had happened in Bulgaria after the liberation of 1878. Once more, Muslim land was thrown cheaply onto the market, or simply abandoned. The burden of maintaining a trade surplus to provide for remittances to

---

[85] M. M. Savić, *Zanati i industrija*, p. 179.
[86] *RCADCF,* 1910 July–Dec., no. 919. Turquie. Le Vilayet de Kossovo . . . en 1909, p. 4.
[87] *BOUCA,* 1909 Üskub p. 78; 1907 (3) Monastir. pp. 6–7.
[88] GBC Macedonia 1907, p. 5.   [89] 'Tkačka industrija', p. 190.
[90] GBC Macedonia 1907, p. 5.   [91] GBC Salonica 1910, pp. 6–7.
[92] *BOUCA,* 1911 bd. 3, Salonich. Handelsbericht 1910, p. 6.
[93] *BOUCA,* 1912 bd. 2, Üskub. Handelsbericht 1911, p. 14.
[94] 'Fabrična industrija', p. 163; *BOUCA,* 1906 bd. 5 Salonich 1906 A XX 13, p. 38.
[95] *BOUCA,* 1912 bd. 2, Salonich. Handelsbericht 1911, pp. 5–7.
[96] Gligor Todorovski. *Makedonija po rasparčuvaneto 1912/13–1915* (Skopje , 1995), pp. 103 ff.

Constantinople[97] was ended, causing prices to rise towards those in Serbia proper.

Maize cultivation, mainly in Hellenic Macedonia, was severely cut back, from around 137,000 hectares pre-war to 81,400 hectares in 1923. For northern Macedonia, the cutback was ascribed to its relative inefficiency and high cost compared with maize produced in Serbia.[98] For rice, of which some 7,000 tonnes were cultivated in northern Macedonia before the Balkan wars, output declined to 6,000 tonnes in 1913–15 and to 1,400 tonnes in 1927. The shrinkage was ascribed to increased wages and a shortage of labour.[99] Tobacco output of Skopje province in 1913 shrank to 1.7 million kg.[100] The opium harvest shrank from 250 tonnes to 150/180 tonnes in 1913–14, allegedly because of trade interference with its export through Salonica in the interest of Greek producers.[101] The reduction in activity also extended to sheep raising. Between 1907 and 1921/2 the flock diminished by 23 per cent, with reductions in the production of milk and wool.[102]

In manufacturing the crisis was especially severe. The surviving cloth mill near Monastir shed three-quarters of its labour force.[103] The difficulties of the textile industries of northern Macedonia would be easy to comprehend were there evidence of a postwar trade depression. But there was none. Annexation of the territory was welcomed by the Belgrade mills, for the excellent protected market it gave them. Such was the demand for *gajtan* that prices rose by 25 per cent, and the firms found it difficult to meet the orders of their clientele.[104] The Ječmenica mill welcomed the 'much better prospects for the penetration of our factory products' which had been created by the 'widening of the frontier', and responded by launching an expansion programme.[105] The struggling Macedonian mills were no match for their new competitors, who dismissed them as 'very primitive'.[106] In 1914 the Diovo, Magarevo and Tetovo woollen enterprises were reportedly still in a weak condition, because they could not withstand the competition of the Belgrade and Leskovac factories, and because of their loss of low-tariff yarn imports from Britain.[107] It seems clear that the textile industries of northern Macedonia had been dangerously dependent on the availability of low cost inputs, both of materials

[97] Iaranoff, *Macédoine*, p. 117.   [98] Ibid., p. 59.   [99] Ibid., p. 62.

[100] Hadži-Vasiljević, *Skoplje*, p. 215, n. 1.   [101] Iaranoff, *Macédoine*, p. 72.

[102] Ibid., p. 113.   [103] Savić, *Zanati i industrija*, pp. 205, 293.

[104] IAB. Minute book of Kosta Ilić sinovi a.d. for 14 Feb. 1914; AS MNP (T), No. 2535, unfasciculated. Ilić–MNP, 14 Feb. 1914, of 17 Feb. 1914.

[105] AS MNP (T) Unfasciculated no. 6424 of 1914. Izveštaj upravnog odbora Milana Ječmenice i Komp. 27 Apr. 1914.

[106] Trgovačka Komora za Kr. Srbiju, *Izveštaj za 1912 i 1913 godinu* (Belgrade, 1914), p. 89.

[107] Savić, *Zanati i industrija*, p. 272.

and labour, to compensate their relatively backward technology; when they lost this advantage they were unable to compete against the relatively mature textile industries of Serbia.

It is unclear whether similar problems were encountered in manufacturing in the areas annexed to Greece and Bulgaria. In 1913, Bulgaria's new territories in Macedonia and Thrace were much depopulated, and producing far below their potential.[108] In Greece, it became an open question as to whether the output of so many new cotton mills could be supported; doubt was expressed as to whether the Macedonian mills could compete with those of Livadia.[109]

The post-1878 experience of Ottoman rule in Macedonia and Thrace does not suggest that Ottoman institutions acted as an economically retarding force. The autocracy of Abdulhamit between 1878 and 1908 remained committed to the principles of the Tanzimat, and pushed through large infrastructure programmes. It was however unable to prevent the descent of Macedonia into anarchy from about 1900, or to restore stability after suppressing the Ilinden uprising of 1903. Even so, the economic effects of disorder were less serious than appeared, and Macedonia, partly thanks to tobacco, was in a prosperous condition on the eve of the overthrow of Turkish rule in 1912. This event probably retarded its further development, in a manner analogous to the effects of 'liberation' on Bulgaria after 1878.

[108] GBC Bulgaria 1913, pp. 7–8.   [109] *RC*, 165 (1913), pp. 465, 470.

12 Summary and conclusions

In 1790 all five territories whose subsequent experience is traced in our text (Bulgaria, Serbia, Bosnia, Macedonia and Montenegro) were (nominally) under Ottoman rule. Economic life was rooted in subsistence farming, and the area was thinly populated (12.5 persons per square kilometre). The temporary fragmentation of the Ottoman Balkans into a shifting mozaic of warlord statelets created new sets of institutions which conditioned the subsequent path of economic evolution.

In Bulgaria and Macedonia, rural insecurity caused peasants to flee into the uplands, to secure a livelihood from scratch cultivation and transhumant stockraising. These migrations to the hills, and subsequent population growth within them, created concentrations of non-agricultural labour in an otherwise thinly settled territory. Even during the most anarchic period, the hill towns acted as small centres of industry.

During the period of anarchy, the Ottomans lost control of Serbia and southern Greece, but, by the 1830s, central government had been reimposed over most of Bulgaria and Macedonia. Feudal land rights were abolished in 1832–4, and much of the lowland farmland was now held as latifundia (*chifliks*). During the *Tanzimat* era, servile tenures were suppressed, and Christians were enabled to buy land. The system exacted perhaps 20–30 per cent of the produce of the tenant cultivator, but burdens became more predictable than in the past.

In Bosnia the Muslim *begs* ruled till 1851 with little reference to Constantinople. After the abolition of *spahiluk*, landowners tended to lease their arable land on sharecropping terms. The low density of population resulted in a shortage of cultivators, so control over servile labour rather than the land was the key to the economic power of the *begs*. Centralized rule began in 1851 and in 1859 a major agrarian reform, the *Safer* law, was implemented. This imposed a regime of administered sharecropping on all *čitluks*. The *Safer* law imposed a high rate of crop surrender on the sharecropper, but it weakened landlord control. This undermined the incentive either of landlord or of tenant to intensify cultivation.

In Bulgaria, plains agriculture languished in the early nineteenth century, partly because of insecurity, and partly because of grain export prohibition. These constraints were removed. The Porte gradually suppressed banditry, reducing internal transactions costs. The Balta-Liman trade treaty (1838) opened international access to Ottoman grain and raw silk. Together these stimuli gave rise to an upswing in Ottoman external and internal commerce, and by the late 1840s, the cropped area was expanding rapidly.

Because of the thinness of lowland settlement, agriculture in Bulgaria in the mid-nineteenth century employed extensive methods of cultivation but yields to seed were surprisingly high, and techniques were improving. Most stockraising was organized on large-scale transhumant lines. Commercial transhumance provided cheap wool for local manufacturing. Bulgarian farm output expanded, probably up to 1877.

In Bosnia, society remained heavily patriarchal in its *mores*. Nevertheless, the territory also experienced strong commercial expansion after mid-century. Although it remained highly dependent on stockraising, the export boom was led by cultivated crops. Comparative figures indicate that farming in Bosnia was less productive than in Bulgaria, possibly because of the inefficiency of the new agrarian code.

Expansion in Ottoman commerce from the 1840s hit the old established guild-ridden city industries, but reintegration into a growing domestic market stimulated the development of pre-modern rural manufacturing in the overpopulated uplands of central Bulgaria and in Hellenic Macedonia. As security improved, the hill villages lost their former refuge function and a slow downward migration from the hills took place, but the expansion of *chiflik* agriculture in the lowlands contained the growing population of the hill settlements, which became increasingly dependent on manufacturing.

The most active manufacturing area was the Sredna Gora, which drew on a longstanding tradition of manufacturing and sheep trading to expand rapidly in population and prosperity. At Koprivshtitsa, sheep trading was combined with textile work and tailoring, and at Trjavna – the 'Bulgarian Nuremberg' – textile making and ikon painting were seasonally alternated with the building trade and itinerant commerce. During the late Bulgarian 'renaissance' textiles, the leading manufacture, co-existed with a mass of other trades.

In textiles, early impetus was given in cotton weaving and block printing and in Hellenic Macedonia cotton piece goods remained the principal textile product. In Bulgaria, however, cotton manufacturing was displaced by the woollen trades. Woollens manufactures employed about 73,000 persons. The women span and wove, the men plaited *gajtan* and sewed and marketed piece goods. Though still at the domestic stage, these manufactures benefited from technical advances. Bulgarian textiles found outlets throughout the Ottoman Empire and were competitive with imports. Sales expanded at least till the 1860s and probably into the mid-1870s. The early textile factories were set up to execute state orders, but were not competitive. Only in the 1870s was there a free market shift into factory production, as rising wages impelled a degree of mechanization.

No real parallel developed in Bosnia to the proto-industrial economy of Bulgaria and southern Macedonia, possibly because of the absence of Christian refuge villages in the mountains, and because cultural influences inhibited proto-industrial development. Industry was mainly of the urban guild type. Natural resources favoured heavy industry but Bosnia's resources remained grossly underexploited.

The lands under direct Ottoman control were significantly urbanized. Bosnia in 1864 was 17.7 per cent urban, northern Bulgaria 15–18 per cent. The relatively high urbanization of Ottoman controlled Europe reflected an agrarian regime in which much land was controlled by non-cultivating rent receivers. The large urban sector in the Ottoman lands and the development both of commercial agriculture and (in Bulgaria) the manufacture of textiles contrasted with conditions in pre-1878 Serbia and Montenegro. After its liberation (1815) Serbia was given over to universal peasant landownership and the absence of rent demands confined commerce to animals driven on the hoof. The now redundant urban sector all but melted away. In 1834, urban population was a mere 4 per cent of the total. Montenegro, with similar institutions, was completely rural.

Like the rest of the Balkans, Serbia was sparsely populated. The cultivated lands (15 per cent of surface area in 1867) were set in a milieu of fertile open range waste, on which the peasants held their animals. Much of the lowland waste was virgin forest. Livestock exports, especially pigs to Austria, provided most of the cash income. Low population pressure had provided a crude abundance, but this was not maintained. Between 1834 and 1867, a decline in livestock numbers struck at the very basis of Serbia's well-being. The diminution of the livestock economy was linked with lowland deforestation. This especially affected pig-raising, because acorns and beech-mast provided the cheapest source of pig fodder needed to bring the animals to export condition.

Deforestation was unchecked because private property rights in unploughed land never received secure recognition. Heavy demands on timber were made for fencing the arable, while forest clearance enabled cultivation continually to shift. Lowland woods only survived at all because stockraisers enclosed fragments of them for grazing. The need to substitute maize feeding for forest grazing rendered the trade decreasingly profitable and the breeding stock fell persistently. Export volume was only maintained by the sacrifice of subsistence consumption. A boost was given to the trade in fattened pigs when the Hungarian Staatsbahn railway reached the Danube in 1856. This made it practicable to deliver pigs to the market in fattened condition but its usefulness was restricted by lack of cheap maize for fattening in Serbia.

To expand cash income other than at the expense of subsistence, Serbia needed to export cultivated produce. As late as 1863, however, peasants brought no more land under cultivation than they needed for subsistence. Despite the still large extent of waste, the average holding had only 3 hectares under arable crops.

The unproductiveness of Serbian farming was attributed by some contempories to the patriarchal culture of idleness. However, effort at the margin was discouraged by inadequacy of market access. The disincentives to self-improvement are evident from the extreme income equality which ruled in the Serbian villages. Despite local equality, the lowlands were relatively affluent, because they could still support themselves by the sale of livestock. However, the hill areas lacked the resources to hold animals and sent grain to the market. This created a perverse flow of grain from upland to lowland. Tax pressures aggravated regional disparities.

After about 1863, the tempo of marketization speeded up as rising Hungarian produce purchases in Serbia dragged Serbian produce prices upward. Yet grain marketing was still restricted by difficulties in securing outlets. In central and western Serbia, grain exports were augmented by the export of prunes and plum jam, and, transiently, silkworm eggs. All these trades were implanted by immigrant entrepreneurs or by foreign merchants. Native enterprise remained passive. During the boom, trade incentives were strengthened by an increasing inflow of imported goods, which improved the terms of trade for farmers. However, access to imports was rendered artificially difficult by the authorities.

In Serbia, upland refuge communities dissolved after the liberation, and no textile trades developed akin to those in Bulgaria. There was little interchange of manufactures between towns and no basis for the spontaneous development of industry.

Like Serbia, Montenegro was cultivated by peasant smallholders, but the amount of arable available provided on average 2.15 hectares per family holding in 1868, without Serbia's margin for expansion. Transhumant stockraising, as in Bosnia, was the key income generator, but scarcity of winter fodder imposed intricate grazing patterns designed to wrest the maximum possible from the pasture reserves. Population pressure forced peasants in winter into downward migration with animals beyond the borders of the Montenegrin state. Consumption of farinaceous food and potatoes was extremely sparing, though compensated by a high intake of milk products. Montenegro was poverty stricken even by Balkan standards, and famine was commonplace.

In this ultra-patriarchal society men were shepherd-warriors, and nothing else. Crop tending was regarded as women's work and manual labour and trade as demeaning. There was no commercial cottage industry. The perennial lack of exchange income elevated banditry to an organized business activity. The inherent unviability of economic life gave rise to increasing external migration, in particular to Serbia, and this evolved into permanent resettlement. Temporary labour migration also developed, as gangs of Montenegrins were sent out to Constantinople to earn money to remit home.

Unintentionally, the Ottoman system during the reform period provided an environment in which an enterprise economy could develop in Bulgaria and southern Macedonia. The 'renaissance' was replicated neither in Bosnia nor in Serbia. Associated as it was with a dynamic enterprise culture, it remained to be seen whether this dynamism would be sustained when Ottoman political and agrarian institutions were shed, as they would be in 1878.

The Balkans 1878–1914

Economic progress in the Ottoman Balkans before 1878 was mainly a by-product of changes in Ottoman institutions and international trade expansion. Peasant Serbia had changed structurally, but only under the negative pressures of population growth and environmental depletion. Both these pressures still operated after 1878, in Bulgaria as well as in Serbia, as the Balkan states continued to grow rapidly in population. Over the long period 1790–1910, Balkan population grew cumulatively at 1.0 per cent per annum, to reach a density by 1910 of 40.1 to the square kilometre, a density which, elsewhere in Europe, was accommodated by a marked shift of resources out of the farming sector. To achieve economic development therefore a structural revolution was going to be needed.

It was unlikely that any such economic revolution would be forthcoming. After Bulgaria was 'liberated' both the Principality and Eastern Rumelia retrogressed. The 'liberation' was to 'serbianize' the Bulgarian economy because *chifliks* were seized by Bulgarian peasants, or sold off to them at distress prices, and under the new regime, rural tax burdens fell. The depression in primary product prices in the 1880s was particularly deleterious to the Balkan economies. Serbia's performance was also weak as was that of the Ottoman Empire.[1] So institutional upheaval was not the only reason for Bulgaria's post-liberation economic collapse. However, the

[1] Sevket Pamuk, 'The Ottoman Empire in the 'Great Depression' of 1873–1896', *JEcH*, XLIV (1984), pp. 107–18.

economy of the Ottoman Empire was to grow from about 1890 till 1913 at a respectable rate.[2] As no such growth occurred in the Balkan states, it is likely that 'serbianization' destroyed Bulgaria's longer run growth dynamic.

Prior to 1878, much of the tithe and rent revenue of Bulgaria had been remitted to Constantinople. As a result the provinces had run large balance of trade surpluses, causing domestic prices to settle at low levels. The diminution of transfers outside the territory released liquidity into the internal economy inflating commodity prices, though the exchange rate remained stable. The export trade dwindled and orientated more than hitherto to cereals. However, transactions costs remained high, so peasant gains were taken out partly in subsistence consumption and partly in a reduction of work effort. The easy availability of land caused a diminution of the supply of labour to the remaining estates, and much land fell out of cultivation.

Crop yields fell heavily from pre-liberation levels. The big commercial flocks disappeared, partly because of woodland destruction, and the ploughing up of lowland pastures. Livestock also regressed qualitatively. Consequently, farm production declined severely, and traded production still more. Muslim emigration also contributed to qualitative deterioration, causing damage to rice growing, sericulture and tobacco growing. Cereal yields and farm output per capita revived in the early 1890s, but the recovery was not maintained, and Bulgarian farm productivity failed right up to the late 1920s to recover to levels attained in the 1860s and early 1870s.

Although Serbia experienced no analogous political upheaval, its output per capita in farming fell in the longer run even more seriously, by 27.5 per cent between the early 1870s and 1910/12, compared with Bulgaria, 14.3 per cent. In Serbia, decline was attended by a pronounced shift in the late 1880s from pastoralism towards the extension of arable. The continued decline of pig raising acted negatively on performance. Export difficulties aggravated a supply side decline caused by the continued erosion of woodland, and the pre-emption of pasture to support the draft needs of the arable.

In Bosnia, progress in farming was constrained by the continued application of the 1859 *Safer* Law. The sharecropper holdings were too large to be cultivated intensively, and returns to landlords fell. Peasants diverted their efforts into lightly taxed animal husbandry. Output both of crops and livestock recovered or expanded rapidly during the 1880s from the low levels of the first post-occupation years, then the familiar Balkan

---

[2] Osman Okyar, 'A New Look at the Problem of Economic Growth in the Ottoman Empire (1800–1914)', *JEEcH*, 16 (1987), pp. 44–6; Caglar Keyder, 'Ottoman Economy and Finances, 1881–1918', *The Social and Economic History of Turkey 1071–1920*, ed. O. Okyar and H. Inalcik (Ankara, 1980), p. 324.

pattern asserted itself, for in the 1890s output per cultivator stabilized then slowly declined. In part this was because there was little marginal land available for exploitation, in part because of forestry laws and Hungarian interference with the Bosnian livestock export.

In Montenegro, Malthusian pressures on agricultural resources became even more acute than in Bosnia. Relative to farm population farm output fell persistently. A crisis developed in transhumant stockraising through lack of access to lowland pastures. Export volumes were only maintained by the sacrifice of subsistence consumption.

In all four territories, farming productivity peaked in the 1880s (in Serbia and Montenegro) or early 1890s (in Bulgaria and Bosnia). From then until World War I, or beyond, all experienced further retrogression. Their long-run performance in farming is displayed in Figure 12(i) and in Table 12.1, which records the data.

Given the rising density of Balkan population and the erosion of extensive pastoralism, intensification in field agriculture offered the only means of raising or even of maintaining farm productivity. In Bulgaria, farmers were able to break in new arable in step with the growth of population but areal yields remained flat. A severe post-1905 fall in livestock holdings caused farm production per capita to stagnate at below 1890s levels. The pressure of settlement in Serbia was higher, and a shortage of potential arable was felt by about 1893. Eventually farmers adopted more intensive systems, and yields started rising after 1900. The raising of sugar-beet, an intensive crop, affirms the contrast. Serbian peasants, though less well remunerated than Bulgarian peasants for beet, were more responsive to the opportunity it offered. However, crop intensification in Serbia was offset by resumed downward pressure on the livestock economy. The intensity of land use also rose in Bosnia, but again more slowly than the farm population.

Montenegro was incapable of maintaining its already inadequate volume of per capita farm output and of feeding its people. Their only exit lay in mass *Gastarbeiter* emigration. External labour migration, after 1900, of young males to the USA, provided a backflow of remittances, which animated urban commerce.

The poor performance of Balkan agricultures invited examination of retardive supply side influences which were common to all of them. The most obvious was the universality of peasant farming, and its adherence to a subsistence base. In Serbia, the monetization of farm produce continued to be checked by official action to constrict peasant access to incentive goods. Supply side adaptation, despite the building of railways, was further retarded by high transactions costs. Into these economies the techniques for rationalizing farming technique were slow to filter.

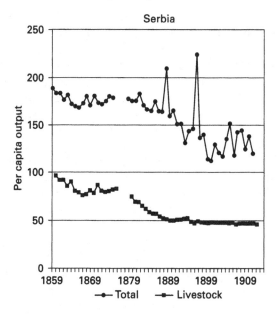

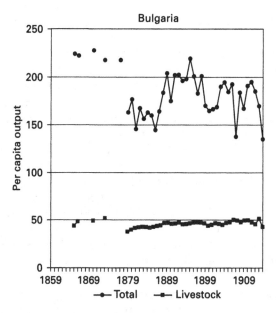

Figure 12.1 Per capita output of Balkan farm populations
in 1910 francs

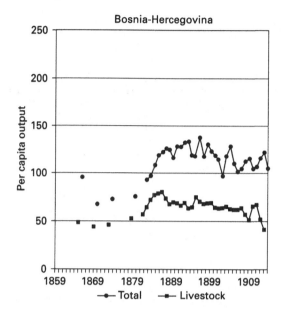

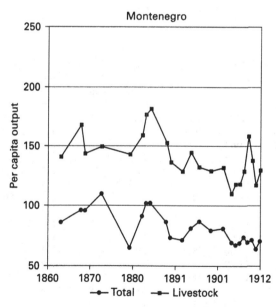

Table 12.1 *Data for Figure 12(i) Per capita output of Balkan farm populations in 1910 francs.*

Year	All farm products				Livestock products			
	Serbia	Bulgaria	Bosnia	Montenegro	Serbia	Bulgaria	Bosnia	Montenegro
1859	188.6	–	–	–	96.0	–	–	–
1860	183.9	–	–	–	91.4	–	–	–
1861	183.5	–	–	–	91.2	–	–	–
1862	176.2	–	–	–	84.6	–	–	–
1863	181.7	–	–	140.8	89.9	–	–	86.4
1864	172.4	–	–	–	80.4	–	–	–
1865	170.3	223.4	95.2	–	78.9	43.1	48.0	–
1866	168.7	221.4	–	–	76.3	47.7	–	–
1867	173.2	–	–	–	77.3	–	–	–
1868	180.6	–	–	167.6	80.7	–	–	96.1
1869	170.2	–	67.5	143.4	78.3	–	43.8	95.5
1870	180.8	227.7	–	–	86.1	49.3	–	–
1871	173.7	–	–	–	80.2	–	–	–
1872	172.3	–	–	–	79.5	–	–	–
1873	175.3	217.1	72.6	150.1	80.3	51.1	45.3	110.3
1874	180.7	–	–	–	81.7	–	–	–
1875	179.0	–	–	–	82.4	–	–	–
1876	–	–	–	–	–	–	–	–
1877	–	217.1	–	–	–	–	–	–
1878	–	–	–	–	–	–	–	–
1879	178.2	163.0	75.6	–	75.1	37.5	52.4	–
1880	176.2	176.6	–	143.1	69.5	39.9	–	64.6
1881	176.2	146.3	–	–	69.1	41.5	–	–
1882	183.6	167.9	93.4	–	65.3	42.2	56.6	–
1883	171.5	156.8	97.2	159.2	62.3	42.9	64.2	91.0
1884	167.4	162.8	108.5	176.9	58.9	42.6	71.6	102.4
1885	165.5	160.2	119.2	181.6	57.3	42.2	76.9	102.5
1886	175.4	144.4	122.5	–	56.9	42.3	78.7	–
1887	165.0	164.3	126.9	–	54.1	43.3	80.2	–
1888	164.4	184.0	125.0	–	52.2	44.5	73.8	–
1889	210.3	204.5	116.3	152.9	51.4	47.4	68.2	86.5
1890	159.9	175.0	128.7	136.9	50.1	47.0	69.5	73.3
1891	166.3	201.9	128.2	–	50.3	45.7	68.8	–
1892	151.8	202.6	132.7	–	50.6	46.5	66.5	–
1893	151.8	195.8	134.0	128.9	51.7	46.7	69.2	71.5
1894	131.3	198.1	119.2	–	52.5	45.5	63.0	–
1895	143.9	219.0	118.0	144.8	48.9	45.4	64.3	81.0
1896	146.8	200.9	138.1	–	47.4	46.8	74.9	–
1897	224.9	183.1	117.9	132.8	49.3	47.6	70.6	87.1
1898	137.4	201.3	130.4	–	48.3	46.9	67.7	–
1899	140.2	170.9	123.2	–	48.1	46.8	68.9	–
1900	114.5	165.0	118.4	129.6	47.5	44.4	68.2	79.1
1901	112.1	167.2	114.5	–	47.8	45.3	63.3	–

Table 12.1 *(cont.)*

| | All farm products | | | Livestock products | | | |
Year	Serbia	Bulgaria	Bosnia	Montenegro	Serbia	Bulgaria	Bosnia	Montenegro
1902	129.9	169.6	96.6	–	48.6	46.7	63.2	–
1903	121.5	190.3	118.4	132.3	48.1	45.4	64.0	81.3
1904	117.4	194.7	128.6	–	48.1	46.7	65.2	–
1905	135.8	184.8	110.0	110.5	47.8	47.9	62.8	69.2
1906	152.4	192.5	101.5	119.0	47.3	50.0	61.4	67.6
1907	117.8	138.2	104.2	118.7	46.3	49.4	62.0	69.1
1908	143.0	184.8	112.3	129.7	47.1	48.2	63.8	74.1
1909	144.9	168.1	115.3	158.6	46.8	49.4	57.1	69.5
1910	124.8	191.3	104.1	138.3	46.9	49.7	51.3	71.9
1911	138.3	195.6	106.7	117.5	47.3	47.3	65.4	64.1
1912	120.3	185.5	115.7	130.4	46.7	45.7	67.1	70.3
1913	–	170.7	122.4	–	–	51.3	52.2	–
1914	–	135.0	106.3	–	–	43.0	41.7	–

Source: BALKSTAT statistics.

Knowledge needed to be more accessible, but peasants were poorly motivated to acquire it. The 'renaissance' legacy caused a stronger response in Bulgaria than in Serbia or Bosnia, but it remained geographically restricted.

The peasantization of lands liberated from Ottoman rule in 1878 caused the flow of rent and tax from villages to towns to diminish, so urban demand for manufactures dropped precipitously. Urban commerce was also hit by the loss of external markets because of the effective upward revaluation of the currency. Prices of imports therefore rose less than those of domestic produce, and craftsmen were pressed by import competition in an urban market whose overall demand for manufactures was shrinking. The crafts decayed precipitously. So towns of their former size became redundant under the new dispensation. In part the problem was solved by the emigration of urban Muslims but subsequent urbanization was minimal or negative. Bulgaria in 1910 was little or no more urban than it had been under Ottoman rule, Bosnia and Montenegro considerably less so.

Urban decline seriously affected the former centres of textile manufacturing in Bulgaria. Not only was domestic demand for textiles reduced, so too was export demand from Serbia and Bosnia, though the Ottoman market remained accessible. It was difficult for unmechanized enterprise to adjust to changed conditions, because of the rise in raw material and wage costs. Textile wages could not rise to match the general rise in prices, so one-time textile workers orientated their effort towards agriculture. Others found employment in the burgeoning new bureaucracies. The woollen output of Eastern Rumelia (by weight) declined by 61 per cent.

Bulgaria's liberation was followed by the building of a rash of small woollen spinning mills in the old proto-industrial towns, especially at Sliven and Gabrovo, which had long been active in the woollen trades. As textile labour supply dwindled, difficulties in securing woollen yarn imports made machine spinning necessary to the survival of the trade. So these woollen mills were erected as defensive investments in the supply chains. Difficulties in procuring woollens, especially *gajtan*, from Bulgaria after its liberation led to the establishment of machine woollen manufacturing in Serbia at Leskovac, in the territory newly annexed. Though Leskovac had not previously manufactured woollens it had a strong proto-industrial base and its entrepot trade in woollens had depended on Bulgarian supplies.

So the early textile factories emerged from a proto-industrial environment. The entrepreneurs lacked access to capital and technical information, so their factories were small and applied obsolescent technology. Nevertheless, they were sufficiently profitable for such shortcomings to be remedied by self-accumulation, which gave rise to a capitalistic culture of personal frugality.

The proto-industrial environment from which the woollen mills emerged did not give rise to obvious external economies. Proto-industry theory gives pride of place to labour endowment, so we would expect entrepreneurs to been advantaged by cheap industrially orientated labour. However, most proto-industrial workers were women who worked at home and could not be transferred into the mills, and the factories had to create their labour forces from scratch. At Sliven, the industry employed urban adult males as fly-shuttle weavers, but availability of this experienced labour encouraged retention of obsolete production methods. At Leskovac labour was cheap but most towns in Bulgaria and Serbia could provide unskilled labour at similar pay. Nor were these towns reservoirs of appropriate labour skills and the factories either had to recruit expensive foreign skills, or accept the inefficiency which flowed from doing without them.

The location of these early factory industries was essentially historic. No in-coming or trans-national firm favoured locating in the old proto-industrial towns. In-coming firms, Münch at Paraćin, Crompton and Michel at Belgrade and the British cotton mill at Varna, located their plant for access to raw material. In the longer run, city and port locations proved at least as advantageous as those of former proto-industrial towns.

In Bulgaria, textile manufacturing was the most important factory industry, accounting in 1907 for 36.5 per cent of net large-scale manufacturing production.[3] Yet woollen manufacturing was a far smaller sector of the economy in 1903 than its proto-industrial predecessor had been in 1867, both in relative and in absolute terms. Table 9.6 showed how great a contraction occurred. A 48 per cent shrinkage of value added was caused partly by the loss after 1878 of the Serbian and Bosnian markets, but the biggest loss was probably of domestic urban demand in the post-liberation upheaval. The unchanging preponderance of the subsistence sector limited mass demand for factory products, and prompted the factories to diversify up-market to compete for urban purchasers. However Bulgarian industry was uncompetitive in this market despite rising tariff protection.

The endogeneously declining Balkan rural economy was inimical to non-agricultural change, and as late as 1910 farming accounted for about half of total output in all three Balkan states. This did not make aggregate economic decline inevitable. Integration of the Balkans into the European economy could induce efficiency improvements outside agriculture, if sufficiently powerful. However, in Serbia and Bulgaria non-farm growth failed to offset decline in agriculture. Neither country exploited the full potential of railways, largely because of resistance by governments to private sector initiatives. Large-scale industry grew rapidly in both countries during the last pre-Balkan War decade, but remained insignificant. Concession laws were designed to attract transnational enterprises, but few such ventures flourished.

The industrial experience of Bosnia-Hercegovina under Habsburg rule provided insights as to what was possible, and what was lacking. The administration launched speedily into resource-based industrialization, commencing with railway construction. Industrialization peaked in intensity under the administration of Count Benjamin Kállay (1882–1903). A complex of large-scale export industries emerged, based on timber, chemical feedstocks, iron and coal. After Kállay's death, industrialization decelerated, but the end achievement was still impressive. Between 1881 and 1913, large-scale industrial output expanded at 12.4 per cent per annum, and came to represent about 54 per cent of the combined large-scale industrial output of Bosnia, Bulgaria and Serbia. The drive for modernization pushed Bosnia's per capita income to well above Balkan levels. In Bosnia, nearly all industrial investment was undertaken by non-native enterprise, and local business interests exhibited the same passivity as in Serbia. A greater pace of achievement could have been attained in Serbia, and possibly in Bulgaria too, if the political environment had been less xenophobic and less hostile to non-native initiatives.

[3] *SGBTs*, 1909, p. 236.

The performance of Macedonia after 1878 provided insights into the likely path of development in Bulgaria, if it had remained under Ottoman rule. As security conditions were especially adverse in the villages, agricultural labour for the *čifliks* was in short supply, and extensive farming methods prevailed. However, estate farming remained profitable, and a boom in tobacco growing sustained rural prosperity.

Much of the hill population and that of the towns sought a livelihood through migrant labouring and small business. In Macedonia and upland Thrace, longstanding woollen proto-industries were boosted after 1878 by the difficulties of their Bulgarian competitors. In the south, cotton manufacturing continued to progress. By 1909, 10 spinning mills in Salonica, Veroia, Naousa and Edhessa with 60,200 spindles span coarse yarn to supply the handloom weavers. Cost pressures developed from around 1905, and weaker manufactures were squeezed out. These pressures further intensified after the Balkan Wars, when events followed a course similar to those experienced in Bulgaria after 1878. Farm production slumped as wages rose and the *čifliks* collapsed. Woollen mills in territories annexed by Serbia could not withstand competition by better equipped factories in the north. Nevertheless, Macedonia was not disadvantaged industrially by its long submission to Ottoman rule. The 'renaissance' culture underpinned a lively market economy.

Looking at the dismal twentieth-century economic performance of Bulgaria and Serbia/Yugoslavia, it is tempting to conclude on a pessimistic note. The period 1904–12 may have marked a bottoming out in long-run per capita product, for Bulgaria at least. During the inter-war years, industrial growth continued to be sustained by promotion of heavily protected light industry. Lampe is highly critical of this policy, which probably slowed structural change.[4] However, subsequent experience under communism shows that shifting resources back into heavy industry was both inefficient and destructive for a country not endowed with subsoil wealth.[5]

I was once asked to extend this study with a post-script into the period since 1918 – and I can see ways of writing a companion volume to link into the theme 'The Balkans: two centuries of economic stagnation'. Its subtitle might well run, 'The triumph of politics over economic rationality'. Continued resource destruction would also rate a dishonourable mention.

[4] Alexander Gerschenkron, 'Some Aspects of Industrialization in Bulgaria, 1878–1939', in his *Economic Backwardness in Historical Perspective* (New York, 1965). A similar standpoint is expressed in 'Industrial Growth without Development', in John R. Lampe, *The Bulgarian Economy in the Twentieth Century* (London, 1986), pp. 68–71 and 93–6.

[5] M. Palairet '"Lenin" and "Brezhnev": Steel Making and the Bulgarian Economy, 1956–90', *Europe-Asia Studies*, XLVII (1995), 493–505.

Select bibliography

ARCHIVAL SOURCES

BELGIUM

Ministère des affaires étrangères, Brussels (BAE)
2911 VI, 4117 V, Dossier 2807 X No. 2161, Film B 24 – Df. 144.

BULGARIA

Tsentralen d'rzhaven Istoricheski Arhiv, Sofia (TsDIA)
E. Rumelia. Oblastno s'branie, f. 20 op. 1 ae. 65, 66, 229.
E. Rumelia. Direktsija na finansite: f. 151 op. 1 ae. 16; f. 158 op. 1 ae. 16, 17, 33, 35; f. 159 op. 1 ae. 191.
Bulgaria. Narodno S'branie 1902, f. 173 op. 2 ae. 674.

Narodna biblioteka Kiril i Metodi, Sofia (M/S dept.)
Hristo Daskalov papers
Fond 129 ae. 112, 166, 186.
Newspapers of the Bulgarian renaissance
Dunav, III (1867) supplement to no. 161, nos. 191, 186, 185, 184, 183; IX (1873) nos. 794, 795, 796, 797.
Turtsija (Constantinople) III (1866) no. 13.
Uchilishte (Ruse) II (1872).
B'lgarija (Constantinople) I and II (1859–60).

FRANCE

Archives nationales, Paris (AN)
F12 Affaires étrangères
7191, 7280.

Ministère des affaires étrangères, Paris (AAE)
Corréspondance Consulaire et Commercial [CC]
Serbie. N.S. 18 Mines I, 1902–10.
Belgrade [B] t. 1–7 (1838–89).

GREAT BRITAIN

Lancashire Record Office, Preston (LRO)
Crompton family of High Crompton [DDCp]
Box 730; box 737.

Oldham Local Studies Library
Crompton Papers. Uncatalogued series box 3.

Public Record Office, Kew (PRO)
Defunct Companies Register
No. 15630 of 1896, box 48413. First Royal Servian Privileged Weaving Co. Ltd.

Foreign Office (FO)
78 (Turkey)
312, 365, 485, 695, 744, 1096, 1377, 1459, 1527, 1681, 1882, 2237, 4953, 5020, 5083, 5298.
105 (Servia)
14, 37, 42, 79, 83, 90, 96, 97, 111, 129, 130, 136, 151.
198 13.
368 (Bulgaria)
278, 394, 518, 800, 942.

YUGOSLAVIA

Arhiv Crne Gore, Cetinje (ACG)
Ministarstvo finansija (MF, MFiG)
Land tax: II/A
2, 15, 17, 21, 23a, 25, 32, 37, 39d, 39e
Ministarstvo unutrašnja dela (MUD)
VII-1, VII-2, VII-17.
Senat (S): -10

Arhiv Srbije, Belgrade (AS)
Ministarstvo finansija (MF)
Administrativno odeljenje (A)
1864 I 118, 1864 I 86.
Ekonomno odeljenje (E) Okrug agricultural reports
1860 II 123, 1862 V 101, 1864 VI 7, 1865 VII 7, 1866 VIII 2, 1867 VIII 137, 1869 XIII 1, 1874 XII 1, 1876 VI 63.
Popisne knjige, 1862–4.
Ministarstvo narodne privrede (MNP)
Statistika (S)
Kut. 5 XXII – 1, kut. 5 XXIII.
Trgovina (T)
1889 X 21, 1894 I 47, 1895 XII 79, 1906 45 6, 1898 VI 2, 1900 IV 63, 1900 XI 42, 1902 1 107, 1906 41 7 1902 I 88, 1903 15 19, 1906 37 8, 1904 13

12, 1905 II 1, 1905 XIV 9, 1904 V 77, 1905 XV 9, 1906 46 37, 1907 38
1, 1907 38 10, 1907 38 32, 1907 38 12, 1914 Nos. 2535, 4876, 6424,
unfasciculated.
Ministarstvo unutrašnja dela, Policajno odeljenje (MUD-P)
1914 XVIII 98.

Istoriski Arhiv Beograda, Belgrade (IAB)
Minute book of Koste Ilića Sinovi a.d. u Beogradu 1910–1914.

Muzej u Smederevu, Smederevo (MuS)
Sava Stanković papers
373/66, 326/66, 518/66, 507/66.

NEWSPAPERS

BELGRADE

Radničke novine
Službeni vojni list
Srbske (later *Srpske*) *Novine*
Trgovinski glasnik
Cetinje
Glas Crnogorca
Plovdiv
Maritsa
Sarajevo
Bosna
Sarajevski Cvjetnik

PRINTED OFFICIAL REPORTS

AUSTRIA

'Hebung der Textilindustrie in Serbien', *Handelsmuseum*, IX (1) 1894
'Jahresbericht pro 1894 der k.u.k. diplomatischen agentie und das k.u.k.
    Generalconsulates in Sofia', *Handelsmuseum*, X (1895) Commercielle
    Berichte
'Salonichs wirthschaftliche Lage', *Handelsmuseum*, II (1887, July–Dec.)
'Wirkwaarenindustrie in Salonich', *Handelsmuseum*, VI (1891)
'Zur wirthschaftslichen Lage Bulgariens III', *Handelsmuseum*, II (1887)
Österreichische Monatschrift für der Orient (Vienna) XI (1885)
Österreichisches Statistisches Handbuch 1913
Statistisches Jahrbuch der Oesterreichischen Monarchie für das Jahr 1863 (Vienna,
    1864)
k.k. Österr. Handelsmuseum, *Serbien. Wirtschaftliche Verhaltnisse, 1909* (Vienna,
    1910); -*1911* (Vienna, 1912)

AUSTRIA-HUNGARY

Berichte der Österr.-Ung. Consular-Ämter. [BOUCA] 1899, bd. 1. Plovdiv; -, 1900
bd. 1 Varna 1900, A II 5; - 1900 bd. 2 Adrianopel 1900, A XX 5; - 1901
Rustchuk 1901 II 3; - 1901 bd. 1 Sofia 1901, A II 1; - 1901 bd. 2 Salonich
1901 A XIX 2; - 1902 bd. 2 (2) Salonich A XVIII 2; - 1902 bd. 1 (1) Sofia
1902, A II 1; - 1902 bd. 2 (2) Adrianopel, A XVIII 4; - 1902 bd. 2 (2) Niš
1902, A XVI 2; - 1902 bd. 2. Üskub XVIII 5; - 1903 bd. 1. Varna A II 5; -
1903 bd. 2 (2) Üskub, 1903, A XX 3; - 1903 bd. 2 (2) Salonich 1903; - 1903
bd. 2 Monastir 1903 A XX 7; - 1903, bd. 2 (2) Adrianopel 1903, A XX 1; -
1904 bd 2 (2) Salonich 1904; - 1904 bd. 1 (1) Varna; - 1904 bd. 2 (2) Belgrad
A XVIII 5; - 1905 Monastir; - 1905 bd. 1 (1) Varna 1905 A II 4; - 1905 bd. 2
(2) Adrianopel 1905 A XX 2; - 1905 bd. 2 (2) Salonich A XX 6; - 1906
Monastir; - 1906 bd. 1 Varna 1906; - 1906 bd. 5 Salonich 1906 A XX 13; -
1906 part 1. Plovdiv 1906; - 1906, bd. 5 Belgrad 1906 A XIX 3; - 1907 (3)
Monastir; - 1907 bd. 1, Varna 1907 A II 4; - 1909 Üskub; - 1909 bd. 1.
Bourgas. Jahresbericht für das Jahr 1908; - 1909 bd. 2. Salonich.
Handelsbericht für das Jahr 1908; - 1910 bd. 2 Salonich. Handelsbericht für
das Jahr 1909; - 1911 bd. 3. Salonich. Handelsbericht für das Jahr 1910; -
1912 bd 2. Üskub. Handelsbericht für das Jahr 1911; - 1912 bd. 1
Adrianopel. Handelsbericht für das Jahr 1911; - 1912 bd. 2 Salonich.
Handelsbericht für das Jahr 1911.

Die Österreichisch-ungarische Monarchie in Wort und Bild. Bosnien und Hercegovina
(Vienna, 1901).

BELGIUM, CONSULAR REPORTS

Reports: *Recueil Consulaire* [RC] Bulgaria, Sofia, CLVI (1912); Serbia 3 Oct.
1887, RC LXI; Salonica, RC LXXV (1892); Adrianople, RC LXXVII
(1892); Philippopoli, 25 Feb. 1886, RC LIII. (1885) Bulgaria, RC LXXVII
(1892); Greece, Macedonia, RC 165 (1913).

BOSNIA-HERCEGOVINA

Bosna i Hercegovina na milenskoj izložbi u Budimpešti godine 1896 (Budapest, n.d.).
Bosnia vilayet *Salname-i vilayet-i Bosna*. Defa V, sene 1287 (=1870); Defa VI,
sene 1288 (1871); Defa IX, sene 1291 (=1874).
La Bosnie-Herzégovine à l'exposition internationale universelle de 1900 à Paris
(Vienna, 1900).
Die Ergebnisse der Viehzählung in Bosnien und die Hercegovina vom Jahre 1910
(Sarajevo, 1912).
Bericht über die Ergebnisse der bos. herceg. Landesbahnen für das Jahr 1909 (Sarajevo,
1910).
Bericht über die Verwaltung von Bosnien und der Hercegovina, 1913 (Vienna, 1914);
1914–16 (Vienna, 1917).
Geschäftsbericht der k.u.k. Militärbahn Banja Luka-Doberlin für das Jahr 1910
(Banja Luka, 1911)

Die Landwirthschaft in Bosnien und der Hercegovina (Sarajevo, 1899).
Statistische Tabellen für Bosnien und die Hercegovina I. Landwirthschaft (Sarajevo, 1896).
Glavni rezultati popisa žiteljstva u Bosni i Hercegovini ot Aprila 1895 sa podacima o teritorijanom razdeljenju, javnim zavodima i rudnim vrelima (Sarajevo, 1896).
Izvještaj o upravi Bosne i Hercegovini, 1906–11 (6 vols. Zagreb, 1908–9, Sarajevo, 1910–11).
Rezultati popisa marve u Bosni i Hercegovini od godine 1895 (Sarajevo, 1896).
Ortschafts und Bevölkerungs-Statistik von Bosnien und Herzegovina (Sarajevo, 1880).
Ortschafts- und Bevölkerungs-Statistik von Bosnien und der Hercegovina nach dem Volkszahlungs-Ergebnisse vom 1 Mai 1885 (Sarajevo, 1886).
Rezultati popisa žiteljstva u Bosni i Hercegovini od 10 Okt 1910 (Sarajevo, 1912).

BULGARIA

Desetogodishna statistika za v'nshnata t'rgovija na B'lgarija 1886–1895 (Sofia, 1906); for 1896–1905 (Sofia, 1912).
Prebrojavane na industriite nas'rchavani ot d'rzhavata 31 Dec. 1904 (Sofia, 1906).
Rezultati ot posevite i rekoltata v knjazhestvo B'lgarija prez zemledelcheskata 1896/7 godina (Sofia, 1901).
Sbornik ot statisticheski svedenija za stopanskoto polozhenie na Zlatishkata okolija (Sofijsko okr'zhije) (Sofia, 1888).
S'krateni protokoli za sasedeniata na I i II redovni sesii na Burgazkata t'rg.-industrialna kamara. (Burgaz, 1909); na III redovnija sesija ... prez Dekemvrij 1909 (Burgaz, 1910).
Statisticheski godishnik na B'lgarskoto Tsarstvo, I, 1909; II, 1910; III, 1911; IV, 1912; V–XIV, 1913–22; XV–XVI, 1923–4; XVII, 1925.
Statistika za srednite pazarni ceni na domasnite zhivotni, po-vazhnite predmeti za zhiveene i nadnicite v B'lgarija prez desetiletieto 1893–1902 (Sofia, 1906).
Statistika za t'rgovijata na Knjazhestvo B'lgarija s cuzhdite d'rzhavi i srednite pazarni ceni ... prez 1906 godina; and similar titles for: 1907; for 1908; for 1909 (Sofia, 1909–10); for 1910 (Sofia, 1911); for 1912 (Sofia, 1911, 1919); for 1913, 1914, 1915 godini (Sofia, 1921).
Svedenija po ikonomichesko s'stojanie na B'lgarija (Sofia, 1888).
Ministerstvo na narodnoto prosveshtenie. *Kratko izlozhenie po zemledelieto i zanajatite v B'lgarija* (Sofia, 1889).
Ministerski s'vet. *Doklad do negovoto velichestvo Ferdinand I Car na b'lgarite po sluchaj 25-godishnata od v'zshestvieto mu na b'lgarskija prestol 1887–1912 ot ministerskija s'vet* (Sofia, n.d.).
Ministerstvo na narodnoto prosveshtenie. *Doklad do g-na Ministra na Narodnoto prosveshtenie ot industrijalna komissija pri Ministerstvo na Narodnoto prosveshtenie za s'stojanieto na zemedelieto i skotov'dstvoto* (Sofia, 1891).
Doklad na v'rhovnata smetna palata do narodnoto s'branie (sesija prez 1911 g.) po izp'lnenie na bjudzheta za 1910 g (Sofia, 1911).
Doklad ot bjuroto na plovdivskata t'rgovsko-industrialna kamara za ikonomicheskoto s'stojanie na rajona ... prez 1895 i 1896 godini (Plovdiv, 1897);
Doklad na plovdivski okr'g upravitel za obshtoto s'stojanie na okr'ga prez g. 1888–98 (Plovdiv, 1889).

Doklad na slivenski prefekt za s'stojanieto na okr'ga i na raznite v nego obshti sluzhbi .. prez Septemvri 1883 god. (Sliven, 1883) and similar titles: for 1889 (Sliven, 1889); for 1894–5 (Sliven, 1895); for 1899–1900 (Sliven, 1900), and see 'S'stojanie . . .'

Doklad za s'stojanieto na sevlievskoto okr'zhie prez 1892–93 godina (Sevlievo, 1893).

Izlozhenie na sevlievski okr. upravitel za s'stojanieto na okr'ga prez 1888 godina (Ruse, 1888) and similar titles for Sevlievo: for 1889–90 (Sevlievo, 1890) for 1890–91 (Sevlievo, 1891); for 1897/8 (Sevlievo, 1898); for 1898/9 (Sevlievo, 1899); for 1899/1900 (Sevlievo, 1900).

Izlozhenie na starozagorskij okr. upravitel za obshtoto s'stojanie na st. zagorskij okr'g (Kazanl'k, 1895)

Izlozhenie za obshtoto s'stojanie na plovdivski okr'g prez 1889–1890 god. (Plovdiv, 1890) and similar titles for 1896–97 (Plovdiv, 1897); for 1899–1900 (Plovdiv, 1900); for 1901–2 (Plovdiv, 1902); for 1906–7 (Plovdiv, 1907).

Izlozhenie za s'stojanieto na slivenskoto okr'zhie prez 1895–1896 godina (Sliven, 1896) and similar titles for 1896–7 (Sliven, 1897).

Izlozhenie za s'stojanieto na burgaskoto okr'zhie prez 1901/02 godina (Burgaz, 1902) and similar titles for 1903/04 (Burgaz, 1904); for 1907/8 (Burgaz, 1908).

Izlozhenie za s'stojanieto na tatar-pazardzhishkoto okr'zhie prez 1890–1891 godina (T-Pazardzhik, 1891) and similar titles: for 1894–5 godina (T-Pazardzhik, 1895).

Izlozhenie za s'stojanieto na t'rnovskoto okr'zhie prez 1898–99 godina (Veliko T'rnovo, 1899) and similar titles for: 1908–9 (v. T'rnovo, 1909); for 1910–11. (Veliko T'rnovo, 1911).

Izlozhenie za s'stojanieto na vratchanskij okr'g 1889–90 g. (Orjehovo, 1890) and similar titles for 1891. (Orjahovo, 1891) for 1891–2 (Plovdiv, 1892); for 1898/9 (Vrattsa, 1899)

Materiali dlya izucheniya Bolgarii (Bucharest, 1877) II/3.

Plovdivsko t'rgovsko-industrialna kamara, *Izvlechenie ot stenografskite protokoli . . . 1897.*

EASTERN RUMELIA

Statisticheski svedenija na direkcijata na financiite na Istochna Rumelija (n.p. n.d.).

Zakono-proekt za dan'chite v'rhu nedvizhimostite i v'rhu prihoda predstaven na Oblastnoto S'branie v obiknovenata mu sesija ot 1883 g.

Godishna statistika za Iztochna Rumelija, 1883.

Raport na komissiata po izuchvanieto na ikonomicheskoto polozhenie na naselenieto v gradovete Karlovo i Sopot (Karlovo, 1883).

Edirne vilayet. *Salname* Defa 3, 1289 (=1873).

FRANCE, CONSULAR REPORTS

'Bulgarie. L'agriculture et l'exploitation du sol en Bulgarie (Ruse 10 Feb. 1884)', *Bulletin Consulaire [BC]* 1884.

'Commerce et navigation de Varna en 1886', *BC*, XV (1888, Jan.–June).

'Situation économique du département de Varna', *BC*, XX (1890), 2nd semester.

'Bulgarie et Roumélie orientale: mouvement commercial pendant l'année 1894', *Rapports commerciaux des agents diplomatique et consulaires de France* [*RCADCF*] no. 304.

'Bulgarie: Bourgas. Mouvement du port de Bourgas en 1893', *RCADCF* (no. 176).

'Commerce et navigation de Roustchouk en 1902', *RCADCF*, 1904 Jan. – June. (no. 339).

'Turquie d'Europe. Commerce de la Roumélie orientale en 1890', *BC*, XXI (1891, 2nd semester).

'Turquie. Importance commerciale de Salonique', *Rapports Consulaire Français*, 1892 (no. 22).

'Turquie. Mouvement commercial du Vilayet de Kossovo pendant l'année 1906', *RCADCF*, 1908 Jan.–June, (no. 686) and similar title for 1909, *RCADCF*, 1910 July–Dec. (no. 919).

'Turquie. Mouvement commercial de Salonique en 1909', *RCADCF*, 1911 (Jan.–June) (no. 927).

GREAT BRITAIN, CONSULAR REPORTS [GBC]

Bosnia 1858, 1867–68, 1871–72, 1874, 1876–81, 1885, 1908–09, 1911–12. Report of Mr Jones, British Acting-Consul in Bosnia, on the Commerce and Present Condition of this province. PP 1859 Sess. 2 XXX and similar titles: for 1867. PP 1867–8 LXVIII; for 1868. PP 1868–9 LX; for 1871, PP 1872 LVIII. for 1872. PP 1873 LXIV; for 1874. PP 1875 LXXV; for 1876. PP 1877 LXXXIII; for 1877. pp. 810–11, PP 1878 LXXIV; for 1878. PP 1878–9 LXXI; for 1879. PP 1880 LXXIII; for 1880. PP 1881 XC; for 1881, PP 1882 LXX; for 1885, Commercial no. 10 of 1886. PP 1886 LXVI; for 1908. (A S.4305) PP 1909 XCII; for 1909 (A S.4446) PP 1910 XCVI; for 1911. (A S. 5009) PP 1912–13 XCIV; for 1912, (A S. 5067) PP 1913 LXIX.

Bosnia 1888. Report on Agriculture in Bosnia and the Herzegovina for the Year 1888 (A. S. 478) PP 1889 LXXVIII.

Bulgaria 1876. Rustchuk. General Report by Consul Reade on the Vilayet of the Danube, PP 1877 LXXXIII.

Bulgaria 1880. Report by vice Consul Dalziel on the Trade and Commerce of Roustchouk for the year 1880, PP 1882 LXX.

Bulgaria 1883, 1890, 1892, 1895, 1897, 1898, 1900, 1903, 1905–06, 1909–10, 1913. Report for the Year 1883 on the Trade and Commerce of Bulgaria (A S. 1) PP 1884 LXXXIII and similar titles: for 1890. (A S. 936) PP 1890–1 LXXXV; for 1892 (A S. 1300) PP 1893–4 XCII; for 1895 (A S. 1826) PP 1897 LXXXIX; for 1897 (A S. 2159) PP 1898 XCIV; for 1898. (A S. 2357) PP 1899 XCVIII; for 1900 (A S. 2642) PP 1901 LXXXI; for 1903. (A S. 3236) PP 1904 XCVII; for 1904. (A S. 3395) PP 1905 LXXXVII; for 1905. (A S. 3630) PP 1906 CXXIII; for 1906. (A S. 3949) PP 1908 CIX; for 1908–9. (A S. 4609) PP 1911 XC; for 1910 (A S. 4817) PP 1911 XC; for 1912–13. (A S. 5320) PP 1914 LXXXIX.

Bulgaria 1884. Position of Peasant Proprietors in Bulgaria (Comm. no 11, 1885) PP 1884–5 LXXXI.

Bulgaria 1885. Report by Vice-Consul Brophy on the Trade and Commerce of Varna for the Year 1885 (A S. 237) PP 1888 C.

Bulgaria 1889. Sofia. Population, Finances, Trade, Agriculture, Industry and General Situation of Bulgaria in 1889 (A S. 752). PP 1890 LXXIV.

Constantinople 1877. Report by Vice-Consul Wrench on the Trade and Commerce of Constantinople for the Years 1876–1877 PP 1878 LXXIV.

E. Rumelia 1876. Notes by Mr Baring on the Exports and Imports etc. from the Sandjak of Philippopolis, Commercial no 17 of 1876, PP 1876 LXXIII.

E. Rumelia 1886, 1887a 1888a. Report for the Year 1886 on the Trade &c of Eastern Roumelia, (A S. 185) PP 1887 LXXXVI and similar titles: for 1887 (A S. 325) PP 1888 CIII; for 1888. PP 1889 LXXVIII.

E. Rumelia, 1887b. Report on the Agricultural Condition of Eastern Roumelia (A S. 358) PP 1888 CIII.

E. Rumelia 1888b. Trade report for the Burgas District in the Year 1888 (A S. 558) PP 1889 LXXVIII.

Edirne, 1868. Report by Mr Vice Consul Blunt on Sheep Husbandry and on the Wool Trade in the Vilayet of Adrianople (Commercial Reports, 1868) PP 1867–8 LXVIII.

Edirne 1911. Report on the Trade of Adrianople Vilayet for the Year 1911 (A S. 5015) PP 1912–13 C.

Greece 1913. Report for the Year 1913 on the Trade of the Piraeus and District (A S. 5290) PP 1914 XCII.

Ionia 1851 Reports Made for the Year 1851 . . . [on] the Past and Present State of Her Majesty's Colonial Possessions (1852). PP 1852 XXXI.

Macedonia 1856, 1867, 1907. Report by Mr Longworth, British Consul at Monastir upon the Trade of that Place and its Dependencies during the Year 1856, Abstract of Reports on the Trade of Various Countries and Places for the Years 1856–1857. PP 1857 Sess. 2 XXXVIII, and similar titles: for 1867 (Command Feb. 1869) PP 1868–9 LIX; for 1907 (A S. 4040) PP CXVI 1908.

Macedonia 1864. Report by Mr Consul Calvert on the Trade and Commerce of the Pashalik of Roumeli for the Year 1864 (Command Feb. 1866) PP 1866 LXIX.

Montenegro 1858, 1895. Report by Mr Rumbold on Montenegro. Vienna, 20 July 1858. PP 1861 LXIII; similar title for 1895 (A S. 1761) PP 1896 LXXXVII.

Montenegro 1887. Report of a Tour in the Neighbourhood of Cettinje (FO Misc. Ser. 1888 No 95) PP 1888 XCIX.

Salonica 1881. Report by Consul General Blunt on the Trade and Commerce of Macedonia and the Port of Salonica for the Years 1879, 1880 and 1881, Commercial no. 6 (1883). PP LXXII 1883.

Salonica 1884, 1888, 1892, 1897, 1903, 1906–1910. Report for the Years 1883–4 on the Trade of Salonica. PP 1887 LXXXVI and similar titles: for 1888. (A S. 623) PP 1890 LXXVII; for 1891–2 (A S. 1310) PP 1893–4 XCVIII; for 1896 and 1897. (A S. 2111) PP 1898 XCIX; for 1903. PP 1904 CI pt. I; for 1906. PP 1907 XCIII for 1907. PP 1908 CXVII; for 1908 (A S. 4359) PP 1909 XCVIII; for 1909. (A S. 4579) PP 1910 CIII; for 1910 (A S. 4797) PP 1911 XCVI.

Serbia 1863, 1872a, 1872b, 1888, 1891, 1892, 1898, 1899. Report of Consul-General Longworth on the Trade of Servia in the Year 1863 (C.3478 of 1865) PP 1865 LIII, and similar titles: Report dated 2 Mar. 1872 (C 563 of June 1872) PP 1872 LVII;for 1872 (Commercial no. 5 of 1874) PP 1874 LXVI; for 1887 and 1888. (A S. 534) PP 1889 LXXX; for 1891 (A S. 1295) PP 1893 XCVI; for 1892 (A S. 1480) PP 1895 C; for 1897–8 (A S. 2207) PP 1899 CII; for 1898 and 1899 (A S. 2383) PP 1900 XCVI.

Serbia 1879. Report by Vice-Consul Baker on the Trade and Commerce of Nisch for . . . 1879, p. 904, PP 1880 LXXIV.

Serbia 1895. Report on the Servian Mines, 1895 (FO Misc. Ser. 350) PP 1895 CIII.

PRUSSIA

'Jahresbericht des Konsulates des norddeutsches Bundes zu Sarajevo für das Jahr 1869', *Preussische Handelsarchiv*, 1870 no. 11.

SERBIA

Državopis Srbije (Belgrade) I (1863); II (1865); III (1869)IV (1870); V (1871); X (1880); XIII (1884) XVI (1889).

La Serbie à l'Exposition universelle de 1911 à Turin (Belgrade, 1911).

Popis domaće stoke u kr Srbiji 31 Dec 1895 godine (*SKS*, XXXII: Belgrade, 1913).

Popis obradjene zemlje u Kr. Srbije 1889g. (SKS, III: Belgrade, 1894); for 1893 (SKS, IX: Belgrade, 1897); for 1897 g. (*SKS*, XVI: Belgrade, 1900).

Popis stanovništva u kr. Srbije 31 Dek 1900 – II (*SKS*, XXIV: Belgrade, 1905).

Prethodni rezultati popisa stanovništva i domaće stoke u Kraljevini Srbiji 31 Dek 1910 godine (Belgrade, 1911), p. 4.

Spomenica Beogradske trgovačke omladine 1880–1930 (Belgrade, 1931).

Statistika pošta telegrafa i telefona kr. Srbije za 1910 god. (Belgrade, 1912).

Statistika cena poljoprivrednih proizvoda u Kr. Srbiji, 1896–1900 (Belgrade, 1902).

Statistika zemljoradnje i žetvenog prinosa u kr. Srbije za 1900g. (*SKS*, XVIII: Belgrade, 1903).

Statistika spoljašne trgovine kr. Srbije za 1900 g. (Belgrade, 1901).

Statistički Godišnjak kr. Srbije. (Belgrade, 1895–) I, 1893; II, 1894–5;III, 1896– 7; IV, 1898–9; V, 1900; VI 1901; VII, 1902; VIII, 1903; IX, 1904; X, 1905; XI, 1906; XII, 1907–8; XIII, 1909–10.

Trgovinski-zanatlijski šematizam za 1911.

Završni račun držav. prihoda i rashoda Kr. Srbije za 1910 god. (Belgrade, 1911).

Zbornik zakona i uredba izdani u Knjažestvu Srbiji, XVII (1864).

Industrijska komora Kraljevine Srbije, *Izveštaj o radu i stanju industrije u 1910 godini* (Belgrade, 1911) and similar title for 1911 (Belgrade, 1912).

Ministarstvo Narodne Privrede. *Izveštaji podneseni Ministru narodne privrede o radu na unapredjenju domaće privrede za god. 1908 i 1909, . . . i merama za dalji rad u tome pravcu* (Belgrade, 1911).

Ministarstvo Narodne Privrede. *Izveštaj o radu odeljenja za poljsku privredu i veteri-narstvo. (Izveštaji podneseni Ministru narodne privrede o dasadašnjem radu na* unapredjenu domaće privrede i merama za dalji rad u tome pravcu.) (Belgrade, 1907).

Ministarstvo Vojno, Statistika država balkanskog poluostrva. I Kr. Srbija (Belgrade, 1890).

Narodna Banka. Narodna Banka 1884–1934 (Belgrade, 1934)

Srpski centralni komitet, Srbija u imovnom pogledu pre za vreme i posle svetskog rata 1914–1918 (Geneva, 1918).

Statistični podatci o Bosni, Hercegovini i jednom kraju Stare Srbije', GSUD, III (O.S. XX) (Belgrade, 1866).

Trgovačka Komora za Kr. Srbiju, Izveštaj za 1912 i 1913 godinu (Belgrade, 1914).

Zavod za statistiku i evidenciju N. R. Srbije, Stanovništvo N R Srbije od 1834–1953 (Belgrade, 1953).

COLLECTED DOCUMENTS

Dokumenti za B'lgarskata istorija. III. Dokumenti iz turskite d'rzhavni arhivi, 1564–1872, ed. Pancho Dorev (Sofia, 1940).

Michoff, Nicolas V., La population de la Turquie et de la Bulgarie. II (Sofia, 1924).

Contribution à l'histoire du commerce bulgare I. Rapports consulaires belges (Sofia, 1941)

Beiträge zur Handelsgeschichte Bulgariens. II Österreichische Konsularberichte (Erster Band) (Sofia, 1943).

Contribution à l'histoire du commerce de la Turquie et de la Bulgarie. III. Rapports consulaires français (Svishtov, 1950)

Beiträge zur Handelsgeschichte Bulgariens. II Österreichische Konsularberichte, 2 (Sofia, 1953)

Naselenieto na Turcija i B'lgarija prez XVIII i XIX v. V (Sofia, 1967)

V'zv'zova-Karateodorova, K. (ed.) Nepres'hvashti izvori (Plovdiv, 1975).

BOOKS AND ARTICLES

Akarli, Engin, 'Ottoman Population in Europe in the Nineteenth Century: Its Territorial, Racial, and Religious Composition' (MA Thesis, University of Wisconsin, 1972)

Akbal, Fazila, '1831 Tarihinde osmanli imparatorlugunda idari taksimat ve nufus', Belletin, XV (1951).

Aleksandrov, Vasil, 'Iz istorijata na edin zapadnal pomin'k (Gajtanzhijstvoto v Karlovsko)', Sp.BID, IX (1905).

Iz istorijata na grad Karlovo (Sofia, 1938)

Aleksić, A., 'Morava, njeno sadašnje stanje i mogućnost plovidbe', GSUD, 2e odeljenje knj. XI (Belgrade, 1879).

Aličić, Ahmed S., Uredjenje bosanskog elayeta od 1789 do 1878 godine (Sarajevo, 1983).

Anderson, Dorothy, The Balkan Volunteers (London, 1968).

Andreades, A., Les progrés économiques de la Grèce (Paris, 1919).

Andreev, Mihail, Istorija na b'lgarskata burzhoazna d'rzhava i pravo, 1878–1917 (Sofia, 1980).

Andrejević, Sevdelin, Ekonomski razvoj Niša od 1830 do 1946 godine (Niš, 1970).

Anon. [J. R. Jolliffe], Narrative of an Excursion from Corfu to Smyrna. . . (London, 1827).

Arbuthnot, G., *Herzegovina; or Omer Pacha and the Christian Rebels* (London, 1862).

Arnaoutovitch, D., *Histoire des chemins de fer yougoslaves, 1825–1937* (Paris, 1937).

Arnaudov, M., *Iz minaloto na Kotel* (Sofia, 1931).

Arsitch, Berissav, *La vie économique de la Serbie du sud au XIXe siècle* (Paris, 1936).

Asboth, J. de, *An Official Tour through Bosnia and Herzegovina* (London, 1890).

Ashworth, William, 'Typologies and Evidence: Has Nineteenth Century Europe a Guide to Economic Growth?' *Economic History Review*, XXX (1977).

Atanasov, I., *Statisticheski sbornik za Knjazhestvo B'lgarija* (Sofia, 1897).

Atanasov, V., 'Kakvo trebva na nashata tekstilna industrija', *Sp.BID*, I (1896).

Ban, Matija, 'Život Majora Miše Anastasijevića', *GSUD*, LXXI (1890).

Barjaktarević, M., 'Neke etnološke zakonitosti kod naših najnovih migracija', *Glasnik etnografskog muzeja u Cetinju*, IV (1964).

Barkan, Omer, 'Essai sur les données statistiques des régistres de récensement dans l'empire Ottoman aux XVe et XVIe siècles', *Journal of the Economic and Social History of the Orient*, I (1957–8).

Barkley, Henry C., *Between the Danube and the Black Sea* (London, 1876).

Begović, Branislav, 'Sedam decenija razvojnog puta industrije šibica u Bosni i Hercegovini u svjetlu arhivske gradje', *Narodni šumar*, XXVI (1972).

Razvojni put šumske privrede u Bosni i Hercegovini u periodu austrougarske uprave (1878–1918) sa posebnim osvrtom na eksploaticju šuma i industrijsku preradu drveta (Sarajevo, 1978).

'Kretanje proizvodnje i eksporta hrastove duge u periodu austro-ugarske uprave u Bosni i Hercegovini', *AHOI*, VI (Zagreb, 1979).

Benko Grado, Arthur, *Migraciona enciklopedija*, sv.1, *Kanada* (Zagreb, 1930).

Berend, Ivan T., and György Ranki, *Economic Development in East Central Europe in the 19th and 20th Centuries* (New York, 1974).

The European Periphery and Industrialization, 1780–1914 (Cambridge, 1982).

Berić, Dušan, 'Problemi propadanja ekonomskog sistema osmanskog carstva u periodu 1848–1878', *IČ*, XXIX-XXX (1982–3).

Berov, Ljuben, *Ikonomicheskoto razvitie na B'lgarija prez vekovete*. (n.p.: Profizdat, 1974).

'Transport Costs and Their Role in Trade in the Balkan Lands in the 16th–19th Centuries', *Bulgarian Historical Review*, 1975.

Dvizhenieto na tsenite na Balkanite prez XVI-XIX v i Evropejskata revoljutsija na tsenite (Sofia, 1976).

'Ravnishte na ekonomichesko razvitie na B'lgarskite zemi po vreme na Osvobozhdenieto', *Trudove na visshija ikonomicheski institut 'Karl Marks'*, I (1979).

Best, J. J., *Excursions in Albania* (London, 1842).

Bianconi, F., *Cartes commerciales, nr. 4. Royaume de Serbie* (Paris, 1885).

Bičanić, Rudolf, *Kako živi narod. Život u pasivnim krajevima* (Zagreb, 1936).

Blau, Otto, *Reisen in Bosnien und der Herzegovina* (Berlin, 1877).

Bobchev, S. S., *Elena i Elensko prez vreme na osmanskoto vladichestvo* (Sofia, 1937).

Bogdanov, Ivan, *Trjavna prez v'zrazhdaneto* (Sofia, 1977).

Bogorov, D., 'Njakolko dena rashodka v Kalofer', *Turtsija* (Constantinople) II, p. 42.

Bogorov, I. A., *Osnova zaradi naprava na edna fabrika da prede i t'che pamuk v Plovdiv* (Constantinople, 1863).

Borchgrave, Emile de, *La Serbie administrative, économique et commerciale* (Brussels, 1883).

Boué, Ami, *La Turquie d'Europe* (Paris, 1840), III.

Recueil d'Itineraires dans la Turquie d'Europe (Vienna, 1854), I.

Bowen, G. F., *Mount Athos, Thessaly and Epirus* (London, 1852).

Brachelli, H. F., *Statistische Skizze der Österreichisch-Ungarischen Monarchie nebst den occupierten-Ländern Bosnien und Herzegovina* ... (Leipzig, 1881).

Bradinska, Radka, 'Navlizaneto na b'lgarskata zhena v promishlenoto proizvodstvo', *Profs'juzni letopisi*, 1968.

Bulajić, Žarko, *Agrarni odnosi u Crnoj gori (1878–1912)* (Titograd, 1959).

Capus, Guillaume, *A travers la Bosnie et l'Herzégovine* (Paris, 1896).

Castellan, Georges, *La vie quotidienne en Serbie au seuil de l'indépendance, 1815–1839* (Paris, 1967).

Chichovski, Georgi, *Srednorodopski problemi* (Asenovgrad, 1935).

Cholakov, V., *Opisanie na selo Panagjurishte* (2nd edn Panagjurishte, 1940).

Cousinery, E. M., *Voyage dans la Macédoine* (Paris, 1831).

Crampton, Richard J., *Bulgaria 1878–1918. A Survey* (Boulder, CO, 1983).

'Political Factors in the Modernization of Bulgaria before the First World War' (Bad Homburg conference on Backwardness and Modernization in Southeastern Europe, July 1989).

Cvetic', Emilo J., 'Povrsˇina, i granicˇna linija Crne Gore', *Delo*, 20 (Belgrade, 1898).

Cvijetić, Leposava, 'Fabrika čohe u Topčideru – Prva beogradska fabrika', *Ekonomski Anali*, XXXI-XXXII (1970).

Cvijić, Jovan, *Osnove za geografiju i geologiju Makedonije i Stare Srbije*, III (Belgrade, 1911).

'Metanastazička kretanja, njihovi uzroci i posledice', *NiPS, XII (Belgrade, 1922)*.

D-va, G. E., 'Znachenieto na v'tr'shnija pazar za nashata v'lnena industrija', *Sp.BID*, XIV (1910).

Damjanov, Simeon, *Frenskoto ikonomichesko pronikvane v B'lgarija 1876–1914* (Sofia, 1971).

D[anailov], G. T., 'P'rvata b'lgarska tekstilna fabrika', *Sp.BID*, VI (1902).

Danailov, G. T., 'Kilimenata industrija v B'lgarija', *Sp.BID*, IV (1900).

Daskalova, N., *Zhivota na Banatchanite B'lgari s. Dragomirovo, Svishtovsko* (Ruse, 1930).

Dedijer, Jevto, 'La transhumance dans les pays dinariques', *Annales de Géographie*, XXV (1916).

Dedijer, Vladimir, *The Road to Sarajevo* (London, 1967).

Dimitrijević, Sergije, *Gradska privreda starog Leskovca* (Leskovac, 1952).

Divljanović, Dragoljub, *Govedja kuga u Srbiji i njenom susedstvu tokom XIX veka (1800–1882)* (Belgrade, 1969).

Djilas, Milovan, *Land Without Justice* (London, 1958).

Djordjević, Dimitrije, 'Balkan Versus European Enlightenment: Parallelisms and Dissonances', *East European Quarterly*, IX (1975).

Carinski rat Austro-Ugarske i Srbije 1906–1911 (Belgrade, 1962).

Djordjević, Tihomir R., *Iz Srbije Kneza Miloša. Stanovništvo, naselja* (Belgrade, 1924).

Srbija pre sto godina (Belgrade, 1946).

'Gradja za istorija i folklor. Nešto statistike Crne Gore s početka XIX veka', *Zapisi*, I (1927).

Djuričić, V. M., et al., *Naša narodna privreda i nacionalni prihod* (Sarajevo, 1927).

Djurović, Mirčeta, *Trgovački kapital u Crnoj gori u drugoj polovini XIX i početkom XX vijeka* (Cetinje, 1958).

Dodov, Al. G., 'Gajtandzhijstvo na gr. Pirdop', *Sp.BID*, VIII (1904).

'Doklad do g.-na Ministra na Narod. Prosveshtenie ot industrijalnata komissija pri Ministerstvoto na Narodnoto Prosveshtenie', *Promishlenost*, III (1890).

Dorze [Dorzée], F., *Zaharnata industrija v B'lgarija* (Sofia, 1904).

Draganova, Slavka, 'De la production agricole, l'imposition fiscale et la différenciation sociale de la population paysanne en Bulgarie du nord-est durant les années 60–70 du XIXe siècle', *Bulgarian Historical Review* (1977).

'Différenciation de fortune dans les villages de la Bulgarie du nord-est durant les années 60 et 70 du XIXe siècle', *Bulgarian Historical Review* (1980).

Materiali za dunavskija vilaet (Sofia, 1980).

'Raspredelenie na pozemnata sobstvenost v severozapadna B'lgarija v navecherieto na Osvobozhdenieto', *Studia balcanica*, XVII (1983).

Berkovsko selo v navecherieto na Osvobozhdenieto (Sofia, 1985).

Dragičević, R. J., 'Prilozi ekonomskoj istoriji Crne Gore (1861–1870)', *Istoriski Zapisi*, X (1954).

Drobnjaković, Borivoje M., 'Jasenica', *NiPS*, XIII (1923).

'Kosmaj', *Srpski Etnografski Zbornik*, XLVI (Belgrade, 1930).

Dučić, Nićifor, *Književni radovi* (Belgrade, 1893), III.

Durham, Mary E., *Through the Lands of the Serb* (London, 1904).

The Burden of the Balkans (London, 1905).

The Struggle for Scutari (London, 1914).

Dvorniković, Vladimir, *Karakterologija Jugoslovena* (Belgrade, 1939).

Džambazovski, Kliment, 'Snabdevanje carigradske pijace sredinom XIX veka sitnom stokom iz Kneževine Srbije', *IČ*, XXIX-XXX (1982–3).

'Uticaj hatišerifa od 1830 i 1833 na režim stočarenja i trgovine stokom na istočnoj granici Kneževine Srbije', *Odredbe pozitivnog zakonodarstva i običajnog prava o sezonskim kretanjima stočara u jugoistočnoj Evropi kroz vekove* (Posebna izdanja Balkanološkog instituta, knj. 4, Belgrade, 1976).

Ekonomski institut N.R. Srbije, *Proizvodne snage N.R. Srbije* (Belgrade, 1953).

Emmanuel, I.-S., *Histoire de l'industrie des tissus des Israelites de Salonique* (Lausanne, 1935).

Erceg, I., 'Stanovništvo Dalmacije na prijelazu iz 18 u 19 st', *AHOI*, II (Zagreb, 1975).

Erdeljanović, Jovan, 'Kuči, pleme u Crnoj Gori', *NSZ*, IV (Belgrade, 1907).

Erdic, Jean, *En Bulgarie et en Roumélie* (Paris, 1885).

Ergil, D., and R. Rhodes, 'Western Capitalism and the Disintegration of the Ottoman Empire', *Economy & History*, XVIII (1975).

Eton, W., *A Survey of the Turkish Empire* (London, 1798).

'Fabrična industrija u evropskoj Turskoj', *Ekonomist* (Belgrade) II (1913).

Felix-Beaujour, *Tableau du commerce de la Grèce formé d'après une année moyenne, depuis 1787 jusqu'en 1797* (Paris, 1800).

Filipović, Milenko, 'Odlaženje na Prehranu', *Glasnik Geografskog društva*, XXVII (Belgrade, 1947).

Frilley, Gabriel, and Jovan Wlahovitj, *Le Monténégro contemporain* (Paris, 1876).

Gandev, Hristo, 'V'lnenieto na sopotskite i karlovskite predachki prez 1883 god', *Profesionalna mis'l*, II (1941).

Problemi na B'lgarskoto v'zrazhdanie (Sofia, 1976).

Gavrilović, Slavko, 'Prilog pitanju trgovine svinjama izmedju Austrije i Srbije u prvoj polovini XIX veka', *Zbornik za istoriju* (Novi Sad) XXVII (1983).

Geshov, Iv. Ev., 'Ovcharite ot Kotlensko i zh'tvarite ot T'rnovsko', *PS*, XXXII-XXXIII (1890).

Giljferding, Aleksandar, *Putovanje po Hercegovini Bosni i Staroj Srbiji* (Sarajevo, 1972, from Russian original St Petersburg, 1859, tr. B. Čulić.)

Ginchev, Tsani, 'Nekolko dumi ot istorijata na nasheto gradinarstvo (bahchovandzhil'k) i uredbata na gradinata', *Trud* (v. T'rnovo) I (1887).

Gonsalves, Priscilla T., 'A study of the Habsburg Agricultural Programmes in Bosanska Krajina 1878–1914', *Slavonic & East European Review*, LXIII (1985).

Good, David F., *The Economic Rise of the Habsburg Empire 1750–1914* (Berkeley, 1984).

'Austria-Hungary', in *Patterns of European Industrialization. The Nineteenth Century*, ed. R. Sylla and G. Toniolo (London, 1991).

Goshev, Iv., 'V Trjavna prez vremeto na poslednite t'rnovski g'rchki vladini (1820–1870)', *B'lgarska istoricheska biblioteka*, III (1930).

Govedarov, Iv. G., *Koprivshtitsa v sv'rzka s duhovnoto ni i politichesko v'zrazhdane* (Sofia, 1919).

Grgašević, Jaša, *Industrija Srbije i Crne gore* (Zagreb, 1924).

Guillaume, Baron, *Grèce. Situation économique* (Brussels, 1900).

Gunchev, Guncho St, *Vakarel. Antropogeografski prouchvanija* (Sofia, 1933).

'Sluginstvoto u Vakarelsko', *Sp.BID*, XXXII (1933).

Güran, Tevfik, *Structure économique et sociale d'une région de campagne dans l'empire Ottoman vers le milieu du XIXe siècle* (Sofia, 1979).

Hadži Vasiljević, Jovan, *Prilep i njegova okolina* (Belgrade, 1902).

'Grad Bitolj', *Brastvo*, XIV (1911).

Južna Stara Srbija. II Preševska oblast (Belgrade, 1913).

Skopje i njegova okolina. Istorijska, etnografska i kulturno politička izlaganja (Belgrade, 1930).

Halpern, Joel M. and Barbara K. Halpern, *A Serbian Village in Historical Perspective* (Prospect Heights, IL, 1986).

Harris, David, *Diplomatic History of the Balkan Crisis of 1875–1878. The First Year* (Stanford, CA, 1936).

Hauptman, Ferdo, 'Borba za bosansko željezo pred prvi svjetski rat', *Godišnjak istorijskog društva Bosne i Hercegovine* (1959), X.

Heuschling, Xavier, *L'Empire de Turquie* (Brussels, 1860).

Hoffman, George W., 'Transformation of Rural Settlement in Bulgaria', *Geographical Review*, LIV (1964).

Holland, Henry, *Travels in the Ionian Islands, Albania, Thessaly, Macedonia etc.* *during the Years 1812 and 1813* (London, 1815).

Hrelja, Kemal, *Industrija Bosne i Hercegovine do kraja prvog svjetskog rata* (Belgrade, 1961).

'Razvoj industrije u Bosni i Hercegovini do drugog svjetskog rata', *AHOI*, I (Zagreb, 1974).

Hristov, Hristo, *Agrarnijat v'pros v B'lgarskata natsionalna revoljutsija* (Sofia, 1976).

Iaranoff, Dimit'r, *La Macédoine économique* (Sofia, 1931).

Ignjić, Stevan, *Užice i okolina 1862–1914* (Titovo Užice, 1967).

Ikonomika na B'lgarija do sotsialisticheskata revoljutsija (2nd edn Sofia, 1989).

Ilić, Radomir M., 'Ibar. Antropogeografska prouchvanija', *NSZ*, III (Belgrade, 1905).

Iliev, A. T., *Staro-zagorski okr'g v narodo-ikonomichesko otnoshenie* (Stara Zagora, 1885).

Ilkov, D., 'Grad Tr'n', *B'lgarska istoricheska biblioteka*, III (1930).

Irechek, Konstantin, 'P'tni belezhki za Sredna Gora i za Rodopskite planini', *PS*, IX (1884).

Knjazhestvo B'lgarija, II (Plovdiv, 1899).

Putovanja po B'lgarija, (Sofia, 1974 edn).

Issawi, Charles, *The Economic History of the Middle East, 1800–1914* (Chicago, 1966).

Economic History of Turkey 1800–1914 (Chicago, 1980).

'Wages in Turkey, 1850–1914', in *Social and Economic History of Turkey 1071–1920*. ed. O. Okyar and H. Inalcik (Ankara, 1980).

Ivanić, Ivan, *Maćedonija i Maćedonci. Putopisne beleške* (Belgrade, 1906).

Maćedonija i Maćedonci, II, *Opis zemlje i naroda* (Novi Sad, 1908).

Ivanov, D. P., 'Spasenieto na B'lgarskata emigracija v Rum'nija', *Nova B'lgarija*, I, 70 (11 Mar. 1877).

'Iz istorije trgovine. Zemljoradnici i trgovci', *Nova trgovina* (Belgrade) April 1952

'Izvoz kudelje i užarije', *Ekonomist*, I (1912).

Jackson, Marvin R., 'Comparing the Balkan Demographic Experience, 1860 to 1970', *JEEcH*, XIV (1985).

'National Product and Income in Southeastern Europe in the First Half of the Twentieth Century: The Problems and the Usefulness of its Measurement' (Conference on Backwardness and Modernization in Southeastern Europe, 1830–1940, Bad Homburg, 3–5 July 1989).

'Quantitative economic history in the Balkans: Observations on the period before 1914', Arizona State University Department of Economics, Faculty working paper EC74–39, 1974, p. 4.

Jakšić, Vladimir, 'Nestajanje srbskoga naroda u Ugarskoj', *Statistična zbirka iz srbski krajeva* (Belgrade, 1875).

'Stanje zemljoradnje u Srbiji', *GSUD*, XLI (Belgrade, 1875).

Janakieva, Zhechka, *Abadzhijstvoto v slivenskija kraj* (Sliven: Okr'zhen istoricheski muzej, 1978).

Janulov, Il., 'Kilimenata industrija v Panagjurishte i nejnite uslovija na truda', *Sp.BID*, IX (1905).

Jelavich, Charles and Barbara, *The Establishment of the Balkan National States, 1804–1920* (Seattle, 1977).

Jergović, F., 'Stočarstvo u Crnoj Gori', *Glas Crnogorca*, 2 Sept. 1891, p. 3.

Jochmus, A., 'Notes on a Journey into the Balkan, or Mount Haemus, in 1847', *Journal of the Royal Geographic Society*, XXIV (1854).

Jovanović, Aleks S., 'Zadruga po propisima našeg gradjanskog zakonika', *GSUD*, XXXVI (Belgrade, 1872).

Jovanović, D., 'U carstvu šljiva i rakije', *Privredni pregled*, III (1925).

Jovanović, Jagoš, *Stvaranje crnogorske države i razvoj crnogorske nacionalnosti*. (Cetinje, 1947).

Jovanović, Ljubomir, 'Mlava. Antropogeografska proučavanja', *NSZ*, II (Belgrade, 1903).

Jovanović, Slobodan, *Ustavobranitelji i njihova vlada* (Belgrade, 1925).

Jovanović, Vladimir, 'Statističan pregled našeg privrednog i društvenog stanja', *GSUD*, L (1881).

Jovičević, Andrija, 'Crnogorsko Primorje i Krajina', *NiPS*, XI (Belgrade, 1922).

Jovičević, Andro, 'Narodni život (Riječka nahija u Crnoj Gori)', *Zbornik za narodni život i običaje južnih slavena*, XV (Zagreb, 1910).

Jubilejna kniga na zheravnenskoto chitalishte 'Edinstvo' 1870–1920 (Sofia, 1921).

Juzbašić, Dž., review of Ferdinand Hauptmann, *Die Österreichish-ungarische Herrschaft in Bosnien und der Hercegovina 1878–1918* (Graz, 1983) in *Godišnjak društva istoričara Bosne i Hercegovine*, XXXV (Sarajevo, 1984).

'Some features of the economic development of Bosnia and Herzegovina between 1878 and 1914', *Survey* (Sarajevo, 1984).

Kanev, Konstantin, *Minaloto na selo Momchilovtsi, Smoljansko. Prinos k'm istorijata na srednite Rodopi* (Sofia, 1975).

Kanitz, Felix, *La Bulgarie danubienne et le Balkan. Études de voyage, 1860–1880* (Paris, 1882).

Srbija. Zemlja i stanovništvo od rimskog doba do kraja XIX veka (tr. by G. Ernjaković of 1904 edn) (Leipzig reprinted Belgrade, 1987), vol. I

Kapidžić, Hamdija, *Bosna i Hercegovina u vrijeme austro-ugarske vladavine* (Sarajevo, 1968).

Kapor, Ambroz, *Prerada duvana u Bosni i Hercegovini od prvih početaka do 1923 godine* (Sarajevo, 1954).

Karić, Vladimir, *Srbija. Opis zemlje, narode i države* (Belgrade, 1887).

Karpat, Kemal, 'Ottoman Population Records and the Census of 1881/82–1893', *International Journal of Middle East Studies*, IX (1978).

Ottoman Population 1830–1914. Demographic and Social Characteristics (Madison, WI, 1985).

Kaser, Karl, 'The Origins of Balkan Patriarchy', *Modern Greek Studies*, VIII (1992).

Keppel, George, *Narrative of a Journey across the Balkan by the Two Passes of Selimno and Pravadi* (London, 1831), I.

Kinglake, Alexander, *Eothen* (Icon edn London, 1963).

Kirov, R., 'Stopansko povdigane na seloto', *Jubilejna kniga na zheravnenskoto chitalishte 'Edinstvo' 1870–1920* (Sofia, 1921).

K'nchov, Vasil, *Izbrani proizvedenija* (Sofia, 1970), II.

Kojić, Branislav D., *Varošice u Srbiji. XIX veka* (Belgrade, 1970).

Komlos, John, *The Habsburg Monarchy as a Customs Union* (Princeton 1983).

K[onstantinov], Hr. P., 'Nekolki dumi za iselvanieto na pomatsite iz rodopskite pokrajnini', *B'lgarska sbirka*, II (1895) no. 1.

Konstantinov, Danail, *Zheravna v minalo i do dneshno vreme* (Zheravna, 1948).

Konstantinov, N., 'Stupanski formi i tehnika na industrijata v B'lgarija predi osvobozhdenieto', *Sp. BID*, VI (1902).

'Zemedelieto v B'lgarija predi osvobozhdenieto', *Sbornik na narodni umotvorenija*, XXVI (1912).

Kosev, D., et al., *B'lgaro Rum'nski vr'zki i otnoshenija prez vekovete. Izsledvanija*, I (XII–XIX v.) (Sofia, 1965).

Kosev, Konstantin, *Za kapitalisticheskoto razvitie na B'lgarskite zemi prez 60–te i 70–te godini na XIX vek* (Sofia, 1968).

Kosier, Lj. St., *Srbi, Hrvati i Slovenci u Americi. Ekonomsko socijalni problemi emigracije* (Belgrade, 1926).

Kostić, Cvetko, *Seljaci industriski radnici* (Belgrade, 1955).

Kostić, K. N., 'Pirot', *Glasnik srpskog geografskog društva*, I (Belgrade, 1912).

Kostić, Milivoje M., *Pisma s puta Beograd – Paraćin – Zaječar* (Belgrade, 1896).

Srpska izvozna trgovina od 1893–1903 godine (Belgrade, 1905).

Kovačević-Bosanac, Jovo Dj., *Raseljavanje Bosne i Hercegovine* (Belgrade, 1901).

Krešeljaković, Hamdija, *Esnafi i obrti u Bosni i Hercegovini* (Naučno društvo N.R. B. i H. Djela, knj. XVII, Sarajevo, 1961).

Lampe, John R., Financial Structure and the Economic Development of Serbia, 1878–1912' (unpublished Ph.D. thesis, University of Wisconsin, 1971).

'Finance and Pre-1914 Industrial Stirrings in Bulgaria and Serbia', *Southeastern Europe*, II (1975).

'Varieties of Unsuccessful Industrialization. The Balkan States before 1914', *JEcH*, XXXV (1975).

'Modernization and Social Structure: the Case of the pre-1914 Balkan Capitals', *Southeastern Europe*, V (1979).

The Bulgarian Economy in the Twentieth Century (London, 1986).

'Imperial Borderlands or Capitalist Periphery? Redefining Balkan Backwardness, 1520–1914', in *The Origins of Backwardness in Eastern Europe*, ed. Daniel Chirot (Berkeley, CA, 1989).

Lampe, John R. and Marvin R. Jackson, *Balkan Economic History, 1500–1950: from Imperial Borderlands to Developing Nations* (Bloomington, IN, 1982).

Lapčević, Dragiša, *Položaj radničke klase i sindikalni pokret u Srbiji* (Belgrade, 1928).

Laveleye, Emile de, *The Balkan Peninsula* (London, 1887).

Lazić, Ant., 'Ekonomski centri Homolja i Zvižda', *Glasnik geografskog društva*, XIV (Belgrade, 1928).

Leake, William M., *Travels in Northern Greece* (London, 1835), III.

McCarthy, Justin, *The Arab World, Turkey, and the Balkans (1878–1914): A Handbook of Historical Statistics* (Boston, MA, 1982).

Macdermott, Mercia, *A History of Bulgaria 1393–1885* (London, 1962).

McGowan, Bruce, *Economic Life in Ottoman Europe. Taxation, Trade and the Struggle for Land, 1600–1800* (Cambridge, 1981).

Mackenzie, G. G. M. and Miss Irby, *Travels in the Slavonic Provinces of Turkey in Europe* (London, 1867).

Magarašević, Djordje, 'Putovanje po Srbiji u 1827 god. 1827', in *Biblioteka baština*, I, ed. S. Velmar-Janković (Belgrade, 1983).

Magocsi, Paul R., *Historical Atlas of East Central Europe* (Seattle, 1993).

Mallat, J., *La Serbie contemporaine* II (Paris, 1902).

Manalov, Iv., 'Kilimenata industrija v Chiprovtsi', *Sp.BID*, V (1901).

Manev, Sv. Iv., 'Kotlensko', *Sp.BID*, VII (1903).

Marković, Svetozar, *Celokupna dela*, II (Belgrade, 1912).

Matuz, Josef, 'Warum es in ottomanischen Türkei keine Industrieentwicklung gab', *Südosteuropa mitteilungen* III (1985).

Meininger, Thomas, 'Teachers and School Boards in the Late Bulgarian Renaissance', in *Bulgaria Past and Present*, ed. Thomas Butler (Columbus, OH, 1976).

Mentelle, Edme, *Géographie comparée ou analyse de la géographie ancienne et moderne – Turquie d'Europe* (Paris, 1785).

Michelsen, Edward H., *The Ottoman Empire and its Resources* (London, 1853).

Mijatović, Stanoje, 'Grad Voden', *Brastvo*, XVIII (Belgrade, 1924).

'Resava', *NiPS*, XXVI (Belgrade, 1930).

Milenković, Vladislav, *Ekonomska istorija Beograda* (Belgrade, 1932).

Milić, Danica, *Trgovina Srbije 1815–1839* (Belgrade, 1959).

'Nemački kapital u Srbiji do 1918', *IČ*, XII-XIII (1961–2).

'Ekonomski potencijal ustaničke Srbije', *Istorijski značaj srpske revolucije 1804 godine* (Belgrade, 1983).

'Šume kao prirodni uslov za neke privredne delatnosti', *AHOI*, X (1983).

Milićević, Milan Dj., *Kneževina Srbija* (Belgrade, 1876).

Kraljevina Srbija (III) *Novi Krajevi* (Belgrade, 1884).

Millet, René, *La Serbie économique et commerciale* (Paris, 1889).

Millman, Richard, 'The Bulgarian Massacres reconsidered', *Slavonic and East European Review*, LVIII (1980).

Milojević, Borivoje Ž., 'Radjevina i Jadar. Antropogeografska ispitivanja', *NSZ*, IX (Belgrade, 1913).

Dinarsko primorje i ostrva u našoj kraljevini. Geografska ispitivanja (Belgrade, 1933).

Visoke planine u našoj kraljevini (Belgrade, 1937).

Milojević, Miroslav D., *Mačva, Šabačka Posavina i Pocerina* (Belgrade, 1962).

Razvoj i osobine stočarstva u istočnoj Srbiji (Belgrade, 1972).

Milošević, S. Dj., *Spoljna trgovina Srbije od 1843–1875 godine* (Belgrade, 1902).

Minces, B., 'Preselencheskijat v'pros v B'lgarija', *B'lgarski Pregled*, IV (1897).

Mishajkov, D., 'Belezhki v'rhu domashnata shaechna industrija v B'lgarija', *Sp.BID*, VII (1903).

'Ocherk na fabrichnata v'lnena industrija v B'lgarija', *Sp.BID*, VIII (1904).

'V'lnenite tekstilni fabriki v B'lgarija i tehnite pazari', *Sp.BID*, XII (1908).

Mladenov, Dimit'r, *Pojava na fabrichen proletariat v B'lgarija* (Sofia, 1961).

Mollov, J. S., and Ju. Totev, *Tseni na zemedelskite proizvedenija u nas prez poslednite 54 godini, 1881–1934* (Sofia, 1935).

'Montenegrin Economics – I', *Montenegrin Bulletin*, no. 4–6 (1 Sept. 1918).

More, Robert J., *Under the Balkans. Notes of a Visit to the District of Philippopolis in 1876* (London, 1877).

Moskov, M., *Emigracija ni v svr'zka s stopanskija ni zhivot* (v. T'rnovo, 1911).

Ljaskovets, minaloto i b'dninata mu. (v. T'rnovo, 1920).

Mouradja D'Ohsson, *Tableau général de l'empire ottoman* (Paris, 1791), IV.

Nachov, N., 'Tsarigrad kao kulturen tsent'r na B'lgarite do 1877 g.' *Sbornik na b'l-garskata akademija na naukite*, XIX (Sofia, 1925).

Kalofer v minaloto, 1707–1877 (Sofia, 1927).

Hristo P T'pchileshtov (Sofia, 1935).

'Nashiti tekstilni fabriki i turskija pazar', *Sp.BID* (1911), XV.

Natan, Zhak, *Ikonomicheska istorija na B'lgarija sled osvobozhdenieto* (Sofia, 1938).

'Neke primedbe o mom putovanju iz Beograda preko Kragujevac u srez Levački', repr. in Petar Ž Petrović, *Putovanja po južnoslovenskija zemljama u XIX veku* (Belgrade, 1954).

Nestorov, Ju., *Grad Kotel* (Kotel, 1933).

Nicolaidy, B., *Les Turcs et la Turquie contemporaine* (Paris, 1859), II.

Nikaschinovitsch, Božidar, *Bosnien und die Herzegovina unter der Verwaltung der österreichisch-ungarischen Monarchie ... Band 1. Berliner Kongress 1878 und die Agrarfrage* (Berlin, 1901).

Nikolchov, V. (ed.), *100 godini b'lgarska industrija 1834–1937* (Sofia, 1937).

Nikolić, Rista T., 'Vranjska Pčinja u slivu južne Morave. Antropogeografska Ispitivanja', *NSZ*, II (1903).

'Okolina Beograda. Antropogeografsko ispitivanje', *NSZ*, II (Belgrade, 1903).

Ognjanović, R., 'Galičnik', *Južna Srbija*, II (1922).

Okyar, Osman, 'A New Look at the Problem of Economic Growth in the Ottoman Empire, 1800–1914', *JEEcH*, XVI (1987).

Ormanov, Iv., 'Gradinari ili gradinarski rabotnici?' *Novo vreme*, XVII (1914).

Oslekov, Luka N., 'Koprivshtitsa', *Jubileen sbornik po minaloto na Koprivshtitsa (1876–1926)*, ed. Arhimandrit Evtimii (Sofia, 1926).

Paić and Scherb, *Cernagora* (Agram [Zagreb] 1846).

Pajakov, L., 'Ekonomicheski pogled v'rhu B'lgarija', *Promishlenost*, I (1888).

'Ekonomicheskoto dvizhenie v Gabrovo', *Promishlenost* (Svishtov) I (1888).

Palairet, Michael, 'The Influence of Commerce on the Changing Structure of Serbia's Peasant Economy 1860–1912' (unpublished Ph.D. thesis, University of Edinburgh, 1976).

'Merchant Enterprise and the Development of the Plum-Based Trades in Serbia, 1847–1911', *Economic History Review*, XXX (1977).

'Serbia's Role on International Markets for Silk and Wine 1860–1890', *AHOI*, IV (1977).

'Fiscal Pressure and Peasant Impoverishment in Serbia before World War I', *JEcH*, XXXIX (1979).

'The 'New' Immigration and the Newest. Slavic Migrations from the Balkans to America and Industrial Europe since the Late Nineteenth Century', in *The Search for Wealth and Stability*, ed. T. C. Smout (London, 1979).

'Land, Labour and Industrial Progress in Bulgaria and Serbia before 1914', *JEEcH*, XII (1983).

'The Decline of the Old Balkan Woollen Industries 1870–1914', *Viertel-jahrschrift für Sozial- und Wirtschaftsgeschichte*, LXX (1983).

'Beet Sugar and Peasant Economy in the Balkans before 1914', *Crisis and Change in the International Sugar Economy*, ed. Bill Albert and Adrian Graves (Norwich: ISC Press, 1984).

'Désindustrialisation à la périphérie: études sur la région des Balkans au XIXe siècle', *Histoire, économie et société*, IV (1985).

'The Culture of Economic Stagnation in Montenegro', *Maryland Historian*, XVII (1986).
'The Migrant Workers of the Balkans and their Villages (18th Century–World War II)', *Handwerk in Mittel-und Südosteuropa*, ed. Klaus Roth (Munich, 1987).
'Farm Productivity under Ottoman Rule and Self-Government in Bulgaria c.1860–1890', in *East European History*, ed. Stanislav J. Kirschbaum (Columbus, OH, 1988).
'Real Earnings and National Product in Yugoslavia (1863–1988)', *10th International Economic History Congress*. Louvain 1990 (Section B 10).
'Rural Serbia in the Light of the Census of 1863', *JEEcH*, XXIV (1995).
Pamuk, Sevket, 'The Ottoman Empire in the "Great Depression" of 1873–1896', *JEcH*, XLIV (1984).
'The Decline and Resistance of the Ottoman Cotton Textiles, 1820–1913', *Explorations in Economic History*, XXIII (1986).
The Ottoman Empire and European Capitalism 1820–1913. Trade, investment and Production (Cambridge, 1987).
Panić, Slavoljub, *Mačvanski pečalbari* (Belgrade, 1912).
Pantelić, Dušan, *Beogradski pašaluk pred prvi srpski ustanak (1794–1804)* (Belgrade, 1949).
Pantić, Dušan M., *Spoljna trgovina i trgovinska politika nezavisne Srbije 1878–1892* (Belgrade, 1910).
Paton, Andrew A., *Researches on the Danube and the Adriatic*, I (London, 1862).
Pavlov, Aleksand'r, 'Ikonomicheskoto razvitie i s'stojanie na gr. Kazanl'k', *Kazanl'k v minaloto i dnes*, I (Sofia, 1912).
Pavlović, Leontije, *Arhiva Arona Despiniča o trgovini Srbije i Austrougarske od 1808–1859* (Smederevo, 1968).
Pejanović, Djordje, *Stanovništvo Bosne i Hercegovine* (Belgrade, 1955).
Pejović, Djordjije, *Iseljavanja crnogoraca u XIX vijeku* (Titograd, 1962).
Peričić, Sime, 'Prilog poznavanju trgovine izmedju Kotora i Crne Gore od 1815 do 1850 godine', *AHOI*, III (1976).
Petrović, D. S., 'Naseljenici i šume u okrugu Topličkom', *Šumarski List*, LI (1927).
Petrović, Jelenko, *Pečalbari naročito iz okoline Pirota* (Belgrade, 1920).
Petmezas, S., 'Patterns of protoindustrialization in the Ottoman Empire – the Case of Eastern Thessaly c.1750–1860', *JEEcH*, XIX (1990).
Pirh [von Pirsch], Otto Dubislav pl. *Putovanje po Srbiji u godini 1829*, tr. Dragiša Mijušković (Belgrade, 1983 edn).
'Po iznos't na nashite shajetsi i gajtani', *Sp.BID*, I (1896).
Popov, Hr. F., *Grad Klisura v Aprilskoto v'zstanie* (Sofia, 1926).
Popov, Kiril G., *Stopanska B'lgarija* (Sofia, 1916).
Popov, Kiril G., [Popoff] *La Bulgarie économique 1879–1911 – Études statistiques* (Sofia, 1920).
Popović, Kosta, *Put licejskih pitomaca po Srbiji godine 1863* (Belgrade, 1867).
Popović, Miroslav D., *Kragujevac i njegovo privredno područje* (Belgrade, 1956).
Popović, N., and D. Mišić, *Naša domaća privreda* (Belgrade, 1929).
Popović, Sreta A., *Na mirisnome Zlatiboru*, 3rd. edn (Belgrade, 1908).
Popović, St., 'Ekonomni izveštaj o putu u Knjaževac, Pirot, Vranju, Leskovac i Niš, *Glasnik Ministarstva Finansija* (Belgrade) II (1883).

Pranchov, Stojan, *Koprivshtitsa ot tochka zrenie istoricheska, sotsialna i ikonomicheska* (Plovdiv, 1886).

Preshlenova, Roumyana, 'Austro-Hungarian Trade and the Economic Development of Southeastern Europe before World War I', in *Economic Transformations in East and Central Europe*, ed. David F. Good (London, 1994).

Quataert, Donald, 'The Economic Climate of the "Young Turk Revolution" in 1908', *Journal of Modern History*, LI (1979) pp. D1147–61.

Ottoman Manufacturing in the age of the Industrial Revolution (Cambridge, 1993).

Radenić, Andrija, 'Izveštaji madžarskih privrednih izaslanika o prilikama u Srbiji 1901–1914', *IČ*, XIV-XV (1963–5).

Radusinović, Pavle S., *Stanovništvo Crne Gore do 1945 godine* (Belgrade, 1978).

Rakovska, A., 'Zhenskijat naemno-rabotnishki trud v B'lgarija i negovoto razvitie', *Novo Vreme*, IX (1905).

Ravenstein, E. G., 'Distribution of the Population in the Part of Europe Overrun by the Turks', *Geographical Magazine*, III (1876);

Ristić, Aristomen, and Svetomir Stojanovic, *Leskovac juče i danas* (Leskovac, 1935).

Roskiewicz, Johann, *Studien über Bosnien und die Herzegovina* (Leipzig, 1868).

Rovinski, P. A., *Chernogoriya v eya proshlom i nastoyashtem. Geografiya – Istoriya – Etnografiya – Arheologiya – Sovremenie polozhenie*. II/1 (St Petersburg, 1897).

Chernogoriya v eya proshlom i nastoyashtem. Gosudarstvenniya zhizn (1851–1907) (Petrograd, 1915).

Sadat, Deena R., 'Rumeli Ayanlari: the Eighteenth Century', *Journal of Modern History*, XLIV (1972).

St Clair, S. G. B., and C. A. Brophy, *A Residence in Bulgaria or Notes on the Provinces and Administration of Turkey* (London, 1869).

Saint Vincent, Bory de, *Histoire et déscription des Iles Ioniennes* (Paris, 1823).

Sak'zov, I., 'Razvitieto na gradskija zhivot i na zanajatite v B'lgarija prez XVIII i XIX vek', *B'lgarija 1000 godini, 927–1927* (Sofia, 1930).

Salaheddin Bey, *La Turquie à l'exposition universelle de 1867* (Paris, 1867).

Sanders, Irwin T., *Balkan Village* (Lexington, KY, 1949).

Savić, Milivoje M., *Zanati i industrija u prisajedinjenim oblastima* (Belgrade, 1914).

Naša Industrija i Zanati I–III (Sarajevo, 1922–3).

Schmid, Ferdinand, *Bosnien und die Hercegovina unter der Verwaltung Österreich–Ungarns* (Leipzig, 1914).

Schwarz, Bernhardt, *Montenegro. Schilderung einer Reise durch das Innere* (Leipzig, 1883).

Sekulović, V., et al., *Kruševački kraj juče i danas* (Kruševac, 1961).

Semerdzhiev, Hr., *Samokov i okolnost'ta mu* (Sofia, 1913).

La Serbie et la Bulgarie en 1876, explorées par un officier d'État Major attaché d'Ambassade (Paris, 1876).

Šerif, Hašim, *Istoriski osvrt na razvoj stočarstva u Bosni i Hercegovini* (Sarajevo, 1963).

Shaw, Stanford J., 'The Ottoman Census System and Population 1831–1914,' *International Journal of Middle East Studies*, IX (1978).

Shaw, Stanford J. and Ezel Kural Shaw, *History of the Ottoman Empire and Modern Turkey*, II, *Reform, Revolution and the Republic* (Cambridge, 1985).

Shishkov, S. N., *Ustovo. Ah Chelebijski okr'g* (Plovdiv, 1885).

Zhivot't na B'lgarite v Srednja Rodopa (Plovdiv, 1886).

Sirakov, Marin St., *Gradinarite ot T'rnovsko v stranstvo* (v. T'rnovo, 1922).

Šobajić, Petar, 'Bjelopavlići i Pješivci. Plemena u Crnogorskim Brdima', *NiPS*, XV (Belgrade, 1923).

Spencer, Edmund, *Travels in European Turkey in 1850* (London, 1851), I.

Spissarevsky, K. D., and R. P. Kossov, *Annuaire international du commerce et de l'industrie du Royaume de Bulgarie* (Sofia, n.d.).

Srdanović-Barac, O., 'Poljoprivreda Srbije pod knez Mihailom prema Feliksu Kanicu', *Ekonomika poljoprivrede*, XXXII (1985).

Srpska Akademija Nauka i Umetnosti (Odeljenje istorijskih nauka), *Istorija Beograda*, I, *Stari srednji i novi vek*, II, *Devetnaesti vek*. (Belgrade, 1974).

St[ajnov], T. B. and M., 'Industrija v Kazanl'k', *Kazanl'k v minaloto i dnes*, III (1928).

Staneff, Stoil, *Das Gewerbewesen und die Gewerbepolitik in Bulgarien* (Ruse, 1901).

Statelova, Elena, *Iztochna Rumelija (1879/1885): Ikonomika, politika, kultura* (Sofia, 1983).

Stavrianos, L. S., *The Balkans since 1453* (New York, 1958).

Stevanović, Živadin M., *Postanak i razvitak gornjeg Milanovca* (Čačak, 1968).

Stipetić, Vladimir, 'Stanovništvo uže Srbije u 19 vijeku i prvi srpski ustanak' *Glas CCXCIV Srpske akademije nauka i umetnosti* (Belgrade, 1975).

(Pop) Stjepo and V. Trifković, 'Sarajevska okolina (1) Sarajevsko polje', *NSZ*, 5 (Belgrade, 1908).

Stoianovich, Traian, 'L'economie balkanique aux XVIIe et XVIIIe siècles' (unpublished doctoral thesis, Faculté des Lettres, University of Paris, 1952).

'Land Tenure and Related Sectors of the Balkan Economy, 1600–1800', *JEcH*, XIII (1953).

'The Conquering Balkan Orthodox Merchant', *JEcH*, XX (1960).

Stojančević, Vladimir, *Miloš Obrenović i njegovo doba* (Belgrade, 1966).

Stojanov, Man'o, *Kogato Plovdiv beshe stolitsa* (Sofia, 1973).

Stojanov, Metodi, *Grad Pirdop v minaloto i sega* (Sofia, 1941).

S[tojanović], T[aso], *Naš ekonomski položaj* (Belgrade, 1881).

Strangford, Viscountess, *The Eastern Shores of the Adriatic in 1863* (London, 1864).

Strauss, Adolf, 'Bulgarische Industrie', *Österreichische Monatschrift für den Orient*, XI (1885).

Sugar, Peter F., *Industrialization of Bosnia-Hercegovina, 1878–1918* (Seattle, 1963).

'The Enlightenment in the Balkans: Some Basic Considerations', *East European Quarterly*, IX (1975).

Southeastern Europe under Ottoman Rule, 1354–1804 (Seattle, 1977).

Sundečić, J. (ed.) *Orlić: Crnogorski godišnjak za . . . 1865* (Cetinje: n.d.; reprint, Cetinje, 1979).

Sundhaussen, Holm, 'Historische Statistik als neues Arbeitsgebiet der Balkanforschung' (manuscript).

'Von der traditionellen zur modernen Rückständigkeit', Bad Homburg conference on Rückständigkeit und Modernizierung in Sudosteuropa 1830–1940.

Svoronos, Nicolas, *Le Commerce de Salonique au XVIIIe siècle* (Paris 1956).

Tabakov, S., *Istorija na grad Sliven*, III, *Ikonomichen razvoj, naroden bit* (Sofia, 1929).

Tamborra, Angelo, 'The Rise of Italian Industry and the Balkans (1900–1914)', *JEEcH*, III (1974).

Teplov, V., *Materialy dlya statistiki Bolgarii Thrakii i Makedonii* (St Petersburg, 1877).

Thömmel, Gustav, *Geschichtliche, politische und topographisch-statistische Beschreibung des Vilajet Bosnien . . .* (Vienna, 1867).

'Tkačka industrija u Evropskoj Turskoj', *Ekonomist* (Belgrade) II (1913).

Todorov, Nikolaj, 'Za naemnija trud v b'lgarskite zemi k'm sredata na XIX v', *Istoricheski pregled BAN*, XV (1959).

'Svedenija za tehnologijata na Slivenskite tekstilni izdelija ot 30te godini na XIX v', *Sbornik za narodni umotvorenija*, L (1963).

'*Balkanskijat grad, XV-XIX vek*. (Sofia, 1972); translated as *The Balkan City, 1400–1900* (Seattle, 1983).

Todorova, Cvetana, 'Kapitalisticheskata industrializatsija na B'lgarija do Balkanskite vojni (1912–1913)', *Izvestija na instituta po istorija*, XXVII (1984).

Todorova, Margarita, 'Za polozhenieto na majstorite stroiteli ot Elensko prez 60-te godini na XIX v', *Muzei i pametnitsi na kulturata*, I (1965).

Todorova, Maria, 'Population Structure, Marriage Patterns, Family and Household (According to Ottoman Documentary Material from North-Eastern Bulgaria in the 60s of the 19th Century)', *Etudes Balcaniques* (Sofia) I (1983).

Todorovski, Gligor, *Makedonija po rasparčuvanjeto 1912/13–1915* (Skopje, 1995).

Tomasevich, Jozo, *Peasants, Politics and Economic Change in Yugoslavia* (Stanford, CA, 1955).

Trajković, Dragoljub, *Istorija leskovačke industrije* (Belgrade, 1961).

Trajković, Ljubica (ed.), *Valjevo i okolina* (Belgrade, 1956).

Trouton, Ruth, *Peasant Renaissance in Yugoslavia, 1900–1950* (London, 1952).

Tsonchev, Pet'r, 'Shivaskijat zanajat v Gabrovo', *Sp.BID*, XIV (1910).

Iz stopanskoto minalo na Gabrovo (Gabrovo, 1929).

Tsonev, Stefan, *D'rzhavno-monopolistichnijat kapitaliz'm v B'lgarija* (Varna, 1968).

Tsouderos, E.-J., *Le relèvement économique de la Grèce* (Paris, 1919).

Ubicini, A., *Letters on Turkey*, I, tr. Lady Easthope (London, 1856).

'L'empire Ottoman, ses divisions administratives et sa population', *L'Économiste français*, V-e année, II no. 30 (28 July 1877).

Ubucini, A. and Pavet de Courteille, *Etat présent de l'Empire Ottoman* (Paris, 1876).

Undzhiev, Ivan, *Karlovo. Istorija na grada do Osvobozhdenieto* (Sofia, 1968).

Urquhart, David, *Turkey and its Resources* (London, 1833).

Usta-Genchov, D., 'Zhetvarskite zadrugi niz T'rnovsko', *Sbornik za narodni umotvorenija nauka i knizhnina* (Sofia) VII (1892).

Vasić, Velimir, 'Pečalbarstvo istočne Srbije' (unpublished doctoral thesis, University of Belgrade, Faculty of Law, 1950).

Vasiliev, Asen, 'Materiali za trjavnanskite narodni majstori-stroiteli i rezbari', *Izvestija na instituta po gradoustrojstvo i arhitektura pri B'lgarska akademija na naukite* (1952).

B'lgarski v'zrozhdenski majstori (Sofia, 1965).

Vasil'ov, T., 'Belezhki v'rhu v'treshnoto s'stojanie na B'lgarija prez 1888 god', *PS*, XXVIII-XXX (Sofia, 1889).

Velj, M. M., 'Debar i njegova okolina', *Brastvo*, VIII (1899).

Vinski, Ivo, 'National Product and Fixed Assets in the Territory of Yugoslavia, 1909–1959', *Income and Wealth*, ser. IX (London, 1961).

Viquesnel, A., *Voyage dans la Turquie d'Europe*, I (Paris, 1868).

Vivian, Herbert, *Servia, The Poor Man's Paradise* (London, 1897).

Vlajinac, Milan, *Rečnik naših starih mera u toku vekova* (Belgrade, 1974).

Vlajkov, Marin T., *Belezhki v'rhu ekonomicheskoto polozhenie na grada Panagjurishte predi i sled v'zstanieto* (Plovdiv, 1904).

Vucinich, Wayne S., *A Study in Social Survival. Katun in the Bileča Rudine* (Denver, CO, 1975).

Vučo, Nikola, *Raspadanje esnafa u Srbiji. Knjiga prva* (Belgrade, 1954).

Položaj seljaštva. Knj. I, Eksproprijacija od zemlje u XIX veku (Belgrade, 1955).

'Razvoj industrije u Beogradu do 1914 godine', in *Istorija Beograda*, II (Belgrade, 1974).

'Železnički saobraćaj kao faktor privrednog razvoja Srbije u XIX veku', *AHOI*, V (1977).

Razvoj industrije u Srbiji u XIX veku (Belgrade, 1981).

'Šume u procesu prvobitne akumulacije kapitala u Srbiji', *AHOI*, X (1983).

Vujanović, Jovan, 'Narodna privreda. Pogled na našu ekonomiju', *Glas Crnogorca*, 29 Jan. 1900, p. 3.

Vukomanović, Mladen, *Radnička klasa Srbije u drugoj polovini XIX veka* (Belgrade, 1972).

Vukosavljević, Sreten, *Istorija seljačkog društva III. Sociologija seljačkih radova* (Belgrade, 1983).

Vulović, Lj., 'Jedna misao – Kako da se pomognemo', *Podrinske Novine* (Šabac) 26 Feb. 1906.

Wallerstein, Immanuel, 'The Ottoman Empire and the Capitalist World Economy: Some Questions for Research', *The Social and Economic History of Turkey 1071–1920*, ed. O. Okyar and H. Inalcik (Ankara, 1980).

Weber, Adolfo, *Put u Carigrad* (Zagreb, 1886).

Wilhelmy, Herbert, *Hochbulgarien. I, Die ländlichen Siedlungen und die bauerlich Wirtschaft* (Kiel, 1935).

Hochbulgarien. II, Sofia. Wandlungen einer Grossstadt zwischen Orient und Okzident (Kiel, 1936).

Wyon, R. and G. Prance, *The Land of the Black Mountain* (London, 1903).

Zahariev, Stefan, *Geografiko istoriko statistichesko opisanie na Tatar Pazardzhishk't kaaz* (Vienna, 1870).

Zannetoff, G., *Die haus-und fabrikmässige Entwicklung der bulgarischen Textilindustrie* (Berlin, 1927).

Živancević, Mihailo M., *Naše zanatstvo i zanatlijski pokret* (Belgrade, 1938).

Zografski, Dančo, *Razvitokot na kapitalističkite elementi vo Makedonija za vreme na turskoto vladeenje* (Skopje, 1967).

Index

Printed in the United States
By Bookmasters